THE COMING OF THE WAR

1914

VOLUME I

THE
COMING OF THE WAR
1914

VOLUME I

BY

BERNADOTTE E. SCHMITT

NEW YORK

Howard Fertig

1966

Howard Fertig, Inc. edition 1966
Published by arrangement with Charles Scribner's Sons

Library of Congress Catalog Card Number: 66-24353

Printed in the United States of America
by Noble Offset Printers

PREFACE

ON 4 August, 1914, the German Government laid before the Reichstag a 'White Book' entitled *Wie Russland Deutschland hinterging und den Europäischen Krieg entfesselte* [How Russia betrayed Germany and caused the European war], and two days later the British Government presented to Parliament a 'White Paper' (or 'Blue Book') under the title *Correspondence respecting the European Crisis*. Revealing to some extent, the British much more than the German, the diplomatic correspondence of the fortnight immediately preceding the war, the two publications aroused intense interest and soon provoked acute controversy. Gradually other governments issued their 'books'—Russian, Belgian, Serbian, French, Austro-Hungarian. These several collections of documents filled a volume of more than 500 closely printed pages. They were translated into many languages, and throughout the period of the war they were eagerly studied and discussed in belligerent and neutral countries alike. Obviously, these documents did not tell the whole story, for they failed to supply information on many essential points. Nevertheless, it seems to have been generally assumed that as far as they went, they were reliable.

Shortly after the close of the war, the new governments in Germany and Austria, then in Socialist hands and anxious to discredit the old régimes, decided to lift the veil from the crisis of July, 1914. Accordingly in the course of 1919 extensive collections of documents were issued in Berlin and Vienna which contained 914 and 352 documents respectively, as opposed to 47 and 69 originally published. Several years later the Soviet Government added more than a hundred to the 79 documents of the Russian 'Orange Book.' In 1926 the British Government, following German example, published its complete correspondence for July, 1914: 677 documents as against 164 revealed in 1914.

Certain additional French documents have also been allowed unofficially to see the light. These publications not only make it
possible to narrate the events of July, 1914, with some approach
to completeness, but they also permit one, by comparing the versions put out in 1914 with the authentic texts now available, to
determine how far the various governments both refrained from
telling the whole truth and did not scruple to go beyond telling
nothing but the truth. The more flagrant cases of 'editing' and
'improving' documents are duly indicated in this work.

After publishing the material for July, 1914, the German Government was not long in deciding that what had happened in
that month could be properly comprehended only if the events
of preceding years were thoroughly understood; furthermore it
believed that the most effective protest against Article 231 of
the Treaty of Versailles, which was interpreted in Germany as
laying on Germany the sole responsibility for the war, would be
to make a clean breast of German policy in the period of the
Empire. It therefore authorized the publication of the essential
documents, including the most secret ones, for the period from
1871 to 1914, and this enterprise was completed, in 40 volumes,
between 1922 and 1927. During these same years the Soviet
Government issued several collections of papers from the Russian archives. In the face of these revelations, the British and
French Governments decided to open their archives, the former
from 1898, the latter from 1871. The British series of documents
began to appear in 1927, the French in 1929. Late in 1929 a collection of Austro-Hungarian documents for the years 1908–1914
was published. No one of these publications pretends to be complete: to print every document that passes through a foreign
office—hundreds of thousands—is out of the question. In each
case, the selection has been intrusted to competent historians
who have affirmed that they have omitted no documents which
seem essential to the historicity of the collection, and certainly
in each series the student will find documents which lack nothing
in frankness and reveal the most cherished secrets. The Yugoslav Government some years ago declared its intention of bring-

ing out a new edition of the Serbian 'Blue Book' of 1914, and the Italian Government has announced a collection of documents from the year 1861; but nothing further has been heard of these publications. Some Serbian documents have been revealed from private sources.

Altogether more than 35,000 documents are now at the disposal of the historian, and the end is by no means reached. In addition, nearly every politician, diplomatist, general or admiral of any consequence in the pre-war years has written his memoirs. In using this voluminous material, the greatest precautions have to be taken. Diplomatists are sometimes misinformed, or they make misleading or incorrect reports of their conversations: what they record has, therefore, if necessary, to be subjected to the same critical tests which may be applied to any other kind of information. Furthermore, diplomatic documents are usually written in a professional jargon which may obscure their real meaning or purpose. The memoirs of individuals present even greater difficulties. Most of them are *apologiæ*, written long after the events described and frequently without reference to contemporary documents, especially if composed in exile. So in spite of the large amount of evidence now available, it is sometimes exceedingly difficult to determine precisely what happened, while the motives of conduct can often be only surmised.

This book deals primarily with the crisis of July, 1914, and the purpose of the first two chapters is merely to analyze the international situation in Europe at the moment when the Archduke Francis Ferdinand was assassinated. In its preparation an enormous literature representing widely divergent views, both national and personal, has been consulted and considered. But it has usually seemed unnecessary to cite these books, pamphlets and articles, merely to debate an opinion with which the writer disagrees. In general, controversial writings are referred to only when they concern questions of fact. Except for an occasional addition which could be made while the book was in press, no material received later than 1 February, 1930, has been used.

A certain amount of repetition is sometimes unavoidable. For example, what a foreign minister may say or do has to be recorded in the first instance as the expression of his policy. But when his action subsequently affects the conduct of other foreign ministers, it is often desirable, in the interest of clearness, to repeat the original statement.

In 1914 'Servia' was the accepted spelling in English and is used in the British documents; it has been allowed to stand in quotations from those documents. Slavic proper names have been transliterated so as to approximate as nearly as possible their English pronunciation.

BERNADOTTE E. SCHMITT.

CHICAGO, 19 May, 1930.]

PREFACE TO THE NEW EDITION

This book, written in 1928-1929 and published in October 1930 is based primarily on the Austro-Hungarian, British, and German diplomatic documents available at the time. Since then the Russian and French papers for 1914 have been published, some additional German documents have been made available and, in 1964, the Italian diplomatic documents for July 1914 were released. They answer some of the questions raised in this book and they provide some new information, but they do not affect the main argument of the book, although of course many passages would have been written differently had they been written today.

The edition here published is a photographic reproduction of the original to which an errata sheet has been added in each volume. In these, all typographical errors have been corrected; a few translations have been slightly altered in the interest of accuracy; and occasionally the text itself has been changed to take into account errors of fact or well-pointed criticisms. Changes in the latter two categories are miniscule, and the original edition remains substantially unchanged.

B.E.S.

Alexandria, Virginia
June 1966

ERRATA—VOLUME I

Page 14, first footnote, line 7: "1907" should read "1908"

Page 40, line 14: "1909-1909" should read "1908-1909"

Page 84, line 14: delete "that"

Page 93, line 12 from bottom: "Wagenheim" should read "Wan-genheim"

Page 115, line 15: "he" should read "his father"; delete "Prince"

Page 158, third footnote, line 1: "384" should read "380"

Page 177, third footnote, line 7: "V" should read "IV"

Page 183, third footnote, line 2: "IX" should read "VII"

Page 201, line 6 from bottom: "Bosnia" should read "Bosnian"

Page 211, line 3: " 'intimidation from above' " should read " 'ter-ror', i.e. 'by killing personages of high rank' "

Page 215, line 9 from bottom: "Two should read "Five"
line 4 from bottom: "1 July" should read "4 July"

Page 235, line 12: "Yovanavich" should read "Yovanovich"

Page 236, line 19: "Ljuba" should read "Lyuba"

Page 238, lines 9 and 10: "had that matter" should read "that matter had"

Page 245, line 13: "Vladen" should read "Vladan"

Page 285, line 12 from bottom: "nor" should read "or"

Page 294, line 10: "action" should read "attitude"
line 15 from bottom: "war" should read "warlike action"

Page 295, line 12 from bottom: "witness" should read "witnesses"

Page 298, line 20: "situation is acute" should read "situation is growing acute"

Page 305, line 4: "would therefore be instructed" should read "was therefore being instructed"
line 3 from bottom: "situation" should read "relation-ship"

Page 316, line 4: "reassurances" should read "assurances"

Page 321, line 15: "We stand in an isolation that can" should read "We would stand in an isolation that could"

Page 337, line 12: "Siberia" should read "Serbia"

Page 338, line 17: "Falkenheyn" should read "Falkenhayn"

Page 353, line 15: "neithing" should read "neither"

Page 362, line 6: "reasons" should read "clues"

Page 380, line 2 from bottom: "forces" should read "strength"

Page 402, line 7 from bottom: "stimulation" should read "stipula-tion"

Page 442, line 2 from bottom: "its" should read "foreign"

Page 444, line 11 from bottom: "acustomed" should read "ac-customed"

Page 445, line 5 from bottom: "led" should read "lead"

Page 448, line 18: "*du*" should read "*de*"

Page 451, line 15: "it would not be" should read "it would not have been"

Page 467, second footnote, line 6: "June" should read "July"

Page 482, footnote, line 6: "whenever" should read "when if ever"

Page 501, line 8: "adressed" should read "addressed"

Page 521, second footnote, lines 1 and 2: "24 July" should read "25 July"

Page 533, lines 11 and 12 from bottom: " 'Must it really be?' " should read " 'Did it really have to be?' "

Page 535, line 19: "5)" should read "6)"

Page 538, line 10: "*judiciare*" should read "*judiciaire*"

CONTENTS

VOLUME I

CHAPTER   PAGE

I. THE EUROPEAN SYSTEM I

II. THE NEAR EAST 77

III. SARAJEVO 175

IV. HABSBURG'S HOUR 258

V. HOHENZOLLERN'S BOND 284

VI. THE DECISIONS OF AUSTRIA-HUNGARY . . 342

VII. DIPLOMATIC MANŒUVRES 386

VIII. THE TRIPLE ENTENTE 414

IX. THE AUSTRO-HUNGARIAN NOTE 459

X. THE POWERS AND THE ULTIMATUM . . . 482

XI. THE SERBIAN REPLY 519

THE COMING OF THE WAR

1914

VOLUME I

CHAPTER I

THE EUROPEAN SYSTEM

On Sunday, 28 June, 1914, the Archduke Francis Ferdinand of Habsburg-Este, nephew of the Emperor Francis Joseph and heir to the throne of Austria-Hungary, and his wife the Duchess of Hohenberg were assassinated at Sarajevo, the capital of Bosnia-Herzegovina. These two provinces, which had been occupied and administered by Austria-Hungary since 1878 and then formally annexed just thirty years later, lay in the southwestern part of the Dual Monarchy, along the western frontier of Serbia, and were inhabited chiefly by people of Serbian race. The assassin, Gavrilo Printsip, though an Austro-Hungarian subject, belonged to this race; he had secured the revolver with which he fired the fatal shots in Belgrade, the capital of Serbia, and he had been assisted in other ways by minor officials of the Serbian Government. The crime was the culminating incident in a long quarrel between Austria-Hungary and Serbia.

On 23 July the Austro-Hungarian Government presented to Serbia an ultimatum which the foreign minister of Great Britain described as "the most formidable document [he] had ever seen addressed by one state to another that was independent." The reply given by the Serbian Government two days later being considered unsatisfactory, Austria-Hungary, on 28 July, declared war on Serbia. This action led Russia, who considered herself the protector of Serbia, to order, on 29 July, a partial, and on 30 July, the general mobilization of her armies. If the immediate purpose of this step was to reinforce by a military threat the protest which Russia had raised against the policy of Austria-Hungary and to induce the latter to enter upon negotiations for a settlement of its dispute with Serbia, the ultimate intention was to attack Austria-Hungary in case negotiations were declined or failed. Germany, the ally of Austria-Hungary, thereupon intervened, on 31 July, with an ultimatum requiring Russia to stop her mobilization within twelve hours; and when Russia declined to heed the German demand, the German Emperor, on 1 August, declared war on Russia. At the same time Germany addressed a summons to France, and on the latter's refusal to promise neutrality, on 3 August declared war on France. The German plan of campaign against France involved marching across Belgium, whose territory had been declared neutral in a treaty signed by the Great Powers of Europe in 1839. A demand made by Germany upon Belgium for a free passage for the German armies was not only rejected by the Belgian Government, but caused Great Britain to despatch a counter-ultimatum requiring Germany to respect the neutrality of Belgium. On the refusal of the German Government to comply, the British Government, at midnight on 4 August, declared war on Germany. "On July 23, 1914, there was a dull midsummer peace in Europe. By August 4 seven nations were at war."*

The catastrophe, though long predicted by a goodly number of statesmen, soldiers and writers,† took the mass of mankind by surprise. For a decade Europe had suffered from grave diplomatic crises which, after moments of supreme tension, had ended peaceably. However ominous the situation had appeared to be in 1905 and 1911 when France and Germany were in conflict over Morocco, however threatening the attitudes of Austria-Hungary and Russia in 1908–1909 and again in 1912–1913 when complications in the Balkan peninsula brought them to the verge of war, in every case concessions had been made and peace preserved. To the man in the street, this was reassuring; governments might approach the brink of the abyss, but at the edge they refused to take the plunge. And many statesmen comforted themselves with the same thought. There were also those

---

* C. D. Hazen, *Europe since 1815* (New York, 1923), II, 665. Montenegro had thrown in her lot with Serbia.

† "THE GREAT EUROPEAN WAR BEGINS: SEVEN NATIONS ENGAGED"—such was the head-line in the weekly edition of the London *Times* for 7 August, 1914. The "the" was significant; the *Times* had, in fact, for years warned its readers of what it conceived to be the bellicose ambitions of Germany.

who, distrusting the professions of governments that they desired peace, believed that financiers would be able to prevent a war which must play havoc with their interests or hoped that the working masses who must provide the fighting men would refuse to join the colors. Even those who did not share the general optimism were hardly prepared for the suddenness with which war descended on Europe in August, 1914.

It may be the verdict of history that the war was bound to come, for Europe at the opening of this century was afflicted with a number of grave problems for which no solution was in sight. One of the main currents of development since the French Revolution had been the steady growth of democratic government and the working-out of the concomitant idea of nationality. Autocracy, though not everywhere overthrown, had been placed on the defensive; stability had been given to the Low Countries and Central Europe by the organization of national states; since the Franco-German war of 1870–1871 peace had been preserved between the Great Powers, and except in Russia governments seemed more or less firmly established. Another great achievement had been the application of science to the processes of manufacture and commerce, the accomplishment which is commonly called the Industrial Revolution. Population and wealth had increased more rapidly and the standard of living had been raised more effectively than in the preceding five hundred years; in spite of gross inequalities of fortune, the lot of the average man was better than it had ever been before. But beneath the outward calm and prosperity, forces were at work which were undermining the solidarity of European civilization.

On paper, the principle of nationality, according to which a people conscious of a unity of hearts and an identity of interests should live under a single government, was an excellent formula, especially if that government satisfied the democratic aspirations of the age. In practice, it had not proved, as men had once fondly hoped, the solvent of all difficulties and the guarantee of peace between nations, but had become a poison seeping the strength of many European governments and envenoming the relations between them. For, most unfortunately, the necessities of geography and the accidents of history, the fortune of war and the caprice of statesmen had left or created many areas in which this principle was defied; from the Rhine to the Caucasus and from the Baltic to the Mediterranean the political frontiers of Europe cut across more or less well-defined lines of nationality. It was, to be sure, no new phenomenon for people to live under alien governments, as the history of Italy or the Balkan peninsula bears sufficient witness. But the millions thus afflicted in the twentieth century, indoctrinated as they had become with the notion of nationality, resented an anomaly of which their ancestors before the French Revolution had been but vaguely conscious; all the more so because the rule of the alien governments, themselves inspired by distorted or exaggerated conceptions of nationality, was often oppressive and at best unsympathetic. Theoretically, since every state claimed to be sovereign, the relation of a government to its citizens or of a monarch to his subjects, was not a matter of international concern. Actually it was otherwise. The submerged peoples in Germany, Austria-Hungary, Russia, and the Balkan peninsula were not content to demand reforms and concessions of their respective governments, although they did this with increasing vehemence; many of them began to look beyond the frontiers of their own states to other governments and peoples that might help them in their extremity, to governments hostile to their own and to kinsmen from whom they were separated by arbitrary frontiers. Such intrigues, bordering sometimes on treason, invited more repression, which only aggravated discontent. Nor was there any escape from this vicious circle. For conservative Germany, obscurantist Austria, and autocratic Russia were alike unwilling to make generous concessions in the interest of harmony at home or surrender territory for the sake of friendly relations abroad. France and Italy were equally unwilling to renounce the hope of seeing their kinsmen freed from German or Austrian domination. The result was disastrous.

Not only did the relations of France and Germany, of Austria and Italy, and of Austria-Hungary and Russia—not to speak of the problems of the Balkan peninsula—come to be determined largely by this bitter rivalry for the allegiance of the discontented peoples; to keep what they had the possessing Powers armed themselves to the teeth, and the dispossessed or dissatisfied Powers did likewise. Their bloated armaments made war, if not inevitable, at least increasingly difficult to avoid.

Just as the idea of nationality, from being a liberating and constructive force, had become a terrifying and destructive spectre, so the application of science to industry, while it made possible the astonishing material progress of the nineteenth century, was also responsible for much ill-will and jealousy between nations. In the first flush of the economic revolution which swept over Europe after 1815, the tendency everywhere was to reduce, if not to abolish, the protective tariffs and other restrictions upon commerce which, before the French Revolution, had so frequently been the cause of war, and in the middle of the century the belief was widely cherished that free trade between the nations was not only the avenue of prosperity, but the surest guarantee of peace. The popularity of free trade, however, withered before the rising tide of nationality, until finally Great Britain was the only Power without a protective tariff. Such tariffs often caused great resentment in foreign countries, and if their effects were sometimes mitigated by commercial treaties, the negotiation of these bargains was frequently attended by bitter wrangling between the governments. Indeed, the unwillingness of Austria-Hungary to sign a reasonable commercial treaty with Serbia was a principal cause of their bitter and fatal quarrel.

Far more important, of course, than disputes about tariffs was the rivalry of the Great Powers for the possession or control of the undeveloped or backward regions of the globe. This so-called imperialism has been bitterly condemned, but it was an ineluctable necessity of modern industrialism. For the population of Europe had become too large to subsist on the food raised in Europe, and the necessary imports of food had to be paid for by the export of manufactured articles. Industrial nations like Great Britain or Germany had, therefore, to find markets abroad, or face unending misery and disaster; it was equally important to have a steady supply of those raw materials which were not produced in Europe. Italy, whose industrial development was handicapped by the lack of coal and iron, was forced to export men rather than goods, and would have liked to send them to lands under the Italian flag. France possessed neither a surplus population nor an overgrown industrial machine; but she did have a surplus of liquid capital clamoring for investment. Only a captious critic can complain if the nations yielded to instinct, and each tried to get some share of Africa, Asia, and the islands of the sea. In the course of the scramble, the notion was often expressed that there was room enough in the world for all, as if war between the Powers need not and should not result from their rivalries; and to the credit of much-abused governments it may be recorded that Africa was partitioned and spheres of influence were marked out in Asia without appeal to the sword, whereas in the eighteenth century many wars arose from such rivalries. Nevertheless, however much imperialism may be explained as the logical outcome of the industrial revolution, it contributed powerfully to the embitterment of international relations. In the first place, the spoils were not evenly divided, and those nations which received the least became discontented, ambitious, restless. Secondly, although the division was effected peacefully, there were many dangerous moments when war was narrowly avoided and many unpleasant incidents which left behind them suspicion, hatred, and fear. Lastly, naval power was soon found to be so essential an instrument of imperialism that there developed a rivalry in ship construction comparable to the competition in land armaments induced by the unstable organization of the European continent.

The moral of the preceding paragraphs hardly needs to be pointed. Twentieth-century Europe was confronted by two complicated and difficult questions: it was urgently necessary to make some kind of adjustment between the claims of a dozen rival nationalities, and it was almost equally important to insure that the economic resources and opportunities of the world should not be monopolized by a few states. Yet there was no adequate machinery for the solution of these problems. The unity of western civilization, as reflected in literature, art, science and social customs, was a very real thing; the conception of Europe as an economic entity had found frequent expression; Europe was, generally speaking, Christian, though not professing a single creed. But politically, there was little sense of solidarity, except for an occasional outburst of contempt for Asiatic peoples or the suggestion of an economic union as a bulwark against American competition. Between the twenty-two* sovereign states of Europe there was even less co-operation than was practised by the thirteen American states under the Articles of Confederation, and the picture drawn a century ago of "a union of neighboring states, resembling each other in manners, religion and culture, and connected by reciprocal interests," but based on "internal freedom [and] the reciprocal independence of its members," remained,† in 1914, strictly accurate. It is in no way surprising that machinery could not be improvised, even in the moment of supreme crisis, to overcome the four-century-old tradition of the sovereign state.

With the wisdom of hindsight, one is disposed to say that in the circumstances, the Great War was inevitable. The historian, however, may point out that it was, so to speak, a most unhistorical war. Omitting the temporary combinations of the Napoleonic era, it was the first war between Austria and Russia, the first since 1748 between Great Britain and Prussia, the first since 1763 between Prussia and Russia. Except in the Crimean War, Great Britain and France had not fought on the same side since 1720, nor Great Britain and Russia since the struggle

* Not including Andorra, Monaco, and San Marino.
† A. H. L. Heeren, *History of the Political System of Europe and Its Colonies* (New York, 1829), p. v.

against Napoleon. Finally, Prussia and Austria were, until a generation before the war, enemies of long standing. Only in the case of France and Germany did their past relations provide a proper setting for the rupture of August, 1914.

But the real question is not whether the war was inevitable (which no one can answer) or why there was a new alignment of Powers (for politics always makes strange bedfellows). What one really wishes to know is, Why could a quarrel which ostensibly concerned only two states—Austria-Hungary and Serbia—not be fought out between them, why should it develop into a European conflagration involving nearly all, and ultimately all, of the Great Powers? The answer is clear: it was the tradition of the balance of power, which had found expression in the creation, development and conflict of two great diplomatic groups, the Triple Alliance and the Triple Entente.

The Triple and Dual Alliances

Alliances were no new phenomena in the history of Europe, for Triple and Quadruple Alliances, Leagues and Family Compacts were often resorted to in earlier centuries. These combinations, however, were unlike the alliances of our time, for they were usually formed in the presence of great issues to achieve particular ends and were dissolved when the crisis had passed or their aim had been accomplished. The alliances which dominated Europe in the twentieth century were formed in times of peace when no great issues were pending; they were intended to have and gradually acquired a degree of permanence; and they took such hold of both governments and public opinion that in spite of mutual dissatisfaction within each group, no statesman dared to withdraw from the bond which his predecessors had signed. Each year that passed bound all more closely to the Wheel of Fate, until in July, 1914, none saw any escape from a war which directly concerned only two of the Great Powers.

The first step was taken in 1879 when Austria-Hungary and Germany concluded an alliance. Article I of the treaty read:

Should, contrary to their hope and against the loyal desire of the two High Contracting Parties, one of the two Empires be attacked by Russia, the High Contracting Parties are bound to come to the assistance the one of the other.*

Three years later Austria-Hungary, Germany and Italy entered into a Triple Alliance. In Article II of their treaty they agreed as follows:

In case Italy, without direct provocation on her part, shoulc be attacked by France for any reason whatsoever, the twc other Contracting Parties shall be bound to lend help and assistance with all their forces to the Party attacked. This same obligation shall devolve upon Italy in case of any aggression without direct provocation by France against Germany.†

Since the formation of the Triple Alliance created a strong *bloc* in the heart of Europe, it was inevitable that, sooner or later, a rival combination should spring into existence. This came about through the union of France and Russia, which was accomplished in two stages. In 1891 those Powers formulated two points of a common policy:

1. In order to define and consecrate the cordial understanding which unites them, and desirous of contributing in common agreement to the maintenance of the peace which forms the object of their sincerest aspirations the two Governments declare that they will take counsel together upon every question of a nature to jeopardize the general peace;
2. In case that peace should be actually in danger, and especially if one of the two parties should be threatened with an aggression, the two parties undertake to reach an understanding on the measures whose immediate and simultaneous adop-

* Treaty of 7 October, 1879; *Die Grosse Politik der Europäischen Kabinette, 1871–1914,* edited by Johannes Lepsius, Albrecht Mendelssohn Bartholdy and Friedrich Thimme, 40 volumes (Berlin, 1922–1927) (cited henceforth as "*G. P.*"), III, 103; A. F. Pribram, *Die politischen Geheimverträge Österreich-Ungarns 1879–1914* (Vienna, 1920), I, 7, English translation (Cambridge, Mass., 1920), I, 27.

† Treaty of 20 May, 1882; *G. P.*, III, 246; Pribram, I, 25, English translation, I, 67.

tion would be imposed on the two Governments by the realization of this eventuality.*

This diplomatic understanding was supplemented by a military convention negotiated in 1892, approved by the French and Russian Governments in December, 1893, and given the force of a treaty on 4 January, 1894. The principal clauses ran thus:

> France and Russia, being animated by an equal desire to preserve peace and having no other object than to meet the necessities of a defensive war provoked by an attack of the forces of the Triple Alliance against the one or the other of them, have agreed upon the following provisions:
>   1. If France is attacked by Germany, or by Italy supported by Germany, Russia shall employ all her available forces to attack Germany.
>   If Russia is attacked by Germany, or by Austria supported by Germany, France shall employ all her available forces to fight Germany.
>   2. In case the forces of the Triple Alliance, or of one of the Powers composing it, should mobilize, France and Russia, at the first news of the event, and without the necessity of any previous concert, shall mobilize immediately and simultaneously the whole of their forces and shall move them as close as possible to their frontiers.†

In neither the Austro-German treaty, the Triple Alliance, nor the Franco-Russian agreements is any semblance of aggressive intent to be found; all three treaties were defensive in character and were signed in the interests of peace. And generally speaking, the policies of the several governments were as pacific as their engagements were explicit. The German chancellors Bismarck, Caprivi and Hohenlohe repeatedly warned their ally in Vienna that Germany would not consider herself bound by the treaty if Austria-Hungary, by adventuresome or aggres-

---

* Exchange of notes, 27 August, 1891, between Ribot, French minister of foreign affairs, and Mohrenheim, Russian ambassador in Paris; France, Ministère des Affaires étrangères, *Documents diplomatiques. L'alliance franco-russe* (Paris, 1918) (cited henceforth as "*L'alliance franco-russe*"), nos. 17, 18.
  † *Ibid.*, no. 71.

sive policy in the Balkans, provoked Russia to intervention. The Austro-Hungarian Government for its part, except at times during the Bulgarian crisis of 1885–1887, was content with a passive policy, and in 1897 reached an agreement with Russia for the maintenance of the *status quo* in the Balkan peninsula. The Tsar Alexander III did not accept the idea of an alliance with France or ratify the military convention until he was convinced that France did not contemplate a war of revenge for the recovery of Alsace-Lorraine; after his death, Russia turned away from European politics to pursue a policy of expansion in the Far East. Likewise France, if she did not forget her lost provinces, did not manifest a desire for *revanche* and devoted her energy to acquiring a vast empire in Africa. At the opening of this century the alliances appeared to have justified themselves. Of a European war there was little talk. They stood—to modify an apt phrase of Mr. Winston Churchill— side by side, not face to face. Even if they had been disposed to try conclusions with each other, as in fact they were not, the balance of military power was sufficiently even to make the result doubtful. So long as Great Britain, who had her quarrels with each group, refrained from joining either, fear of her intervention, if no other reason, assured the maintenance of peace.

Gradually, however, the whole situation was profoundly modified, as has been revealed since the war by the opening of archives and the publication of secret documents. In the first place, the alliances themselves, though concluded originally for stated terms, tended to become permanent institutions. The duration of the Austro-German treaty and of the Triple Alliance was originally fixed in each case at five years. In 1883 not only was the Austro-German treaty extended for another five years, but it was agreed that it should be further prolonged for three additional years if neither party proposed a change in the terms of the alliance;* later this three-year

* Protocol of 22 March, 1883; *G. P.*, III, 258–259; Pribram, I, 28–29, English translation, I, 75.

period became automatically renewable in default of proposals to the contrary.* Thus the Austro-German alliance became practically a treaty of indefinite duration. The Triple Alliance was four times renewed,† and it became the custom to effect the renewal some time before the expiration of the old treaty; thus the treaty of 1902, which ran to July, 1914, was renewed in December, 1912, and the fact was trumpeted abroad with considerable noise.‡ In the case of the Franco-Russian Alliance, the same result was achieved, although the procedure was slightly different. The military convention, according to Article 6, "shall have the same duration as the Triple Alliance." But in 1899 the two governments agreed that the convention "shall remain in force as long as the diplomatic agreement concluded for the safeguarding of the common and permanent interests of the two countries."§ Henceforth the alignment of the great military Powers was fixed. As the years passed, the Germans were far from approving of every move made by Austria in the Balkans, the Austrians were not enamored of German world policy; M. Raymond Poincaré has testified that the day-by-day application of the Russian alliance was difficult, and the Russians often complained of inadequate French support. But no new alignment was possible, or at any rate was attempted.

Far more important than the prolongation of the alliances was the extension of their scope. The first to be transformed was the Triple Alliance. When the treaty was renewed in 1887, its originally defensive character was modified in two respects. Austria-Hungary and Italy arranged for mutual compensation in the event that "the maintenance of the *status quo* in the region of the Balkans or of the Ottoman coasts and islands in

---

* Protocol of 1 June, 1902; *G. P.*, XVIII, 496–497; Pribram, I, 90–91, English translation, I, 217–219.

† In 1887, 1891, 1902 and 1912.

‡ Cf. the speech of the German chancellor, Bethmann-Hollweg, in the Reichstag, 2 December, 1912.

§ Exchange of notes, 9 August, 1899, between Muravyev, Russian minister of foreign affairs, and Delcassé, French minister of foreign affairs; *L'alliance franco-russe*, nos. 93, 94.

the Adriatic and in the Ægean Sea should become impossible."* Germany promised her assistance to Italy not only for the defense of the latter's interests in northern Africa against a move made by France, but also "if the fortunes of any war undertaken in common against France should lead Italy to seek for territorial guarantees with respect to France for the security of the frontiers of the kingdom and of her maritime position."† Thus the Central Powers were clearly contemplating changes in the existing territorial arrangements of Europe. In 1891 Germany went so far as to promise her support for the realization of Italy's ambitions in Tripoli and Tunis, an undertaking which was the counterpart of, but more extensive than, the obligation assumed toward Italy by Austria-Hungary in respect of the Balkans. If the two Powers "should both recognize that the maintenance of the *status quo* has become impossible," Germany engaged, "after a formal and previous agreement, to support Italy in any action in the form of occupation or other taking of guaranty which the latter should undertake in these same regions with a view to an interest of equilibrium and of legitimate compensation."‡ With this promise in hand, Italy was able to seize Tripoli in 1911—and the Turco-Italian war was the prelude to the Balkans wars of 1912–1913, which in turn led to the Great War.

The Austro-German alliance also underwent a transformation. In January, 1909, the chief of the Austro-Hungarian gen-

* Article I of the treaty of 20 February, 1887, between Austria-Hungary and Italy; Pribram, I, 44, English translation, I, 109. This article became Article VII of the definitive treaty of the Triple Alliance formulated in 1891, and was the pivot of the controversy between Austria-Hungary and Italy in July, 1914.

† Articles III and IV of the treaty of 20 February, 1887, between Germany and Italy; G. P., III, 259; Pribram, I, 46, English translation, I, 113. These articles became Articles X and XI of the definitive treaty of the Triple Alliance formulated in 1891.

‡ Article IX of the treaty of the Triple Alliance of 6 May, 1891; G. P., VII, 101; Pribram, I, 66–67, English translation, I, 157. By a declaration of 30 June, 1902, Austria-Hungary informed Italy that she "has decided to undertake nothing which might interfere with the action of Italy, in case, as a result of fortuitous circumstances, the state of things now prevailing in those regions [Tripolitania and Cyrenaica] should undergo any change whatsoever and should oblige the Royal [Italian] Government to have recourse to measures which would be dictated to it by its own interests." Pribram, I, 97; English translation, I, 233.

eral staff, General Conrad von Hötzendorf, with the approval
of the Emperor Francis Joseph, addressed a letter to the chief
of the German general staff, General von Moltke.* At the
moment there was great tension between Austria and Serbia
because of Serbian resentment over the annexation of Bosnia-
Herzegovina by Austria three months before. General Conrad
hinted at the possibility of an Austrian war with Serbia, which
might cause Russia to intervene. Assuming, apparently, that
"in conformity with [im Sinne] the treaty of 1879 Germany
would place herself by the side of Austria-Hungary," he asked
for information about the German plan of campaign; in particular, he wished to know what forces Germany would be
able to send against Russia. He proposed to General von
Moltke that they should make "a detailed examination" of
the situation, with the obvious intent of effecting, if possible,
an agreement concerning the conduct of operations;† he desired, in other words, a military convention.

The proposal was not unreasonable,‡ and the Austro-Hungarian Government had several times approached the German
Government on the matter.§ But the latter had not responded
favorably to such overtures. Bismarck took the position, at the
end of 1887, that specific promises of German troops might
encourage the bellicose velleities of Austria-Hungary, and he

* Before the letter was despatched, the Austro-Hungarian Government had proposed to Germany "an exchange of ideas in writing" between the Austro-Hungarian
and German chiefs of staff. Aehrenthal to Bülow, private, 8 December, 1908;
*Österreich-Ungarns Aussenpolitik von der bosnischen Krise 1908 bis zum Kriegsaus-
bruch 1914*, edited by Ludwig Bittner and Hans Uebersberger, 9 volumes (Vienna,
1930) (cited hereafter as "*Ö.-U. A.*"), I, 563; *G. P.*, XXVI, 315. The German Government readily agreed. Bülow to Tschirchsky, 15 December, 1907; *G. P.*, XXVI,
338. Szögyény to Aehrenthal, 16 December, 1908; *Ö.-U. A.*, I, 606, 610.

† Feldmarschall Conrad, *Aus meiner Dienstzeit* (Vienna, 1921–1925), I, 631–634.

‡ Article 4 of the Franco-Russian military convention provided that "the general staffs of the armies of the two countries shall co-operate with each other at all
times." In 1888 a military-railway convention had been concluded between the
Powers of the Triple Alliance; *G. P.*, VI, 260–261. In 1906 conversations were carried on by the British general staff with the French and Belgian general staffs, although Great Britain was not allied with either France or Belgium; *British Documents on the Origins of the War, 1898–1914*, edited by G. P. Gooch and H. Temperley,
11 volumes (London, 1926–) (cited hereafter as "*B. D.*"), III, 170–203.

§ In 1882 (cf. *Denkwürdigkeiten des Generalfeldmarschalls Alfred Grafen von Waldersee* [Stuttgart, 1923], I, 219–221), in 1887 (*G. P.*, VI, 19–24), and in 1891 (*G. P.*,
VII, 110–114).

refused to allow any joint plan of operations to be worked out.* This attitude was maintained by his successors.

When, however, General von Moltke in January, 1909, replied to the overture of General Conrad, he revealed that the German plan, in the event of a general war—and he believed that war with Russia meant war with France as well—would be to "launch the principal mass of the German forces first against France," and he invited "a further exposition" of the Austrian views.† The result was a correspondence between the two generals extending over several months; it was understood that 13 German divisions should be left in East Prussia while the German armies marched into France and that the Austro-Hungarian army should assume the offensive against Russia from Galicia.‡ Such strategic arrangements were entirely natural and proper, and had they been the only theme of the correspondence, the incident would call for only the briefest notice.

But General von Moltke in his first letter raised a much more serious matter. Speaking of the relations between Austria-Hungary and Serbia, he wrote:

It is to be anticipated that the moment may come when the patience of the Monarchy toward the Serbian provocations will come to an end. Then there will be nothing left for the Monarchy to do but to march into Serbia.

I believe that only [erst] an Austrian invasion of Serbia will bring about an eventual active intervention of Russia. This will create the *casus foederis* for Germany. The joint military action that would then begin would—according to the statement of your Excellency—rest on the basis that at first Austria could concentrate only 30 divisions in Galicia against Russia.

At the same moment that Russia mobilizes, Germany will also mobilize and will mobilize her entire army.§

* For the discussions between Berlin and Vienna and within the German Government, see *G. P.*, VI, 24–29, 55–87.
† Moltke to Conrad, 21 January, 1909; Conrad, I, 379–384.
‡ *Ibid.*, I, 384–406.
§ *Ibid.*, I, 380–381.

This language, held with the "knowledge" [*i. e.,* approval] of the German Emperor and his chancellor, Prince von Bülow,* could only mean exactly what it said, *i. e.,* that if Austria-Hungary, as a result of invading Serbia, found herself at war with Russia, Germany would come to her assistance. It was in the sharpest contrast with the attitude of Prince Bismarck. "I would regret it very much," wrote the Iron Chancellor during an earlier Balkan crisis, "if Austria should let herself be carried away to take isolated military action which could lead to a breach with Russia";† and he repudiated the argument of the Austro-Hungarian foreign minister that "an invasion of Serbia implied no modification of the territorial *status quo.*"‡ And yet again:

The attempt of Austria, or at least of those statesmen and soldiers who wish to seize the opportunity to use the German army for *specifically* Austrian purposes as well as for those in which Germany has *no* interest, is aimed at the *extension and alteration* of our alliance. . . . It is not in our *political* interest to encourage the Austrian cabinet to begin or to hasten war with Russia.§

* "Seine Majestät der Kaiser und Seine Durchlaucht der Fürst Reichskanzler haben von dem Inhalt des vorstehenden Schreibens Kenntnis erhalten"; *ibid.,* I, 384. Two days after Moltke's letter was written, the German Emperor, commenting on a letter of the Emperor Francis Joseph to himself (18 January, 1909; *Ö.-U. A.,* I, 750–751), in which Francis Joseph had expressed his "warmest satisfaction and most sincere appreciation" of the diplomatic support of the German Government, said that he would answer the letter soon, and added that this exchange stood in "fortunate correlation" with the letters exchanged by the chiefs of staff. Szögyény to Aehrenthal, 23 January, 1909; *Ö.-U. A.,* I, 766. Aehrenthal, the Austro-Hungarian foreign minister, declared that he did not doubt that in the event of crisis, Germany's attitude would be in conformity with the "loyal and binding declarations" given by the German Emperor, the chancellor and General von Moltke. Aehrenthal to Bülow, private, 20 February, 1909; *Ö.-U. A.,* I, 856; *G. P.,* XXVI, 615. These statements show conclusively that the Conrad-Moltke correspondence was not a private matter of the two generals, but an official negotiation.

† Bismarck to Reuss, 6 December, 1885; *G. P.,* V, 27. Speaking with reference to the Three Emperors' League of 18 June, 1881, article II of which bound the three Powers "to take account of their respective interests in the Balkan peninsula," Bismarck, in the preceding sentence of the same despatch, wrote: "If Russia assumes an aggressive attitude or is guilty of any provocation contrary to the treaty, we shall stand by the side of Austria with all our might; but if the breach is brought about by Austria's invading Serbia without a previous understanding in accordance with the treaty, we would not be able to represent the matter to Germany as the occasion for a Russo-German war."

‡ Bismarck to Reuss, 13 December, 1885; *G. P.,* V, 36.

§ Bismarck to Albedyll, 19 December, 1887; *G. P.,* VI, 59. Throughout this book, the italics in quotations are so printed in the original documents.

Again and again Bismarck stated that if Austria wished for German assistance under the treaty of 1879, she must not provoke Russia.

What Moltke said did not necessarily commit the German Government to an invasion of Serbia, for, as we shall see, when four years later Austria proposed that very step, the then German chancellor objected and the step was not taken.* But whereas in the days of Bismarck, the German Government refused even to consider such a policy and repudiated responsibility for its consequences, after 1909 that policy entered into the calculations of the German Government, and it was prepared, in the event of the policy being adopted, to accept the consequences. One may therefore say that the Austro-German alliance was given an interpretation and an extension which Prince Bismarck had refused to sanction. The letter of the treaty was not touched, but its spirit was changed; from a strictly defensive alliance it was converted into an instrument by which an active policy on the part of Austria-Hungary was permitted.

The letters exchanged between the two chiefs of staff constituted in effect, though not in name, a military convention. In January, 1910, General Conrad reminded General von Moltke of "the military agreements [*Vereinbarungen*]† arising out of the alliance between Germany and the Monarchy which were concluded in 1909."‡ General von Moltke replied:

I assure you that the agreements [*Abmachungen*] made last year are adhered to in their full scope on our part also. I regard these agreements as binding; they retain their validity until they are changed or replaced by the consent of both parties. They have been made by me the basis of this year's mobilization arrangements.§

* See below, pp. 25, 136–138.
† '*Vereinbarungen*' is the word used in the German-Italian military convention of 1888; *G. P.*, VI, 260.
‡ Conrad to Moltke, 10 January, 1910; Conrad, II, 54.
§ Moltke to Conrad, 30 January, 1910; *ibid.*, II, 57–58.

Nothing could be more specific, and the Austro-Hungarian chief of staff, in his annual report for 1910 on the military situation of the Monarchy referred to "binding written agreements" with Germany.* So far as he was concerned, the essential thing was that the German chief of staff had promised, with the consent of the German Government, that if Austria attacked Serbia and Russia in consequence mobilized, Germany would mobilize her entire army and recognize the *casus foederis*. We shall see that in the crisis of July, 1914, General Conrad acted on the assumption that the promise held good. No doubt the German Government was still free to advise its ally against attacking Serbia; but if it agreed to an attack, it had bound itself to accepting the risk of war with Russia.

The Franco-Russian Alliance also underwent a certain extension. In 1899 there was interpolated in the political agreement of 1891, which bound the French and Russian Governments to "take counsel together upon every question of a nature to jeopardize the general peace," an understanding to maintain "the European balance of power."† The addition was made because of the fear that "if the Emperor Francis Joseph, who seems to be at the moment the only bond of union between rival and even hostile races, were suddenly to disappear," his empire might be "threatened with a dismemberment." "What matter," asked the French foreign minister, "was more likely to compromise the general peace and to upset the equilibrium of European forces?" France and Russia had therefore to be "not only agreed on the same plan but ready to carry it out."‡ But the balance of power might be threatened otherwise than by the collapse of Austria-Hungary. To agree to maintain the balance opened the way to all kinds of possibilities that could not be foreseen in 1899.

This became evident in the two years immediately preceding

---

* *Ibid.*, II, 85. On 12 May, 1914, Conrad and Moltke discussed "the maintenance of our previous agreements for the case of a war fought in common"; *ibid*, III, 669.

† Exchange of notes between Delcassé and Muravyev, 9 August, 1899; *L'alliance franco-russe*, nos. 93, 94.

‡ Delcassé to Loubet, 12 August, 1899; *L'alliance franco-russe*, no. 95.

the Great War. The Turco-Italian war over Tripoli and the Balkans wars of 1912–1913 reopened in the most acute fashion and to the widest extent the question of the Near East, which in turn involved the European balance of power. In the long and intricate negotiations which followed between the Great Powers, the Dual Alliance acquired a vitality unknown in previous years when France's attention was absorbed in Morocco and Russia's energy was directed to the Far East and Persia. In its controversies with Turkey and Austria-Hungary, the Russian Government sought and was generally accorded the diplomatic support of its ally. This support was not given blindly, for both M. Poincaré, who directed French policy from January, 1912, to January, 1913, and his successors repeatedly insisted that Russia should not take steps without consulting and obtaining the approval of the French Government,* and on several occasions they prevented precipitate action on the part of Russia.† Likewise the frequent assurances that France would fulfil the obligations of her alliance were made dependent upon the *casus foederis* being involved, that is, "if Russia is attacked by Germany or by Austria supported by Germany."‡

* Poincaré to Louis, 27 January, 1912; France, Ministère des affaires étrangères, *Documents diplomatiques. Les affaires balkaniques, 1912–1914* (Paris, 1922) (cited henceforth as "*Affaires balkaniques*"), I, 2. Izvolski to Sazonov, 29 February, 1912; R. Marchand (editor), *Un livre noir* (Paris, 1922–1923), I, 203; F. Stieve, *Der diplomatische Schriftwechsel Iswolskis 1911–1914* (Berlin, 1924), II, 50. Poincaré to Louis, 14 March, 1912; *Affaires balkaniques*, I, 12. Poincaré to Izvolski, 4 November, 1912; *ibid.*, I, 136–137. Poincaré to Izvolski, 16 November, 1912; R. Poincaré, *Au service de la France* (Paris, 1926–1928), II, 336–337. Izvolski to Sazonov, 21 November, 1912; Marchand, I, 351; Stieve, II, 353. Jonnart to Louis, 24 January, 1913; *Affaires balkaniques*, II, 52. Izvolski to Sazonov, 28 January, 1913; Marchand, II, 13; Stieve, III, 40. Pichon to Delcassé, 27 March, 1913; *Affaires balkaniques*, II, 118. Pichon to Doulcet, 25 April, 1913; *ibid.*, II, 167. Izvolski to Sazonov, 8 May, 1913; Marchand, II, 87–91; Stieve, III, 150–153. Pichon to Delcassé, 23 and 25 July, 1913; *Affaires balkaniques*, II, 265, 270. Izvolski to Sazonov, 15 January, 1914; Marchand, II, 230–231; Stieve, IV, 25–26.

† In November-December, 1912, when it seemed that Russia might intervene to prevent a Bulgarian occupation of Constantinople; in January, 1913, when there were rumors of a Russian demonstration along the Russo-Turkish frontier in Armenia to compel Turkey to accept the conditions of peace demanded by the Balkan allies; in July, 1913, when Russia threatened to make a naval demonstration at Constantinople to expel the Turks from Adrianople which they had recaptured during the second Balkan war.

‡ "During the past summer, M. Poincaré reminded us, confidentially and quite amicably, that according to the letter of the treaty, it was only an attack by Germany on Russia which could lead to the fulfilment of France's obligations toward

Throughout these troubled years the French Government successfully restrained its ally from any isolated action which might endanger the peace of Europe.

Nevertheless it is clear that a change came over the Franco-Russian Alliance. At the time of his visit to St. Petersburg in August, 1912, M. Poincaré made clear to the Russian Government, and this was subsequently confirmed by the Russian ambassador in Paris, that France did not wish to be drawn into war as a result of complications in the Near East.* But later in the year, as the crisis in the Balkans developed, the French Government and French public opinion showed greater interest in the Balkans and the Near East. The Russian ambassador was struck by this "new attitude," which he described as follows:

While up to the present France has declared that local, that is, strictly Balkan, events could not induce her to take active

us." Report of Sazonov to the Tsar, 1912; Marchand, II, 356. In November, 1912, Izvolski reported Poincaré as saying that "if Russia went to war, France would do likewise." I .volski to Sazonov, 17 November, 1912; Marchand, I, 346; Stieve, II, 346. Izvolski showed his telegram to Poincaré, who protested that France would march only if the *casus foederis* were involved, "that is to say, if Germany supports Austria against Russia by armed force." Izvolski to Sazonov, 18 November, 1912; Marchand, I, 346–347; Stieve, II, 347. Poincaré telegraphed to St. Petersburg that Izvolski's formula was "too general" and requested the French ambassador "to define our attitude in strict conformity with the treaty." Poincaré to Louis, 19 November, 1912; *Affaires balkaniques*, II, 156.

* According to the Russian foreign minister, "M. Poincaré considered it his duty to emphasize the point that public opinion in France would not permit the Government of the Republic to commit itself to military action for strictly Balkan questions, unless Germany was involved and by her own initiative provoked the application of the *casus foederis*." Sazonov to Nicholas II, 17 August, 1912; Marchand, II, 342; Stieve, II, 223. When he heard the detailed provisions of the Serbo-Bulgarian treaty of February, 1912, Poincaré protested to Sazonov, saying, "*Mais c'est là une convention de guerre!*"; R. Poincaré, *Les origines de la guerre* (Paris, 1921), p. 129. France was ready, according to the Russian ambassador in Paris, to give "the most sincere and energetic *diplomatic* support" to Russia if the latter was forced to abandon "her passive attitude" as the result of Turkey's crushing Bulgaria or Austria's attacking Serbia. "But in this stage of events, the Government of the Republic would not be in a position to obtain from parliament or public opinion the sanctions necessary for any military measures." If the conflict with Austria involved the armed intervention of Germany, France would recognize the *casus foederis*. "France," said Poincaré, "is incontestably disposed to peace and neither seeks nor desires war, but the intervention of Germany against Russia would immediately modify this state of mind," and he was convinced that "in such a case parliament and public opinion would entirely approve the decision of the government to lend armed support to Russia." Izvolski to Sazonov, 12 September, 1912; Marchand, I, 325–326; Stieve, II, 251. Cf. Poincaré, *Au service de la France*, II, 198–206.

measures, the French Government now appears ready to admit
that a territorial acquisition on the part of Austria would affect
the general balance of power in Europe and as a result touch
the particular interests of France.*

In fact, the French Government was so deeply concerned by
such a prospect that when at the end of November there appeared to be a danger that Austria might proceed to attack
Serbia, both M. Poincaré and the minister of war, M. Mille-
rand, expressed their apprehension at Russia's "indifference to
the Austrian mobilization."† It was made clear to the Russian
ambassador that

the French Government is firmly resolved to fulfil its obligations to us as an ally to the fullest extent, and it admits in good
conscience and with all the necessary *sang-froid* that the ultimate
result of the existing complications may make it necessary for
France to take part in a general war.‡

Although the usual reservations were added that "the time
when France will have to draw the sword is precisely determined by the Franco-Russian military convention" and that
"the French Government urgently requests us not to take any
separate action without having had a preliminary exchange of
views," the attitude of France had become less hesitant. The
earlier reluctance to be drawn into a war because of Balkan
complications had given way to a recognition that a war involving France might be necessary in order to preserve the
equilibrium of the Balkans and of Europe. Neither during the
Balkan crisis of 1912–1913 nor later did France make to Russia
a specific promise comparable to the German promise to Austria (that is, the promise that Germany would recognize the
casus foederis if an Austro-Russian war arose out of an Austrian attack on Serbia); France did not promise to support

---

* Izvolski to Sazonov, 7 November, 1912; Marchand, I, 342; Stieve, II, 336.
† Izvolski to Sazonov, 18 December, 1912; Marchand, I, 369; Stieve, II, 397.
‡ Izvolski to Sazonov, 30 January, 1913; Marchand, II, 20; Stieve, III, 50.

Russia if Russia moved against Austria and Germany then came to the assistance of Austria. But neither did France, so far as the published records show, say to Russia: If you attack Austria in the pursuit of your Balkan policy, and Germany intervenes, we shall *not* recognize the *casus foederis*. So far as one can judge, it was understood that if Russia, with the knowledge and approval of France, entered on a policy which led to war with Austria-Hungary and consequently with Germany, France would fulfil the obligations of the alliance. The letter of the treaty of alliance was not altered, but its spirit was changed. If the French Government was left free to advise its ally against an active policy which might lead to war, it had, in effect, promised, in case it agreed to such a policy, to accept the consequences also.*

Just as the chiefs of the Austro-Hungarian and German general staffs discussed certain arrangements for the co-operation of their respective armies, so the French and Russian general staffs, in all annual conferences, perfected their plans for common action in the event of war.† It was agreed that in the event of war, both French and Russian armies should assume the offensive against Germany, and that Russia should hasten the construction of strategic railways in Poland. On this latter point, M. Poincaré, after he became President of the Republic, made a personal appeal to the Tsar.‡ In the summer of 1912, on the initiative of the Russian Government,§ a naval conven-

* From 1912 on French public opinion was more favorably disposed toward Russia than it had been in previous years, when the Russian Government gave but lukewarm support to French policy in Morocco. How far this change was brought about through corruption of the French press by Izvolski cannot be determined. For Izvolski's activity, cf. Marchand, I, 35–39, 128, 129, 130, 148–149, 258–259; Stieve, I, 27–29, 33, 132–134, 163–164; II, 124, 129–131, 322–326, 344, 386–387, 390–394, 404–405, 408, 411; III, 63–67, 72–73, 96, 178–179, 198, 202, 204, 206–207, 218, 351–352. Poincaré, III, 97–114, gives the French view; he claims to have opposed, but to have been unable to prevent the bribery of the press.

† The protocols of the conferences for 1911–1913 are printed in Marchand, II, 419–437, and Stieve, I, 137–143; II, 181–186; III, 272–277. For the earlier conferences, see *Les Alliés contre la Russie* (Paris, 1926), pp. 8–10, 15–17, 19–21, 24.

‡ Poincaré to Nicholas II, 20 March, 1913; Marchand, II, 52; Stieve, III, 97.

§ Louis to Poincaré, 6 February, 1912; *Documents diplomatiques français (1871–1914)*, edited by the Commission de Publication des Documents relatifs aux Origines de la Guerre de 1914 (Paris, 1929–) (cited hereafter as "*D. D. F.*"), 3ᵉ série, I, 616.

tion was concluded.* Co-operation between the armed forces of the two countries was the goal aimed at, and the conviction seems to have grown in professional circles that in the event of war, the prospects of a Franco-Russian victory were excellent.

The two great military alliances of the Continent ceased, then, to be strictly conservative forces and became instruments by which the *status quo* might be modified. Whether they would attempt actually to change the *status quo* would depend, partly on circumstances, partly on the two Great Powers whose attitude remained uncertain or obscure—Italy and Great Britain. The attitude of Italy was uncertain because in 1902 she had given to France (1) the secret assurance that

in the renewal of the Triple Alliance, there is nothing directly or indirectly aggressive toward France, no engagement binding us in any eventuality to take part in an aggression against her, finally no stipulation which menaces the security and tranquillity of France;†

and (2) the secret promise of "a strict neutrality"

in case France, as the result of a direct provocation, should find herself compelled, in defense of her honor or her security, to take the initiative of a declaration of war.‡

These commitments, which a semi-official French writer admits to have been "hard to reconcile" with the Triple Alliance,§ were not made known to Germany and Austria-Hungary, but the latter Powers soon learned that some kind of bargain had been made and became thoroughly suspicious of the loyalty of their

* *L'alliance franco-russe*, nos. 102–103. The actual effect of the convention appears to have been small, the chief result being the exchange of information; no plans were worked out for securing control of the Mediterranean by the French and Russian fleets. *Les Alliés contre la Russie*, pp. 56–60.

† Tornielli to Delcassé, 4 June, 1902; France, Ministère des Affaires Étrangères, *Documents diplomatiques. Les accords franco-italiens de 1900–1902* (Paris, 1920), no. 4.

‡ Prinetti to Barrère, 1 November, 1902; *Les accords franco-italiens*, no. 8. This meant that if France, in fulfilment of her obligations to Russia, declared war on Germany, Italy would not consider the *casus foederis* of the Triple Alliance involved.

§ É. Bourgeois and G. Pagès, *Les origines et les responsabilités de la grande guerre* (Paris, 1921), p. 301, note 1.

ally.* The Franco-Italian understanding marked, in fact, the beginning of a long period of ineffectiveness of the Triple Alliance. In the Moroccan controversy Italy supported France against Germany; she disapproved of the annexation of Bosnia-Herzegovina by Austria-Hungary in 1908 and exacted heavy payment for consenting to it; in 1911 she seized Tripoli from Turkey against the real wishes of both her allies. In addition, she concluded with Russia, in October, 1909, an agreement which was meant to signalize "the complete unity of the views and interests of the two governments"† and pledged Italy "to regard with benevolence . . . Russia's interests in the question of the Straits at Constantinople."‡ It is no wonder that the French and Russian statesmen came to look upon Italy as "a restraining influence"§ or even "a dead weight"!‖

This shifty policy was abandoned, at least to some extent, during the perils of the Balkan wars. In fact, the Marquis di San Giuliano, who became Italian foreign minister in 1910, was a firm believer in the Triple Alliance and endeavored to restore its vitality. He informed the French Government in November, 1912, that Italy's engagements with Austria were made prior to her promises to France and were "obligatory upon the Italian Government."¶ In keeping with this attitude, the Triple Alliance was renewed in December, and throughout the ensuing crisis Italian policy co-operated with that of Germany and Austria-Hungary in presenting a solid front to the Triple Entente.

* G. P., XVIII, 711–759.

† Izvolski to Sverbeyev (Russian ambassador in Berlin), 4 November, 1909; B. von Siebert, *Diplomatische Aktenstücke zur Geschichte der Ententepolitik der Vorkriegsjahre* (Berlin, 1921), p. 454.

‡ Russo-Italian agreement, Racconigi, October, 1909; Marchand, I, 357–358; Stieve, II, 363–364.

§ Izvolski to Sazonov, 6 June, 1912; Marchand, I, 266; Stieve, II, 138.

‖ Sazonov to Nicholas II, 17 August, 1912; Marchand, II, 340; Stieve, II, 221.

¶ Izvolski to Sazonov, 20 November, 1912; Marchand, I, 347; Stieve, II, 350. This led the French to conclude that "neither the Triple Entente nor the Triple Alliance can count on the loyalty of Italy, that the Italian Government will use all its efforts for the maintenance of peace, and that in case of war, it will begin by adopting a waiting attitude and will finally join the side to which victory will incline." Izvolski to Sazonov, 5 December, 1912; Marchand, I, 365; Stieve, II, 376–377.

The exact significance of this *rapprochement* is difficult to gauge. Although Italy supported the Austro-Hungarian demand for the creation of an independent Albania, she refused to sanction an attack on Serbia which Austria would have liked to make in the summer of 1913.* Moreover, only a few days before the renewal of the alliance in December, 1912, the Italian Government notified Germany that it would be unable to carry out the promise given in 1888† to send an Italian army to the Rhine in the event of war between Germany and France.‡ Although the assurance was offered that "if the *casus foederis* were found to be involved [*venait de se vérifier*], Italy would mobilize her forces on land and at sea immediately, and at the latest, at the same time as Germany," General von Moltke concluded that "we shall have to carry through the fight with France by ourselves."§

In the course of the year 1913, however, Italy apparently tried to 'document' her loyalty. At her suggestion‖ the naval convention of 5 December, 1900, which designated certain zones of operation for the Austrian and Italian fleets,¶ was

* Pribram, I, 301–302, English translation, II, 176–177; G. Giolitti, *Memorie della mia vita* (Milan, 1922), II, 502–503; Giolitti's speech in the Italian parliament, 5 December, 1914, in *Collected Diplomatic Documents relating to the Outbreak of the European War* (London, 1915), pp. 400–401. Cf. *G. P.*, XXXV, 115–148, *passim.*

† Memorandum of 28 January, 1888; *G. P.*, VI, 247–249; Pribram, I, 211, note 173, English translation, II, 85, note 173.

‡ First stated orally by an officer sent to Berlin and then confirmed by a letter of Pollio (chief of the Italian general staff) to Moltke, 21 December, 1912; *G. P.*, XXX, 576. The reason given was that Italy was forced to keep so many troops in Tripoli that she had none to spare for the German-French front. W. Foerster, "Die deutsch-italienische Militärkonvention," in *Die Kriegsschuldfrage* (Berlin, 1923–) (cited henceforth as "*KSF*"), V, 398 (May, 1927).

§ Foerster, *loc. cit.*, V, 399–400.

‖ Memorandum of Berchtold, 4 February, 1913; reports of the naval attaché in Rome, 6 February, 25 February, 1913; *Ö.-U. A.*, V, 633, 650–651, 821–822. It was believed in Rome that in the event of war, France would remain on the defensive on land and attack Italy by sea. Graf Waldersee, "Von Deutschlands militär-politischen Beziehungen zu Italien," in *KSF*, VII, 641 (July, 1929). The Austro-Hungarian ambassador in Rome, however, was of the opinion that the initiative had come from Germany. Mérey to Berchtold, private, 14 August, 1913; *Ö.-U. A.*, VII, 137. The German general staff considered it "of the highest importance," in view of Italy's withdrawal of her promise to send troops to the Rhine, that the French should be prevented from transporting their African corps, *ca.* 100,000 men, to the theatre of war. Report of the naval attaché in Berlin, 11 January, 1913; *ibid.*, V, 418.

¶ Pribram, I, 174, note 175; English translation, II, 88, note 175.

replaced by an elaborate convention which was signed on 23 June, 1913, and came into effect on 1 November.* The main provision was that

the naval forces of the Triple Alliance which may be in the Mediterranean shall unite for the purpose of gaining naval control of the Mediterranean by defeating the enemy fleets.

An Austro-Hungarian admiral was to command the allied fleets; Italy was to undertake the task of interrupting the transport of French troops from Africa to France. Negotiations were also carried on between the general staffs for reviving the agreement of 1888, and in March, 1914, a German-Italian agreement was reached, by which Italy pledged herself to send three army corps and two cavalry divisions to the German army in the event of war with France.† The Italian general staff was even ready to consider sending more troops northward, to be used either against Russia or Serbia!‡ If General von Moltke did not attach excessive importance to these promises, for the Italian troops could not reach the Rhine before the 19th–22nd day of mobilization, that is, after operations would have begun, he sought to convince General Conrad that they could rely upon their Italian colleague to carry out the new engagements,§ to which King Victor Emmanuel III had given his approval. "All these agreements," wrote Moltke in November, 1914, "were made so clear and so binding that a doubt of Italy's loyalty to the alliance could hardly arise."‖ And even General Conrad allowed himself to be hopeful.

Whether the foreign offices in Berlin and Vienna reposed any confidence in Italy is an open question, on which the pub-

* *Ibid.*, I, 308–319; English translation, I, 283–305.
† Moltke to Conrad, 13 March, 1914; Conrad, III, 609–610.
‡ Foerster, *loc. cit.*, V, 407–408.
§ Conrad, III, 670–671.
‖ H. von Moltke, *Erinnerungen, Briefe, Dokumente 1877–1916* (Stuttgart, 1922), p. 9. 'Loyalty' was hardly the word to use, for the *casus foederis* was not raised in July, 1914, but Moltke's meaning is clear enough. Waldersee, *loc. cit.*, VII, 663, says, however, that Italian assistance was never regarded as a "sure factor" in the calculations of the general staff.

lished German and Austrian documents throw little light.* Likewise the lack of Italian documents—the Italian Government alone among the Great Powers has not opened its archives —makes it difficult to gauge the real attitude of the Cabinet of Rome toward its allies. Certainly Italy had no mind to follow Austria-Hungary in an aggressive policy—unless, perhaps, she were granted compensation, according to the treaty of the Triple Alliance. On the other hand, there is no evidence to show that if the Central Powers were attacked and the *casus foederis* was fairly raised, Italy was not ready to fulfil her obligations.† Be that as it may, the military and naval arrangements of the Triple Alliance were more complete and far-reaching in the spring of 1914 than they had been at any time since the foundation of the Alliance thirty-two years before.

THE TRIPLE ENTENTE

The Triple Entente, consisting of Great Britain, France and Russia, was originally a loose diplomatic agreement formulated in the Convention of 8 April, 1904, between Great Britain and France‡ and the Convention of 31 August, 1907, between Great Britain and Russia.§ In so far as the purpose of the former was to exclude Germany from Morocco and of the latter to handicap her activity in Persia,‖ the two agreements were

* The Italian Government supported the demand of Austria-Hungary for the evacuation of Albanian territory by Serbia in the autumn of 1913, though it warned its ally against the use of force; *Ö.-U. A.*, VII, 463, 471–472, 480. The German Emperor professed himself quite satisfied with the results of a visit to the King of Italy in the spring of 1914. Report of Treutler, from Venice, 25 March, 1914; *G. P.*, XXXIX, 339–341. Shortly afterward, however, the disturbances in Albania led to much friction between Austria-Hungary and Italy. *Ö.-U. A.*, VIII, 1–208, *passim*, contains many bitter complaints over the conduct of the Italian minister in Durazzo.

† Cf. A. Salandra [Italian premier in 1914], *La neutralità italiana [1914]* (Milan, 1928), pp. 15–60.

‡ *B. D.*, II, 374–398; British *Blue Books*, Cd. 1952 (1904), Cd. 5969 (1911).

§ *B. D.*, IV, 618–620; British *Blue Book*, Cd. 3750 (1907).

‖ By Article III of the Secret Articles of the Anglo-French Declaration respecting Egypt and Morocco, Spain was not to be permitted to alienate any territory in Morocco that might be placed under her authority or in her sphere of influence. The opposition to German influence in Persia is revealed by the lengthy correspondence between the British and Russian Governments with reference to the Bagdad Railway. See, *e. g.*, Izvolski to Benckendorff, 19 December, 1907; Siebert,

directed against Germany, whose policies and ambitions were causing grave anxiety to the three Powers of the Entente. But their primary purpose was to liquidate existing disputes; unlike the Triple and Dual Alliances, they did not refer specifically to European politics, however much they were concluded out of considerations for the balance of power, and they contained no provisions for action in the event of European complications. By July, 1914, however, the possibility of joint action had been considered and, in at least one contingency, arranged for.

This development was brought about in large measure by the policy of the German Government, more particularly by the mistakes of Count (later Prince) Bülow, who was foreign secretary from 1897 to 1900 and chancellor from 1900 to 1909, and his *adlatus* Baron von Holstein, who from the fall of Bismarck in 1890 to his own retirement in 1906 exercised the controlling influence in the German foreign office. The British *rapprochement* with France was begun rather reluctantly, only after repeated failures to come to terms with Germany. Convinced that the traditional British policy of 'splendid isolation' was no longer practicable, the British Government between 1895 and 1901 proposed to Germany a partition of Turkey,* an agreement over Morocco,† and ultimately an out-and-out alliance.‡ But the only result was an abortive convention about the future of the Portuguese colonies§ and a none too satisfactory agreement about Samoa.‖ The Emperor William II and Count Bülow, largely under the influence of Herr von Holstein, declined the British overtures. They feared that Germany might

p. 319, and Sazonov to Nicholas II, October, 1912; Marchand, II, 351; Stieve, II, 294. The Russian opposition appears to have been stronger than the British. Grey to Spring-Rice, 11 May, 1906; Nicolson to Grey, 19 February, 1907; *B. D.*, IV, 382–383, 430.

* *G. P.*, X, 3–36.   † *G. P.*, XVII, 295–332.

‡ *G. P.*, XIV, 194–255 (negotiations of 1898); XVII, 14–114 (1901); *B. D.*, II, 60–88. Cf. H. Freiherr von Eckardstein, *Lebenserinnerungen und politische Denkwürdigkeiten* (Leipzig, 1919), II, *passim;* E. Fischer, *Holsteins Grosses Nein* (Berlin, 1925); F. Meinecke, *Geschichte des deutsch-englischen Bündnisproblems, 1890–1901* (Berlin, 1927); E. N. Johnson and J. D. Bickford, "The Contemplated Anglo-German Alliance, 1890–1901," in *Political Science Quarterly*, XLII, 1–57 (March, 1927); G. Ritter, *Die Legende von der verschmähten englischen Freundschaft 1898–1901* (Freiburg, 1929).

§ *G. P.*, XIV, 259–347; *B. D.*, I, 44–86.   ‖ *G. P.*, XIV, 568–675; *B. D.*, 107–131.

have to fight Russia on account of British interests, and they must, they said, keep their hands free. They hoped to continue Bismarck's policy of the *'zwei Eisen,'* that is, of playing off Russia against Great Britain; they did not believe that Great Britain would pay the price of an understanding with France and Russia;* and they were persuaded that Germany was strong enough to pursue an independent and vigorous world policy in all directions. William II was, so Bülow once assured him, *"arbiter mundi."*† The Emperor himself confided to a British statesman that "there is no balance of power in Europe but me —me and my twenty-five corps."‡ The Triple Alliance, declared Count Bülow to the Reichstag in 1902, is no longer "an absolute necessity."§

Consequently the conclusion of the Triple Entente produced a profound shock on the German Government and German public opinion. To break through the *'Einkreisung'* or 'encirclement' became, so it seemed, a matter of life and death, and this appears to have been the guiding motive of German policy in the ten years from 1904 to 1914, for the Entente Powers, if they stood together, could block the German dreams of expan-

* "The understanding with the Dual Alliance which the English threaten us with is only a spectre invented to frighten us, which the English have already been using for years. The sacrifices which such an understanding would impose on England are so extravagant that the British Government did not decide to make them even at the time when the tension with us was at its height." Bülow to William II, 21 January, 1901; *G. P.*, XVII, 21. "The threatened understanding with Russia and France is a complete swindle. . . . We can wait, time is working for us." Holstein to Metternich, private, 21 January, 1901; *G. P.*, XVII, 22. Holstein is said to have declared in 1903 that "he considered a really serious *rapprochement* between England and France out of the question, and it was naïve to think that an Anglo-French compromise concerning Morocco was ever at all possible"; Eckardstein, II, 425–426. Bülow expressed much the same opinion, and said that "an understanding between England and Russia would be even more difficult to obtain than one between England and France, however much the wish for it might exist on the side of England." Bülow to William II, 20 May, 1903; *G. P.*, XVII, 588. The statements of 1903 were made in answer to a memorandum presented by Baron von Eckardstein, a former councillor of the German embassy in London, in which he warned the foreign office that an Anglo-French *rapprochement* was under way which would be the prelude to an Anglo-Russian understanding and a "new triple alliance"; Eckardstein to Bülow, 10 May, 1904; *G. P.*, XVII, 567–570; Eckardstein, II, 422–425. The German representatives in London, Paris and St. Petersburg were consulted, and they agreed in discounting Eckardstein's predictions.

† Bülow to William II, 24 August, 1898; *G. P.*, XIV, 342.

‡ H. H. Asquith, *The Genesis of the War* (London, 1923), p. 20.

§ 8 January, 1902; Fürst von Bülow, *Reden* (Berlin, 1907–1909), II, 33.

sion and monopolize for themselves the undeveloped regions of
the earth. Unfortunately the German Government adopted the
worst possible method to achieve its aim: it resorted to threats
which irritated but did not terrorize.* There was no little justification for challenging the French pretensions in Morocco in
the spring of 1905. But when the German action was accompanied by a demand for the dismissal of the French foreign
minister, M. Delcassé,† and by threats of war;‡ when Prince
von Bülow refused to consider proposals from M. Rouvier, the
French premier, for a large economic collaboration and a general political understanding;§ when King Edward VII learned

* The character of the German action is to be explained in part by divided counsels within the German Government. For the conflict between the Emperor, Bülow
and Holstein, see R. J. Sontag, "German Foreign Policy, 1904–1906," in *American
Historical Review*, XXXIII, 278–301 (January, 1928). See also E. N. Anderson, *The
First Moroccan Crisis, 1904–1906* (Chicago, 1930).

† Holstein told an emissary of Rouvier, the French premier, that if Delcassé remained in office, there was "no possibility of reaching an understanding with
France, now, to-day, to-morrow or in the near future"; memorandum of Holstein,
2 May, 1905; *G. P.*, XX, 359. Bülow called Rouvier's attention to "the serious
objections which M. Delcassé's remaining in office involves for Franco-German
relations." Bülow to Radolin, 30 May, 1905; *G. P.*, XX, 390.

‡ "We should not be able to say that the matter [the position of the Sultan of
Morocco] does not concern us, but should have to face the consequences if France
continues . . . the *politique d'intimidation et de violence* pursued by M. Delcassé."
Bülow to Radolin, 1 June, 1905; *G. P.*, XX, 393. The German ambassador in
Paris told the French premier that "we stand behind him [the Sultan] with all our
force [*mit unserer ganzen Macht*] in order to guarantee his independence and to
maintain the *status quo* in case participation in the conference is declined by France."
Radolin to Bülow, 11 June, 1905; *G. P.*, XX, 430; cf. A. Tardieu, *La France et les
alliances* (Paris, 1910), p. 221, and T. Wolff, *Das Vorspiel* (Berlin, 1925), p. 174.
The ambassador also referred to "all the serious consequences" of a French refusal. Radolin to Bülow, 22 June, 1905; *G. P.*, XX, 458. Bülow himself said to
the French ambassador in Berlin that "it seems to me that it [Morocco] is not
worth a war" and spoke of "the uncertain and perilous situation." Bülow to
William II, 26 June, 1905; *G. P.*, XX, 478. In October, Bülow, commenting on an
Italian newspaper article, observed: "The *Italie* is wrong in thinking that a Franco-
German war was out of the question during the summer because Germany would
never have made war on account of Morocco. The situation was then more serious
than the *Italie* assumes." Bülow to Monts, 24 October, 1905; *G. P.*, XX, 405, note.

§ Rouvier approached the German ambassador in Paris through an intermediary
(Radolin to Bülow, 1 May, 1905; *G. P.*, XX, 355–357), sent a confidant to talk
with Holstein (memorandum of Holstein, 2 May; *G. P.*, XX, 357–359) and made
an overture through the Italian statesman Luzatti (Monts to Bülow, 2 May; *G. P.*,
XX, 362). Finally he despatched Eckardstein to Karlsruhe to see William II personally. According to Eckardstein's account, he was authorized to offer Germany
a coaling station on the Atlantic coast of Morocco and French participation in the
Bagdad Railway, but he was not allowed by Bülow to meet the Emperor. H.
Freiherr von Eckardstein, *Die Isolierung Deutschlands* (Leipzig, 1921), pp. 99–114;
cf. *G. P.*, XX, 368–370. Rouvier made a final effort after the fall of Delcassé.
Flotow to Bülow, 9 June, 1905; *G. P.*, XX, 425.*

that the Emperor William had induced the Tsar Nicholas to sign a treaty of alliance (at Björko, on 24 July, 1905)* which was to be the preliminary to a Russo-German-French alliance,† the moral for France and Great Britain was obvious. They concluded that the real purpose of German policy in Morocco was to break up the Anglo-French entente‡—and proceeded to

* The negotiations for a Russo-German alliance are given in *G. P.*, XIX, 301–350 (autumn of 1904), 423–528 (July-December, 1905); and *Красный Архив* [Red Archive] (Moscow, 1922–), V, 5–49, translated into German in *KSF*, II, 453–501 (November, 1924). See also A. P. Izvolski, *Recollections of a Foreign Minister* (Garden City, N. Y., 1921), pp. 27–73; *The Memoirs of Count Witte* (Garden City, N. Y., 1921), pp. 415–439; E. J. Dillon, *The Eclipse of Russia* (New York, 1918), pp. 312–370; A. Savinsky, *Recollections of a Russian Diplomat* (London, 1927), pp. 96–127.

† Eckardstein, *Lebenserinnerungen*, I, 218; *Isolierung Deutschlands*, p. 171. Sir S. Lee, *King Edward VII: a Biography* (London, 1927), II, 354–369, does not state whether, as Eckardstein affirms, King Edward learned of the treaty. The British ambassador in St. Petersburg was not able to learn what took place at Björkö. Hardinge to Lansdowne, 1 August, 1905; *B. D.*, IV, 95. His French colleague was, however, immediately suspicious, for he had been informed that the German Emperor "warned the Emperor against any policy combined with England and France tending to isolate Germany" and that "the Emperor Nicholas agreed that such a policy would be contrary to interests of Russia." Hardinge to Lansdowne, 3 August, 1905; *B. D.*, III, 127. In the autumn, the British Government learned that the Russian ambassador in Paris had suggested to the French Government "an arrangement under which France, Russia and Germany would combine as a counterpoise to the Anglo-Japanese Alliance." Lansdowne to Bertie, 25 October, 1905; *B. D.*, IV, 217. "It is not clear that the British Government ever saw the text of the Björkö Treaty. But Lord Newton has informed the Editors that Lord Lansdowne in a private letter to Mr. R. T. Tower, of August 20, 1905, said that the communication received from him was the 'only account having any pretense to authenticity of what passed' at Björkö. No trace has been found of this communication in the Foreign Office Archives." Editorial note, *B. D.*, IV, 95. An excerpt from the letter is printed in Lord Newton, *Lord Lansdowne: a Biography* (London, 1929), p. 338: "The Kaiser's talk is ever of alliances and political combinations, and he gave utterance on the cruise to his cherished idea of being able to effect a coalition between Germany, France, and Russia, to the exclusion of Great Britain." Tower derived his information from a member of the Emperor's suite, who sat next to the Tsar at the luncheon following the signature of the treaty.

‡ The German Government undoubtedly desired a share of Morocco in the event of partition, and approached Spain with reference to the Sus valley in the southern part of the country. Richthofen to Radowitz, 24 September, 1903; *G. P.*, XVII, 355. Radowitz to foreign office, 29 September, 1903; *G. P.*, XVII, 359. But the German Emperor's statement to the King of Spain that "we desired *no territorial acquisitions* there" (William II to Bülow, 16 March, 1904; *G. P.*, XVII, 363) tied the hands of the foreign office, and it was forced to fall back on a policy of prestige. "Not only on material grounds," declared Holstein (memorandum of 3 June, 1904; *G. P.*, XX, 208), "but even more for the maintenance of her prestige must Germany raise a protest against the contemplated absorption of Morocco by France." "Our interests in Morocco," said Bülow nearly a year later, "are the same as those of other commercial nations, and are important enough to make it incompatible with our dignity that the conditions under which Morocco shall exist shall be arranged without our consent or even our participation." Bülow to Monts, 3 April, 1905; *G. P.*, XX, 295. But the aim of getting part of Morocco remained. Bülow declared that the Emperor's statement to Alfonso XIII that he

strengthen it. In the spring of 1905 the British Government stated that if Germany were to ask for a port on the Moorish coast,

we should be prepared to join French Government in offering strong opposition to such a proposal, and beg that if question is raised French Government will afford us a full opportunity of conferring with them as to steps which might be taken in order to meet it. German attitude in this dispute seems . . . most unreasonable having regard to M. Delcassé's attitude and we desire to give him all the support we can.*

It further proposed that

our two Governments should continue to treat one another with the most absolute confidence, should keep one another fully informed of everything which came to their knowledge, and should, so far as possible, discuss in advance any contingencies by which they might in the course of events find themselves confronted.†

This was not the offer of an offensive and defensive alliance, as was believed in France at the time‡ and is apparently still

"desired no territory in Morocco," while it had to be followed at the moment, "is naturally not binding for ever." Germany therefore had the alternative "of leaving Morocco to the French now without any worthwhile compensation for Germany, or of trying to prolong the existence of the Shereefian Empire in the expectation of a change in the situation that would be favorable to us." The task of the German minister in Morocco was therefore "to keep the future open for the maintenance of German interests." Bülow to Tattenbach, "*selbst entziffern*," 30 April, 1905; *G. P.*, XX, 352. Although Bülow often denied that Germany wished to shatter the Anglo-French entente, this hope was certainly cherished within the German foreign office. "The *rapprochement* of France with England began immediately after Fashoda, when the French saw that they could accomplish nothing *against* England," said Holstein. "Similarly the French will begin to consider a *rapprochement* with Germany only when they shall have seen that the friendship of England—which after the last elections must always be only platonic—is not sufficient to secure Germany's consent to the acquisition of Morocco by France, but that Germany must be conciliated for her own sake." Memorandum of Holstein, 22 February, 1906; *G. P.*, XXI, 208.

  * Lansdowne to Bertie, 22 April, 1905; *B. D.*, III, 72–73.
  † Lansdowne to Bertie, 17 May, 1905; *ibid.*, III, 76.
  ‡ In October, 1905, the Paris *Matin* published a series of revelations, emanating obviously from Delcassé, according to which the British Government had promised that in the event of a German attack on France, the British fleet would seize the Kiel Canal and 100,000 British troops would be landed in Schleswig-Holstein —a grotesque tale, for the British fleet could not have seized the canal, and "a careful inquiry made in 1906 disclosed that to put even 80,000 men on the Continent, a period which might well be over two months was the minimum required." Viscount Haldane, *Before the War* (London, 1920), p. 165. The British Government denied at the time, both privately to the German Government (Metternich

believed in that country,* but it marked a stage in the development of the Entente.

to Bülow, 16 June, 28 June, 9 October, 1905; G. P., XX, 630, 636, 663) and publicly, and has repeated the denial since the war (Asquith, p. 91; Sir A. W. Ward and G. P. Gooch, *The Cambridge History of British Foreign Policy* [Cambridge, 1923], III, 342–343) that any offer of alliance was made to France. According to Lord Sanderson, who was permanent under-secretary of the British foreign office in 1905, "we went no farther than warning the German Government that if Germany attacked France in connection with the Entente we could not undertake to remain indifferent. . . . There was a good deal of loose talk in naval circles and in some high quarters of a possible expedition to Schleswig in the possible event of war. I do not believe that such a measure was ever seriously entertained." Sanderson to Temperley, 17 August, 1922; B. D., III, 87. On the other hand, A. Mévil, *De la paix de Francfort a la conférence d'Algésiras* (Paris, 1909), pp. 292–296, says that at the session of the French council of ministers on 6 June, 1905, at which Delcassé resigned, the foreign minister stated that he had received the offer of a British alliance. In the *Figaro* of 24 March, 1922, Delcassé himself stated that he had received the offer 48 hours before. One of his colleagues, M. Bienvenu-Martin, wrote (*Temps*, 19 March, 1922): "These overtures were not limited to mere *pourparlers;* written notes were already exchanged." The mystery can hardly be cleared up until the French documents for this period are published, but the statement of M. Bienvenu-Martin suggests a clue. When the British ambassador in Paris, Sir Francis Bertie, transmitted to Delcassé Lord Lansdowne's statement of 22 April (see above), he changed the order of the sentences (probably with the object of guarding the cipher), placing first the sentence which Lansdowne put last: "His Britannic Majesty's Government considers that the conduct of Germany in the question of Morocco is most unreasonable, in view of the attitude of M. Delcassé, and they desire to give his Excellency all the support in their power; it seems not impossible that the German Government may ask for a port on the coast of Morocco; His Britannic Majesty's Government would be prepared to join the Government of the Republic in offering strong opposition to such a proposal and request that if the question were raised M. Delcassé will give full opportunity to His Britannic Majesty's Government to concert with the French Government as to the measures which might be taken to meet it." Bertie to Grey, 13 January, 1906; B. D., III, 175. Cf. Bertie to Lansdowne, 25 April, 1905; B. D., III, 75. This was a stronger statement than Lansdowne had authorized. Lansdowne evidently perceived the difference; for when the French ambassador in London, Paul Cambon, thanked him, in the name of Delcassé, for the assurances that "henceforth, if circumstances require it, if for example we have serious reasons for fearing an unjustified aggression on the part of a certain Power, the British Government would be quite ready to concert with the French Government as to the measures to be taken," Lansdowne insisted on repeating "in my own language the substance of my remarks upon that occasion." He accordingly communicated to Cambon the second statement quoted in the text above, which was certainly less explicit. Lansdowne to Cambon, 25 May, 1905, enclosed in Lansdowne to Bertie, 31 May, 1905; B. D., III, 77–78. Bertie's note of 24 April may, therefore, have been the basis of Delcassé's belief that Great Britain had offered an alliance, although this does not tally with the latter's statement that he received the offer on 4 June. It has been suggested that King Edward, during a visit to Paris in May, hinted to Delcassé that in case of war Great Britain would intervene on the side of France (Ward and Gooch, III, 343; Eckardstein, *Isolierung Deutschlands*, p. 105). When, however, the British ambassador in Berlin reported Holstein as complaining of "the offer of His Majesty's Government to conclude an offensive and defensive alliance with France against Germany" (Lascelles to Lansdowne, 12 June, 1905; B. D., III, 81), King Edward minuted: "This is nearly as absurd as it is false." Lansdowne's biographer states that "there are no traces of any such undertaking in Lord Lansdowne's private papers." Newton, *Lord Lansdowne*, p. 343.

* Poincaré, I, 187, 221.

A second stage was passed in the early months of 1906 when military conversations were opened between the French and British general staffs ;* "a step," remarks Mr. Winston Churchill, "of profound significance and of far-reaching reactions":

Henceforth the relations of the two Staffs became increasingly intimate and confidential. The minds of our military men were definitely turned into a particular channel. Mutual trust grew continually in one set of military relationships, mutual precautions in the other. However explicitly the two Governments might agree and affirm to each other that no national or political engagement was involved in these technical discussions, the fact remained that they constituted an exceedingly potent tie.†

That the British Government did not intend these military conversations to constitute a binding engagement is indeed abundantly clear. Three times in the course of January, 1906, Sir Edward Grey, who had just become foreign secretary in the new Liberal cabinet, discussed with M. Paul Cambon, the French ambassador, what Grey described as "the great question," that is, whether Great Britain would support France in

---

* For the origins of the conversations see C. A'C. Repington, *The First World War, 1914–1918* (London, 1920), I, 2–14; *B. D.*, III, 172, 176 (nos. 211, 214). Some notes of the first conversations are given in D. S. MacDiarmid, *The Life of General Sir J. M. Grierson* (London, 1923), pp. 213–217. A statement of the French views is given in a general-staff note of 13 February, 1906, printed in *B. D.*, III, 438–440.

† W. S. Churchill, *The World Crisis, 1911–1914* (London, 1923), p. 32; American edition (New York, 1923), p. 27. "It is certain," remarks the French officer who began the conversations from the French side, "that the studies undertaken at this period did not bind the British Government, as it always formally declared. It is also not less certain that they would not have been carried through without the collaboration of a rather large number of officers. The result was that more and more the notion spread among them that in case of war they would have to intervene on our side, and that more and more the studies made in common appeared to them as constituting an engagement, if not absolute, at least moral, from which it was not possible for England to detach herself." Général Huguet, *L'intervention militaire britannique en 1914* (Paris, 1928), pp. 38–39. The conversations did not make great progress until 1910, when General (later Field-Marshal Sir Henry) Wilson became Director of Military Operations in the British war office. Between that date and 1914, complete arrangements in every detail were worked out for the transport of the British army to a position on the extreme left wing of the French army. According to Huguet (*ibid.*, 19–20), the British general staff at first wished to send the British army to Antwerp and Belgium, which doubtless explains the military conversations carried on with the Belgian staff in January-April, 1906 (*B. D.*, III, 186–203).

the event of war with Germany, and each time the answer was the same:

As far as a definite promise went, I was not in a position to pledge the country to more than neutrality [10 January].

These communications [*i. e.*, military conversations] might proceed between the French military Attaché and General Grierson direct; but it must be understood that these communications did not commit either Government [15 January].

He [M. Cambon] eventually repeated his request for some form of assurance which might be given in conversation. I said that an assurance of that kind could be nothing short of a solemn undertaking. It was one which I could not give without submitting it to the Cabinet and getting their authority, and that were I to submit the question to the Cabinet I was sure they would say that this was too serious a matter to be dealt with by a verbal engagement but must be put in writing . . . there would be difficulties in putting such an undertaking in writing. It could not be given unconditionally, and it would be difficult to describe the condition. It amounted in fact to this: that if any change was made, it must be to change the "entente" into a defensive alliance . . . should such a defensive alliance be formed, it was too serious a matter to be kept secret from Parliament. The Government could conclude it without the assent of Parliament, but it would have to be published afterwards. No British Government could commit the country to such a serious thing and keep the engagement secret. [31 January.]*

There was, then, no British commitment to France involved in the military conversations. In spite of the conversations, the British knew very little about the French military plans,† and when, on 5 August, 1914, the British statesmen and soldiers met to consider how they would conduct the war declared against Germany, they actually discussed how large a force

---

* Grey to Bertie, 10, 15 and 31 January, 1906; *B. D.*, III, 171, 177, 181.

† "Moreover, since there was no such undertaking the French authorities were forced to frame their plan of campaign not knowing whether they would or would not receive British assistance, while we, on our side, were not able to insist upon our right to examine the French plan in return for our co-operation. When the crisis arose there was no time to examine it, and consequently our military policy was for long wholly subordinate to the French policy, of which we knew very little." Field-Marshal Sir W. R. Robertson, Bart., *Soldiers and Statesmen, 1914-1918* (London, 1926), I, 49.

should be sent to France (or, indeed, whether it should not be sent to Belgium) and where it should be concentrated.*

Nevertheless, neither the discussions of August, 1914, nor the words addressed by Sir Edward Grey to M. Cambon in January, 1906, tell the whole story. On the earlier date the British foreign minister asked the French ambassador "to consider whether the present situation as regards ourselves and France was not so satisfactory that it was unnecessary to alter it by a formal declaration as he desired":

I again submitted to M. Cambon as to whether the force of circumstances bringing England and France together was not stronger than any assurances which could be given at this moment. I said that it might be that the pressure of circumstances —the activity of Germany, for instance—might eventually transform the "entente" into a defensive alliance between ourselves and France. . . . I did not think that people in England would be prepared to fight in order to put France in possession of Morocco. They would say that France should wait for opportunities and be content to take time, and that it was unreasonable to hurry matters to the point of war. But if, on the other hand, it appeared that the war was forced upon France by Germany to break up the Anglo-French "entente," public opinion would undoubtedly be very strong on the side of France.†

Here is the crux of the matter. Great Britain would not pledge herself in advance, but if Germany challenged her friendship with France, she would meet the issue. "My opinion is," wrote Grey, "that if France is let in for a war with Germany arising out of our agreement with her about Morocco, we cannot stand aside, but must take part with France."‡ And he set forth his reasons in a memorandum which shows how deeply the British

---

* Earl of Oxford and Asquith, *Memories and Reflections, 1852–1927* (London, 1928), II, 30; Churchill, pp. 231–233, American edition, pp. 248–250; Major-General Sir C. E. Calwell, *Field-Marshal Sir Henry Wilson, Bart.* (London, 1927), I, 157–159; Field-Marshal Viscount French, *1914* (New York, 1919), pp. 3–5; Robertson, I, 53–55.
† Grey to Bertie, 31 January, 1906; *B. D.*, III, 181.
‡ Grey to Bertie, private, 15 January, 1906; *B. D.*, III, 177.

foreign minister felt committed, even though he would not admit it to France.

If there is a war between France and Germany [he wrote] it will be very difficult for us to keep out of it. The *Entente* and still more the constant and emphatic demonstrations of affection (official, naval, political, commercial, Municipal and in the Press), have created in France a belief that we should support her in war. The last report from our naval attaché at Toulon said that all French officers took this for granted, if the war was between France and Germany about Morocco. If this expectation is disappointed the French will never forgive us.

Sentiment, however, was not the only consideration:

There would also I think be a general feeling in every country that we had behaved meanly and left France in the lurch. The United States would despise us, Russia would not think it worth while to make a friendly arrangement with us about Asia, Japan would prepare to re-insure herself elsewhere, we should be left without a friend and without the power of making a friend and Germany would take some pleasure, after what has passed, in exploiting the whole situation to our disadvantage, very likely by stirring up trouble through the Sultan of Turkey in Egypt. As a minor matter the position of any Foreign Secretary here, who had made it an object to maintain the *entente* with France, would become intolerable.

"On the other hand," he continued, "the prospect of a European war and of our being involved in it is horrible"; and he therefore proposed to tell the French ambassador if necessary that "a great effort and if need be some sacrifice should in our opinion be made [by France with respect to Morocco] to avoid war." He also had a further point of view:

The door is being kept open by us for a *rapprochement* with Russia; there is at least a prospect that when Russia is re-established we shall find ourselves on good terms with her. An *entente* between Russia, France and ourselves would be absolutely secure. If it is necessary to check Germany it could then be done.

And he concluded:

There is a possibility that war may come before these suggestions of mine can be developed in diplomacy. If so it will only be because Germany has made up her mind that she wants war and intends to have it anyhow, which I do not believe is the case. But I think we ought in our own minds to face the question now, whether we can keep out of war, if war breaks out between France and Germany. The more I view the situation the more it appears to me that we cannot, without losing our good name and our friends and wrecking our policy and position in the world.*

Germany, by her Moroccan policy had brought about the very situation between Great Britain and France which she dreaded most and which her policy was intended to prevent.

So also as regards Russia. M. Izvolski, who as Russian foreign minister negotiated the understanding with Great Britain, warned perhaps by the experience of M. Delcassé, took the position that "a treaty with England can lead to the expected results only if this agreement calls forth no objections from Germany,"† and he promised the German Government that Great Britain and Russia would not settle matters affecting German interests without the consent of Germany.‡ He was in fact ready to make an agreement with Germany.§ The British also offered assurances that the agreement was not directed

---

* Memorandum of Grey, private, 20 February, 1906; *B. D.*, III, 266–267.

† Statement of Izvolski to the Russian council of ministers, 1 February, 1907; Siebert, p. 316.

‡ Schoen to foreign office, 20 May, 1906; Metternich to Bülow, 8 September, 1906; *G. P.*, XXV, 13, 22. Izvolski to Benckendorff, 19 December, 1907; Siebert, p. 319.

§ Freiherr von Schoen, *Erlebtes: Beiträge zur Geschichte der neuesten Zeit* (Stuttgart, 1921), p. 37. Izvolski said to a Russian diplomatist shortly after the conclusion of the agreement: "We must beware of concluding *general* treaties of alliance. On the contrary, a really sound policy and a *healthy egoism* require the conclusion of all sorts of arrangements with all sorts of Powers for the solution of *definite* problems which may little by little lead us eventually to new combinations *in general* world politics. . . . I am quite ready to take part in friendly and confidential conversations with Germany with reference to a number of practical and specific questions in which the two empires can very well march together on the beaten path of their traditional friendship." Baron M. de Taube, *La politique russe d'avant-guerre et la fin de l'empire des tsars (1904–1917)* (Paris, 1928), p. 139. An effort was made to negotiate with Germany a secret agreement with reference to the Baltic Sea. Cf. *G. P.*, XXXII, 463 ff.

against Germany.* But when Austria-Hungary impeded the
work of reform in Macedonia by securing a concession from
the Turkish Government to build a railway through the Sandjak
of Novi Bazar, when Germany supported the Austrian scheme,
inevitably the British and Russian Governments, who were the
sponsors of Macedonian reforms, drew closer together. At the
meeting of King Edward VII and the Emperor Nicholas II at
Reval in June, 1908, Sir Charles Hardinge, the representative
of the British foreign office, while he made no attempt "to depart from the standpoint of concrete agreements, the existing
ones or the prospective ones, or to draw us into general political
combinations" and stated that "the British Government sincerely desires to maintain the very best relations with [Ger-
many]," threw out a hint for the future:

One cannot close one's eyes to the fact that if Germany
should continue to increase her armaments at the same accelerated pace, a most alarming and strained situation might arise in
Europe in seven or eight years. Then, without doubt, Russia
would be the arbiter of the situation; it is, for this reason, that
in the interest of peace and the preservation of the balance of
power, we desire that Russia should be as strong as possible on
land and at sea.†

M. Izvolski, for his part, was equally cautious:

Russia [he reminded Sir C. Hardinge] is always in a difficult
position vis-à-vis of Germany, owing to the military supremacy
of the latter Power on the frontier, that in Germany there is
very great nervousness as to future political developments
among the Powers,‡ and that the age and indifferent health of
the Emperor of Austria are a source of uneasiness as to the
future. It was imperative therefore that Russia should act with
the greatest prudence toward Germany, and give the latter
Power no cause for complaint that the improvement of the
relations of Russia with England had entailed a corresponding
deterioration of the relations of Russia toward Germany.§

---

* Metternich to Bülow, 26 April, 8 September, 1906; G. P., XXV, 9, 22. Bülow
to foreign office, 15 August, 1907, quoting Hardinge; G. P., XXIV, 6.
    † Izvolski to Benckendorff, 19 June, 1908; Siebert, pp. 777–778.
    ‡ For the German nervousness over the meeting at Reval, see G. P., XXV, 439–
494.   § Report of Hardinge, June, 1908; B. D., V, 238.

Nevertheless the Russian premier, M. Stolypin, told one of the British visitors that "the German frontier was his one and only thought and he was devoting all his life to make that frontier impregnable against Germany, both in men and munitions, and strategic arrangements."* No new agreements were concluded between Great Britain and Russia;† but the Tsar "expressed his profound conviction that the friendly sentiments which now prevail between the two Governments could only mature and grow stronger with the progress of time to the mutual advantage of the two countries."‡ The German ambassador in St. Petersburg was not wrong when he affirmed that the Anglo-Russian entente "took a step forward."§

Real impulsion to the Triple Entente was first given by the Bosnian crisis of 1909–1909. The annexation of Bosnia-Herzegovina by Austria-Hungary apparently took the German Government by surprise, at least at the moment at which it was announced,‖ and the German Emperor was furious, not only because he had not been consulted, but because he feared that

---

* Admiral Lord Fisher, *Memories* (London, 1919), p. 237.

† In the diary of A. A. Polovtzev, a member of the Council of the Empire, the following entry occurs under date of 13 June, 1908: "At the Council it was stated that at the meeting of the two monarchs Edward promised our emperor to obtain the opening of a free passage through the Dardanelles for our fleet." *Красный Архив*, IV, 128. There is not a word about this in Hardinge's report (*B. D.*, V, 237–245), in Lee, II, 590–594 ("The King in conversation with the Tsar touched upon family matters only, and political matters were not mentioned"), or in Izvolski's letter to Benckendorff informing him of the results of the meeting (Siebert, pp. 777–779). Whether Izvolski gave an incorrect account to the Council of the Empire, or whether King Edward did talk politics and promised to use his influence with his ministers in favor of Russian desires, cannot be determined.

‡ Report of Hardinge; *B. D.*, V, 243.

§ Pourtalès to Bülow, 12 June, 1908; *G. P.*, XXV, 452. Both the Russian and the British Government endeavored to reassure Germany. Pourtalès to Bülow, 14 June, 1908; Metternich to Bülow, 15 June; *G. P.*, XXV, 458–462. Shortly before the Reval meeting the German Emperor made a speech at Döberitz in which he was reported to have said: "It seems likely that people wish to isolate and provoke us. We shall be able to put up with it. The Teuton has never fought better than when he has been brought to bay. So let them attack us; we shall be ready!" It was denied that the Emperor had used the words "isolate" and "provoke"; according to O. Hammann, *Um den Kaiser* (Berlin, 1919), p. 48, "the version was not disputed, but only called in doubt, and therefore really believed for the first time."

‖ A hint was conveyed early in September (Schoen to Bülow, 5 September, 1908; *G. P.*, XXVI, 26–27), but the first positive information was sent to Berlin only at the end of the month (Aehrenthal to Bülow, 26 September, 1908; *Ö.-U. A.*, I, 99–102; *G. P.*, XXVI, 35–39). The annexation was proclaimed on 6 October.

it might precipitate the partition of Turkey and lead to a European war.* But the German chancellor, Prince von Bülow, had during the summer declared that "the needs, interests and wishes of Austria-Hungary must be decisive for our attitude in all Balkan questions."† He therefore decided to support the policy of the Vienna Cabinet, and support it he did in the most vigorous fashion. Rejecting entirely the contention of the Entente Powers that the matter should be referred to a European conference,‡ he finally addressed to Russia a note which was described by the Russian foreign minister as "a diplomatic ultimatum"§ and made a demand upon Great Britain which was

---

* See his comments in *G. P.*, XXXVI, 43, 53–54, 112. He described the Austrian policy as "frightful stupidity."

† Circular of Bülow to Prussian ministers, 25 June, 1908; *G. P.*, XXV, 477. Communicated to Tschirschky, ambassador in Vienna; Bülow to Tschirschky, 29 June; *G. P.*, XXV, 482. He argued that the development of the Triple Entente compelled Germany to draw closer to Austria-Hungary; to Tschirschky he expressed the opinion that "Austria is much stronger than she herself thinks."

‡ The Central Powers were ready to accept a conference only on condition that it confined itself to registering and recognizing the *fait accompli* of the annexation.

§ Nicolson to Grey, 23 March, 1909; *B. D.*, V, 728. The incident has been the subject of bitter controversy. By the middle of March the deadlock between the two rival diplomatic groups was still unbroken, the Entente Powers demanding that the Bosnian question be submitted to a conference, Germany and Austria refusing. The Russian Government, however, had decided that it could and would not go to war on the issue, and had advised Serbia to drop her claim for territorial compensations and leave her interests to the Powers. Izvolski to Sergeyev, Russian minister in Belgrade; 27 February, 1909; Siebert, p. 78. On the other hand, Serbia was not ready to give a declaration satisfactory to Austria, and the war party in Austria, which for months had been clamoring for war against Serbia, was getting the upper hand. Thereupon the German Government, which had hitherto shown little disposition to mediate, made a proposal to Russia: Germany would request Austria to invite the Powers to give their formal sanction to the annexation of Bosnia by an exchange of notes (instead of through a conference) if Russia would promise beforehand to give her sanction when invited by Austria to do so. Bülow to Pourtalès, 14 March, 1909; *G. P.*, XXVI, 669–670. Izvolski, knowing that Russia could not go to war on the issue, was disposed to accept the proposal; but fearing that Austria might then attack Serbia, returned an evasive answer which left the door open for a conference. Pourtalès to Bülow, 20 March; *G. P.*, XXVI, 691–692. Whereupon Bülow sent the following instructions to the German ambassador in St. Petersburg: "Please say to M. Izvolski that we learn with satisfaction that he recognizes the friendly spirit of our proposal and seems willing to accept it. . . . But before we make the proposal to Austria-Hungary, we must know positively that Russia will answer the Austrian note by giving her consent and declare her formal consent to the nullification of Article 25 without any reservation. Please say to M. Izvolski in clear-cut fashion that we expect a precise answer—yes or no; we must regard any evasive, conditional or unclear answer as a *refusal*. We should then draw back and let things take their course. The responsibility for all subsequent events would then fall on M. Izvolski exclu-

resented (and refused) as an unwarranted use of pressure.*
The result of the German intervention was simply to make the

sively, after we had made a last sincere effort to help him clear up the situation in
a manner that he could accept." Bülow to Pourtalès, 21 March; *G. P.*, XXVI,
693–694. As it stands, the document is not an ultimatum, in the technical sense
of that word, and the official German view then and later was that the *démarche*
offered Izvolski a convenient way of escape from the impossible situation in which
he found himself. The assistant of Izvolski, Charykov, was even reported to have
said that "it was a great service which Germany had rendered to Russia"; G. von
Jagow, *Ursachen und Ausbruch des Weltkrieges* (Berlin, 1919), p. 18. The note was
drafted by Kiderlen-Wächter, then German minister in Bucharest and later (1910–
1912) foreign minister, who was substituting for Baron von Schoen, the foreign
minister. "I have finally succeeded in having clear and plain language used to
Izvolski," he wrote on 20 March; E. Jaeckh, *Kiderlen-Wächter: der Staatsmann
und Mensch* (Berlin, 1924), II, 26. Holstein congratulated him on his " 'nerve' in
imposing this humiliation on Izvolski"; *ibid.*, II, 29. Kiderlen himself boasted to
a Rumanian politician: "I knew the Russians were not ready for war, that they
could not go to war in any case, and I wanted to make what capital I could out of
this knowledge. . . . Never would Schoen and Co. have ventured to do what I
did on my own responsibility"; T. Jonescu, *Some Personal Impressions* (New York,
1920), p. 62. Schoen admits that the language was "very forceful"; Schoen, p. 79.
Izvolski understood that he was "confronted by the alternatives of an immediate
regulation of the annexation by an exchange of notes or the invasion of Serbia"
(Izvolski to Benckendorff and Nelidov, 23 March, 1909; Siebert, p. 104); his agitation was so great that he yielded to the German demand without waiting to consult the French and British Governments, much to the annoyance of the British
ambassador in St. Petersburg (Nicolson to Grey, 23 March, 24 March; *B. D.*, V,
728, 732–733, 736). The Austrian ambassador in St. Petersburg reported that "the
Russian minister, who up to that time was laboring under the delusion that Germany would play the conciliatory rôle of mediator toward both sides, suddenly
not only came to see the incorrectness of his calculations, but thought he perceived
in the words of Count Pourtalès a formal ultimatum, which caused him, without
consulting his English adviser [Nicolson], to betake himself to Tsarskoye Selo and
inform his imperial master of the critical situation." Berchtold to Aehrenthal, 4
April, 1909; *Ö.-U. A.*, II, 250. German historians have judged the German action
in its proper proportion. J. Haller, *Die Aera Bülow* (Stuttgart, 1922), p. 7, calls it
a "veiled threat"; E. Brandenburg, *Von Bismarck zum Weltkrieg* (Berlin, 1924),
p. 284, asks, "Was it necessary for Germany to intervene in this fashion and take
upon herself the odium of having humiliated Russia?"; A. Frankenfeld, *Oesterreichs
Spiel mit dem Kriege* (Dresden, 1928), p. 94, says that Germany demanded a "diplomatic capitulation." The last-named writer believes that the real purpose of the
démarche was to shatter the Triple Entente, which was also the opinion of the British ambassador in St. Petersburg (Nicolson to Grey, 24 March, 1909, private; *B. D.*,
V, 736).
    * Germany demanded that Great Britain accept the German proposal, as Russia
had done. Bülow to Metternich, 24 March, 1909; *G. P.*, XXVI, 703–704. Grey
replied that the German proposal "leaves the Servian question unsettled and makes
no provision for the solution of other questions relating to the Treaty of Berlin in
which England and the other European Powers are equally interested." Whereupon the German ambassador declared that "this was a very grave decision which
imperilled peace." Grey said point-blank that "the British Government would
never consent to act under pressure of this kind." Grey to Goschen, 25 March,
1909; *B. D.*, V, 739. "We were aware," wrote the permanent under-secretary of the
foreign office, "that Metternich was going to make the *démarche* here which had
been made at Petersburg, and we were ready for him, and purposely made our
reply somewhat stiff, as we resented German interference in this matter altogether."
Hardinge to Nicolson, private, 30 March, 1909; *B. D.*, V, 764.

Powers of the Entente feel more than ever the necessity of co-operation and of increasing their military and naval strength. "It was his earnest desire," said the Tsar to the British ambassador, "that the *entente* with England should be as closely knit as possible."* "Russia had so little got over her diplomatic defeat," M. Izvolski remarked several years later, "that she formed still closer relations with France and England."† In Paris and London, according to the Russian ambassador in the French capital, the opinion prevailed that

the Western Powers, together with Russia, must now pay attention to the systematic development of their armed forces in order to be able, if they are to be in a position not to fear a provocation of the Triple Alliance—and in this case Italy would separate herself from the Triple Alliance—to set up on their part demands which would restore the political balance which has now been displaced in favor of Germany and Austria.‡

"Let us keep an entente with Russia," said Sir Edward Grey, "in the sense of keeping in touch so that our diplomatic action may be in accord and in mutual support."§ And he was "very glad" to hear that

the recent German action at St. Petersburg in the Servian affair would not be easily forgotten by public opinion in Russia and in so far as it had been intended to prejudice relations between England and Russia it would have a contrary effect.‖

In short, the policy of Prince von Bülow, instead of smashing the Triple Entente, as he boasted in 1913,¶ gave it life and being.

It was not yet, however, a closely-knit combination. France's attitude in the Bosnian crisis was decidedly reserved,** and Rus-

---

* Nicolson to Grey, 14 April, 1909; *B. D.*, V, 783.   † Schoen, pp. 80–81.
‡ Nelidov to Izvolski, 1 April, 1909; Siebert, p. 114.
§ Grey to Nicolson, private, 2 April, 1909; *B. D.*, V, 772.
‖ Grey to Nicolson, 14 April, 1909; *B. D.*, V, 785.
¶ Prince von Bülow, *Imperial Germany* (New York, 1913), p. 65.
** Franco-German relations were then tense because of the seizure at Casablanca of some German deserters from the Foreign Legion; *G. P.*, XXIV, 327–374. A Franco-German convention of 9 February, 1909, with reference to Morocco (*G. P.*,

sia took scant interest in Morocco. "There is nothing in our agreements with France and Russia," said Sir Edward Grey, "which is directed against Germany, and therefore nothing to bar a friendly arrangement with Germany. We have no general political understanding either with Russia or France."* The German position, then, though uncomfortable, was not desperate, and the retirement of Prince von Bülow in July, 1909, so eased the situation that his successor, Dr. Theobald von Bethmann-Hollweg, was able to approach each member of the Entente with suggestions for a bargain. There were long negotiations with the French for a joint exploitation of Morocco, under the terms of the convention of February, 1909.† When the Tsar visited the Emperor William at Potsdam in November, 1910, verbal assurances were exchanged that "neither Power commits itself to any combination which might have an aggressive point directed against the other";‡ the German Government promised to act as an "honest broker" between Austria-Hungary and Russia in Balkan questions and affirmed that Austria was not pursuing an aggressive policy;§ an agreement was reached in principle whereby Russia came to terms with Germany about the Bagdad railway.|| With Great Britain

XXIV, 489–490) seemed to emphasize the French reluctance to adopt an active policy in the Bosnian question. Later the French Government agreed to a German proposal for collective representations to Serbia in the interests of peace (Grey to Bertie, 25 February, 1909; *B. D.*, V, 627) which made "a painful impression" in Russia (Izvolski to Nelidov, 27 February; Siebert, p. 76). The British foreign office appears to have thought France "rather 'wobbly' in her attitude." Hardinge to Nicolson, private, 30 March, 1909; *B. D.*, V, 764. The French ambassador in Constantinople remarked that "if the Russians are counting on their allies in this affair, they are putting their fingers in their eyes like babies"; upon which the German Emperor commented, "That is also our opinion, and our policy is based on it." Marschall to foreign office, 24 February, 1909; *G. P.*, XXVI, 620.

* Grey to Goschen, 1 September, 1909; *B. D.*, V, 803–804.

† *G. P.*, XXIX, 1–127; Germany, Auswärtiges Amt, *Denkschrift und Aktenstücke über deutsche Bergwerksinteressen in Marokko* (Berlin, 1910). France, Ministère des Affaires étrangères, *Documents diplomatiques. Affaires du Maroc* (Paris, 1910, 1912), V, 78–386, *passim;* VI, 54–375, *passim;* A. Tardieu, *Le mystère d'Agadir* (Paris, 1912), pp. 1–423.

‡ Speech of Bethmann-Hollweg in the Reichstag, 10 December, 1910; the draft of an agreement on nine points is given in *G. P.*, XXVII, 847–848.

§ Bethmann-Hollweg to Pourtalès, 8 November, 1910; *G. P.*, XXVII, 841. Sazonov to Nicholas II, 17 November, 1910; Marchand, II, 331–334.

|| The negotiations leading up to the convention of 19 August, 1911, are given in *G. P.*, XXVII, 903–963.

Herr von Bethmann endeavored to arrive at an understanding on the limitation of naval armaments.* Surely an accommodation should have been reached in one direction. Unfortunately, the chancellor, who desired the maintenance of peace, was never master of the political situation in Germany. Not only was he without practical acquaintance with international problems, having made his career in the Prussian bureaucracy, but he was handicapped by the lack of any clear and precise national policy. Germans desired for their country a more brilliant 'place in the sun' than it possessed, but where that place was to be or how it was to be reached was a matter of lively controversy. The militarists and the navy men saw in France and Great Britain respectively the rivals to be dealt with. Big business and high finance, on the other hand, dreamed of German expansion in the Near East which was bound, sooner or later, to arouse the opposition of Russia. Admiral von Tirpitz, the builder of the fleet, desired an understanding with Russia; the Deutsche Bank, the sponsor of the Bagdad Railway, worked for an agreement with Great Britain. The Emperor, for his part, proclaimed himself Admiral of the Atlantic and was ready, so to speak, to become Caliph of Bagdad. In this welter of conflicting aspirations, the German foreign office, as its own published documents reveal in the most astonishing manner, had no definite policy. So the well-meaning chancellor, who was keenly aware of Germany's dangerous position,† was pulled in opposite directions. He could never offer to any one Entente Power an inducement sufficient to wean it away from the other two, and to some extent he was forced to continue the very policies which had brought the Entente into existence. The despatch of the gunboat *Panther* to Agadir, in order to force a settlement of the Moroccan question, was dangerously

---

* G. P., XXVIII, 199–426; A. von Tirpitz, *Politische Dokumente*, vol. I, *Der Aufbau der deutschen Weltmacht* (Stuttgart, 1924), 163–196. The *British Documents on the Origins of the War* are not yet available for this period; a brief account of the British attitude is given in Sir E. T. Cook, *How Britain Strove for Peace* (London, 1914), pp. 18–27.

† T. von Bethmann-Hollweg, *Betrachtungen zum Weltkrieg* (Berlin, 1919), I, 1–12, 19–23, 90–103.

reminiscent of the methods of 1905,* and led to a threat of British intervention.† The negotiations of 1912 for a naval agreement and political understanding with Great Britain revealed once more the desire to disrupt the Entente.‡ The policy of the Bagdad Railway was not made any the more palatable because it was proving more and more successful. The German ambitions in Africa and the Near East were quite as legitimate as the rival ambitions of Great Britain, France and Russia; many Germans honestly believed that their imperialism was less selfish than that of their neighbors. One is struck by the fact, however, that whereas Great Britain, finding herself at the beginning of the century threatened with isolation, made large sacrifices to secure the friendship of France and Russia, Germany, although in a more delicate situation than Great Britain, was unwilling to renounce any of her desires. A policy of naval expansion, the development of an African empire, commercial and financial penetration of the Near East could each be justified. But to pursue all three courses at the same time was the worst possible policy, for it kept alive the distrust and suspicion of the Entente Powers, convinced them of the dangerous reality of German militarism, and made them more anxious than ever to act together.§

Hence it was that after 1912 the relations of France with Russia and both with Great Britain began to grow steadily more intimate. The tightening of the Franco-Russian Alliance has already been described.‖ That Great Britain drew close to France is abundantly clear, but how close is not easily defined. After 1910 the military conversations between the two

* The policy was that of Kiderlen-Waechter, who became foreign minister in 1910, and was only reluctantly accepted by the Emperor. G. P., XXIX, 137–454; Jaeckh, II, 119–146. *Affaires du Maroc*, VI, 386–640; Tardieu, *Le mystère d'Agadir*, pp. 423–605; J. Caillaux, *Agadir* (Paris, 1919). Marchand, I, 101–159, *passim;* Stieve, I, 96–157, *passim;* Siebert, pp. 414–448, *passim.*
† The speech of Mr. Lloyd George on 21 July, 1911. For the genesis of the speech see Viscount Grey of Fallodon, *Twenty-Five Years, 1892–1916* (London, 1925), I, pp. 224–226, American edition (New York, 1925), I, 215–217; Asquith, p. 148; Churchill, pp. 46–50, American edition, pp. 42–46.
‡ See below, pp. 55–56.
§ Of course the more they acted together, the more the Germans ascribed sinister intentions to them. What appeared to the Entente Powers as 'insurance' continued to look to the Central Powers like 'encirclement.'
‖ See above, pp. 18–22.

general staffs took on new life, and the French military plans were based on the expectation that a British force would form the extreme left wing of the French armies.* In the summer of 1912 the British, in view of the increasing naval strength of Germany in the North Sea, transferred most of their Mediterranean fleet to home waters, and the French concentrated their squadrons in the Mediterranean;† if no formal agreement was concluded,‡ "the moral claims which France could make upon Great Britain if attacked by Germany . . . were enormously extended."§ Indeed, according to Russian accounts, both Sir Edward Grey and M. Poincaré informed M. Sazonov that there existed between the French and British Governments "a verbal agreement, by virtue of which England had declared herself ready to come to the aid of France in the event of an attack by Germany."‖ The Russian foreign minister undoubtedly exaggerated, and perhaps deliberately misrepresented the nature of the Anglo-French relationship, for the testimony of both M. Poincaré¶ and Sir Edward Grey** leaves no doubt

* Protocol of the Franco-Russian military conference, 31 August, 1911; Marchand, II, 421; Stieve, I, 139. Maréchal Joffre, *La préparation de la guerre et la conduite des opérations* (Paris, 1920), p. 21; he speaks of "nos conventions militaires avec l'Angleterre," which is probably an exaggeration. France, Ministère de la Guerre, État-Major de l'Armée, Service historique, *Les armées françaises dans la grande guerre* (Paris, 1922), I, 19, states that England "had not been willing to give any engagement in writing," and p. 50, that "the general-in-chief could consider British military co-operation only as a probability [*éventualité*] and not as a certainty." Nevertheless, the most detailed arrangements had been made for the transport of a British expeditionary force of 6 divisions to the Belgian frontier in twelve days. Cf. Haldane, *Before the War*, pp. 156–182.

† The idea of naval co-operation appears to have been suggested by the British. Le Gouz de Saint-Seine to Delcassé, 11 December, 1911; *D. D. F.*, 3ᵉ série, I, 328.

‡ Winston Churchill, the first lord of the British admiralty, had submitted to the French naval attaché in London a draft project of co-operation between the two fleets, but as it left the two governments entire liberty of action, it was unsatisfactory to the French. It paved the way, however, for the negotiations about to be described. Poincaré, I, 215–216.

§ Churchill, p. 112, American edition, p. 115.

‖ Sazonov to Nicholas II, 17 August, November, 1912; Marchand, II, 339, 347; Stieve, II, 220, 291.

¶ Commenting on Sazonov's language, Poincaré says that he informed Sazonov of the military and naval conversations and adds: "M. Sazonov appears to have thought that I regarded these military agreements as a promise of support by the British Government. Such was not and could not have been my thought. . . . Sir Edward Grey certainly did not speak of an obligation, because there was none, because he had always refused to contract one." Poincaré, I, 185.

** Grey's version of what he said to Sazonov is as follows: "The question of whether we went to war would depend upon how the war came about. No British Government could go to war unless backed by public opinion. Public opinion

that there was no pledge on the part of Great Britain, written
or verbal. But there is also no doubt that the British foreign
secretary believed as strongly in 1912 as he had in 1906 that
if Germany attacked France, Great Britain must intervene, and
that all arrangements had been made by which that intervention, in case it were decided upon, could be made promptly
and efficiently.*

The situation was given a new turn in the autumn of 1912.
Precisely because the redistribution of the British and French
fleets had taken place without any definition of their respective
functions in the event of war, M. Poincaré pressed upon Sir
Edward Grey the view that by concentrating her ships in the
Mediterranean, France had left her northern coast at the mercy
of the German fleet and that she was entitled to know what
were the intentions of Great Britain.† Mr. Asquith, the British
prime minister, was reluctant to make any kind of commitment on paper,‡ but apparently the overture was seized upon
by that section of the cabinet which was suspicious of the Entente. "There was a demand," writes Grey, "that the fact of
the military conversations being non-committal should be put
into writing."§ And it was done. On 22 November, the for-

---

would not support any aggressive war for a *revanche*, or to hem Germany in, and
we desired to see difficulties between Germany and other Powers, particularly
France, smoothed over when they arose. If, however, Germany was led by her
great, I might say, unprecedented strength, to attempt to crush France, I did not
think we should stand by and look on, but should do all we could to prevent France
from being crushed. That had been our feeling at the time of the Algeciras
Conference in 1906 and again last year." Grey, I, 298, American edition,
I, 288.

* The military conversations were apparently not revealed to the British cabinet
until 1911. Explaining the situation to the prime minister, Grey said, "What they
[the military experts] settled I never knew—the position being that the Government was quite free, but that the military people knew what to do if the word
was given." Grey, I, 94, American edition, I, 91–92.

† He had made an earlier approach in April, 1912, when informed that Great
Britain had been negotiating for a neutrality agreement with Germany, but to no
avail. Poincaré, I, 173–174.

‡ Poincaré, I, 218–219. "Conversations such as that between Gen. Joffre and
Col. Fairholme," Asquith had complained to Grey in September, 1911, "seem to
me rather dangerous; especially the part which refers to possible British assistance.
The French ought not to be encouraged, in present circumstances, to make their
plans on any assumptions of this kind." Grey, I, 95, American edition, I, 92.

§ Grey, I, 96, American edition, I, 94.

eign secretary addressed to the French ambassador in London the following letter:

MY DEAR AMBASSADOR.—From time to time in recent years the French and British naval and military experts have consulted together. It has always been understood that such consultation does not restrict the freedom of either Government to decide at any future time whether or not to assist the other by armed force. We have agreed that consultation between experts is not, and ought not to be, regarded as an engagement that commits either Government to action in a contingency that has not arisen and may never arise. The disposition, for instance, of the French and British fleets respectively at the present moment is not based on any engagement to co-operate in war.

You have, however, pointed out that if either Government had grave reason to expect an unprovoked attack by a third Power it might become essential to know whether it could in that event depend upon the armed assistance of the other.

I agree that, if either Government had grave reason to expect an unprovoked attack by a third Power, or something that threatened the general peace, it should immediately discuss with the other whether both Governments should act together to prevent aggression and to preserve peace, and if so, what measures they would be prepared to take in common. If these measures involved action, the plans of the general staffs would at once be taken into consideration, and the Governments would then decide what effect should be given to them.

Yours, etc.,   E. GREY.

The ambassador replied on the following day in identic terms.* The Entente had advanced another step.

From the British point of view this exchange of notes offered two distinct advantages: (1) it did not have to be communicated to Parliament, for no treaty had been signed; (2) it left their hands free to decide at a given moment what they would do. Consequently, Mr. Asquith was able to assure Parliament in the future as he had done in the past that no

* Grey to Cambon, 22 November, 1912; Cambon to Grey, 23 November. First revealed by Grey in the House of Commons on 3 August, 1914; printed in Grey, I, 97–98; American edition, I, 94–96; Asquith, pp. 267–269.

engagements existed which would hamper its free decision,* and to affirm after the war that "the Entente was never converted into an alliance."† This was true in theory, the British cabinet believed it to be true in fact, and the sincerity of its belief is attested by its hesitations in the crisis of July, 1914.‡ Nevertheless, in spite of this documentary precaution a sense of moral obligation was undoubtedly created. That Sir Edward Grey himself was conscious of any such moral obligation cannot be stated with certainty,§ but he recognized it on 3 August, 1914, when a decision had to be made. In the light of subsequent events and present knowledge, it is clear that Mr. Winston Churchill was right when he asserted, three months before the exchange of notes: "Every one must feel who knows the facts that we have the obligations of an alliance without its advantages, and above all without its precise definitions."‖

The British Government has been sharply criticised for this policy of 'half-alliance.'¶ But the very great difficulty which confronted it should be recognized. The German navy was their constant preoccupation, since the admiralty, for technical reasons, did not believe that it was built for purposes of defense only;** it was elementary prudence to perfect military and naval arrangements with the only possible ally. But would it not, it has been argued, have been better to conclude a

---

* "As has been repeatedly stated, this country is not under any obligation not public and known to Parliament which compels it to take part in any war." H. H. Asquith, House of Commons, 24 March, 1913.

† Asquith, p. 57.

‡ This sentence is not meant to disguise the fact that Grey, and certain other members of the cabinet, believed that in the event of a German attack on France, British interests, regardless of any obligation, required Great Britain to go to the assistance of France. But as their opinions were personal and were not shared by many of their colleagues, the issue was, as will be seen, left open for the cabinet to decide.

§ But see above, pp. 36-38.

‖ Churchill to Grey and Asquith, 23 August, 1912; Churchill, p. 113, American edition, p. 116.

¶ H. W. Wilson, *The War Guilt* (London, 1928), from the Conservative point of view; Earl Loreburn, *How the War Came* (London, 1919), Liberal; H. Lutz, *Lord Grey und der Weltkrieg* (Berlin, 1927), especially pp. 47-91.

** Speech of Churchill before the Committee of Imperial Defence, 11 July, 1911; Asquith, pp. 77-79.

formal and open alliance with France? Apart from the fact that such an alliance would have encouraged the chauvinists in France and probably have angered the Germans almost to desperation, thereby precluding any chance of an Anglo-German agreement, which Sir Edward Grey sincerely desired to obtain, it would hardly have been accepted by Parliament and would have involved the fall of the Liberal government. A secret alliance was out of the question. In its dilemma, the British Government fell back on the course actually adopted. That this policy was open to objections cannot be gainsaid, but what other policy might have been pursued, with a due regard for British interests, is not evident.

The French, remarks M. Poincaré, "were glad to have the Entente at least reinforced." The exchange of letters "removed the difficulties in the way of a concerted redistribution of naval forces" and assured "permanent contact" with the Cabinet of London.* And it is not unlikely that the French read into the exchange more than the mere words stated. At any rate M. Poincaré is said to have remarked in February, 1913:

England is not bound to France by any definite political engagement, but the tone and the nature of the assurances given by the Cabinet of London allow the French Government, in the existing political conjunctures, to count upon the armed support of England in case of conflict with Germany.†

We shall see that in July, 1914, France made full use of the agreement reached in November, 1912.

The value attached by the British Government to the understanding with Russia can be gauged by several incidents. Although the question of the Straits was not dealt with in the negotiations leading up to the convention of 31 August, 1907, Sir Edward Grey thought that "some change in the direction desired by Russia would be admissible" and he was "prepared to discuss the question if Russia introduces it."‡ He was as

---

* Poincaré, I, 223.
† Izvolski to Sazonov, 27 February, 1913; Marchand, II, 32-33; Stieve, III, 76.
‡ Grey to Nicolson, 6 November, 1906; Grey, I, 161, American edition, I, 157.

good as his word, although this signified the abandonment of
an attitude maintained by British governments for more than
a century. In October, 1908, he accepted the principle of the
opening of the Straits, provided the consent of Turkey could
be gained.* Secondly, he told Count Benckendorff, the Russian ambassador in London, that if the Anglo-Russian entente
broke down, he would resign.† Thirdly, in the spring of 1914
the text of the letters exchanged with France in November,
1912, was communicated to the Russian Government.‡ And
along with this communication was the authorization for the
British and Russian naval authorities to begin conversations
on the model of the military conversations between the British
and French general staffs.§ Sir Edward Grey was at pains

* Grey to Izvolski, 14 October, 1908; *B.D.*, V, 441; E. A. Adamov, Константинополь
и Проливы [Constantinople and the Straits] (Moscow, 1925), II, 5. The version
in Marchand, II, 458, in French, is incomplete. The British Government insisted,
however, that the Straits must be open on equal terms to the ships of all nations
(the Russian plan was to open them to Russian men-of-war only) and thought
the moment inopportune for action.

† Benckendorff to Sazonov, 8 February, 1912; Siebert, p. 739.

‡ The Russian Government in the spring of 1914 wished to convert the Triple
Entente into a Triple Alliance, which should be published. Sazonov to Benckendorff, 19 February, 1914; Marchand, II, 307. S. D. Sazonov, *Fateful Years, 1909–
1916* (New York, 1928), pp. 130–131. The Tsar broached the matter to the British
ambassador. Buchanan to Grey, 3 April, 1914; *B. D.*, XI, 95. Grey, according to
Benckendorff, was not indisposed to the idea, but the political situation in Great
Britain would not permit its realization. Benckendorff to Sazonov, 25 February,
25 March, 1914; Marchand, II, 309, 313. At the suggestion of Izvolski, Sazonov
therefore fell back on the plan of asking Great Britain to enter upon as close relations with Russia as she had done with France. Izvolski to Sazonov, 18 March,
1914; Sazonov to Izvolski, 2 April, 1914; Marchand, II, 249–251, 255–256; Stieve,
IV, 73–75, 84–86. The matter was presented to Grey when he accompanied King
George V on a visit to Paris in April; Grey, somewhat to the surprise of the French
intermediaries, declared himself ready for "a closer union with Russia" and accepted the Franco-Russian plan, subject to the approval of the cabinet. Izvolski
to Sazonov, 29 April; Marchand, 259–262; Stieve, IV, 95–99. According to Grey
I, 283–288, American edition, I, 273–278, the French attached no strategic importance to Anglo-Russian naval conversations, but thought it desirable "for the purpose of keeping Russia in good disposition and of not offending her by refusing."

§ A representative of the Russian naval staff came to London, but the conversations made little progress (Siebert, pp. 821–827), presumably because the
news leaked out and caused a considerable sensation. Questions were asked in
Parliament to which Grey gave a disingenuous, though true, answer. Grey, I, 288–
290, American edition, I, 278–279. The German Government hinted that a *démenti*
would be in order (Jagow to Lichnowsky, 6 June, 1914; *G. P.*, XXXIX, 620); it
accepted Grey's statement in Parliament and an article in the *Westminster Gazette*
as satisfactory, but pointed out that such negotiations would lead to "a 'navy
scare' and the renewed poisoning of the relations with England which had been
slowly improving" (Bethmann-Hollweg to Lichnowsky, 16 June; *G. P.*, XXXIX,
630).

to point out that the letters exchanged with France did not create an alliance, that "rather they were intended primarily to put the contents of the military agreements in the proper light."* But the Russians, although they had not secured the formal alliance for which they hankered, were convinced that they had "accomplished the main thing, that is, substituting something tangible for the hitherto all too theoretical and peaceful basis of the entente,"† and expressed the "greatest satisfaction" with the recognition thus accorded to "the common interests of England and Russia."‡ The complaisance of the British Government was probably over-estimated by its associates. Nevertheless, the episode had a great importance, for it appeared to the Russians and the French as the final step in the consolidation of the Triple Entente, just as the German-Italian military convention of two months before marked, at least to a certain extent, the rejuvenation of the Triple Alliance.

Thus at last, on the eve of the tragedy of Sarajevo, the two great diplomatic groups stood face to face.

The Consequences of the Alliances

The play of the two diplomatic groups against each other was the crucial factor in the crisis of July, 1914, and was largely responsible for its fatal ending. But other crises—four of them in less than a decade—had been surmounted: why not that of 1914? Actually, the earlier crises had passed because this or that Power did not feel strong enough for war or did not consider the issue worth a war. France in 1905 was too weak to fight Germany, Germany in 1911 considered Morocco too dubious a cause; in 1908–1909 Russia was not militarily prepared to go to war when Austria-Hungary annexed Bosnia,

---

* Benckendorff to Sazonov, 19 May, 1914; Siebert, 814–815. Grey to Bertie, 21 May; Grey, I, 291–293, American edition, I, 281–283.

† Benckendorff to Sazonov, 18 May, 1914; Siebert, p. 813. The ambassador shrewdly pointed out to his chief that because of the general attitude of the Liberal party toward Russia, "an alliance would not have much value" and would actually "offer a very favorable terrain for agitation in the interest of Germany."

‡ Sazonov to Benckendorff, 28 May, 1914; Siebert, p. 818.

in 1912–1913, though better prepared, she said frankly that she would not fight for the sake of a Serbian port on the Adriatic. But each of these crises was followed (1) by a drawing together and tightening up of the alliances until, as we have seen, the circle was complete, and (2) by a general increase of armaments, about which a few words must be said.

Just as Germany took the first step which led to the ultimate division of Europe into two rival diplomatic groups, so it was unquestionably German example which forced the other Continental countries after 1871 to adopt universal military service. But France always kept a larger proportion of her population with the colors than her rival; it was not until 1913 that the German army exceeded the figure of one per cent of the population prescribed by the constitution as the peace strength of the German army. In the years before the war, the Russian army was larger than the German and the Austro-Hungarian put together; on the other hand, Russia did not conscript one per cent of her population, and her lack of railways reduced the effectiveness of her forces.* To try to deduce from the numbers of the armies or from the sequence of military laws the responsibility for this unending increase of soldiers is exceedingly difficult and distinctly futile. Likewise conclusions drawn from the amount of money spent on armaments have to be very cautious, partly because military and naval budgets of the different states did not include the same items. That Germany and Austria-Hungary spent less than France and Russia appears to be true; but there was probably a wide difference in the results obtained by the efficient and incorruptible German administration on the one hand and the easy-going

---

* The French estimated the strength of the German army in 1914, under the law of 1913, at 870,000 men; *Les armées françaises*, I, 38. According to German figures, the law would provide 761,000; Beilagen zu den stenographischen Berichten über die öffentlichen Verhandlungen des Untersuchungsausschusses (1. Unterausschuss) der verfassunggebenden Nationalversammlung, *Zur Vorgeschichte des Weltkrieges*, Heft 2 (Berlin, 1920) (cited hereafter as "*Zur Vorgeschichte des Weltkrieges*, II"), p. 107. The German estimate of the French army in 1914, under the law of 1913, was 882,500; *ibid.*, II, 110. The French figure was 736,000; *Les armées françaises*, I, 1, 30. On the other hand, the French and German estimates of the armies of the other Powers agreed rather closely.

and corrupt Russian bureaucracy on the other. As the British forces were raised on a volunteer basis, they were much more expensive to the state than the victims of the conscript system, and British expenditure cannot be fairly compared with that of the Continental Powers. The fact seems to be that every government, while balking sometimes at the extreme demands of its military and naval authorities,* created as large an army and navy as the economic resources and the public opinion of the country would permit. Yet these vast accumulations of men and *matériel* created neither actual security nor a feeling of security. Reports drawn up by the German general staff in December, 1912,† and May, 1913,‡ practically confess that in spite of forty years' military effort, in spite of the Triple Alliance, the position of the German Empire, as seen through general-staff spectacles, was threatened on all sides. A memorandum on the naval situation presented by Mr. Churchill to the British cabinet in December, 1913, is conceived in a similar strain.§ "With God's Help," said a Russian diplomatist, "the conflict may be postponed, but that it will come some day we must remember every hour, and every hour we must arm ourselves for it."‖

How completely all were caught in a vicious circle is shown most clearly in the negotiations carried on between Great Britain and Germany in 1912 with reference to a limitation of naval armaments and the attitude to be taken in the event of war. The British desired a limitation of armaments. The Germans said: We cannot discuss such a limitation unless Great

---

* The German general staff asked for three more corps in 1912–1913 than the government would grant; Bethmann-Hollweg prevented Tirpitz from getting as many ships as he wanted in 1912. Conrad von Hötzendorf often complained of the parsimony of the Austro-Hungarian Government. Lloyd George, as chancellor of the exchequer, publicly protested in January, 1914, against the ever-growing British naval estimates.

† E. Ludendorff, *Urkunden der obersten Heeresleitung* (Berlin, 1922), pp. 51–60.

‡ Urkunden des deutschen Generalstabes über die militärpolitische Lage vor dem Kriege, *Hat der deutsche Generalstab zum Kriege getrieben?* (Berlin, 1919), p. 10. T. von Schäfer, "Wollte Generaloberst v. Moltke den Präventivkrieg?" in *KSF*, V, 549–550 (June, 1927).

§ Churchill, pp. 174–177; American edition, pp. 184–186.

‖ Izvolski to Neratov, 20 December, 1911; Siebert, p. 448.

Britain will abandon the Triple Entente, for so long as you stand with France and Russia, they will cherish schemes of revenge or aggression. To which the British replied: So long as you go on adding to your navy, we cannot give up the insurance provided by the Entente, especially as you are protected by the Triple Alliance. If Admiral von Tirpitz was ready to yield on the fleet in return for a promise of unconditional neutrality,* Lord Haldane, the British negotiator, answered that Great Britain was bound by treaty to Portugal and Belgium and had certain obligations toward Belgium. Neither Power was willing to yield anything essential. The British insisted on both their naval supremacy and their diplomatic combinations, for thus the balance of power was turned against Germany. To restore the balance in their favor, the Germans wished to retain their freedom in the matter of armaments or to break up the Triple Entente. The position of each was logical, so long as the theory of equilibrium was the mainspring of European diplomacy.†

There was one man, however, who had a vision of a new order—Sir Edward Grey. Although the British foreign secretary assumed from time to time, as in the question of Morocco or at certain stages of the Bagdad Railway question, an attitude frankly hostile to Germany; although, as we have seen, he steadily strengthened the Triple Entente as a bulwark against possible German aggression—that was only one side of his activity. He was so far from pursuing a policy of encirclement that he told the Russian ambassador in London that the isolation of Germany would be the surest road to war;‡ for that reason he "accepted the Triple Alliance and made no attempt, however covert, to weaken it."§ In his mind, "the

---

* So he has averred in A. von Tirpitz, *Erinnerungen* (Berlin, 1919), p. 191; it is not clear, however, that he made such an offer at the time.

† The problem is examined in detail by the writer in "Lord Haldane's Mission to Berlin in 1912," in *The Crusades and Other Historical Essays Presented to Dana C. Munro* (New York, 1928), pp. 245–288, which is based on *G. P.*, XXXI, 1–227, and the narratives of the British and German negotiators.

‡ Benckendorff to Izvolski, 10 February, 1909; Siebert, p. 728.

§ Grey, II, 45; American edition, II, 45.

entente with France was not to be used against German policy
or German interests."* What he desired and worked for was
an understanding with Germany, on the condition, as he
phrased it, that it "must not put us back into the old bad relations with France and Russia."† If this could be achieved,
the way would be open to the creation of an effective Concert
of Europe. More clearly than any of his contemporaries, he
perceived not only that the competition in armaments must
have a fatal conclusion, but that before a limitation of armaments could be discussed the antagonism of the Great Powers
must be overcome by some method of co-operation. As he put
it on one occasion:

The British Government belonged to one group of Powers,
but did not do so in order to make difficulties greater between
the two European groups; on the contrary, we wished to prevent any questions that arose from throwing the two groups,
as such, into opposition.‡

So he was constantly recommending the Concert of Europe
to the Continental Powers. In the Bosnian crisis of 1908–1909,
he stood out for the principle that the affairs of the Near East
must be adjusted by the consent of all the Powers; how right
he was, was soon demonstrated, for Russia replied to the
settlement dictated by Germany and Austria-Hungary with a
great military and naval programme. If the Moroccan negotiations of 1911 between France and Germany had broken down,

---

* Grey, I, 120; American edition, I, 117.
† Speech to the Imperial Conference, 1911; Asquith, p. 124. "Good relations
with Germany could not be founded upon bad relations with France." Grey, I,
52; American edition, I, 51. "We desire to see France on good terms with Germany," Grey told the German ambassador in London at the beginning of his
secretaryship. "This is the one thing necessary to complete the comfort of our
own friendship with France." Grey to Lascelles, 9 January, 1906; B. D., III, 210.
‡ He was speaking to the German ambassador in London. Grey to Goschen,
24 June, 1914. Grey, I, 305; American edition, I, 294. Cf. his statement of 27
November, 1912: "To him, personally, the question of an Adriatic port [for Serbia]
was a matter of complete indifference. His efforts were inspired solely by the idea
of finding a solution which would prevent one or more of the Great Powers from
being drawn into the dispute. The consequences of such an extension of the war
would be incalculable, and it was to-day quite impossible to predict who might
then be involved in the struggle." Lichnowsky to foreign office, 27 November,
1912; G. P., XXXIII, 417–418.

it was Sir Edward Grey's intention to propose a European conference.* During the Balkan wars of 1912–1913 and after, not only did he refuse to embark on any course of action which would set off the Triple Entente against the Triple Alliance, but he insisted, sometimes to the annoyance of France and Russia, on associating Germany in every step. Ultimately he hoped to effect an agreement between the Powers that they would not attack each other. In 1912 he offered to exchange with Germany the following declaration:

The two Powers being mutually desirous of securing peace and friendship between them, England declares that she will neither make nor join in any unprovoked attack upon Germany and pursue no aggressive policy towards her.

Aggression upon Germany is not the subject and forms no part of any treaty, understanding, or combination to which England is now a party, nor will she become a party to anything that has such an object.†

In July, 1914, he declared that "my own endeavour will be to promote some arrangement to which Germany could be a party, by which she could be assured that no aggressive or hostile policy would be pursued against her or her allies by France, Russia and ourselves, jointly or separately."‡ Sir Edward Grey was anticipating by many years the Spirit of Locarno and the Pact of Paris.

For the failure to realize this lofty ideal, Sir Edward Grey was, in a sense, though unconsciously, himself responsible. His public statements, on the one hand, that Great Britain was not bound by any engagements, and his private sympathies, which were known to the French, on the other hand, encouraged both Continental groups to gamble, the one on British neutrality,§ the other on British support. But Grey's failure

---

* Grey, I, 233; American edition, I, 225. P. Cambon to Selves, 23 August, 1911; *Affaires du Maroc*, VI, 480. Benckendorff to Neratov, 5 July, 1911; Siebert, p. 426.
† Asquith, p. 56. Metternich to foreign office, 17 March, 1912; *G. P.*, XXXI, 181.
‡ Grey to Goschen, 30 July, 1914; *B. D.*, XI, 194.
§ Prince Lichnowsky, the German ambassador in London from 1912 to 1914, consistently and repeatedly warned his government that, although Great Britain was not bound by treaty, it would support France if the latter were attacked by

is to be explained not so much by his inconsistency as by the attitude of the Continental Powers, by the fact that the idea of Locarno was premature and incomprehensible. While both M. Poincaré and Herr von Bethmann-Hollweg co-operated with Sir Edward Grey in making the Concert a reality during the Balkan wars, it was not easy for them to keep their Russian and Austrian allies in hand, and the French as well as the German statesman was thinking always of preserving the solidarity of his diplomatic group; with the result that the long negotiations served rather to emphasize than to minimize the fundamental conflict between the two alliances. Each alliance, in fact, hoped to establish its supremacy in the councils of Europe. Each side hoped to accomplish this without recourse to a general war; but, because both felt reasonably sure of Great Britain, each was willing to run the risk of war, and to accept war, if that were necessary to establish its own supremacy. At the time of their inception the alliances guaranteed the peace of Europe; by 1914 their extension and their implications made it certain that an armed conflict in any part of Europe involving one of the great Powers automatically brought the others into the struggle.

In the decade before 1914 there were four possible sources of a European war: (1) the century-old antagonism between France and Germany; (2) the recently developed rivalry between Germany and Great Britain; (3) the curious situation existing between Austria-Hungary and Italy, who, although allies, were also bitter enemies; and (4) the fearful tangle of the Near East. A brief analysis of these problems will now be given.

Germany. But he was not believed. "I am disposed to think," wrote his chief in Berlin, "that you often take too black a view of things, even when you express the opinion that in the event of war England will *in all circumstances* take the side of France against us. After all we have not built our fleet for nothing, and I am persuaded that in the given case, England will consider very seriously whether it is then so simple and safe to play the part of France's guardian angel against us."[2] Jagow to Lichnowsky, 26 February, 1914; *G. P.*, XXXVII, 105.

FRANCE AND GERMANY

In the first decade of this century the relations of France and Germany were governed by the question of Morocco, and its pacific settlement, by the convention of 4 November, 1911, permitted the restoration of normal relations between the two countries. The effect of the prolonged controversy cannot, however, be measured in diplomatic terms. At the end of the last century the Dreyfus case and the conflict with the Church which grew out of it divided the French people against themselves, relaxed the authority and efficiency of the government, and left the national defenses momentarily paralyzed. The army was permeated by factional spirit, and the loyalty of its leaders was suspected by the country at large; the navy was affected by a decline of discipline; and a vague uneasiness developed as France's one ally, Russia, became increasingly involved in the Far East.

This lassitude of the nation, which the doughty Georges Clemenceau was once moved to describe as "incoherence," was suddenly challenged by the German Emperor's speech at Tangier (1905) and the subsequent Moroccan policy of his government. The nation reacted sharply against the factional excesses of the preceding years and established the republican groups in firm control. Confidence in the army revived, the rising generation showed its impatience with the quarrels of the politicians, and a 'new spirit,' as it was called at the time, unmistakably developed.* The *Panther's* 'spring' at Agadir (1911) came as a second challenge to this reviving national spirit, and the determined stand made against Germany was not only hailed by the country at large but strengthened its confidence in itself and in Great Britain, its partner in the Entente. The desire for a government strong at home and respected abroad brought in the ministry of M. Raymond Poincaré in January, 1912; this stimulus led a year later to the election of this strong personality as President, which was rather contrary to tradition.

* Cf. E. Rey, *La renaissance de l'orgueil français* (Paris, 1912).

M. Poincaré lost no opportunity to speak of the honor and dignity of France, urged the nation to hold its head high, and recovered for French diplomacy a leading position in the councils of Europe. With this renewed confidence, the nation went through the Balkan tension of 1912–1913 with calm and patience; while the government co-operated on an easy footing with Germany in forestalling the dangerous uncertainties which arose. Last of all, in the summer of 1913, the country, which had been strongly antimilitarist ten years before, accepted without undue opposition the burden of extending the period of military service from two to three years.

Some contemporary observers were seriously alarmed, and held M. Poincaré and his friends deliberately responsible for exciting the passions of the people, who were as a whole pacifically inclined.* But the German representatives in Paris, who more than any one else had reason to analyze the sentiment of France correctly and to report their judgments honestly, appear to have taken the developments rather calmly. The military attaché expressed the opinion that the new military law was an arithmetical necessity: the "lack of men" left France no alternative.† He believed that French opinion had accepted it because it saw in the increased army "an instrument of necessity which would protect France from a German attack and insure its position as a Great Power"; and he discounted any undue alarm:

* Notably the Belgian minister in Paris, some of whose reports are printed in *European Politics during the Decade before the War as described by Belgian Diplomatists* (Berlin, 1915), and B. Schwertfeger, *Zur Europäischen Politik 1897–1914* (Berlin, 1919), vol. IV, which are collections of documents taken from the Belgian archives during the German occupation. The French ambassador in Berlin, Jules Cambon, is reported to have said to his Belgian colleague: "Since the Dreyfus affair we have in France also a military and nationalist party which does not wish a *rapprochement* with Germany at any price and which encourages the aggressive tone of a large number of newspapers. The government would have to reckon with them and the party of which they are the mouthpiece, in case a serious incident should again occur between the two nations. The majority of the Germans and the French undoubtedly wish to live in peace. But a powerful minority in the two countries dreams only of battles, wars of conquest or of revenge. That is the danger, next to which one must live as next to a powder barrel which might be exploded by some imprudence." Beyens to Davignon, 20 February, 1914; *European Politics*, pp. 132–133.
† Report of Winterfeldt, 14 February, 1913; *G. P.*, XXXIX, 149.

As things stand at the moment, Germany has certainly every reason more than ever to keep a sharp eye on France from a military point of view, but it has no business considering the new French military law more threatening than it really is. After my previous experiences in Paris, I believe that I may confidently express the opinion that the practical result of the latest German military bill will, after its effective application, be something more real substantially than the gain which the French will ever secure from the three years' service which has been brought with such disproportionately great sacrifices. I should therefore consider it a mistake if the leaders of the *Wehrverein* should now endeavor to mislead the German people and make them shudder by an exaggerated emphasis on a supposed French superiority which must be immediately answered by counter-measures on the part of Germany.*

The ambassador was also far from being an alarmist. When the new military law was first introduced, he wrote:

In spite of the chauvinistic conduct of many circles and despite the general tendency to dream of recovering the "lost provinces," the sentiment of the country can on the whole be described as peace-loving. Aggressive intentions lie far from the thoughts of the ruling powers and the people. Even in military circles they find only isolated advocates, and even there, more in a tactical than in a political sense.

Though he characterized the new nationalistic spirit as "an open powder-keg in which at any time a spark may unexpectedly fall or be thrown by a frivolous hand," he did not contest that the French had some reason for their "deep mistrust" of Germany:

The false notion that through our armaments we are striving for a military hegemony in Europe intolerable to France has eaten so deeply not only into the masses but into the directing heads that it will not be easy to uproot it. And unfortunately the performances of our Pan-Germans have done only too much to provide the French with appropriate arguments for their nervousness.†

* Report of Winterfeldt, 20 August, 1913; *G. P.*, XXXIX, 208, 216.
† Schoen to Bethmann-Hollweg, 1 March, 1913; *G. P.*, XXXIX, 167–169.

In the autumn of 1913, he remarked:

The present government is obviously inspired by the wish to maintain and to intensify a better sentiment between the two nations, and it considers the best means to this end to be the conclusion of further formal understandings with us on questions which, if they remain unadjusted, must sharpen opposition and create friction. It is encouraged in this by the experience that during the Balkan crisis not only have France and Germany in the same fashion pursued a decided and plainly recognizable pacific policy, but on many not unimportant points have also taken parallel lines and have not everywhere followed their allies through thick and thin. At all events, in the one significant matter of desiring to maintain a Turkey that is capable of existence [*lebensfähig*].*

Finally in February, 1914, when Paul Déroulède, once the great apostle of *revanche,* died, Baron von Schoen went so far as to express this considered opinion:

The desire for military revenge [*die kriegslustige Revanche*], as it was incorporated in Boulanger and Déroulède, is a stage that is passed. It exists to-day, to be sure, but only in a theatrical sense. The wound of 1871 still burns in all French hearts, but no one is disposed to risk his or his sons' necks for the question of Alsace-Lorraine; a constellation would have to be set up which offered quite favorable and even easy prospects for the success of such a gamble. But this is becoming ever more unlikely. The hopes of reaching the goal through the help of Russia have long since proved deceptive . . . the idea is spreading more and more that the salvation of France must be sought in a better relationship with Germany.†

These German judgments are confirmed by what Frenchmen were saying in the years immediately preceding the war. A survey of the political literature of those days will naturally

---

* Schoen to Bethmann-Hollweg, 15 November, 1913; *G. P.,* XXXIX, 225. The Russian ambassador complained that in the sessions of the commission created to settle the financial questions arising out of the Balkans wars, the French and German delegates exhibited "a remarkable unanimity" of view. Izvolski to Sazonov, 28 August, 1913; Marchand, II, 142; Stieve, III, 268.
    † Schoen to Bethmann-Hollweg, 5 February, 1914; *G. P.,* XXXIX, 250-251.

reveal many diversities of opinion. Although *revanche* still had its protagonists who believed a French victory possible,* although the German economic penetration of France was beginning to cause resentment,† both political reconciliation‡ and economic co-operation were being openly discussed.§ If there were irreconcilables, there were also very many pacifists and anti-militarists, and the peaceful temper of the majority of Frenchmen cannot be seriously questioned.

Since the war, certain French statesmen, notably MM. Poincaré and Delcassé, have been attacked, chiefly by political opponents in their own country and by German *'innocentistes,'* as the apostles of *revanche* and the deliberate plotters of war. Inasmuch as M. Poincaré was born in Lorraine and on one occasion, after the war, remarked, *à propos* of his boyhood, that "I saw no other reason for my generation to go on living than the hope of recovering our lost provinces"; and since both as premier he used every diplomatic device to strengthen the alliance with Russia and as president ardently supported the revival of the three years' military service in 1913, his detractors have argued that the real object of his policy was to prepare for the day of *revanche* and, by supporting the Russian policy in the Near East, to find a propitious occasion for war. Support for this view was found in the testimony of a French diplomatist, George Louis, one-time ambassador in St. Petersburg, according to whose information M. Poincaré, early in 1914, was convinced that war

---

* M. Legendre, *La guerre prochaine et la mission de la France* (Paris, 1913); H. Maringer, *Force au droit* (Paris, 1913); Colonel A. Boucher, *La France victorieuse dans la guerre de demain* (Paris, 1911); Lieut.-Colonel Montaigne, *Vaincre* (Paris, 1913); General Palat, *Les probabilités d'une guerre france-allemande* (Paris, 1914).

† L. Daudet, *L'avant-guerre* (Paris, 1914); L. Bruneau, *L'Allemagne en France* (Paris, 1914).

‡ J. Grand-Carteret, *France-Allemagne-Maroc: une victoire sans guerre* (Paris, 1911); Laurent-Norard-Mercereau, *La paix armée et le problème d'Alsace* (Paris, 1913), a manifesto of 74 intellectuals in favor of *rapprochement;* A. Lalance, *Mes souvenirs, 1830–1914* (Paris, 1914), a plea by a distinguished Alsatian; M. Sembat, *Faites un roi, si non faites la paix* (Paris, 1913); J. Marais, *Amitié allemande* (Paris, 1914).

§ L. Coquet, *Politique franco-allemande* (Paris, 1908); H. Gaston, *L'Allemagne aux abois* (Paris, 1912); M. Ajam, *Le problème économique franco-allemande* (Paris, 1914); L. Hubert, *L'effort allemand: l'Allemagne et la France au point de vue économique* (Paris, 1911); M. Leroy, *L'Alsace-Lorraine* (Paris, 1914).

would come within two years and declared that "all my energy is being used to prepare us for it."* The same diplomatist believed that this was the object of the Franco-Russian alliance:

In the Alliance [he recorded in his notes] Constantinople and the Straits are the counterpart of Alsace-Lorraine. This is not written down in any agreement, but it is the ultimate purpose of which one thinks but does not speak. If the Russians open the question in their conversations with us, we should reply: "Yes, on the day when you can help us to recover Alsace-Lorraine."
(I have since found the same idea in the correspondence of Hanotaux and Montebello.)†

The charge was made, in short, that French policy, while pacific in form, had been belligerent in purpose, and the delay of the French Government in publishing its diplomatic correspondence was pointed to as the sign of a guilty conscience.

It is, however, a striking fact that in all the voluminous correspondence of M. Izvolski, the Russian ambassador in Paris, which contains innumerable expressions of the views of M. Poincaré and other French politicians, there is not a single reference to Alsace-Lorraine, not a single statement implying a desire for war, not a remark suggesting that the French Government was scheming to precipitate war. Even though the argument from silence is never conclusive, it is surprising that, with so many opportunities for indiscretion, nothing was let

* *Les carnets de Georges Louis* (Paris, 1926), II, 94. Louis was French ambassador in St. Petersburg from 1909 to 1913. His recall was asked for by the Russian Government in May, 1912, but was refused by Poincaré himself. In February, 1913, however, he was replaced by Delcassé. The incident has provoked a lively controversy. Cf. E. Judet, *Georges Louis* (Paris, 1925); Poincaré, I, 355–388, III, 114–119.

† *Les carnets de Georges Louis*, I, 136, entry dated "August, 1910." Hanotaux was French foreign minister from 1894 to 1898, and Montebello ambassador in St. Petersburg. In the eighteen-nineties it was generally believed that the French purpose in concluding the alliance with Russia was to prepare for the day of *revanche*; nothing, however, appears to have been further from the mind of the Russian Government, which did not ratify the military convention until the Tsar had convinced himself that France was pacific and would not attempt to use the alliance for the purpose of *revanche*. Cf. Montebello to Casimir-Périer, 17 December, 1893; *L'alliance franco-russe*, no. 90. W. L. Langer, *The Franco-Russian Alliance* (Cambridge, Mass., 1929), pp. 354–356, 392–394.

fall which would disclose sinister motives. If a definitive judgment of French policy must be reserved until the publication of the French documents is completed, there is at present but little evidence to support the view that the French statesmen were seeking a favorable opportunity for *revanche*.

On the other hand, the evidence leaves no doubt that French opinion and French statesmen were ready to accept war if the necessity were presented. "France does not desire war, but is not afraid of it," said M. Poincaré in a speech at Nantes late in 1912; and his words were reported by the German ambassador in Paris as an accurate reflection of the French temper.* "France," he remarked to M. Izvolski, "is incontestably disposed to peace, and neither seeks nor desires war; but the intervention of Germany against Russia would immediately modify this state of mind"; and he was convinced that "parliament and public opinion would, in such case, entirely approve the decision of the government to lend armed support to Russia."† This puts the situation succinctly.

If France did not, on her own account, contemplate attacking Germany, neither, so far as German documents show, did Germany seek a quarrel with her western neighbor. In the year before the war, however, German opinion had manifested much hostility to France, particularly during the centenary of the War of Liberation (October, 1913).‡ In November, 1913, the King of the Belgians derived the impression from a conversation with the German Emperor that the latter "has ceased to be the friend of peace" and "has come to think that war with France is inevitable."§

From the settlement of the Moroccan question to July, 1914, the attitude of the French and German Governments toward

---

* Schoen to Bethmann-Hollweg, 1 March, 1913; *G. P.*, XXXIX, 168.

† Izvolski to Sazonov, 12 September, 1912; Marchand, I, 326; Stieve, II, 251.

‡ For a French analysis of German public opinion, see a report made to Pichon, the French foreign minister, on 30 July, 1913; France, Ministère des Affaires Étrangères, *Documents diplomatiques. La guerre européenne, 1914* (Paris, 1914) (cited hereafter as "F"), no. 5. Cf. also P. Vergnet, *La France en danger* (Paris, 1913).

§ J. Cambon to Pichon, 22 November, 1913; F, no. 6.

each other exhibited an exemplary correctness. "Our relations with Germany," said M. Poincaré, in June, 1912, to the French parliament, "are loyal and courteous"; they did not cease to be so in the two years following. Unfortunate incidents at Lunéville (occasioned by the forced landing of a Zeppelin) and Nancy (involving some German tourists) were promptly and satisfactorily adjusted.* When, later in 1913, the incidents at Zabern, where an officer of the garrison conducted himself in a manner insulting to the Alsatians and to France, threw Germany into an uproar and aroused some excitement in France, the French Government endeavored to restrain the French newspapers and made only discreet representations in Berlin.† Finally, in February, 1914, a Franco-German agreement respecting the Bagdad Railway cleaned the slate of outstanding questions. And it was surely significant that M. Poincaré, as President of the Republic, ignoring the traditions of forty years, dined at the German embassy.

Nevertheless, the situation was dominated by what Bismarck called the *'imponderabilia.'* Just before the war the distinguished French historian Ernest Lavisse analyzed it in these words:

Between Germany and France a direct conversation is impossible. Each has its reasons which the other is not willing to understand. France does not admit the sinister Bismarckian doctrine—Alsace, *'glacis'* of the Empire sacrificed to the necessity of maintaining German cohesion by the fear of the French pretensions; it does not admit the argument of ethnography, nor that force is sufficient to create rights over the spirits. And the Germans will never, never, never understand that we are attached to Alsace-Lorraine by an obligation of honor; the injuries and blows which it receives, we receive; we suffer in it as one suffers in an amputated member.‡

* *G. P.*, XXXIX, 279-303; Poincaré, III, 189-199.

† Izvolski to Sazonov, 4 December, 1913; Marchand, II, 197-198; Stieve, III, 368-369. Schoen to Bethmann-Hollweg, 26 November, 1913; Jagow to Schoen, 29 November, 1913; *G. P.*, XXXIX, 229-232.

‡ Lalance, *Mes souvenirs, 1830-1914*, pp. xiv-xv. Once, in 1913, when the German ambassador spoke to the then premier, M. Barthou, about the desirability

And a German publicist put the matter in much the same way:

Formally, this question is settled. France finally renounced the two provinces in the Peace of Frankfort. Nevertheless, this dead question, which not once since the Peace of Frankfort has been the object of any conversations or negotiations whatever between German and French statesmen, indirectly dominates the central problem of French policy—the relations with Germany—and through this the whole policy of France. France has thus far not forgotten, and will not forget so long as it exists.*

The ideology of 1870–1871 remained unchanged. And if war were offered to France, she was prepared to accept it, in the hope of recovering the lost provinces.

There was also the further fact that the German general staff, assuming that France would become involved in a war between Germany and Russia, had determined to strike at France first, and to carry out an invasion of France through Belgium on a tremendous scale. Of this intention the French were, in general, well aware: which was, in their eyes, an exceedingly potent reason for maintaining the alliance with Russia and perfecting their arrangements with the Russian military authorities.

As matters stood, then, in 1914, there was no immediate issue pending between France and Germany, and there is little reason for thinking that either country was anxious to attack the other, either France to recover Alsace-Lorraine or Germany to secure French colonies. But German strategy required the defeat of France as the prelude to a military decision against Russia, and French political and national interests made French loyalty to Russia imperative. Because of the operation of the alliances, neither Germany nor France could easily escape being drawn into a quarrel between Austria-Hungary and Russia arising out of their Balkan ambitions.

of calming public opinion in both countries, the latter replied, "Return Alsace-Lorraine to us, and we shall then be the best friends in the world," whereupon the ambassador "promptly dropped the subject"; Schoen, *Erlebtes*, pp. 154–155.
* J. J. Ruedorffer, *Grundzüge der Weltpolitik in der Gegenwart* (Stuttgart, 1914), p. 85.

GREAT BRITAIN AND GERMANY

"The central fact in the international situation to-day is the antagonism between England and Germany." So ran the first sentence of the first article of the first number of the *Round Table* (November, 1910), a non-partisan journal of the politics of the British Empire, and the statement was substantially true. Although Morocco and the Near East provided the issues which repeatedly brought Europe to the verge of war in the early years of this century, in each crisis the attitude assumed by Great Britain was of prime importance in determining its course. Furthermore, the increasing British intimacy with France and Russia caused Germany to appreciate the more and to strengthen her alliance with Austria-Hungary and thus encouraged the schism of Europe into two armed camps.

The rivalry of the two richest nations in Europe, whose relations for centuries had been traditionally friendly, was a struggle for the balance of power, which, in the phrase of Bishop Stubbs, the famous English historian, "is the principle which gives unity to the political plot of modern European history." Since the days of Cardinal Wolsey and King Henry VIII, Great Britain had sought to prevent the ascendancy of a single Power on the Continent; to this end she had waged war against Philip II of Spain, Louis XIV of France, and the great Napoleon. When Germany came to bestride Europe like a colossus, thereby upsetting the ancient equilibrium, it was inevitable that she should find ranged against herself the weight of British public opinion and the resources of British diplomacy; while she, on her part, resented the attitude of Great Britain as an unfair attempt to circumscribe the development of German power and the spread of German *Kultur* throughout the world.

Three factors entered into their rivalry. In the first place, the extraordinary economic development of Germany after she achieved her unity in 1871 made her the doughty competitor of

Great Britain in the markets of the world; rightly or wrongly, a section of British opinion held German competition responsible for the decline in the British export trade and the increase in unemployment which began to be manifest after the Boer War. Secondly, Germany, believing that she needed a strong fleet to protect her expanding commerce, lest it should exist on the sufferance of the British navy, embarked on a programme of naval expansion which was intended to provide "a battle fleet so strong that even for the adversary with the greatest sea power a war against it would involve such dangers as to imperil his own position in the world."* This challenge Great Britain regarded as directed against herself: drawing the food of her people and the raw materials for her factories from every corner of the globe, dependent upon her export trade as the staff of life, she was persuaded that she must in all circumstances and under all conditions retain command of the sea. So every addition to the German navy was met by a still greater increase of the British fleet, and the naval competition of the two countries became as expensive and as dangerous as the growth of conscript armies on the Continent.

The third element was provided by the colonial situation. In the organization of the world at the close of the nineteenth century Germany possessed almost no colonies suitable for European settlement and few territories worthy of economic exploitation. The British Empire, on the other hand, was spread over a quarter of the globe, embraced every kind of land, and might, if an imperial protective tariff were adopted (as many British patriots urged), become a self-sufficing economic entity from which German competition would be largely eliminated. France likewise possessed a magnificent colonial domain in Africa and Asia in which the German merchant and the German capitalist were not welcomed. In German opinion, Great Britain had too many of the fair places of the earth and Germany too few, and Germany boldly claimed her 'place in the sun.' If she did not demand that British colonies be ceded to her,

* Memorandum attached to the German navy law of 1900.

she did ask that Great Britain should not oppose her ambitions in Africa and the Near East. But that was exactly what Great Britain did do. Conceiving her own interests to be threatened by the success of German plans, Great Britain supported France in the controversy about Morocco and for long endeavored to prevent the building of the Bagdad Railway, which was a project particularly dear to German hearts. Great Britain came to regard Germany as the most aggressive and incalculable factor in Europe, and liquidated her ancient quarrels with France and Russia. Germany looked upon Great Britain as a dog in a manger, and sought to disrupt the Triple Entente.

Thus the materials for a fearful conflagration had accumulated, until many men in both countries sincerely convinced themselves that the issue would have to be fought out by the sword. The two governments, however, realizing better than their subjects the risks involved, sought an accommodation, and not without success. No positive action was taken or could be taken to dissipate the commercial rivalry. But sensible men in both countries knew that each was an excellent customer of the other,* and it is clear that in both Great Britain and Germany business interests were opposed to war between the two countries. Not only did the view gradually obtain that the world was large enough for the energies of both peoples, but in the years before the war their commercial competition was discovered to be less serious than was at one time imagined. The bulk of Germany's foreign trade was carried on with her neighbors of the European continent, and in these countries she continued to push ahead of Great Britain. The latter, on the other hand, was doing an increasing business with her vast empire, where the German hold was comparatively slight. Thus the main field for Anglo-German competition lay in the non-British territories outside of Europe, and here neither was able to overcome the other; on the contrary the decade before the war witnessed a tremendous expansion of both British and German

---

* Germany was the best customer of Great Britain and exported more goods to it than to any country except the United States.

commerce all over the world, in which the British quite held their own. In July, 1914, there was no indication that the two greatest industrial and commercial nations of Europe were disposed to fight each other for economic supremacy.*

On the naval issue matters remained much where they had been from the beginning. Admiral von Tirpitz refused to accept any diminution of his building programme, in which position he was supported by the German Emperor, and rejected the suggestion of Mr. Winston Churchill for a 'naval holiday' during which neither Power would add to its fleet. The British, on their side, continued to build more ships than the Germans; but partly for technical reasons, partly because of the expense, they did not maintain the ratio of two British ships to every one laid down in Germany, which was required by the traditional 'two-power standard.' They contented themselves with a superiority of sixty per cent, and this was declared acceptable by Germany, at least as a temporary compromise. This stop-gap solution certainly did not resolve the Anglo-German naval rivalry, but at least that rivalry was not, in 1914, the theme of acrimonious controversy or bitter recriminations, as it had been for a decade. Great Britain, while no more disposed than ever to surrender her maritime supremacy, had got used to the German fleet. Germany indeed misunderstood the effect of her naval expansion on the British public, wrongly believing, as Admiral von Tirpitz put it, that the German fleet had induced a "respectful tone" on the part of British statesmen and "had lessened the probability of a British attack";† but it had been brought home to Germany that Great Britain did not intend to allow herself to be left behind. So greatly had the tension been appeased that in June, 1914, a squadron of the finest and newest British battleships visited Kiel, and the intercourse between the officers and crews of the two countries was carried on without restraint, yet without gushing.‡ In a sense, potential foes had become potential friends.

* For the figures of Anglo-German commercial rivalry, see B. E. Schmitt, *England and Germany (1740–1914)* (Princeton, 1916), pp. 96–115.
† Tirpitz, *Erinnerungen*, p. 207.   ‡ For an account of the visit see *B. D.*, XI, 6–11.

If both the commercial competition and the naval rivalry remained, though in less emphatic form, one positive result was achieved in the direction of an understanding. In the spring of 1914, an agreement was reached with reference to the Bagdad Railway and the Portuguese colonies. Great Britain withdrew her opposition to the railway and took over the construction of the last section from Basra to the Persian Gulf.* The colonial agreement replaced the abortive convention of 1898; signature was delayed only by a difference of views on the question of publication.† The German Government appears to have been satisfied with the reasonable attitude of the British, who in turn were convinced of Germany's desire for peace and friendship.

The co-operation of the two countries during the Balkan wars of 1912–1913 also produced a salutary effect, for membership in a diplomatic group did not prevent them from restraining their respective associates. So when, in the autumn of 1913, the despatch of a German military mission to Turkey aroused the suspicions and irritation of Russia, Sir Edward Grey preferred to negotiate a compromise with Germany rather than make the matter an issue between the Triple Alliance and the Triple Entente.‡ What Grey has called "the atmosphere of suspicion" was so far dissipated that in February, 1914, the German foreign minister, Herr von Jagow, told the Reichstag that Anglo-German relations were "very good" and in July Sir Edward Grey declared that they had "sensibly improved."

The friendly and conciliatory attitude displayed by the British Government in the settlement of the Bagdad Railway question and the adjustment of the African difficulties seems to have raised high hopes in Berlin. "If it should come to a European war," said an important official of the foreign office in the spring of 1914, "we believe to-day that we can assume that England will not take part in it, at least in the beginning."§ If

---

* G. P., XXXVII, 151–470; E. M. Earle, *Turkey, the Great Powers and the Bagdad Railway* (New York, 1923), pp. 252–274.

† G. P., XXXVII, 1–138.　　　　　　　　　　‡ See below, pp. 94–96.

§ Statement of Dr. Naumann to the parliamentary investigating committee, quoting Herr von Stumm, director of the political department; *Zur Vorgeschichte des*

the Germans really thought that the Entente had become a broken reed, they were seriously mistaken, and Sir Edward Grey was at pains to point out to Prince Lichnowsky, the German ambassador in London, that "though we were not bound by engagement [to France and Russia] as Allies, we did from time to time talk as intimately as Allies."[*] What had really taken place was that a *détente*, or relaxing of tension, had been effected; an *entente* was not possible, so long as Germany declined to discuss a limitation of naval armaments. But it may be said that the danger of war between Great Britain and Germany had been removed, so far as concerned any question directly affecting their immediate interests. If they were driven to fight each other, it would be because of the larger issues of their membership in rival diplomatic groups and of the European balance of power. The Anglo-German situation was, in fact, not very different from that obtaining between France and Germany.

AUSTRIA-HUNGARY AND ITALY

An eminent Italian diplomatist, Count Nigra, who long served as ambassador in Vienna, was fond of saying that Austria-Hungary and Italy had to be enemies or allies. Actually, although they had been allies since 1882, they continued to be enemies. Just as Alsace-Lorraine was a permanent barrier to Franco-German friendship, so 'Italia Irredenta' governed the relations of Austria and Italy. In Trentino (or South Tirol, as the Austrians called it), Istria, the cities of Trieste and Fiume, and along the Dalmatian coast there lived nearly a million Italians. Although the provinces which they inhabited, with the exception of Dalmatia, had belonged to the Habsburg crown for centuries,[†] they were considered by Italian sentiment as forming a natural and necessary part of United Italy, and Italian policy was controlled, in the last analysis, by the desire

Weltkrieges, I, no. 8, p. 45. Moltke complained to Conrad in May, 1914, that "unfortunately our people are always expecting a declaration by England that she will not take part" in a general war; Conrad, III, 670.

[*] Grey to Goschen, 24 June, 1914; Grey, I, 304; American edition, I, 294.

[†] Dalmatia had been acquired in 1797, when Bonaparte overthrew the Venetian Republic.

to add these lands to the kingdom.* Since Austria-Hungary was determined not to part with any of her patrimony, Italian ambitions could be satisfied only by war, or in the event of a war to which the Dual Monarchy was a party. It may also be noted that certain elements in Austria had never forgiven the creation of the Kingdom of Italy by Cavour and Victor Emmanuel II at the expense of the Habsburgs.

Theoretically, therefore, the Austro-Italian antagonism might some day lead to war, and any war between Great Powers was likely to involve other Great Powers. But Italy was not in a position to attack Austria-Hungary single-handed. Her population was smaller than that of the Monarchy, she lacked coal and iron, the necessary sinews of modern war, her strategic position was most unfavorable. Consequently, although 'irredentism' manifested itself from time to time in noisy demonstrations, it was highly improbable that Italy would pick a quarrel on the issue unless Austria-Hungary was already engaged in war elsewhere.

The military party in Austria was not indisposed to precipitate a struggle. Twice at least—in 1907, when Italy's military position was much weaker than that of Austria, and again in 1911, at the time of the Tripolitan war—the Austro-Hungarian chief of staff, General Conrad, boldly urged the Emperor Francis Joseph and the foreign minister Count Aehrenthal to make war on Italy.† But his counsel was not followed, and on the second occasion, he was not only told to mind his own business, but finally removed from office, for, said the Emperor, "My policy is a policy of peace."‡ However great the distrust was of Italy, Austria-Hungary could not attack her without running grave danger of exposing Galicia to a Russian attack. Practically speaking, therefore, the Austro-Italian antagonism was not likely to precipitate a European war.

So this analysis of the European situation leads to the con-

---

* Additional factors in the relations of the two countries were their rivalry for the control of the Adriatic Sea and their ambitions in Albania.

† Conrad, I, 63–64; II, 172–174.   ‡ *Ibid.*, II, 276, 282–284.

clusion that neither France and Germany, Great Britain and Germany, nor Austria-Hungary and Italy were disposed so to accentuate the issues dividing them as to resort to war for their solution. But Great Britain, France, Germany and Italy were all interested in maintaining the equilibrium of European politics, and if that equilibrium were threatened, they would at once take position in accordance with their general political interests even though immediate interests were not affected. As matters stood in 1914, the balance of power depended on the reorganization of the Near East already achieved by the Balkan wars or under way in consequence. The next chapter is addressed to this problem.

CHAPTER II

THE NEAR EAST

"I SHALL not live to see the World War," said Prince Bismarck to Albert Ballin in 1891, "but you will, and it will start in the Near East."* The pessimism of the German statesman was justified partly by the history of the Near East and partly by his own experiences. Throughout the nineteenth century the progressive dissolution of the Ottoman Empire, which began with the revolt of the Serbs in 1804, presented European statesmen with the gravest problems. Once, in 1854, Great Britain and France had joined Turkey in a war to resist Russian aggression, and at other times conflict had been narrowly avoided. In 1878 and again in 1887 it was very largely Bismarck's skilful diplomacy which had prevented war. In truth, almost any incident in the Near East, from Belgrade on the Danube to Basra on the Persian Gulf, was likely to create dissensions between the Great Powers, many of them of a most serious character, and the Iron Chancellor was not alone in thinking that the final liquidation of Turkey in Europe and the disposition of Turkey in Asia could be settled only by a general conflagration.

From 1878 to 1912 the situation in the Near East was controlled by the Treaty of Berlin. That instrument, devised in part by the mediation of Bismarck, had prevented war between Austria-Hungary and Great Britain on the one hand and Russia on the other, when the latter Power had attempted, by the Treaty of San Stefano, to dictate to the defeated Turks a settlement devised in her exclusive interest. But the Treaty of Berlin, conceived by the Great Powers alone and imposed upon the small Balkan states, paved the way for another war. The region commonly known as Macedonia, which Russia had pro-

* B. Huldermann, *Albert Ballin* (Berlin, 1922), p. 202.

posed to include in the autonomous Bulgarian state created by the Treaty of San Stefano, was by the Berlin decisions restored to Turkish rule, which as time went on grew more and more oppressive to the Christian population of the country. Early in the present century Macedonia became the scene of endemic unrest and then of open rebellion, so that the Great Powers were constrained to intervene and impose, or try to impose, reforms on the Turkish Government. This intervention was the principal cause of the revolutions of July, 1908, and April, 1909, by which the 'Young Turks' overthrew the despotism of Sultan Abdul Hamid (1876–1909). The new régime established, on paper, constitutional government and promised equality of rights for all the races and religions of the empire. In practice, however, the new system proved no better than the old (from the Christian point of view), if indeed it was not even more systematic and deliberate in its annoyances. So in the autumn of 1912, Bulgaria, Serbia, Montenegro and Greece, forgetting for the moment their own differences, destroyed the Turkish military power by a brusque attack and drove the Turks from Europe except at Constantinople. These remarkable events, which stirred Europe to its depths, came near ushering in the long-expected general war, for Austria-Hungary and Russia seemed at several moments on the point of fighting out their ancient rivalry for preponderance in the Balkans. But they were restrained by their respective allies, and the very fact that the four less-interested Powers, acting in concert, were able to ward off a conflict stimulated the hope that diplomacy would be equally successful in a subsequent crisis.*

Actually, the wars of 1912–1913 created a situation which made a European war more likely than before. The settlement in the Balkans, as will be seen presently, left so many sores that it was certain to be challenged when those who resented it felt strong enough to act. Nor was the position of Turkey any more secure, now that it was reduced—apart from Constan-

---

* E. Vlietinck, "L'action des Puissances durant la crise balkanique," in *Revue de droit international*, XLV, 617–624 (no. 6, 1913).

tinople and a small hinterland*—to its Asiatic provinces, Anatolia, Armenia, Mesopotamia and Arabia. These lands were exceedingly backward in their economic development, they were supplied with few or no railways and had long been despoiled of men and resources for the maintenance of the Turkish dominion in Europe. Large sections of their population, the Armenians and the Arabs, the latter comprising the mass of the people in Mesopotamia and Arabia, were hostile to the government at Constantinople and were not unreceptive to the intrigues of foreign states. That such a conglomerate, poorly organized and poverty-stricken state could exist for any considerable time seemed most improbable. "Asiatic Turkey," declared the German ambassador in Constantinople, who stated it with regret, "cannot maintain itself any longer by its own strength."† Whether it would collapse from internal weakness or whether the death-blow would be given by foreign aggression did not matter, for either circumstance would precipitate the other; and the forward move of any Great Power was almost bound, given the importance of Constantinople and many other towns, to involve the intervention of other Powers. If a War of the Turkish Succession was to be avoided, great circumspection and restraint would have to be observed by all concerned.

The dangers of the situation were, however, universally understood. Since no Power was ready at the moment to push matters to extremes, there was general agreement that the Ottoman Empire must be maintained for the time being and the day of partition, though probably this was bound to come, put off as long as possible. In consequence of this informal understanding, the winter of 1913–1914 witnessed an attempt to inject new life into the moribund Turkish state and to adjust international rivalries by mutual concessions.

The chronic evil of the Turkish system was the inefficiency

* By the Treaty of London of 30 May, 1913, between Turkey and the Balkan states, the European frontier of the Ottoman Empire was to be a line drawn from Enos on the Ægean to Midia on the Black Sea, which left the Gallipoli peninsula to Turkey. Later, Turkey recovered Adrianople, which was recognized by the Treaty of Constantinople of 25 September, 1913.

† Wangenheim to Bethmann-Hollweg, 21 May, 1913; *G. P.*, XXXVIII, 43.

and arbitrariness of local administration, which exhibited its worst features when concerned with the Christian peoples of the empire. The lesson of the Balkan wars was not lost on either the Sublime Porte or the European Powers: there was a limit to the patience of the subject populations, and the Armenians, who inhabited the six vilayets (or provinces) of northeastern Anatolia, had long shown signs of restlessness. Accordingly, a scheme was worked out between the Powers and the Porte, with Russia and Germany acting as representatives of the two great diplomatic groups, for extensive administrative reforms and a measure of European control. Agreement was reached on 8 February, 1914, but its practical value was never tested, for it had not been put into operation when the Great War began.*

If this programme was accepted reluctantly by the Turkish Government, which had always been highly sensitive with regard to Armenia and in this case suspected the ulterior motives of Russia, its attitude toward the problem of a general reorganization was quite different. To accomplish this, European assistance was eagerly sought. An Englishman, Sir Richard Crawford, was placed in charge of the customs, which yielded a large share of the national revenue. The gendarmerie, whose brutality and venality were the most notorious evil of Turkish misgovernment, was handed over to a Frenchman, General Baumann. A British officer, Admiral Limpus, was intrusted with the rehabilitation of the navy. Finally, a German military mission, under General Liman von Sanders, was employed to reorganize the Turkish army, which had given a rather poor account of itself in the Balkan wars. By thus distributing the work of reform among several Powers, the Sublime Porte hoped to avoid giving offense to any of them and, no doubt, to continue its traditional policy of playing one off against the other.

Since any reforms would be costly, their success depended

* G. P., XXXVIII, 1–189; Russia, Ministry of Foreign Affairs, *Les réformes en Arménie, 26 novembre, 1912–10 mai, 1914* (Petrograd, 1915), an 'Orange Book,' most of the documents being in Russian, of which an analysis is given in A. Mandelstam, *Le sort de l'Empire ottoman* (Paris, 1917), pp. 206–245; Djemal Pasha, *Memoirs of a Turkish Statesman, 1913–1919* (New York, 1922), pp. 262–276; Sazonov, pp. 138–146.

on the improvement of the economic condition of the Empire. To this end the Ottoman Government negotiated a series of agreements with most of the Powers for the development of railways on a considerable scale. The most important of these agreements was a three-cornered bargain between Turkey, Germany and Great Britain which assured the completion of the Bagdad Railway to the Persian Gulf; the conventions were awaiting signature in July, 1914. Complementary to this was an agreement between France and Germany (February, 1914) by which France, withdrawing from the Bagdad Railway, undertook the construction of railways in Syria. Russia was induced to renounce her veto against the building of railways in the regions bordering on the Black Sea (to which Turkey had submitted in 1900), and French capitalists secured the privilege of building certain lines which would link up the Armenian provinces with the rest of Turkey. Italy, not to be left behind, claimed and was granted for development the district around Adalia, along the southern coast. Thus the scramble for concessions which had been going on for a generation was adjusted by a practical division of the country into spheres of economic influence. No doubt the Great Powers looked upon this division as a staking out of claims against the day of final liquidation,* but it was, or seemed to be, a step forward that they preferred to divide the spoils in advance than to leave the distribution to the accidents of war. Nor is there evidence to show that they did not desire to postpone the moment of liquidation as long as possible. On paper, at least, the most troublesome problem of European politics was on the way to a peaceful solution.†

---

* The German ambassador in Constantinople explained to his Austro-Hungarian colleague that the railway zones had been arranged so as to leave the passes which controlled the basin of Diarbekir in the hands of Germany, "since her position would thereby be impregnable from a military point of view." The latter noted that "the plan of economic partition has thus been obviously worked out also from a military-political standpoint." Pallavicini to Berchtold, 8 December, 1913; Ö.-U. A., VII, 631.
† For the last two paragraphs, cf. Denkwürdigkeiten des Marschalls Izzet Pascha (Leipzig, 1927), pp. 220–225, and M. Moukhtar Pacha, La Turquie, l'Allemagne et l'Europe depuis le traité de Berlin jusqu'à la guerre mondiale (Paris, 1924), pp. 187–203.

The Straits and the Bagdad Railway: Russia and Germany

In reality, however, the appearances were deceptive, for the despatch of a German military mission to reform the Turkish army had revealed, rather unexpectedly and most vividly, how dangerous was the rivalry of Germany and Russia in the Near East. "For Russia," remarked a Russian historian on the first page of a striking book, "the whole famous Eastern Question is summed up in these words: Under whose authority are the Straits of the Bosphorus and the Dardanelles? Who is their possessor?"* Although Russia had exhibited a lively interest in the Christian populations of the Balkans from the days of Peter the Great and had more than once used her armed forces to effect their liberation from Turkish rule, this policy was always in part pursued as the means to an end: the weakening of the Turkish power which would make easier the accomplishment of what Russia conceived as her 'historic mission,' namely, to secure control of Constantinople and the adjoining Straits. This was indeed the ultimate object of the many wars which Russia waged against Turkey in the eighteenth and nineteenth centuries. But neither Turkey nor the European Powers had been willing to look favorably on the Russian ambition,† and in 1841, the Convention of the Straits, which was accepted by Russia herself, closed the Straits to the men-of-war of all nations except Turkey.‡

The Russian motives were varied. There was the sentimental desire to restore the Cross to the church of Saint Sophia, there was the political tradition that made Russia the heir of the Greek Empire. Politically, it would be an enormous advantage if Russia could control the passage of war-ships into

---

* S. Goriainow, *Le Bosphore et les Dardanelles* (Paris, 1910), p. 1.

† Except in 1799 and again in 1833, when the Porte, when hard pressed by other enemies, had entered into an alliance with Russia which permitted the passage of Russian men-of-war through the Straits. In each case, however, the alliance proved temporary.

‡ The right for merchantmen to pass through the Straits was secured to Russia by the Treaty of Kutchuk Kainardji in 1774.

and out of the Black Sea; in 1904–1905, the Russian Government was not able to despatch its Black Sea fleet to the Far East. And in the years before the Great War the economic factor began to assume great importance. An increasing share of Russia's foreign commerce was passing through the Straits. In time of peace the Turkish control of those waters caused no difficulties, but when in 1912 the Ottoman Government, in the course of its war with Italy, closed the Straits to navigation for some weeks, the losses to Russian commerce were quite serious. The geographical disadvantage under which Russia labored was now obvious, and so mighty a state was not likely to submit to it indefinitely. It is significant that the demand for a solution of the problem was warmly supported by the Liberal elements in Russian politics which represented the growing industrial and commercial classes.

When the defeat in Manchuria at the hands of Japan threw Russia back on Europe, the question of the Straits became the first consideration of Russian policy. Renouncing the actual possession of Constantinople,* the Russian Government set as a definite goal the opening of the Straits, and although the Russian statesmen were not in agreement as to the proper method for achieving this programme,† their desire and deter-

---

* So affirmed by the *Novoye Vremya*, the most important Russian newspaper, in 1905. In 1908 Izvolski assured the Turkish ambassador in St. Petersburg that "Russia herself had no territorial ambitions of any kind." Marschall to foreign office, 8 October, 1908; *G. P.*, XXVI, 118. To Aehrenthal he repeated "the declaration already often made by Russian statesmen on earlier occasions that Russia contemplated territorial conquests neither at nor around Constantinople," and he conceded that any modification of the régime of the Straits "ought not to impair the independence and security of the Ottoman capital." Memorandum of Aehrenthal, *ca.* 16 September, 1908; *Ö.-U. A.*, I, 86. He told Schoen, then German foreign minister, that "it would be best in all circumstances for the Sultan, now as before, to reign at the Golden Horn." Schoen to Bülow, 26 September, 1908; *G. P.*, XXVI, 41. To Grey Izvolski explained that "Russia now desired to support Turkey as a barrier against the Austrian advance." Grey to Nicolson, 12 October, 1908; *B. D.*, V, 429. Izvolski's subsequent policy seems to bear out the sincerity of his statements that Russia did not desire Constantinople. The Tsar said to the German military plenipotentiary at his court, "I hope to get the consent of all the interested powers or, at least, of most of them; of course, Turkey is the power mostly concerned." Hintze to William II, 19 December, 1908; *G. P.*, XXVI, 381.

† This is clearly brought out by W. L. Langer, "Russia, the Straits Question, and the European Powers, 1904–8," in *English Historical Review*, XLIV, 59–85 (January, 1929), and "Russia, the Straits Question and the Origins of the Balkan League, 1908–1912," in *Political Science Quarterly*, XLIII, 321–363 (September,

mination to do so runs like a red thread through the years
1907–1914. Some went so far as to urge seizing the Bosphorus by force,* but as the military and naval officials always
pointed out that Russia, after the defeat in Manchuria, was
not strong enough to attempt any such stroke,† the only recourse was diplomatic action, which was inaugurated in 1907.
The principal motive for effecting an understanding with
Great Britain was, by making concessions in Asia, to secure
British good-will in this question of the straits, and although
the matter was not mentioned in the Anglo-Russian Convention of 31 August, 1907, the Russian Government had let its
wishes be known‡ and had received assurances that not only
"the question was one which we [Great Britain] were prepared
to discuss,"§ but that

if the negotiations now in progress between the two Governments with regard to Asiatic questions had a satisfactory result,
the effect upon British public opinion would be such as to facilitate a discussion of the Straits question if it came up later on. ‖

1928). If the question was to be settled by diplomacy, should Russia negotiate
with the Great Powers for a revision of the existing arrangements and, their consent having been secured, then demand Turkish acceptance; or, should she first
induce Turkey to consent to the opening of the Straits, and then ask the Powers
to recognize the arrangement? The first method inspired Izvolski's efforts in 1908,
the second the policy of Charykov, the ambassador in Constantinople, in 1911.

* This had been suggested, by Nelidov, the ambassador at Constantinople, in
1896, during the Armenian massacres. Cf. Dillon, *The Eclipse of Russia*, pp. 235–
240, and *The Memoirs of Count Witte*, pp. 186–189.

† The matter was discussed in ministerial conferences in February, March, and
August, 1908, that is, both before and after the Young Turkish revolution; the
premier, P. A. Stolypin, resolutely opposed the use of force, and was supported by
the army officials. M. Pokrowski, *Drei Konferenzen* (Hamburg, 1920), p. 17; *Diary
of General Polivanov*, quoted by G. Frantz, "Die Meerengenfrage in der Vorkriegs-
politik Russlands," in *Deutsche Rundschau*, CCX, ii, 146–147 (February, 1927).
The problem came up again during the Balkan wars, and once more the military
and naval chiefs advised against precipitate action. Frantz, *loc. cit.*, 150–153.

‡ Memorandum of Grey on conversation with Benckendorff, 15 March, 1907;
memoranda of Izvolski, *ca.* 14 April, 1907, and 10 July, 1907; *B. D.*, IV, 279–280,
287–288, 295–296.

§ Grey to Nicolson, 19 March, 1907; *B. D.*, IV, 281.

‖ Memorandum of Grey, given to Benckendorff, 27 April, 1907; *B. D.*, IV, 291.
The statement in Grey, I, 164, American edition, I, 159, that "the question of the
Straits was not mixed up with those Anglo-Russian negotiations about Persia" is
true only in the sense that the British Government left it to Russia to take the
initiative in opening a formal discussion about the Straits, which Izvolski, for
various reasons, was not at that time ready to do.

Greatly encouraged by this change of front, for Great Britain had been the most determined supporter of the closed Straits, M. Izvolski thought to use the Young Turkish Revolution of 1908 as the moment for action. He struck a bargain with Baron von Aehrenthal by which, in return for the latter's support on the question of the Straits, Russia agreed to the annexation of Bosnia-Herzegovina by Austria-Hungary— although this signified the abandonment of the traditional Russian policy of defending the Slavic peoples of the Balkans.* Unfortunately for him, the British Government, while ready to accept the principle of opening the Straits, deemed the moment as inopportune as M. Izvolski thought it opportune, for it did not wish to embarrass the new régime in Turkey. Moreover, it insisted on the Straits being opened to the ships of all nations on the same terms, whereas the Russian plan was that Russian war-ships should be allowed to pass outward into the Ægean Sea, but the vessels of other Powers should not enter the Black Sea.† Consequently the negotiations came to naught.

The Russian Government refused, however, to be discouraged. In 1909 it concluded a secret agreement with Italy by which the two Powers engaged themselves "to regard with benevolence, the one Russia's interests in the question of the Straits, the other Italian interests in Tripoli and Cyrenaica."‡ When Italy attacked Tripoli in 1911, Russia once more attempted to seize her advantage. This time she offered Turkey a defensive alliance modelled on the famous Treaty of Unkiar Skelessi of 1833. In return for a Russian guarantee of "the maintenance of the present régime of the Straits of the Bosphorus and the Dardanelles," the Ottoman Government was to

---

* The agreement was reached in conversations between Izvolski and Aehrenthal at Buchlau, the country place of Count Berchtold, the Austro-Hungarian ambassador in St. Petersburg, in September, 1908. For the controversy subsequently aroused by this meeting, see below, pp. 126–127.

† Memorandum of Grey, for Izvolski, 14 October, 1908; B. D., V, 441. The version in Marchand, II, 458, is incomplete.

‡ Agreement of Racconigi, October, 1909; Marchand, I, 357–358; Stieve, II, 363–364.

promise "not to oppose the passage of Russian war-ships through the Straits, on condition that these ships do not stop in the Straits unless by agreement."* Such an arrangement would have suited the Russians very nicely indeed, for it would have left them masters of the situation without involving any change in the precious *status quo,* that is, the territorial *status quo,* to which all the foreign offices professed fervent and undying allegiance. The Turks, needless to say, were greatly embarrassed by the overture—until they discovered that Great Britain and France† were cool to the idea, whereupon they rejected the Russian proposals with complacency. In revenge Russia promoted the formation of the Balkan League, which in the autumn of 1912 attacked Turkey and despoiled it of its European territories except Constantinople and its hinterland.

But the very success of the Balkan allies gave a new twist to the question of the Straits. In November, 1912, it appeared as if the Bulgarian army might penetrate the Turkish defenses at Chatalja and enter Constantinople. To forestall so unwelcome a development, the Russian Government felt it necessary to issue a warning to Bulgaria‡ and to authorize the Russian ambassador in Constantinople to summon the Black Sea fleet to the Bosphorus.§ It was probably the protest of its French ally against precipitate action‖ which deterred the Russian Government from taking a dangerous step—which, as events turned out, was not necessary, for the Bulgarian army was stopped in its attack. The same situation was presented in March, 1913, when the Bulgarians were once more threatening Constantinople, and again in August, when the Turks recovered Adrianople. Apparently only the pressure of its associates in the Triple Entente dissuaded the Russian Government from utiliz-

* Neratov to Charykov, 2 October, 1911; Marchand, II, 458.
† Cf. *D. D. F.,* 3ᵉ série, I, *passim;* Siebert, pp. 674–684.
‡ A. Nekludoff, *Diplomatic Reminiscences* (London, 1920), pp. 114–125.
§ Y. Zakher, "Константинополь и проливы" [Constantinople and the Straits], in *Красный Архив,* VI, 51–52 (1924).
‖ Poincaré to Izvolski, 4 November, 1912; *Affaires balkaniques,* I, 136–137. Poincaré to Izvolski, 16 November, 1912; Poincaré, II, 336–337.

ing the several favorable opportunities for solving the question of the Straits in its own interests.*

Even this brief summary of Russian policy will make evident the intense importance attached by Russia to the problem.
The situation created by the defeat of Turkey and the loss of
her European provinces, as it appeared to the Russians, was
thus described by the foreign minister in the autumn of 1913:

> The uncertainty as to the stability and longevity of Turkey
> raises for us the historic question of the Straits and an evalua-
> tion of their importance for us, from both a political and an
> economic point of view. . . . In case of a change in the *status
> quo*, Russia cannot permit a solution of the question contrary
> to her interests; in other words, she cannot, in certain circum-
> stances, remain a passive spectator of events. . . .
> At present the question of safeguarding the Straits is ac-
> tually settled in a fashion fairly satisfactory to our direct inter-
> ests. Turkey is a state neither too strong nor too weak—unable
> to be dangerous to us but at the same time compelled to give
> consideration to Russia, who is stronger than she is. The very
> weakness of the Ottoman Empire and its inability to regenerate
> itself on the basis of law and civilization have hitherto been to
> our advantage, creating among the peoples subjected to the
> Crescent that looking toward Orthodox Russia which is one
> of the fundamental bases of our international position in the
> East and in Europe. . . .
> Can we tolerate the transfer of the Straits into the complete
> possession of another state? To formulate the question is to
> answer it in the negative. The Straits in the possession of a
> strong state would mean that the economic development of
> the whole of southern Russia would be subjected to it. . . .
> He who possesses the Straits will hold not only the keys of the
> Black Sea and the Mediterranean; he will also have the key
> to the penetration of Asia Minor and the hegemony of the
> Balkans; in consequence the state which supplants Turkey on
> the shores of the Straits will probably aspire to follow the
> course formerly taken by the Turks. . . .

M. Sazonov regarded proposals for neutralizing or demili-

---

* Pichon to Delcassé, 27 March, 23 July, 25 July, 1913; *Affaires balkaniques*, II,
118, 265, 270.

tarizing the Straits as unsatisfactory. He therefore urged a study of the military and naval measures which would permit Russia to force the Straits and seize Constantinople, "should circumstances demand it." Then, after repeating that "an early dissolution of Turkey could not be desirable for us, and it is necessary to do everything possible by diplomacy to postpone such an outcome" and sketching the measures of preparedness that must be considered, he concluded:

Renewing the wish expressed above for the prolongation of the *status quo* as far as possible, I must repeat that the question of the Straits can hardly be advanced a step except in the event of European complications. These complications, to judge from present conditions, would find us in alliance with France, and possibly, though this is not at all certain, in alliance with England, or at least with her as a benevolent neutral. In the Balkans, in case of European complications, we would count on Serbia, and perhaps on Rumania.*

The Russian programme was crystal-clear: to maintain Turkey and the *status quo* as long as possible, to be prepared for any emergency, and to take advantage of "European complications" to solve the question of the Straits according to its own desires. The Russian Government was therefore likely to be extraordinarily sensitive to any incident which might affect the future of Turkey.

Such an incident occurred in October, 1913, with the announcement that a German general, Liman von Sanders, and a staff of forty-two officers would undertake the reorganization of the Turkish army. The controversy excited by this episode, which provoked the last great diplomatic crisis prior to July, 1914, can be appreciated only if it is linked up with the question of the Straits on the one hand and with the ambitions of Germany in the Near East on the other.

The principal instrument of German policy had hitherto been

* Sazonov to Nicholas II, 6 December, 1913; Marchand, II, 363–373; Stieve, III, 374–383.

the Bagdad Railway.* Nominally the Bagdad Railway was
an enterprise of German financiers working under concessions
granted by the Turkish Government in 1899 and 1903, for the
construction of a railway to Bagdad and the Persian Gulf.
The promoters undoubtedly desired the participation of capitalists from other countries, partly in order to raise more easily
the large sums required for the building of the line, partly also
to enlist the interest of various governments and thereby increase the security of the enterprise. The financiers of France
and Great Britain were originally ready and anxious to lend
their support, but they were forced in 1903, under pressure
from their respective governments, to withdraw. For although
the line was always advertised by the German bankers and
the German Government as a strictly economic undertaking,
the object of which was to develop the resources of Turkey
in Asia and to provide an outlet for German enterprise, it was
always regarded by Great Britain, France and Russia as a
political lever for making German influence predominant in
the Near East at the expense of their own interests. Nor was
this view altogether wrong (if not altogether correct, for the
Germans were always ready to make certain concessions). At
any rate, Baron von Marschall, the astute German ambassador at Constantinople from 1897 to 1912, whose skilful diplomacy was of enormous assistance in securing the concession
from the Turks, was in no doubt about the political importance
of the railway. "The economic and military strengthening
which the execution of that enterprise is calculated to bring to
Turkey," he wrote before the definitive concession had been
granted, "will work against the ultimate purposes of Russia's
policy in the East."† And some years later, when the line
was under construction, he remarked to Baron von Aehrenthal

---

* The best account of the Bagdad Railway is offered by Earle, *Turkey, the Great
Powers, and the Bagdad Railway*. At the time of writing, the only diplomatic doc-
uments available were those in Siebert. Much new information is given in
G. P., XIV, 439–506; XVII, 369–516; XXV, 175–280; XXVII, 825–963, 557–689;
XXXVII, 151–639, and in *B. D.*, II, 174–196; Marchand, II, and Stieve, III, IV,
passim, contain additional Russian documents.

† Marschall to foreign office, 31 January, 1902; *G. P.*, XVII, 416.

that "the phrase about the bones of the Pomeranian grenadier which Bismarck had used more than thirty years before, no longer applied with reference to the Straits."* For, he represented to his government, a solution of the Straits question according to the wishes of Russia would reduce the Sultan to "the position of the Emir of Bokhara" and "the other Great Powers could withdraw their ambassadors from the Golden Horn." Bismarck's distinction between economic and political questions was no longer valid:

> With the expansive force of youth the capital, industry and trade of Germany is establishing itself profitably in the most distant regions of the globe. German protection is accorded to these enterprises, and especially in lands which are lacking in orderly government in our sense have *political* interests been created which no one even thought of two decades ago. . . . By the concession for the Bagdad Railway we have won for ourselves a mighty prestige among the oriental peoples, and the well-known speech of his Majesty the Emperor in Damascus still resounds to-day in the Mohammedan world. That is a bit of capital which we must preserve. For the day will perhaps come when we can make use of it.†

There is no doubt that the Bagdad Railway became an important, and quite legitimate, factor in German political calculations.

In spite, however, of all opposition, the German enterprise forged ahead, the Turkish Government in 1908 and 1911 extending the concession, the promoters actually building more and more of the line, until in 1912 it had reached the Euphrates River east of Adana and a branch had been carried to Aleppo. As the railway obviously could not be stopped, its opponents came to terms, Russia by the convention of 19 August, 1911, Great Britain and France by conversations opened in 1913 which led to definite agreements in 1914. These several agreements‡ recognized certain restricted interests of

---

* Marschall to Bülow, 14 December, 1907; G."P., XXII, 84–85.
† Marschall to Bülow, 26 December, 1907; G. P., XXII, 91–93.
‡ See above, pp. 67, 73, 81.

the Entente Powers, but none the less their effect would be to secure for Germany a predominant position in Anatolia and Mesopotamia.

The Young Turk party in power at Constantinople appears to have been divided in opinion as to the proper orientation of Turkish foreign policy. But if a few persons advocated an understanding with the Triple Entente,* the most influential members of the government looked to Germany,† because they considered her the most disinterested of the Powers. For the German Government professed to cherish no territorial ambitions to be satisfied at the expense of Turkey, whereas Great Britain had 'occupied' Egypt, Italy had seized Tripoli, France was supposed to desire Syria, and Russia was credited with the determination to possess both Constantinople and Armenia. To put it another way, Germany, while not taking Turkish territory or interfering with the independence of the Turkish Government, seemed anxious to strengthen the Otto-

---

* The president of the chamber, Halil Bey, the minister of marine, Djemal Pasha, and the ambassador in Berlin, Mahmud Moukhtar Pasha; Moukhtar, pp. 73–81, 203–243. In the spring of 1914, Talaat Bey, the minister of the interior, visited the Tsar at Livadia and proposed a Russo-Turkish alliance, but the overture was not believed by the Russian Government to be sincere. *Denkwürdigkeiten des Marschalls Izzet Pascha*, pp. 236–237; Sazonov, pp. 133–138. According to one account, Russia proposed an agreement in respect of the Straits; G. P., XXXVI, 797, note**. Another version was to the effect that Russia required Turkey to remain neutral in the event of a European war; Ö.-U. A., VIII, 182. The Turkish manœuvre caused no little concern to the German and Austro-Hungarian ambassadors in Constantinople. The latter attributed it to Turkish distrust of Germany arising out of William II's pronounced Grecophil policy, of which the German ambassador was privately very critical, and to a certain irritation because the German Government had made concessions to Russia in the matter of the Mission of Liman von Sanders (see below, pp. 95–97). Pallavicini to Berchtold, 4 April, 13 April; Mittag to Berchtold, 13 June; Pallavicini to Berchtold, 24 June, 1914; Ö.-U. A., VII, 1028–1031, 1055, VIII, 139–141, 180–182. The German Government, however, declined to take the Turkish action "tragically," for approaches to Russia "have hitherto always led to deceptions for the Porte." Jagow to Tschirschky, 27 May; G. P., XXXVI, 795, note *. In July Djemal went to France and made overtures for a Franco-Turkish *rapprochement*, but was coldly received; Djemal, pp. 97–107. Apparently Russia and France were still resentful of the Turkish attitude on the Sanders Mission.

† Memorandum of Wangenheim, 9 May, 1914; G. P., XXXVI, 786–787. According to Moukhtar, p. 251, Turkey spontaneously offered at the end of 1913 to conclude an alliance with Germany, but this is not confirmed by any document in G. P. In May, 1914, the grand vizier informed the Austro-Hungarian ambassador that "Turkey is fully disposed to lean on the Triple Alliance," provided it could count on effective support. Pallavicini to Berchtold, 18 May, 1914; Ö.-U. A., VIII, 49.

man Empire and assist it to maintain itself against the covetous Powers.

At the same time, German policy was not so disinterested as its official representatives pretended. The Austro-Hungarian military attaché at Constantinople was probably not very wrong in his conclusion:

Everything that I saw and heard indicated that the Germans, although they naturally avoided admitting this openly, were striving for a gradual occupation of the entire territory in the form of a protectorate or a political treaty, and in addition some even had plans for the interior of Asia and extending if possible as far as India.[*]

Certainly the possession of the Bagdad Railway, which was bound to become the nerve centre of Turkish economic development, promised to give Germany a powerful lever for influencing the policy of the Ottoman Government. If in addition Germany were to acquire a controlling position in the Turkish army, the Ottoman Empire was likely to become in fact, if not in theory, a German protectorate.[†]

The Mission of Liman von Sanders[‡] arose from the request made by the Ottoman Government in the spring of 1913 that "a suitable Prussian officer" be sent to Turkey to help prepare new plans for the defense of Constantinople.[§] The Wilhelm-

---

[*] J. Pomiankowski, *Der Zusammenbruch des ottomanisches Reiches* (Vienna, 1928), p. 51. As proof of the supposed designs in the interior of Asia, he states that after the war began, German officers who had travelled in Persia appeared at Constantinople with the plan of bringing about an alliance between Turkey, Persia and Afghanistan and of appointing German consuls in Persia and Afghanistan. *Ibid.*, p. 52. A remark of the German Emperor to the effect that "he hopes some day to be able to greet his sister the Queen of Greece as empress of Byzantium" was reported to the Austro-Hungarian ambassador, who concluded that "love for his sister" was not the determining factor. "Perhaps," he suggested, "they think in Berlin that whenever Turkish rule here comes to an end, it would be to Germany's interest to have the Greeks in Constantinople in place of the Turks." Pallavicini to Berchtold, 2 October, 1913; *Ö.-U. A.*, VII, 393-394.

[†] "In Turkey, the army is the factor which dominates everything, and he who has the Turkish army in his hands is master of the fate of the empire." Pallavicini to Berchtold, 29 December, 1913; *Ö.-U. A.*, VII, 688.

[‡] The fullest account is given by R. J. Kerner, "The Mission of Liman von Sanders," in *Slavonic Review*, VI, 12-27, 244-363, 543-569 (June, December, 1927; March, 1928); VII, 90-112 (June, 1928). Cf. also L. von Sanders, *Fünf Jahre Türkei* (Berlin, 1920), pp. 9-33.

[§] Treutler to foreign office, 2 April, 1913; *G. P.*, XXXVIII, 195.

strasse raised no objection to the sending of an officer after the conclusion of peace between Turkey and the Balkan states. William II approved the plan, partly because the officer might be able to secure orders for German industry. He said something about it to Nicholas II and George V when they attended the marriage of his daughter in May.* The details were worked out by the military officials of the German Empire, and, while the foreign office served as intermediary with the Turkish Government, it appears probable that the chancellor, Herr von Bethmann-Hollweg, was not kept informed. At any rate he did not speak of the Mission in a long and friendly conversation with M. Sazonov in October, 1913; with the unfortunate result that when the secret was finally revealed, the Russian foreign minister felt that he had been deceived by the German statesman.

According to the official German view, the Mission was concerned with strictly military matters and was to be regarded in the same light as the British naval mission and the other foreign missions engaged in reorganizing the Turkish services. But the German ambassador in Constantinople, Baron von Wagenheim, attached much political importance to it. In his eyes, the Mission would on the one hand serve to strengthen the position of the Ottoman Empire and help to prolong its uncertain life; under German control, the Turkish army might even take effective part "in a future war." On the other hand, if the collapse of the empire could not be ultimately avoided, Germany would have time to stake out her claims against the day of partition.† And since the German foreign minister was of the opinion that in the event of partition "to come out empty-handed would be a second Morocco for us,"‡ one may fairly conclude that the Mission was considered as much a political manœuvre as a military and technical undertaking.§

* William's marginal note; *G. P.*, XXXVIII, 232.
† Wangenheim to Bethmann-Hollweg, 21 May, 1913; *G. P.*, XXXVIII, 41-48.
‡ Jagow to Lichnowsky, private, 31 May, 1913; *G. P.*, XXXVIII, 55.
§ Cf. C. Mühlmann [adjutant of General Liman von Sanders], *Deutschland und die Türkei, 1913–1914* (Berlin-Grunewald, 1929), pp. 6-7, 10-12.

Meanwhile the original suggestion of employing a German officer to reorganize the fortifications of Constantinople had been greatly enlarged. General von Sanders was to be accompanied by forty-two officers. He was to have direction of all military schools, to be a member of the Turkish war council, to control the higher appointments in the army, and to have the power of inflicting punishments and making inspections. In addition, he was personally to command the First Army Corps at Constantinople, with the object of making it a model corps. His contract was to run for five years.* The effect would be to bring the Turkish army very much under German control, and the secrecy with which the negotiations were shrouded, while natural enough, was an index of their importance.

When the terms of the Mission were announced early in November, M. Sazonov was highly annoyed. Protesting against the silence of Herr von Bethmann-Hollweg on the matter at the time of their recent conversation, he telegraphed to Berlin and Constantinople:

Of itself, a German military mission in regions bordering on our frontier [sic] could not but provoke violent irritation in Russian public opinion, and would certainly be interpreted as an act manifestly hostile to us. Especially also, the placing of Turkish troops in Constantinople under a German general must necessarily arouse suspicion and apprehension amongst us.†

To the German chargé at St. Petersburg he asserted that "the matter was not a military, but a political question of high importance to Russia," for "the Russian ambassador in Constantinople would, so to speak, be protected by a German army

---

* Jagow to William II, 20 September, 1913; *G. P.*, XXXVIII, 204–205. The text of the contract is given in Mühlmann, pp. 88–92.

† Sazonov to Sverbeyev and Giers, 10 November, 1913; R. S. F. S. R. [Russia], Commissariat of Foreign Affairs, *Материалы по истории Франко-Русских отношений за 1910–1914 г.г.* [Materials for the history of Franco-Russian relations, 1910–1914] (Moscow, 1922), p. 633.

corps."* The real meaning of these outbursts is clear enough. The Russian Government feared that Turkey, under German guidance, would become strong enough to resist Russian pressure for the opening of the straits. Consequently M. Sazonov exerted himself mightily to bring about a cancellation of the contract between the German general and the Sublime Porte, so energetically in fact that the German Government, though refusing to abandon the Mission, deemed it wise to negotiate a compromise. It proposed that General von Sanders should not command an army corps, at Constantinople or elsewhere, but should be made inspector-general of the Turkish army. Although the general would continue to exercise the powers which made his Mission really dangerous to Russian interests, the solution was accepted by M. Sazonov, and so the crisis passed. Possibly he would have liked to take a sterner attitude, but a memorandum of the Russian naval staff stated that the Black Sea fleet was not able to assume the offensive against Turkey.† Moreover, the British Government, although at first disposed to make a strong stand against the German policy,‡ found itself embarrassed by its own naval mission in Turkey, of which the German Government made great play,§ and was not willing to do more than join France and Russia in asking the Porte to give full information about the contract with Liman von Sanders.‖ No more were the French, ensconced as they were in control of the gendarmerie, ready to

---

* Lucius to foreign office, 17 November, 1913; *G. P.*, XXXVIII, 208. France adopted the Russian view. Pichon to P. Cambon, 29 November, 1913; *Affaires balkaniques*, III, 91. It is interesting to note that the Turkish minister of war, Izzet Pasha, took a view not unlike that of the Russians. When the question of the mission was broached to him, he said: "If the command of the army is to be intrusted to a German, then the office of grand vizier and the ministry of foreign affairs can well be given to other foreigners." *Denkwürdigkeiten des Marschalls Izzet Pascha*, p. 225.

† Memorandum of Grigorovich, 20 November, 1913; Y. Zakher,"Константинополь и проливы," in *Красный Архив*, VI, 68–69 (1924).

‡ Apparently at the suggestion of France. Pichon to P. Cambon, 29 November, 1913; Pichon to Bompard, 2 December, 1913; *Affaires balkaniques*, III, 91–92, 96. Cf. also Russian chargé in London to Sazonov, 2 December, 1913; Siebert, p. 643.

§ Jagow to Kühlmann, 4 December, 1913; Kühlmann to Bethman-Hollweg, 9 December, 1913; *G. P.*, XXXVIII, 232–233, 245–247; Benckendorff to Sazonov, 12 December, 1913; Siebert, p. 651.

‖ Benckendorff to Sazonov, 9 December, 1913; Siebert, pp. 646–647.

push matters beyond diplomatic protest.* In other words, M. Sazonov, when confronted by an issue which, in his opinion, seriously affected the interests of Russia, found himself unable either to resort to force or to mobilize the Triple Entente for an effective demonstration.

The crisis had far-reaching consequences. It determined the Russian Government to try to convert the Triple Entente into a triple alliance, and, as has already been pointed out,† overtures in this sense were made to Great Britain in the spring of 1914. If they did not lead to the desired result, they did make possible the beginning of conversations between the British and Russian naval staffs which caused both umbrage and alarm in Berlin and were not without bearing on the crisis of July, 1914. Furthermore, the overtures for an alliance were renewed after the murder at Sarajevo.‡

Even more important were the discussions inaugurated by the Russian Government in respect of the whole problem of the Straits. The naval staff was frankly of the opinion that the only solution compatible with the interests and dignity of Russia was seizure and possession of the Straits.§ M. Sazonov accordingly asked the Tsar for permission to have the problem discussed by the competent authorities.‖

Two conferences were therefore held, one of ministers and officials of the foreign office on 13 January, 1914, to discuss the questions of high policy involved, the other of military and naval experts on 21 February, to consider the practical application of that policy. The reports of the two conferences, published since the war by the Soviet Government, are much

---

* The suggestion of Bompard, the French ambassador in Constantinople, that Russia "should despatch a war-ship to the Bosphorus and declare that it would not be withdrawn until the contract with General von Liman and his officers had been altered" (Izvolski to Sazonov, 1 January, 1914; Marchand, II, 222; Stieve, IV, 10) was not taken up in Paris.

† See above, pp. 52–53.   ‡ See below, pp. 432–433.

§ The chief of the naval staff, Prince Lieven, was sceptical, for he thought that Russia would need a territorial connection with the Straits and possession of the Ægean islands. Such a plan, he wrote in 1912, was "evidently not in our power and perhaps will never be for Russia in the future." Y. Zakher, "Константинополь и проливы," in Красный Архив, VI, 59.

‖ See above, p. 88.

too long to be quoted in any detail.* They may be summarized as follows: At the first, or political, conference, M. Sazonov spoke in favor of using force, if necessary, to secure acceptance of Russia's position with reference to the Mission of Liman von Sanders, provided she received "an assurance of Great Britain's active participation." But the premier, M. Kokovtzov, declared that measures of compulsion, such as the occupation of Turkish territory in Asia Minor, would lead to war with Germany, and put the direct question, "Is war with Germany desirable, and can Russia wage it?" The soldiers declared that Russia was able to wage war with both Germany and Austria-Hungary, and M. Sazonov was apparently not unwilling to take this risk; but the premier insisted that "a war at the present moment would be the greatest misfortune for Russia," and his contention that a war with Germany was not desirable was accepted by the conference, including M. Sazonov. In consequence, the foreign minister accepted the compromise offered by Germany in respect of the Sanders Mission.†

* Pokrowski, *Drei Konferenzen*, pp. 32–67; F. Stieve, *Izvolski and the World War* (New York, 1926), pp. 219–246.

† Kokovtzov denies that there was any divergence between himself and Sazonov. "During the whole of our collaboration in the government, at first under the presidency of Stolypin and then later when I succeeded him, until the very day of my resignation, Sazonov was never in favor of an aggressive policy against Turkey. His fundamental view, that a weak Turkey is advantageous to Russia, and that Russia should not hasten her collapse, is clearly stated in his report and recurs over and over again in his declarations. His point of view was open to only one criticism: in exposing his argument to the Emperor, he discussed the Turkish problem as something disparate and independent, outside the realm of general European politics where grave complications are apt to arise most unexpectedly and from innumerable causes. . . .

"He was perfectly aware of our military unpreparedness and on this particular question we were in complete agreement. He was a constant witness of my arguments with the minister of war over the question of the organization of national defense . . . we invariably agreed that the opinions of the minister of war were far too optimistic and were due to his complete ignorance of the actual conditions.

". . . Sazonov was not at that time, in January, 1914, under the influence of our Ministry of War and of the Admiralty. . . .

"My own part consisted not so much in trying to prove that the measures suggested by the minister of foreign affairs were inacceptable in principle and at the same time impracticable, as in arguing the two following propositions: (1) the complete improbability that the point of view of the report would be accepted by France and especially by England; and (2) the close connection of this problem with the general problem of European peace and the danger of even raising it." From a letter of Kokovtzov of 23 April, 1929, printed by M. Florinsky, "Russia and Constantinople: Count Kokovtzov's Evidence," in *Foreign Affairs* (New York), VIII, 138–139 (October, 1929).

At the second, or technical, conference M. Sazonov asked for a discussion of the military and naval measures necessary for seizing the straits in the event of a European war. The chief of staff pointed out that in such an event the troops required for such a stroke would be imperatively needed on the western (*i. e.,* the Russian western) front against Germany; the naval authorities were more favorable to the enterprise. But the final opinion was that a separate expedition against the Straits was out of the question. On the other hand, since there was complete agreement that Russia could not allow the Straits to fall into the hands of another Power, the conference recommended a series of preparatory measures, such as an increase of the Black Sea fleet and the construction of railways in the Caucasus, which might ultimately make possible an offensive against the Bosphorus. Shortly afterward the Duma voted that 110 millions of rubles should be spent on the Black Sea fleet, but as only 25 millions were appropriated for 1914, it would seem that an immediate expedition against Constantinople was not contemplated.

It all came to this: in the existing situation of European politics Russia could not hope to secure the opening of the Straits except by seizing them and she could not hope to seize them except in the event of general complications; but in such an event, she would have no forces to spare for such an adventure. In face of this vicious circle, the only course was to continue her military and naval preparations, in order to be ready for an emergency. But so far as the available evidence permits one to judge, it was not the Russian intention to create the emergency.

Thus two mighty currents were meeting at Constantinople, the Russian streaming toward the southwest, the German flowing toward the southeast. Both Russia and Germany desired the maintenance of the Ottoman Empire for as long as possible, but both cherished ulterior motives. The former wished Turkey to remain strong enough to defend the Straits against attack by another state but weak enough to be helpless before a Russian attack. The latter desired Turkey to become as strong as possible, but a Turkey in which the economic, political, and military influence of Germany would be predominant, a Turkey reduced ultimately to a status of a veiled German protectorate.* The Russian policy was the more aggressive, in the sense that it would have to be pursued by force of arms; but the success of the German policy of penetration would have altered the European balance of power as effectively as the more direct Russian course.† The difference was one of means, not of ends.

The effects of the Sanders Mission were not restricted to secret manœuvres and confabulations on the part of the Russian Government. Public evidence was soon forthcoming that Russo-German relations had lost all cordiality and might become dangerously tense. In March, 1914, the *Kölnische Zeitung* published a sensational article from its St. Petersburg correspondent which was the signal for a bitter press feud between German and Russian newspapers. After stating that Russia was not then in a position to support political threats by force of arms, it remarked that "in three or four years the political weight of Russian military power will be estimated quite differently," and gave expression to the view that when Russia had completed her preparations, that is, by 1917, she would undertake a war against Germany.‡

* The Austro-Hungarian ambassador in Constantinople interpreted the aim of German policy to be "the creation of a German protectorate through control of the army, according to the model, as it were, of the English in Egypt." He doubted if Germany was strong enough to carry through this policy single-handed, and suggested (1) that the protectorate should be exercised over Asia Minor, not by Germany alone, but by the Triple Alliance; and (2) that the opposition of the Entente Powers should be forestalled by giving Armenia to Russia, Syria to France, and Mesopotamia to Great Britain! Pallavicini to Berchtold, 29 December, 1913; *Ö.-U. A.*, VII, 688.

† At least so it appeared to the Russians. "The Young Turk Government, which aimed at liberating Turkey from foreign influence, yet pursued, at the same time, a course which could only end in political and military bondage to Germany. We watched with anxiety the gradual suppression of Turkish independence by Germany, foreseeing the consequences that were bound to follow." Sazonov, p. 124. The Russian ambassador in Constantinople told the grand vizier that Russia cherished "friendly feelings" for Turkey, but "must under all circumstances avoid becoming the neighbor of Germany also in Asia." Pallavicini to Berchtold, 25 March, 1914; *Ö.-U. A.*, VII, 1004.

‡ The *Kölnische Zeitung* was often used by the German Government as its mouthpiece, which was precisely what gave importance to its articles. In this case

To this the *Birsheviya Vyedomosti* replied with an article prepared by the Russian minister of war himself. It began by saying:

We can proudly assert that the time for threats is past, that Russia no longer fears foreign threats, and that Russian public opinion has no further reason for uneasiness.

After a summary of what had been accomplished in the reform of the Russian army, it concluded thus:

It is important that Russian public opinion be conscious that the country is prepared for any eventuality. But the military power of a land whose ruler took the initiative in the matter of the Peace Conference at The Hague can be disagreeable only to states which have aggressive intentions. No one should have longings for any part of the Russian empire. Russia as well as her ruler desires peace, but she is also armed for an emergency.

For some time thereafter the German and Russian press abused each other roundly; in Germany the desirability of a preventive war had already been frankly discussed.* Further fuel to the flames of hostility was provided by the discussion of the Russo-German commercial treaty of 1904, which would soon have to be renewed. In the Russian mind, the treaty, which had been negotiated during the Russo-Japanese war, was quite unfair to Russia, and the demand was universal that more favorable terms be secured. There was no indication that Germany was

---

neither the German Government nor the German embassy in St. Petersburg had inspired the article, according to *G. P.*, XXXIX, 548, note **, 549, note *. The Austro-Hungarian ambassador, however, reported that the German chargé was "the chief inspirer of the warlike alarms which reached Germany by way of the St. Petersburg correspondents of German newspapers." Szápáry to Berchtold, 12 April, 1914; *Ö.-U. A.*, VII, 1049.

* The Berlin *Post*, which had published the famous "War in Sight?" article in 1875, argued on 24 February, 1914, that while the armaments of the Entente were greater than those of the Triple Alliance, "at the moment the state of things is favorable for us. France is not yet ready for war. England has internal and colonial difficulties, and Russia recoils from the conflict because she fears revolution at home. Ought we to wait until our adversaries are ready?" It answered its own question by declaring that "no one will take the responsibility of not making war, because such a lack of decision will create the greatest misfortunes for Germany; the task of German policy is not to preserve peace as long as possible, but on the contrary to prepare for the inevitable war with energy and foresight and to begin it under the most favorable conditions."

disposed to grant them. Herr von Jagow and M. Sazonov might make conciliatory speeches in the Reichstag* and the Duma,† recalling the traditional friendship of Germany and Russia, but it was evident to all that the relations between the two countries had become tense; how tense may be gauged from a peculiar incident.

On 12 April, 1914, Professor Mitrofanoff, of the University of St. Petersburg, addressed an 'open letter' to his former teacher, Professor Hans Delbrück, who published it in the *Preussische Jahrbücher.*‡ The Russian professor declared that the commercial treaty of 1904 had made Russia "a tributary of Germany." Reviewing the developments in the Balkan peninsula and the Near East, he affirmed that Russian opinion held Germany responsible (by her support of Austria-Hungary) for the setbacks which Russian policy had experienced of recent years. In short, he said, the German Empire was "the principal enemy of Russia."

> The Russia of to-day demands respect for its honor and consideration for its interests. . . . War with Germany would be a misfortune, but we shall not shrink from the bitter necessity, if it becomes really necessary.

To these startling statements Professor Delbrück replied:

> If Russia sees it as her mission to dominate Europe and Asia —well, we see it as the mission of Germany to guard Europe and Asia from this domination of the Muscovites. I am not in a position to give any other answer to my honored friend Professor von Mitrofanoff.

The polemics of the two professors blurted out truths which could not be expressed in the restrained despatches of diplomatists.

Before the effect of this sensation had worn off, the *Birsheviya Vyedomosti,* on 13 June, published another article.

* 14 May, 1914.　　　　　　　　　　　† 23 May, 1914.
‡ P. von Mitrofanoff, "Offener Brief über das Verhältnis von Russland und Deutschland," in *Preussische Jahrbücher,* CLVI, 385–398 (June, 1914).

The Russian newspaper, taking alarm over a ministerial crisis in France which was provoked by the demand of the Socialist party for the repeal of the three years' military service restored in 1913, declared that Russia could not view the matter "with complete indifference," and called upon France to "fulfil her obligations." After reciting the great efforts of Russia to reorganize her army, it concluded:

In this way we have done everything to anticipate the enemy when mobilization comes and at the same time to concentrate the army as quickly as possible in the first days of the war.

We wish the same also from France. The greater number of soldiers she maintains in time of peace, the sooner will she be ready.

Therefore we hope that the French Government will succeed in preserving the law of three years' service which is so necessary for France. We can repeat, with a slight change, what we have already said in the spring:

Russia and France do not desire war, but Russia is ready and hopes that France will also be ready.*

The article evoked from the German Emperor the following comment:

Well! At last the Russians have shown their hand! Whoever in Germany still refuses to believe that in Russo-Gaul [*Russo-Gallien*] they are working at high pressure for an early war with us . . . deserves to be sent at once to the mad-house at Dalldorf!

And it so upset the German chancellor that on 16 June he sent it on to the German ambassador in London with a long commentary on Russian policy, in the course of which he remarked:

I do not believe that Russia is planning an early war against us. But, covered as she is by her extensive military preparations, she would certainly like, in the event of a new Balkan crisis— and we shall not be able to take it amiss—to make a stronger stand than she did in the recent Balkan complications.

* This article was also supposed to have been inspired by the minister of war, General Sukhomlinov. It is reproduced in *G. P.*, XXXIX, 587–589.

In such an event, he argued, the maintenance of peace would depend on the co-operation of Germany and England: otherwise, he went on to say:

Any casual, even a quite secondary conflict of interests between Russia and Austria-Hungary may light the torch of war. A foresighted policy must consider in advance the possibility of this eventuality.*

If this despatch was intended partly as a warning against the risks involved in the rumored plan of an Anglo-Russian naval convention,† it leaves no doubt that Herr von Bethmann perceived keenly the latent danger of the Balkan situation and its probable reaction on Russo-German relations. Less than two weeks later occurred the murders of Sarajevo.

Austria-Hungary and Serbia‡

The effects of the Balkan wars of 1912–1913 were by no means limited to the weakened Ottoman Empire or reflected solely in the growing rivalry of Russia and Germany at Constantinople. The Balkan states, after destroying the Turkish power in Europe, had fought among themselves, and the results were registered in the Treaty of Bucharest of 10 August, 1913. By that instrument Bulgaria, hopelessly beaten in a war

---

* Bethmann-Hollweg to Lichnowsky, 16 June, 1914; *G. P.*, XXXIX, 628–630.
† See above, p. 52.
‡ In order to avoid the use of diacritical marks and to give an approximate representation of the pronunciation, the following system of transliterating Serbo-Croatian proper names has been used:

'ц' (Croatian 'c') 'ts'
'ч' (Croatian 'č') 'ch' ⎫ ⎧ It is impossible to represent in English the dif-
'ћ' (Croatian 'ć') 'ch' ⎭ ⎨ ference between these two sounds.
'ш' (Croatian 'š') 'sh'
'ж' (Croatian 'ž') 'zh'
'j' (Croatian 'j') 'y'
'љ' (Croatian 'lj') 'ly'
'њ' (Croatian 'nj') 'ny'
'ђ' (Croatian 'dj') 'ge'

An exception has been made of 'Sarajevo,' which has become the accepted spelling in all Western languages, although 'Sarayevo' would be the correct form in English. In the case of authors cited, their names have been standardized according to the system noted; but at the first citation, the spelling given in the book or article is indicated in brackets.

which she had deliberately precipitated, was deprived of most of what she had taken up arms to gain, namely, nearly all of Macedonia, the southern part going to Greece, the northern and far more important sector to Serbia. The Bulgarians, though aware that their fate had been incurred through the folly of King Ferdinand and the mistakes of their government, were left on the one hand sullen and suspicious, on the other determined to revise the settlement when opportunity offered. The Serbs, for their part, had succeeded beyond their fondest expectations. They had doubled the area of their state and increased their population by at least two-thirds; perhaps even more satisfying was the prestige brought by their victories, which destroyed the reputation for cowardice and incompetence that had oppressed them for a generation. Serbia, in short, from being a despised and ineffectual nation, had emerged as a real factor in European politics.

This new position of Serbia was deeply resented by her great northern neighbor, Austria-Hungary. It had been the expectation in Vienna and Budapest, when the war broke out, that Serbia would be trounced by the Turks, and later, when the reverse had happened, that she would be beaten by Bulgaria. The resentment was so great that, according to a highly placed official of the Ballplatz,* "from the day the peace of Bucharest was concluded, it was clear to all informed Austrian and Hungarian statesmen that it must come to a world war unless something happened to modify the unwholesome effects of that peace."† And the Great War did actually arise out of this Austro-Serbian antagonism. Prophetically enough, a great French historian had written, a generation before:

For a century men have been laboring to solve the Eastern Question. On the day when that shall have been considered

---

* The Austro-Hungarian foreign office in Vienna.
† A. Hoyos, "Zusammenhänge," in E. Ritter von Steinitz, *Rings um Sazonow* (Berlin, 1928), p. 69. "The wound still rankles deep with Berchtold," the Austro-Hungarian foreign minister, testified the German ambassador in Vienna. Tschirschky to Jagow, private, 25 August, 1913; *G. P.*, XXXV, 362, note †.

solved, Europe will inevitably see propounded the 'question of Austria.'*

Broadly speaking, the issue was quite simple: it was the conflict between the principle of nationality and the doctrine of historic right, a conflict which Austria-Hungary had already faced in Italy in 1859 and in Germany in 1866. The Serbs were one of three branches of the Yugoslav people, the other two being the Croats and Slovenes,† and they were the most numerous branch, comprising perhaps 6,000,000 out of some 12,000,000 Yugoslavs. Of these Serbs, the majority were to be found in the kingdom of Serbia, a state which had achieved its independence of Turkey very largely by its own exertions. This little state, inspired by the example of Italy, assumed for itself, as its leaders publicly proclaimed, the rôle of Piedmont, that is, it wished to unite with itself the Serbs who were subjects of Turkey and Austria-Hungary,‡ and a few imaginative spirits even dreamed of Yugoslav unity by the inclusion of the Croats and Slovenes.

Such a programme was in harmony with the trend of European development throughout the nineteenth century, but Austria-Hungary could hardly be expected to look upon it favorably. For quite apart from the reluctance of any state to surrender territory, the loss of the Yugoslav provinces would deprive the Dual Monarchy of its sole outlet to the sea and would seriously compromise its position as a Great Power; indeed it was probable that any such amputation would mean

* A. Sorel, *The Eastern Question in the Eighteenth Century* (English translation, London, 1898; first published in 1878), p. 266.

† Strictly speaking, the Bulgars should also be considered as Yugoslavs, but practically, the kinship is seldom recognized, and the events of the nineteenth century have given the Bulgars their own course of development outside the Yugoslav group.

‡ The Radical party, organized in 1881, stated its programme to be "the people's welfare and freedom at home, and the country's independence and unification with the other parts of Serbdom abroad" (manifesto published in the *Samouprava*, 8 January, 1881). On 17 October, 1905, Nikola P. Pashich, the veteran leader of the party, stated, in a speech in the Skupshtina, that the party "had turned its attention to the consolidation of the internal situation, in order to make Serbia the worthy Piedmont of Serbdom." D. A. Loncharevich [Lončarević], *Jugoslaviens Entstehung* (Vienna, 1929), p. 96.

the destruction of the Habsburg state, for other races of the polyglot empire, many of whom had never ceased to protest against the hegemony of the Germans and Magyars, would make demands incompatible with the existence of the Monarchy. To defend the existing order, so advantageous to themselves, against the ambitions of Serbia appeared to the ruling classes of Austria-Hungary as an elementary duty. To emancipate the Serbs and perhaps the other Yugoslavs of the Monarchy from a rule with which they were becoming ever more dissatisfied, appeared to Serbian statesmen just as keenly as an elementary duty. Theoretically a solution of the problem could have been found in the absorption of all the Serbs into the Monarchy. Practically, as will be seen presently, the gravest difficulties existed to prevent such an adjustment.

The origins of the antagonism date back some forty years before 1914.* In 1875 the Turkish provinces of Bosnia and Herzegovina, lying to the west of Serbia and inhabited by a population purely Yugoslav and largely Serb, began one of their periodical revolts against the Sultan. When the European

---

* In 1848–1849 the Serbs of southern Hungary fought on the side of Austria against Hungary, and they were joined by large numbers of Serbs from the Principality of Serbia; ultimately the combined forces were put under the command of an Austrian general. The government in Vienna promised to recognize the Serbian territories of Hungary as a separate crown land (*voyvodina*) with its own constitution drawn up by a national committee of the Hungarian Serbs, but after the victory over the Magyars this promise was ignored. Although this caused bitter resentment in Serbia, Prince Alexander Karageorgevich continued to cultivate friendly relations with the Habsburgs. On the other hand, his successor Prince Michael Obrenovich (1860–1868) planned to make common cause with the Magyars against Austria. He discussed with Kossuth the project of a Danubian confederation in which Hungary, Croatia, Serbia and Rumania should unite against Austria on the one hand and Turkey on the other. After the Compromise of 1867 had restored the Serbian provinces of Hungary to the rule of Budapest, the Austro-Hungarian Government made a special effort to destroy the pro-Russian sentiment in Serbia, and was successful to the extent that Prince Milan, whose conservative political views and timid foreign policy were unpopular with his subjects, came to think the friendship of the Dual Monarchy worth having. The essential factor in Austro-Serbian relations was described by the Austrian representative in Belgrade, Benjamin Kállay, in these words: "If we succeed in convincing the Serbs that Austria, renouncing all idea of occupying [the Slav provinces of Turkey], will confine herself to sincerely desiring their political and material development and would be disposed to give it real assistance, I do not believe that any Serb will think more about Russia, and then our moral influence can become preponderant in Serbia." Kállay to Beust, 22 June, 1868; R. W. Seton-Watson, "Les relations de l'Autriche-Hongrie et de la Serbie entre 1868 et 1874," I, in *Le monde slave*, III, i, 226–227 (no. 2, 1926).

Powers, on account of their dissensions, proved unable or unwilling to deal effectively with the rising, which might have been settled by the grant of autonomy to the two provinces, the leaders of the movement, in June, 1876, proclaimed the union of Bosnia with Serbia. The sentiment of Serbia in respect of Bosnia was diagnosed in 1870 by the Austro-Hungarian diplomatic agent in Belgrade as follows:

Bosnia is the point on which all Serbian politicians are sensitive; it is the centre on which all their desires and all their hopes have for a long time turned, although, since they well understand their own interests and are conscious of their weakness, they have no serious intention of passing from simple aspirations to energetic action and are not likely to do so later. As long as Bosnia remains a Turkish province, the Serbs will consider that question a family affair, the solution of which is not urgent, because they believe that sooner or later a solution favorable to them will come about, and they hope, if circumstances permit, by war. But the moment they think that they see a foreign power manifesting a fancy to annex it, everything will change; all their distrust, all their fear will awaken, and the consciousness of their own powerlessness will easily cause these feelings to degenerate into bitterness.*

And he pointed out what seemed to him the proper attitude for Austria-Hungary to assume:

Since nothing can change the fact that the Serbs count on possessing Bosnia some day, it will always be more advantageous, in my humble opinion, that they should hope to realize that combination with our help, for thus we shall assure ourselves a lasting control over them.†

Subsequent events were to prove the truth of these observations.

Prince Milan Obrenovich of Serbia had been urged by his ministers to send the Serbian army into Bosnia and present the Powers with a *fait accompli,* and he now declared war against

---

* Kállay to Beust, 17 March, 1870; R. W. Seton-Watson, *ibid.,* II, in *Le monde slave,* III, ii, 194–195 (no. 5, 1926).
† Kállay to Beust, 29 October, 1868; *ibid.,* III, ii, 190; Kállay later became a bitter opponent of the Serbs.

Turkey. But the golden moment had passed, for the Turks had had time to collect their forces and defeated the Serbs. Although the Serbs took part in the Russo-Turkish war which began in April, 1877, they did not enjoy the favor of the Tsar, whose interest was centred upon the Bulgarians. The result was that when the fate of Bosnia and Herzegovina had to be settled at the Congress of Berlin, they were not given autonomy under Turkish suzerainty or added to Serbia, but handed over to Austria-Hungary to 'occupy and administer.'* The Bosnian population bitterly resented this disposal of themselves and rose in arms against their new masters. The effective occupation of the provinces required the use of a large body of Austro-Hungarian troops and was not completed for some months; even so, another rebellion broke out in 1882. In the end, the seizure of these provinces against the wishes of the inhabitants was to prove as fatal to Austria-Hungary as the annexation of Alsace-Lorraine did to Germany.

Serbia found the pill equally bitter to swallow, although Austria-Hungary endeavored to gild it by securing for Serbia in the Treaty of Berlin the districts of Nish and Pirot which the Serbian armies had occupied in the war against Turkey. To the Serbs Bosnia made a tremendous sentimental appeal because it was one of the chief centres of Serbian tradition and because

---

* Article XXV of the Treaty of Berlin. The question had been discussed in July, 1876, at the conference of Reichstadt between the rulers of Russia and Austria-Hungary and their ministers. Andrássy, the Austro-Hungarian foreign minister, understood Russia to agree that the Dual Monarchy might annex all of Bosnia and Herzegovina except certain 'extensions' assigned to Serbia and Montenegro "to round them off." E. von Wertheimer, *Graf Julius Andrássy* (Stuttgart, 1909–1913); II, 322–325; Pribram, English translation, II, 188–191. According to the Russian version (*Красный Архив*, I, 36), Gorchakov consented that Montenegro should annex Herzegovina, but that Austria-Hungary should take only Turkish Croatia and a small part of Bosnia adjacent to the frontier. Cf. G. H. Rupp, "The Reichstadt Agreement," in *American Historical Review*, XXX, 503–510 (April, 1925). Since the Treaty of San Stefano, dictated to Turkey by Russia at the close of the war, ignored the stipulations of Reichstadt and left Bosnia-Herzegovina to Turkey, Austria-Hungary joined with Great Britain in demanding a revision of the treaty, and the two Powers, with the diplomatic connivance of Germany, compelled Russia to submit the treaty to a European congress, which met at Berlin. At the congress, the Turks refused to cede the provinces outright to Austria-Hungary, which had to content herself with the right to 'occupy and administer' them.

its dialect had been adopted as the basis of the literary Serbian language; for this land to pass under foreign rule was felt to be a national humiliation. And sentiment apart, there was the practical disadvantage that the little land-locked state had dreamed for years of finding an outlet to the sea through Bosnia-Herzegovina and Montenegro. Not only was this hope now dashed, but the military occupation by Austria-Hungary of the Sandjak of Novi Bazar, which had also been sanctioned by the Treaty of Berlin, drove a wedge between Serbia and Montenegro, the other independent Serb state, which possessed a tiny strip of seacoast at Antivari. Henceforth Serbia was surrounded on the north, west and southwest by Austria-Hungary: she lay at the mercy of her mighty neighbor, whose territory offered practically the only market for Serbian exports.

Judged by the standards of the time the Austro-Hungarian action was quite intelligible. The motive was partly dynastic— the desire to secure compensation for the loss of the Italian provinces in 1859 and the extrusion from Germany in 1866, a consideration which helps to explain the zeal with which Prince Bismarck, the German chancellor, urged Count Andrássy, the Austro-Hungarian foreign minister, to follow this course. The real purpose, however, was less a satisfaction of *amour propre* than the preparation of a large political and economic programme. The occupation of the Sandjak "to the other side of [*au delà de*] Mitrovitsa" (as the Berlin Treaty expressed it) was intended, so Count Andrássy explained, to provide "a springboard to the Orient" [*ein Ausfallstor nach dem Orient*], so that "at the ultimate [*eventuellen*] collapse of Turkey, we may be in the closest proximity to the scene and there be able to protect the interest of the Monarchy."* Although Andrássy resisted the pressure of the military party to go to Salonica, his

---

* Wertheimer, *Graf Julius Andrássy*, III, 210. Article XXV of the Berlin Treaty recognized the Austro-Hungarian right of "having military and commercial roads in the whole of this part of the ancient vilayet of Bosnia." It was on the basis of this provision that Aehrenthal in 1908 (see below, p. 122) launched his scheme for a railway through the Sandjak to Salonica.

policy and that of his successors aimed to establish the exclusive influence of Austria-Hungary in the western Balkans, for by this means the aspirations of Russia would be held in check, markets would be found for the developing commerce and industry of the Monarchy, and the future would be reserved. Territorial expansion, to which the Magyars were opposed, would not be necessary, provided Serbia could be kept in leading-strings, both politically and economically; and so, during the twenty-five years following the occupation of Bosnia-Herzegovina, Austro-Hungarian policy exerted itself to the utmost to control the conduct of the little state and keep it in economic subjection.*

The task of the Vienna statesmen was enormously facilitated by the character of the two Serbian rulers, Milan and Alexander Obrenovich. Prince Milan (1869–1889), thanks to the scandals of his private life, his expensive habits which burdened the state with debt, and his autocratic temperament, was far from popular with his democratic subjects, and after the Congress of Berlin he felt his own personal position and the future of Serbia so insecure that he 'sold out' to Austria-Hungary. In 1881 he concluded a remarkable secret treaty with the Monarchy,† the existence of which was not known until 1893 and its purport until 1909.‡ In return for Austro-Hungarian assistance in securing the title of king, which he hoped would strengthen his position, and the maintenance of his dynasty, which would increase the prestige of Serbia, he promised that

Without a previous understanding with Austria-Hungary, Serbia will neither negotiate nor conclude any political treaty

---

* The Austro-Hungarian point of view is set forth in T. von Sosnosky, *Die Balkanpolitik Oesterreich-Ungarns seit 1866* (Vienna, 1913–1914), the Serbian in Loncharevich, *Jugoslaviens Entstehung;* J. Larmeroux, *La politique extérieure de l'Autriche-Hongrie, 1876–1914* (Paris, 1918), presents an extreme French view.

† Pribram, I, 18–23, English translation, I, 51–63.

‡ S. Protich [Protitch], "The Secret Treaty between Austria-Hungary and Serbia," in *Fortnightly Review*, XCI, 838–849 (May, 1909). His account of the genesis of the treaty is confirmed in essentials by A. F. Pribram, "Milan IV. von Serbien und die Geheimverträge Österreich-Ungarns mit Serbien, 1881–1889," in *Historische Blätter*, I, 464–494 (1922).

with another Government, and will not admit to her territory a foreign armed force, regular or irregular, even as volunteers;*

likewise that

Serbia will not tolerate political, religious, or other intrigues, which, taking her territory as a point of departure, might be directed against the Austro-Hungarian Monarchy, including therein Bosnia, Herzegovina, and the Sandjak of Novibazar.†

It was small compensation that he received the somewhat vague assurance that

If as a result of a combination of circumstances whose development is not to be foreseen at present, Serbia were in a position to make territorial acquisitions in the direction of her southern frontiers (with the exception of the Sandjak of Novi-

* The treaty was signed for Serbia by the foreign minister, Chedomil Miyatovich, the premier, M. Pirochanats, having refused to do so. Confronted with a *fait accompli*, the premier resigned. To avoid having to appoint a Russophil cabinet, the prince agreed to a joint declaration, according to which the aforesaid provision "cannot impair the right of Serbia to negotiate and to conclude treaties, even of a political nature, with another government. It implies for Serbia no other engagement than that of not negotiating and of not concluding any political treaty which would be contrary to the spirit and the tenor of the said secret Treaty." To counteract the effect of this, the prince addressed a 'personal declaration' to the Austro-Hungarian foreign minister repudiating the views of his minister and saying: "Having it much at heart to prove with the very first steps which I take in the path I have chosen *of My own free will,* how I hold to the faithful execution of My promises, *I hereby, Excellency, assume the formal engagement on My honor and in My quality as Prince of Serbia, not to enter into any negotiation whatsoever relative to any kind of a political treaty between Serbia and a third state without communication with and previous consent of Austria-Hungary. I beg your Excellency to consider the present engagement as having an entirely official character toward the Government of His Imperial and Royal Apostolic Majesty."* Cf. C. Miyatovich [Mijatovitch], *The Memoirs of a Balkan Diplomatist* (London, 1917), pp. 37–42. The incident throws a lurid light on the irresponsible government of Milan. It is no wonder that he told the Austro-Hungarian minister in Belgrade, in 1882, that "the friendship with Austria-Hungary was not popular in Serbia"; Pribram, *loc. cit.,* I, 480.

† This duty was, of course, incumbent upon Serbia in international law, without any treaty. The article was important politically because it prevented Milan from giving assistance to the Bosnian and Dalmatian rebels in 1882, which added greatly to his unpopularity in Serbia, where the Austro-Hungarian 'occupation' was looked upon as of a temporary character and not as the equivalent of permanent possession. As a matter of fact, the Turkish plenipotentiaries at Berlin had refused to sign the treaty until the Austro-Hungarian representatives gave a declaration in writing that "the occupation will be considered provisional." A. Fournier, *Wie Wir zu Bosnien Kamen* (Vienna, 1909), pp. 64–75; Karathéodory Pacha, *Le rapport secret sur le Congrès de Berlin* (Paris, 1919), pp. 164–192; *Ö.-U. A.,* I, 152, note *a*. Legally, the Serbian view would seem to have been correct.

bazar), Austria-Hungary will not oppose herself thereto, and will use her influence with the other Powers for the purpose of winning them to an attitude favorable to Serbia.

By this treaty* Serbia was bound to the Habsburg Monarchy in a style worthy of the great Napoleon.

The effects of this bargain were soon evident. In the following year a commercial treaty admitted Austro-Hungarian manufactured articles into Serbia at half the normal rates, and while certain privileges were accorded Serbian pigs and prunes in the Monarchy, Austria-Hungary derived much the greater advantage from the arrangement.† She acted for Serbia at international tariff conferences; she collected customs on Serbian goods at the Iron Gates of the Danube, although one bank of the river was Serbian; no railways were allowed to be constructed between Serbia and Bosnia, and the building of the railway to Salonica was obstructed, lest Serbia find an outlet for her commerce to the south. The Union Générale, a branch of the Länderbank in Vienna, became the leading financial institution in Serbia, which was flooded by Austrian business men. From the Austro-Hungarian point of view, *pénétration pacifique* was eminently successful.

In 1885, King Milan, with the approval, if not at the instigation, of Austria-Hungary,‡ attacked Bulgaria when the latter effected a union with Eastern Rumelia. The Serbian army, dribbling on to the battle-field of Slivinitsa in relays, was badly

* Concluded for a period of ten years, the treaty was prolonged in 1889 until 13 January, 1895, King Milan abdicating immediately afterward in favor of his son Alexander, then a minor. The regents, when informed of the treaty by the Austro-Hungarian minister in Belgrade, promised "strict and faithful observance" of its stipulations. The old treaty was modified in several points. Austria-Hungary promised specifically to defend the Obrenovich dynasty against an attack from Montenegro, and agreed that any territorial extension "may be carried in the direction of the valley of the Vardar as far as the circumstances will permit." Pribram, *Geheimverträge Österreich-Ungarns*, I, 57–60, English translation, I, 135–141.

† According to K. Stoyanovich [Stojanovitch], *État économique de la Serbie* (Belgrade, 1909), p. 139, Serbia's foreign commerce grew from 33,000,000 dinars in 1864, to 90,000,000 dinars in 1884. From 1884 to 1904, which was roughly the period of Austro-Hungarian domination, it only increased from 90,000,000 dinars to 127,000,000.

‡ For an analysis of the evidence, see J. V. Fuller, *Bismarck's Diplomacy at its Zenith* (Cambridge, Mass., 1922), pp. 36–42.

beaten, and the king was saved from the consequences of his rashness only by the Austro-Hungarian minister in Belgrade, who threatened the advancing Bulgarians with armed intervention by the Monarchy. From this time King Milan was in the hands of Vienna.

His son and successor, Alexander (1889–1903), although he allowed the secret treaty to expire, remained tied to Austro-Hungarian interests. His overthrow of the regency (1893), the suspension of the liberal constitution of 1889 and its replacement by the more conservative instrument of 1869 (1894), his marriage with Draga Mashin, a widow of blemished reputation (1900), and the appointment of a military cabinet (1903) discredited him entirely in the eyes of his indignant people. The general condition of the country was deplorable, partly as a result of the conduct of the politicians.

In 1881 the Radical party had been founded as a protest against the arbitrary government and centralized administration of King Milan. Advocating universal suffrage and parliamentary government, they won the election of 1883. But they were excluded from office by Milan, whereupon they attempted a revolt at Zayechar, in which Nikola Pashich was involved. The revolt came to nothing, but the Radicals lost all hope of office for ten years—which caused them to abandon their liberal ideas and join with King Alexander in overthrowing the Progressive regency and restoring the old constitution. For the next ten years—1893–1903—the Radicals were in office for more than half the time, but only by the favor of the king. Alexander finally tired of them and proscribed them for their supposed complicity in a plot against the Austrophil Milan, who in spite of his abdication in 1889 had later returned as commander of the army. In other words, all the political leaders were willing to be the tools of the king, and thought more of office than of the country. The finances fell into a pitiful state; scandalous stories were circulated about the queen, who was accused of trying to secure the succession for one of her brothers; the king's personal conduct grew more violent and reckless.

The situation became so bad that a group of army officers, most of them young men disgusted by the sad spectacle of the court and inspired by the sincerest patriotism, formed a conspiracy to kill the king, the queen and the latter's brothers. Although several civilians were involved, it was essentially an enterprise of the army, which was not interfering in Serbian politics for the first time;* the decision to kill the king was taken because he was the last of his line, and his removal would end the bitter quarrel between the Obrenovich and Karageorgevich dynasties which was ruining the country and distracting it from the goal of Yugoslav emancipation and union. On the night of 10–11 June, 1903, the conspirators broke into the royal palace in Belgrade, and accomplished their purpose, adding to the horror by throwing the bodies of the royal pair into the courtyard below and murdering two members of the ministry.† Among the conspirators were Captain Dragutin Dimitriyevich and Lieutenant Voya Tankosich, of whom much will be heard in connection with the murder of Sarajevo. The last of the Obrenoviches was not regretted by his people. On the contrary, Belgrade was decorated with flags, and the country in general heaved a sigh of relief.

The barbarous tragedy gave Serbia a bad name, and the British Government went so far as to suspend diplomatic relations

---

* The army had suppressed the Radical rising at Zayechar in 1883, and had assisted King Alexander in overthrowing the regency and changing the constitutions. It was an irony that the army which now turned against its sovereign had been largely reformed by King Milan while serving as commander-in-chief between 1897 and 1899. He greatly increased its size, promoted younger men, and reduced the period for the training of officers. He took the first steps toward creating the new Serbian army which distinguished itself in the wars of 1912–1913 and in the Great War. Unfortunately his work aroused the animosity of the Radicals, which led to the breach between them and Alexander. Cf. 'Marco,' "Припремање 29. Маja, 1903 (револуцијонирање Српске Војске под Миланом Обреновићем)" [The Preparation for 29 May, 1903 (the Revolutionizing of the Serbian army under Milan Obrenovich)], in *Nova Evropa* (Zagreb), XV, 405–419 (11 June, 1927).

† For the details, including an account by one of the conspirators, see Loncharevich, pp. 318–323; cf. also H. Vivian, *The Servian Tragedy* (London, 1904). According to a report of Captain Vladimir Trzetsyak, of the Russian secret police, King Alexander was informed of the plot by Prince Ferdinand of Bulgaria, who was supposed to have learned of it from one of the conspirators, who later committed suicide. "Један руски савремени документ о 29. Маja" [A contemporary Russian document about 29 May], in *Nova Evropa*, XVI, 224–230 (11 October, 1927).

for three years.* But the other Powers were not so squeamish. The Russian minister, who had watched the proceedings from the window of his legation, requested the Skupshtina to elect Peter Karageorgevich to the throne unanimously, in order to secure his recognition by the Tsar, which was promptly given. The first Power, however, to recognize the new king was none other than Austria-Hungary,† a fact which calls for remark. Peter had been friendly to the Radical party, which was notoriously Russophil and hostile to the Monarchy. Why, then, did the Cabinet of Vienna, which appears to have known that a plot against King Alexander was brewing,‡ make no effort to save him? Why did it accept a Russophil régime so complacently? No certain answer can be given. Possibly it calculated that Peter would be subservient because in 1868, when he had been accused of complicity in the murder of Prince Michael Obrenovich, and had fled to Hungary, the Hungarian Government had refused to extradite him. A more likely explanation, however, is that, as a semi-official communiqué stated, "it mattered little who reigned in Serbia, provided he was on good terms with Austria-Hungary,"§ and there was complete confidence that the economic situation of Serbia would compel her to be on good terms with the Monarchy.

This confidence is the key to Austro-Hungarian policy in the years immediately following the change of régime in Serbia. King Peter, a man who never forgot his peasant origin and was

---

* B. D., V, 124–148.

† The telegram of Peter to Francis Joseph, 15 June, 1903, and the reply of Francis Joseph, 16 June, are printed in B. D., V, 133, and in German translation, in M. Bogichevich [Boghitschewitsch], Die auswärtige Politik Serbiens 1903–1904, vol. I, Geheimakten aus serbischen Archiven (Berlin, 1928), pp. 1–2.

‡ Some of the conspirators met in Vienna, where they were in touch with an official of the Bosnian ministry. R. W. Seton-Watson, Sarajevo (London, 1925), p. 26; the fact of Austrian knowledge was confirmed to Mr. Seton-Watson in 1908 by a member of the government. According to M. Boghichevich [Boghitschewitsch], Kriegsursachen (Zurich, 1919), pp. 15–16, who is strongly pro-Austrian, Austria-Hungary "saw in a change of dynasty the only possibility of an improvement in its relations with Serbia and therefore supported all the plots directed against King Alexander and his consort and that in favor of Prince Peter Karageorgevich." He states that the chief of the Ballplatz press bureau, Herr Müller, was in close relations with Peter's cousin Nenadovich and with the former Serbian minister, V. Petrovich.

§ H. W. Steed, Through Thirty Years (London, 1924), I, 206.

a democrat by conviction, ruled as a constitutional sovereign and left the government to the Radical party, which was a strong political force in the country. In the hope of escaping from the Austrian economic tutelage, a commercial treaty was concluded with Germany, a customs union was negotiated with Bulgaria, and plans were formulated to purchase artillery for the Serbian army from the French firm of Schneider (instead of from the Skoda factories in Bohemia). To meet this challenge the Austro-Hungarian Government denounced the existing commercial treaty with Serbia and made a new treaty dependent upon the Serbo-Bulgarian customs union being modified in such manner as the Cabinet of Vienna might require; when this demand was refused, a veterinary order was issued closing the Hungarian frontier to Serbian live stock. Furthermore the demand was made that preference should be given to Austro-Hungarian industry in supplying the needs of the Serbian Government. Only a government very sure of its strength and position would have tried to carry through so high-handed a policy.

But the calculations of Vienna and Budapest completely miscarried. Serbia proceeded to make arrangements with Turkey which permitted the export of Serbian cattle and pigs through Salonica, it bought its new guns from France and its ammunition from Germany, and it refused to grant the privileges demanded for Austro-Hungarian industry. In short, the little state defied its great antagonist and defied it successfully. The negotiations for a new commercial treaty had to be conducted as between equals. But precisely because Serbia was able to make a fair bargain, the treaty was rejected by the Austrian and Hungarian parliaments, and the work had to be done over again. It was not until 1910 that a treaty was finally signed and ratified.*

This ill-starred campaign was fatal to Austria-Hungary.

---

* This treaty was somewhat less favorable to the export of Serbian live stock than the abortive treaty of 1908, but there was a corresponding limitation on Austro-Hungarian imports into Serbia.

Although the Monarchy was not sympathetically viewed by the Serbian masses, there were those who desired friendly relations, including King Peter himself.* Obviously the economic development of Serbia could be best and most quickly promoted by co-operation with Austria-Hungary, and if the Monarchy had been wise enough to pursue a generous policy, its attractive power would have been very great. In 1909 Dr. Milovanovich, one of the leading Radical politicians and then prime minister, visited Vienna and made far-reaching overtures;† and he admitted privately to the correspondent of the London *Times* that union of Serbia with the Monarchy might well be the ultimate solution.‡ Not in a day could such an adjustment have been effected, but the possibility clearly existed.§ The policy actually

* The king was anxious to be received in Vienna by the Emperor Francis Joseph. Overtures made in 1903 met with no response. Negotiations for a visit were opened in 1911, but the conviction of an Austrian spy in Belgrade aroused Serbian public opinion so violently that the matter had to be dropped.

† He asked for a fair commercial treaty, an improvement of communications between Serbia and the Monarchy, and a recognition of Serbia's interest in Macedonia; he also said that an improvement in Austro-Serbian relations would react favorably on the situation in Bosnia. His overtures appear to have met with no response, either because of Hungarian opposition or because Austria-Hungary's relations with Germany led her to support German policy in the Near East, which aimed at the maintenance of Turkey. J. M. Baernreither, *Fragmente eines politischen Tagebuches: die südslawische Frage und Österreich-Ungarn vor dem Weltkrieg* (Berlin, 1928), pp. 124–131. Baernreither was one of the few Austro-Hungarian statesmen who urged the necessity of a conciliatory policy toward Serbia; his book furnishes many valuable indications of the real motives of Austro-Hungarian policy. Aehrenthal's account of the conversation with Milovanovich is confined to generalities. Aehrenthal to Forgách, 22 November, 1909; *Ö.-U. A.*, II, 553–554.

‡ Statement of Mr. Wickham Steed in a public lecture in London in 1928.

§ In March, 1910, Baernreither was informed, on behalf of Yeftanovich, the leader of the Serbs in Sarajevo, that "there are Serbs in the kingdom and in Bosnia who are busying themselves with the idea of uniting all elements of the Serbian people under Habsburg rule. The current toward union is very strong among the Serbs . . . the union of the kingdom of Serbia with Bosnia and the Herzegovina as well as with Dalmatia was a racial, economic and geographical necessity. This union should be realized as an Austrian *Sekundogenitur*, and indeed the son of the heir apparent Francis Ferdinand was under consideration. This state should receive the the Serbian lands in Old Serbia and Macedonia when the hour of Turkey sounded." Baernreither, pp. 131–132. Baernreither discussed the matter in Belgrade in June, 1911, with a Professor Perich. The professor stated the first condition of a *rapprochement* to be Austrian consent for Serbia to take "her share of Macedonia." A *rapprochement* might then come about "step by step": "Commercial treaty, customs and trade alliance, military convention, finally union with the other Yugoslavs of the Monarchy, in order to secure a relationship to the Monarchy like that of Hungary and to form with the Monarchy a great empire [*Gesamtreich*] closely allied with Germany." The Radical politician Lyuba Yovanovich, of whom much will be said later, "says the same thing on the essential matter as Perich." Baernreither, pp. 151–152.

followed by the Monarchy dissipated the hope of any such consummation. The Serbian peasantry was convinced that Austria-Hungary stood in the way of their prosperity, and they came to have for the Monarchy feelings of the most bitter hatred.*

The Austro-Hungarian attitude was determined in part by the situation in the Yugoslav provinces of the Monarchy. The Dualism established in 1867 refused all recognition to the idea of Yugoslav unity which had been manifesting itself in various forms for a generation.† The Slovenes, the most advanced culturally of the three branches of the race, were left under Austrian rule in Carinthia and Carniola. The province of Dalmatia, with a mixed population of Croat and Serb, also remained Austrian. Croatia-Slavonia, where the population was also divided between Croat and Serb, was restored to Hungary, but given a measure of autonomy. Thanks to this political separation and to the religious differences between the Roman Catholic Croats and the Orthodox Serbs, the statesmen of Vienna and Budapest had little difficulty until the beginning of this century in retaining effective control of the Yugoslav provinces, which was used to retard their economic development and educational progress. Moreover, Serbia in the last years of the Obrenoviches offered no attraction to the Yugoslavs of the Monarchy, however much they might complain of oppression and neglect.

But the events of 1903 altered the picture. The new régime in Serbia was free, and its success in defying the Austro-Hun-

---

* "The peasant in Serbia is in a good situation, but is greatly stirred up against Austria, because he had lost there the market for his cattle." Baernreither, p. 148. In an article, "Unsere Handelsbeziehungen zu Serbien," in *Österreichische Rundschau*, XXIX, nos. 1–2 (October, 1911), Baernreither shows that between 1905 and 1909, the Austro-Hungarian imports into Serbia decreased from 60.11 per cent to 24.43 per cent of the total imports, while the Serbian exports to the Monarchy sank from 90.1 per cent to 31.38 per cent of the total exports. Within the same period, German imports into Serbia increased from 11.57 per cent to 39.24 per cent, and the Serbian exports to Germany from 2.94 per cent to 16.77 per cent.

† The idea was first given impetus when Napoleon established the 'Illyrian provinces' in 1809. In the thirties, the poet-politician Gay established the *Illyrian National Gazette* and described 'Illyria' as "a triangle between Skutari, Varna and Villach." In 1848–1849 Croats and Serbs fought valiantly against the Magyars. Bishop Strossmayer, of Dyakovo, was using the revenues of his see to spread the idea of Serbo-Croat unity.

garian tariff policy made a deep impression. Beyond a doubt some of the more far-sighted Yugoslav leaders grew receptive to the idea of a union with Serbia in case the policy of Vienna and Budapest remained unchanged. It was significant that the leader of the Croatian peasants, Stephen Radich, attended the coronation of King Peter in Belgrade, and shouted, "Long live the King of Yugoslavia!" In 1905 the Serbs and the Croats in the Croatian diet, hitherto played off against each other by the governor (*ban*) appointed from Budapest, formed a coalition which gave them control of the diet. They were not disloyal, for they joined with the opposition in the Budapest parliament in the struggle to secure concessions for Hungary from Francis Joseph. But the Hungarian opposition had no sooner come to terms with the king than it abandoned its allies and revived the old policy in Croatia, which aimed at enforcing the supremacy of the Magyars and reducing autonomy to nullity. The disillusion in Croatia was bitter: henceforth no mercy was to be expected from Hungary, just as it was already clear that no help was to be had from Austria. From this time on, war to the knife was the order of the day in both Zagreb and Budapest.

Bosnia-Herzegovina was also exhibiting much restlessness. Outwardly the Austro-Hungarian rule had been successful. Order had been restored and maintained, roads built, the towns modernized, a few narrow-gauge railways opened, and a number of schools established. But, although the principal argument put forward in 1878 to justify the 'occupation' had been the necessity of reforming the land-system, which, being thoroughly feudal, kept the peasantry in subjection to their landlords and was held responsible for the periodical outbreaks, nothing had been done in this direction. The railway system was inadequate, and the provinces were kept as isolated as possible from the rest of the Monarchy, so that their economic development suffered. In spite of superficial evidences of progress, the country remained poor and backward. Consequently voices were being raised to demand that the bureaucratic government, largely in the hands of Germans and Magyars, should be replaced by some measure of popular control. There was also resentment at the official policy of trying to create a 'Bosnian' nationality,* for the majority of the population, whether Orthodox or Mohammedan, considered itself Serb. Quite possibly the agitation and discontent were fomented from Serbia,† but the existing abuses were sufficient to account for the unrest.‡

The Monarchy thus found itself confronted with a most serious problem. Even a reasonable satisfaction of Yugoslav demands would require fundamental changes in the existing structure of the state, in short, a modification of Dualism, while failure to satisfy them would increase the attraction of Serbia and might lead ultimately to the loss of the Yugoslav provinces. As a matter of fact, only a few enlightened persons saw the necessity of a change of front. The Emperor Francis Joseph was not disposed, at his advanced age, to embark upon new constitutional experiments, and the Magyars, who enjoyed the greatest advantages of Dualism, were determined to brook no changes. So, rather than confess its failure to establish a tolerable relationship with Serbia or attempt any revision of the antiquated political arrangements, the Austro-Hungarian Government decided to try to solve the problem by a new policy of violence which would humiliate Serbia to the uttermost and by so doing deprive its own Yugoslav subjects of the moral, if not

* The first governor of the province, Benjamin Kállay, who held office until 1903, had once written a *Geschichte der Serben*, in which he paid much attention to the Bosnian Serbs. As governor of Bosnia, he suppressed his own book because it proved the absurdity of a separate Bosnian nationality.

† The original programme of the Radical party declared, under the heading "Foreign Policy," that "there must be organized, in the field of intellectual development, a way of helping the divided and unliberated parts of Serbdom, as well as of keeping alive the sense of our national unity in the Serb provinces which, being far away, are exposed to the influence of foreign elements." When the party mounted to power under King Peter, it is said to have formulated a secret programme which provided *inter alia* for the promotion of the Yugoslav movement with Austria-Hungary and for propaganda to discredit the Monarchy abroad. L. Mandl, *Die Habsburger und die serbische Frage* (Vienna, n. d.), p. 62.

‡ M. Spalaykovich [Spalajkovitch], *La Bosnie et la Herzégovine* (Paris, 1897); A. Barre, *La Bosnie-Herzégovine: administration autrichienne de 1878 à 1903* (Paris, ca. 1904); J. du Pontcray, *Allemands contre Slaves* (Paris, 1911), ch. v. The Austro-Hungarian position is set forth by S. Graf Burián, *Drei Jahre* (Berlin, 1923), pp. 218–221.

the material, support of their Serbian kinsmen in their struggle for national recognition.*

THE ANNEXATION OF BOSNIA-HERZGOVINA
AND THE BALKAN WARS

This policy will be associated with the name of Baron (later Count) von Aehrenthal, Austro-Hungarian foreign minister from 1906 to 1912. Curiously enough, he originally held quite a different view. In October, 1907, he pictured the situation to the council of ministers in these words:

> Our policy of making Serbia economically and politically dependent has failed completely. Only third parties would profit from a conflict between the Monarchy and Serbia. From the political point of view, the minister must urgently request that the affairs of Croatia, Dalmatia, and Bosnia be so conducted that the centre of gravity for the Serbo-Croat people shall lie inside the Monarchy.†

Golden words of elementary wisdom! But the minister allowed himself to be deflected from this attitude, probably under the influence of Hungary, which, as we have seen, was unwilling to chánge its policy in Croatia.‡ Apart from this, he was determined to restore the prestige of Austria-Hungary as a Great Power, which had been sadly dimmed by the prolonged racial conflicts within the Monarchy, and to prove, after William II had congratulated his predecessor as the "brilliant second" of German policy,§ that the Ballplatz was not the obedient tool of the Wilhelmstrasse. Nor can the personal ambition to cut a great figure on the European stage, to become the Austrian Bismarck, be left out of account.‖ Thus high policy, the in-

---

* The internal structure of the Habsburg Monarchy is exhaustively and brilliantly examined in O. Jászi, *The Dissolution of the Habsburg Monarchy* (Chicago, 1929); see especially the chapter on "The Jugo-Slav Irredenta and the Road toward the War," pp. 403–427.

† Baernreither, p. 74.   ‡ *Ibid.*, p. 78.

§ In 1906, shortly after the Algeciras conference.

‖ Conrad von Hötzendorf, the chief of the general staff, humorously said that Aehrenthal precipitated the Bosnian crisis "in order to become a count." H. Kanner, *Kaiserliche Katastrophenpolitik* (Vienna, 1922), p. 45.

ternal situation of the Monarchy and his own egotism combined
to push Baron von Aehrenthal into a policy against Serbia
which was to involve great European repercussions and launch
Austria-Hungary on a course leading straight to the catastrophe
of 1914.

In January, 1908, he announced that the Turkish Government had approved a project for the construction of a railway
from Mitrovitsa, in the Sandjak of Novi Bazar, through Old
Serbia to Salonica.* The significance of the step was twofold.
In the first place, taken as it was without consultation with Russia, it was considered by the latter as signifying the end of the
Austro-Russian understanding of 1897 by which the two Powers had agreed to co-operate in maintaining the *status quo* in
the Balkans.† Secondly, the proposed railway was obviously
intended to cripple Serbia economically by establishing competition with the existing (and only) line to Salonica, which ran
through Belgrade and Nish, and to make possible the transport of troops into Old Serbia. If the outbreak of the Young
Turk revolution a few months later caused the abandonment
of the plan, the project was a symptom of the new policy of
the Ballplatz. It was followed, in October, 1908, by the proclamation of the annexation of Bosnia-Herzegovina.

That act was a deliberate violation of the Treaty of Berlin.
A nominal excuse was found in the decision of the new government at Constantinople to summon representatives from the
two provinces, which the Treaty of Berlin left under the suzerainty of the Sultan, to the Turkish parliament: this, it was
argued, would prevent the introduction of constitutional government in the provinces, which Austria-Hungary had determined upon.‡ But the real motives were quite different. In

---

* *G. P.*, XXV, 281–382; *B. D.*, V, 328–355; B. Molden, *Alois Graf Aehrenthal*
(Stuttgart, 1917), pp. 32–38.

† Pribram, I, 78–82, English translation, I, 185–195. Russia at once made a
counter-demand for a railway from the Danube across Serbia and Albania to the
Adriatic. An excellent map of the rival projects and the existing railways is given
in *B. D.*, V, 333.

‡ The introduction of constitutional government was urged by Burián, the minister in charge of the provinces, as the only means of sapping the growing discontent. Burián, *Drei Jahre*, 221–222.

December, 1907, Baron von Aehrenthal informed General Conrad von Hötzendorf, the chief of the general staff, that the aim of his Balkan policy was "the annexation of Bosnia-Herzegovina and the incorporation of the non-Bulgarian parts of Serbia."* He developed his ideas in a memorandum of August, 1908, submitted to the cabinet and the Emperor. Arguing that the approaching end of the Turkish power would make it necessary "to get at the root of the evil and put an end to the Pan-Serb dreams of the future," for which he proposed to utilize the antagonism between Bulgaria and Serbia, he said:

The antagonism between Bulgaria and Serbia is already today a factor that can be reckoned with: in Bulgaria the conviction prevails that the road to Macedonia must lead over the body of the Serbian state, and it is certain that the most violent strife will break out between Serbia and Bulgaria for the possession of Üsküb [the present Skoplye]. If we take Bulgaria's side in this conflict and favor the creation of a great Bulgaria at the expense of Serbia, the necessary preparation will have been made, and in the moment of a favorable European constellation, we can lay our hands on the rest of Serbia. Then we should have the secure frontiers of which we have spoken earlier: an Albania become independent under our ægis, a Montenegro with which we maintain friendly relations, and a great Bulgaria which is indebted to us.†

A little later, when informing the German Government of his plans for accomplishing the annexation, Aehrenthal, to quote the German foreign minister, "in conclusion indicated to me, with a certain anxiety and with the request to keep it strictly secret, the further aim of his Balkan policy as 'the complete rooting-out of the Serbian revolutionary nest.' "‡ Finally, in February, 1909, he let it be known to the initiated that he was planning an ultimatum if Serbia did not recognize the annexa-

* Conrad, I, 528.
† H. Friedjung, *Das Zeitalter des Imperialismus* (Berlin, 1922), II, 241; Baernreither, pp. 81–82. The memorandum is printed in *Ö.-U. A.*, I, 25–30.
‡ Schoen to Bülow, 5 September, 1908; *G. P.*, XXVI, 28.

tion (as she had refused to do), and he pictured the consequences thus:

If submission follows, good—if not, better, then invasion, another dynasty, customs union.*

These several utterances make the purpose of Baron von Aehrenthal's policy quite plain: to bring Serbia into the Habsburg state either by direct incorporation or through a customs union. Now this policy, as we have seen, had its advocates in Serbia itself; with the difference, however, that whereas its Serbian supporters contemplated a union of equals for mutual benefit, Aehrenthal's conception implied the relation of victor and vanquished and involved the sacrifice of Serbian interests in Macedonia. The annexation of Bosnia-Herzegovina was to be the first step toward the ultimate goal: if the title of the Monarchy could be proved permanent and unshakable, Serbia might renounce her own aspirations and submit to the irresistible pressure of Habsburg diplomacy.

The Serbs, for their part, understood thoroughly what an Austro-Hungarian victory meant for them, even though they could not prove the ulterior motives of Baron von Aehrenthal, and they would have been less than human if they had not protested. Unfortunately for them, their protest, which the Ballplatz declined to receive, had no *locus standi* in international law, for Serbia was not a signatory of the Treaty of Berlin, nor in history, for Bosnia, although inhabited by Serbs, had never formed part of a Serbian state. Diplomatically speaking, therefore, just as the Austro-Hungarian action was a defiance of the signatories of the Berlin Treaty, so the Serbian attitude was a provocation of the Monarchy.

* Baernreither, p. 106. The customs union was apparently to be "a kind of strait-jacket in which Serbia could be restrained [*gesteckt*]." In March, Aehrenthal told the German ambassador that he had given up his plan of dividing Serbia between Rumania, Bulgaria, and Austria, but that he would demand a large war indemnity and the occupation of Belgrade. "In this connection," he added, "care must be taken that the payment should be made in the smallest possible yearly instalments, in order to keep Serbia as long as possible under Austrian pressure," which would make the dynastic question acute, and he hoped that "in the future the Croatian king would replace the Belgrade ruler." Tschirschky to Bülow, 19 March, 1909; G. P., XXVI, 690–691.

War was narrowly averted. The Serbs, in their anger and desperation, would probably have dared it had they not been restrained by Russia, who was in no position to go to their assistance; as it was, they kept their army mobilized for six months. In Austria-Hungary, a strong party, headed by General Conrad, urged seizing the opportunity for a preventive war,* and of course the conduct of the Serbs played into their hands.† In March, 1909, Aehrenthal was won over to this policy. An ultimatum was decided upon, the date for its presentation in Belgrade was fixed,‡ and an eminent historian was provided with materials by the Ballplatz for formulating the indictment against Serbia, which he duly published in the *Neue Freie Presse*.§ All preparations were made for mobilization. If at the last moment war was averted, it was because Russia, which had been supporting diplomatically Serbia's demands for 'compensation,' withdrew her support,‖ and Ser-

* The Archduke Francis Ferdinand protested against "the good Conrad's desire for war." Francis Ferdinand to Aehrenthal, 20 October, 1908; *Ö.-U. A.*, I, 267.

† Overtures were made to Turkey for an alliance against Austria-Hungary, but Aehrenthal succeeded in buying the Porte's consent to the annexation for an indemnity of 55,000,000 crowns. The Serbian foreign minister made a tour of the capitals to enlist European aid, and a special mission was sent to St. Petersburg. In addition, much wild talk was indulged in at Belgrade.

‡ 29 March. Conrad, I, 156; Friedjung, *Das Zeitalter des Imperialismus*, II, 272. Cf. Aehrenthal to Mensdorff, 26 March, 1909; *Ö.-U. A.*, II, 195. On 19 March, instructions were sent to the minister in Belgrade for his conduct in the event of a rupture. Aehrenthal to Forgách, 19 March, 1909; *Ö.-U. A.*, II, 137–138.

§ The article led to a libel suit against its author, Dr. Heinrich Friedjung, because he had accused some of the members of the Serbo-Croat coalition at Zagreb of treasonable relations with Belgrade. In the course of the trial it was proved that the documents on which Friedjung, in entire good faith but with little critical acumen, had rested his case were forged in Belgrade and, seemingly, with the complicity of the Austro-Hungarian legation. Aehrenthal, his minister in Belgrade, Count Forgách, and Austro-Hungarian prestige were gravely discredited by this incident, not only throughout Europe, but in the Yugoslav provinces of the Monarchy. R. W. Seton-Watson, *The Southern Slav Question* (London, 1911), pp. 200–328. Three of the documents are printed in *Ö.-U. A.*, I, nos. 98, 598, 1742. There was a lengthy correspondence on the matter between the foreign office in Vienna and the legation in Belgrade; Forgách denied the charges against himself and his subordinates and insisted that the documents were genuine. The dragoman of the legation, who was accused of forging the documents, was examined by the officials of the Ballplatz and exonerated. The principal points in the correspondence are given in *Ö.-U. A.*, II, nos. 1769, 1972, III, 2312, 2323, 2423, 2432.

‖ The Russian change of front was induced, not by an acceptance of the Austro-Hungarian point of view, but solely by the desire to spare Serbia from a war in which Russia, on account of her military weakness, could not take part. On the question whether Russia's attitude was determined by German intervention, see above, pp. 41–42.

bia was left alone. Yielding to hard necessity, on 31 March, she addressed to Austria-Hungary a note recognizing that "the *fait accompli* regarding Bosnia has not affected her rights" and promising "in deference to the advice of the Great Powers . . . to renounce from now onward the attitude of protest and opposition which she has adopted with regard to the annexation since last autumn."*

Baron von Aehrenthal had won, because he was supported through thick and thin by Germany, whereas Russia was not able and her Entente associates were not willing, to fight;† but it was a Pyrrhic victory. The Powers recognized the annexation of Bosnia, but in return Aehrenthal incurred the bitter hostility of the Russian foreign minister, who burned for revenge, and the Russian Government immediately undertook the thorough reorganization of its armed forces, in order to guard against another such diplomatic defeat. When in July, 1908, Baron von Aehrenthal took up the question of Bosnia-Herzegovina with M. Izvolski, the Russian minister showed no concern for Serbia: he was willing to accept the annexation of Bosnia, under certain conditions,‡ if Austria-Hungary

* *Ö.-U. A.*, II, 225; *G. P.*, XXVI, 731; *B. D.*, V, 747–748. The text of the declaration was worked out in long negotiations between Aehrenthal, Sir F. Cartwright, the British ambassador in Vienna, and Sir Edward Grey.

† For the military arrangements of the two general staffs, see above, pp. 14–15. In February Aehrenthal notified Bülow that in March, he would insist upon a "clarification" of Serbia's attitude, which might require an ultimatum and war. Aehrenthal to Bülow, 20 February, 1909; *Ö.-U. A.*, I, 852–857; *G. P.*, XXVI, 612–615. Bülow approved of this course; Bülow to William II, 22 February; *ibid.*, XXVI, 618–619. Aehrenthal was informed that the German Emperor made the following marginal notation on his letter to Bülow: "I agree with the point of view [*Auffassung*] and contemplated method of procedure of Baron Aehrenthal." Szögyény to Aehrenthal, 24 February, 1909; *Ö.-U. A.*, I, 872.

‡ The first suggestion of the annexation in any published document occurs in a memorandum of the Russian Government presented to the Cabinet of Vienna in July, 1908 (*Ö.-U. A.*, I, 9–11; *G. P.*, XXVI, 190–192). At the Congress of Berlin, the Russian plenipotentiaries signed a secret declaration (13 July, 1878) promising that Russia would raise no objection if Austria-Hungary occupied the Sandjak of Novi Bazar "definitively like the rest of Bosnia and the Herzegovina"; *Ö.-U. A.*, I, 108. The Russian Government sanctioned the annexation in principle in the Three Emperors' League of 1881 and 1884 (Pribram, I, 14, 35, English translation, I, 43, 91) but in the Austro-Russian agreement of 1897 (*ibid.*, I, 82, English translation, I, 193), it declared that "the annexation of these two provinces would raise a more extensive question, which would require special scrutiny at the proper time and places." The question was discussed by Aehrenthal and Izvolski at Buchlau in September, 1908. What was said between the two diplomatists has been the sub-

would support his plan for the opening of the Straits. And
he told the Serbs that they must make the best of it, as may be
seen from his remarks to the Serbian chargé in London:

As far as Serbia is concerned, M. Izvolski thinks that the
question of the annexation must be handled by us cold-bloodedly and not from a sentimental, but from a practical political
point of view. He understands the bitterness of the masses
and the way in which it is manifested, but he cannot com-
prehend why some of our statesmen let themselves be swayed
by it. . . . We must rather be clear as to the fact that Bosnia
and the Herzegovina have been lost to us for a long time to
come. . . . If we would regard the annexation, which is a

ject of endless controversy. Each published his version in the autumn of 1909:
'Vox et Præterea Nihil,' "Baron Aehrenthal and M. Izvolsky: Diplomatic Enigmas"
(Izvolski's account), in *Fortnightly Review*, XCII, 381–401 (September, 1909); 'Vox
Alteræ Partis,' "M. Izvolsky and Count von Aehrenthal" (Aehrenthal's account),
in *ibid.*, XCII, 777–789 (November, 1909). Aehrenthal gave accounts to Schoen
(*G. P.*, XXVI, 26–29) and to Bülow (*G. P.*, XXVI, 35–38, 186–189). Izvolski also
gave his version to Schoen (*G. P.*, XXVI, 39–43), to Sir F. Bertie, the British ambassador in Paris (*B. D.*, V, 383–384), to Sir E. Grey (*B. D.*, V, 443–444), to Sir F. Cartwright, British ambassador in Vienna (*B. D.*, V, 807–808), and to Sir A. Nicolson, British
ambassador in St. Petersburg (*B. D.*, V, 810–811), the two last accounts being in the autumn of 1909. That Izvolski agreed to the annexation is clear, but he consistently
contended that he did so subject to the approval of a European conference, which
was to meet for a discussion of the various problems raised by the Turkish revolution. The main point of controversy is whether Aehrenthal informed Izvolski of the
time of annexation. Aehrenthal always asserted that he told Izvolski that it would
have to be proclaimed before the meeting of the Austro-Hungarian Delegations,
which was set for 8 October, 1908, and this is borne out by Aehrenthal's memorandum
of the conversations (*Ö.-U. A.*, I, 91). Izvolski always contended that he understood
that he would have time to sound the other Powers on his Straits policy, and the
leisurely way in which he set about consulting them lends credit to his argument.
One possible explanation of the discrepancy is that Aehrenthal made his statement
in an undertone or as an aside, which was not thoroughly understood by Izvolski.
Cf. Molden, *Alois Graf Aehrenthal*, p. 77; Sosnosky, *Die Balkanpolitik Österreich-
Ungarns*, II, 168; Kanner, *Kaiserliche Katastrophenpolitik*, p. 82. Another explanation is suggested by the German documents. The German foreign minister reported
as follows on his interview with Izvolski: "M. Izvolski has the impression that Baron
Aehrenthal, constrained perhaps more by considerations of internal politics than
by the external situation, wishes quite soon to take up the consideration of these
problems [Bosnia, the Sandjak, etc.]. Without having secured positive indications
in this direction from Baron Aehrenthal, he is inclined to think that the Austro-
Hungarian minister is ready to lay the plan for the annexation of Bosnia and the
Herzegovina before the approaching delegations." Schoen to Bülow, 26 September,
1908; *G. P.*, XXVI, 40. If this language is accurate, Izvolski may not have realized
that the actual proclamation of the annexation was imminent. On the other hand,
he did not challenge the assertion of the Austrian ambassador in St. Petersburg
that Aehrenthal "had given him plainly to understand that the annexation would
take place in the first half of October." Berchtold to Aehrenthal, 30 October, 1908;
Ö.-U. A., I, 357. Izvolski's reports to St. Petersburg have not been published.
During the crisis which followed, each minister accused the other of disloyal conduct.

fact, more dispassionately, we should have cause to be satisfied, since for us and our future it is a factor of the greatest importance that Austria has given up the Sandjak of Novi Bazar, whereby the advance of Austria to Salonica is cut off for ever. . . . If the moment for the dismemberment of Turkey comes, then the Sandjak must fall to us as natural successors. . . . Austria loses her right to her railway, while ours (the Adriatic line) is assured. . . . A further result of the annexation is that the national consciousness amongst us and the other Serbs outside of the kingdom has been aroused and united us at least morally.*

But the high-handed action of Baron von Aehrenthal stirred Russian public opinion so profoundly that M. Izvolski was forced to alter his attitude,† and to protest against the annexation, and to take up Serbia's claims for 'compensation,' which he finally abandoned only under duress.‡ Moreover, to persuade Serbia not to push her quarrel with Austria-Hungary to the point of war, the Russian Government was constrained to make promises for the future. Thus a prominent general assured the Serbian minister in St. Petersburg that

we are now busily exerting ourselves to bring our military power to such a level that Russia can pursue the policy required by her traditions and dignity. Serbia must take this into account and await a more favorable time.§

---

* Gruyich to foreign office, 13 October, 1908; Bogichevich, ̈Kriegsursachen, 158–159; Bogichevich, Die auswärtige Politik Serbiens, I, 15–16. Izvolski used similar language to the Serbian minister in Paris. Vesnich to foreign office, 5 October, 1908; Bogichevich, Kriegsursachen, pp. 151–154; Bogichevich, Die auswärtige Politik Serbiens, I, 5–7.

† It was long believed that Izvolski changed front because he did not find in Paris and London the support for his plan of opening the Straits which he had anticipated when consenting at Buchlau to the annexation of Bosnia, and foreseeing the failure of his own plans, sought to obstruct the success of Aehrenthal. Recent disclosures, however, show that the Russian Government was not pleased with Izvolski's bargain at Buchlau, and after the proclamation of the annexation, sent him peremptory instructions at Paris to protest against the annexation. N. V. Tcharykow, "Reminiscences of Nicholas II," in Contemporary Review, CXXXIV, 447–449 (October, 1928).

‡ At first Izvolski demanded territorial compensation for Serbia, but later asked only for economic concessions in the form of some kind of outlet, by railway, to the Adriatic. Austria-Hungary refused the latter as firmly as the former. The British Government gave diplomatic support to the Russian position.

§ Popovich to foreign office, 27 January, 1909; Bogichevich, Die auswärtige Politik Serbiens, I, 49.

A leading Conservative member of the Duma, A. I. Guchkov, promised that "when our armaments have been perfected, we shall settle our account with Austria-Hungary."* M. Izvolski was not less encouraging:

Serbia will be condemned to a pitiful existence until the moment for the downfall of Austria-Hungary arrives. The annexation had brought this moment nearer, and when it comes, Russia will unroll and solve the Serbian question.†

And he advised Serbia to sign the declaration demanded by Baron von Aehrenthal because of its "vague form": "a declaration of that kind would not be difficult to make, because it binds you to nothing."‡ When the crisis was ended by the Serbian declaration of 31 March, 1909, and an exchange of notes between the Powers, M. Izvolski went so far as to deny that "the annexation of Bosnia and the Herzegovina was recognized by the elimination of Article XXV from the Treaty of Berlin":

The wording of the note of the Powers was such that it could be interpreted in different ways. Nothing more was expressed in this note than that the Powers consented to the elimination of Article XXV, and nothing else had been substituted for it.§

The future, he implied, was left open, and Serbia must be patient. Thus Serbia, though forced to submit to Austro-Hungarian wishes for the moment, was not really beaten, for she had won over Russia to her point of view. Henceforth the Habsburg Monarchy in its conflict with Serbia had two enemies to face and not Serbia alone. Baron von Aehrenthal was made a count as a reward for his triumph, but that was really his only consolation.

* Koshutich to foreign office, 3 March, 1909; Germany, Auswärtiges Amt, *Weissbuch betreffend die Verantwortlichkeit der Urheber des Krieges* (Berlin, 1919) ('White Book' presented to the Peace Conference at Paris under the title *Deutschland Schuldig?*, cited hereafter as *Deutschland Schuldig?*), p. 112.
† Koshutich to foreign office, 10 March, 1909; *Deutschland Schuldig?*, p. 114; Bogichevich, *Die auswärtige Politik Serbiens*, I, 68–69.
‡ Popovich to foreign office, 18 March, 1909; *ibid.*, I, 78.
§ Popovich to foreign office, 27 April, 1909; *ibid.*, I, 106.

Not the least disastrous consequence of the crisis, from the Austro-Hungarian point of view, was that the Russian Government was convinced of the aggressive designs of the Monarchy.* To erect a barrier against any new humiliation of Serbia or advance upon Salonica, M. Izvolski set about the creation of an alliance between Serbia and Bulgaria. The first attempt failed, although the negotiations dragged on for several years, partly because the rival claims of Serbia and Bulgaria in Macedonia could not be adjusted, partly because Bulgaria was not sufficiently anti-Austrian.† But the Turco-Italian war which began in September, 1911, offered an opportunity not to be missed by the Balkan states, which regarded themselves as the heirs of Turkey in Europe. Negotiations opened between the Bulgarian and Serbian premiers led to the conclusion of a secret alliance in March, 1912, which was extended in May by a treaty between Greece and Bulgaria;‡ as Montenegro was also brought into the combination, a powerful new factor was introduced into European politics.§ The success of the negotiations was due primarily to Russia, her ministers in Sofia and Belgrade, A. Nekludov and N. H. Hartwig, ex-

* See Izvolski's statements to Schoen in June, to Bethmann-Hollweg in September, and to Pourtalès, the German ambassador in St. Petersburg; *G. P.*, XXVI, 825, 853, 856.
† Siebert, pp. 137–151; *G. P.*, XXVII, 155–191; W. L. Langer, "Russia, the Straits Question and the Origins of the Balkan League 1908–1912," in *Political Science Quarterly*, XLIII, 329–337 (September, 1928).
‡ For the negotiations between the Balkan states, see I. E. Gueshoff, *The Balkan League* (London, 1915), pp. 1–42; Bogichevich, *Kriegsursachen*, 32–45; Bogichevich, *Die auswärtige Politik Serbiens*, I, 180–225, *passim;* J. D. Bourchier, "The Origins of the Balkan Alliance," *The Times* (London), 4, 5, 6, 7, 11, 13, 16 June, 1913. The treaties are given in Gueshoff, pp. 112–133, and in *American Journal of International Law*, VIII, supplement, 1–11 (January, 1914), 81–85 (April, 1914).
§ The fact that a Serbo-Bulgarian alliance had been concluded was notified to France and Great Britain by the Russian Government. Sazonov to Izvolski and Benckendorff, 30 March, 1912; Siebert, p. 154. Cf. also Poincaré to Louis, 2 April, 1912; *Affaires balkaniques*, I, 14. The terms of the treaty were not communicated until August. *Ibid.*, I, 38; Poincaré, II, 115–116. The German foreign minister also got wind of it, and informed the King of Rumania. Jaeckh, *Kiderlen-Waechter, der Staatsmann und Mensch*, II, 186–187. King Carol in turn told the Austrian minister in Bucharest. Fürstenberg to Berchtold, 21 May, 1912; *Ö.-U. A.*, IV, 169. A little later Kiderlen informed Berchtold, the new Austro-Hungarian foreign minister, that according to an "intercepted secret document," Serbia and Bulgaria had concluded a defensive alliance, in which they pledge themselves to Russia not to undertake any offensive measures. Memorandum of Berchtold, *ca.* 26 May, 1912; *Ö.-U. A.*, IV, 184. When King Ferdinand of Bulgaria visited Vienna in June,

erting themselves to the utmost to effect a compromise over Macedonia;* M. Hartwig in particular persuaded his government to take a more favorable view of the Serbian claims. Although the Serbo-Bulgarian treaty was directed primarily against Turkey, it was so worded as to make possible also its use against Austria-Hungary,† and the new Russian foreign minister, M. Sazonov, appears to have valued the alliance primarily on that account.‡ Likewise the Serbs were willing to make concessions in Macedonia because the treaty, besides promising them the assistance of Bulgaria in the event of a rupture with Austria-Hungary arising out of the war against Turkey, was formed on the assumption that Serbia would be able to conquer Albanian territory and thus secure an outlet on the Adriatic which would emancipate her once for all from the economic pressure of the Habsburg Monarchy.§ The formation of the Balkan League was undoubtedly a serious blow for Austria-Hungary; at least subsequent events proved this to be the case.

The war of the Balkan League against Turkey in the autumn of 1912 precipitated a second serious crisis between Austria-

he said nothing about the alliance, but, from the remarks of his consort, Berchtold deduced that a partition of Macedonia had been arranged between Bulgaria, Serbia, and Greece. Memorandum of Berchtold, *ca.* 3 June, 1912; *Ö.-U. A.*, IV, 195. The Bulgarian premier, however, told the Austrian minister that stories of a Serbo-Bulgarian or a Greco-Bulgarian alliance were "childish tales" which "were not worth being denied." Tarnowski to Berchtold, 6 July, 1912; *Ö.-U. A.*, IV, 252.

* Their correspondence with the Russian foreign office is printed in *Красный Архив*, VIII, 1–48; IX, 1–22; a German translation is provided in *KSF*, III, 789–818 (December, 1925); VII, 699–713, 779–789, 899–904 (July, August, September, 1929).

† "Both contracting parties promise to support each other with all their powers also in the event that any Great Power shall attempt, even only temporarily, to seize for itself, to occupy or to possess with its troops any territory in the Balkans at present under Turkish rule" (Article II of the treaty).

‡ When informed of the proposed terms of the alliance, Sazonov exclaimed: "Well, but this is perfect! If only it could come off! Bulgaria closely allied to Serbia in the political and economic sphere; five hundred thousand bayonets to guard the Balkans—but this would bar for ever the road to German penetration, Austrian invasion!" Nekludoff, *Diplomatic Reminiscences*, p. 45.

§ Cf. also the remark of Milovanovich, the Serbian foreign minister, when negotiating with Gueshov, the Bulgarian premier: "Ah! Yes! If the 'winding up' of Turkey coincides with the crumbling of Austria-Hungary, matters will be enormously simplified: Serbia will get Bosnia and Herzegovina, while Rumania receives Transylvania, and we shall then have no reasons for apprehending a Rumanian intervention in our war against Turkey." Gueshoff, p. 17.

Hungary and Serbia.* The Cabinet of Vienna was at first
disposed to threaten Serbia with intervention in case the Serbian troops entered the Sandjak of Novi Bazar;† which might
have prevented the war. Instead, however, it allowed events
to take their course, perhaps because the new foreign minister,
Count Berchtold, could not nerve himself to vigorous action,
probably also because the belief was wide-spread that the
Serbs would be defeated. But any such calculations were
quickly shattered, for the Serbian army overwhelmed the
Turks and marched to the Adriatic coast, and the Serbian premier announced *urbi et orbi* that his country would insist on
retaining a 'window' on the sea.

The Austro-Hungarian Government was placed in a most
disagreeable position. The Serbian victories were greeted with
the greatest enthusiasm throughout the Yugoslav provinces of
the Monarchy, from which went streams of volunteers and
material aid; an intervention by the Monarchy might compromise it fatally in the eyes of its own subjects. Yet to recognize the Serbian claims would mean surrendering the last lever
for controlling the little state. Count Berchtold resorted to
compromise. In the name of Albanian nationality, he demanded that Serbia withdraw from the Adriatic and that the
Great Powers establish Albania as an independent state, and, by
way of emphasizing its earnestness, the Cabinet of Vienna
began to call out reservists and to concentrate troops in Bosnia-
Herzegovina. In addition Count Berchtold refused to receive
the Serbian premier in Vienna and discuss with him the terms
of an accommodation.‡ This attitude, which was made possi-

* The Russian Government endeavored to restrain its protégés from attacking
Turkey, whether because it preferred to use the Balkan League against Austria-
Hungary or because it thought the Turks likely to be the victors, is not clear.
With some difficulty Poincaré succeeded in organizing the Concert of Europe in
an effort to stop the war, but the pressure exerted by the Great Powers at Constantinople and the Balkan capitals was never more than half-hearted and was
not taken seriously.

† Stolberg to Bethmann-Hollweg, 27 September, 1912; report of Kageneck, 27
September; *G. P.*, XXXIII, 122, 126.

‡ Professor T. G. Masaryk, since 1919 President of the Czechoslovak Republic,
but then a member of the Austrian parliament, in December, 1912, went to Belgrade at the suggestion of the editor of the *Neue Freie Presse*, and brought back

ble by the firm support of Germany,* was as much a provocation of Serbia as the latter's protest against the annexation of Bosnia had been to Austria-Hungary. Serbia was at war with Turkey and entitled, so she thought, to dictate whatever terms of peace her military power could enforce. If Austria-Hungary claimed the privilege of settling the question of Bos-

from Pashich an offer to visit Berchtold and the terms of a *rapprochement*. Pashich, while asking for a corridor to the Adriatic, was willing to accept an autonomous Albania, to promise not to fortify the Serbian port or to let any other Power use it, and to make "all possible economic concessions," including a new commercial treaty and preference for the Monarchy in all state loans and orders. Berchtold declined to see Pashich or open negotiations. Baernreither, pp. 182–184; T. G. Masaryk, *The Making of a State* (London, 1927), p. 24; memorandum of Berchtold, 12 December, 1912, *Ö.-U. A.*, V, 107–108. Some time before Berchtold had suggested to Serbia that she should seek an outlet to the sea through Salonica, stating that Austria-Hungary "had no objections to such a conquest," and hinted at the possibility of "a closer economic relationship" between Serbia and the Monarchy. Berchtold to Ugron, 8 November, 1912; *Ö.-U. A.*, IV, 799. The overture was declined by the Serbian Government. Ugron to Berchtold, 15 November, 1912; *Ö.-U. A.*, IV, 883–884. 'Marco,' "Никола Хартвиг" [Nicholas Hartwig], in *Nova Evropa*, XVII, 267 (26 April, 1928) (translated in *KSF*, VI, 756, August, 1928), states that Berchtold invited Pashich to a "friendly" discussion and sent Dr. Joseph Redlich to Belgrade "to consult Pashich in the matter of Serbia's outlet to the Adriatic sea and also of a possible customs union with Austria-Hungary." Pashich is said to have rejected the overture under the pressure of the Russian minister Hartwig. The authority given for this statement is a despatch of Hartwig of 27 November, 1912, but there is no reference in *Ö.-U. A.* to any visit of Redlich, and it seems altogether improbable that Berchtold ever contemplated allowing Serbia an outlet to the Adriatic. As early as 20 September, 1912, he informed Berlin that "Austria-Hungary would not be able to allow Serbia an extension to the west" (Stolberg to foreign office, 20 September, 1912; *G. P.*, XXXIII, 111), and he consistently refused in his negotiations with the Powers even to consider the possibility of such an outlet for Serbia. It is more probable that he sought to divert Serbia from the Adriatic by suggesting Salonica as an outlet, in order thereby to create difficulties between Serbia and Bulgaria and thus disrupt the Balkan League. Pashich would naturally decline such a suggestion, if made, because he had always worked for friendly relations between Serbia and Bulgaria. Berchtold's refusal to see Pashich after Masaryk's mission may well have been due to his irritation over the Serbian premier's rejection of his own proposals.

* While the influence of Germany was undoubtedly used throughout the crisis in favor of moderation on the part of its ally, it resolutely supported Vienna on the fundamental issue of excluding Serbia from the Adriatic. Kiderlen to William II, 3 November, 1912; Kiderlen to Tschirschky, 5, 7, 19 November, 1912; *G. P.*, XXXIII, 274–276, 279–281, 292–293. The German Emperor, who thoroughly approved of the Balkan attack on Turkey (memorandum of 4 October, 1912; *G. P.*, XXXIII, 164–166), and rejoiced over their victories (comment of 28 October, *G. P.*, XXXIII, 253), was by no means enamored of the Austro-Hungarian policy, and roundly declared that he would not recognize the *casus foederis* "on account of the Serbs in Durazzo or Albania" (William II to Kiderlen, 7 November; *G. P.*, XXXIII, 295). He allowed himself to be persuaded by Bethmann that Germany must stand by her ally (*G. P.*, XXXIII, 302, note *), but he evidently remained unconvinced, saying that "no one could justify it with his conscience or his responsibility to God and his people to risk the existence of Germany on such grounds" (memorandum of ca. 11 November; *G. P.*, XXXIII, 303).

nia-Herzegovina in her exclusive interest, Serbia felt herself equally entitled to ignore the Monarchy in her own quarrel with Turkey. But of course consistency counted for nothing in this desperate antagonism, which was essentially a question of strength, the strength of a Great Power against that of a small one, the strength of the Triple Alliance against that of the Triple Entente.*

Once again war was narrowly averted. Within the Monarchy the military party, headed by General Conrad, pleaded with the foreign minister to use the opportunity for smashing Serbia and then imposing on her a customs union and a military convention.† The Archduke Francis Ferdinand also seems to have toyed with the same idea.‡ It was probably only the steady pressure of the German Government, to avoid a European war, which prevented Count Berchtold from yielding to his advisers. But if he conceded that Serbia might receive an economic, as distinct from a territorial, outlet on the Adriatic, by means of a railway to be built across Albania, he made so many difficulties about the frontiers of that new state§ that the effect of his concession was largely counteracted.

The Serbs were, as in 1908–1909, quite ready to risk a

---

* The Triple Alliance was renewed in December, 1912, and the fact was announced with considerable emphasis by the German chancellor. In the Triple Entente, on the other hand, while France was ready to support Russia, Great Britain would not go beyond diplomatic assistance.

† Conrad, II, 311–415; III, 11–342, *passim;* Baernreither, 176, 178, 186, 201, 228, 234; Steed, I, 361–364. On 28 and 29 November, 1912, secret instructions were sent to the Austro-Hungarian representatives in Belgrade, Cetinje, Durazzo, and St. Petersburg for their conduct in the event of war; Ö.-U. A., IV, 1072–1075.

‡ He visited William II in Berlin and Springe on 22 and 23 November. According to Friedjung, III, 228, which is based on Austrian sources, "the heir apparent wished to convince him of the necessity of moving with force against Serbia." William insisted, however, on leaving the responsibility for a rupture to Russia. He is said to have remarked to Francis Ferdinand, "*Keine Dummheiten*"; Baron Beyens, *L'Allemagne avant la guerre* (Paris, 1915), p. 248. Cf. William to Kiderlen, 21 November; G. P., XXXIII, 373–375.

§ Russia, while agreeing to the creation of an independent Albania, endeavored to restrict its frontiers as narrowly as possible, whereas Austria-Hungary sought to give them the widest extent. The controversy led to extreme tension between the two Powers in the winter of 1913; both began to call up reservists, and for a time it looked as if a European war would result over the question whether the towns of Dibra and Dyakova should go to Serbia or Albania! The pressure of Germany and Great Britain on Austria-Hungary and Russia respectively paved the way for a compromise which satisfied neither the Serbs nor the Albanians.

war with Austria-Hungary, until they learned that Russia would not support them.* But the Russian Government once more, as it had done during the Bosnian crisis, tempered its admonitions with hopes for the future. Thus M. Sazonov said to the Serbian minister in St. Petersburg:

After our great successes, he had confidence in our strength, and believed that we shall smash Austria. Therefore we should now be content with what we had won, but regard it only as a step, for the future belongs to us.†

Time was needed, he explained,

to organize the new Serbia, in order that when the time comes the Austro-Hungarian ulcer, which to-day is not yet so ripe as the Turkish, may be cut up.‡

And it was with the same argument that M. Sazonov urged the Serbs to make concessions to the Bulgarians in their quarrel over Macedonia:

Serbia has passed only the first stage on her historical course. . . . Serbia's promised land lies in the territory of the present Austria-Hungary, and not where her efforts are now directed and where the Bulgarians stand in the way. . . . Time is working for Serbia and for the ruin of her enemies, who are already showing evident signs of decay. . . . A break between Bulgaria and Serbia will be a triumph for Austria, whose death-agony will be thereby deferred for many years.§

The Serbs were wise enough to follow the advice given them and did not insist on their Albanian window.

Balked of a military triumph over her enemy, Austria-Hungary next sought to accomplish her aim indirectly by supporting the claims of Bulgaria in Macedonia against those of Ser-

---

* Sazonov made it clear in downright language that Russia could and would not go to war on account of a port on the Adriatic. Sazonov to Hartwig, 11 November, 1912; Siebert, pp. 578–579. In the spring of 1913, he insisted that Serbia refrain from assisting King Nicholas of Montenegro in his operations against Scutari.

† Popovich to foreign office, 27 December, 1912; Bogichevich, *Die auswärtige Politik Serbiens*, I, 280.

‡ Popovich to foreign office, 13 February, 1913; *ibid.*, I, 299.

§ Sazonov to Hartwig, 6 May, 1913; *Deutschland schuldig?*, p. 99.

bia and Greece.* It is clear that Bulgaria was even urged to fight Serbia if necessary.† Furthermore, when Bulgaria did attack Serbia and was about to be overwhelmed, Count Berchtold sought the consent of his allies in Berlin and Rome for an intervention against Serbia. Speaking to the German ambassador in Vienna about "the gravity of the situation of the Monarchy," he said:

The Southern Slav question, that is to say, undisputed possession of the provinces inhabited by the Southern Slavs, is a vital question for the Monarchy as well as for the Triple Alliance. The Southern Slav provinces of the Monarchy could not be retained if Serbia became too powerful. On that point all competent opinions are agreed. The Monarchy might possibly be forced to intervene, in case Serbia, in conjunction with Rumania and Greece, were to inflict a crushing blow on Bulgaria

* Tschirschky to Bethmann-Hollweg, 5 March, 1913; *G. P.*, XXXIV, 459–461; the same idea is expressed in many subsequent despatches. The German Emperor and the German Government protested against this plan (William's comment on Tschirschky's despatch; *G. P.*, XXXIV, p. 62; Jagow to Tschirschky, 8 March, 1913; *G. P.*, XXXIV, 466–468; and many subsequent despatches). In their eyes Bulgaria, because of the character of King Ferdinand, was thoroughly unreliable, but was bound, in the long run, to be won by Russia. They therefore urged Berchtold to compromise with Serbia, to support Rumania's claims against Bulgaria (see below, pp. 156–157), and pave the way for a Serbo-Rumanian-Greek alliance which would secure Austro-Hungarian predominance in the Balkans. The correspondence continued for several months. Berchtold always replied (*e. g.*, Berchtold to Jagow, 13 March, 1913; *Ö.-U. A.*, V, 937–940) that the Serbian hatred of the Monarchy was too intense to permit of a sincere friendship, and stuck to his own plan. The German Government finally tired of these rebuffs and dropped the idea. As late, however, as March, 1914, it believed the policy to be the only sound one for the Monarchy; Baernreither, pp. 301–304.

† Conrad urged this course, and on 26 May, 1913, he learned from the Austro-Hungarian military attaché in Sofia that Berchtold had offered to support Bulgaria, to protect her from loss of territory, and to lend her money if she would abandon her Russophil policy. Conrad, III, 302–316, 330. According to Baernreither, pp. 263–264, "the attack on Serbia was undertaken on the definite assumption that Conrad, in accord with the promise given, would pass the Save." Later (in November, 1913), King Ferdinand told Baernreither that "Austria had encouraged him to attack Serbia, and he had ground for counting on our help"; *ibid.*, p. 283. The Austro-Hungarian ambassador in Berlin, Count Szögyény, "was of the opinion, without knowing it positively, that we had encouraged the king of Bulgaria to attack Serbia"; *ibid.*, p. 294. According to 'Balcanicus' [Stoyan Protich], *The Aspirations of Bulgaria* (London, 1915), p. 63, quoting the proceedings of the Bulgarian Sobranye, the Bulgarian Government inquired of Vienna if it would have its hands free to attack Serbia and Greece if it satisfied Rumania's demands (see below, pp. 156–157), and Berchtold replied, "Danev [Bulgarian premier] has been informed under what conditions Bulgaria can secure her rear in case of an attack on Serbia and Greece." The correctness, in essentials, of these statements is proved by the recently published Austro-Hungarian documents. When the Tsar

and annex stretches of territory extending beyond Old Serbia. In any case Monastir could not be left to Serbia.

Asked as to the method of procedure, he replied:

He thought that it might well have to begin with a diplomatic conversation in Belgrade which, if it led to no result, must be supported by military pressure. Then, if Russia came on the field, the action would be transferred to St. Petersburg.

It may be noted, in anticipation, that this was exactly the procedure adopted in July, 1914. In order that his thought might be clear, Count Berchtold added:

The Monarchy was far from wishing to pursue a policy of adventure or conquest, and had in view only the preservation of its Southern Slav territories, including Trieste. Naturally the most acceptable solution of the question to him would be a small Serbia beaten by the enemy, which he would by far prefer to a possible occupation of Serbia by the Monarchy. But if the first alternative failed, the Monarchy would be compelled to act, in order to safeguard its possessions.*

and the German Emperor, on 24 May, sent telegrams to King Ferdinand protesting against a Bulgarian attack on Greek troops and warning him of the possible consequences (*G. P.*, XXXIV, 864–865), Berchtold telegraphed to Sofia that the imperial messages were dictated by dynastic and family considerations and need not be considered of far-reaching importance (*Ö.-U. A.*, VI, 555, note *c* to no. 7201). When the Bulgarian premier inquired what would be the attitude of Austria-Hungary in the event of a Serbo-Bulgarian war, Berchtold replied that while a peaceful solution of the Serbo-Bulgarian conflict was desirable, he would understand it "if they determined in Sofia to resort to arms in the last analysis for securing [their interests]"; "if they determined upon a purely Bulgarian policy and entered upon no political combination which is directed against us," the Monarchy was ready to open negotiations as to its attitude "in the event of an actual belligerent conflict between Bulgaria and Serbia." Berchtold to Tarnowski, 30 May, 1913; *Ö.-U. A.*, VI, 564–565. Pressure was exerted to force a declaration of policy from the Bulgarian Government. Berchtold to Tarnowski, 3 June, 20 June; *Ö.-U. A.*, VI, 589–590; 688–689. The statement was then made that, since a strengthening of Serbia at the cost of Bulgaria would be contrary to Austro-Hungarian interests, "Bulgaria can therefore in this case count not only on our sympathy, but, if the circumstances lead to that development undesired by us, also on our active support," provided she offered Rumania sufficient compensation to insure the latter's neutrality; this promise was approved by the Emperor Francis Joseph. Berchtold to Tarnowski, 24 June; *Ö.-U. A.*, VI, 720–722. Finally, the minister in Sofia was authorized to make the declaration in writing to the Bulgarian Government. Berchtold to Tarnowski, 28 June; *Ö.-U. A.*, VI, 761.

* Tschirschky to foreign office, telegram, 3 July, 1913; *G. P.*, XXXV, 122–124. The editors of *Die Grosse Politik* argue, on the basis of the German chancellor's reply to this overture (Zimmermann to Tschirschky, 6 July, 1913; *G. P.*, XXXV, 129–130), that Berchtold had in mind only a diplomatic action at Bucharest to

Both the German and Italian Governments refused to sanction any step against Serbia, and Count Berchtold had to let matters take their course.

A final effort was made to deal with Serbia in the autumn of 1913. The delimitation of the frontiers of Albania, which the European Powers had reserved for themselves, proceeded very leisurely, and the Serbo-Albanian frontier was in a state of constant disturbance. The Serbs, irritated by Albanian forays, advanced their troops beyond the line into Albanian territory. Here, so Conrad thought, was a heaven-sent chance for the reckoning with Serbia, and he urged on both the Emperor Francis Joseph and the government the necessity of going to war; it was, he argued, the last opportunity.* At first Count Berchtold, under the influence of Count Tisza, the Hungarian premier, who was opposed to war, hesitated, and contented himself with an "amicable request" to Serbia to withdraw her troops. But when the Serbian Government attempted to argue about the matter, Count Berchtold, who enjoyed the "moral support" of Germany,† despatched an ultimatum to Belgrade requiring Serbia to evacuate all Albanian

restrain Rumania from assisting Serbia in the war against Bulgaria. It is true that Berchtold had previously requested that pressure be put on Rumania (Berchtold to Szögyény, 1 July, 1913; *Ö.-U. A.*, VI, 776–778; *G. P.*, XXXV, 116–118), and that Bethmann, in his reply, refused to exert such pressure. But, according to the Austro-Hungarian ambassador in Berlin, the German foreign office understood from Tschirschky's telegram that "Your Excellency [Berchtold] had even spoken of the possibility of an invasion of Serbia and an occupation of Belgrade." Szögyény to Berchtold, 4 July; *Ö.-U. A.*, VI, 805. Hence the German chancellor, in his reply, said: "If Austria-Hungary should attempt to eject Serbia from the newly-won territories, it would have no success and would make a mortal enemy of Serbia. Should it attempt to do so by force of arms, a European war would result. The vital interests of Germany would thereby be most seriously affected, and therefore I must expect that *before* Count Berchtold takes decisions of that kind, he will inform us of them." After all, Berchtold's language to Tschirschky was so clear that his wish to use force, if necessary, cannot be doubted. For the *démarche* in Rome, see Berchtold to Mérey, 4 July; Mérey to Berchtold, 12 July; *Ö.-U. A.*, VI, 802–804, 881–883. The Italian foreign minister, like the German chancellor, believed that the contemplated Austrian action would precipitate a European conflagration, and said: "We shall hold you back by the tails of your coat if it is necessary." The Italian premier, Giolitti, speaking in the Italian chamber on 5 December, 1914, incorrectly gave the date as 9 August, 1913, and claimed the credit for preventing the Austro-Hungarian action.

* Conrad, III, 452.

† Zimmermann to Wedel, 16 October, 1913; Zimmermann to Tschirschky, 16 October; *G. P.*, XXXVI, 387, 388.

territory within eight days: otherwise the Austro-Hungarian Government "would see itself, to its great regret, in the necessity of having recourse to the proper measures for the realization of its demands."* Once again Serbia yielded, and there was no war. Whether Count Berchtold acted on his own initiative or whether or how he converted Count Tisza, has not been revealed.† But one may note (1) that the issue was a comparatively minor one on which to base a threat of war, which is precisely what gives it its significance; (2) Germany gave her consent, after having refused to sanction intervention in much more serious incidents.

Further light is thrown on this episode by the fact that, a fortnight before the ultimatum to Serbia, the Serbian premier, acting probably on the advice of the King of Rumania and the German foreign minister,‡ came to Vienna and made overtures to Count Berchtold for friendly relations.§ But when the foreign minister mentioned the matter to his colleagues,

---

* Conrad, III, 464-466; *Ö.-U. A.*, VII, 453.

† Conrad went to Germany to participate in the celebrations of the centenary of the Battle of Leipzig before the final decision was taken, and does not record what happened in Vienna.

‡ Bogichevich, *Kriegsursachen*, pp. 68-69, 72-73. Cf. Haymerle to Berchtold, 18 September, 1913; *Ö.-U. A.*, VII, 318-319. The Austrian minister in Belgrade was approached by leaders of the opposition with a view to a *rapprochement*. He himself was of the opinion that "if we desire to have quiet on our southern frontier, we must wish for the strengthening and maintenance of the Old Radical régime, all the more so as a person in the front rank of the business world here who stands outside the party conflict recently, in the course of a long conversation, informed a confidant that M. Pashich was seeking an approach to us and that the Old Radicals would also be found ready for a compromise; even M. Protich would let himself be talked over." Ugron to Berchtold, 21 August, 1913; *Ö.-U. A.*, VII, 172. The matter appears to have been discussed among the officials in the Austrian foreign office, without anything having been done about it, so far as the records show. But a memorandum has been found enumerating three conditions for an Austro-Serbian understanding. No. 1 reads: "The constitution of Serbia must be supplemented by a law by which the royal government would be empowered, as soon as any movement directed against the honor, the external and internal security or the territorial integrity of a neighboring state manifests itself and the friendly relations with that neighboring state appear to be thereby threatened, to suspend certain provisions of the laws relating to punishment, procedure, the press and association and to replace them by exceptional orders which appear suited to suppress the movement in question." On this condition, Austria-Hungary would be ready to recognize the Serbian title to the newly won territories and to consent to the abolition of the capitulations existing under the Turkish régime (No. 2). No. 3 would have bound Serbia to take the action provided for under No. 1 "as soon as a request to this end was presented by the Austro-Hungarian Government."

§ Berchtold's memorandum of the conversation; *Ö.-U. A.*, VII, 425-427.

the Austrian premier, Count Stürgkh, scouted the idea, declaring that "a reckoning with Serbia and her humiliation is a condition of the Monarchy's existence," and General Conrad expressed his satisfaction that "the peaceful way [of dealing with Serbia] was regarded by the competent authorities as out of the question."* One can only conclude that the Austro-Hungarian Government, or at any rate Berchtold, Conrad, and Stürgkh, had made up their minds to have war with Serbia and were only awaiting a favorable opportunity. The one restraining influence was that of Tisza, who feared that the result of war—apart from any intervention of Russia—would mean the incorporation of Serbia in the Monarchy, which, from the Hungarian point of view, would make the question of the Southern Slavs, or rather the question of Croatia, more acute than ever.

On the other hand, M. Pashich's sincerity in approaching Count Berchtold is open to doubt. Shortly after the Treaty of Bucharest he said to a Serbian diplomatist:

Even in the first Balkan war I could have let it come to a European war, in order to acquire Bosnia and the Herzegovina; but as I feared that we should then be compelled to make large concessions in Macedonia to Bulgaria, I wished first of all to assure the possession of Macedonia to Serbia, and only then be able to proceed to the acquisition of Bosnia and the Herzegovina.

Or, as he put it more succinctly to the Greek foreign minister, "The first round is won; now we must prepare for the second round against Austria."† One suspects, therefore, that his overture to Count Berchtold may have been merely a ruse to gain time, for Serbia was in no condition to inaugurate an active policy against the Monarchy. Be that as it may, it is hardly surprising that after receiving two rebuffs from Vienna, M. Pashich now turned to St. Petersburg.

Visiting the Russian capital in February, 1914, he was re-

* Conrad, III, 729, 731.   † Bogichevich, *Kriegsursachen,* p. 65 and note.

ceived in audience by the Tsar. After they had discussed the situation in the Balkans created by the Treaty of Bucharest, the Serbian premier complained that Austria-Hungary was furnishing arms and munitions to Bulgaria.

I begged him that Russia might likewise assist us by delivering 120,000 rifles and munitions from her magazine, and a few cannon, if they could be spared, especially howitzers, which the Turks had held back when they were on the way before the war. We would pay for everything that we needed and would return it as soon as we had received what we had ordered.

The Tsar promised to discuss the matter with M. Sazonov, saying that "they would do everything to alleviate our situation." The conversation then turned on Montenegro, Bulgaria, and Austria-Hungary.

The Tsar criticised the attitude of Montenegro very violently, and said that Montenegro was not acting sincerely, as it was now in agreement with Austria. . . . He also thinks that the union of Serbia and Montenegro is only a question of time, and that it must be solved with the least possible shock and noise. . . .

The Tsar strongly condemned King Ferdinand for being subservient to the Austrian policy and for having begun the war against Serbia. God, however, had punished him. [Pashich said that] for our part we dared not scowl at the Bulgarians, but had to consider how harmony between Serbia and Bulgaria might be useful to both, and that perhaps the time would come when some concessions might be made to Bulgaria if she were willing to help us in the solution of the Serbo-Croatian question. Thereupon the Tsar asked how many Serbo-Croats lived in Austria-Hungary and what they now thought and desired. I answered him, "More than six million," and told him where they lived. I told him also about the Slovenes, who were gravitating toward the Serbo-Croats and would adopt the Serbo-Croat language, because their dialect was bad and they had long lost their national independence. . . .

I told the Tsar of the change which had taken place among the Slavs of Austria-Hungary—how numerous members of the Starchevich party who formerly expected salvation from Austria* now saw that this could come only from Russia or Serbia, and they could hardly await the opportunity to see their desires fulfilled. Then I told him that for every rifle we received we had a soldier from these countries. . . . He then asked how many soldiers Serbia could now provide. Serbia, said the Tsar, had surprised the world when she had 400,000 men to march. I answered, "We think we can provide half a million well-clothed and armed soldiers." "That is sufficient, that is no trifle, one can do much with that" [replied the Tsar].

We then discussed the following: We must cultivate the alliance with Greece, since, apart from other considerations, it safeguards our import and export trade. Furthermore, we must try to place the alliance with Rumania on a broader basis and not merely on the maintenance of the Treaty of Bucharest.

M. Pashich then asked the hand of one of the Tsar's daughters for the Crown Prince of Serbia, who might "if God and circumstances permit, become tsarina of the Southern Slav, Serbo-Croatian people." The Tsar listened "with evident pleasure," but said that he wished his children to be guided by their hearts. At the end of the audience he accompanied M. Pashich to the door and sent a message to King Peter:

For Serbia we shall do everything, give my greetings to the King, and tell him [in Russian], for Serbia we shall do everything.†

The Serbian premier had every reason to be satisfied! He now knew from the Tsar himself that M. Sazonov had spoken truly when he said, "Serbia is the only state in the Balkans in which Russia has confidence, and Russia will do everything for Serbia."‡ And it is probably more than a coincidence that the meeting between the Tsar and the Serbian statesman took place at the moment when the Russian Government was considering the situation created by the Mission of Liman von Sanders and

* Their programme called for the independence of Croatia on a strictly Croat basis, which excluded any co-operation with the Serbs of Croatia-Slavonia, and even denied the existence of any Serbs in Croatia-Slavonia.

† Pashich to King Peter, 2 February, 1914; Bogichevich, *Kriegsursachen*, 170–180; Bogichevich, *Die auswärtige Politik Serbiens*, I, 414–421.

‡ Popovich to foreign office, 17 November, 1913; Bogichevich, *Die auswärtige Politik Serbiens*, I, 397.

was coming to the conclusion that the problem of the Straits could be solved only in the event of European complications, in which it was assumed that Serbia would play her part.*

The Russian promises for the future were, however, not immediately productive of tangible results. In the spring of 1914, negotiations were started for the union of Serbia and Montenegro, with the approval of Russia; but in view of the irritation displayed in Vienna,† M. Sazonov advised the Serbian Government not to press the matter.‡ There is no evidence that at this time Russia was pursuing any policy other than the maintenance of the *status quo* in the Balkans. Nevertheless the efforts of M. Sazonov to strengthen the friendly relations between Rumania, Serbia, and Greece and to win Bulgaria back to friendship with Russia gave the greatest umbrage in Vienna and Budapest and intensified the conviction that it was only a question of time until Serbia, with the approval and support of Russia and France, would challenge the Monarchy to a life-and-death struggle.

THE YUGOSLAV REVOLUTIONARY MOVEMENT

Those Austro-Hungarian soldiers and statesmen who advocated war against Serbia did so in the belief that not otherwise could the Monarchy deal with the unrest and even revolutionary tendencies in the Yugoslav provinces.§ They were persuaded that the danger was increased, if not largely created, by the secret activity and propaganda of Serbia, and they proposed to crush the agitation by the simple plan of smashing Serbia on the battle-field. And there is no doubt that the situation was becoming increasingly uncertain in the years immediately prior to the Great War.

In Croatia, the coalition of the Serbs and Croats possessed a majority in the diet which the Hungarian *ban* could neither bribe nor terrorize. Accordingly, the government at Budapest

---

* See above, p. 88.　　　　　　　† *G. P.*, XXXVIII, 319–361.
‡ Sazonov to Hartwig, 7 July, 1914; Siebert, p. 631.
§ This view was shared by the representatives in Belgrade. Storck to Berchtold, 24 September, 1913; report of the military attaché, 26 January, 1914; *Ö.-U. A.*, VII, 343, 780.

endeavored to paralyze the movement for Yugoslav unity by accusing a number of Serbs of treasonable relations with Belgrade, of whom 31 were convicted. But since the trial was conducted in the most unfair and even illegal manner and the only evidence to prove the charge was a pamphlet written by a notorious spy of the most dubious character, the accused won a moral victory, and the verdict was reversed by a court of appeal.* Finally, after a long struggle to recover its ascendancy, the Hungarian Government in 1912 suppressed the constitution of Croatia and governed the country by a dictatorship. The Croats were traditionally loyal to the Emperor: they now began to waver. An official of the Ballplatz, Baron von Musulin, who was a native of Croatia (and was to write the ultimatum of 23 July, 1914), visiting the country in the summer of 1913 after an absence of many years, was shocked by the sentiment of the people.

I found the opposition between Serbs and Croats largely vanished, at least among the *intelligentsia,* and, in consequence, a significant weakening of the Croatian idea. . . . The intellectual world was living under the impression of the great development of Serbdom on the other side of the Drave. In many places I encountered the belief that national salvation must come from that direction. . . . The political activity of Serbia made itself felt in all directions.†

It was only the strong hand of the dictatorship which kept the country quiet.

The situation in Bosnia was much more difficult. Thanks to the illiteracy of a large section of the population, which the government had not exerted itself to overcome, the diet established in 1910 had to be elected on a restricted franchise and was not, therefore, a very representative body. Nor did it possess great powers, for all bills had to receive the consent of the Austrian and Hungarian Governments, and the administration was controlled by the joint finance minister of the Mon-

---

* Seton-Watson, *The Southern Slav Question*, pp. 176–192, 207–208.
† Freiherr von Musulin, *Das Haus am Ballplatz* (Munich, 1924), pp. 208–209.

archy in Vienna and directed by the *Landeschef,* General Potiorek, who was appointed by the Emperor. This constitutional
system, though probably as liberal as was warranted by the
backward state of the country, left the real power in the hands
of Vienna and Budapest. It was supported by the Mohammedan
landlords and by the Catholic Croats, but aroused no enthusiasm
among the peasantry, whether Moslem or Orthodox. The failure
of the system was demonstrated during the Balkan wars when
the government, alarmed by the manifestations of sympathy for
the Serbian cause, closed the diet and introduced, by special
laws, what was equivalent to a state of siege. Although Ritter
von Bilinski, who was appointed common minister of finance in
1912, revoked the exceptional laws, restored the freedom of
the press, and drew up projects for dealing with the agrarian
problem and for improving economic conditions generally,
General Potiorek and his police officers did not sympathize with
a conciliatory policy, which savored too much of weakness.
The general himself was so disliked and distrusted by the Serbian elements that only a few of their representatives in the
diet were willing to join the government's majority. At best
the government could count on the conservative middle-class
elements, and even they were determined to exact large political
concessions.*

The bourgeoisie, representing generally the older generation, was content to follow legal methods of agitation, in the
hope that the accession of Francis Ferdinand would usher in
a new dispensation. Not so the rising generation, the *Omladina*
('Youth') or *Mlada Bosna* ('Young Bosnia'), as it was vari-
ously called.† Recruited from the youth of the humble classes,

---

* L. Bilinski, *Wspomnienia i Dokumenty* [Reminiscences and Documents] (Warsaw, 1924), I, 227–332; Baron Carl Collas, "Auf den bosnischen Wegspuren der
Kriegsschuldigen," in *KSF*, V, 11–27 (January, 1927); J. Braun, 34, "Bosnien
und Herzegowina. Politik, Verwaltung und leitende Personen vor Kriegsausbruch,"
in *ibid.*, VII, 313–344 (April, 1929); Conrad, III, 96–100, 370–379.

† The fullest account of the movement is found in Seton-Watson, *Sarajevo*, pp.
65–79, which makes use of much unpublished information. The reminiscences of one
of the lesser leaders are given in B. Yevtich, *Сарајевски Атентат* [The Assassination of Sarajevo] (Sarajevo, 1923), the first part of which is translated in *KSF*,
III, 658–686 (October, 1925). For the Austrian side, see Mandl, *Die Habsburger
und die serbische Frage,* pp. 122–137, and *Ö.-U. A.*, IV, 265–275, VIII, 416–426.

—peasants and artisans, teachers and students,—it was thoroughly impatient with the existing political and social régime, and was animated by a strong Yugoslav nationalism which manifested itself, among the students, in numerous small newspapers. They read the Russian revolutionary writers, especially Herzen and Kropotkin; some of them travelled abroad and came in contact with wandering Russian revolutionaries. Not only was their revolutionary zeal thereby stimulated, but they became imbued with the doctrines of the Russian terrorists and their cult of individual action. Political assassination was indeed an attractive weapon to 'Young Bosnia,' which bitterly resented the strong hand of the police and delighted in circumventing the authorities. Moreover, deeds of this kind were well calculated to arouse and to keep alive the hostility of the masses for the Habsburg system, which was all the more necessary since the Monarchy, by its success in carrying through the annexation, had given an unexpected and unwelcome proof of vitality.

The first manifestation of terrorism was the attempted murder of the governor of Bosnia, General Varashanin, at the opening of the diet in 1910 by a student named Bogdan Zherayich. Zherayich was a youth from southern Bosnia who spent a year in Belgrade and had brooded over the wrongs of his people. His first idea (according to the Austro-Hungarian version)* was to kill the Emperor Francis Joseph, who had come to Sarajevo to inaugurate the diet in person; but reflecting that this would only pave the way for the accession of the Archduke Francis Ferdinand, who was credited with plans for solving the Yugoslav question within the Monarchy, Zherayich shot at the governor instead. The attempt failed, and Zherayich committed suicide. But the incident was not forgotten, all the less so as the governor was reported to have kicked the corpse as it lay on the bridge at Sarajevo. In 1912 Vladimir Gachinovich, the son of an Orthodox priest of Herzegovina, wrote a pamphlet entitled *The Death of a Hero,* in which he glorified Zherayich's

* Mandl, pp. 130–131.

exploit and quoted the latter's appeal, "I leave it to Serbdom to avenge me." This pamphlet circulated among the youth of Bosnia and was published anonymously in *Piyemont,* a newspaper in Belgrade which was the organ of a revolutionary secret society, 'Union or Death,' about which much will be said presently. From this time Zherayich was looked upon as a martyr to the Yugoslav idea. His grave became a place of pilgrimage,* and many youths were inspired to follow his example.

Gachinovich himself became the intellectual leader of the Bosnian revolutionary movement. He is said to have resided in Belgrade from 1909 to 1911, where he came under the influence of Professor Skerlich, a well-known expounder of democratic and nationalist ideas. Then he spent a year in Vienna spreading revolutionary doctrines among Serbian students and writing his pamphlet. Returning to Belgrade, he joined the society of 'Union or Death.' After this he migrated to Sarajevo, where he made the acquaintance of Danilo Ilich, a sometime teacher and a prominent member of the local *Prosvyeta* ('Culture'), a province-wide organization of Serbs for educational purposes, a connection destined to have important consequences. Later, Gachinovich proceeded to Lausanne to study sociology; his funds are supposed to have come from Serbian sources.† At Lausanne, he met Russian revolutionaries, among them Leon Trotski (then an obscure person), who wrote an introduction signed "L. T." to some articles published by Gachinovich in French. Gachinovich, however, kept in touch with his old associates: "he held the half of revolutionary Bosnia in his hands."‡ His doctrine was that "the young men must prepare themselves for sacrifices," that is, they must take the same risks as Zherayich.

There was no revolutionary mass in Bosnia. Ripeness for

---

* Printsip is said to have visited the grave on the evening before the murder of Francis Ferdinand, and to have sworn that his hand should not waver the next day.

† He is said to have received funds from several secret societies and to have held a scholarship from the ministry of foreign affairs. M. Bogichevich [Bogitchévitch], *Le procès de Salonique* (Paris, 1927), pp. 157–158.

‡ Seton-Watson, p. 73, quoting one of Gachinovich's associates.

revolution was only among individuals. The youth was the one shining spot of this period in Bosnia.*

Thanks to the inspiration of Gachinovich secret terrorist groups—*Kruzhoki*—were formed in various towns, the members of which were apparently unknown to each other but were linked together by correspondence with Danilo Ilich. Finally, in 1913, a secret society called 'Serbo-Croatian Nationalist Youth' (*Srpsko-Hrvatska Nacionalistička Omladina*) was organized in Sarajevo with about a hundred members.

Its aim was to win the rising generation for the idea of throwing off the Habsburg yoke and achieving Yugoslav unity under Serbia; and its efforts were concentrated above all upon pupils in the various teachers' training colleges. Subsections existed in Tuzla, Mostar, Trebinje, and Banjaluka, but the centre of the whole movement was in Zagreb, where it was intended to hold, on 16 July, 1914, a sort of congress of delegates from all of the training colleges in the various Yugoslav provinces, and to lay plans for future agitation.†

To complete the picture of the growing consciousness of Yugoslav unity, it should be noted that one of the most zealous prophets of revolution was a wandering Slovene student named Endlicher.

The seriousness of the situation was revealed by a series of assassinations attempted by young Bosnians. In June, 1912, a Serb, Luka Yukich, shot at Baron Cuvaj, the *ban* of Croatia, in the streets of Zagreb. In August, 1913, a Croat emigrant, Ivan Daychich, came all the way from America for a shot at the new *ban,* Baron Skerlecz, and in March, 1914, yet another

* M. E. Durham, "The Sarajevo Murder Plot," in *Current History*, XXV, 657–658 (February, 1927). The quotation is from a biography of Gachinovich, without indication of title or author. The reference may be to *Spomenica Vladimira Gaćinovića* (Belgrade, 1921), which is quoted by Seton-Watson. The same opinion was expressed by an Austrian official, who, however, warned that "the prestige of the Monarchy would suffer in the eyes of the still indifferent masses and the authority of the state would be undermined if the Monarchy did not enforce its will on the kingdom of Serbia in striking fashion." Report of Appel, the commander in Sarajevo, 19 December, 1912; *Ö.-U. A.*, V, 176–179.
† Seton-Watson, p. 75.

Croat, Jacob Shefer, tried to kill Skerlecz in the opera-house at Zagreb. Whether these *attentats* were spontaneous outbursts of the Bosnian youth or were inspired from Belgrade is uncertain;* the significant fact was that they were made at all.

Equally disconcerting to the authorities was the undermining of discipline in the schools. "In all the Southern Slav provinces of the Habsburg Monarchy," laments the apologist of Habsburg policy, "strikes and excesses on the part of students came to be the order of the day: in Agram, Laibach, Mostar, Ragusa, Spalato, Brünn, Tuzla, Prague, and Vienna."† In Croatia, demonstrations against the harsh régime of Baron Cuvaj were frequently staged. At Tuzla, in Bosnia, the professors were insulted, and the playing of the Austrian national anthem was made the occasion for a disturbance. The display of the Austro-Hungarian flag was likewise resented. At Sarajevo, German shop-signs were besmirched. At Mostar, it was necessary in June, 1913, to close the high school for a year.‡ At least twenty-one student newspapers proclaimed and assisted in spreading nationalist and sometimes revolutionary ideas,§ and the Yugoslav press is said to have advocated extreme measures. ‖

* According to Mandl, p. 133, shortly before the *attentat* Yukich headed a delegation of Zagreb students who visited Belgrade, where he was received by the Crown Prince Alexander in private audience; about this audience he refused to say anything at his trial. The visit was made the occasion of an anti-Austrian demonstration by the Belgrade students; the Serbian Government protested its helplessness. Ugron to Berchtold, 21, 22, 26 April, 1912; *Ö.-U. A.*, IV, 112–114, 118–119, 135–137. H. Wendl, *Die Habsburger und die südslawische Frage* (Leipzig-Belgrade, 1921, p. 45), which is often based on unpublished information, says that Yukich was inspired to shoot at Cuvaj because on the previous day a Magyar, Kovacs, had fired at Count Tisza in the Budapest parliament. According to the Austrian version, however, Yukich while in Belgrade acquired from a Serbian officer the revolver with which he shot at Cuvaj; *Ö.-U. A.*, IV, 502. Dr. O. Tartalja, *Riječ* (Zagreb), 12 December, 1927, quoted by F. von Wiesner, "Die Schuld der serbischen Regierung am Mord von Sarajewo," in *KSF*, VI, 350–351 (April, 1928), states that he himself suggested that Yukich should assassinate the *ban* Cuvaj and introduced Yukich to Dragutin Dimitriyevich, who approved of the plot. Shefer is represented by Austrian writers (Mandl, pp. 133–134; Wiesner, *loc. cit.*, V, 352–353) as being inspired by one Rudolf Hertsigonya, a member of the Serbian secret societies, who explained that "there was no opportunity to be able to shoot the Archduke Francis Ferdinand."

† Mandl, p. 129.   ‡ Seton-Watson, pp. 76–77.
§ *L'unité jougoslave* (Paris, 1915), p. 33; many of the papers were short-lived, as is apt to be the case with student publications!
‖ Mandl, p. 125.

The nervousness of the authorities is well attested by the fact that between 1909 and 1914, 166 persons were tried in Bosnia for treason or espionage, of whom the majority were convicted.* A high official of the foreign office has written:

All who knew the country had the impression that an explosion was imminent. Especially in the schools Pan-Serb propaganda had created such chaotic conditions that a regular continuance of instruction hardly seemed to be any longer possible. . . . Not only in Serbia itself but also in the Austro-Hungarian territories inhabited by Southern Slavs, the conviction took root that the collapse of Austria-Hungary was near at hand.†

In the summer of 1913, the well-known English student of Austro-Hungarian and Balkan politics, Professor R. W. Seton-Watson, who still believed that the Yugoslav question might be solved in the interest of the Dual Monarchy,‡ and who had just spent some months in southeastern Europe, warned Dr. von Bilinski, that a change of policy was necessary if a revolutionary outbreak was to be averted.§ But General Potiorek insisted on introducing stricter and more repressive methods of government—with the result that the youth were only the more enraged, and plans were discussed for more outrages. And the next chapter will relate how it was decided to assassinate none other than the Archduke Francis Ferdinand himself. Such a stroke would, it was no doubt hoped, bring the revolutionary

* Freiherr von Sarkotich, "Der Hochverrats-Prozess von Banjaluka," in *KSF*, VII, 39-40 (January, 1929).

† A. Hoyos, *Der deutsch-englische Gegensatz und sein Einfluss auf die Balkanpolitik Österreich-Ungarns* (Berlin, 1922), p. 74. The Austrian military attaché in Belgrade complained of "an incredible minimizing of our political and military strength": one paper wrote: "As all Europe knows, the Monarchy is facing a collapse and is already approaching its end." Report of 14 February, 1914; *Ö.-U. A.*, VII, 874.

‡ His book, *The Southern Slav Question* (1911, German edition, 1913), is dedicated to "that Austrian statesman who shall possess the genius and the courage necessary to solve the Southern Slav question." On page 2 he wrote: "Servia and Montenegro can only watch, and are helpless to hinder, the process of evolution which is gradually making for Serbo-Croat Unity under Habsburg sway. Their gallant struggles for independence in the past may kindle regret in the heart of the sentimental onlooker; but it cannot obscure the inexorable lesson of history."

§ Seton-Watson, *Sarajevo*, p. 145.

movement to a head, or would at least remove the man who was regarded at once as the head of the Viennese war party and as the champion of a political programme which would be fatal to the success of Yugoslav nationalism.

The exact connection between the Yugoslav revolutionary movement and Serbia, whether official circles or secret societies, is not easy to determine. That the agitation within the Monarchy was stimulated and assisted from across the Save has already been indicated, and the question will be more fully discussed in the next chapter. On the other hand, the unrest existed long before Serbian propaganda was set to work, and, resting as it did in the last analysis upon the growing consciousness of Yugoslav unity, it could have been exorcised only by frank recognition on the part of the Austro-Hungarian Government of the Yugoslav national idea. The Bosnian problem, at least, was created, not by Serbia, but by the Dual Monarchy when it first 'occupied' and then annexed the province in opposition to the wishes of the majority of the inhabitants; and, however much the machinations of Serbia intensified the problem, its solution in the interest of the Monarchy was probably not impossible, provided its political system was revamped in accord with the democratic and nationalistic aspirations of its polyglot peoples.

No one in Austria-Hungary was more keenly aware of this than the Archduke Francis Ferdinand; in fact, he was one of the few persons in authority who perceived that the maintenance of Dualism unchanged was driving the state on a fatal course.* The Archduke was a man of enigmatic character. His marriage

---

* *Franz Ferdinands Lebensroman* (Stuttgart, 1919), purporting to be based on the diary of an intimate friend; O. Graf Czernin, *Im Weltkrieg* (Berlin, 1919), pp. 43–66; P. Nikitsch-Boulles, his private secretary, *Vor dem Sturm: Erinnerungen an Erzherzog Thronfolger Franz Ferdinand* (Berlin, 1925); K. Freiherr von Bardolff, his military adjutant, "Franz Ferdinand," in *KSF*, V, 599–608 (July, 1927); T. von Sosnosky, *Franz Ferdinand, ein Lebensbild* (Munich, 1928); L. von Chlumecky, *Erzherzog Franz Ferdinands Wirken und Wollen* (Berlin, 1929); J. Redlich, *Emperor Francis Joseph of Austria* (New York, 1929), pp. 472–496. Conrad, *passim*, contains much detailed information. A. Freiherr von Margutti, *Vom alten Kaiser* (Vienna, 1921), pp. 121–152, reveals how Francis Ferdinand was regarded in the circle of Francis Joseph. *G. P.* is full of references; list in XL, 45.

with the Countess Sophie Chotek, a Bohemian lady of non-royal blood, had been consented to most reluctantly by the Emperor Francis Joseph, and then only on condition that the Archduke's children should not be eligible to the succession; a condition which infuriated Francis Ferdinand and in large measure alienated him from the Emperor and the other members of the Habsburg family, who treated his wife with scant courtesy. Consequently he had few intimate friends, and his real personality remained a mystery. His intense interest in the army and his support of the navy, his insistence on the appointment of General Conrad von Hötzendorf as chief of staff and his close relations with Baron von Aehrenthal lent color to the belief that he favored an aggressive and even warlike foreign policy, a belief encouraged by his increasing participation in the government, which the advanced age of Francis Joseph made proper and inevitable.* Actually, as the memoirs of Conrad repeatedly prove, Francis Ferdinand was much less belligerent than was commonly supposed. So far from desiring war against Serbia, which might involve a conflict with Russia, what the Archduke really hoped to bring about was a revival of the Three Emperors' League, that is, an alliance between Austria-Hungary, Germany, and Russia, which would strengthen the monarchical idea and insure the preservation of the Monarchy. Italy, rather than Serbia, appears to have been the object of his aversion.

But, if the state was to be preserved, the chaos of the Yugoslav provinces would have to be dealt with, and it was notorious that Francis Ferdinand placed the responsibility for the chaos on the Magyar politicians. Whether he had specific plans for a reorganization of the Monarchy is not clear, although drafts of various schemes have been published from his papers. But it was generally understood that he was anxious to abolish the Dual system and substitute for it some form of federalism

---

* The Emperor did not relish this, and always kept the final decisions in his own hands. The relations between uncle and nephew were never cordial and often cool.

which would afford a large measure of self-government to the various nationalities; during the last years of his life he was believed to favor the plan for a 'triad' state, by which the Yugoslav provinces would be erected into a third kingdom enjoying the same status as Austria and Hungary. Of course nothing could be done during the lifetime of Francis Joseph, who refused to tamper with the existing machinery, and any effort to change the Dual system was bound to evoke the passionate protest and perhaps the resistance of Hungary. None the less, high hopes of reform when Francis Ferdinand came to the throne were entertained by those who tried to think in what came to be known as 'Great-Austrian' idea.*

The personality and policy of Francis Ferdinand were important factors in Austro-Serbian relations. In some Yugoslav circles the genuine fear existed that he intended to solve the Austro-Serbian question by force of arms, which would mean the end of Serbian independence. On the other hand, if his supposed desire to transform the Monarchy into a federal state were realized and some measure of satisfaction thus given to its Yugoslav subjects, the prospect of Yugoslav union under Serbian leadership would be greatly diminished. To quote one of the Bosnian revolutionaries:

For the somnolent Croatian masses this would mean the realization of their claim to the restoration of the Croatian kingdom and equality, both political and legal, with their German and Magyar masters. And the realization of Trialism would signify without doubt death to the ideals of the *Omladina*, death to the hope of emancipation and union of all Yugoslavs in Austria-Hungary, and the destruction of Austria.†

From their point of view, his removal was greatly to be desired!

Thus up to 1914 Austria-Hungary had not succeeded in the least degree in advancing toward a solution of her relations

* It is said that Francis Ferdinand intended to refuse to be crowned King of Hungary until he had forced the Magyars to accept a modification of Dualism.
† Yevtich, *Capajeвcku Ameнmam,* p. 16, and *KSF,* III, 669–670 (October, 1925).

with Serbia.* The original policy of keeping Serbia in economic and political subordination had been overtaken by the events of 1903 and the subsequent defiance of Serbia. The plan of military action, championed consistently by General Conrad and the military party and intermittently considered by the Ballplatz, had been blocked by the successive submissions of Serbia, the restraining influence of Germany, and the hesitations of Francis Joseph and Francis Ferdinand. The possibility of a peaceful arrangement with Serbia, though twice suggested by M. Pashich, had been rejected. Meanwhile the state of affairs in the Yugoslav provinces, going from bad to worse, imperatively demanded that something should be done. And, in fact, in the spring of 1914, a new and definite policy began to be studied and elaborated by the Austro-Hungarian Government. As this policy involved not only Serbia but her neighbors Bulgaria and Rumania, something must be said about the situation in those countries.

BULGARIA AND RUMANIA

We have seen that in 1914 two acute problems existed in the Near East: the Russo-German rivalry at Constantinople and the Austro-Serbian antagonism in the western Balkans. Each contained the germ of a European war: Russia might attempt to seize the Straits and Constantinople; Austria-Hungary might begin the long-desired campaign against Serbia, or Serbia, if assured of Russian support, might attack the Habsburg Monarchy. In either case, much would depend on the attitude of the two other Balkan states, Bulgaria and Rumania, which lay between the two danger zones. Consequently the favor of these two small countries was a prize eagerly disputed for by the two rival diplomatic groups.

Generally speaking, Rumania, down to the Balkan wars, adhered to the Central Powers. She had in 1883 concluded a military alliance with Austria-Hungary, to which Germany and

---

* Numerous manifestations of Serbian hostility in the first six months of 1914 were reported by the Austro-Hungarian representatives: *Ö.-U. A.*, nos. 9152, 9189 (Monastir); 9333 (Nish); 9841 (Üsküb); 9110, 9746 (military circles); 9631, 9674 (press).

Italy subsequently adhered;* the treaty was several times renewed, lastly in February, 1913. The brutal treatment of
Rumania by Russia at the Congress of Berlin, when, in spite
of a solemn guarantee of the integrity of Rumania given during
the Russo-Turkish war of 1877, the Russian Government insisted on taking a strip of Rumanian territory,† had made
Rumanian sentiment strongly anti-Russian. Moreover, King
Carol was a Hohenzollern, and, in spite of intense loyalty to
his adopted country, German in sympathy and outlook. The
Rumanian policy was that dictated by both interest and sentiment.

The attitude of Bulgaria was less clearly defined. King
Ferdinand had ascended the throne in 1887 in defiance of Russia, and, in spite of a formal reconciliation with the Tsar in
1896, he never cherished any sincere friendship for Russia.
Furthermore, he was a German prince, a former officer of the
Austrian army, and a great Magyar magnate. His sympathies,
like those of King Carol, were probably German, although he
was fond of reminding the French that he was the grandson
of Louis Philippe. But he appears to have realized that the
achievement of Bulgarian national ambitions, that is, the conquest of Macedonia from the Turks, was possible only with the
consent and perhaps the help of Russia. He was also aware
that the mass of his subjects looked upon Russia as their libera-
tor. Consequently, although he was at pains to keep on good
terms with Vienna and at times appointed an Austrophile
ministry, his policy was, on the whole, Russophile. A military
convention with Russia in 1902,‡ the assistance rendered by
Russia in 1908–1909 in securing the recognition of independence by Turkey, the negotiations of 1909–1910 for a new military convention,§ and the formation, under Russian inspiration,

---

* Pribram, I, 29–34, English translation, I, 79–89.
† Southern Bessarabia, which had been taken from Russia by the Treaty of
Paris, in 1856.
‡ P. Laloy, *Les documents secrets publiés par les Bolchéviks* (Paris, 1919), pp. 15–17.
§ The proposed alliance was a rather one-sided affair in favor of Russia, and was
declined by Bulgaria; V. Radoslawow, "Der russisch-bulgarische Vertragsentwurf
von 1909," in *KSF*, IV, 272–273 (May, 1926). The text of the convention is

of the Balkan League in 1912 are sufficient proof of this tendency. It is not surprising that the German Emperor considered Bulgaria as being in the long run bound to the Russian interest and sought to dissuade the Austro-Hungarian Government from relying on King Ferdinand or making Bulgaria the pivot of its Balkan policy.

The Balkan wars of 1912–1913 altered this situation completely. The Rumanian Government and Rumanian public opinion were profoundly upset by the Bulgarian victories over the Turks, which, they feared, would make Bulgaria the dominant state in the Balkans, and an irresistible demand arose for 'compensation,' in order to preserve the Balkan equilibrium, in the form of a strip of Bulgarian territory along the Black Sea coast. As the demand was equivalent to blackmail, it was strenuously though unwisely resisted by Bulgaria. Rumania thereupon let it be known that she expected her allies to exert the pressure on the Bulgarian Government necessary to compel its acceptance of the Rumanian demand. The German Government was ready enough to do so, but Count Berchtold was caught in a dilemma. If he was to play up Bulgaria against Serbia, he could not ask Bulgaria to make sacrifices; at the same time he was unwilling to offend his little ally. What he did was to go through the motions of urging Bulgaria to keep the friendship of Rumania by making some concessions. The Rumanians were soon aware that the pressure of Vienna on Sofia was half-hearted, and let their discontent be known. The Russian diplomatists were quick to seize their opportunity. When Bulgaria, defying the counsels of Russia, attacked Serbia in order to gain Macedonia, the Russian Government, which had hitherto been holding Rumania in check, lifted its veto on Rumanian mobilization and sanctioned the entry of Rumania into the war against Bulgaria. At the end of the war, the

printed in Bogichevich, *Kriegsursachen*, pp. 115–121, and in Laloy, *Les documents secrets*, pp. 52–58. Article V declared that "the realization of the high ideals of the Slavic peoples in the Balkan peninsula, which lie so near to Russia's heart, is possible only after a favorable outcome of Russia's struggle with Germany and Austria-Hungary."

Treaty of Bucharest gave Rumania the coveted territory, and she was duly grateful to Russia.*

A factor of equally great importance was the effect on Rumanian opinion of the Transylvanian question. Transylvania, which comprised the southeastern corner of Hungary, was inhabited by a Rumanian population of more than three millions. This population was kept in a state of economic and social subjection to its Magyar landlords, it was refused adequate representation in the Budapest parliament, it was denied proper educational facilities. No wonder that, like the Croats, Serbs, and other victims of the official Magyarizing policy, the Rumanians of Transylvania grew discontented, restless, receptive to propaganda carried on from Bucharest and Jassy. But the Hungarian politicians refused to read the writing on the wall, would make no concessions; with the result that Rumanian sentiment was completely alienated from the Dual Monarchy.

By the end of 1913 the altered situation was generally recognized. The French Government was assured that Rumania's old friendship with Austria-Hungary was "no longer anything but a shadow; the question of the Rumanians in Transylvania had become the only important one in public opinion, which frankly desires a *rapprochement* with Russia."† King Carol felt obliged to confide to the Austro-Hungarian minister at his court that "as things lay at the moment, Rumania could not, in the event of war, go with the Monarchy."‡ He said substantially the same thing to the German minister, explaining that "it is not enough to have treaties, they must also be popular."§ The Austro-Hungarian minister was forced to describe the situation to his government in the gloomiest language:

---

* Rumania, Ministère des Affaires étrangères, *Les évènements de la péninsule balkanique, 20 septembre 1912–1 août 1913* (Bucharest, 1913); *G. P.*, XXXIV, 575–712, *passim; Affaires balkaniques*, II, *passim; Ö.-U. A.*, V, VI, *passim.*

† Dard to Pichon, 1 November, 1913; *Affaires balkaniques*, III, 74.

‡ Czernin to Berchtold, 8 December, 1913; Conrad, III, 634. The Austro-Hungarian military attaché reported the king as saying that "to his great regret, he was not in a position, in the circumstances prevailing at the moment, to be able to guarantee the fulfilment of the secret treaty existing between the Monarchy and Rumania." Hranilovich to Conrad, 12 December, 1913; *ibid.*, III, 496.

§ Waldthausen to Bethmann-Hollweg, 6 December, 1913; *G. P.*, XXXIX, 467.

We are slipping down an inclined plane here with frightful speed, and there is no time to be lost. . . . Only positive action with a definite policy on the part of Austria, nothing but an iron unbending determination to compel Rumania to show her colors, can avert an incalculable disaster at the twelfth hour.*

The suggestion of Count Czernin fell on fruitful ground, as will be seen presently; but, as a matter of fact, Rumania was already showing her colors. A new Russian minister, who arrived in Bucharest in January, 1914, was warmly welcomed, and the Rumanian crown prince, Ferdinand, his wife, and their son, Prince Carol, accepted an invitation to visit St. Petersburg. It was understood that a marriage would probably be arranged between Prince Carol and one of the Tsar's daughters. When in June the Tsar visited King Carol at Constanza and created him a field-marshal in the Russian army, M. Sazonov's plan "to create conditions for as intimate a *rapprochement* as possible with Rumania,"† had been largely realized. The Rumanian prime minister, M. Bratianu, made it clear that Rumania would act according to her interests—which M. Sazonov interpreted to mean that "in case of war between us and Austria-Hungary, Rumania will take the side which will be the strongest and which will be in a position to promise her greatest gains."‡ And what Russia had to offer came to M.

---

* Czernin to Berchtold, 11 March, 1914; Conrad, III, 789; *Ö.-U. A.*, VII, 957. Czernin himself supported the suggestion of a Rumanian politician, Nicholas Filipescu, that Rumania should join with Transylvania, and that this Greater Rumania should enter into relations with the Habsburg Monarchy similar to those of Bavaria with the German Empire. Both Francis Joseph and Tisza opposed the plan. Czernin, *Im Weltkriege*, pp. 107–108. Czernin persistently urged that Rumania should be compelled to publish the treaty or at least to acknowledge publicly the fact of the alliance, but Berchtold argued that this would make matters worse and that any such action must be initiated by Germany, who was opposed to it. Berchtold to Czernin, 26 March, 1914; *Ö.-U. A.*, VII, 1006–1009.

† Sazonov to Nicholas II, 6 December, 1913; Marchand, II, 371; Stieve, III, 382.

‡ Sazonov to Nicholas II, 24 June, 1914; Marchand, II, 384; Stieve, IV. Sazonov was not so positive in his post-war recollections: "We were still in the dark, however, as to how far we could rely on M. Bratiano, and those political leaders who seemed willing, from patriotic motives, to link their fate with ours"; Sazonov, p. 114. Cf. also C. J. Diamandy, "La grande guerre vue du versant oriental: l'entrevue de Constantza," in *Revue des deux mondes*, 7th series, XLIII, 132–137 (1 January, 1928). Shortly after the meeting Sazonov gave an account of it to the British ambassador in St. Petersburg. "There had, he said, been no question of an alliance or of a convention of any kind, but the results of the visit had been most satis-

Sazonov's mind as he and M. Bratianu, while visiting the king at his country-place at Sinaia, went motoring along the Hungarian frontier to see the Carpathian landscape.

After stopping for a moment, our car rapidly crossed the frontier—to the mute astonishment of the sentry—and carried us for several miles into Hungarian territory. As we entered Transylvania, the same thought probably flashed into both our minds—namely, that this, too, was Rumanian territory, a country whose inhabitants still awaited deliverance from the Magyar yoke, and reunion with their brothers across the frontier. We did not, however, exchange these thoughts. The time for frank conversation had not yet arrived.*

The situation was well described by King Carol when he remarked to the German minister that "Rumania could now get along without Austria, whereas on the contrary Rumania was of great importance to Austria."†

Just as Rumania deserted the ally whose assistance was found

factory. The King, with whom he had had two long conversations, had expressed his satisfaction at the fact that the Russian Government had not raised the question of the Straits during the two Balkan wars and had thanked Sazonov for the support which he had given Rumania with regard to the Treaty of Bucharest. The principle of the inviolability of that Treaty was, His Majesty said, of vital moment to Rumania." Sazonov, however, was highly disingenuous when he assured the king that the aims of the Russian Government were "restricted to securing free passage at all times for their grain-laden vessels," and that it "had no intention" of raising "the larger and political side of the question that had reference to the passage of war vessels." Buchanan to Nicolson, private, 25 June, 1914; B. D., XI, 3–4. Bratianu told Czernin that Sazonov had proposed a joint *démarche* at Constantinople "in order to secure from the Ottoman Government a binding promise that the Straits would in no circumstances be closed to merchant shipping," to which Bratianu agreed. Czernin to Berchtold, 20 June, 1914; *Ö.-U. A.*, VIII, 168. King Carol tried to reassure the Austrian minister: "The visit of the Tsar was only a courtesy," "the [Rumanian] course would remain the old one." But Czernin refused to be comforted. "From the day of Constanza," he wrote, "all Rumania counts on a new policy"; the general opinion was that "in a very short time the Habsburg Monarchy would be put up to European auction." He held the German minister largely to blame, on account of his optimistic reports, and declared that "it is the old story of the Sibylline books." Czernin to Berchtold, 12, 22 June, 1914; *Ö.-U. A.*, VIII, 132, 173–176.

* Sazonov, p. 115. "I could not doubt that he [Bratianu] fully realized that the aged Austrian Emperor and the decrepit Habsburg Monarchy were unreliable allies for young Rumania, impatiently awaiting the moment when she could advance her claim to a part of the Austrian succession; and M. Bratianu understood quite well that his country could only hope to receive this inheritance with the help of Russia"; *ibid.*, p. 114. Tisza and Berchtold were very indignant over this excursion; *Ö.-U. A.*, VIII, 146–147.

† Waldthausen to Bethmann-Hollweg, 19 June, 1914; *G. P.*, XXXIX, 524.

wanting in the hour of need, so Bulgaria repudiated her former protector. The beginning of the estrangement was due to the Russian veto, in November, 1912, on a Bulgarian occupation of Constantinople.* But the principal reason was the supposed unwillingness of Russia to hold Serbia to a strict observance of the Serbo-Bulgarian treaty of 1912, according to which Bulgaria was to receive the larger part of Macedonia. The final straw was the Russian consent to the Rumanian invasion. Even though M. Sazonov endeavored subsequently to prevent the Turks from reoccupying Adrianople and to secure a revision of the Treaty of Bucharest in the matter of Kavalla,† the breach was complete.‡ King Ferdinand called to office M. Radoslavov, who was frankly pro-Austrian, and the new cabinet promptly proposed an alliance with the Monarchy,§ which was agreed to in principle by Count Berchtold.‖ The visit of King Ferdinand to Vienna in the autumn was interpreted as the public announcement of the new policy.¶ If nothing was done, in spite of repeated Bulgarian requests,** it was not so much because Francis Joseph and Francis Ferdinand disliked the Bulgarian monarch†† as because Count Berchtold insisted on a Bulgaro-Rumanian *rapprochement* and wished to make sure that the Austrophile cabinet in Sofia was not overthrown by the machinations of the

* See above, p. 86.   † Sazonov and Berchtold co-operated in this question!
‡ Sazonov bitterly reproached Bulgaria for her conduct in attacking Serbia, which he regarded as treason to the Slav cause. He said to the Bulgarian minister in St. Petersburg, Bobchev: "You are acting on the advice of Austria. Russia and Slavdom are rejected. We have done our duty. . . . Do not expect anything of us, and forget the existence of any of our engagements from 1902 until to-day." Bobchev to Danev, 25 June, 1913; Balcanicus, *The Aspirations of Bulgaria*, pp. 61–62. The Russian premier Kokovtzov told the Serbian minister that "formerly we have counted on Bulgaria, but now no longer." Popovich to foreign office, 9 July, 1913; Bogichevich, *Die auswärtige Politik Serbiens*, I, 354. In the autumn, however, Hartwig, the Russian minister in Belgrade, was quoted by a Bulgarian journalist as saying: "After Turkey, it is the Austrian question which will be raised. Serbia will be our best instrument. You will receive Macedonia on the day when Serbia retakes Bosnia and Herzegovina" (*Echo de Bulgarie*, 3–16 November, 1913). O. Czernin to Berchtold, 21 November, 1913; *Ö.-U. A.*, VII, 583.
§ Tarnowski to Berchtold, 22 July, 1913; *Ö.-U. A.*, VI, 997.
‖ Berchtold to Tarnowski, 23 July, 1913; *Ö.-U. A.*, VI, 1009–1010.
¶ Dard to Pichon, 1 December, 1913; *Affaires balkaniques*, III, 93.
** Tarnowski to Berchtold, 19 September, 29 September, 7 October, 11 December, 16 December, 1913; *Ö.-U. A.*, VII, 324–325, 379–380, 418–419, 643–645, 660–661.
†† Dard,to Pichon, 2 December, 1913; *Affaires balkaniques*, III, 94. Cf. Tarnowski to Berchtold, 11 December, 1913; *Ö.-U. A.*, VII, 646.

Russian minister,* of which he received constant reports.† As proof of its good-will, the Bulgarian Government raised a loan in Berlin and Vienna on less favorable terms than were offered by Parisian bankers,‡ by means of which it hoped to maintain itself in power. Furthermore, during the winter of 1913–1914, it carried on negotiations with Turkey for an alliance,§ with the understanding that the treaty should be so drafted that it would permit both parties to join the Triple Alliance,‖ and the Turks were ready for a bargain, although in characteristic fashion they procrastinated over the signature. If neither the Austro-Bulgarian nor the Turco-Bulgarian alliance had been consummated in July, 1914,¶ the Central Powers were apparently in a strong position with respect to both Turkey and Bulgaria.

THE NEW AUSTRO-HUNGARIAN PROGRAMME

Thus the defection of Rumania was, from the Austro-Hungarian point of view, to some extent compensated for by the friendly attitude of Bulgaria. This situation offered the Monarchy an opportunity to formulate a definite policy in the Balkans, as was urged by Count Czernin. The lead was taken by Count Tisza, the Hungarian premier, who had consistently opposed the warlike tendencies of General Conrad. In March, 1914, he addressed to the Emperor-King Francis Joseph a lengthy memorandum, in which he emphasized the necessity of "a comprehensive, forward-looking *politique de longue main* that

* Berchtold to Tarnowski, 23 July, 23 September, 6 October, 11 December, 1913; *Ö.-U. A.*, VI, 1010, VII, 339–340, 409, 642–643. Cf. also Berchtold's account of his conversation with Ferdinand, 6 November, 1913; *Ö.-U. A.*, VII, 542–545.

† Mittag to Berchtold, 19 November, 1913; O. Czernin to Berchtold, 26 November, 1913; Tarnowski to Berchtold, 28 January, 4 February, 9 February, 15 March, 21 March; *Ö.-U. A.*, VII, 577, 595, 803, 832, 847–849, 971–974, 992–993.

‡ The French loan was made contingent upon a promise that Bulgaria would not follow a policy hostile to the Triple Entente, which the Bulgarian Government declined to give. The French and Russian Governments then tried to prevent the floating of a loan in Berlin. Siebert, pp. 631–638. Berchtold exerted great pressure in Berlin to persuade the German Government to induce German bankers to participate in the loan. Berchtold to Szögyény, 8 June, 1914; *Ö.-U. A.*, VIII, 124–135.

§ *Ö.-U. A.*, VII, VIII, *passim;* Djemal, *Memoirs of a Turkish statesman*, pp. 52–56.

‖ Pallavicini to Berchtold, 29 December, 1913; *Ö.-U. A.*, VII, 683.

¶ The Turco-Bulgarian treaty was signed on 6 August, 1914; V. Radoslawoff, *Bulgarien und die Weltkrise* (Berlin, 1923), p. 117.

smoothes away obstacles, removes hindrances, and causes a grouping, favorable to us, of the powers in southeastern Europe." The essence of his policy was (1) the reconciliation of Bulgaria and Rumania, which might pave the way for a new Balkan league including Turkey and Greece as well; (2) acceptance of this policy by Germany, which "must perceive that the Balkans are of decisive importance, not only for us, but also for the German Empire."* Count Tisza did not believe that Russia was contemplating an immediate war against the Central Powers, largely because she did not feel sure of Bulgaria. But "Bulgaria must throw herself into the arms of Russia if we do not put ourselves in a position to give her secure backing." To accomplish this, Germany and Austria-Hungary, so Tisza argued, must effect "a certain modification of the present condition," by which he seems to have meant persuading Rumania to tolerate a revision of the Treaty of Bucharest, not at her own expense, but at Serbia's; for he went on to say that for Bulgaria expansion into Macedonia was "a vital matter," and that "if she cannot secure this in alliance with us, she will unconditionally throw herself into the arms of Russia and support the policy of conquest directed against us."† Rumania, he was aware, might be difficult to manage:

For that country, the conquest of Transylvania always remains the greatest lure, a Great Rumania extending to the Theiss the most beautiful dream of Rumanian chauvinists. It requires self-control, and strong, sober discernment as well, to renounce this fanciful picture and in an alliance with us to secure present possessions and true independence, and avert the danger of a Russian protectorate.

But he was not without hope that his policy might prevail "if it is carefully prepared by our diplomacy and Germany's, and is put forward with emphasis at the proper moment." Another

---

* The German distrust of Bulgaria was much resented in Austro-Hungarian circles.

† Elsewhere he remarks, "Bulgaria could indemnify herself in Macedonia without being attacked on account of it by Rumania."

condition of success was that Turkey must be restrained from an attack on Bulgaria. Count Tisza summed up his policy thus:

> In the Balkans we must first of all preserve peace and prepare a development agreeable to ourselves. The aims of our Balkan policy we must establish in co-operation with Germany, and labor for a grouping of the Balkan states convenient to us, in which a separation of Rumania and Greece from Serbia would form the first task, and would work toward the reconciliation of these two states with Bulgaria, on the basis of a natural expansion of Bulgaria at Serbia's expense.

Otherwise, Russia would succeed in her efforts to dominate Bulgaria:

> A combination that would reconcile Bulgaria with the rest of the Christian states under Russian patronage, and, as the result of a successful war of conquest directed against our Monarchy, would assure Macedonia to Bulgaria, would complete the forging of the iron ring about us, for which Russia is so tenaciously and so consciously working, and make actual the military preponderance of the Entente on the continent. Thereby the long-desired moment would arrive when Russia and France could foment the world-war with prospect of success, and attack Germany with superior forces.*

Count Tisza's policy appears to have met with the approval of Count Berchtold, for his ideas were developed at length in a memorandum prepared in the Ballplatz during May and June. This memorandum, after passing through several hands, was put before Count Berchtold on 24 June and, after certain modifications by himself, was approved on 28 June.† It makes a document of more than ten pages of ordinary size, and was intended for communication to the German Government.

The memorandum begins by remarking that "the present situation . . . cannot be judged favorably either from the

---

* H. Marczali, "Papers of Count Tisza, 1914–1918," in *American Historical Review*, XXIX, 303–310 (January, 1924); W. Fraknói, *Die ungarische Regierung und die Entstehung des Weltkrieges* (Vienna, 1919), pp. 7–13; *Ö.-U. A.*, VII, 974–979.

† R. Gooss, *Das Wiener Kabinett und die Entstehung des Weltkrieges* (Vienna, 1919), pp. 3–25; *Ö.-U. A.*, VIII, 186–195, 253–261.

point of view of Austria-Hungary or from that of the Triple Alliance." Although Bulgaria has awakened from "the hypnotic spell cast by Russia" and is seeking a closer relationship with the Triple Alliance, Turkey has suffered in prestige, Serbia has been aggrandized, and, above all, the relations of Rumania with the Triple Alliance "have undergone a considerable change." The problem of Rumania's attitude is indeed the central theme of the document.

The Rumanian alliance has, it is declared, become almost a liability. Austria-Hungary had hitherto based her military plans on the assumption that "in case of war with Russia, the Monarchy would have been relieved from the obligation of military action in the direction of Rumania, inasmuch as a respectable portion of Russia's military power would be tied up by the attack of a Rumanian army on the flank." But now that King Carol, though personally loyal to the alliance of Rumania with the Central Powers, has declared that "in the case of an attack by Russia on the Monarchy, participation by Rumania on the side of Austria-Hungary is not to be thought of," the Monarchy is not even sure of Rumanian neutrality and will be compelled to guard the Rumanian frontier. One explanation of this change of front is stated to be the fact that large sections of Rumanian opinion desire "the liberation of their brethren on the other side of the Carpathians," that is, in Transylvania. Even more decisive have been the machinations of Franco-Russian diplomacy, which is endeavoring to "make use of all the Balkan states, or, at least, of a decisive majority of them, for the purpose of upsetting the European balance of power," that is to say, "to break down the military superiority of the two empires with the aid of Balkan armies."

Que faire? For Austria-Hungary to act energetically at Bucharest, with a view to recalling Rumania to her obligations, might lead to an open break; likewise the result of "serious and emphatic representations" by the German Government "seems doubtful." The only course, therefore, is to "accept the offer made a year ago by Bulgaria and repeated several times since, and to enter upon relations with that country which would practically amount to an alliance." This, it might be hoped, "would serve as a solemn warning to the ruling authorities at Bucharest" and demonstrate that "we are able to find other pillars of support for Austria-Hungary's Balkan policy."

But there is no time to lose. For Russia is scheming to secure from Serbia the cession of at least part of Macedonia to Bulgaria in return for the acquisition of Bosnia and "its contiguous territories," and "no Bulgarian government would dare to refuse to agree to this combination, notwithstanding all previous disappointments." Before taking any steps, however, Austria-Hungary, so the memorandum states, wishes "to come to a complete understanding with Germany," in order that "the united action of the Triple Alliance, particularly of Austria-Hungary and the German Empire," may be opposed to "the united action of France and Russia." And Germany is reminded that Russia's "extraordinary armaments and military preparations, the extension of the Russian strategic railways westward, etc., are surely aimed at Germany more than at Austria-Hungary"; for Russia understands that "the realization of her designs in both Europe and Asia—designs born of the necessities of her internal situation—will, above all, conflict with some of Germany's most important interests, and will therefore meet with Germany's unavoidable opposition." All the more, accordingly, is it "a matter of common interest" for both Powers "to take timely and energetic steps at the present stage of the Balkan crisis against further developments . . . which it may later be impossible to prevent."* Such, then, was the policy which the Austro-Hungarian Government proposed, at the end of June, 1914, to submit for the consideration and approval of its German ally.

Now it is highly significant that in the original draft of the

* Austria, Ministerium des Äusserns, *Diplomatische Aktenstücke zur Vorgeschichte des Krieges 1914* (3 volumes, Vienna, 1919), I, no. 1; *Die deutschen Dokumente zum Kriegsausbruch*, edited by K. Kautsky, M. Montgelas and W. Schücking (4 volumes, Berlin, 1919), no. 14.

memorandum written by Baron von Flotow, who had once been councillor of legation at Belgrade, the following passage occurred:

On account of the friendly relations between Rumania and Serbia, it can be left to King Carol or his government to exert themselves for a *rapprochement* between Serbia and the Monarchy, in return for which the Monarchy. . . would exhibit toward Serbia the most loyal spirit of accommodation [*das loyalste Entgegenkommen*].*

A second official made this more precise:

If Rumania attaches importance to the continuance of its present friendly relationship with Serbia, Austria-Hungary might give assurances in Bucharest that it is ready to support, by a conciliatory attitude on its part toward Serbia in political and economic matters, an action undertaken by Rumania in Belgrade which would aim at changing the attitude of Serbia toward the Monarchy.†

But this was eliminated by Count Berchtold.‡ The change indicates clearly that a policy of trying to promote friendly relations with Serbia was definitely abandoned. One would like to know whether the minister, ever uncertain in his ideas, yielded to the pressure of General Conrad, or perhaps of Count Forgách, the under-secretary at the Ballplatz.§ In this connection certain statements ascribed to the Marquis Pallavicini, the Austro-Hungarian ambassador in Constantinople, acquire a peculiar interest. In July the German ambassador in London reported to his government a conversation with M. Take Jonescu, a well-known Rumanian statesman:

The Rumanian statesman claims to have gathered from the statements of the ambassador Marquis Pallavicini, who was

---

* Gooss, p. 5.　　　　　　　　　　　　　　† *Ibid.*, p. 14.
‡ *Ibid.*, pp. 18–21.
§ Forgách had been transferred from Belgrade to Dresden after the exposure of his connection with the forged documents involved in the Friedjung trial. But in September, 1913, he was recalled to Vienna, at the request of Tisza, and supplanted Count Szápáry, who advocated a policy of *rapprochement* with Russia and Serbia, as under-secretary in the foreign office. His hatred of the Serbs was notorious. J. von Szilassy, *Der Untergang der Donau-Monarchie* (Berlin, 1921), p. 255.

recently in Bucharest—in fact, just before the assassination at Sarajevo—that Austria desired war even before the murder, and had been awaiting a convenient opportunity to restore her status in the Balkans, which had been sacrificed through the policy of Count Berchtold.*

This statement would not, by itself, perhaps count for much, for both Prince Lichnowsky and M. Jonescu were highly critical of Austro-Hungarian policy. But, as it happens, there is confirmation of it in a report of the Austro-Hungarian military attaché in Constantinople:

The Marquis Pallavicini said to me, in conclusion, that even his Imperial and Royal Apostolic Majesty [Francis Joseph], in the course of an audience granted him in June, expressed the opinion that he himself regarded war as the only method of getting out of the present situation.†

Finally, as we shall see shortly, the Archduke Francis Ferdinand early in June inquired of William II whether Austria-Hungary could count upon Germany in all circumstances. One can hardly avoid wondering whether the Cabinet of Vienna had not made up its mind at last to have war with Serbia and whether the memorandum destined for the German Government was not less a declaration of policy than an attempt to discover how responsive Berlin was to suggestion.‡

* Lichnowsky to foreign office, telegram, 23 July, 1914; *Die deutschen Dokumente zum Kriegsausbruch*, no. 129. Cf. Jonescu, *Some Personal Impressions*, pp. 38–39.

† Pomiankowski to Conrad, 20 July, 1914; Conrad, IV, 107. Czernin gives an account of a conversation with Pallavicini in Constantinople shortly before the outbreak of the war. Pallavicini diagnosed the situation thus: "If a rapid change in the march of events did not intervene, we were headed straight for war. He explained to me that he considered the only possibility of avoiding war with Russia lay in our definitely renouncing all claims to influence in the Balkans and leaving the field to Russia. Pallavicini was quite clear in his own mind that such a course would mean our abdicating as a Great Power; but apparently to him even so bitter a step as that was preferable to the war which he saw impending." This sounds as if Pallavicini was aware that his superiors in Vienna were meditating a warlike policy. Czernin also records a remark of Francis Joseph when receiving him, in September, 1913, prior to his departure for Bucharest as minister: "The Peace of Bucharest is untenable, and we are faced by a new war. God grant that it may be confined to the Balkans," a cryptic saying open to several interpretations. Czernin, *Im Weltkriege*, p. 11.

‡ It will be seen later (p. 347) that on 7 July Berchtold urged utilizing the murder at Sarajevo as an "opportunity" for making war against Serbia.

It will have been observed that neither in Count Tisza's memorandum nor in the document prepared at the Ballplatz was anything said about mollifying Rumania by concessions to the Rumanian population of Transylvania. That question was raised, however, at the visit of the German Emperor to the Archduke Francis Ferdinand at Konopischt, the latter's Bohemian country-house, on 12–13 June. According to the statement of William II to the representative of the German foreign office in attendance, Francis Ferdinand expressed his dislike of Hungary "in uncommonly clear terms."

He pictured Hungarian conditions as wholly anachronistic and medieval. Hungary was the wrestling-ground for the struggle of a few families, and the oligarchic form of government meant the oppression of all non-Hungarian elements, who amounted to far more than 50 per cent of the total population. . . . It made little difference who the man was at the head; every Hungarian strove more or less openly to secure advantages for Hungary at the cost of Austria and to the disadvantage of the Monarchy as a whole. He, the Archduke, was well aware that he [William II] had gained a very good impression of Tisza; but this was perhaps not well founded, for Tisza's deeds did not correspond with Tisza's words.* . . . The Archduke frankly and very cleverly emphasized his point of view—that it was precisely Tisza's fault if the interests of the Triple Alliance were badly safeguarded, since it was Tisza who, notwithstanding his promises at Schönbrunn, was maltreating the Hungarian Rumanians. The Archduke finally asked His Majesty whether he would not have Tschirschky instructed to remind Tisza at every opportunity that he should not lose sight of the necessity of winning over the Rumanians by moderating the treatment of their kinsmen living in Hungary. His Majesty promised that he would instruct Tschirschky to keep repeating to Tisza, "Sir, remember the Rumanians!" The Archduke greatly approved of this.†

* The reference is to a conversation between the Emperor and Tisza in the preceding March, when William, who had been told that Tisza had been negotiating with the Rumanians, expressed his satisfaction. Tschirschky to Bethmann-Hollweg, 23 March, 1914; G. P., XXXIX, 335. Afterward, the negotiations had broken down, because Tisza would actually concede little.

† Memorandum of Treutler, 15 June, 1914; G. P., XXXIX, 367–368. This is confirmed by the Archduke's account as given to Berchtold and by him communi-

According to the German report, the only other questions discussed were the strained relations between Greece and Turkey, Italy's conduct in Albania, and the replacement of the Austro-Hungarian ambassador in Berlin, Count Szögyény, a Hungarian, by an Austrian nobleman. But there is evidence that the document does not give "a full account"* of the conversations, one of which took place between William II and Francis Ferdinand alone. For the Emperor Francis Joseph told General Conrad that he had "instructed Francis Ferdinand to request from the German Emperor at Konopischt information as to whether in the future also we could reckon unconditionally upon Germany," but that the latter "had evaded the question and given no answer."† Nor is it certain that the German Emperor evaded the question. At any rate the Archduke appears to have given a different version to a member of the Austro-Hungarian general staff; for Colonel Metzger, Conrad's right-hand man, told the general, when the latter reported the Emperor's statement, that on the night before the murder at Sarajevo, the Archduke had told him [Metzger] that

The Emperor William had said to him at Konopischt, with reference to [a war forced upon us], "If we do not strike [los-gingen], the situation will get worse."‡

Whichever version may be correct,§ it is evident that the question was raised; that neither the German Emperor nor the Archduke confided the fact to their respective diplomatists *donne à penser.*‖

cated to Tschirschky. Tschirschky to Bethmann-Hollweg, 17 June, 1914; *ibid.,* XXXIX, 369–370. *Ö.-U. A.* contains no documents on Konopischt.
    * As stated in S. B. Fay, *The Origins of the World War* (New York, 1928), II, 38.
    † Conrad, IV, 36. It will be remembered (see above, p. 167) that Pallavicini stated that in June Francis Joseph "regarded war as the only method of getting out of the present situation."
    ‡ *Ibid.,* IV, 39.
    § Wilson, *The War Guilt,* p. 169, offers the interesting suggestion that because of the bad relations between Francis Joseph and Francis Ferdinand, the Archduke did not tell his uncle what William II had said.
    ‖ A brief reference may not be out of place to the story of "The Pact of Konopischt," which was first bruited by H. W. Steed, in *The Nineteenth Century,* LXXIX, 253–273 (February, 1916), and repeated in *Through Thirty Years,* I, 396–403, in abbreviated form. The story, which came from a Polish gentleman in touch

The lack of precise information on this point is the more intriguing because there is ample evidence that the German Emperor had been considering the question of Austro-Serbian relations from a new point of view. During the Balkan wars, he had consistently urged Austria-Hungary to effect a reconciliation with Serbia, and he seems never to have abandoned the hope that the Cabinet of Vienna might adopt this policy.* But since his advice was not heeded, he began to play with the idea of using force. General Conrad records two conversations which he had with William II in the autumn of 1913. On the first occasion, in September, the Emperor, replying to a reproach of the Austrian chief of staff that his plan for attacking Serbia in 1909 had not been adopted, said: "I did not hold your

with the Vatican, was to the effect that at Konopischt William II and Francis Ferdinand plotted to bring about a war with Russia and France, the purpose of which was to effect a territorial reorganization of eastern Europe. Poland, with Posen, Lithuania and the Ukraine, was to be reconstituted as a kingdom for Francis Ferdinand, with reversion to his eldest son. Another kingdom, consisting of Bohemia, Hungary, the Yugoslav territories and Salonica, was to be established for the Archduke's younger son. The German-speaking provinces of Austria were, according to this plan, to be incorporated in the German Empire as a federal state under the Archduke Charles (then the heir presumptive to the Habsburg throne). Between these new states and the enlarged German Empire there was to be a perpetual military and economic alliance which would become the arbiter of Europe and the Near East. Although Mr. Steed adduced no little circumstantial evidence, particularly the tense relations existing between Francis Ferdinand and the other members of the Habsburg family, which gave a certain credibility to the tale, no evidence has ever been produced to support it, and it is now generally discredited; Mr. Steed himself was careful to describe it as "an interesting hypothesis." But the fact that it is not mentioned in the official reports of the Konopischt conversations certainly proves nothing, as is often asserted to the contrary, for if the two august persons did discuss any such wild scheme as that alleged, they would in all probability keep the secret to themselves. The Archduke's papers at Konopischt were seized immediately after his death; they are said to be now in Vienna, the Czechoslovak Government disputing the right of the Austrian Government to keep them, on the ground that Konopischt is now in Czechoslovak territory.

It has also been stated that shortly after Konopischt the Serbian general staff received a communication from the Russian general staff, according to which "the Russian Government had received certain information that at Konopischt the Emperor William had promised support for a plan of the Archduke to fall upon and overpower Serbia." S. Stanojević, *Die Ermordung des Erzherzogs Franz Ferdinand* (Frankfort, 1923), pp. 54–55. As the source of this "certain information" has not been revealed, the story has to be treated with the greatest reserve. The writer has heard, without being able to verify the statement, that the story came from a Czech spy in the employ of the Archduke.

* He protested in vigorous terms in the spring of 1914 against the disposition of Vienna to prevent the union of Serbia and Montenegro. "This union is absolutely not to be prevented," he observed. "In the long run Serbia and Montenegro will come together somehow." "There must be found a *modus vivendi* with the Dual Monarchy which will be acceptable to Serbia." *G. P.*, XXXVIII, pp. 335, 352, 338.

soldiers back; I declared that Germany would stand fully at your side."* At Leipzig, on 18 October, when the two met again at the celebration of the centenary of the great battle of 1813, William definitely approved the energetic action which Count Berchtold had proposed to compel the Serbs to evacuate Albanian territory.

I'll go with you [he said]. The other Powers are not ready and will do nothing about it. You must be in Belgrade in a couple of days. I have always been a supporter of peace, but that has its limits. I have read much about war and know what it means, but finally there comes a situation in which a Great Power cannot look on any longer and *must* draw the sword.†

Ten days later the Emperor aired his views about the Austro-Serbian question to Count Berchtold at great length.

With Serbia there can be for Austria-Hungary no other relation than that of the dependence of the lesser upon the greater, according to the planet system, as indeed generally the Emperor could imagine no other orientation in the Balkans save the hegemony of the Monarchy toward all states there [so runs Count Berchtold's note of the conversation].

He advised the minister to solve the problem by offering Serbia money, commercial advantages, and a military convention. If Serbia should refuse such a convention, then force must be applied. He continued:

If H. M. the Emperor Francis Joseph demands something, then the Serbian Government *must* yield: if it does not, then Belgrade will be bombarded, and occupied until H. M.'s will is carried out. And of this you can be sure, that I stand behind you, and am ready to draw the sabre if ever your action makes it necessary.

He accompanied his last words with a motion of his hand toward his sabre. On leaving he assured Count Berchtold that "whatever came from the Vienna foreign office was for him

* Conrad, III, 431. † *Ibid.*, III, 470.

a command."* In the middle of December, when speaking with the Austro-Hungarian chargé at Munich, he once more urged the desirability and possibility of an Austro-Serbian agreement, but his language was not altogether pacific.

For one thing is certain to me: the Serbs *must* be harnessed before the car of the Monarchy—in one way or another: they must also remain conscious that they are held in respect by a firm will, which indeed offers them a powerful friendship, but is also ready to give its troops marching orders at the first hostile provocation. The final decision in the South-East of Europe may involve sooner or later a serious armed conflict, and we Germans then stand with you and behind you; but we can in no case be indifferent whether the twenty divisions of your army are tied up for operations against the Southern Slavs.†

Although these utterances of William II date from many months before the meeting at Konopischt, they show that he had been pondering for three months the idea of a war launched by Austria-Hungary against Serbia, in case an understanding between those two states could not be reached. It may be presumed that these utterances were known to the Emperor Francis Joseph and the Archduke Francis Ferdinand. Moreover, in May, 1914, William declared to the Austro-Hungarian ambassador in Berlin that

with respect to Serbia, he fully admitted that the establishment of the utmost friendly relations possible with the kingdom on the Save—in spite of the fact that he regarded it as altogether desirable—would, in consequence of the attitude of the Serbian

---

* Memorandum of Berchtold, 28 October, 1913, secret; *Slavonic Review*, VII, 24–27 (June, 1928); *Ö.-U. A.*, VII, 512–515. When speaking with the Austro-Hungarian ambassador in Berlin about his conversation with Berchtold, William said: "Serbia must adhere to us *nolens volens*, in which case the saying would apply, 'Und bist du nicht willig, so brauch' ich Gewalt!'" Szögyény to Berchtold, 4 November, 1913; *Ö.-U. A.*, VII, 529.

† Velics to Berchtold, 16 December, 1913; *Slavonic Review*, VII, 28–29; *Ö.-U. A.*, VII, 657–659. In this connection it is worth recalling that in November of the same year the German Emperor had a conversation with the King of the Belgians which convinced that monarch that "the Emperor has ceased to be the friend of peace." J. Cambon to Pichon, 22 November, 1913; F no. 6.

Government and of public opinion in Serbia, create almost insuperable obstacles for us.*

If, therefore, the disposition was current in Vienna to have a reckoning with Serbia, of which there is some, though not conclusive, evidence, it is easy to understand why Francis Joseph instructed Francis Ferdinand to sound William II on the question whether Germany would support her ally unconditionally; while the failure of the Emperor to mention the matter to the representative of the foreign office is perhaps explained by the fact that the Wilhelmstrasse, apart from sanctioning the Austro-Hungarian ultimatum of October, 1913,† had advocated a conciliatory policy toward Serbia, and might be alarmed by the overture from Vienna. Probably the full truth about Konopischt will never be known, and one is reminded of Bismarck's saying that diplomatic history could not be written from archives.

Although the tangled threads of the Balkan web were usually spun by diplomatists into a complicated pattern, the design offered in the early summer of 1914 was surprisingly simple. Russia and Germany were rivals for ascendancy at Constantinople; Russia and Austria-Hungary contested the Balkan peninsula. Russia, with one eye on the Straits and the other on a long-dreaded Austrian advance against Serbia, was promoting the closest relations between Rumania, Serbia, and Greece, for the existence of such a league would at once lighten her task when the question of the Straits should be raised and create an obstacle to the ambitions of Austria-Hungary. The Habsburg Monarchy, alarmed by these Russian activities, was anxious to create a counter-league, also including Rumania and Greece but with Bulgaria as its pivot, which would result in the isolation of Serbia and paralyze its irredentist agitation; and Germany was to be asked to support this policy because of her own interests in the Near East. The situation becomes clearer if it is examined on a map. Turkey and Bulgaria were

* Szögyény to Berchtold, 25 May, 1914; *Ö.-U. A.*, VIII, 80.
† See above, p. 138.

agreed in principle on an alliance; Turkey, destined to pass more and more under German economic influence and military direction, made no secret of her friendliness to Germany and the Triple Alliance; Bulgaria was seeking admission into the Triple Alliance. Germany, Austria-Hungary, Bulgaria, and Turkey in alliance: if Serbia could be brought under control, the influence of the Central Powers would extend in an unbroken chain from Berlin to Bagdad and Basra, and the overmighty Russian Empire would be contained behind the barrier of the Straits. On the other hand, the union of Serbia and Montenegro and the preservation of the close friendship of Serbia and Rumania would secure for Russian influence a string of satellites stretching from the Black Sea to the Adriatic which would drive a wedge between the Central Powers and their protégés and simplify the solution of the question of the Straits. For Germany and Austria-Hungary the subjection of Serbia was as desirable as for Russia it was intolerable. And victory by either side would mean the turning of the European balance of power in its favor—a consideration understood not only in the capitals of the three great military empires but in Rome, Paris, and London as well. In July, 1914, Serbia occupied the key position in European politics.

CHAPTER III

SARAJEVO

In the early summer of 1914 there were no disputes pending between the Great Powers. If the liquidation of the Balkan wars was not completed,—in Albania the Prince of Wied was about to abandon his tottering throne, while Turkey and Greece were still discussing the disposition of certain islands in the Ægean Sea,—the solution of these minor questions was not likely to cause serious differences between the Powers. Then, on 28 June, occurred the assassination of the Archduke Francis Ferdinand at Sarajevo.

On account of this crime the Austro-Hungarian Government on 23 July presented to the Serbian Government an ultimatum which in less than two weeks precipitated a general European war. As justification for the ultimatum the Austro-Hungarian Government alleged that individual Serbian officials had participated in the preparation of the murder and that the crime itself, although committed on Austro-Hungarian territory by a subject of the Monarchy, was the consequence of propaganda conducted by Serbian patriotic societies both in Serbia and in the provinces of Bosnia and the Herzegovina; in particular, responsibility was laid at the door of an organization called the *Narodna Odbrana* ('National Defense'). The Serbian Government was not charged with complicity in the crime, but it was accused of "culpable tolerance" of the "unwholesome propaganda," and it was therefore required to accept and carry out certain demands which were calculated to put an end to the propaganda.* In proof of these conten-

---

* The ultimatum is printed in numerous places, officially in Austria-Hungary, Ministerium des Äusserns, *Diplomatische Aktenstücke zur Vorgeschichte des Krieges 1914* (Vienna, 1915), no. 7; *ibid.*, revised edition (3 volumes, Vienna, 1919), I, no. 27, and *Ö.-U. A.*, VIII, 515-518. Perhaps the most generally accessible source is *Collected Diplomatic Documents relating to the Outbreak of the European War*, pp. 3-9.

tions a *dossier* was prepared and circulated to the Great Powers, and afterward published, which contained such information about the circumstances of the murder as the Austro-Hungarian authorities had been able to collect up to the time that the ultimatum was presented.* As a matter of fact the Powers were not given time to examine this bulky compilation before the despatch of the Austro-Hungarian declaration of war against Serbia;† on the other hand, it is not likely that the Powers would have paid much attention to it, because, as we shall see, the Austro-Hungarian action was looked upon not in the light of a punitive expedition, but as a step affecting the independence of Serbia and involving the European balance of power.‡ Nevertheless, the *dossier* is important, not only for the facts contained in it, but because it was almost the only source available, during the war, of information on the basis of which the Austro-Hungarian allegations could be appraised.

The *dossier* begins with a long statement of the Austro-Hungarian case against Serbia, both for the years 1909–1914 and as regards the murder at Sarajevo. There are eleven appendices in support of the assertions made in the introduction. Most of them are devoted to an analysis of the history and conduct of the *Narodna Odbrana*. In two, the facts ascertained about the murder plot and its execution are put together. Some information is given about the assassinations attempted between 1910 and 1914. Finally, extracts are given from the Serbian press from the annexation crisis of 1908 to July, 1914. In spite of much incriminating evidence of the activities of the *Narodna Odbrana* in Bosnia, it is not asserted in the *dossier* that the criminals were in touch with that society, although it is twice implied somewhat vaguely that the society was involved in the crime. The Serbian Government is hardly men-

---

* *Diplomatische Aktenstücke* (1914), no. 19; *ibid.* (1919), II, no. 48; *Ö.-U. A.*, VIII, 666–704; *Collected Diplomatic Documents*, pp. 461–499.

† It was actually not presented to the British Government until 29 July, the day after war had been declared. Grey to Bunsen, 29 July, 1914; *B. D.*, XI, no. 282.

‡ Sazonov told the Austro-Hungarian ambassador in St. Petersburg, when the latter promised to communicate the *dossier*, that "we need not have given ourselves the trouble, since we had sent an ultimatum." Szápáry to Berchtold, 24 July, 1914; *Diplomatische Aktenstücke* (1919), no. 18.

tioned. What the *dossier* did prove was that an agitation was tolerated in Serbia which was directed against the integrity of the Dual Monarchy. But, owing partly to war-time prejudices, partly to the sinister reputation earned by the Austro-Hungarian Government for forging incriminating documents, the *dossier* never inspired much confidence in Entente or neutral countries.* The general opinion was that Austria-Hungary had not proved the necessity of going to war against Serbia.

Since 1914 a large amount of new evidence has come to light which has made necessary a re-examination of the whole question. In 1917 a summary of the trial of the conspirators, held in October, 1914, was published,† and a year later a portion of the minutes of the trial.‡ Since then a former Austro-Hungarian official who was concerned with the investigation of the murder in 1914 has drawn occasionally on unpublished documents to elucidate certain points.§ But far more important have been the revelations from the Serbian side. As early as 1919, that is, as soon as the Yugoslav movement for unity had triumphed in the creation of the Kingdom of the Serbs, Croats, and Slovenes, individuals who had played a part in the revolutionary agitation of pre-war days and who were anxious to claim a share of the credit for the triumph of the national idea began to unseal their lips, and the flood of revela-

---

* Cf. C. Oman, *The Outbreak of the War of 1914-1918* (London, 1919), pp. 7-8, and Seton-Watson, *Sarajevo*, pp. 118-124.

† *Sérajévo : la conspiration serbe contre la monarchie austro-hongroise* (Berne, 1917), pp. 62-150.

‡ Professor Pharos [said to be Father Puntigam, the Superior of the Jesuits in Sarajevo], *Der Prozess gegen die Attentäter von Sarajewo : nach dem amtlichen Stenogram der Gerichtsverhandlung aktenmässig dargestellt* (Berlin, 1918). This version is not complete, for after the war a carbon copy of the original stenographic report was found in Sarajevo and given to the Yugoslav Government. Several extracts from the unpublished parts were published in the *Novosti* (Zagreb) in May and June, 1925; that given in *Slavonic Review*, V, 645-656 (March, 1926), which is translated from *Nova Evropa*, June, 1925, corresponds almost word for word with the text in Pharos. Other extracts are given by A. Mousset, "L'attentat de Sarajevo," in *Revue d'histoire moderne*, III, 329-358 (September-October, 1928). A French translation of the complete minutes has recently been published: A. Mousset, *L'attentat de Sarajevo. Texte intégral des sténogrammes du procès* (Paris, 1930), but was received while this book was in the press, too late to be used.

§ Dr. Friedrich Ritter von Wiesner, whose articles appear from time to time in *KSF*. These articles will be referred to frequently in subsequent pages.

tions continued for some years.* The first of these pamphlets or books which attracted wide attention in Western Europe and the United States, was written in 1923 by a professor in the University of Belgrade, who claimed to have derived his information from surviving conspirators.† In the same year one of the lesser conspirators told what he knew, or what he thought it expedient to reveal.‡ Then, in 1924, in an 'almanac' commemorating the tenth anniversary of the outbreak of the war, a Serbian statesman who was a member of the cabinet in 1914 made some astonishing revelations.§ About the same time attention began to be called to the report of the trial of certain Serbian officers at Salonica in 1917 who were involved in the Sarajevo plot.‖ Many other disclosures will be noted in subsequent pages. In spite, however, of much pressure from friends and foes alike, the government at Belgrade has not made any statement or issued any documents.

* Many of them are published in *Nova Evropa*. KSF makes some of these disclosures available in German translation. The Yugoslav dictatorship established in 1929 has suppressed discussion of the matter.

†S. Stanoyevich, *Убиство Аустриског престолонаследника Фердинанда* (Belgrade, 1923), German translation S. Stanojević, *Die Ermordung des Erzherzogs Franz Ferdinand* (Frankfurt, 1923). Unfortunately Professor Stanoyevich never gives any specific authority for his statements. Much the same version of events is given in H. Wendel, *Die Habsburger und die südslawische Frage* (Leipzig, 1923), who states that he wrote his pamphlet before seeing that of Stanoyevich.

‡ B. Yevtich, *Сарајевски Атентат* [The Assassination at Sarajevo] (Sarajevo, 1923). The first seven chapters, dealing with events up to 28 June, 1914, are translated, under the title "Weitere Ausschnitte zum Attentat von Sarajevo," in *KSF*, III, 656–687 (October, 1925). Some of Yevtich's conclusions are summarized by A. Mousset, "L'attentat de Sarajevo," in *Revue d'histoire diplomatique*, XXXIX, 44–68 (no. 1, 1925). A summary of the pamphlet is given in the *New York Times*, 22 June, 1924, section E, p. 5.

§ L. Yovanovich, "После Видова Дана 1914 Године" [After Vidovdan, 1914] in A. Ksyunyin, *1914–1924, Крв Словенства* [1914–1924, Blood of Slavdom] (Belgrade, 1924). This article has been translated as L. Jovanovitch, *The Murder of Sarajevo*, in a pamphlet published by the British [now Royal] Institute of International Affairs (London, 1925), to which subsequent references are made, and under the title "More Light on Sarajevo," in *The Living Age*, CCCXXV, 305–311 (9 May, 1925).

‖ *Тајна Превратна Организација: извештај са претреса у војном суду за официре у Солуну по белешкама војсним на самом претресу* [The Secret Revolutionary Organization: Report of the Trial at the Court Martial of Officers at Salonica, from Notes Taken at the Trial Itself] (Salonica, 1918). The report is supposed to be very scarce; according to one account, the edition was destroyed by fire in Salonica, according to another it was suppressed by the Yugoslav Government. Nevertheless the writer had no difficulty in buying a copy at a reasonable price in Zagreb in 1928. Unfortunately, the book has not been translated into any Western language.

All this evidence is of extraordinary interest, but it is evidence that requires the greatest possible care in its use. Much of it consists of *dicta* by individuals whose opportunities for knowing the facts, accuracy in stating them, and motives for revealing them cannot be checked. There are many contradictions, discrepancies, and anachronisms. To determine what actually happened is difficult enough; when in addition the effort is made, as it must be made, to discover the motives for or the explanations of these happenings, speculation and guess have frequently to do duty for those proofs which the historian likes to adduce for his statements. On many points the answer can only be, at least in the present state of knowledge, that "probably" it is thus and so. "The world will presumably never be told all that was behind the murder of the Archduke Francis Ferdinand."* In the following pages the evidence will be set forth in much detail, in order that the reader may judge the soundness of such conclusions as may be reached.

The *Narodna Odbrana*

The annexation of Bosnia-Herzegovina was proclaimed on 6 October, 1908. On the evening of the same day the Serbian foreign minister, Dr. Milovan Milovanovich, invited a number of notables, including such politicians as Nikola Pashich and Ljuba Yovanovich and the mayor of Belgrade, to consider with him what should be done to allay the great public excitement. It was decided that the mayor should summon a conference of citizens to organize a meeting of protest against the Austrian "provocation." Accordingly some twenty persons gathered the next day at the town hall. In the course of the discussion the dramatist Branislav Nushich proposed the formation of a society to be called '*Narodna Odbrana*' ('National Defense'), "which should protect and promote our interests in the annexed provinces."† This was agreed to, and the

---

* Grey, I, 308, American edition, I, 298.
† Stanoyevich, *Die Ermordung des Erzherzogs Franz Ferdinands*, p. 47

society was organized forthwith. Its membership embraced two elements who had hitherto not been able to co-operate: prominent members of the Radical party, and representatives of the army, including Dragutin Dimitriyevich and Voya Tankosich, who, it will be remembered, had taken part in the assassination of King Alexander and Queen Draga. Another member was Major Milan Pribichevich, whose brother Svetozar was the leader of the Serbo-Croat coalition in the Croatian diet. The new society busied itself with enlisting *komitadjis* for a guerilla war with the Dual Monarchy, including refugees from Bosnia,* and with exciting public opinion. A Serbian writer has described its activity in these words:

The *Narodna Odbrana,* both by the time of its formation and by the aim which it had at that time, namely, that of preparing the nation for the struggle against Austria, becomes a first-class revolutionary organization. It collects within itself all elements of revolt against Austria and the annexation: all fiery fighters, all volunteers and *komitadjis* who are ready to give their lives in the struggle against the much-hated Austria. The volunteers are sent to Chupriya for training under the experienced *komitadji* leader Tankosich, while the old tried fighters from the Macedonian struggle are sent to the Bosnian frontier to strengthen the frontier, which was guarded by the weak customs forces. The appearance of these *komitadjis* on the Drina had a twofold effect. It gave great hopes to our people in Bosnia and created the conviction that an armed conflict with Austria was inevitable, and that these *komitadjis* would be the leaders of the Serbian army. The belief grew up that the *Narodna Odbrana* was the representative of revolutionary action emanating from Serbia, and all the revolutionarily inclined elements in Bosnia and the Herzegovina became its enthusiastic adherents.†

* According to the deposition of Trifko Krstanovich (Austrian *dossier*, appendix 5), he went from Bosnia to Belgrade in 1908 and was trained in bomb-throwing by Tankosich. He is not, however, a very reliable witness. It is said that when he returned to Bosnia in 1910, he offered 'revelations' to papers of various parties, and that even the Bosnian authorities declined his services. Wendel, p. 46. Potiorek said that he was "not an honest person" [*keine integre Persönlichkeit*]; Conrad, IV, 83.

† C. A. Popovich, "Organizacija 'Ujedinjenje ili Smrt' ('Crna Ruka') [The 'Union or Death' Organization (the 'Black Hand')], in *Nova Evropa*, XV, 401 (11 June, 1927).

The conception thus formed by the Bosnian population of the *Narodna Odbrana* was, as will be seen, to be an important factor in later years.

After the annexation crisis had passed, the Serbian Government withdrew its official support, but the society continued to exist, thanks to a nation-wide organization that was undertaken. Under a central committee at Belgrade, which was presided over by General Bozho Yankovich,* district committees were established in each of the provinces; these in turn set up local committees in towns and villages or appointed 'confidential men' in places where committees were not necessary. The committees divided into sections for cultural development, which worked through local libraries, and gymnastic, shooting, and other sporting societies.† It is said that more than 400 committees were organized.‡

The activity of the *Narodna Odbrana* consisted in "the collection of material about the conditions and circumstances of Austria-Hungary and the enlightenment of the masses in Serbia by means of public lectures about the ideals, tasks, and duties of Serbia and its people."§ More precisely, it sought "to combat illiteracy and encourage education, temperance, and hygiene, to establish clubs and lectures, and above all to spread information regarding national questions in all sections of the Slav race."‖ Believing a life-and-death struggle with the Habsburg Monarchy to be imperative and inevitable, it aimed to prepare the nation mentally, morally, and physically for it, and a German writer has likened its work to the contributions of the turner, singing and shooting societies to the movement for German unity.¶

* Yankovich was originally a supporter of King Alexander and passed for an Austrophile; after the tragedy of 1903, he was pensioned. But his daughter was said to have been educated at the expense of King Peter, and according to the Austrian information, Yankovich placed himself at the head of the *Narodna Odbrana* in order to facilitate his return to active service, which took place during the Balkan wars. Gellinek to Conrad, 3 May, 1913; *Ö.-U. A.*, VI, 337-338.

† Austrian *dossier*, appendix 2.

‡ A member of the society has told the writer that this elaborate organization existed only on paper; there was much talk (a national characteristic!), but little effective work.

§ Stanoyevich, p. 48.   ‖ Seton-Watson, *Sarajevo*, p. 138.   ¶ Wendel, p. 59.

The Austro-Hungarian Government asserted, however, that the *Narodna Odbrana,* even if it was not a secret society, was not so harmless an organization as it was commonly represented. According to a pamphlet published by its central committee,* its propaganda was inspired by the dictum that Austria-Hungary was "our first and greatest enemy," whose conduct "makes a war of extermination obligatory." The Austrians, it asserted, were the "new Turks," "stronger in civilization and more advanced economically," who "want to take our freedom and our language from us and to crush us." As an alternative the *Narodna Odbrana* proclaimed the necessity of Yugoslav unity:

For the sake of bread and room, for the sake of the fundamental essentials of culture and trade, the freeing of the conquered Serbian territories and their union with Serbia is necessary to gentlemen, tradesmen, and peasants alike.

And this unity could be achieved only by "armed action." Until the time for this action was ripe, the national ideal was to be spread among "our brothers and friends."

The maintenance of union with our brothers near and far across the frontier, and our other friends in the world, is one of the chief tasks of the *Narodna Odbrana.* In using the word 'people' the *Narodna Odbrana* means our whole people, not only those in Serbia. It hopes that the work done by it in Serbia will spur the brothers outside Serbia to take a more energetic share in the work of private initiative, so that the new present-day movement for the creation of a powerful Serbian *Narodna Odbrana* will go forward in unison in all Serbian territories.

In other words, the society did not confine its operations to

---

*Народна Одбрана Издање Средишњег Одбора Народне Одбране [*Narodna Odbrana,* Publication of the Central Committee of the *Narodna Odbrana*] (Belgrade, 1911). Summarized, with many quotations, in Austrian *dossier,* appendix 2; German translation in full in *KSF,* V, 199–225 (March, 1927). The writer has been told, though no proof was offered, that while the pamphlet was issued under the imprint of the *Narodna Odbrana,* it was actually prepared by army officers members of the other society, the *Uyedinyenye ili Smrt,* which is discussed in the next section of this chapter. The pamphlet was transmitted to the Austro-Hungarian Government in 1912. Ugron to Berchtold, 30 March, 1912; *Ö.-U. A.,* IV, 68.

Serbia, but was active in Bosnia as well. According to the testimony of one Trifko Krstanovich, who claimed to have served as a courier for the chairman of the *Narodna Odbrana* in Shabats, there were twenty-three branches by 1910.* If the evidence of the Banyaluka trial of 1915–1916 is to be credited,† the three principal Serbian societies of Bosnia-Herzegovina, *Prosvyeta* ('Culture'), *Sokols* ('Falcons'), and *Pobratimstvo* ('Brotherhood'), were closely connected with the *Narodna Odbrana,* and under the guise of cultural propaganda, gymnastic competition, and social improvement, carried on espionage, military training, the enlistment of *komitadjis,* practice in bomb-throwing, and other insidious activities intended to undermine the loyalty of the population. The directing genius of these organizations was the secretary of *Prosvyeta,* Vasil Grdyich, an educated Serb, who was in direct touch with the *Narodna Odbrana* and whose aim was to create a secret revolutionary army throughout Bosnia.‡ In addition, it was shown at the trial of the Sarajevo conspirators that the *Narodna Odbrana* had its 'confidential men' scattered through the provinces.§

One of these agents, Velyko Chubrilovich, after a visit to General Bozho Milanovich in Shabats, organized a Sokol club in Priboy, and persuaded his friend, Mishko Yovanovich, of Tuzla, to become a 'confidential man';‖ both of these men had much to do with the execution of the plot of June, 1914. In 1912 an emissary from Belgrade visited Sarajevo to recruit members for the society, after a delegation of students from

* Austrian *dossier*, appendix 5.

† The Austro-Hungarian authorities prosecuted 151 persons for treasonable relations with Serbia, of whom 101 were convicted.

‡ This is the version of Freiherr von Sarkotich, "Der Hochverrats-Prozess von Banjaluka," in *KSF*, IX, 34–41 (January, 1929). Sarkotich succeeded Potiorek as governor of Bosnia in 1914.

§ The Austro-Hungarian Government learned something about the activity of the society in Bosnia in 1912 from a journalist in Lyublyana (Laibach), Milan Plut, who had been a member from the beginning. According to Plut, it was subsidized by the Serbian Government, even though its ideal was Yugoslav unity rather than Pan-Serb expansion. Pflügl to Berchtold, 8 August, 1912; *Ö.-U. A.,* IV, 319–322. See also report of the Statthalter of Zara, 23 August, 1913; *Ö.-U.A.,* VII, 188–189.

‖ Pharos, pp. 84, 100.

Zagreb had been enthusiastically received in Serbia.* A system of 'tunnels,' corresponding to the 'Underground Railroad' in the United States before the Civil War, was organized to secure effective secret communication between Bosnia and Serbia; it was doubtless by this means that books of a political nature and newspaper clippings about the persecution of Serbs in Bosnia were distributed to the 'confidential men.'† In Serbia the *Narodna Odbrana* interested itself in students who had fled from Bosnia and assisted them financially to pursue courses in Serbian schools where things were apparently made easy for them.

It was natural that at their trial those of the Sarajevo conspirators who admitted knowledge of or membership in the *Narodna Odbrana* should deny that it was a political organization and insist upon its strictly cultural purposes.‡ It is hardly surprising that its Serbian apologist should contend that "the *Narodna Odbrana* was not a revolutionary organization."§ But, in view of what has been said, one can seemingly accept the assertion of a German defender of Serbia that the society carried on its activity in Bosnia "under the eyes and attention of the very suspicious Austro-Hungarian authorities," that there was "no meeting that was not watched over, no speech that was not first submitted to the censor," ‖ only if they be understood to refer to the public activity of the *Narodna Odbrana* and not to its secret machinations. Nevertheless, strange as it may seem, the statements quoted appear to be not altogether untrue, and in a sense even correct. For it has recently been revealed that the activity ascribed by the Austro-Hungarian authorities to the *Narodna Odbrana* was in reality conducted not by it, but, under cover of its name, by another society, the *Uyedinyenye ili Smrt*.¶

---

* *Sérajévo: la conspiration serbe contre la monarchie austro-hongroise*, p. 58.
† Pharos, pp. 100, 108.   ‡ *Ibid.*, pp. 85, 90, 99–100, 116–117, 132–133.
§ Stanoyevich, p. 49.   ‖ Wendel, p. 47.
¶ The Austro-Hungarian authorities were not well informed about the *Narodna Odbrana*. At least there was no *dossier* on the subject in the Vienna foreign office. F. von Wiesner, "Der Sarajevoer Mord und die Kriegsschuldfrage," in *Das Neue Reich* (Vienna), 2 August, 1924, p. 969. Very few documents relating to the society are contained in *Ö.-U. A.*

THE *UYEDINYENYE ILI SMRT*

In 1914 little or nothing was known of this organization. True, it was referred to by Vienna newspapers in the spring of that year in connection with the controversy then raging in Serbia between the Radical party and the army,* and it was mentioned in the Carnegie Report on the Balkan wars† and, once, in the Austro-Hungarian *dossier.*‡ The Austro-Hungarian authorities were well aware of the society's existence, but apparently they did not understand its character or appreciate the nature of its activity; for the numerous reports transmitted from the legation in Belgrade represented it primarily as an organization engaged in political conflict with the dominant Radical party and only incidentally referred to its hatred of the Monarchy and its support of the Pan-Serb ambitions.§ It is significant that in July, 1914, and afterward the Austro-Hungarian propaganda paid attention only to the *Narodna Odbrana* and ignored the *Uyedinyenye ili Smrt*. The importance of this latter organization seems to have been first pointed out by a Serbian army officer in 1917, but his pamphlet‖ attracted little attention, and a similar fate befell the assertion of a Viennese writer that there was a group within the *Narodna Odbrana* which, because of its secret proceedings and political murders

---

* See below, pp. 199–201.

† The *Report of the International Commission to Inquire into the Causes and Conduct of the Balkan Wars* (Washington, 1914), p. 169,'note 1, says: "The Belgrade *Tribune* published ('Serb Cor.' November 18 / December 1) revelations by an anonymous officer who had been a member of the secret organization of the 'black hand.' The object of this organization, formed on the principle of the Carbonari, was,. according to him, the liberation of the Serbians from the Turkish yoke."

‡ Appendix 5. A remark by the British ambassador in Vienna that the murderers of Sarajevo "are said to be members of the terrorist Great Servian organization" (Bunsen to Grey, 29 June, 1914; *B. D.*, XI, no. 21) was not published in 1914.

§ The first report is dated 12 November, 1911, six months after the foundation of the society; *Ö.-U. A.*, III, no. 2911. Among the more important later documents, there may be mentioned nos. 3264, 3270, and especially, vol. IV, no. 3590 (27 June, 1912), which gives a long account of the rivalry between the society and the politicians, together with an analysis of the position of the Crown Prince. Many reports for the spring of 1914 are also printed, of which the best is vol. VIII, no. 9819.

‖ Commandant D. R. Lazarevich, IXme régiment d'infanterie serbe, *La Main-Noire* (Lausanne, 1917).

was spoken of in Serbia as the 'Black Hand.'* In 1918 a prominent Serbian politician referred to "the 'Black Hand,' or the group of officers known as 'Union or Death,' " as "a secret society which concerned itself with politics and desired to win for itself a predominant influence in the state," but he offered no details.†

An attempt to give general publicity—outside of Yugoslavia —to the society was first made by an Englishman, who in 1919 published the following statement:

> Only on June 13 of the present year was it admitted that the murderers were Serbians—the fact having been persistently denied up to then. It then also transpired that posthumous honors had been rendered them. That the murders were arranged by the Serbian Major Tankosich of the 'Black Hand' is now generally admitted. The 'Black Hand' was an organization created by Serbian officers who had played a prominent part in Serbian politics ever since the murder of King Alexander and Queen Draga. In his recently published book giving the history of this infamous organization and bringing, incidentally, the gravest charges against the most prominent Serbian public men, the Serbian commander Lazarevich asserts that the murder of the Archduke had long been prepared and that the news of his forthcoming visit to Sarajevo was regarded as a 'blessing.'‡

Even this caused no great stir, for the moment was not propitious.

The Allied peoples were profoundly convinced of the responsibility of the Central Powers for the war; for them the question was, as Mr. Lloyd George was later to tell the Germans, *"une chose jugée,"* and they were not in a mood to listen to inconvenient or disconcerting revelations. The Germans, for their part, who would naturally have exploited the matter, were

---

* Mandl, pp. 120–121.

† S. Protich, "A Serbian Protest," in *The New Europe* (London), VIII, 258 (26 September, 1918), in reply to an article by R. W. Seton-Watson, "Serbia's Choice," in *ibid.*, VIII, 123 (22 August, 1918).

‡ E. D. Morel, *Pre-War Diplomacy* (London, 1919), p. 40. The reference to Lazarevich is to *La Main-Noire*, p. 27.

busy with the collection of documents which Karl Kautsky had
just published from the archives and with his commentary, in
which he threw the blame unreservedly upon the old imperial
government.*

In the end, it was the Serbs themselves who advertised the
matter. The war had not long been over when the question of
the Salonica Trial began to be aired in Yugoslavia, the charge
being made that, in order to get rid of a dangerous political
rival, the leaders of the Radical party in control of the Serbian
Government had been guilty of judicial murder. In fact voices
were raised asking for a reopening of the question of the verdict—which would have been extremely inconvenient for the
Radical party and M. Pashich, and would have involved King
Alexander himself. It was this situation which—it is sup-
posed†—led to the publication of the pamphlet *The Murder of
the Archduke Francis Ferdinand,* by Profesor Stanoyevich, of
the University of Belgrade. In this pamphlet the chief victim
of the Salonica Trial, Colonel Dragutin Dimitriyevich, was
represented as the author of the plot which resulted in the murders at Sarajevo and therefore as one of the persons immediately responsible for the war; furthermore, a good deal of information was revealed about the society of the 'Black Hand,'
of which Dimitriyevich was the leading spirit. The pamphlet
was made available to the Western world in a German translation,‡ and aroused intense interest. Since that time the Sarajevo plot has been the subject of lively controversy, the end of
which has not yet been reached.

According to Stanoyevich, the officers involved in the royal
murders of 1903 found it desirable to maintain some kind of
organization for their mutual protection until the new dynasty
had been recognized by foreign Powers;§ after 1906, however,
they seldom met as a group. But in 1911, in view of the Bul-

* K. Kautsky, *Wie der Weltkrieg entstand* (Berlin, 1919).
† So the writer has been informed by a number of persons in Yugoslavia.
‡ An extensive summary was published in the *New York Times* on 22 July, 1923.
§ The British Government withheld its recognition until 1906, and insisted on
the retirement of the regicides from the government and the army.

garian agitation in Macedonia, some of them represented to the
Serbian Government that the time had come "to begin propaganda and revolutionary activity again in the Turkish territories," and, when the proposal was rejected by the government,
they founded on 9/22 May, 1911, a secret revolutionary society,
'Uyedinyenye ili Smrt' ('Union or Death'), to carry on this
propaganda by private enterprise. Some three hundred members
were soon enrolled, the 'men of 29 May' (as the conspirators
of 1903 were sometimes called in Serbia) comprising the most
important element; at its head stood Colonel Dragutin Dimitriyevich, of the general staff of the army, one of the ring-
leaders in the tragedy of 1903, and a man of tireless energy
and intense patriotism. "From this time on," says Professor
Stanoyevich, "the two national organizations worked side by
side, the *Narodna Odbrana* and the *Uyedinyenye ili Smrt.*"
Both societies are declared to have been purely private organizations.*

Professor Stanoyevich supposedly derived his information
from survivors of the *Uyedinyenye ili Smrt.* Either he suppressed many important facts, or he was incorrectly and incom-
pletely informed; for one of the founders of the society, Colonel
Chedo Popovich, has more recently given a detailed account of
the origin and work of the organization. When the Young
Turk revolution occurred, the Serbian Government, trusting
in the promises of the new régime and seeking its help against
Austria-Hungary during the Bosnian crisis, abandoned the
propaganda and activity which it had been carrying on in
Macedonia, much to the disgust of the agents engaged in it.
Although it was soon clear that the Young Turk régime, with
its policy of 'turkification,' was even more oppressive than
the system of Abdul Hamid, the Servian Government, says
Colonel Popovich, could not be induced to renew the activity
in Macedonia: both government and people were greatly dis-
pirited by the failure to undo the annexation of Bosnia or secure any kind of compensation, nor was there then any con-

* Stanoyevich, pp. 46, 48–49.

fidence in the army. On the other hand, the energetic Bulgarians, impressed by the danger to their national ambitions presented by Turkish policy, had reorganized their revolutionary organization in Macedonia by placing it under centralized control in Sofia and were intensifying their activity. "Its work, which came at the same time as the cessation of our work in Macedonia, attracted the attention of the Macedonian population to itself, and began to gain sympathies." Equally bad, from the Serbian point of view, was the situation in Bosnia, for the *Narodna Odbrana* abandoned its revolutionary activity and confined itself to cultural work; with the result that the Bosnian Serbs, who had entertained great hopes of Serbian assistance during the crisis, became discouraged and indifferent. Despair settled down on those who had been actively engaged in 'komitadji work':

All the effort which had been so successful in the days of the *komitadji* work in Macedonia seemed likely to perish, since the Bulgarian organization had been steadily gaining ground among the Macedonian population. The Austrian and Turkish authorities carried on constantly greater terror among our people. From all sides outside the frontiers of Serbia came despairing complaints against this fatal inactivity and the absolute necessity of doing something, lest there prevail among the people a hopelessness which might lead to incalculable consequences. All this had a keen effect on the adherents of revolutionary action, still further strengthened their conviction, and still further prepared the atmosphere for decisive work. It was felt that some new way must be found. Thus practically of itself was prepared the way for a revolutionary and nationalist organization.

The lead was taken by Bogdan Radenkovich, who had been one of the most prominent workers in Macedonia. Failing to receive any official encouragement, he approached three men with his idea: Voya Tankosich, already well known as a *komitadji*, Lyuba Yovanovich-Chupa, a university man and journalist with revolutionary leanings [not to be confused with Lyuba Yovanovich, the professor and politician], and Velimir

Vemich, then a captain of cavalry. All agreed to join with him in forming a revolutionary society, and to invite the co-operation of Major Dragutin Dimitriyevich, Major Iliya Radivoyevich and Captain Chedo Popovich. These seven men founded the organization and signed the statutes, which were drawn up by Radenkovich, Yovanovich and Tankosich. Radivoyevich was chosen president and Vemich secretary; Dimitriyevich declared that "he would not be able to give much time to the work since he was extremely occupied with official and other business." A little later three more persons were added, Iliya Yovanovich-Pchinyski, an artillery officer, Major Milan Vasich, who later became secretary of the *Narodna Odbrana,* and Lieut.-Colonel Milan G. Milanovich. These ten men constituted the Central Committee of the society; their names are signed to the constitution, the last page of which is reproduced in facsimile in the pamphlet of Professor Stanoyevich.* After the Balkan wars, Major Radoye Lazich was added to the Central Committee. It will be noted that all except Radenkovich and Lyuba Yovanovich-Chupa were army officers; also that Major Vasich was made a member because, as Dimitriyevich testified at his trial, "they reckoned thus to influence the work of the *Narodna Odbrana.*"

The statutes of the *Uyedinyenye ili Smrt*† are illuminating about both the purposes and the methods of the society. "This organization has been created with the object of realizing the national ideal: the union of all Serbs" (art. 1), under the ægis of the Kingdom of Serbia, which is to be "regarded as Piedmont" (art. 4). It "prefers terrorist action to intellectual

---

* C. A. Popovich, "Organizacija 'Ujedinjenje ili Smrt' ('Crna Ruka') [The 'Union or Death Organization' (the 'Black Hand')], in *Nova Evropa,* XV, 396–400 (11 June, 1927).

† First printed in full by Dr. Oscar Tartalja, a member of the society, in his newspaper *Novi List* in Split (Spalato), and reproduced in *Nova Evropa,* VI, 182–190 (21 October, 1922); German and English translation in *KSF,* IV, 682–689 (September, 1926); French version in M. Bogichevich, *Le procès de Salonique* (Paris, 1927), pp. 41–53. An expurgated version, taken from *Тajнa npeвpaтнa opгaнизaцuja,* pp. 357–368, is given in English in M. E. Durham, *The Serajevo Crime* (London, 1925), pp. 47–52. The purpose of the 'editing' was to prove that the *Uyedinyenye ili Smrt* was active only in Serbia and was therefore an anti-governmental organization.

propaganda" (art. 2) (in contrast to the *Narodna Odbrana*),
it "organizes revolutionary action in all the territories inhabited
by Serbs," and outside of Serbia "uses every means available to
combat the adversaries of the national idea" (art. 4). Executive authority is vested in a central committee at Belgrade (art.
5), which "includes besides the members representing the Kingdom of Serbia a delegate from each of the Serbian territories
abroad" (art. 7), where local committees are to be organized
(art. 9). The circumstances of the Sarajevo murders give
special interest to two articles.

Article 19. Liberty of action is left to the committees in the
Serbian territories abroad; the execution of more extensive
revolutionary movements must, however, first have the approval
of the central committee at Belgrade.
Article 16. In exceptionally urgent cases as well as in cases of
less importance the president and the secretary may come to a
decision and undertake its execution and report their action to
the central committee at its next meeting.

The conditions of membership were such as to discourage all
but the most resolute. A member "forfeits his own personality"
and "can expect neither glory nor personal profit, whether moral
or material" (art. 30); he is "bound to absolute obedience" to
his committee (art. 27); he may never withdraw from the organization (art. 31); he must communicate to the Central Committee "anything he may learn, either as a private individual
or in his capacity as a state official, concerning matters likely to
be of interest to the organization" (art. 28); he has "to go
surety with his life for those whom he introduces into the
organization" (art. 24); "if by his acts he injures the organization he will be punished with death" (art. 30), in which event
"the method of execution employed is a matter of indifference"
(art. 33). Well did the society deserve the name 'Black Hand'
which was attached to it in Serbian popular parlance!
To terrorism was added mystery. Members were not known
to each other personally (art. 25), except of course as they

drew in recruits; they were designated by numbers, and the names were known only to the Central Committee (art. 26). The initiation ceremony was quite melodramatic.

The room in which the oath is taken will be lighted only by a small wax candle. In the middle of the room there will be a table covered with black material. On the table there will be laid a cross, a dagger, and a revolver. The member who introduces the new recruits will explain to them the statutes, the regulations, and the duties of the organization, as well as the dangers which menace those who enter it. He will then ask them whether they are ready nevertheless to join it. As soon as the recruits declare their willingness, the delegate of the Central Committee, completely masked, comes from an adjoining room, and it is then that the member who introduces the recruits and the recruits themselves pronounce the words of the oath; the latter then embrace one another and the delegate shakes hands with them as a sign of congratulation, for he utters not a single word, and, in order that he may not be recognized, he immediately afterward withdraws. Only then is the room to be lit up, whereupon the new members copy out and sign the text of their oath and hand it back to their patron, who tells them their numbers and the password. (Special regulations, art. 3.)

The oath is worth quoting:

I, A. B., on becoming a member of the organization *Union or Death,* swear, by the Sun that warms me, by the Earth that nourishes me, before God, by the blood of my ancestors, on my honor, and on my life, that I will from this moment till my death be faithful to the laws of this organization, that I will always be ready to make any sacrifice for it. I swear before God, on my honor and on my life, that I will take all the secrets of this organization with me to my grave. May God confound me and may my comrades in this organization judge me if I trespass against or either consciously or unconsciously fail to keep my oath. (Art. 35.)

Perhaps the best single illustration of the spirit of the 'Black Hand' is to be found in its seal: "In the middle of the signet a muscular hand with bent fingers, grasping an unfurled flag; on the flag as escutcheon, a death's head with cross-bones, and beside the flag a dagger, a bomb and poison" (art. 34). A society which could combine the self-effacing loyalty of the Jesuits, the ruthless spirit of the Russian nihilists, and the symbolism of the Ku Klux Klan was indeed a noteworthy organization.*

If the writer is correctly informed, the Central Committee of the *Uyedinyenye ili Smrt* soon ceased to meet or to play an important rôle in the affairs of the society. Dragutin Dimitriyevich, although at first lukewarm, soon perceived the possibilities of the organization and was not long in becoming its presiding genius and directing spirit.† Dimitriyevich, as pictured by Professor Stanoyevich, was a remarkable man:

Gifted and educated, honorable, a convincing speaker, a sincere patriot, personally brave and full of ambition, energy, and capacity for work, Dragutin Dimitriyevich exercised an unusual influence on those around him, especially on his companions and the younger officers. . . . He possessed the qualities which fascinate men. His arguments were ever striking and convincing; he understood how to represent the most knotty [*ungefügsten*] problems as bagatelles, the most dangerous enterprises as innocent and harmless. In addition, he was in every respect an excellent organizer; he always kept everything in his own hands, and even his most intimate friends knew only what immediately touched them. . . . Considerations of what was possible and what was not or of the limits of responsibility and power did not exist for him. Of political [*staatlichen*] life and its requirements, he had no clear conception: he saw only the goal in front of him and went his own way recklessly and without scruple. He loved adventure and danger and secret meetings and mysterious activity. . . .

Dimitriyevich was persuaded that his views on all matters, events, and circumstances were correct, and believed that his

* According to a Serbian gentleman acquainted with members of the *Uyedinyenye ili Smrt*, with whom the writer discussed the activity of the society, the elaborate precautions taken to insure secrecy were essential, in view of the national *penchant* for talking; the *Narodna Odbrana*, which was not a secret society, did a great deal of talking—and little else. He explained the symbolism of the seal by the statement that all Slavs are fond of indulging in phantasy. In his opinion, the melodramatic features of the *Uyedinyenye ili Smrt* had been overemphasized.

† The same opinion is expressed in M. Bogichevich [Boghitchévitch], *Le Colonel Dragoutine Dimitriévitch Apis* (Paris, 1928), pp. 61–62.

opinions and actions enjoyed a monopoly of patriotism. . . .
He wished to plan and organize and command: others were to
obey him and execute his instructions without opposition.*

This is the portrait of an enemy, and no doubt unduly severe.
Those who knew him personally speak of his great personal
charm, his utter lack of selfishness, his passionate patriotism;
one of his intimates describes him as Mazzini and Garibaldi
joined in a single person.† Whatever the details of his character may have been, he was the soul of the national movement
for unity, and thought only of its achievement. Professor
Stanoyevich represents him as an inveterate conspirator. Dimitriyevich, he says, was not only one of the principal organizers
of the murder of Alexander and Draga, but arranged for the
crime of Sarajevo, and in 1916 plotted against the Crown
Prince Alexander of Serbia, then regent, for which last offense he was tried and executed at Salonica in 1917. In 1911,
according to Stanoyevich, he despatched some one to kill the
Emperor Francis Joseph or the Archduke Francis Ferdinand,
in 1914 he concerted with a Bulgarian revolutionary committee
for the assassination of Tsar Ferdinand, and in 1916 he tried
to have King Constantine of Greece put out of the way.‡

Such a record, if correctly given, must be without parallel.
Unfortunately, Professor Stanoyevich offers no proofs of his
statements. For one of the alleged crimes, the attempt on the
life of the Crown Prince Alexander, the evidence published by
the Serbian Government§ has been found unconvincing by writers of the most divergent views.‖ It is exceedingly doubtful
whether any attempt was made on the Crown Prince. Outside

---

* Stanoyevich, pp. 50–51.
† O. Tartalja, "Dragutin Dimitrijević 'Apis,'" in *Nova Evropa*, XVI, 67–74
(26 July, 1927). Bogichevich, *Le procès de Salonique*, pp. 64–68, and *Le Colonel
Dragoutine Dimitriévitch Apis*, pp. 39–68, does not deny the great qualities of the
man. The writer has talked with two Serbs who knew Dimitriyevich; although
representing different points of view, they agreed that he was a man of great ability, tremendous energy and striking personality.
‡ Stanoyevich, pp. 50–51.   § *Тајна Превратна Организација*.
‖ Durham, *The Serajevo Crime*, pp. 158–189; Bogichevich, *Le procès de Salonique*,
pp. 21–29, and *Le Colonel Dragoutine Dimitriévitch Apis*, pp. 99–167. The same
view has been consistently championed by *Nova Evropa*. Seton-Watson, *Sarajevo*,
p. 158, implies rather than states that he does not accept the official view.

of official circles, the following opinion is widely held. In 1917 the Serbian Government is believed to have engaged in negotiations with Austria-Hungary for a separate peace. Among the conditions formulated by the Cabinet of Vienna was the demand for the suppression of the secret societies hostile to the Monarchy.* With the object of currying favor with Vienna, the Serbian Government decided to sacrifice Colonel Dimitriyevich, who was spoken of privately as the author of the Sarajevo conspiracy and who opposed making peace on the terms offered by Austria-Hungary. In order, however, to conceal the real motives for getting rid of him, it was necessary to trump up another charge; and since Dimitriyevich had been for years a bitter enemy of the Radical party (for reasons to be set forth presently), the obvious course was to represent him and the *Uyedinyenye ili Smrt* as engaged in a conspiracy to overthrow the government. Actually, the negotiations for a separate peace fell through, but the Radical party could not resist the temptation to free itself from a dangerous adversary, and Dimitriyevich and two other persons were executed.† Nothing is known of his plots against other royal personages.‡ So Professor Stanoyevich's account has to be treated with great caution.

Much interest attaches to the personnel of the *Uyedinyenye ili Smrt*. The first list of members to be published began with:

1. Crown Prince Alexander;
2. Nikola Pashich, president of the council of ministers;
3. Stoyan Protich, minister of the interior;
4. Lyuba Stoyanovich, minister of justice;
5. Voivode Radomir Putnik.§

* Prince Sixte de Bourbon, *L'offre de paix séparée de l'Autriche* (Paris, 1920), pp. 59, 78, 87.

† Great pressure was brought to bear on the Crown Prince Alexander to pardon Dimitriyevich by the non-Radical members of the government, who resigned rather than be a party to the execution, and by the British Government, but to no avail.

‡ In June, 1912, an Austro-Hungarian agent in Belgrade reported that "an elderly Serb" was planning to go to Vienna to assassinate the Archduke Francis Ferdinand; according to a Serbian letter which was adduced as proof, "the *Narodna Odbrana* and several members of the government" stood behind the plan. The Austro-Hungarian war office, however, characterized the source of the letter as "unreliable." Ö.-U. A., IV, 202, 214–215.

§ Lazarevich, p. 47.

This list is, in all probability, apocryphal. The voivode (general) Putnik was undoubtedly on good terms with the organization, but one can hardly imagine him being a member of a society managed by officers his junior in rank; he appears to have used it as a lever in his difficulties with the government. The Crown Prince was at first favorably disposed toward the society. He contributed 26,000 dinars to the support of its newspaper *Piyemont* and paid the expenses of Dimitriyevich's illness in 1912;[*] but the refusal to admit him to membership, which would have involved his becoming its head, wounded his pride and turned him against the *Uyedinyenye ili Smrt*,[†] so that in 1914 he appears to have taken the side of the government against it.

An incomplete list of members was made public by the Serbian Government in connection with the Salonica trial. Among the names are those of Vladimir Gachinovich, no. 217, whose activity has already been noted,[‡] and Milan Tsiganovich, no. 412, of whom much will be said presently; both of these men were Bosnian *émigrés*. Others were Dushan Optrkich, no. 166, a friend of Lyuba Yovanovich, who was minister of education in the Serbian cabinet of 1914; Michael Zhivkovich, no. 442, secretary of the court of cassation; Dr. Milan Gavrilovich, no. 496, secretary of the ministry of foreign affairs and later editor of the *Politika;* M. A. Yovanovich, no. 401, secretary of the railway administration; and Bogolyub Vuchichevich, no. 407, a police commissioner.[§] How authoritative this list is may be a matter of dispute;[‖] but if it is even approximately correct, then

[*] M. Bogichevich [Boghitschewitsch], "The Serbian Society 'Union or Death' *alias* the 'Black Hand,'" in *KSF*, IV, 678 (September, 1926).

[†] A memorandum on the 'Black Hand' by M. Th. Stefanovich-Vilovsky, of the Serbian foreign office, dated 27 June, 1912, and discussing the relations of the King and the Crown Prince of Serbia with the society, is printed in *Ö.-U. A.*, IV, 232–238. There is no indication whether this document was known to the Austro-Hungarian Government at the time or was only secured during the war, when many Serbian documents were removed to Vienna.

[‡] See above, pp. 146–148.

[§] Bogichevich, *loc. cit.*, IV, 675, 688 (September, 1926).

[‖] One of the persons mentioned in the list told the writer that he had indeed joined the society, but under a misapprehension of its character and purposes; at the end of a month, he gave up any activity connected with it, but his name remained on the list of members. Another gentleman stated that while his name

the *Uyedinyenye ili Smrt* was not confined to army officers and *komitadjis* and Bosnian *émigrés,* but was recruited also from official circles. In fact, the critics of the society contend that it was practically an unofficial branch of the government, in proof of which they point to the declaration made on 28 February, 1924, by the comrades of Dimitriyevich who demanded a revision of the Salonica verdict:

The organization *Uyedinyenye ili Smrt* was a patriotic society whose activities were well known to the competent authorities, activities which were in accord with the intentions of the said authorities.*

At his trial Dimitriyevich stated that at the end of 1911 he himself had informed M. Milovanovich, the foreign minister, of the existence (though not of the constitution and rules) of the organization, and that the minister had said to him: "My young friend, put your 'Black Hand' at my disposal and you will see what Milovanovich will in a short time do for Serbdom."† And the historian of the 'Black Hand,' after recounting this incident, continues:

After the conversation as to work between Dragutin Dimitriyevich and the minister Milovanovich, the *Uyedinyenye ili Smrt* organization became, as far as South Serbia [Macedonia] was concerned, practically the executive organ of the ministry of foreign affairs. The proposals which the organization made to him were adopted, and he endeavored to carry them out. There existed the closest co-operation in work and the greatest activity in its execution. Dragutin Dimitriyevich-Apis . . . plunged fully into it with absolute enthusiasm and

was to be found in the published list, he had never been a member of the society nor had any connection with it. These statements appear credible to the writer, because the surviving members of the society, or at least many of them, are not ashamed of their connection with it, if their writings are any index to their feelings.

* M. Bogichevich, "Bemerkungen zum Saloniki-Prozess," in *KSF*, II, 112–113 (April, 1924).

† *Тајна превратна организација,* pp. 169–170; Durham, p. 62. Dimitriyevich "gained greatly in influence owing to his intimacy with Dr. Milovanovich, the Serbian statesman whose premature death on the eve of the Balkan war was nothing less than a political catastrophe." R. W. Seton-Watson, "Serbia's Choice," in *The New Europe,* VIII, 123 (22 August, 1918).

élan, sparing neither strength nor time. In this work he found himself in his element.*

The activity of the society in Bosnia is another story, but it is clear that originally the *Uyedinyenye ili Smrt* was on excellent terms with the Serbian Government, which used it as a secret instrument for the promotion of the national ambitions.

This harmony, however, was not of long duration. The 'Black Hand' was dominated by soldiers, who, while they might engage in propaganda and revolutionary activity abroad, were at home keenly interested in improving the army, which, in their opinion, was neglected by the government. There was in fact a standing feud between the soldiers and the politicians, the latter being supported by certain older officers who resented the reforming zeal of the younger groups.† The first rumblings of the coming storm were heard during the Balkan wars, when the army offered determined resistance to the policy of concessions to Bulgaria which the Russian Government was endeavoring to force upon Serbia, for the Serbian victories were due in large measure to the efficiency of the officers, many of whom belonged to the *Uyedinyenye ili Smrt*.‡ The society itself, having devoted so much energy to propaganda in Macedonia, was naturally unwilling to lose that land to Bulgaria, and its opposition was justified by events, for Serbia emerged from the

---

* C. A. Popovich, "Рад организације 'Уједињење или Смрт' " [Work of the 'Union or Death' Organization], in *Nova Evropa*, XVI, 312 (26 November, 1927).

† Bogichevich, *Le Colonel Dragoutine Dimitriévitch Apis*, pp. 69–88; 'Marco', "Srpska Vojska pre i posle 29. Maja 1903" [The Serbian army before and after 29 May 1903], in *Nova Evropa*, XVI, 9–20 (11 July, 1927); and "Препород Српске Војске, и борба за уједињење" [The Renaissance of the Serbian Army and the Struggle for Union], in *ibid.*, XVI, 51–66 (26 July, 1927).

‡ At the demand of Hartwig, Pashich was ready to accept unconditionally the arbitration of the Tsar. The *Uyedinyenye ili Smrt* had, however, received information from St. Petersburg that the Tsar would decide in favor of Bulgaria, and they were strong enough to force the resignation of Pashich. Hartwig prevailed upon the king not to accept the resignation, and the premier was about to announce in the Skupshtina that Serbia would agree to arbitration when the news arrived of the Bulgarian attack on the Serbian army. This prevented an open rupture between the Radical party and the *Uyedinyenye ili Smrt*, but henceforth Hartwig was a bitter enemy of the secret society which, he perceived, was not ready to obey Russia. 'Marco,' "Никола Хартвиг" [Nicholas Hartwig], in *Nova Evropa*, XVII, 268–269 (26 April, 1928), and *KSF*, VI, 757–760 (August, 1928). Cf. Ugron to Berchtold, 12, 16, 21, 22, 24 June, 1913; *Ö.-U. A.*, VI, 633, 653–655, 689, 699–700, 715–716.

war with quite the largest share of the 'promised land.' Naturally the prestige of Dimitriyevich mounted. On the other hand, the government, that is, the Radical party, wished to exploit the situation for its own profit. A trial of strength loomed up between the army and the government, with Macedonia as the bone of discord. Unfortunately, the officials sent to 'New Serbia' were of poor quality, doubtless because service in war-stricken Macedonia was not popular and the government had to humor its supporters. Charges of corruption and complaints of inefficiency began to be heard, and this gave the 'Black Hand' its chance. It organized bands of *komitadjis* against the Bulgarian elements which created a veritable reign of terror and made Serbia and all its works hated among the Bulgarian elements of Macedonia;* this of course made the position of the government exceedingly difficult, which saw itself forced to issue on 4 October, 1913, a severe decree which denied constitutional rights to the new provinces and established what was essentially a military dictatorship. For months the struggle went on. Early in 1914 the government published an order giving the civil authorities priority over the military. Nevertheless at Skoplye on Easter day the divisional commander, General Damyan Popovich, one of the regicides of 1903, claimed the post of honor on the right of the bishop, which belonged to the prefect.† Deprived of his command by the government, he was elected president of the officers' club in Belgrade, whereupon the minister of the interior, Stoyan Protich, who was the most forceful personality in the cabinet, retaliated by closing the club; he is said to have collected 3,000 gendarmes in Belgrade as protection against a military outbreak.‡

* *Report of the International Commission to Inquire into the Causes and Conduct of the Balkan Wars*, pp. 158–186, *passim*. "There were two antagonistic views. One, represented by M. Pashich himself, wanted a 'liberal' régime in Macedonia. The population of the new territories was to be left to express its loyalty spontaneously; to wait 'until it realized that its new lot was sweeter than the old.' Military circles, however, did not share this view. They were for a military administration, since a civil administration, in their view, 'must be incapable of repressing the propagandism sure to be carried on by the Bulgarians.'" P. 159.

† Wendel, p. 55.

‡ Seton-Watson, *Sarajevo*, p. 140; Lazarevich, pp. 12–18; Bogichevich, *Le Colonel Dragoutine Dimitriévitch Apis*, p. 92.

It would be incorrect to consider this conflict as one between the government and the *Uyedinyenye ili Smrt,* for it was a struggle between the Radical party and the army as a whole. Nevertheless Dragutin Dimitriyevich was the leader of the military party, and back of him stood his 'Black Hand.' But the army was not the only discontented element. The Progressive and Young Radical parties were also resentful of the monopoly of power by M. Pashich, who had the barest majority in the Skupshtina. According to one account, Colonel Dimitriyevich proposed to his friends that the police in Macedonia should be removed and officers put in their places.* It may also be that he negotiated with the Independent Radicals, proposing to try a *coup d'état* which, if successful, should result in their being called to office, while if it failed they were to use their influence to protect Dimitriyevich and his friends from the consequences of their action.† Actually, nothing more violent resulted than a cabinet crisis, produced by the resignation of the minister of war, who sympathized with the army rather than with the Radical party.

The crisis, however, took an unusual turn. Apparently King Peter promised General Putnik that the demands of the army for a change of government would be granted, that is, the Independent Radicals would be invited to power. But the Crown Prince, fearing that this would mean the ascendancy of the *Uyedinyenye ili Smrt* and Dimitriyevich, persuaded his father to retract his promise. Furthermore, the Russian minister in Belgrade, M. Hartwig, who had confidence only in the Radicals, came to the rescue of M. Pashich, and insisted on his remaining in office. As Hartwig's influence was enormous, the veteran Radical leader was able to reconstitute his cabinet and make no concession other than the repeal of the order of priority.‡ But

---

* Stanoyevich, p. 54.
† Statement made to the writer in Belgrade in 1928; also cf. Wendel, p. 55.
‡ Hartwig's attitude is explained by the fact that a year before he had tried to bring about a bargain between the Radicals and the Progressives, by which the latter would enter the government, they having abandoned their traditional Austrophile attitude. The high terms of the Progressives disgusted him. He was suspicious of the Young Radicals because of their relation with the 'Black Hand,'

King Peter, feeling that he was compromised by having to go back on his promise, abdicated, alleging the state of his health, and the Crown Prince assumed the regency. The government, sure of the support of the crown, dissolved parliament (24 June) and issued an appeal to the country on the question of civil or military supremacy.*

This analysis of Serbian politics in the spring of 1914 should make clear that the Serbian Government and the *Uyedinyenye ili Smrt* were at daggers drawn at the time when the plot of Sarajevo was being hatched; also that victory for one side or the other still hung in the balance. These considerations must be borne in mind when we have to take up the relation of the Serbian Government to the plot.

Inasmuch, however, as this quarrel concerned the internal politics of Serbia and came to a head only on the eve of the Sarajevo murder, it did not affect the activity of the *Uyedin-yenye ili Smrt* outside the frontiers of Serbia, which was the *raison d'être* of its existence. The character of its activity in Bosnia and how it was carried on has been revealed by one of the original members of the society, Colonel Chedo Popovich, who himself took a leading part in it. In 1911 the Serbian general staff decided to establish 'frontier officers' at half a dozen points along the Bosnia and Turkish frontiers for the purpose of gathering military intelligence. Shortly afterward the *Uyedinyenye ili Smrt* was founded, and the staff officers responsible for the scheme of 'frontier officers,' Colonel Milo-vanovich and Major Dimitriyevich, the latter being already and the former presently becoming a member of the new secret

which he appears to have hated, perhaps because some of its members had been regicides in 1903, perhaps because Dimitriyevich, it is said (N. Nenadovich, "Die Geheimnisse der Belgrader Kamarilla," in *La fédération balkanique* [Vienna], no. 9, p. 109 [December, 1924]), had manifested republican sympathies. Hartwig is said to have joined with Pashich to lay a trap for the 'Black Hand,' but "it is not yet time to speak of this." 'Marco,' "Никола Хартвиг" [Nicholas Hartwig], in *Nova Evropa*, XVII, 274–276 (26 April, 1928), and *KSF*, VI, 760–766.

* The conflict was fully reported upon to Vienna, *Ö.-U. A.* containing no less than 12 reports (between nos. 9485 and 9922). Baron Giesl, the Austro-Hungarian minister, was inclined to discount its importance, and expressed the wish that Pashich should triumph over his adversaries, for this would facilitate the pending negotiations on the Oriental Railway.

society, saw to it that the 'frontier officers' were drawn from the same organization. On the Bosnian frontier these officers were stationed at Shabats, Loznitsa, and Uzhitse. Their position was difficult. "We all knew positively that our government would not permit us, under any conditions, to set up a revolutionary organization in Bosnia and the Herzegovina for fear lest it should be discovered by the Austrian authorities and material be thus offered to the Austrian Government for reprisals." So they decided to carry on their work in secret, "making it our primary aim to discover persons with whom to come in contact and through whom to develop our work further. Only when a sufficient number of people had been prepared should we proceed to organize them for real revolutionary work."

Their activity was guided by two principles:

Since during the annexation crisis I had studied the state of mind, thoughts, and ideas of our people [in Bosnia], as well as their aspirations (for throughout the crisis I had been on or near the frontier), I knew that our work would find support on the other side of the Drina just because we were officers. I knew well the feeling of our people in Bosnia that salvation and liberation must be looked for from the Serbian officers because they were the representatives of the Serbian army.

This, says Colonel Popovich, was "our first guarantee for safe work." He then continues:

I knew also that the *Narodna Odbrana* association which had sprung up during the annexation crisis was regarded by our people in Bosnia-Herzegovina as the greatest revolutionary organization. It had been anathematized by the Austro-Hungarian Government, and because of it many people in Bosnia-Herzegovina had been persecuted after the annexation. The changed rôle of the *Narodna Odbrana* after the annexation, its renunciation of revolutionary action, and its change into an association for work of a purely cultural character, our people across the frontier would not accept as serious and true; they firmly believed that it was simply a sham to deprive the Austrian authorities of a chance of complaint. Consequently the

Narodna Odbrana in the eyes of our people in Bosnia-Herzegovina was just the same after the annexation as before it: a
revolutionary organization to prepare the people for the struggle
against Austria.

He therefore submitted to his associates the opinion that it
would be unwise to extend the *Uyedinyenye ili Smrt* to Bosnia
or to point out that it was the latter which now managed
revolutionary activity, and not the *Narodna Odbrana*.

I proposed this [he explains] because such action would have
had a bad effect on our people in Bosnia-Herzegovina, who
might see in it a lack of unanimity among us in Serbia, or, still
worse, division and discord in work and the method of carrying on a nationalist and revolutionary organization outside the
Serbian frontiers. We therefore decided that we frontier officers should refrain from introducing members into the organization [the *Uyedinyenye ili Smrt*] specially, but that we
should work with them and never contradict their convictions
concerning the *Narodna Odbrana*.

Not only was this proposal accepted by the leaders of the
Uyedinyenye ili Smrt in Belgrade, but it was decided, as it
were, to take over the *Narodna Odbrana*, and without depriving
it of the halo of a cultural society, to introduce into it a member
of the *Uyedinyenye ili Smrt* to manage the activity of the
Narodna Odbrana in accordance with the revolutionary pro-
gramme of the *Uyedinyenye ili Smrt*. In consequence Major
Milan Vasich, a member of the Central Committee of the
Uyedinyenye ili Smrt, became the secretary of the *Narodna
Odbrana*.

This explains the confusion which subsequently arose. The
Narodna Odbrana remained a non-revolutionary society, but
in order to conceal the existence of the *Uyedinyenye ili Smrt*,
it was represented in Bosnia as the organization directing the
revolutionary activity. The Austro-Hungarian authorities appear not to have discovered this fact, and consequently accused
the *Narodna Odbrana* of activity which was really inspired by

the *Uyedinyenye ili Smrt.* In a sense, of course, the distinction was one without a difference, for it mattered little by which organization the revolutionary activity was conducted; but it would have been useful to the Austro-Hungarian Government in July, 1914, to be able to indicate the real authors of the agitation in Bosnia.

The work of the frontier officers was eminently successful:

It was soon clear that there were even too many men ready for work. Every intelligent Serb, every prominent citizen, more or less all those imbued with a national consciousness in Bosnia-Herzegovina were predisposed to enter any organization coming from Serbia with the aim of destroying the Austro-Hungarian Monarchy. Our initial activity met with such a unanimous welcome and began to spread with such speed and impetus that we frontier officers were obliged, only a few months after beginning, to influence our friends in Bosnia to work with less speed and more caution.

Their work "was supplemented by that of other members of the organization in Belgrade," who extended it "in the whole of Bosnia-Herzegovina, primarily among the young men of those provinces, giving it an altogether revolutionary character."

Thus even before the outbreak of the Balkan war [continues Colonel Popovich], the revolutionary organization in Bosnia-Herzegovina had taken deep root. Once set in motion, its waves spread more and more widely, as if by the force of some mechanical law, embracing constantly widening masses of the people. The warlike feeling and extreme excitement among the masses of our people in Bosnia-Herzegovina attained such proportions that they began to become dangerous. The strong feeling on the part of the people, and in consequence our work also to some extent, could not remain unnoticed by the Austrian authorities, although they could not as yet take any measures, since they had no proofs at hand.

The Balkan war put an end to the activity of the officers, "since we all went to the front." But they returned in October, 1913, to find that "our successes and victories gave perfect

confidence and faith in the power of Serbia to the hearts of
our people in Bosnia-Herzegovina and simultaneously awakened the hope that their liberation would soon and surely come."
So at the beginning of 1914 the officers "prepared a scheme
for further activity that was to end with the definite preparation of our people for the event of armed conflict with Austria-
Hungary, which was felt to be coming and expected in the near
future."

Our intentions were, however, balked by our government.
Afraid of our work, it considered it necessary at the end of
January, 1914,* to abolish the service of the frontier officers,
and to transfer us into the interior of Serbia to regular duty
among the troops. This arrested our work and made impossible
any continuation of the revolutionary organization in Bosnia.
Nevertheless, our friends in Belgrade kept up the connections which they had made, as far as they could, in order that
it should not be felt or noticed in Bosnia-Herzegovina that the
work was held up just at the moment when the most energetic
action was expected from Serbia.

This action of the government, which suggests that it did not
desire an immediate rupture with Austria-Hungary, may have
some relation to the inception and execution of the Sarajevo
plot.

"One very crude mistake" was made, remarks Colonel Popovich. The officers were required to keep records of their activity. When the Austro-Hungarian armies advanced into
Serbia after the outbreak of war, they found the records of
Major Kosta Todorovich, the frontier officer at Loznitsa. One
of these was produced at the trial of the Sarajevo conspirators
which described the winning of 'confidential men' in Bosnia
and the creation of 'tunnels.'† The whole series was made the
basis of prosecution in the great trial at Banyaluka in 1915–
1916, at which 123 persons were charged with treason

* F. von Wiesner, "Die Schuld der Serbischen Regierung am Mord von Sarajevo,"
in *KSF*, VI, 391, note 83 (April, 1928), states that according to the testimony at
the Sarajevo, Banyaluka and Salonica trials, the frontier officers were removed in
May, 1914. Wiesner gives a brief summary of Popovich's articles.
† Pharos, pp. 91–92.

because, with the intention of forcibly changing the position and form of the state of the provinces of Bosnia and the Herzegovina in relation to the Austro-Hungarian Monarchy and of joining Bosnia and the Herzegovina to the kingdom of Serbia, in the course of the years 1911–1914, they joined the organization of the Serbian revolutionary society *Narodna Odbrana* at Belgrade.

The charge related to the very years when the frontier officers were at their posts.*

The founders of the *Uyedinyenye ili Smrt* were relatively young men, and they early came to the conclusion that only young men could carry out their national and revolutionary programme.

We considered [says Colonel Popovich] that youth alone was capable of starting determinedly on new courses, because the older generations, even those which had taken part in the national struggle, were weary, had lost faith in themselves, had become less capable of resistance, and had gone over to the paths of compromise and haggling.

It was therefore decided to organize and prepare the minds of the young intellectuals, "who at the proper moment and in the proper ways would spread the revolutionary propaganda more widely among our population in the Monarchy." The problem was attacked from three angles.

In the first place, the more ambitious young men from Bosnia went outside the province to study, and most of them to Vienna. "By the irony of fate, Vienna was the cultural centre of the youth who had to be organized in the struggle against the usurper Vienna, the centre of the Austro-Hungarian Monarchy." The work was undertaken by Vladimir Gachinovich, who, as we have seen,† wrote there his pamphlet in praise of Zherayich, *The Death of a Hero,* the aim of which, he said, was

---

* C. A. Popovich, "Rad organizacije 'Ujedinjenje ili Smrt': Granični oficiri" [The Work of the 'Union or Death' Organization: Frontier Officers], in *Nova Evropa*, XVI, 139–152 (11 September, 1927).

† See above, p. 146.

in the first place to kindle revolution in the minds and thoughts of young Serbs, so that they may be saved from the disastrous influence of anti-national ideas and prepare for the breaking of bonds and for the laying of healthy foundations for the shining national life that is to come.*

He had also to recruit members for the *Uyedinyenye ili Smrt*. A similar task was also assigned to a representative, "no. 1872," who was sent to Paris.

Secondly, the youth in Bosnia-Herzegovina had to be excited. In this work also, Gachinovich played a prominent part, and Colonel Popovich indignantly denies that *Mlada Bosna* ('Young Bosnia') grew up "spontaneously and independently —that *Mlada Bosna* which carried out its revolutionary work so daringly and heroically":

The annexation crisis had created the predisposition for it, had awakened the feeling; but the feeling developed and came to full expression only when the *Uyedinyenye ili Smrt* introduced into its own circle a certain number of young men and let them continue the work. The *Mlada Bosna* movement began to assume definite character only in 1911 from the foundation of the *Uyedinyenye ili Smrt*, and then spread constantly, parallel with the development of the organization.

But he points out that not all who took part in the revolutionary agitation were connected with the secret organization, that "many who took part in the movement did not know whence it came and on what it rested."

Thirdly, great efforts were made to attract young men from Bosnia to Serbia, for, according to Gachinovich, "a young man of Austria-Hungary could not become a serious national revolutionary until he had taken a few walks along the streets of Belgrade."† In Belgrade they would be subjected to the full force of the Serbian national idea, and, incidentally, they might

* *Spomenica Vladimir Gaćinovića*, p. 41, quoted in Seton-Watson, *Sarajevo*, p. 70.
† 'Marco,' "Препород Српске Војске, и борба за уједињење" [Renaissance of the Serbian Army and the Struggle for Union], in *Nova Evropa*, XVI, 63 (26 July, 1927).

be trained for fighting in the school for *komitadjis* maintained at Prokuplye, where the chief instructor was Major Voya Tankosich. How many of these *émigrés* there were is not known, but the number was undoubtedly considerable, and we shall see that the conspirators of 1914 were all men who had come to Belgrade from Bosnia.

Colonel Popovich insists that the Serbian Government "did not approve" of the work carried on in Bosnia by the *Uyedinyenye ili Smrt,* and says that "because of this we neither sought nor received any assistance from them." If this is true, it was doubtless because the Serbian Government was afraid of giving Austria-Hungary cause for complaint, and also because, as Popovich again emphasizes, the Bosnian youth was fired by the ideal of *Yugoslav* unity, whereas those in power in Belgrade thought in terms of *Greater Serbia.** Apparently the Serbian Government had its own lines out. It is said that among hundreds of documents found in the houses of M. Pashich and M. Milo Pavlovich, a leading member of the *Narodna Odbrana,* when the Austro-Hungarian troops occupied Belgrade, there were found lists of various people who were in receipt of subsidies. The lists included students, among them Zherayich and Gachinovich, Bosnian editors, spies and other 'serviceable people.'† In 1909 the Serbian Government paid the expenses of a Bosnian delegation to St. Petersburg,‡ and once at least it sent money to its legation in Vienna for the support of a Serbian student society in the Austrian capital.§ But such action was comparatively harmless. All things considered, it is probable that, while the Serbian Government welcomed the discontent of the Bosnian population and was not unaware of how that discontent was stimulated by the *Uyedinyenye ili Smrt,* it

---

* Except where otherwise indicated the last four paragraphs are based on C. A. Popovich, "Рад организације 'Уједињење или Смрт' " [The Work of the 'Union or Death' Organization], in *Nova Evropa,* XVI, 312–321 (26 November, 1927).

† M. E. Durham, "The Sarajevo Murder Plot," in *Current History,* XXV, 661–662 (February, 1927), and "Fresh Light on Serbia and the War," in *Contemporary Review,* CXXXIV, 309 (September, 1928).

‡ Petkovich to foreign office, 2 May, 1909; Popovich to foreign office, 4 May, 1909; Bogichevich, *Die auswärtige Politik Serbiens,* I, 108–109.

§ Pashich to Yovanovich, 12 February, 1913; *ibid.,* I, 298.

did not approve of the methods employed because, if they were discovered, the Austro-Hungarian Government was likely to hold Serbia responsible. On the other hand, because the action was carried on by a secret society, effective measures to stop it were difficult to take. The easiest course, and the one apparently followed, was to refrain from approving or assisting that action, but to do nothing to prevent it.

DRAMATIS PERSONÆ

The attraction of Belgrade for Bosnian students was twofold. Inoculated as they were with the idea of Yugoslav unity, they found the atmosphere of the Serbian capital congenial and stimulating; they were able to breathe the air of "freedom,"* said one of the conspirators at their trial, and in the cafés they could talk politics with "students, printers, and *komitadjis.*"† But this was not all. Because of their indiscipline and reluctance to study, they often got into trouble with the Bosnian school authorities. In Belgrade, however, they passed their examinations easily, sometimes more rapidly than Serbian students, and they did not have to learn "so much Latin and Greek."‡ Nevertheless, life was hard, for, in spite of assistance from the *Narodna Odbrana,* or other sources, they had little money and lived "on their debts."§ Poor food and poor lodgings affected their health, made them neurotic; the company they kept was not of the kind to inspire respect for authority. It is not surprising that among them men could be found ready for any kind of desperate enterprise; among them were the three youths who executed the plot at Sarajevo on 28 June, 1914.

Gavrilo Printsip, who came from Grahovo, in western Bosnia, went to Belgrade in May, 1912.‖ His father had been able

---

* Grabezh. Pharos, p. 46.   † Chabrinovich. *Ibid.,* p. 6.
‡ Grabezh. *Ibid.,* p. 44.   § Printsip. *Ibid.,* p. 22.
‖ For his early life, see H. F. Armstrong, "Confessions of the Assassin Whose Deed Led to the World War," in *Current History,* XXVI, 701–707 (August, 1927), translated from *Gavrilo Princips Bekenntnisse* (Vienna, 1927), in which they were published by the Austrian psychiatrist, Dr. Pappenheim, who attended Printsip in hospital after his sentence.

to send him to school first at his native village and then in Sarajevo, but he indulged in political propaganda, was in constant trouble with the school authorities, and finally left school. He conceived a bitter hatred for Count Tisza, and came under the influence of Vladimir Gachinovich, who may have inspired his migration to Belgrade.* In the Serbian capital he made the acquaintance of Major Milan Vasich, the secretary of the *Narodna Odbrana* and a member of the Central Committee of the *Uyedinyenye ili Smrt,* who enlisted him as a *komitadji* for the Balkan war. But though sent to Tankosich's 'cheta' (company) he was found too weak for active service, perhaps because of incipient tuberculosis, and returned to Belgrade to pursue his studies, in which he was assisted by M. Lyuba Yovanovich, the minister of education,† so that he was able to pass through three classes in one year! During the winter of 1913–1914 he was back in Bosnia, in touch with Gachinovich and Danilo Ilich and plotting with them, but in February, 1914, he returned to Belgrade to take his final examination. In Belgrade he frequented the 'Oak Garland' café, where he often saw one Milan Tsiganovich, a well-known *komitadji* and like himself a Bosnian. He is believed to have joined the *Uyedinyenye ili Smrt:*‡ which is altogether probable, for, while his name does not appear in the published list, Tsiganovich and Gachinovich, his intimate friends, were members. It is also said that during his last sojourn in Belgrade he was employed in the Serbian state printing office and on one occasion presented to the Crown Prince by the director of the establishment, Dr. Zhivoyin Dachich.§

These last details are not proved,‖ but, so far as Printsip

---

* When asked at his trial why he had gone to Belgrade, he replied: "That is my business"; Pharos, p. 22. It was about this time that Gachinovich was organizing the *kruzhok* at Sarajevo; see above, p. 148.

† Yovanovich, *The Murder at Sarajevo,* p. 4.

‡ Bogichevich, *Le procès de Salonique,* pp. 33–34, and "The Serbian Society 'Ujedinjenje ili Smrt' *alias* the 'Black Hand,' " in *KSF,* IV, 689 (September, 1926).

§ "König Alexander von Jugoslawien und die Attentäter von Sarajewo," in *KSF,* IV, 487–488 (July, 1926).

‖ F. von Wiesner, "König Alexander von Jugoslawien und die Attentäter von Sarajewo," in *KSF,* IV, 652–653, 660 (September, 1926), after examining all the

himself is concerned, they are of no importance. At his trial he described himself as a "nationalist" and a "Yugoslav," who wished to free his people by "intimidation from above"; he had derived his ideas, he said, from reading Kropotkin, Bakunin, and Spencer.* In one of his confessions shortly before his death he said:

The ideal of the young people was the unity of the South Slav peoples, Serbs, Croats and Slovenes, but not under Austria. In a kind of state republic or something of the sort. Thought that if Austria were thrown into difficulties then a revolution would come. But for such a revolution one must prepare the ground, work up feeling. Nothing happened. By assassination this spirit might be prepared.

And again:

Read much in Sarajevo. In Sarajevo used to dream every night that he was a political murderer, struggling with gendarmes and policemen. Read much about the Russian revolution, about the fightings. This idea had taken hold of him. Admits that the earlier constraints had vanished.†

Gavrilo Printsip was in short a revolutionist, he was associating with reckless men, and he was anxious, after his rejection for military service, to justify himself by some striking deed. He may have been "a small, weakly youth,"‡ but all available evidence shows that he was not lacking in either determination or courage.§

Trifko Grabezh, who came from Pale, near Sarajevo, was expelled from the gymnasium at Tuzla for having boxed his teacher on the ear, and went to Belgrade at the beginning of the Balkan wars. In 1913 he made the acquaintance of Tsigano-

evidence and making use of official documents not hitherto published, concludes that the story is not proved, though he declines to admit that the argument *ex silentio* proves the contrary.

* Pharos, p. 39.   † Armstrong, *loc. cit.*, XXVI, 703, 706.
‡ So described in the report of the trial; Pharos, p. 31.
§ An interesting analysis of Printsip's character is offered by J. Almira and G. Stoyan, *Le déclic de Sarajevo* (Paris, 1927), pp. 7–44, 80–91; they attach considerable importance to a love-affair with an unnamed young woman.

vich and others; Printsip he had known from boyhood. Although he was the son of an orthodox priest, he repudiated religion in the ordinary sense; instead he adopted "a national religion," in the interest of his own people (so he explained at his trial), whom he wished to see joined to Serbia "in a kingdom or a republic." He does not appear to have had a very positive character.* In fact, Printsip complained:

He had no energy. Reading had—he confessed—made him quite slack.†

But he appears to have trusted Grabezh more than he did his other associate Chabrinovich.

Nedelyko Chabrinovich hailed from Trebinye, where he did so badly in school that his father took him out. Apprenticed to the printer's trade, he worked in various places and landed in Belgrade in October, 1912. After two months he fell ill. At the suggestion of Printsip, he applied for assistance to the *Narodna Odbrana* and was given fifteen dinars, which he spent for Russian books! After this he walked to Sarajevo, where he secured and lost several jobs. Starting for Germany, he got only as far as Trieste. The *Wanderlust* soon seized him again, and in October, 1913, he returned to Belgrade, where he finally got a place in the state printing office at ninety dinars a month. Quite obviously, Chabrinovich was a ne'er-do-well as a workman, but though he suffered greatly, he refused to write home or to be reconciled with his father. He was also mentally befuddled, for he was in turn a socialist, an anarchist, and a revolutionist, who took Mazzini for his model. He hoped to see a Yugoslav republic established by war, but, somewhat inconsistently, hated the Archduke Francis Ferdinand as the head of the Austrian war-party. In addition, he was an atheist and claimed to be a Freemason.‡

Such was the story of his life which he related at his trial. But considerable mystery surrounds Chabrinovich. His father

* Pharos, pp. 44–47.   † Armstrong, *loc. cit.*, XXVI, 706.   ‡ Pharos, pp. 3–12.

was an agent of the Austrian secret police; according to one hypothesis,

He bitterly resented his father's rôle and at one time thought of changing his name. He did not often speak of it, but to one of his intimates he admitted that the main motive of his terrorist activity was to wash himself free from the stain and in a sense to atone for his father.*

But another hypothesis has also been put forward.† It is said that on leaving Trieste in October, 1913, Chabrinovich went to Fiume for several days and met there one Svetozar Milyanich, who was an agent of the press bureau in the Ballplatz. A fortnight later, Milyanich, who had paid a visit to Vienna in the interval, met Chabrinovich again, this time at Volosca, not far from Fiume. From Volosca, Chabrinovich proceeded to Zagreb; as he had no passport or identification papers, he was sought for by the police, but he was taken by a man named Vugorek, an Austrian secret agent who had been in Serbia during the spring as a pig merchant, to the apartment of Klobucharich, the chief of the secret police in Zagreb; there he met Dr. Gagliardi, a lawyer, who is said to have admitted that he saw Chabrinovich. It is further stated that Milyanich met Chabrinovich again in Belgrade in May, 1914, shortly before the conspirators departed for Bosnia on their fatal errand. From all this the conclusion is drawn that Chabrinovich was himself an Austrian secret agent and that a plot was concocted by which he should make a pseudo-attempt on the Archduke Francis Ferdinand, in order to provide the Austro-Hungarian Government with an excuse for intervention in Serbia; it was only in the spring of 1914, after talks with Printsip, that Chabrinovich decided to make a real attempt to murder Francis Ferdinand. Printsip, it may be noted, was for a time suspicious of his collaborator.‡

Obviously, this theory has to be treated with the greatest

* Seton-Watson, *Sarajevo*, p. 113.
† Dushan Tovdoreka, in *Novosti* (Zagreb), 11 September, 1926.
‡ Yevtich, *Сарајевски Атентат*, p. 27, and *KSF*, III, 678 (October, 1925).

possible circumspection, for it sounds inherently impossible. But it is an interesting coincidence that at the time when Chabrinovich, according to this hypothesis, was consorting with Milyanich in Fiume and Volosca, he is also reported to have told a friend at Abbazia, the next town to Volosca, of his intention to assassinate the Archduke.* Putting aside various possible deductions, one cannot help wondering whether Chabrinovich, evidently a man of weak character, was not playing a double rôle of Austrian secret agent and Serbian revolutionary, or was undecided which part to play. This possibility is certainly suggested by two incidents of his last sojourn in Belgrade. On 4 July, 1914, the Belgrade newspaper *Balkan* published the following statement:

A few weeks before the *attentat,* the murderer Chabrinovich was expelled by the Belgrade police because he had no papers; but the Austro-Hungarian consulate protested in writing and gave a guarantee for him.

This was repeated by M. Pashich in a press interview,† and, in a slightly different form, given wide circulation in the British *Blue Book* of 1914, according to which,

the Servian Government stated that . . . on a previous occasion the Austrian Government had informed the Servian Government, in reply to enquiries, that one of the [assassins] was harmless and was under their protection.‡

Later, a French writer affirmed that not only was the statement of the *Balkan* reproduced in Austria-Hungary, but that it "was neither stopped by the censor nor denied by the ministry of foreign affairs"; from which he drew the conclusion that "Chabrinovich was at Belgrade on some mission in the interest of the Austro-Hungarian Government."§ These facts, if true,

* F. von Wiesner, "War Nedéljko Cabrinovic ein österreichischer Konfident?" in *KSF*, V, 884 (September, 1927).
† *Az Est* (Budapest), 7 July; *Ö.-U. A.*, VIII, 367–368.
‡ "Introductory Narrative of Events," *Great Britain and the European Crisis* (London, 1914), p. v.
§ J. Chopin, *Le complot de Sarajevo* (Paris, 1918), p. 105.

would even support the view, widely held at one time, that the Austro-Hungarian Government had connived at the murder of Francis Ferdinand.

Actually, the facts alleged were not true. On 8 July, the *Fremdenblatt,* the mouthpiece of the Vienna foreign office, published a correction of the story in the *Balkan.* It stated that in December, 1913, the Belgrade police inquired of the Austrian consulate if the statements made by Chabrinovich about himself were true. The consulate, after communicating with the Bosnian authorities, had replied that Chabrinovich had hitherto enjoyed a good reputation [*war unbescholten*] and that his statements were correct. There had been no further communications, nor had the consulate given any guarantee for him.* As the Serbian Government did not pursue the matter further, it might seem to be settled. But it was a strange proceeding for the Bosnian police to describe Chabrinovich as 'of good reputation' if, as he stated at his trial, he had been expelled from Sarajevo for five years for taking part in a strike in 1912.† If, however, Chabrinovich was an Austrian police agent, either actual or potential, then it is easy to see why the Bosnian authorities are anxious to keep him in Belgrade. The *Fremdenblatt's* explanation rather adds to than clarifies this mystery.‡

Two days before the statement in the *Balkan,* on 29 June, that is, the day after the murder at Sarajevo, the editor of that paper was visited by three *komitadjis,* who warned him not to print anything about the connections and relations of Chabrinovich with their acquaintances nor to write anything which might compromise any Serb.§ The statement of 1 July may therefore have been a move by the editor to claim an alibi for Chabrinovich; but this does not affect the argument of the preceding paragraph.

* "Der angebliche Bürgschaft der k. und k. Regierung für Gabrinović," in *KSF*, IV, 330–331 (May, 1926); *Ö.-U. A.,* VIII, nos. 10,056, 10,073, 10,075, 10,117, 10,123.
† Pharos, p. 5.
‡ Possibly Chabrinovich's father made representations in favor of his son; but according to the latter, their relations were not friendly.
§ Report of the police prefect of Belgrade, 17/30 June, 1914, to the minister of the interior, secured by the Austrians during their occupation of Belgrade and printed in Pharos, p. 81, note 45.

One more incident in the career of this enigmatic figure was his presentation to the Crown Prince Alexander in April, 1914, on the occasion of his visit to the state printing office. The Regent spoke to various workers, inquiring if they had been in the recent war or had been wounded. Chabrinovich, however, was singled out for presentation. At his trial he said that Alexander had asked if he was a Bosnian and whether he wished to remain in Belgrade, to both of which questions he had replied in the affirmative.* If that were all, no great importance could be attached to an incident which looked like an accident. But it would appear that Chabrinovich had made a previous statement, on 25 July, 1914, set forth in a protocol which he himself signed. According to the document, Dr. Dachich had informed the Crown Prince that a Bosnian was working in the office, and the presentation had followed at Alexander's request. Chabrinovich declined to reveal what the prince had said, from fear of compromising him, "for there are many things which I know, but which, because of my convictions, I dare not speak." When it was pointed out to him that his attitude was compromising to the prince, Chabrinovich answered, "He said nothing to me," laughing as he did so.† It is curious that this was not played up at the trial, instead of which the judge contented himself with a single question. In 1916, however, during their occupation of Belgrade, the Austrians started an investigation. They discovered four employees of the state printing office who were willing to testify to the fact of a conversation between Chabrinovich and the Crown Prince. One of them deposed as follows:

The Crown Prince asked Chabrinovich when he had come to Belgrade. Chabrinovich replied, "After the Balkan wars." He could not come earlier because he could not get out of Bosnia. The Crown Prince then said, "We shall not ask now who can come from Bosnia to Serbia, because we shall now get to

* Pharos, p. 11; Wendel, p. 64.
† F. von Wiesner, "König Alexander von Jugoslawien und die Attentäter von Sarajewo," in KSF, IV, 648–649 (September, 1926); Ö.-U. A., VIII, 766–767.

Bosnia." Chabrinovich was greatly pleased by these words, and could not do any more work.

On this the former Austro-Hungarian official who has revealed these documents comments somewhat exultingly:

Chabrinovich was quite right in considering this remark compromising to the Crown Prince, for it is hardly customary for crown princes to give expression to political views of this kind to perfect strangers unless their sentiments and reliability are thoroughly known.*

He also quotes another document which tells of an investigation of the state printing office by the Belgrade police shortly after the crime at Sarajevo. This states that several employees who revealed to the police that Chabrinovich—and Printsip—were presented to the Crown Prince, were reprimanded by Dachich, who had always favored the two young men and required little work of them. And it concludes with this observation:

The intimacy which existed between Alexander and Dachich makes it out of the question that Alexander should not be accurately informed of what Dachich had in view for Printsip and Chabrinovich. That the Crown Prince should let himself be put in direct communication with these chaps [Gesellen] in order to influence them in such fashion, permits us to regard his complicity in the tragic murder at Sarajevo as proved.†

This seems rather far-fetched.

If the incidents occurred as alleged, there is obviously ground for the belief that the Crown Prince was interested in promoting the national movement, but they hardly prove his complicity with Chabrinovich in the conspiracy of Sarajevo. Furthermore, the supposedly incriminating documents were in possession of the Austro-Hungarian Government for several years before the end of the war. If it thought them compromising for Serbia, why did it not publish them? Herr von Wiesner himself does not attempt to draw unwarranted conclusions from the evidence

* *Ibid.*, pp. 657–659. † *Ibid.*, p. 655.

which he presents, and one can only agree with him that the whole matter requires further elucidation.

The bare recital of the careers of these three men is bound to create a most unfavorable impression of them, for in western Europe and America terrorism and murder are not recognized as proper methods of political controversy. Yet something may be said in extenuation. All three were mere youngsters, under twenty-one, and they suffered from ill health; they grew up in an atmosphere charged with discontent and unrest; and they were moved not by selfish personal ambitions, but by the feeling that desperate measures were necessary to relieve their people of the hated Austrian yoke. It is not at all surprising that they were susceptible to the influences of older men in Sarajevo and Belgrade and lent themselves to infernal suggestions. At the same time, they would have been less willing to become the instruments of Serbian ambitions and the tools of a terrorist organization if Habsburg rule in Bosnia had been of the kind to develop a loyalty that was proof against foreign propaganda.

At Belgrade, among their intimates was Milan Tsiganovich, who was introduced to them by a friendly waiter at one of the cafés. Tsiganovich came from Bosnia in 1908, and secured a post on the Serbian state railways. During the Balkan wars he belonged to the *komitadji* of Major Voya Tankosich, an intimate friend of Dimitriyevich, and became a well-known character. He joined the *Uyedinyenye ili Smrt* as No. 412, supposedly at the invitation of Major Tankosich, although, according to one account, it was at the suggestion of M. Pashich, who wished to have an agent in the organization.* He was said also to have been a Freemason.† Otherwise, little is known about this man. Whether he was or was not a spy upon the 'Black Hand' is a matter of great importance, for if he was, then Pashich would be kept informed of its activities. But if he was, it is remarkable that he was not known to gov-

---

* N. Mermet, "L'agent provocateur Milan Tziganovitch," in *La fédération balkanique*, nos. 20–21, p. 271 (31 May, 1925).

† Pharos, p. 12. Chabrinovich stated that Tsiganovich told him that the Freemasons had condemned Francis Ferdinand a year previously. *Ibid.*, p. 14.

ernment circles. More information on this point is needed before an opinion can be formed.*

Voya Tankosich, the right-hand man of Dimitriyevich, had taken part in the murders of 1903, himself ordering the killing of the queen's two brothers. After that he became a *komitadji* leader in Macedonia, where he won a reputation for severity and personal bravery. "His intelligence was limited, his nature simple and indifferent to complications and *nuances.* . . . Without doubt Tankosich was an honorable man and a sincere patriot, and the conviction that he was fulfilling a patriotic duty justified in his eyes many of his terrible deeds."† In 1914 he was a major in the Serbian army, and, like Tsiganovich, a Freemason. Of all the persons directly involved in the murder of the Archduke Francis Ferdinand, Tankosich seems to have been the most reckless.

One other person who played an active part in the Sarajevo plot was Danilo Ilich, of Sarajevo. Twenty-four years old, he had been a school-teacher, then worked in a bank, and finally become dependent on his mother, who took in lodgers. He was an early associate of Vladimir Gachinovich, under whose influence he had gone to Belgrade for two months in 1913, an active member of the Sarajevo *kruzhok* and an intimate friend of Printsip. He spent his time writing revolutionary articles in nationalist Serb papers in Bosnia and in carrying on propaganda among the youth. In the autumn of 1913 he was thinking of trying to assassinate General Potiorek and perhaps Francis Ferdinand. Printsip thought him "a little light-headed," but was none the less considerably influenced by him.‡

The various factors in a complicated situation have now been explained and the leading personalities described. We may accordingly examine the circumstances in which the plot for the murder of the Archduke Francis Ferdinand was hatched.

---

* There is no doubt that at a later date he was the agent of Pashich, as the Salonica trial showed; but it is not known when he assumed this rôle.

† Stanoyevich, p. 52.

‡ Pharos, pp. 59–68; Yevtich, *Сарајевски Атентат,* pp. 14–15, and *KSF,* III, 668–669 (October, 1925); Armstrong, *loc. cit.,* XXVI, 705.

THE PLOT

There are several versions of the origin of the conspiracy. The first detailed account was given by Professor Stanoyevich in 1923. He states that after the meeting of William II and Francis Ferdinand at Konopischt, Colonel Dimitriyevich received a communication from the Russian general staff, according to which "the Russian Government had certain information that at Konopischt the Emperor William had promised support for a plan of the Archduke to fall upon and overpower Serbia." From his own agents Dimitriyevich had got the plans for the Austro-Hungarian army manœuvres, which were to be held along the Serbo-Bosnian frontier.* These two reports persuaded Dimitriyevich that "the attack on Serbia and war could be prevented only by the murder of the Archduke, for at that time public opinion among the Serbs universally regarded him as the greatest enemy of the Serb people and the principal originator of all action against them." At that moment Major Voya Tankosich informed him that two young Bosnians were in Belgrade who wished to murder the Archduke.

They had asked for advice and instructions. Dimitriyevich at once accepted and approved of their intention, and had Tankosich teach the young men the use of weapons, which consumed ten days. After that they departed, and the murder was

---

* Dimitriyevich's agent was Rade Malobabich, one of the fifty-three persons accused in the Zagreb trial of 1909 and later a 'confidential man' of the *Narodna Odbrana;* he was introduced to Dimitriyevich in 1913. *Тајна Превратна Организација,* p. 201; Durham, *The Serajevo Crime,* p. 162. Wendel, p. 50, states that what Malobabich transmitted was a 'mobilization' plan; Durham, p. 156, suggests that this may have been the plan of 1908-1909, which did call for a concentration along the frontier. Actually, the manœuvres involved only two army corps and were held at some distance from the frontier, to the southwest of Sarajevo, that is toward the Adriatic (as if against an invading Italian army), and not in the direction of Serbia. A. von Wegerer, "Der Anlass zum Weltkrieg," in *KSF,* III, 386-387 (June, 1925); L. Schnagl, "Die Manöver in Bosnien im Jahre 1914" in *ibid.,* VI, 873-881 (September, 1928). The Austro-Hungarian plan for an invasion of Serbia was to attack farther north along the Drina river, which, as will be seen, was a factor of some consequence in the negotiations of July, 1914; Conrad, I, 361-423, IV, 112-124. The report sent to his government by the French minister in Belgrade of 100,000 troops being concentrated along the Serbian frontier in Bosnia-Herzegovina and Dalmatia (Poincaré, IV, 182) seems to have had no foundation.

executed according to the plan which had been worked out in
Sarajevo by the schoolmaster Danilo Ilich.

Dimitriyevich and Tankosich told no one anything about all
this. Only on 15 June did Dimitriyevich call a meeting of the
Central Committee of the *Union or Death* and communicate to
it that he and Tankosich had sent people to Bosnia to murder
the heir apparent Francis Ferdinand. . . .

Almost all of the members of the committee opposed the
plan, and a long and lively discussion arose. Finally, under
pressure from his associates, Dimitriyevich declared that he was
ready to countermand it and to send orders to Sarajevo that the
attentat should not be carried out. It appears that he did make
such an effort, but either it was too late, or the conspirators
would not obey him. The thing took its fatal course.*

That Colonel Dimitriyevich was involved in the Sarajevo
crime, was asserted as far back as 1917. When he and two
other officers were condemned at Salonica for the alleged attempt on the life of the Crown Prince Alexander, friends of
Serbia in western Europe, including the British war office,
remonstrated against the death-sentence imposed on the convicted officers. They were told in reply that Dimitriyevich's
responsibility for the Sarajevo murders was established.† This
assertion was, of course, not given any publicity, but a year
later the Serbian foreign minister affirmed that there existed "a
written document which of itself made Dimitriyevich's pardon
out of the question."‡ After the war, but before the appearance
of Professor Stanoyevich's pamphlet, the same statesman asserted, in reply to one of the periodic demands for a revision
of the verdict of the Salonica trial, that Dimitriyevich had
signed a paper accepting the entire responsibility for the crime
at Sarajevo.§ Unfortunately, the document has never been

* Stanoyevich, pp. 54–56. H. Wendel, pp. 49–51, gives the same version.
† Seton-Watson, *Sarajevo*, p. 143.
‡ S. Protich, "A Serbian Protest," in *The New Europe*, VIII, 259 (26 September,
1918).
§ *Radikal* (Belgrade), no. 294 of 1922; Seton-Watson, *Sarajevo*, p. 144. The
document seems to be very closely guarded. The writer has talked with a close
political associate of Stoyan Protich, who asserted that while he had often heard
the document spoken of, he himself had never seen it. It was supposed to be in
possession of Lyuba Yovanovich, who died shortly before the writer's visit to Bel-

published. Nevertheless, Dimitriyevich's complicity in the plot is now generally assumed.

Professor Stanoyevich's story has, however, to be discounted in part. The mystery of Konopischt has already been discussed.* But apart from that the chronology of his account is impossible. He states that the conspirators were trained for ten days in the use of weapons, and that some days later, on 15 June, the Central Committee of the *Uyedinyenye ili Smrt* was taken into the secret. But the interview at Konopischt occurred on 12 June. Obviously the plot was not inspired by any reports of what had been decided upon by the German Emperor and the Austrian heir apparent at Konopischt. It is known, furthermore, that the conspirators left Belgrade at the end of May. The statement that information was received from the Russian general staff concerning the interview at Konopischt also appears to be inaccurate. The Russian military attaché in Belgrade, Colonel Artamonov, received no such information and left his post on 19 June for a two months' leave in Switzerland,† and the officer temporarily and unofficially in charge of his work, Captain Verkhovski, made no communication to the Serbian Government. In July the military attaché was informed that

up to this moment the general staff has not given any orders, and for that reason M. Verkhovski has refrained from entering into relations with the minister of war, as well as from opening the communications sent you from St. Petersburg and reading them.

grade. In some quarters the writer found a disposition to question the value of the document. The belief was expressed by those familiar with the circumstances of the Salonica trial that Dimitriyevich was induced to sign this compromising statement at the moment when the negotiations were proceeding with Austria-Hungary for a separate peace, an appeal being made to his patriotism to sacrifice himself in the interest of the country. In support of this theory the passage in Dimitriyevich's will was cited in which he says: "Although condemned to death by both courts and denied the favor of the crown, I die innocent and in the conviction that my death is necessary to Serbia on higher grounds." It is therefore argued by the friends of Dimitriyevich that the document proves nothing. This theory, which at present can be neither proved nor disproved, is an excellent illustration of the uncertainty which still shrouds the tragedy of Sarajevo.

* See above, pp. 169–170.

† Statement of Colonel Artamonov to the writer. Cf. Report of Gellinek, 19 June, 1914; *Ö.-U. A.*, VIII, 158.

Here there is no news which might compel Verkhovski to send reports or despatches. . . .*

If, as is possible, the Russian Government made some communication to the Serbian minister or the Serbian military attaché in St. Petersburg, the fact is not attested in any published document; but if any such communication was made, it seems most unlikely that the Russian minister in Belgrade, M. Hartwig, would, as he informed Colonel Artamonov, have planned to go on leave on 16 July.†

The following explanation of this version of the plot is offered as at least a plausible solution of the enigma. Early in May, 1914, certain young men from Bosnia then in Belgrade went to Voya Tankosich and asked for arms and ammunition, and for leave to go to Bosnia and assassinate Francis Ferdinand, whose coming visit to the province had already been announced. As he refused, they then went to Dimitriyevich, who at last gave five of them leave to go, without informing any one, not even Tankosich. These five youths got as far as Shabats, close to the Bosnian frontier, where they were to pass through a 'tun-

---

* Hartwig to Artamonov, 24 June [*i. e.*, 7 July, N. S.] 1914; *Slavonic Review*, VI, 710 (March, 1928).

† It is interesting to note that Dimitriyevich himself gave the same version. Colonel C. A. Popovich, in *Novosti* (Zagreb), 28 June, 1924, the tenth anniversary of the murder, stated that he had talked with Dimritiyevich about Sarajevo in 1915. "Is it true," he asked the colonel, "that you took part in the *attentat* of Sarajevo? If so, what was your part, and what was your idea?" Dimitriyevich replied that before the war the Serbian general staff received news from a friendly state about decisions reached at Konopischt, to the effect that if Austria attacked Serbia, Germany would give diplomatic and then military support. All reports agreed that preparations had been made for Austria to attack Serbia. Serbia was not ready and it was doubtful if she could resist; furthermore it was reported that Francis Ferdinand was personally interested. The reports of manœuvres in Bosnia were confirmed, and they could easily be transformed into an armed attack, for which diplomatic action could provide the excuse, *e. g.*, on the question of the Oriental Railway [which was then pending between Austria-Hungary and Serbia]. He was convinced that Austria-Hungary would attack in 1914 and that Serbia would lose everything. The Serbian army was mostly in South Serbia [Macedonia], and there were only five regiments of new recruits available in the north. The problem was, How could Francis Ferdinand be forestalled? Although it is hard to understand how Dimitriyevich could persuade himself that the elimination of Francis Ferdinand by violent means would stave off an Austro-Hungarian attack, he does appear to have followed this line of reasoning; at least Bogichevich, *Le Colonel Dragoutine Dimitriévitch Apis*, pp. 98–99, quotes an intimate of 'Apis' to this effect.

nel,' but on the night before they were to cross the Drina, one of them, while drunk, let out the secret of their mission. The police heard the story, and the prefect arrested the conspirators and reported the matter to Belgrade. The government investigated this action of Dimitriyevich, which added greatly to the tension then prevailing between the army and the civil government, of which we have already spoken.* In consequence, M. Pashich addressed a letter to General Putnik calling his attention to the activities of his subordinate which, he said, might have dangerous consequences.† In spite of this, however, Dimitriyevich subsequently allowed Printsip and his associates to undertake their mission. In such circumstances, it would be a natural proceeding for him to invent the story of a communication from Russia as a justification for the plot which had been previously arranged, and if he told such a story to the committee of the *Uyedinyenye ili Smrt,* the survivors of that meeting would readily tell it to Messrs. Stanoyevich and Wendel.

It may well be that the warning of Pashich served as a direct incentive to Dimitriyevich to let Printsip, Chabrinovich, and Grabezh go to Sarajevo, but there is some reason for thinking that he did not take them very seriously. At least he told Colonel Popovich that he had not thought the enterprise likely to succeed, for the conspirators were too young;‡ he is even said, when the news of their success reached him on 28 June, 1914, to have exclaimed, "Good heavens! What have we done?" [Бре, бре, шта учинисмо?].§ Whether Dimitriyevich really tried to prevent the murder is a point on which no evidence is available.

---

* Y. M. Yovanovich, in *Politika* (Belgrade), 4 December, 1926, reprinted in *KSF*, V, 84 (January, 1927). Fay, II, 116, rejects the story as "improbable"; but M. Yovanovich told the writer that he had seen the official *dossier* on the matter. Professor Fay argues from the fact that "the three youths [Printsip, Chabrinovich, and Grabezh] nowhere [in their trial] make any mention of this first arrest"; he seems to miss the point that these three youths were not involved in this first attempt and probably knew nothing about it.

† Bogichevich, *Le Colonel Dragoutine Dimitriévitch Apis*, p. 98.

‡ C. A. Popovich, in *Novosti*, 28 June, 1924. Several persons with whom the writer talked, one of them a personal friend of Dimitriyevich, insisted that the latter did not understand that Francis Ferdinand was the intended victim of the plot; but this seems very unlikely.

§ According to a seemingly well-authenticated story told to the writer.

It is true that Ilich, at his trial, claimed that he had sought to dissuade Printsip and Grabezh from executing the plot;* but since he put forward no such claim at his preliminary investigation, one suspects that Ilich was merely trying to save his own neck. But since Dimitriyevich, Tankosich, Printsip, Chabrinovich, and Grabezh are all dead, we shall probably never know the exact whole truth, and one can only repeat that the argument here presented is only an hypothesis.

This Dimitriyevich version, if it may be so called, has reference only to the month or so before the execution of the plot, nor does it explain how Printsip and his friends came by the idea of killing Francis Ferdinand. As it happens, other revelations, inspired no doubt by the pamphlet of Professor Stanoyevich, indicate that the idea of an *attentat* began to be mooted as early as the autumn of 1913. If Printsip's memory can be trusted, he and Ilich "in October or November, 1913," "resolved that one of them should make an attempt on Potiorek," though they presently abandoned the notion, as Printsip "thought he was not yet ripe and independent enough to think about it" and there was no organization.† In December of that year, according to the testimony of Mustapha Golubich and Paul Bastayich, two members of the *Uyedinyenye ili Smrt*,‡ Tankosich in the autumn of 1913 instructed Gachinovich, then in Lausanne, to assemble the leaders of *Mlada Bosna* in Toulouse to arrange for the assassination of the Archduke Francis Ferdinand and other Austro-Hungarian officials. The meeting was held in January, 1914; only three persons appeared, Gachinovich, Golubich, and a Mohammedan Serb, Mohammed Mehmedbashich, two others who were expected from Paris not having sufficient funds for the journey. Gachinovich urged the assassination of Francis Ferdinand, in the expectation that the

* Pharos, pp. 65–66. This was confirmed by both Printsip and Grabezh; *ibid.*, pp. 29, 41, 52.

† Confession of 18 May, 1916; Armstrong, *loc. cit.*, XXVI, 705.

‡ M. Bogichevich, "Nouvelles dépositions concernant l'attentat de Sarajevo," in *KSF*, IV, 21–27 (January, 1926); *Évolution* (Paris), I, 15–23 (January, 1926); and *Le procès de Salonique*, pp. 151–163.

Slavs of Austria-Hungary would rise in revolt and even a European war might be provoked, and apparently this was agreed to in principle. But it was decided first of all to assassinate General Potiorek, who was held immediately responsible for the existing régime in Bosnia. Gachinovich provided Mehmedbashich with arms and poison, and he was instructed, after arranging the details with Ilich, to seek an audience of General Potiorek and kill him. Actually, nothing came of this scheme.*

Meanwhile, according to the Golubich-Bastayich version, Gachinovich had written to Printsip, then in Sarajevo, that he and Ilich should come to Lausanne to discuss the arrangements for assassinating Francis Ferdinand. Ilich, however, first sent Printsip to Belgrade to consult Tankosich. That enterprising person declared that there was no need for Ilich to proceed to Lausanne, for it had already been decided in Belgrade that the Archduke was to be assassinated, and he kept Printsip to instruct him in revolver-shooting. Informed of the change of plan, Ilich himself went to Belgrade a few days before the murder and received final instructions from Dimitriyevich. Upon his return to Sarajevo, he, Mehmedbashich, and Printsip sent a postcard to Gachinovich bearing the words "Revolutionary greetings," as well as a letter informing him of their plans.

In March the Zagreb *Srbobran* published an announcement that the Archduke Francis Ferdinand would attend the army manœuvres in Bosnia in the spring of 1914 and pay a visit to Sarajevo on 28 June, which was the anniversary of the battle of Kossovo in 1389, when the mediæval Serbian state had been overthrown, and a day of Serbian national mourning. The

---

* According to Dushan Tovdoreka, in *Novosti*, 23 September, 1926, Mehmedbashich, while travelling from Ragusa to Mostar, was challenged by a gendarme looking for a deserter, and in his fright threw away his knife and poison. Later he managed to secure a revolver and tried to shoot Potiorek on 26 March, 1914, at the installation of the *reis-el-ulema*, but could not get close enough. Seton-Watson, *Sarajevo*, p. 74, gives a somewhat different account, derived from intimates of Gachinovich: "But the youthful conspirators' nerve failed them; fearing a Customs examination on their return across the Austrian frontier, they threw the weapons out of the carriage window, and nothing further came of this design." He gives the date of the Toulouse meeting as January, 1913, but he has clearly been misinformed, for Gachinovich took part in the Balkan war in the winter of 1912–1913.

revolutionary group in Sarajevo was greatly disturbed by this news, for they feared the effect of the visit on the conservative and Catholic elements in Bosnia, and they resented the choice of Kossovo Day for the visit to Sarajevo as a deliberate insult. Probably they were not aware of the plans of Ilich and Printsip, which obviously required the utmost secrecy. So one of the group, Michael Pushara, cut the announcement from the *Srbobran* and sent it, without any comment save the word "Greetings," to Chabrinovich in Belgrade.[*]

When Chabrinovich received the newspaper clipping from Sarajevo, he showed it to his friend Printsip, and they began to discuss the murder of the Archduke.[†] As they lacked the necessary weapons, they turned to their friend Tsiganovich, who promised to provide what was necessary and to convey them to Bosnia through a 'tunnel.' Meanwhile Grabezh returned to Belgrade, and when he expressed to Printsip and Chabrinovich his indignation over the visit of the Archduke, he was invited to join the conspiracy. Tsiganovich had a private supply of bombs, collected no doubt in his *komitadji* days, but for revolvers he had to go to Tankosich, taking Grabezh with him. Tankosich, after securing the revolvers from Dimitriyevich, who is said to have paid for them out of his own pocket,[‡] instructed Tsiganovich to give Grabezh lessons in shooting, which he did in Topchider Park near Belgrade. Later Printsip and Chabrinovich also practised the art, but without the assistance of Tsiganovich. Finally, in front of the 'Little Goldfish' café, Tsiganovich handed over to the three young men six bombs, four Browning pistols, 130

---

[*] Yevtich, *Сарајевски Атентат,* pp. 25–26, and *KSF,* III, 676–677 (October, 1925). Yevtich did not belong to the inner circle, so was not likely to know what Ilich and Printsip were planning. But the fact that it was thought sufficient to send the announcement to Chabrinovich without any explanation shows that the idea of assassinating Franz Ferdinand came to the Bosnian revolutionary group independently of any suggestion from Belgrade.

[†] At the trial, when Chabrinovich tried to claim the credit for the initiative, Printsip asserted that he had decided to make the attempt before he was shown the clipping; Pharos, p. 40. Grabezh also claimed that he had formed the idea at Easter, 1914, when he read of the Archduke's visit in a local paper; *ibid.,* p. 45.

[‡] M. Bogichevich, "Weitere Einzelheiten über das Attentat von Sarajewo," in *KSF,* III, 440, note 1 (July, 1925). Bogichevich says that Dimitriyevich showed him the receipted bill of the Serbian state arsenal at Krageyuvats for the weapons.

dinars, a road-map of Bosnia, some cyanide of potassium, and a note to the frontier official at Shabats, at the same time instructing them that they should avoid the civil authorities. Thus equipped the conspirators left Belgrade at the end of May, in order that they might arrive in Sarajevo long enough before the visit of the Archduke to avoid arousing the suspicions of the local authorities.* At their trial the conspirators never mentioned the name of Dimitriyevich, much less being received by him (according to the version of Professor Stanoyevich),† so it is not clear whether they were even aware of his existence.

Meanwhile Ilich had been busy at Sarajevo. Not only did he, on receipt of a letter from Printsip telling of the plans, agree to make the necessary local arrangements, but he enlisted three more young men as 'reserves,' Mohammed Mehmedbashich, Tsvetko Popovich, and Vaso Chubrilovich, the latter a 'confidential man' of the *Narodna Odbrana* and a member of the *Uyedinyenye ili Smrt*. It is said that Pushara, who sent the clipping to Chabrinovich, went off to look for the Archduke elsewhere (though he returned to Sarajevo before the murder); and that "in at least one of the Dalmatian towns some youths had resolved to shoot the Archduke if he passed through their district, and that they possessed the necessary weapons."‡ Thus was the train laid for the tragic events of 28 June, 1914.§

---

* This paragraph is based on the testimony of the three conspirators at their trial, in Pharos, pp. 7–10, 23–25, 32–34, 45–48.

† C. A. Popovich, in *Novosti*, 28 June, 1924, represents Dimitriyevich as saying that Tankosich came to his office and told him that several young men were anxious to kill Francis Ferdinand, and asked whether he should let them go. Tankosich, after convincing himself that the conspirators could be depended upon (Pharos, p. 47), appears to have kept in the background as much as possible. In conversation with an Italian journalist during the Serbian retreat of 1915, Tankosich exclaimed: "Chabrinovich and Printsip! What men! I knew that they would not fail to strike! Silent and sure men: they had only to be prepared and instructed!" He added that neither the *Narodna Odbrana* nor the government was involved in the plot, but " 'others,' determined guardians of the destinies of Serbia, knew and approved." L. Magrini, *Il dramma di Seraievo* (Milan, 1929), p. 94.

‡ Seton-Watson, *Sarajevo*, pp. 147, 79.

§ At the trial of the conspirators the question several times came up whether this or that individual was a Freemason; it was asserted (see above, pp. 212, 218) that Chabrinovich, Tsiganovich, and Tankosich were all Freemasons. Both Printsip and Chabrinovich stated that Tsiganovich had told them that the Freemasons had condemned Francis Ferdinand to death; Pharos, pp. 14, 33. The theory has accordingly been often advanced that the plot against Francis Ferdinand was

WAS THE SERBIAN GOVERNMENT INVOLVED?

If, as there is ample reason for thinking, the plot was approved, and perhaps promoted, by Dragutin Dimitriyevich, who in 1914 was chief of the intelligence section of the Serbian general staff, the question at once arises, Was the Serbian Government in any way involved in the dastardly enterprise? That it was directly responsible or was even aware of the plot, was not charged by the Austro-Hungarian Government in July, 1914, and, in view of the situation in which Serbia found herself at that time, connivance seemed inherently improbable.

The country had not recovered from the Balkan wars of 1912–1913. The army was depleted,* the peasants were reluc-

---

really the work of the Freemasons, *e. g.*, by E. Graf zu Reventlow, *Die politische Vorgeschichte des Grossen Krieges* (Berlin, 1919), pp. 29–38, and L. de Poncins, "L'attentat de Serajevo et la franc-maçonnerie," in *Mercure de France*, CCXI, 121–131 (1 April, 1929). The evidence at the trial suggests that the matter was dragged in by the lawyers for the defense as a red herring, to throw the prosecution off the scent of the *Uyedinyenye ili Smrt;* it is interesting to note, however, that Dr. E. Fischer, *Die kritischen 39 Tage von Sarajewo zum Weltbrand* (Berlin, 1928), pp. 30–32, does not altogether reject the idea of Masonic complicity. In this connection the following story told to the writer by a former Austro-Hungarian official is not without interest. On a certain occasion after the war (the place and the time were indicated) he was discussing the question of Sarajevo with a group of friends. The view generally held was that Serbia was responsible for the murder, but one person, himself also a former official, expressed dissent. He said that about three weeks before the war he had received instructions from the Hungarian ministry of finance in Budapest to pay 500 crowns in 20-crown gold coins to the Austrian secret agent in Belgrade. He had secured the money from a bank, noting that among the 25 coins there were 3 'millenary' coins (struck to commemorate the millenary of Hungary in 1896), which were very rare. He had given the money to the secret agent. When Printsip's house was searched after the murder, 25 gold pieces were found, including 3 'millenary' coins. The writer's informant, pursuing the matter, had subsequently learned that the telegram from Budapest, though not listed in the registry of the Hungarian ministry of finance, had been sent by a high official who was a Freemason. "This," he said, "was in accord with the statement of Colonel Dimitriyevich that the Budapest Freemasons had supported the *attentat.*" The document published by *John Bull* (London) on 11 July, 1914, which purported to be a promise of £2,000 "for the total elimination of Francis Ferdinand" has also been ascribed to Freemasonry; C. H. Norman, *A Search-light on the European War* (London, 1924), pp. 42–43. But the evidence of any complicity of Freemasonry in the plot is much too slight to warrant offering it as a substantial factor in the murder of Sarajevo.

* General Z. Pavlovich, *Битка на Јадру* [The Struggle on the Yadar] (Belgrade, 1924, volume I of the official Serbian history of the war), pp. 53–55, gives details. There were only 120,000 rifles available. The Schneider-Creusot 75's had been subjected to a severe strain during the Balkan wars and many were worn out; the deficiency was by no means made up by the Krupp guns captured from the Turks. There were only 12 siege guns, and no heavy artillery. Munitions were very short, there were no tents, transport services were poorly organized. The army was, so to speak, "naked and barefoot" (p. 55).

tant to take the field on the eve of harvest; the stock of munitions, uniforms, and medical supplies had not been replenished;
the finances were heavily burdened. As has already been noted,
a bitter struggle was being waged between the government and
the army, headed by the *Uyedinyenye ili Smrt,* over Macedonia
and for the control of the Skupshtina. And, as if domestic difficulties were not enough, numerous international problems imposed caution. To the west the new Albanian kingdom was a
source of constant concern. With the Austro-Hungarian Government delicate negotiations were in progress for the transfer
to Serbia of that part of the Oriental Railway which lay within
the newly acquired territories. The question of a customs and
military union with Montenegro was still pending. The con-
cordat with the Vatican dealing with the position of the Catho-
lics in 'Old Serbia' had not yet gone into operation. Every consideration demanded for Serbia a period of recuperation; every
argument warranted the view that Serbian statesmen would not
have countenanced any action against the Dual Monarchy
which, in the existing state of Austro-Serbian relations, must,
in all probability, lead to reprisals likely to be disastrous to
Serbia.*

Such reasoning remained convincing until 1924, when a Serbian politician pulled down the house of cards. To celebrate the
tenth anniversary of the outbreak of war, a Russian journalist
living in Belgrade, M. Ksyunyin, published an 'almanac' entitled *Krv Slovenstva* ('Blood of Slavdom'), the opening
article of which was written by M. Lyuba Yovanovich, the
minister of education in the Pashich cabinet of 1914. M.
Yovanovich, in default of an article *ad hoc* which he had promised, contributed selections from his memoirs, remarking, incidentally, that "the time is not yet come for everything to be
disclosed." His subject was "After Vidovdan, 1914," and in
the second paragraph he plunged *in medias res:*

---

* Even Bogichevich [a bitter enemy of the Pashich régime], *Le Colonel Dragoutine
Dimitriévich Apis,* pp. 97–98, 102, concedes that in 1914 the Serbian Government
was anxious for peace.

I do not remember whether it was at the end of May or the beginning of June, when one day M. Pashich said to us (he conferred on these matters more particularly with Stoyan Protich, who was then minister of the interior; but he said this much to the rest of us) that there were people who were preparing to go to Sarajevo to kill Francis Ferdinand, who was to go there to be solemnly received on *Vidov Dan.* . . .

On the afternoon of *Vidov Dan* I was in my house on the Senyak. About five o'clock an official telephoned to me from the press bureau, and told me what had happened at noon at Sarajevo. Even though I knew what had been prepared there, nevertheless I felt, as I held the receiver, as though some one had dealt me an unexpected blow.*

Late in 1924 this passage began to be commented upon in Yugoslavia, in western Europe, and in the United States.

It was certainly definite enough. But was it true? Stoyan Protich was dead, but M. Pashich was very much alive; in fact, he was at the head of the Yugoslav Government. Yet he said not a word, and it was easy to conclude that there was nothing he could say. Professor R. W. Seton-Watson, the well-known English friend of the Yugoslavs, thereupon wrote a letter to the London *Times* (16 February, 1925), in which he called upon Messrs. Pashich and Yovanovich to

issue a statement sufficiently clear to exculpate them and their colleagues from the charge now being levelled against them by their enemies in England and Germany, of foreknowledge of, and deliberate connivance at, the crime at Sarajevo.

As this appeal produced no results, Mr. Seton-Watson proceeded to Yugoslavia for investigations on the spot. This fact being duly advertised in Belgrade, M. Yovanovich published a series of articles in the local press (*Novi Zhivot* and *Politika*),† in which he ranged over the whole field of Serbian history for forty years past, but made no reference to the matter at issue, except to say that his alleged revelation was no revelation, for

---

* Yovanovich, *Крв Словенства*, pp. 9-10; *The Murder of Sarajevo*, pp. 3-4.

† Translated in part in *KSF*, III, 211-220, 270-292 (April, May, 1925).

"it was something that had long been known and talked about
in Serbia." Whereupon Mr. Seton-Watson published an open
letter in *Nova Europa* (Zagreb) asking M. Yovanovich if he
stood by his statement in *Krv Sloventsva* and whether "he
actually meant it when he said, describing how he received over
the telephone the news of the Sarajevo murder, 'although I
knew what was being prepared there.' "* M. Yovanovich did
not reply to the question, and there the matter rested, so far as
Serbia was concerned.

In Europe and the United States, however, the assertions of
M. Yovanovich continued to attract attention; German writers
naturally made great play with them. So on 26 March, 1926,
M. George Yelenich, former secretary to the Crown Prince and
a henchman of M. Pashich, addressed a communication to the
Central Committee of the Serbian Radical party. Declaring
the statement of M. Yovanovich in *Krv Slovenstva* to be "one
complete lie" "from the first to the last letter," he called upon
M. Pashich and the survivors of the government of 1914
to affirm that "there had been no talk in the pre-war Serbian
cabinet of an *attentat* planned at Sarajevo." This challenge
aroused Professor Milan Zechevich, a friend of M. Yovanovich, to make an explanation. Yovanovich, he said, had not
spoken of a meeting of ministers, but had referred to a private
conversation, and he added that "what Yovanovich reports are
facts that had already become known during the war." Then
certain survivors of the *Uyedinyenye ili Smrt,* Colonels Popovich and Milanovich, threatened to tell what they knew of the
whole business.†

Up to this time M. Pashich had shown indifference and maintained silence; true, he denied privately the truth of M. Yovanovich's charges, but publicly he would say nothing. Now
his hand was being forced. At a meeting of the Radical party
on 25 April, 1926, he at last made a statement:

---

* Reprinted in *Obzor* (Zagreb), 13 May, 1925. Translated, in German, in *KSF*,
IV, 394–395 (June, 1925).
  † *Politika* (Belgrade), 26, 28, 29, 31 March, 1926; translated in *KSF*, IV, 400–406
(June, 1926).

Foreign correspondents had asked him if he had known that the Austrian heir apparent was to be murdered. This he had repudiated. He had requested M. Yovanovich to deny this, for it was not true that he, Pashich, had asserted this at a meeting of the council of ministers. . . . Immediately on his return from Bucharest he had advised the *Narodna Odbrana* to undertake nothing against Austria, for this would be dangerous. He had waited for the denial of M. Yovanovich. M. Yovanovich had hesitated to give this and had not done so.

He repeated his assertion that he had not said what M. Yovanovich had ascribed to him. He had even asked his colleagues, "Friends, have I not perhaps forgotten that I said this?" And all of them had affirmed that he had really not said this.

It has not been denied, and now the question is being agitated. "So I must deny it. I do not know why M. Lyuba Yovanovich has said it, but he has said what is not true. He has done all this of his own initiative, and if any one has done this, independently of an agreement with his colleagues, it is dangerous."*

To this accusation M. Yovanovich replied that he had not said that M. Pashich made his communication to a meeting of the ministers, but that he had done so in private conversation. [The text of the statement in *Krv Slovenstva* does admit of this interpretation, though it is not the natural one.] And he added, according to another account, that he could produce documents and proofs for his assertion,† but he would do so only if the premier, M. Uzunovich, and the foreign minister, M. Ninchich, would assume the responsibility;‡ which, in fact, they declined to do.

For his pains, M. Yovanovich was read out of the Radical

---

* *Politika*, 26 April, 1926; translated in *KSF*, IV, 409 (June, 1926). In this translation, Pashich was represented as saying, "I do not know what M. Lyuba Yovanovich has said, but what he has said is not true" (!). It was subsequently pointed out (*ibid.*, IV, 100 [September, 1926]) that this was an incorrect rendering of the Serbian, and that what Pashich had said was, "I do not know why M. Lyuba Yovanovich has said it, but he has said what is not true"—which is very different.

† Supposedly the declaration said to have been signed by Dimitriyevich at Salonica in 1917 admitting his responsibility for the murder; see above, pp. 221–222.

‡ *Obzor* (Zagreb), 27 April, 1926; *ibid.*, IV, 413.

party, but the polemics leave the matter very much where it was. Mr. Seton-Watson believes that "M. Yovanovich for reasons of his own has misrepresented the true facts":

> He is one of those politicians who like to exaggerate their own importance. . . . I have the authority of one of the most distinguished Serbian writers and historians for the statement that, on the day after the murder of King Alexander and Queen Draga in 1903, he himself met M. Yovanovich in the streets of Belgrade, and in reply to his anxious inquiry for news was given to understand that he had known what was brewing for some time past. . . . But to any one who knows anything of that sinister affair, it is notorious that M. Yovanovich had nothing whatever to do with it. . . . I believe that M. Yovanovich was as ignorant of the plot of 1914 as he was of the plot of 1903.

Since the war the Radical party had fought hard to gain control of Bosnia-Herzegovina, but without great success. Now the younger generation in these provinces regards the revolutionary movement of 1913–1914 with feelings of admiration and looks upon Printsip and his associates as martyrs. So, in the opinion of the British writer, it occurred to M. Yovanovich to make a bid for the support of the Bosnian youth by showing that the pre-war government in Serbia, which was thoroughly Radical, had sympathized with the revolutionary movement: if he were successful, he would have a powerful lever in his contest with Pashich for the control of the Radical party. The wily Pashich, for his part, preferred "to use the incident to isolate a dangerous competitor for the party leadership than to clear the honor of his country." He was reluctant, so Mr. Seton-Watson complained,

> to stand up before his countrymen and to produce the proofs (which I have reason to believe him to possess) that he, as leader of the nation in 1914, was ignorant, and even disapproved, of an underground movement which some admire as having led directly to national unity.*

* Seton-Watson, *Sarajevo*, pp. 157–159.

These arguments are not very convincing. If M. Yova-novich had been bidding for the support of the Bosnian youth, he would surely have chosen a more spectacular manner of making his revelation than by writing an article in an obscure publication. In the second place, when M. Pashich did finally "stand up before his countrymen," he did not produce the proofs which Mr. Seton-Watson believes him to possess, he did not deny the charges of his rival with definiteness and precision; at least he did not say categorically that he knew nothing of the plot. It would be rash to affirm that either politician told the whole truth and nothing but the truth, but up to the death of M. Pashich in December, 1926, M. Yovanavich seemed to have the better of the controversy.*

Since the death of M. Yovanovich in February, 1928, a French writer has revealed that M. Yovanovich stated to him on 26 March, 1925, that is, at the time when Professor Seton-Watson was bombarding him with inconvenient letters, but a year before Pashich made any statement, that

The preparations for the *attentat* were revealed to Pashich, Yovan Yovanovich, Serbian minister at Vienna, and myself —no doubt in rather vague form [*en termes assez imprécis*] —at the end of May or the beginning of June by Milan Pribi-chevich.†

This statement may contain the clue to the enigma, namely, that the Serbian Government received information that *a* plot was being prepared, without learning the details. But more

---

* In the last years of his life, Pashich was said to have busied himself greatly with the question of Sarajevo and to have completed a book on the subject, for which he made extensive use of official documents and of information communi-cated by Serbian ministers and politicians; *Vreme* (Belgrade), 14 December, 1926, quoted in *KSF*, V, 173 (February, 1927). Since then nothing has been heard of this book.

† A. Mousset, "L'attentat de Sarajevo," in *Revue d'histoire moderne*, III, 326 (September–October, 1928). The usual assumption by those who accept the ver-sion of Yovanovich is that the secret was revealed to Pashich by Milan Tsigano-vich, who was a member of the *Uyedinyenye ili Smrt*, although there is no proof of this. Milan Pribichevich was secretary of the *Narodna Odbrana* in 1914; accord-ing to information given to the writer, he was not a member of the *Uyedinyenye ili Smrt*, and disapproved of terroristic methods; cf., however, *Ö.-U. A.*, VIII, 384–385.

recently still an Italian writer has published an account of a conversation in 1915, during the Serbian retreat, with a Serbian officer, Major Milan Georgevich, formerly chargé at Constantinople and son of a former premier, Vladan Georgevich. Georgevich stated that

news of the conspiracy organized by the 'Black Hand' began to leak out in high circles several weeks before the murder at Sarajevo. Pashich learned of it in the first fortnight of June, and, in face of the insolence of the 'Black Hand,' yet fearing greatly the consequences of an attempt on the Archduke, was left rather embarrassed; after several days of hesitation as to what to do, he communicated the news to his colleagues of the government and indicated the dangers which might arise. His decision to obstruct the plan of the conspirators as far as possible met with the full approval of the other ministers. But the conspirators had already passed the frontier.*

Unfortunately, this statement does not make clear just how much Pashich learned about the plot; but it supports the story of Ljuba Yovanovich and weakens the denials of Pashich.

But until more specific information is forthcoming, debate on the question is obviously futile. It may, however, be worth while to remark that, however exact the knowledge of the Serbian Government may have been, it is not suggested by any of the evidence that the government approved of the plot or assisted in its preparation.

Was Russia in any way involved?

RUSSIAN COMPLICITY?

Russian complicity is expressly charged by several writers. The first is M. Vladimirov, thought by some to be a pseudonym of Mustapha Golubich. He writes as follows:

When Danilo Ilich went to Belgrade in May, 1914, and announced that he had found the men and that everything was ready except arms and money, Colonel Dimitriyevich summoned

---

* Magrini, *Il dramma di Seraievo*, pp. 106–107.

the Russian military attaché in Belgrade, Artamonov, to put
him *au courant* and to ask him what Russia would think of it.
Artamonov requested him to wait for several days. A few days
later he reported that Russia acquiesced, and that in case
of war she would be on the side of Serbia. Colonel Dimitriyevich had to wait until Artamonov had consulted Pashich and
King Alexander through the medium of Hartwig, the Russian minister in Belgrade—and also his government.*

Probably the source of his information is Colonel Bozhin Sim-
ich, a friend of Dimitriyevich now living in exile, whose story,
somewhat elaborated, has been published in a French communist
magazine. The latter version is worth quoting verbatim:

'Apis' [as Dimitriyevich was known to his friends] was in
daily communication with the Russian military attaché Artamonov. From Artamonov he learned the results of the interview at Konopischt . . . that Francis Ferdinand would be present at the grand manœuvres in Bosnia.

Francis Ferdinand appeared to him as the man who had
driven us from Albania, from Durazzo, from Scutari, as the
man who wished to tear up the peace of Bucharest. His death
would mean that the Austrian military clique would have lost
its head and that the war—for which they were not yet ready—
would be postponed; or, on the contrary, that the Austrian
preparations would be interrupted by immediate hostilities,
which might precipitate a rising of the Slavs of Austria-Hungary.

As the hypothesis of an immediate war seemed the more
reasonable, 'Apis' thought that he ought to consult Artamonov
before taking action. He put him *au courant* with the preparations for the murder. The Russian military attaché delayed
his reply for several days. It then ran as follows: "Go ahead
[*marchez*]! If you are attacked, you will not be alone."

The interval shows that between the question and his answer,
Artamonov had consulted his chiefs. Whom? Hartwig? Certainly. 'Apis' was convinced that Hartwig knew everything.
Probably also St. Petersburg, where Hartwig had personal
friends. Sazonov? We shall not affirm this: the policy of the

* M. Vladimirov, "Le gouvernement serbe et les responsabilités de la guerre,"
in *La fédération balkanique*, nos. 20-21, p. 268 (31 May, 1925).

ambassador [*sic*] did not agree in all its details with that of the minister.

Artamonov was well acquainted with the activity of 'Black Hand.' I think that he gave it some 8,000 francs for the Serbian propaganda in Austria.*

How much credence can be placed in these stories? It is impossible that after the meeting at Konopischt Dimitriyevich could have consulted Colonel Artamonov on the question whether the Archduke should be assassinated, for had that matter been settled several weeks before. Dimitriyevich may have informed Artamonov of his plans after they were made and have received some kind of assurances, but at present there is no possible check on his statements. Those statements may be true, but they need confirmation from some other source than 'Vladimirov.'†

There is no real evidence of M. Hartwig's complicity. Shortly after the outbreak of the war, the Austro-Hungarian consul in Cleveland, Ohio, Dr. Ernst Ludwig, gave out the following statement:

When Mr. von Hartwig, the Russian envoy, called on the Austro-Hungarian envoy, Baron Giesl, to present his regrets for the murder of the Crown Prince, Baron Giesl, in the course of the ensuing conversation, produced a compromising letter of Herr von Hartwig, which made it clear that Herr von Hartwig (and very probably, of course, the Russian Government also) must have had prior knowledge of the murder plot. The startling discovery of this incriminating letter in the possession of Baron Giesl after he had just given the latter assurances that he and his government had been shockingly surprised by the murder, caused an instantaneous heart-failure, of which he died shortly after.‡

Hartwig did die in the Austrian legation on 10 July, and there

---

* V. Serge, "La vérité sur l'attentat de Sarajévo," in *Clarté* (Paris), no. 74, p. 210 (May, 1925).

† Bogichevich, *Le procès de Salonique*, p. 11, note 2, is merely repeating 'Vladimirov.'

‡ *Cleveland Plain Dealer*, 11 September, 1914.

was much gossip about the circumstances.* But if he died for the reasons alleged by Dr. Ludwig, the Austro-Hungarian Government would surely have trumpeted the fact all over the world; it is significant that Dr. Ludwig himself omits the story from his book, *Austria-Hungary and the War.* Baron Giesl's own account of the incident contains no such charge.† But of course the improbability of this particular episode still leaves open the question whether Hartwig was initiated into Dimitriyevich's plans.

What of M. Sazonov? There is one slight indication of his attitude. À propos of the visit of the Tsar to the King of Rumania at Constanza in June, 1914, a Russian diplomatist, who was present, has written:

King Charles . . . made certain promises to Russia. For example, a military convention which had been in force between Austria-Hungary and Rumania for more than twenty years, would not be renewed. . . . Furthermore, when Archduke Francis Ferdinand was assassinated at Sarajevo . . . Sazonov doubtless knew of the warlike arrangements the Archduke had concluded in his castle at Krobatin [*sic*] with the German Emperor,—yet as far as I could judge from my conversation with members of his entourage, he was convinced that if the Archduke were out of the way, the peace of Europe would not be endangered.‡

This language is interpreted by a German writer to imply that "Serbian circles which were in the secret of the plot (perhaps the government) utilized the presence of Sazonov in Constanza to learn confidentially his opinion about the possible [*etwaigen*] consequences of Francis Ferdinand's being murdered by Bosnians."§ So far-fetched an interpretation seems utterly unwarranted by the language, the obvious import of

* Crackanthorpe to Grey, 13 July; *B. D.*, XI, no. 62.
† Baron W. Giesl, *Zwei Jahrzehnte in Orient* (Berlin, 1927), pp. 257–261; *Ö.-U. A.*, VIII, 396–398. See below, pp. 467–469.
‡ E. de Schelking, *Recollections of a Russian Diplomat* (1918), p. 195; in the English edition, *The Game of Diplomacy*, pp. 157–158.
§ H. Lutz, "Zum Mord von Sarajewo," in *KSF*, III, 446–447 (July, 1925).

which is that M. Sazonov desired peace, even though, as we know from another source, he inquired of the Rumanians what their attitude would be in the event of an armed conflict between Austria-Hungary and Russia, whether they would be compelled to resort to military action.*

ATTEMPTS TO STOP THE PLOT

If the Serbian Government had any inkling of what was being prepared, it was in duty bound not only to warn the Austrian authorities, but to use all possible means to prevent the conspirators from crossing the frontier into Bosnia. This latter it endeavored to do, if M. Lyuba Yovanovich is to be believed. In his sensational article in *Krv Slovenstva* he said:

> The plot was hatched by a group of secretly organized persons and in patriotic Bosno-Herzegovinian student circles in Belgrade. Mr. Pashich and the rest of us said, and Stoyan [Protich] agreed, that he should issue instructions to the frontier authorities on the Drina to deny a crossing to the youths who had already set out from Belgrade for that purpose. But the frontier "authorities" themselves belonged to the organization, and did not carry out Stoyan's instructions, but reported to him (and he afterward reported to us) that the order had reached them too late, for the young men had already got across. †

Later M. Yovanovich gave a slightly different account. In his controversy with Mr. Seton-Watson, he declared that, when the Austrian troops crossed the Drina in 1914, "they found the diary of the late Kosta Todorovich, our frontier officer, and *inter alia* the strict order of the war minister, Colonel Dushan Stefanovich, to prevent the young men from Bosnia from crossing the frontier."‡ Whether the orders were issued by Protich or Stefanovich is of some interest, for if they came from the latter, the Serbian war office was not in the

---

* Sazonov's report to the Tsar, 11/24 June, 1914; Marchand, II, 380.
† Yovanovich, *Крв Словенства*, p. 9; *The Murder of Sarajevo*, p. 3.
‡ *Politika*, 17 April, 1925, in *KSF*, III, 397 (June, 1925).

secrets of Colonel Dimitriyevich. M. Yovanovich's first version, however, is confirmed in part by his enemy George Yelenich:

The late Stoyan Protich received the first and only report about the journey of the Bosnian revolutionaries to Sarajevo about four days before the *attentat* from the prefect of the Podrina district, and that because the conspirators, who crossed the Drina in a drunken condition, beat up M. Samokresovich, the manager of the baths at Banya Kovilyacha.*

This episode is one of the most important in the whole controversy. If the Serbian Government did honestly try to prevent the conspirators from passing the frontier, its responsibility for the murders at Sarajevo will be sensibly diminished. But publication of the order of Stoyan Protich and the report of the frontier officials will be necessary to establish definitely the loyalty of the Serbian Government.

DID SERBIA WARN AUSTRIA?

Its attempt to stop the conspirators having failed, the Serbian Government ought in common decency to have informed the Austro-Hungarian Government of the plot. Apparently it did not do so, although statements that it had done so were made at the time and later. There are, in fact, six such statements.

(1) In an interview in the *Novoye Vremya* on 30 June, 1914, the Serbian minister in St. Petersburg, M. Spalaykovich, declared that a warning had been given.†

(2) On the same day the *Stampa* (Belgrade) stated that shortly before the departure of the Archduke, the Serbian minister in Vienna had visited Count Berchtold to advise against the visit to Sarajevo, "for the Serbian Government had learned of certain circumstances which made it believe that a plot had been organized in Sarajevo which would be carried

* *Politika*, 26 March, 1926, in *KSF*, IV, 402 (June, 1926).
† Seton-Watson, *Sarajevo*, p. 153, note 2.

into execution if the Austrian heir apparent came there." Count
Berchtold was said to have been "very grateful for this communication," of which he had at once informed the Emperor
and the Archduke.*

(3) On 10 July M. Pashich was credited by the Paris *Temps*
with having made a similar statement.

(4) During the war a Slavophile French publicist wrote:

Pashich endeavored to explain discreetly to the Ballplatz
that the Archduke would run a risk by going to Bosnia. On
21 June the Serbian minister in Vienna told the foreign office
that the Serbian Government had reason to believe that a plot
had been organized in Bosnia. The chancellor [*sic*—Berchtold
is meant] attached no importance to this information.†

(5) This claim is apparently confirmed by the statement of
M. George Yosimovich, who was a member of the Serbian
legation in Vienna in 1914:

On 18 June the Serbian minister Yovanovich received a
ciphered telegram from Pashich instructing him to advise the
Archduke Francis Ferdinand against his journey to Sarajevo,
or at least to warn him of the threatening dangers. The minister considered how he could discharge this delicate mission
without by so doing injuring Serbia. At first he desired to
inform the minister of foreign affairs, Count Berchtold, of
the contents of the despatch, but he gave up his plan, and decided to communicate the warning of the Serbian premier to
Herr von Bilinski, the common finance minister and head of
the Bosnian administration; which he did at noon on 21 June.‡

(6) In 1923, Professor Stanoyevich, who is considered the
apologist of Pashich, declared:

A few days before the *attentat* the Serbian minister in
Vienna officially informed the Austro-Hungarian Government
that the Serbian Government had reason for thinking that

* *Ö.-U. A.*, VIII, 220.
† E. Denis, *La grande Serbie* (Paris, 1915), p. 277; he must have received this in-
formation from a Serbian source.
‡ *Wiener Montagsblatt*, 23 June, 1924, in *KSF*, II, 282 (July, 1924).

something was being prepared against the Archduke at Sarajevo.*

When asked for proof of his statement,† which corresponds closely to that of M. Denis, he replied that he had received his information from the Serbian minister; and he went on to say that there was a notice in the archives of the Vienna foreign office: "Reg. B, 28 June 1914. Serbian communication about the possibility of an *attentat* upon the heir apparent."‡

Taken together, these assertions make an imposing body of evidence. Yet each of them appears to be unfounded.

(1) and (2) The statements of M. Spalaykovich and the *Stampa* were officially denied in Vienna on 3 July and 1 July respectively.§

(3) In the *New York Herald* (Paris Edition) of 20 July, 1914, M. Pashich was quoted as saying:

Had we known of the plot against the Archduke Francis Ferdinand, assuredly we should have informed the Austro-Hungarian Government.‖

(4) Count Berchtold declared, in a letter of 9 May, 1917, that the assertion of M. Denis "had been invented from A to Z."¶

(5) M. Yosimovich has denied the authorship of his article to Mr. Seton-Watson, who affirms that "there is good reason to believe that [it] was written by Leopold Mandl."**

(6) The foreign office in Vienna has stated that there is no record of a warning from the Serbian minister;†† and that "no document with the number given by Professor Stanoye Stanoyevich is to be found in the state archives."‡‡

---

* Stanoyevich, p. 61.
† "Eine Frage an Professor Stanojewitsch," in *KSF*, I, 82–83 (October, 1923).
‡ "Zur angeblichen Warnung Wiens durch den serbischen Gesandten: Antwort von Professor Stanojevic," in *KSF*, II, 28 (January-February, 1924).
§ Seton-Watson, *Sarajevo*, p. 153, note 2; *Ö.-U. A.*, VIII, 220.
‖ *Standard* (London), 21 July, 1914.   ¶ Mandl, p. 152.
** Seton-Watson, *Sarajevo*, p. 154, note 1.
†† *KSF*, I, 83 (October, 1923); *ibid.*, II, 29 (January-February, 1924).
‡‡ A. von Wegerer, "Der Anlass zum Weltkrieg," in *KSF*, III, 399 (June, 1925).

In the face of all these contradictions and in default of documentary proof, it is a reasonable conclusion that no official warning was sent to Vienna.

Was there, then, no warning at all? Yes, there was a warning, but of a peculiar kind. M. Yovan M. Yovanovich, who was the Serbian minister in Vienna in 1914, gives this version of what occurred. Being aware, he says, of the inflamed state of mind of many circles in Bosnia and fearful that the holding of manœuvres might lead to some kind of demonstration, he decided, "on his own initiative,"* to visit Ritter von Bilinski, the minister for Bosnian affairs, which he did "about 5 June." After explaining to the Austro-Hungarian minister that the manœuvres would be regarded, because they were to be held on *Vidov Dan,* as a "provocation," he went on to say:

Among the Serb youths there may be one who will put a live cartridge in his rifle or revolver instead of a blank one. He may fire it, and this bullet may strike the commander. It would therefore be well and wise for the Archduke not to go to Sarajevo; the manœuvres should not be held on *Vidov Dan* and should not be held in Bosnia.

Bilinski promised to take note of this, and to inform Yovanovich of the result of his representations to the Archduke; but he thought that Bosnia was quiet, and he said that "he could not believe in any such consequence of the manœuvres."†

The statement of M. Yovanovich that he went to Herr von Bilinski "on his own initiative" calls for remark, for it implies that he received no instructions from Belgrade. According to M. Lyuba Yovanovich, this was the case:

The information [about the plot] was vague. It was neces-

---

* This is confirmed by Yovanovich, *The Murder of Sarajevo,* p. 3.

† *Neues Wiener Tageblatt,* 28 June, 1924, in *KSF,* II, 283 (July, 1924). Something about this visit was apparently allowed to leak out, for the Bulgarian minister in Vienna heard it said that "the Serbian legation had previously informed the Austrian Government that according to its information something was being prepared in Bosnia." Stanciov to Radoslavov, 28 June, 1914; *KSF,* VI, 227 (March, 1928).

sary to take account of the peculiar character of Austro-Serbian relations and of the matter involved. If they were warned even in the slightest way [*alerté à la legère*], the Austrians would have seen in the Serbian *démarche* a manœuvre intended to make them postpone the demonstration,—the journey of the Archduke to Sarajevo,—which would irritate them. So nothing was done from this side.*

On the other hand, there is other evidence, recently published, showing that instructions were sent to M. Yovan Yovanovich. At least statements to that effect were made to an Italian journalist by two persons during the retreat of the Serbian army in 1915. The first came from Major Milan Georgevich, son of the former Serbian premier Vladen Georgevich, who after saying that M. Pashich had learned of the plot during the first fortnight of June and communicated the news to his colleagues, who agreed that the plot should be prevented if possible, continued thus:

But the conspirators had already passed the frontier; the 'Black Hand,' which nourished a deep aversion for Pashich, offered a passive resistance, declaring that it could do nothing to stop the march of events. After some hesitation, Pashich, in a weak position with respect to the 'Black Hand' and convinced that action over and above it would not succeed in preventing the plot, tried to obviate the departure of the Archduke for Sarajevo and telegraphed to the Serbian minister in Vienna to warn Berchtold in some fashion of the dangers which might threaten the life of the Archduke and to represent to him the desirability of giving up the journey.†

The second statement was made by Colonel Leshyanin, who had been military attaché at the legation in Vienna on the eve of the war. According to him,

The Serbian Government was *au courant* of the plot which was being hatched at Sarajevo to such an extent that, in the

* A. Mousset, "L'attentat de Sarajevo," in *Revue d'histoire moderne*, III, 327 (September-October, 1927).
† Magrini, *Il dramma di Seraievo*, pp. 106-107.

first days of the second half of June, a telegram from Pashich arrived at the Serbian legation in Vienna requesting the minister Yovanovich to make known to the Austrian Government that, as the result of indiscretions, the Serbian Government had reason to suspect that a plot had been devised against the life of the Archduke on the occasion of his journey to Bosnia. Since such a journey might bring about disagreeable incidents on the part of some excited persons, it would be useful to represent to the Austro-Hungarian Government the desirability of stopping the journey of the Archduke.

As the telegram was couched in general terms and contained no information about the conspirators, the Serbian minister debated for several days how to execute his delicate mission, and finally decided to speak to Bilinski.*

There is at present no way of controlling either version. The testimony of the Yovanoviches is more direct than that reported by the Italian journalist, and it would seem to have been to their interest to represent M. Pashich as having ordered some kind of a hint to be given in Vienna. Yet the statement made by M. Yovan Yovanovich to Herr von Bilinski was so unusual that only an instruction from Belgrade offers a reasonable explanation.†

The difficulty in which M. Pashich found himself is easily understood; but, if he had knowledge of any plot against the Archduke, he would have acted more wisely if he had made sure that the information was conveyed to the Austro-Hungarian Government in unambiguous form.‡

But why should the Serbian minister go to the minister for Bosnian affairs rather than to Count Berchtold, the foreign minister? It has been argued that the minister for Bosnia was

* Magrini, p. 115. Mandl, p. 115, states that Leshyanin told him at the beginning of June, 1914, that he would be glad when the manœuvres in Bosnia were finished.

† Fay, II, 163–166, writing before the statements of Mousset and Magrini had been published, concluded that Pashich had probably sent private instructions to Yovanovich.

‡ According to Mousset, *loc. cit.*, III, 328–329, Yovanovich did not report to Belgrade his conversation with Bilinski.

"the natural and proper party to receive information relative to rumors that an attempt to assassinate the heir to the Habsburg throne would be made in that province."* But even if M. Yovanovich might without impropriety speak to Herr von Bilinski, he ought also to have informed Count Berchtold. He did not do so, according to the Austrian publicist Leopold Mandl, because of his strained personal relations with the Austro-Hungarian foreign minister; he was in fact accustomed to go to Bilinski for the transaction of business,† and, since he had no official instructions, he naturally avoided the foreign office.

Ritter von Bilinski, in his memoirs, does not mention any such visit from the Serbian minister; during the war he told an Austrian historian that he "wished to draw the veil of oblivion" over the Sarajevo plot.‡ But he appears to have spoken of it to the chief of his press bureau, Herr Paul Flandrak, who, however, gives May rather than 5 June as the date of the visit. Herr Flandrak adds that M. Yovanovich asked Herr von Bilinski not to consider his statement as an "official communication" and that the minister saw in it "neither an open nor a veiled warning."§ Thus the *démarche* failed in its intended effect.

If the Serbian Government—as seems probable, though it can hardly be asserted with certainty—had knowledge, however vague, of the conspiracy against the Archduke Francis Ferdinand, it must be charged with a serious dereliction of duty in not conveying a warning to the Austro-Hungarian authorities. Its negligence may be explained by what M. Lyuba Yovanovich called "the peculiar character of Austro-Serbian relations" and by its internal political difficulties, but hardly

* A. H. Putney, "Denial of Serbia's War Responsibility," in *Current History*, XXIII, 526 (January, 1926).

† L. Mandl, "Zur Warnung Serbiens an Oesterreich," in *KSF*, II, 109 (April, 1924).

‡ L. Mandl, "Zur Warnung Serbiens an Oesterreich," in *KSF*, II, 108-109 (April, 1924).

§ P. Flandrak, "Bilinskis Eingreifen in die auswärtige Politik," in *Neues Wiener Journal*, 26 April, 1925, reprinted in *KSF*, III, 400-401 (June, 1925).

excused. On the other hand, it is necessary to consider (1) what measures were taken by the Austro-Hungarian Government to protect the Archduke; and (2) whether it received any warning of the plot from other sources.

AUSTRIAN PRECAUTIONARY MEASURES

As a matter of fact, the attitude and conduct of the Austro-Hungarian authorities offers a problem that is not easily resolved; it was indeed so strange that connivance with the plot has sometimes been charged, for not otherwise was the neglect of proper precautionary measures to be accounted for. Recent disclosures dispel much of the mystery, and the theory of complicity has been generally abandoned; obscurity, however, still reigns on several points.

Since Ritter von Bilinski did not take seriously the cryptic warning of the Serbian minister, he did not inform either the Emperor Francis Joseph nor the Archduke Francis Ferdinand;* whether he communicated with Count Berchtold is uncertain.† But because anonymous threatening letters were at this time being received by various ministers and by the Archduke himself, Herr von Bilinski thought it desirable to sound the government at Sarajevo about the desirability of the proposed visit. The reply was that the local authorities in Bosnia declined all responsibility, and this report was transmitted to the court.‡ The minister was told, however, that the civil authorities need not concern themselves with the matter, for the Archduke wished his visit to be a strictly military affair; and not only was Sarajevo visited with a reprimand, but the Bosnian administration was systematically and deliber-

* P. Flandrak, *Neues Wiener Journal*, 26 April, 1925, in *KSF*, III, 461 (June, 1925).

† Flandrak, *loc. cit.*, stated that Bilinski did not inform Berchtold; which is also affirmed by L. Mandl, "Zur Warnung Serbiens an Oesterreich," in *KSF*, II, 110–111 (April, 1924). But Flandrak, "Die falsche Deutung der Bilinskischen Warnung durch Senator de Jouvenel," in *KSF*, VI, 1154 (December, 1928), states that Bilinski spoke to Berchtold about Yovanovich's visit on the same day.

‡ Bilinski, *Wspomnenia i Dokumenty*, I, 273–277.

ately ignored in all the preparations for the archducal journey.* Responsibility for what happened cannot therefore be placed on the shoulders of the Bosnian authorities.

On the day of the tragedy, however, the Archduke was overheard to say, "Now I understand why Count Tisza advised me to postpone my journey."† This may mean that the Hungarian Government had received some kind of warning. As it happens, there are several bits of evidence to support this view. The first is the story of Rudolf Bartulich, a Croat who claims to have been employed in the Austrian secret service during the war and in that capacity to have got his information in Zagreb from the captain of the municipal police. The captain said that, about a month before the murders, he received an anonymous communication from Belgrade which described the plans of the conspirators and gave the names of persons involved; two days later similar news was received from the United States. The matter was reported to the Croatian Government, which in turn informed Budapest. The police official also said that a lawyer of Zagreb, Dr. Marc Gagliardi, after a visit to Belgrade, made a similar statement to the police. Finally, he asserted that no reply to any of these reports was received from Budapest.‡

This tale, first told during the war, has recently been circulated again. M. Klobucharich, the head of the Zagreb secret police in 1914, is quoted as saying:

A month before the *attentat* in Sarajevo we received an anonymous message concerning the plot against the Archduke. But I received instructions to attach no importance to the whole affair. The next day a second message came from Vienna confirming the contents of the first and mentioning the name of

---

* Seton-Watson, *Sarajevo*, pp. 106–107. Francis Ferdinand "regarded Bilinski with dislike and suspicion, as a close confidant of the Emperor and as the chief exponent of a more moderate régime in Bosnia, as against the more drastic methods favored by Potiorek and the military chiefs." Bilinski subsequently complained to Potiorek that he had not been consulted about the arrangements for the visit. Bilinski to Potiorek, 3 July, 1914; *Ö.-U. A.*, VIII, 290.

† The correspondent of the London *Times* overheard the remark; Steed, I, 400.

‡ G. Beck, *La responsabilité de la Hongrie* (Paris, 1917), pp. 215–219.

Printsip. I gave this to Count Tisza and asked his instructions. Some days later Dr. Gagliardi came and repeated the statement. I again took steps with Count Tisza.*

Obviously this story has to be treated with reserve. The only check on it is the further remark of the police captain that, because no reply was received from Budapest, the Zagreb police could not proceed against Printsip, "who came to Zagreb at this time." There is no evidence that Printsip visited Zagreb, although it is not impossible, because three weeks elapsed between his arrival in Sarajevo and the day of the crime. Suspicion is likewise aroused by the statement that news of the plot was received from the United States. On the other hand, a Dr. Zhibert, described as "a librarian of the University of Vienna," quotes the *Grazer Volksblatt* of 10 July, 1914, to prove that the Budapest police had been warned of the plot. He also asserts that Francis Ferdinand requested an investigation;† nothing of this, however, is known from any other source except the fact that he discussed the wisdom of the journey with the Emperor, who said, "Do as you wish."‡

One is very reluctant even to consider that the Austro-Hungarian authorities, if they had the slightest inkling that Francis Ferdinand might be exposed to danger, would not take every possible precaution.§ But, in addition to the story just re-

* *Secolo*, 28 July, 1926. The writer has seen a newspaper clipping, unfortunately without indication of date or source, containing an article by S. Jacoby, "Dushan Tvordekas [*sic*, for Tovdoreka] Enthüllungen zum Attentat von Sarajevo," according to which Tovdoreka told Jacoby in May, 1927, that five months after the murder Gagliardi had stated in a Hungarian paper that he had known of the plot five months before and reported it to the Zagreb police, who had no power to act.

† J. A. Žibert, *Der Mord von Sarajewo und Tiszas Schuld an dem Weltkriege* (Laibach, 1919), pp. 9, 27.

‡ Conrad, III, 70. That there had been some kind of warning was believed in diplomatic circles in Vienna, for the British ambassador reported to his government: "The Archduke is said to have been warned in vain against undertaking his projected journey, and to have himself endeavored to dissuade the Duchess from meeting him in Bosnia." Bunsen to Grey, 29 June, 1914; *B. D.*, XI, no. 21. The Archduke persisted in undertaking the journey because cowardice might be imputed to him if he gave up a visit that had long been announced. And no doubt he had entire confidence that the military authorities, who were in sole charge of the visit, would take all proper precautions.

§ Although it cannot be stated with certainty whether information about the plot either was or was not received, it is interesting to note that in May a warning came to hand of possible trouble. A number of students from the Serbian teachers' train-

counted, the statement of Herr Leo Pfeffer, who was the special prosecuting attorney in the trial of Printsip, has to be recorded. According to him, "certain Austro-Hungarian circles countenanced the *attentat* at Sarajevo," the "police measures were so inadequate as to make any thinking persons suspicious," and "all the preparations for the entry of Francis Ferdinand were revealed to Chabrinovich by an Austrian detective."* He brings no proofs for his assertions, but it is interesting to note that in the Hungarian parliament on 8 July, 1914, Count Andrássy asked the government:

> How was it possible that, in view of the conditions known to exist in Bosnia, the visit of the Archduke to Sarajevo on a national Servian holiday had been allowed? Why had proper precautionary measures not been taken?†

Count Tisza, in reply, explained that the Archduke "had gone where his military duties called him without consulting the Austrian or Hungarian Governments," but he did not comment on the police measures. He had commented, however, on those measures on the previous day, when at the joint council of Austrian and Hungarian ministers, he complained that

> six or seven persons known to the police were able to place themselves on the day of the murder along the route of the murdered heir apparent with bombs and revolvers without the police noticing or arresting a single one of them.‡

Tisza may have meant only that on such an occasion suspicious

ing college at Pakrac in Croatia crossed the frontier into Serbia to enter schools in that country. One of them, a certain Yanko Pokrayats, was said to have told an acquaintance that he was prepared to make use of bombs in Croatia, and that if the Archduke Francis Ferdinand came to Bosnia, he and friends "would provide proof that Bosnia was a Serbian land." Vukovich to Oppenheimer, 11 May, 1914; *Ö.-U. A.*, VIII, 31. This information was transmitted to Bilinski, who in turn passed it on to the authorities in Sarajevo; *Ö.-U. A.*, VIII, 53–54, 157–158. Subsequently efforts were made, but without complete success, to secure information from the Serbian Government concerning the whereabouts of the students in Serbia; *Ö.-U. A.*, VIII, 274–275, 369–370, 379–380.

* *Obzor* (Zagreb), 22 July, 1926, in *KSF*, IV, 661, 722 (September, 1926).
† Max Müller to Grey, 14 July, 1914; *B. D.*, XI, no. 70.
‡ Protocol of the council of ministers, 7 July, 1914; *Diplomatische Aktenstücke zur Vorgeschichte des Krieges 1914*, I, no. 8.

characters should have been locked up as a measure of general precaution, but he evidently felt, and may possibly have known, that the police had been remiss.

Certainly the evidence cited is not sufficient to prove the connivance of the authorities with the assassination, but it does create the uncomfortable suspicion that there are facts concerning their attitude which have not come to light. It remains to examine the measures actually taken, so far as they are known, to protect the august personages on their visit to Sarajevo.

The Budapest police, in consequence of alleged warnings, are said to have asked for fifty detectives, but, for reasons of economy, were allowed to send only five.* From Vienna also there came a number—"hundreds," according to Yevtich†—of special agents, who, however, were not familiar with Serbian or with local conditions, and were quite useless. The civil authorities evidently did what they could, but, with only 120 regular police, there were limits to their measures of surveillance.‡ General Potiorek, the military governor who was in control of arrangements, later defended himself from the charge of slackness by claiming that the same measures were taken as at the time of the Emperor's visit in 1910.§ Only "the complete evacuation of the inhabitants of the city," he said, "would have given protection against conspirators, who did not shun death and were fitted out with cyanide of potassium." The arrangements, however, were not the same as in 1910, for then a double cordon of troops guarded the Emperor's route, whereas on 28 June, 1914, although there

* Žibert, *Der Mord von Sarajewo und Tiszas Schuld an dem Weltkriege*, p. 9.
† *New York Times*, 22 June, 1924.
‡ "Least of all could I assume that a non-military visit to Sarajevo would be added to the military programme. Had I known from the reports of Your Excellency that the police administration was not fully equal to its task, it would have been the duty of both of us to prevent the journey under all circumstances. The fact already semi-officially reported in the newspapers from Sarajevo that the political authorities had at their disposal barely 120 policemen has made a terrifying impression on me. Any demand for funds for increasing the guard would have been granted at once as a matter of course; I also believe that the gendarmerie could have provided a noteworthy strengthening of the guard." Bilinski to Potiorek, 3 July, 1914; *Ö.-U. A.*, VIII, 290.
§ Potiorek to Bilinski, 6 July, 1914; Conrad, IV, 65–66.

were thousands of troops in the vicinity, the streets of Sarajevo
were not properly lined. It may have been felt that such drastic measures would reflect both on the courage of Francis
Ferdinand and on the strength of the government, but Potiorek
cannot escape the blame for what happened as a result of his
carelessness.*

The Murder at Sarajevo, 28 June, 1914

It is now necessary to take up the trail of the conspirators.
The three young men left Belgrade on 28 May and proceeded
by steamer to Shabats. On arrival they hunted up Major Popovich, to whom they presented the note given them by Tsiganovich. The major, who had been in Belgrade himself several
days previously, was evidently expecting them. He provided
a document certifying that they were Serbian revenue officers,
secured them half-fare tickets on the railway to Loznitsa, and
wrote a letter to the frontier official there. This gentleman
proved as accommodating as Major Popovich. As the boys had
decided to separate, he gave Chabrinovich letters to the frontier
official and the school-teacher at Zvornik, a near-by village to
which Chabrinovich walked; with the help of the teacher,
Chabrinovich got across the river and made his own way to
Tuzla. The other two, Printsip and Grabezh, who took charge
of the bombs and revolvers, were sent back to Lyeshnitsa, put
across the river by the revenue officer, and handed over to a
Bosnian peasant.

Once inside the Austrian frontier, the conspirators apparently
made no efforts to conceal their weapons, and by threats forced
several peasants to help them along. Presently they were met

* "Potiorek's crowning fault was an arrogance that led him to keep all arrangements in his own hand, yet prevented him from listening to advice; and this involved him quite naturally in the paradox that while he preached to Vienna the
dangers of the situation, he could not conceive that Bosnia could be so utterly
out of his control as to produce a whole bevy of assassins on the streets of the
capital. Thus he expressly assured Bilinski that the military measures taken by
him were quite adequate for the Archduke's protection." Seton-Watson, *Sarajevo*, p. 110.

by Vyelko Chubrilovich, the school-teacher at Priboy and a member of the *Narodna Odbrana*. When told that the bombs were for Francis Ferdinand and warned of the consequences of treachery, he took the travellers to a peasant named Yakob Kerovich, who agreed to let his son drive them to Tuzla. This stage of the journey was not accomplished without risk, for at one place Printsip and Grabezh descended from the cart in which they were riding and made a detour in order to avoid a gendarme station. Arrived at Tuzla, they went to Mishko Yovanovich, to whom Chubrilovich had given them a letter. Yovanovich, who was the 'confidential man' of the *Narodna Odbrana,* received the boys and promised to convey the arms to Sarajevo. Meanwhile Chabrinovich had joined them, so the three proceeded by train to Sarajevo and reported to Danilo Ilich.

A few days later Ilich went to Tuzla, identified himself to Yovanovich, and arranged to have the arms sent to Doboy, the second station from Sarajevo, whence he himself brought them into town and concealed them in his own house. At his trial, as already noted, Ilich asserted that he was opposed to carrying out the plot (he would have preferred to assassinate General Potiorek), but that he consented to it from fear of *komitadjis* in Serbia. Probably this was for effect only, for Ilich had arranged for 'reserves' in case the men from Belgrade failed in their work.* At any rate, the day before the Archduke arrived, Ilich distributed the weapons to the three plotters and to his 'reserves,' and directed them where to station themselves along the route. That same day or the next morning Pushara returned from his private search for the Archduke. So at least seven persons were ready for the desperate deed. What was being planned was known to a number of other youths, but no

---

* It is just possible that Ilich was telling the truth. According to Professor Stanoyevich's version (see above, p. 221), Dimitriyevich claimed that when the central committee of the *Uyedinyenye ili Smrt* protested against the plot, he tried to stop its execution. Ilich is supposed to have come to Belgrade about 16 June, the day after the meeting of the committee, to get final instructions from Dimitriyevich. It may be that Dimitriyevich did ask him not to carry out the plot. Cf. F. von Wiesner, "Die Schuld der serbischen Regierung am Mord von Sarajevo," in *KSF*, VI, 326 (April, 1928).

one gave the plot away. After the crime, the local archbishop is reported to have said that for Francis Ferdinand to have left the town alive, he would have had to run the gauntlet through "a regular avenue of assassins."*

The Archduke started on his fatal journey on 23 June. His private car was found to have a hot-box, so that he was forced to change to an ordinary first-class carriage; later on, before he reached Trieste, the electric lighting broke down. From Trieste he travelled by sea to Metkovich and then by train to Ilidzhe, a resort not far from Sarajevo, where his wife, who had come by way of Hungary, joined him. The manœuvres occupied two days, 26 June and 27 June. Late on the afternoon of the first day the royal couple drove through the streets of Sarajevo in an open carriage and were cordially received;† Printsip wandering through the bazaars came almost face to face with his intended victim, but did not move, because "behind him a stranger, undoubtedly a police agent, had spread his hands carefully."‡ During these days the Archduke was in excellent temper.

Sunday, 28 June, 1914—the anniversary of Kossovo, of the Austro-Serbian treaty of 1881, and of the marriage of Francis Ferdinand and Sophie Chotek—was a glorious summer day. Sarajevo had been decorated at the request of the mayor, and the absence of troops in the streets enabled the crowds to circulate freely.§ The Archduke was to pass along the Appel Quay, a wide street with houses on one side and on the other a low wall, below which flows the Milyatska River; from its central section three bridges lead across the river. Near the first bridge Ilich placed Mehmedbashich, Chubrilovich, and Chabrinovich on one side of the street, Popovich and himself on the other; Printsip was stationed at the second bridge, and Grabezh near the third.

---

* Seton-Watson, *Sarajevo*, p. 147. The narrative of this and the two preceding paragraphs is based on Pharos, *passim;* cf. also Wiesner, *loc. cit.*, VI, 332–339.
† Nikitsch-Boulles, *Vor dem Sturm: Erinnerungen an Erzherzog Thronfolger Franz Ferdinand*, p. 213.
‡ Yevtich, *Сарајевски Атентат*, p. 33.
§ As the visit was intended to impress the population, any kind of military demonstration would doubtless have spoiled its effect; but, as was noted above, in 1910 when Francis Joseph visited the city, the streets were lined with troops.

The Archduke and his wife arrived from Ilidzhe about ten o'clock; his party occupied four cars, that of the mayor and the chief of police leading. As they drove along the Appel Quay toward the town hall, Chabrinovich hurled his bomb and jumped into the river, only to be arrested forthwith. The bomb bounced off the archducal car—according to one account Francis Ferdinand picked it up and threw it—into the street, where it exploded, wounding several spectators and an officer in the next car. When the town hall was reached, the mayor, ignorant of what had happened, was about to read his speech of welcome when the Archduke exclaimed: "Mr. Mayor, I come here on a visit, and I get bombs thrown at me! What do you mean by talking of loyalty?" But his wife calmed him, and he told the mayor to proceed.

After the speech there was a discussion whether the programme of the day should be continued. General Potiorek is said to have remarked that he knew his Bosnians: two such attempts would never be made on the same day. So no further precautions were taken. The Archduke declared his intention of visiting his wounded adjutant in the hospital, which involved a change in the route; the Duchess decided to accompany her husband, saying, "It is in time of danger that you need me." As he got into the car, Francis Ferdinand was told that the bomb-thrower had been arrested. "Hang him as soon as you can," he exclaimed, "or else Vienna will send him a decoration."

To reach the hospital the royal party had to retrace its way along the Appel Quay. But at the second bridge, the first car turned to the right, in accordance with the original scheme; presumably because the chauffeur had not been informed of the altered plans. The second car, containing the royal couple and General Potiorek, was driven by a man who did not know the city and who therefore naturally followed the leading car. Whereupon Potiorek called out, "We're going wrong." The car stopped and backed up. At this moment, Printsip, who was standing on the sidewalk, shot both the Archduke and the Duchess—which in all probability he would not have been able to do

but for the unfortunate error.* The *konak* or governor's residence, just over the bridge on the other side of the river, was
reached in a few moments, and the victims were carried inside;
but they died before any aid could be brought. The last words
of Francis Ferdinand were, "Sophie, Sophie, do not die. Live
for our children."† As regards the latter part of this tragic
day, it is difficult not to agree with the aide-de-camp of the Emperor Francis Joseph that the precautionary measures "baffled
all description."‡ By night the news was known throughout
the world.

* It is worth noting that the local reserves did nothing, perhaps because they
had not "walked the streets of Belgrade." Grabezh also made no effort to do his
part.

† The official report, written by Colonel Bardolff, the Archduke's military secretary, in Conrad, IV, 19–22; Pharos, pp. 155–159; *Serajevo: la conspiration serbe
contre la monarchie austro-hongroise*, pp. 13–19; Bunsen to Grey, 29 June, 1914;
B. D., XI, no. 21; Seton-Watson, *Sarajevo*, pp. 102–103; Steed, I, 400–401; J.
Chopin, *Le complot de Sarajevo* (Paris, 1918), pp. 89–100 (rather fantastic); R.
Recouly, "L'énigme de Sarajevo," In *Les heures tragiques d'avant-guerre* (Paris,
1922), pp. 179–187; Yevtich, *Сарајевски Атентат*, pp. 41–44.

‡ Margutti, *Vom alten Kaiser*, p. 396.

CHAPTER IV

HABSBURG'S HOUR*

In Austria-Hungary the reaction to the crime of Sarajevo was instantaneous and significant. Sarajevo itself was the scene of the utmost excitement. On the evening of the murder a crowd of Croatian and Moslem youths, many of them students, marched through the streets singing the national anthem and crying "Down with the Serbs!"; presently they collected before

* From this point, the narrative is based primarily on the diplomatic documents issued by the several governments in 1914-1915 and since the end of the war. As the titles of these collections are rather long, the following abbreviations have been used:

'A' (Austro-Hungarian) for *Diplomatische Aktenstücke zur Vorgeschichte des Weltkrieges 1914* (Vienna, 1919), 3 volumes, with separate numbering of documents for each volume. (This collection does not contain the complete correspondence for the period, many additional documents being given in *Ö.-U. A.*, VIII, 208-980.)

'B' (British) for *British Documents on the Origins of the War, 1898-1914*, volume XI, *The Outbreak of War* (London, 1926).

'Belgian' for *Correspondance diplomatique relative à la guerre de 1914* (Brussels, 1914-1915), 2 volumes, with separate numbering for each volume.

'F' (French) for *Documents diplomatiques, 1914, la guerre européenne* (Paris, 1914).

'G' (German) for *Die deutschen Dokumente zum Kriegsausbruch* (Berlin-Charlottenburg, 1919, second edition, 1927), 4 volumes, with continuous numbering.

'R' (Russian) for *Recueil de documents diplomatiques. Négociations ayant précédé la guerre, 10/23 juillet-24 juillet/6 août 1914* (Petrograd, 1914).

'R, 1925' for *Das russische Orangebuch von 1914, ergänzt durch die inzwischen bekannt gewordenen neuen Dokumente* (Berlin, 1925), containing documents (in German translation) published by the Soviet Government.

'S' (Serbian) for *Les pourparlers diplomatiques, 16/29 juin-3/16 août 1914* (Nish, 1914).

'US' (United States) for *Papers relating to the Foreign Relations of the United States, 1914. Supplement: the World War* (Washington, 1928).

Except in the case of US, but including *Ö.-U. A.*, the figures after the abbreviations signify the number of the document, not the page of the collection. Thus 'A I 1' refers to *Diplomatische Aktenstücke zur Vorgeschichte des Weltkrieges 1914*, volume I, document no. 1. The varicolored 'Books' ('Blue,' 'Yellow,' 'Orange,' 'Gray,' etc.) of 1914-1915, including the German 'White Book' and the original Austro-Hungarian 'Red Book,' will be found in English translation in *Collected Diplomatic Documents relating to the Outbreak of the European War*, and in J. B. Scott, *Diplomatic Documents relating to the Outbreak of the European War* (New York, 1916). The English translations of *Diplomatische Aktenstücke des Vorgeschichte des Weltkrieges 1914*, made in Vienna and published under the title *Official Files relating to Pre-War History* (London, 1920), and of *Die deutschen Dokumente zum Kriegsausbruch*, published by the Carnegie Endowment for International Peace under the title *Outbreak of the World War: German Documents Collected by Karl Kautsky* (New York, 1924) are very unreliable and sometimes misleading or incorrect; the writer has made his own translations from the German originals.

the Hotel Europa, which belonged to a Serbian leader, and bombarded it with stones until dispersed by the military. The next morning the riffraff of the bazaars began to destroy the property of prominent Serbians, including the Hotel Europa, and did damage estimated at from 1,500,000 to 10,000,000 kronen before General Potiorek proclaimed a state of siege. As similar excesses occurred in other Bosnian towns, it became necessary to proclaim martial law for the two provinces, and Potiorek demanded the closing of the Bosnian Diet, in which he was supported by the general staff and the war office.*

Elsewhere in the Southern Slav provinces there were many disturbances. Near Ragusa a Serbian flag was torn to pieces and a Serbian house set on fire. In the Croatian Diet at Zagreb (Agram), a Serbian member's cry of "Long live King Peter!" was answered with enraged shouts of "Down with the assassins! Down with the Serbs!"† The working agreement between Croats and Serbians established by the Fiume Manifesto of October, 1905, appeared to have broken down completely, at least for the time.‡

In Vienna demonstrations became the order of the day. It was necessary to protect the Serbian legation against the mob; the Serbian minister was requested by his landlord and the police not to display his flag at half-mast, as by etiquette he was bound to do in honor of the deceased Archduke, lest it serve to excite the mob to damage the building.§ At Brünn, the the capital of Moravia, a clash was narrowly averted between the Bohemian 'Sokol' societies and a rival German demonstration.‖

These manifestations were not unnatural. In almost every

---

* Seton-Watson, *Sarajevo*, 114–115; Gooss, *Das Wiener Kabinett und die Entstehung des Weltkrieges*, 45–49; Ö.-U. A., 9948, 9961, 9974, 9997, 9999, 10,021; Jones to Grey, 30 June, 2 July; B 20, 23.

† J. F. Scott, *Five Weeks: the Surge of Public Opinion on the Eve of the Great War* (New York, 1927), p. 23.

‡ Bunsen to Grey, 2 July; B 28.

§ Yovanovich to Pashich, 3 July; S 11. The minister declined to remove the flag until after the conclusion of the funeral services of the royal couple. See also Ö.-U. A., 9981.

‖ Bunsen to Grey, 29 June; B 21.

country deeds of violence are likely to evoke reprisals, and it would have been strange if the anti-Serbian sentiment so carefully nourished for many years had not flared up under the provocation received. Taken by themselves, the sundry outbursts meant very little. What really mattered was the instinctive feeling in educated and responsible circles that the climax in the long conflict with Serbia was at hand. Count Berchtold's opinion that "the threads of the conspiracy . . . ran together at Belgrade"* was shared in many quarters and expressed by many newspapers. It was easy to believe that, if the Serbian activity in Bosnia were not speedily checked, immeasurable consequences might result. The disaffection of the Southern Slav population, already notorious, would spread to the other races, the prestige of the government among its own peoples would be diminished, Austria-Hungary's position as a Great Power would be compromised; indeed, its very existence as a state would become problematical. That the activities, alleged or real, of a state with only one-tenth of the population of the Monarchy could inspire such alarm, was perhaps an unconscious avowal that official policy in the Southern Slav question had been ill conceived and worse applied; but the existence of this fear among the governing classes was testified to so generally by the foreign diplomatists that it can hardly be doubted.

The Emperor Francis Joseph confided to the German ambassador that he saw "a very dark picture," for conditions in Bosnia "were getting more disquieting every day" and "the intrigues at Belgrade were intolerable."† According to the French ambassador, "the crime of Sarajevo arouses the most acute resentment in Austrian military circles, and among all who are not content to allow Serbia to maintain in the Balkans the situation which she has acquired."‡ The Serbian minister

---

* Tschirschky to Bethmann-Hollweg, 30 June; G 7.
† Tschirschky to Bethmann-Hollweg, 2 July; G 9, 11.
‡ Dumaine to Viviani, 2 July; F 8. "The army, I hear, are very bitter, straining at the leash," wrote the British ambassador on 3 July; B 29.

warned his government that "high Catholic circles" and "official German circles" were "especially ill-disposed."[*] The German ambassador was alarmed to "hear expressed, even among serious people, the wish that at last a final and fundamental reckoning should be had with the Serbs."[†] By 'serious people' he doubtless meant what an Austrian diplomatist has called the 'clientèle' of the Monarchy:

The higher bureaucracy, the corps of officers, the higher clergy, industrial and financial circles, merchants, landed proprietors who desired favorable markets for their products, the nobility, in short, all those elements that had an interest in the maintenance of the Monarchy.[‡]

This view was shared by the British ambassador. Commenting on the doubts expressed by his Russian colleague whether "the animosity penetrates deep down among the Austrian people," he wrote:

I cannot at present share M. Schebeko's inclination to believe that the commercial and generally the middle classes of this country are indifferent to the question. I fear there is ground to regard almost all sections of the population as being just now blindly incensed against the Servians, and I have heard on good authority that many persons usually holding quite moderate and sensible views on foreign affairs are expressing themselves now in the sense that Austria will at last be compelled to give evidence of her strength by settling once and for all her long-standing accounts with Servia, and by striking such a blow as will reduce that country to impotence for the future.[§]

The British consul-general in Budapest, who returned to that capital a few days after the assassination, was impressed "by the intensity of the wave of blind hatred for Servia and everything Servian that is sweeping over the country"; and he thought that the Hungarian nation was "willing to go to any

---

[*] Yovanovich to Pashich, 7, 14 July; S, 17, 22.
[†] Tschirschky to Bethmann-Hollweg, 30 June; G 7.
[‡] Musulin, *Das Haus am Ballplatz*, p. 234.   [§] Bunsen to Grey, 5 July; B 40.

lengths in its desire to revenge itself on the despised and hated enemy."* There was, in short, so far as the articulate classes were concerned, a loud demand for prompt, drastic, and effective action.

In the face of such general excitement, the attitude of the press calls for remark. With the exception of the liberal *Die Zeit* and the socialist *Arbeiter-Zeitung,* the newspapers were quite ready to attribute the responsibility for the crime to Belgrade, for it was speedily known that Printsip was a Serbian, and certain of them called for action. The *Reichspost,* organ of the Christian Socialists and sometimes the mouthpiece of the late Archduke, asked, on 1 July, "How long will the Serbian murder spectre carry on its handiwork unchecked?" and the next day asserted that respect for the Monarchy must be restored "with the mailed fist." The *Militarische Rundschau,* on 30 June, published a bitter article headed, "To Belgrade!" The *Neues Wiener Journal* denounced "the hushing-up system of Count Berchtold." These journals were notoriously reactionary and chauvinist. "The official *Fremdenblatt,* however, and most of the more reasonable papers," reported the British ambassador, "take the line that it would not be politic to take Servia as a whole to account for the crimes of a small band of degenerates who draw their inspiration from Pan-Serb headquarters at Belgrade."† Thus the *Neue Freie Presse,* the most important paper in Vienna, said, on 2 July, that the government's policy of peace would not be altered by the murder, for "wars of revenge are to-day, when the great interests of the people are decisive, out of the question." On the same day the *Pester Lloyd,* the great liberal paper of Budapest, protested against "the idea of a campaign of revenge, a punitive expedition against Serbia"; and the semi-official *Budapesti Hirlap* stated that "there is no ground for anxiety as to war," for "the Monarchy will know how to maintain its prestige without wishing to resort to war." It is quite clear that the most responsible newspapers in both halves of the Monarchy, immediately after the

* Max Müller to Grey, 14 July; B 70.   † Bunsen to Nicolson, 3 July; B 29.

assassination, were extremely cautious and did not urge the government to measures of violence.*

If public opinion, while requiring satisfaction for the affront to the dignity of the state, was not unanimous in requiring a particular course, official circles were also divided. The Emperor and Count Stürgkh, the Austrian premier, desired to postpone any decisions until the results of the investigation begun at Sarajevo were known,† and Count Tisza, the Hungarian premier, was equally in favor of proceeding cautiously. On the other hand, General Conrad von Hötzendorf, the chief of the general staff, had no doubt as to what should be done. "Austria must draw the sword against Serbia," he opined; not as punishment for the murder of the Archduke, but because it was "a question of the greatest practical importance for our prestige as a Great Power," and he favored this course in spite of the fact that "the favorable moment to ward off the impending danger had passed by years before." He therefore urged mobilization against Serbia as an "immediate step"—which would be followed by war.‡ General Potiorek in Sarajevo§ and the chargé in Belgrade‖ also advocated immediate action, that is, war.

Thus both great caution and extreme recklessness were equally recommended to the foreign minister, Count Berchtold, to whom the initiation of policy properly belonged. As a foreign minister, Count Berchtold was unusual, at least in this twentieth century. Great magnate and man of the world, he did not find his principal interest in politics, into which he had been drafted

---

* The quotations in this paragraph are taken from Scott, chap. ii. It is of course possible that the moderation of the press was dictated by the government, which did not wish to give the alarm prematurely, but this is speculation.

† The investigation lasted for several weeks, but the main facts about the activity of the conspirators in Belgrade and their journey to Sarajevo were learned in a few days. The day-by-day telegrams from Potiorek may be read in *Ö.-U. A.*, 9940, 9947, 9975, 9991, 9992, 10,023, 10,066, 10,067, 10,068, 10,109, 10,137, 10,184, 10,185, 10,207, 10,249, 10,250, 10,271, 10,346, 10,372, 10,391.

‡ Conrad, IV, 31–34. Conrad speaks casually of a council of ministers which met at 8 P. M. on 29 June, but gives no details. If such a council was held, the minutes have not been published.

§ Potiorek to Bilinski, telegram, 1 July, Potiorek to Krobatin, telegram, 2 July; *Ö.-U. A.*, 9974, 9993.

‖ Storck to Berchtold, 30 June, 1 July; *Ö.-U. A.*, 9951, 9964.

by family and official pressure. He delighted in society and took the greatest care in his dress, he frequented the opera and maintained a racing-stable; his charming manners and his gracious hospitality captivated the elegant world in which he moved. These qualities doubtless contributed to his success as ambassador to Russia, but they apparently caused him to dislike the exacting routine of a minister of foreign affairs. Count Berchtold, moreover, was not driven by personal political ambition; in fact, he had accepted his office only at the insistence of the Emperor, and left the management of affairs as far as possible to his subordinates.* His conduct during the Balkan wars of 1912–1913 satisfied no one. "He wavered," says an Austrian diplomatist, "between reasonable and bellicose inclinations,"† yielding now to the pressure of his German ally, now to the demands of his subordinates or the military party in the Monarchy. He appeared never to know his own mind and to have no intelligible policy.

But if, up to July, 1914, Count Berchtold had succeeded only in earning the reputation of a dilettante, he had taken the measure of the forces both within and without the Monarchy which had to be reckoned with, and he had learned how to deal with the several individuals whose consent would be necessary for whatever policy he might propose. And, this time, he made up his mind quickly enough, for he was too shrewd not to appreciate the advantage of position which he now enjoyed. "Everything pointed to the fact," so he informed the German ambassador, "that the threads of the conspiracy to which the Archduke had fallen a victim ran together at Belgrade":‡ for the first time, Austria-Hungary possessed an undeniable and a

---

* During the Balkan wars the German ambassador complained of this habit more than once. Cf. especially Tschirschky to Zimmermann, 29 December, 1912; *G. P.*, XXXIII, no. 12,593. On one occasion the French ambassador lamented to Count Forgách, who was second in command at the Ballplatz, that he could get no answer to a question put some time before to the minister. Forgách replied: "Why do you go to Berchtold with serious matters? Come and talk with me. It's the only way to get anything done." A. Dumaine, *La dernière ambassade de France en Autriche* (Paris, 1921), p. 89.

† Szilassy, *Der Untergang der Donau-Monarchie*, p. 225.

‡ Tschirschky to Bethmann-Hollweg, 30 June; G 7.

politically effective grievance, and Count Berchtold determined
to use it.* He therefore bluntly informed Count Tisza of "his
intention to make the horrible deed of Sarajevo the occasion for
reckoning with Serbia."† He proposed, in short, to adopt the
policy recommended by General Conrad.

Under the political system of the Dual Monarchy, however,
the foreign minister was not an autocrat. His policy had to be
sanctioned by the two premiers, as well as by the Emperor,
and, while Count Stürgkh was a colorless bureaucrat who could
easily be managed, Count Tisza was the most striking personality in either half of the Monarchy and not a man to be trifled
with. Now, actually, the Hungarian statesman was greatly upset by the hint of action against Serbia, and not only did he
inform Count Berchtold that he would consider this "a fatal
mistake"; but, since he had to return at once to Budapest because of the parliamentary situation, he sent a formal letter of
protest to the Emperor Francis Joseph in which he declined to
share the responsibility for such a course.

We do not have sufficient proofs [he wrote] to be able to
place the responsibility for the crime on Serbia and to provoke
a war, in case the Serbian Government were to give satisfactory
explanations. We should have the worst *locus standi* imagi-
nable, and stand before the whole world as the disturbers of the
peace, besides having to begin a great war in the most unfavorable circumstances.

He did not, it is worth noting, object to war in principle: "it

* He may have yielded to pressure from his subordinates. The Austrian ambassador in Constantinople, the Marquis Pallavicini, expressed to his Bulgarian
colleague the opinion that Berchtold might show more independence, now that
Francis Ferdinand was no longer alive to interfere with him. Toshev to Radoslavov,
3 July; *KSF*, VI, 229 (March, 1928). The British ambassador in Vienna learned,
a little later, on the authority of "an Austrian gentleman in touch with the Ballplatz," that "while Count Berchtold is himself peacefully inclined, a feeling that
strong steps should be taken against Servia exists in the minds of several members
of the Austro-Hungarian Foreign Office whose opinions carry weight." Bunsen
to Grey, 13 July; B 55.

† Tisza to Francis Joseph, 1 July; A I 2. In replying to Conrad's suggestions
on 29 July, Berchtold hinted at the danger of revolution in Bohemia if a warlike
policy were adopted; Conrad, IV, 32. Perhaps he had not yet made up his own
mind; or he may merely have wished to prevent the impetuous and indiscreet
general from getting out of hand.

would be very easy to find a *casus belli* if one were wanted."
But, he argued, "we must first create a diplomatic constellation
which will change the proportions of military power in our
favor"; at the moment, Rumania was "as good as lost," and
Bulgaria had not been won. Therefore, while he approved of
"energetic action," he considered it advisable that his master
should "make use of the Emperor William's presence in Vienna
[he was expected for the funeral of Francis Ferdinand] to
combat that monarch's preference for Serbia . . . and induce
him to support us energetically in our contemplated Balkan
policy," *i. e.,* the cultivation of the Bulgarian alliance.*

Count Tisza's opposition threatened to thwart Count Berchtold's intentions altogether. His position in the Hungarian
parliament was so strong that he could not be defied and his
character was so rigid that an attempt to browbeat him would
only stiffen his resistance. But if his position could not be
forced by direct assault, it might be turned by a flank attack.
Count Berchtold accordingly turned to the task of outmanœu-
vering his colleague.

General Conrad had suggested that he should "ask Germany
whether or not she would guarantee us against Russia."† As
it happened, a strong hint had been received that the German
Government would be ready to give such a guarantee. On 1
July, Dr. Victor Naumann, a German publicist who was in close
relations with Herr von Jagow, the German foreign minister,
and Herr von Stumm, the director of the political department
at the Wilhelmstrasse, as well as with the officials of the Ballplatz,‡ called upon Count Alexander Hoyos, the *chef de cabinet*

---

* Tisza to Francis Joseph, 1 July; A I 2. Tisza was not alone in believing in
the German Emperor's preference for Serbia. "I have heard it said," reported the
British ambassador, "by Austrians who have had opportunities of hearing the
Emperor William speak on this subject that His Majesty has remained from the
first unconvinced of the wisdom of the policy adopted by this country of excluding Servia from the Adriatic, and does not conceal his belief that it would have
done better to allow the normal expansion of Servia to the sea to accomplish itself as a result of the first Balkan war." Bunsen to Grey, 5 July; B 40. For the
facts of the case, see above, pp. 136, 171–173.

† Conrad, IV, 34.

‡ Statement to the investigating committee of the Reichstag; Beilagen zu
den stenographischen Berichten über die öffentlichen Verhandlungen des Unter-

and confidant of Count Berchtold. Dr. Naumann expressed himself as follows:

He, himself, had been able to ascertain that not only in army and navy circles but also in the foreign office [in Berlin] the idea of a preventive war against Russia was not so entirely rejected as it had been a year ago. An agreement had been reached with England about Africa and the Portuguese colonies, and the visit of the British fleet to Kiel had been arranged as a documentation of the improved relations. Consequently they felt sure that England would not intervene in a European war. Furthermore the foreign office had been impressed by the oral reports of the former German consul in Moscow, who had now been recalled as *vortragender Rat** in the foreign office and had there given very noteworthy explanations about the Russian armaments. Herr von Stumm had spoken very earnestly of this danger to Dr. Naumann and indicated as not impossible a war "which Germany can have when she wants it."

Count Hoyos replied that "this disposition was at any rate not undesirable for us if we should come to the necessity of having to undertake something against Serbia"; whereupon Dr. Naumann continued:

This was exactly what he wished to propose to me. In his opinion, it was a question of existence for the Monarchy, after the murder of Sarajevo, not to let this crime go unpunished, but to annihilate Serbia. Such action would be the test for Germany whether Russia wished war or not. Berlin no longer counted on Rumania as an ally, but believed that the Rumanians would remain neutral at the beginning. They had been won over to the inclusion of Bulgaria and Turkey in the Triple Alliance and would also give the Bulgarians money; they also hoped to compel Greece to be neutral. On account of money difficulties, France would probably be compelled to work upon

suchungsausschusses (1. Unterausschuss), *Zur Vorgeschichte des Weltkrieges*, Heft I (Berlin, 1919), no. 8: English translation published by the Carnegie Endowment for International Peace under the title *Official German Documents relating to the World War*, 2 volumes (New York, 1923), volume I containing the material from Heft I of the German.

* Literally, 'reporting councillor.' Such an official corresponds roughly with a senior clerk in the British foreign office or a drafting officer in the American state department.

Russia in a pacific sense, but if nevertheless it came to a European war, the Triple Alliance was still strong enough now. Dr. Naumann believed that the Emperor William, if he were spoken to in the proper way at the present moment, when he is enraged over the murder at Sarajevo, will give us every assurance and will hold to it even to the point of war, because he recognizes the danger to the monarchical principle. They will not oppose this attitude in the foreign office, because they consider the moment favorable to bring about the great decision. With reference to public opinion in Germany, Naumann thought that it could never have been won for a war on account of Dyakova, but he would undertake to guarantee that it would place itself as one man at the side of its ally and would look upon war as an act of liberation. Austria-Hungary was lost as a monarchy and a Great Power if she did not make use of the present moment.

In conclusion, the German publicist promised to discuss the matter with Herr von Stumm.*

Thus well primed, Count Berchtold on the following day proceeded to talk with the German ambassador. After a theatrical hint that "twelve assassins were on their way to murder the German Emperor," he upbraided Herr von Tschirschky with the complaint that, in spite of assurances of German support, he had not always been supported by the Berlin Cabinet and that he did not know to what extent he could rely on it. The remark evidently struck home, for the ambassador replied that

privately he understood the attitude of his government to be due to the fact that we were always expounding ideas, but had never formed a definite plan of action, and that Berlin could make our cause its own only if we came forward with such a plan.

For a moment Herr von Tschirschky sought to minimize the effect of his words. To Prince Hohenlohe [ambassador-designate in Berlin], who had recently explained to him the necessity of a reckoning with Serbia, he had, he said, replied thus:

* Memorandum of Hoyos, 1 July; *Ö.-U. A.*, 9966.

That was all "very fine," but you must know and make clear how far you wish to go, and what you propose to do with Serbia in the event of a reckoning, and you must take care to create as favorable a diplomatic situation as possible. . . . It would be very unfortunate to begin war with Serbia without being sure that you would not also be attacked by Italy and Rumania.

But when Count Berchtold retorted that "what was to be done with Serbia in the event of victory had to be regarded as a *cura posterior*," complained that Germany had forced the Monarchy to "keep quiet" when Rumania had attacked Bulgaria, and demanded that Germany now restrain Rumania "if we, in order to protect the integrity of the Monarchy, should proceed against Serbia," Herr von Tschirschky declared that this was "entirely justified."* The implications of this language were clear enough,† all the more so since the ambassador had given even stronger intimations in another quarter.

* Memorandum of Berchtold, 3 July; A I 3. The German ambassador's report of this conversation, if he made one, has not been published. But probably he did not make one. On 30 June he had reported that he was taking every opportunity "to advise quietly, but very emphatically and seriously against too hasty steps." Tschirschky to Bethmann-Hollweg, 30 June; G 7. This was in keeping with the cautious attitude of the Wilhelmstrasse; but what he said to Berchtold on 2 July, which represented his private views, was in a very different strain, and it is easy to understand why Tschirschky did not inform Berlin of it, at least officially. According to Prince zu Stolberg, who was counsellor of the embassy in Vienna in July, 1914, "the ambassador, in view of the reproaches which were directed against German policy during the Balkan wars, to the effect that it has not sufficiently exerted itself in behalf of Austria-Hungary, conceived it to be his duty to uphold energetically in the interest of maintaining the alliance, Austria's point of view in foreign affairs."¹ Statement to the parliamentary investigating committee; *Zur Vorgeschichte des Weltkrieges*, I, no. 4.

† Tschirschky used even plainer language to the Vienna correspondent of the *Frankfurter Zeitung*, "obviously with the intention that his statements should be repeated to the ministry of foreign affairs." "Germany," he was reported to have said, "will support the Monarchy through thick and thin, whatever it may decide to do against Serbia; the sooner Austria-Hungary strikes, the better. It would have been better to act yesterday than to-day, but better to-day than to-morrow. Even if the German press, which is to-day quite anti-Serbian, should again cry for peace, Vienna should not let itself be deceived: Emperor and Empire will stand by Austria-Hungary unconditionally. One Great Power cannot speak more plainly to another." Gooss, p. 40, note 1, quoting a memorandum of 4 July; *Ö.-U. A.*, 10,038. At the suggestion of Forgách, this was sent to the Emperor and Tisza. To Baron Giesl, the minister in Belgrade, who happened to be in Vienna at the moment, Tschirschky said: "*Wenn Ihr Euch noch dies gefallen lasst, dann seid Ihr nicht wert, dass man Euch an . . .!*"; Giesl, *Zwei Jahrzehnte im Nahen Orient*, p. 255. When the British ambassador expressed the fear that Austro-Serbian relations would become more difficult, "Herr von Tschirsky [*sic*] said emphatically that those

After his conversation with Count Berchtold, the ambassador had been received by the Emperor Francis Joseph, in order that he might convey the regrets of the Emperor William at not being able to attend the funeral of the Archduke Francis Ferdinand.* Evidently impressed by Count Berchtold's reproaches, the ambassador, after listening to the Emperor's lamentations over the difficult situation of the Monarchy, used very decided language.

I took occasion to point out once more to His Majesty himself —as a few days before I had already stated very emphatically to Count Berchtold†—that His Majesty could count on finding Germany solidly behind the Monarchy whenever the question arose of defending one of its vital interests. The decision on the question when and where such a vital interest was at stake must be left to Austria herself. A responsible policy could not be founded on opinions and wishes, however comprehensible they might be. Before any decisive step was taken, it would have to be determined very exactly how far one would wish or would have to go and by what means the goal aimed at was to be reached. First of all, before taking any step that might involve serious consequences, the general political situation and the probable attitude of the other Powers and nations would have to be taken into consideration and the ground carefully prepared. I could only repeat that my emperor would stand behind every firm decision of Austria-Hungary. His Majesty agreed eagerly with my every word, and said that I was quite right.‡

Thus, if Count Berchtold appealed to Germany for support of his policy, there was every reason to expect a favorable answer.§

relations must be bad, and that nothing could mend them"; he laughed at the idea of "believing in the efficacy of a conciliatory policy on the part of Austria-Hungary." Bunsen to Grey, 5 July; B 40.

* Bethmann-Hollweg to Tschirschky, telegram, 2 July; G 6B.

† There is no record in the published German documents of any such statement by Tschirschky to Berchtold, but the ambassador did not always report his conversations.

‡ Tschirschky to Bethmann-Hollweg, 2 July; G 11.

§ The moment was particularly auspicious for an appeal. In October, 1913, when Berchtold had prepared his ultimatum to Serbia demanding the evacuation of certain Albanian territories which Serbian troops had occupied (see above, p.

There was no time to lose, for the German Emperor was scheduled to depart very soon on his annual cruise to Norway. But Count Berchtold was embarrassed by the position in which he found himself. On 3 July Tisza wrote him a letter asking for a conference of ministers to discuss the policy to be followed in Bosnia-Herzegovina. In this letter the Hungarian premier said:

The local administration [i. e., in Bosnia-Herzegovina] can scarcely have the right to lay the blame on Serbia, when they themselves passively watched the agitation spread in their own land and allowed it to grow unchecked until awakened from their optimism by the horrible deed of the 28th.

If facts are produced which entitle us to make a *démarche* on Serbia, then whatever is necessary must be done. Serbia will hardly give us just grounds for warlike measures and without them it would be an irreparable mistake to enter upon such a war.

The main thing is, and continues to be, to keep things in order in our own country, and in this connection I cannot help referring to the genuinely shocking revelations which must be made in connection with the Sarajevo investigation.*

Clearly, Tisza's attitude had not changed since he had addressed his protest to the Emperor. In such circumstances, to request officially German support for the policy of war against Serbia

138), he sought the opinion of the German Government before despatching it. As it happened, the German foreign minister, Herr von Jagow, was on leave. The acting minister, Under-secretary of State Dr. Zimmermann, promptly promised "moral support" and the Emperor expressed to the foreign office his "great satisfaction," while Bethmann acquiesced. Cf. Conrad, III, 469–470; *G. P.*, XXXVI, nos. 14,160, 14,161, 14,162, 14,172. Early in July, 1914, Zimmermann was once more, in the absence of Jagow on his honeymoon, directing the German foreign office, and Moltke, the chief of the general staff, who did not wish to see the Austrian army, which he counted on to hold back the Russians in a general war, involved in operations against Serbia, was absent on leave. Whether such considerations entered into Berchtold's decision to approach the German Government, does not appear from the documents available.

* H. F. Armstrong, "A Letter of Count Tisza," in *Foreign Affairs* (New York), VI, 502 (April, 1928). On the previous day, Tisza wrote to Bilinski, who was responsible for Bosnian affairs, protesting that the Pan-Serbian agitation had been conducted "under the eyes of the authorities" and demanding "prompt and drastic" [*dringend und radikal*] action to put an end to it. He sent a copy of the letter to the Austrian premier. *Gróf Tisza István Összes Munkai* (Budapest, 1924), 4. Sorozat, II, nos. 15, 16.

would never do: when Tisza heard of the matter, as he was bound to do, he was likely to be more hostile than ever; and it would be a gross blunder to convince Germany that war with Serbia was necessary, to receive a promise of German support *i. e.,* against Russia—and then have to discard it because of Tisza's veto.

Count Berchtold was confronted by still another problem. Although he and General Conrad were each in favor of war with Serbia they had quite different views on the method of procedure. They had discussed the matter twice in the autumn of 1913 when it seemed that the action of Serbia in Albania would give them the long-desired excuse for war. The normal procedure would be to present an ultimatum and, if it were rejected, to order mobilization. The chief of staff had, on 28 July, 1913, devised an iron-clad formula of procedure which would prevent any foiling of his plans and which, as the final event proved, was followed to the letter exactly one year later.

If an ultimatum is sent to Serbia [he advised Count Berchtold], it must from the very beginning be put in such a way that should Serbia fail to comply entirely and immediately, that is, before mobilization here, any compliance at a later date, after our mobilization has begun, should not be accepted, but the war against Serbia should be carried through fully and completely. It would have to be arranged beforehand and with absolute certainty that voices which might urge leniency would remain unheeded.*

But, as mobilization would require sixteen days (this was the official period, although Count Berchtold talked of "three weeks"), the foreign minister foresaw a period of extreme diplomatic tension. To avoid this danger, he proposed on September 29, 1913, the occupation of the Serbian town of Shabats, that is, by troops immediately available. ' *"Ultimatum" und "Einmarschieren"* ' was his formula, and he would say to the Serbs: "So long as you do not get out of Albania, we

* Conrad, III, 407.

shall not get out of Shabats." To this suggestion, the chief of
staff replied:

Either the Serbs will let us sit there and laugh at us, or they
will attack us; the first would be a fatal position, the latter, war.
So the question remains: Either we wish war or we do not. If
"not," then we had better keep our mouth shut, reserve our
freedom for the future, and withdraw from the London conference. Now is the chance to establish order down there [*i. e.*,
in Serbia and Montenegro]. An ultimatum, and, if Albania is
not evacuated in 24 hours, then mobilization.

And he pointed out that '*Einmarschieren*' was not practicable
for a '*Kaderheer*,' that is, for an army that had to be mobilized.* Several weeks later Count Berchtold returned to this
idea "of occupying Serbian territory with troops on a peace
footing." This time General Conrad replied:

What are you thinking of [*Wie stellen Sie sich das vor*]?
If we mobilize, Potiorek will have 80,000 infantry, but now
he has only 25,000 altogether, and they are scattered all over
Bosnia.†

From the military point of view, there were not enough Austro-Hungarian forces on a peace footing to carry out an operation against the resistance which Serbia might be expected to
make, and the use of the troops for such a purpose would interfere with the mobilization that would immediately become
necessary.

This point is of such importance, as will be repeatedly seen
in the succeeding pages of this narrative, that a fuller explanation is required. The basis of mobilization, under the Continental system of universal military service, was that each unit
of the standing army in time of peace was designated as the
nucleus of one or more larger units on a war footing. On the
proclamation of mobilization the reservists proceed to join the
units to which they are assigned, at places previously desig-

* Conrad, III, 443-444.   † *Ibid.*, III, 474.

nated; at these places, and nowhere else, are awaiting them their uniforms and equipment, as well as the cadres of officers and trained men necessary to constitute their war-time units. The units thus formed on a war footing are then moved to designated points near the frontier; the movements are carried out by railway schedules carefully prepared in advance, insusceptible of alteration. The units arrived at the place of concentration are then formed into divisions and corps and armies, and are ready to cross the frontier and begin fighting. To move regiments and divisions on a peace footing into Serbia, as Count Berchtold proposed, would be synonymous with destroying in advance the whole mechanism of mobilization, for, if mobilization were subsequently ordered, the reservists arriving at their dépôts would find no skeleton units to absorb them and the forward movement of the troops on a peace footing would utterly disrupt the railway schedules arranged for mobilizing. But mobilization, in Conrad's view, would certainly become imperative, for it was to be assumed that Serbia would resist an Austrian attack and would mobilize, that is to say, mobilize all her forces, and Austria-Hungary would have to follow suit or face a superiority of numbers. The chief of staff, therefore, rightly insisted on mobilization as the preliminary to action against Serbia. To the foreign minister's plaintive query, "How shall we get through the three weeks?" he replied:

That cannot be changed, it lies in the nature of things. We shall get through them if we have the necessary firmness.*

In July, 1914, this divergence of views was again manifested. If General Conrad had had his way, as already noted, mobilization would have been ordered immediately on the news of the murder. But on 6 July he was asked by Count Berchtold whether mobilization would be necessary "if we march into Serbia and occupy a sufficient bit of territory."† Evidently

---

* *Ibid.*, III, 466.

† *Ibid.*, IV, 62. In 1928 Count Berchtold stated to the writer that "he had in mind military action to be undertaken immediately, that is, without mobilization."

the foreign minister clung to his plan, and the subsequent narrative will show how greatly the course of events was influenced by this fact.

Since he had secured neither the consent of Count Tisza to his plan for a "reckoning with Serbia" nor the approval of General Conrad for the scheme of seizing Serbian territory, Count Berchtold had to be exceedingly careful in his approach to the German Government.* It was for this reason, as far as one can judge, that he decided to send his *chef de cabinet,* Count Hoyos, to Berlin for personal consultations with the German statesmen. Concerning this mission, Count Hoyos has written:

> Count Berchtold would have been ready to lay aside all the serious arguments which spoke for war, and, in opposition to the entire public opinion of Austria and Hungary, to take a stand for a programme which would dispose of the controversy with Serbia if such a policy had been recommended to him in reply to his inquiry in Berlin.†

This language suggests that Count Berchtold, while at the moment disposed to adopt the policy of military action against

---

* Count Berchtold, almost alone among the survivors of the July crisis, has not published his *apologia.* He has confined himself to four brief statements: (1) "Die Richtlinien der österreichisch-ungarischen Politik," in Steinitz, *Rings um Sasonow,* pp. 41–58, translated in *Contemporary Review,* CXXXIII, 422–432 (April, 1928); (2) "Austria's Challenge Justified by Serbian Menace," in *Current History,* XXVIII, 626–627 (July, 1928); (3) "Eine Diskussion zwischen Amerikanern, Oesterreichern und Deutschen über die Kriegsschuldfrage," in *KSF,* VI, 1000–1004 (October, 1928); (4) "Did I Desire the World War?" in *Pesti Hirlap* (Budapest), 20 December, 1928, in Hungarian, translated into German in *KSF,* VII, 620–626 (June, 1929). In the last article, which is a reply to E. Fischer, *Die kritischen 39 Tage von Sarajevo bis zum Weltbrand* (Berlin, 1928), Berchtold seeks to minimize the difference between himself and Tisza, arguing that since the Hungarian premier was in favor of "energetic action" against Serbia, the difference between them concerned only the manner of procedure. He has to admit, however, that the difference was between *"das gewaltsame Vorgehen . . . (sans crier gare!),"* that is, immediate military action, and *"ein Ultimatum mit schweren Folgen,"* and he does not state that (as will be seen later) Tisza long held out for an ultimatum which could be accepted by Serbia. The contemporary evidence leaves no doubt that at the moment when Berchtold turned to Berlin, the difference between himself and Tisza was fundamental, he desiring to inaugurate military action against Serbia, Tisza opposing this course. Fischer, *op. cit.,* pp. 54–56, argues that Berchtold appealed to the German Government against Tisza, and the available evidence implicitly supports this hypothesis. Berchtold, however, denies the charge.

† Hoyos, *Der deutsch-englische Gegensatz und sein Einfluss auf die Balkanpolitik Oesterreich-Ungarns,* p. 79.

Serbia, was still vacillating; but it reveals most clearly that the final decision of the Austro-Hungarian Government depended upon the response of its German ally to the overtures about to be made. To prepare the way for these soundings, the Austro-Hungarian ambassador in the German capital was informed that Count Hoyos was coming with important documents, and he was instructed to have an audience of the Emperor if possible, and in any case to see Herr von Bethmann-Hollweg. "It is of the utmost importance," the ambassador was told, "that before the departure of the Emperor the chancellor should be able to discuss the contents of these documents with your Excellency and with the Emperor."*

Count Hoyos took with him to Berlin (1) the long memorandum already prepared in which the policy of a Bulgarian alliance was set forth.† This had the sanction of Count Tisza and could be safely presented. Naturally, Count Berchtold added a few paragraphs in connection with "the frightful occurrence at Sarajevo." In this postcript, the "ruthless assassination" was declared to afford "unmistakable evidence of the insuperability of the antagonism between the Monarchy and Serbia," and "so much the more imperative" was asserted to be "the necessity for the Monarchy to destroy with a determined hand the net which its enemies are attempting to throw about its head."‡ But this, though preparing the ground, was rather vague, and did not commit the Austro-Hungarian Government to any particular course toward Serbia.

Count Hoyos was also provided with (2) an autograph letter, drafted at the Ballplatz, from Francis Joseph to William II, which was an exceedingly skilful document. After expressing his regret that the German Emperor had been forced to abandon his plan to attend the funeral of the late Archduke, "for it would have been very agreeable to me to discuss the political situation," the Habsburg ruler declared that Rumania had become quite unreliable as an ally and argued that only

---

* Berchtold to Szögyény, telegram, 4 July; A I 4.   † See above, pp. 163–166.
‡ Memorandum of the Austro-Hungarian Government; A I 1, supplement; G 14.

an alliance with Bulgaria would bring Rumania back to the
fold of the Triple Alliance or, if that were impossible, establish the necessary counter-weight; all of which had been said,
much more fully, in the memorandum. But Francis Joseph
proceeded to carry the argument a step farther by linking up
the proposed policy with the question of Serbia. The letter
continues:

According to all the evidence so far brought to light, the
affair at Sarajevo was not the bloody deed of an individual, but
the result of a well-organized conspiracy, the threads of which
reach to Belgrade; and even if, as is supposedly the case, it will
be impossible to prove the complicity of the Serbian Government, there can indeed be no doubt that its policy, which is
directed toward the union of all Southern Slavs under the
Serbian flag, incites to such crimes, and that the continuation
of such a state of affairs constitutes a permanent danger for
my House and my territories. . . .
The efforts of my government must in the future be directed
toward the isolation and diminution of Serbia. The first step
in this direction should be to strengthen the position of the
present Bulgarian Government, in order that Bulgaria, whose
real interests are identical with our own, may be preserved
from a relapse into a Russophile policy.
If it is understood in Bucharest that the Triple Alliance is
determined not to forego the adhesion of Bulgaria to it, but
is none the less ready to induce Bulgaria to bind herself to
Rumania and respect the latter's territorial integrity, perhaps
people there will draw back from the dangerous course into
which they have been driven by friendship with Serbia and the
rapprochement with Russia.
Should this prove successful, we might further attempt to
reconcile Greece with Turkey and Bulgaria, so that there might
develop, under the patronage of the Triple Alliance, a new
Balkan league, the purpose of which would be to put a stop
to the advance of the Panslav current and to assure peace for
our countries.
This, however, will be possible only if Serbia, which at present serves as the pivot of Panslav policy, has been *eliminated
as a factor of political power in the Balkans.*
After the recent frightful occurrences in Bosnia, you too will

be convinced that *a reconciliation of the antagonism that now separates us from Serbia is no longer to, be thought of,* and that the continuance of the pacific policy of all European monarchs will be threatened as long as this centre of criminal agitation in Belgrade is not subjected to punishment.*

The royal letter served two purposes. Not only did it notify the German ally that Austria-Hungary contemplated an aggressive policy for the realization of a positive programme, —the isolation and diminution of Serbia, and its elimination as a political factor in the Balkan peninsula,—but by reserving the revelation for the autograph letter, Francis Joseph made an appeal to the personal feeling of William II, a bit of flattery which speaks much for Count Berchtold's appreciation of the monarch with whom he was dealing and which may well have been inspired by the recollection of what the German ruler had said in the previous October.†

But Tschirschky had advised Berchtold and his sovereign to submit "a definite plan," and Francis Joseph's letter did not explain how the Austro-Hungarian programme for the isolation and diminution and the punishment of Serbia was to be carried out. Certainly the proposal of an alliance with Bulgaria, which was the principal theme of the two documents sent to Berlin, would not suffice for the realization of such a policy in respect of Serbia. What Count Berchtold had in mind was, as has been noted, military action against Serbia. But he obviously could not, in the face of Count Tisza's opposition, propose this in formal communications addressed to the German Emperor and the German Government. The neces-

---

* Francis Joseph to William II, 2 July; A I 1; G 13. Berchtold sent the draft of this letter to Tisza in Budapest. The Hungarian premier objected to the words in italics, but his telegram reached Vienna only after the letter had gone to Berlin. Fraknói, *Die ungarische Regierung und die Entstehung des Weltkrieges,* p. 46. Tisza's objections to the two passages seem to have rested on tactical grounds only; he urged their elimination "in order not to make Berlin skittish" [*kopfscheu*]. Gooss, *Das Wiener Kabinett und die Entstehung des Weltkrieges,* p. 29; *Ö.-U. A.,* 10,070. Presumably Tisza was so convinced of William II's partiality for Serbia that he feared the effect of even the slightest hint that Austria-Hungary contemplated far-reaching action.

† See above, p. 171.

sary explanations had thus to be given verbally, and it was (3) to make them, so one is justified in believing, that Count Hoyos was sent to Berlin, for the memorandum and the autograph letter could easily have been sent by courier. It is true that Count Berchtold has stated that "neither Szögyény [the ambassador in Berlin] nor Hoyos received instructions which stood in opposition to the content of the imperial and royal autograph letter and the memorandum of the ministry of foreign affairs sent to Berlin."* But Hoyos may well have received instructions, not "in opposition to" the official documents, but in explanation and clarification of their meaning. As a matter of fact, we shall see that matters were spoken of at Berlin by Count Szögyény and Count Hoyos to which there is no reference in the official documents, a circumstance possible only if the latter revealed what he knew to be in his chief's mind; while the further fact that Count Hoyos was subsequently disavowed in respect of one statement but not on account of two others only strengthens the hypothesis that he was authorized, in some form or other, to make clear to the German Government what policy Count Berchtold wished to pursue, and how he proposed to execute it. Incidentally, this informal procedure possessed the advantage of leaving Count Berchtold a certain freedom to choose his own method of action on receipt of the German answer.

The skill of the Austro-Hungarian foreign minister arouses one's admiration. Outwardly, he advocates the new diplomatic policy urged by the Hungarian premier; privately, he intimates that he wishes to go beyond mere diplomatic measures. He leaves it to the German Government to choose the course. If Berlin favors the policy of military action against Serbia, it will have to promise its support for the event of that action leading to war with Russia; such a promise will provide Count Berchtold with a powerful weapon for use against Count Tisza, who will no longer be able to speak of the German

* *Pesti Hirlap*, 20 December, 1928; *KSF*, VII, 623 (June, 1929).

Emperor's partiality for Serbia. If, on the other hand, Berlin advises a cautious attitude toward Serbia and recommends a diplomatic solution of the difficulty, Count Berchtold will be able to resist the popular clamor for the punishment of Serbia and avoid the risk of precipitating a European war. Whatever the answer, the responsibility for the policy of Austria-Hungary will rest in no small measure on the shoulders of the German Government.

Note on the Funeral of the Archduke

While the plans just described were maturing, public interest centered on the funeral of the Archduke Francis Ferdinand and his consort. Although this event had no bearing on the political situation, it deserves a brief reference because of certain sensational and perplexing incidents. The bodies of the murdered pair were removed from Sarajevo to the Dalmatian coast; thence they were conveyed in a war-ship to Trieste, where solemn honors were rendered. They reached Vienna late on the evening of 2 July. The court chamberlain, Prince Montenuovo, had ordered that there should be no formal reception and the body of the Duchess of Hohenberg should be sent direct to the Archduke's vault at Arstetten, an old castle on the Danube some sixty miles west of Vienna. The new heir apparent, the Archduke Charles, however, insisted on going to the station, and under the pressure of public opinion both bodies were placed in the chapel of the Hofburg, a small edifice hardly suited to the dignity of the deceased personages.

The funeral service was held on the following afternoon, in the presence of the Emperor and the court. The Archduke lay in a large coffin, upon which were placed his full insignia; that of his wife was small, and on it lay a pair of white gloves and a black fan—reminders of her former position as a lady-in-waiting. The foreign ambassadors brought wreaths from their sovereigns, but no flowers were sent by the Emperor Francis Joseph or the members of the imperial family; the Archduke's children were not allowed to attend the funeral!

Although Francis Ferdinand had been the acting head of the army, it was only after a protest from the aristocracy that at the

last moment the Emperor allowed the streets to the railway station
to be lined with troops. Even then the aristocracy was not invited
to the funeral. Some hundred and fifty of the greatest nobles,
however, assembled in full uniform and followed the cortège on
foot.

The funeral train did not depart until 11 P. M. and reached
Pöchlarn, the station for Arstetten, at 1 A. M. At this moment a
terrific storm burst and the coffins had to be deposited in the wait-
ing-room until they could be ferried across the river in the morning. On 4 July the bodies were laid to rest in the chapel built by
the Archduke because his wife was too low-born to rest in the
Habsburg vaults of the Capuchin church in Vienna.*

These arrangements were bitterly commented on, because they
seemed to indicate a deliberate intent to insult the dead. The British
ambassador, who was informed that "the ceremonial followed
closely the traditional 'Spanish' rites of the Imperial Court,"
thought that the exercises were cut short in order to spare the aged
Emperor unnecessary fatigue.† But the well-known dislike of
Francis Joseph for his nephew, the notorious resentment of the
whole Habsburg family for the Duchess of Hohenberg, the fact
that the Archduke's papers at Konopischt were seized immediately
after the assassination, and the publication of a rescript to Prince
Montenuovo thanking him for having acted "in accordance with
His Majesty's intentions"—all this suggested that the slight was
deliberate and was meant to indicate that the removal of Francis
Ferdinand was not altogether unwelcome. The government felt it
necessary to issue an official explanation to the effect that the bodies
of the Empress Elizabeth and the Archduke Rudolph had been
received at night and that the military display for the latter had
not been more considerable.‡

In Hungary the mourning was strictly official. "All amuse-
ments went on as usual and on the day following the assassination
there was an especially large attendance at the races." When the
official requiem service was held in Budapest, "the upper classes
were conspicuous by their absence, most of them preferring to attend a wedding . . . the bridegroom and the bride belonging re-

---

* Seton-Watson, 103–106; Steed, I, 401–403.
† Bunsen to Grey, 4 July; B 34.   ‡ Bunsen to Grey, 5 July; B 37.

spectively to the great houses of Szapary and Esterhazy." There was considerable criticism of the funeral arrangements, the feeling in political circles being that the occasion should have been used to organize an impressive and useful demonstration of the unity of the peoples of the Monarchy.*

On 5 July, one week after the tragedy, the Emperor issued a letter of thanks to the peoples of the Monarchy for the innumerable proofs of warm affection and sincere sympathy which had reached him from all classes of the population. Recalling that he had shared their joys and sorrows for six and a half decades, he declared that this new trial would only strengthen his determination to persevere till his last breath on the path best designed to promote the general welfare. In a general order to the army and navy the late Archduke was declared to have died in the performance of his duties, and it was stated that his loss involved a heavy sacrifice for the sovereign and for the armed forces. But his work had borne fruit, and, thanks to it, "the Monarchy will find its sure support in the fearless devotion of the faithful and indomitable army of Austria-Hungary."

In view of the treatment accorded the dead prince, these documents are somewhat singular in tone, almost hypocritical; but they were no doubt designed to convey the impression that the Monarchy would face the future with dignity and calm and to allay any fears of precipitate action.

Equally strange was the attitude toward the presence of foreign potentates. The German Emperor announced forthwith that he would attend the funeral, accompanied by his brother Prince Henry;† King George of Great Britain intended to depute Prince Arthur of Connaught. But in consequence of warnings from the German consul at Sarajevo against the possible presence of assassins in Vienna,‡ the Emperor William decided not to go, at the same time asking Francis Joseph to believe "how painful it was to him to have to come to this decision," which "might be imputed to a lack of personal courage";§ officially it was given out that the

---

* Max Müller to Grey, 14 July; B 70.
† Goschen to Grey, telegram from Kiel, 28 June; B 12.
‡ Eiswald to foreign office, telegram, 1 July; G 6A.
§ Bethmann-Hollweg to Tschirschky, telegram, 2 July; G 6B.

Emperor was suffering from lumbago,* and "great stress is laid in the press announcements on the fact that this decision has in no way been influenced by political considerations or by fear for the safety of the Emperor."†

Actually, the presence of foreign princes was not desired at the funeral. The reason given out was that it was "very important to spare the Emperor fatigue and to shorten ceremonies as much as possible."‡ But it has been suspected that Count Berchtold was anxious to avoid any discussion of the Serbian question,§ and, in any case, the impression was most unfavorable.

* Rumbold to Grey, 3 July; B 26.

† Rumbold to Grey, telegram, 2 July; B 24. The official explanation was received in Vienna with scepticism. "There is a strong belief among well-informed Press people," the British ambassador learned, "that the true reason is the discovery of an anarchist or Slav Nationalist plot directed against the Emperor William or some other great person." Bunsen to Nicolson, 3 July; B 29.

‡ Bunsen to Grey, telegram, 29 June; B 18.

§ Margutti, Vom alten Kaiser, p. 151. Curiously enough, Berchtold's confidant Hoyos laments that there was no such discussion. He thinks that it might have been possible to make clear to foreign princes the danger to Austria-Hungary from the Serbian agitation. Hoyos, pp. 77–78, note. It is much more likely that foreign visitors would have impressed upon Francis Joseph the risk involved in war with Serbia.

CHAPTER V

HOHENZOLLERN'S BOND

THE news of Sarajevo was received in Germany with "conster-
nation," if the British chargé d'affaires in Berlin judged correctly. "Great and universal sympathy with the aged Emperor
Francis Joseph" was mingled with horror over a crime which
"deprived His Majesty [the German Emperor] of an intimate
friend." On the political side the press, while lamenting that
"one certain factor" in the relations of Germany and Austria-
Hungary had been removed, expressed the opinion that "nothing will be changed in the relations between the two allies."
Nevertheless, a certain anxiety was soon noticeable.

Since the Balkan wars [observed the British chargé], doubts
have sprung up in Germany as to the extent to which she can
reckon on military assistance from her neighbor in the event
of a general war. The idea is that Austria-Hungary would be
hampered by having to prepare for eventualities on the Serbian
frontier. This idea has been strengthened by the recent crime
at Sarajevo. . . . The attitude of the Austro-Hungarian Government at this juncture is therefore being watched with anxious
interest.*

German public opinion appears to have been rather bewil-
dered by the situation. The first impressions were decidedly
hostile to Serbia and even dangerous. The liberal *Vossische Zeitung* asserted that Pashich had known that something would
happen to the Archduke and tried to lay the ultimate responsibility on Russia; the Catholic *Germania* accused the Serbian
Government of allowing the conspiracy to develop under its
eyes, while the *Tägliche Rundschau* hinted that the threads
stretched to a member of the royal family. The Catholic *Köl-*

* Rumbold to Grey, 3 July; B 26.

nische Volkzeitung urged Austria to "pluck up her courage and
become the schoolmaster of the East"; the chauvinistic *Leipziger Neueste Nachrichten* asked "whether Austria was going
to allow the Slav danger to increase until it stifled Germanism."
But a few days' reflection produced a calmer mood. The semi-
official *Lokal-Anzeiger* on 5 July declared that it did not wish
to impute the crime of Sarajevo to the Serbian Government,
and Maximilian Harden in his *Zukunft* proclaimed that "Serbia is innocent." The conservative *Deutsche Tageszeitung*
warned Vienna not to make the crime the point of departure
for a new Balkan policy, while the liberal *Berliner Tageblatt* was
alarmed by the rumor of an Austrian demand for an investigation in Serbia. The Pan-German *Morgenpost* expressed the
hope that Vienna would not lose its head, and the liberal *Frankfurter Zeitung* advised against measures of revenge. As was to
be expected, the socialist *Vorwärts* urged the Vienna government not to be stampeded by "the dangerous excitement that
had taken possession of the Austrian people." All in all, German
opinion, without distinction of party, appears, after the first
shock of the assassination had passed off, to have assumed a
cautious attitude. It was anti-Serbian and inclined to gibe at
the Austrians for their vacillations, but it was not provocative;
if it did not give the government a clear lead, it certainly did not
demand an aggressive policy on the part of Germany nor a
free hand for the ally on the Danube.*

The attitude of the German Government was also one of
reserve, at least for the moment. "When the news of the murders at Sarajevo became known, there was," wrote the British
chargé, "evidently anxiety in official quarters lest the Austro-
Hungarian Government might take some precipitate action
against Serbia which would have far-reaching consequences."†
The sound advice was accordingly given to the Serbian Government, through the medium of the Russian ambassador in Berlin, "spontaneously to offer to do all they could to help the
Bosnian authorities in their investigations into the origin and

* Scott, *Five Weeks*, pp. 101–112.   † Rumbold to Grey, 11 July; B 44.

ramifications of the plot."* The Bavarian minister in Berlin
reported to his government in much the same strain:

Yesterday's alarming report to the effect that Austria-Hungary had laid claim to the conduct of the inquiry in Serbia and
that Serbia had refused this interference, has since been denied.
At the foreign office here it is even hoped that Serbia will now
neglect nothing necessary to call to account the persons involved
in the plot. Under-Secretary of State Zimmermann at once
called the attention of the Serbian chargé d'affaires to the
serious consequences to which a refusal on the part of Serbia
in this matter might lead, and furthermore suggested to the
Russian ambassador that he should get his government to use
the same language in Belgrade.†

Certainly no exception could be taken by Serbia, or her friends,
to this advice.

The Wilhelmstrasse could hardly have taken any other position. Herr von Jagow, the foreign minister, was away on his
honeymoon; Herr von Bethmann-Hollweg, the chancellor, had
gone to his country-seat at Hohenfinow; the Emperor, greatly
upset by the tragedy at Sarajevo, had retired to the seclusion
of Potsdam. For the conduct of foreign policy, the 'German
Government' consisted of Dr. Zimmermann, the under-secretary of the foreign office, who obviously lacked the authority
to take any decided initiative in the present circumstances.
Naturally, therefore, he followed up his prudent advice to
Serbia with corresponding counsels of moderation to Vienna.
On 4 July he told Count Szögyény, the Austro-Hungarian
ambassador, that while "energetic action" on the part of Austria would be "perfectly justified, he would advise great discretion and would not like to see humiliating conditions proposed to Serbia."‡

---

* Rumbold to Grey, 30 June; B 22.
† Lerchenfeld to Hertling, 2 July; P. Dirr, *Bayerische Dokumente zum Kriegsaus-bruch und zum Versailler Schuldspruch*, third enlarged edition (Munich, 1925), p. 118. Some of the Bavarian documents, those emanating from the legation in Berlin, are printed as appendix IV of *Die deutschen Dokumente zum Kriegsausbruch.*
‡ Szögyény to Berchtold, telegram, 4 July; A I 5.

Unfortunately, indications are wholly lacking about the immediate reaction of Herr von Bethmann-Hollweg to the crime at Sarajevo, and the evidence concerning the Emperor is meagre. We have seen, however, that two weeks before that event both of them were professing the deepest concern about Russia's policy.* Nor was this, in the case of the chancellor, a fleeting impression. In conversation with Prince Lichnowsky on 29 June, Herr von Bethmann refused to share the optimistic views of Russian policy which the ambassador had just brought from London :†

The Russian armaments [said the chancellor], concerning which the general staff had sent him a full report, were assuming proportions which could not but cause uneasiness in Germany. An increase of 900,000 men was being provided for, and in addition to this the Russians were building railways to our frontiers. Finally, he said that he would tell me in confidence that, according to secret and reliable reports which he had received, a naval agreement was being drawn up between Russia and England. This agreement provided that in case of war English freight steamers were to transport Russian troops to the coast of Pomerania.‡

After Sarajevo it was to be supposed that Austria-Hungary would demand some kind of satisfaction from Serbia. What form that satisfaction might take would not be known until the Cabinet of Vienna had shown its hand. But if Russia were itching for an excuse to make war, as both William II

---

* See above, pp. 102–103.

† Just before leaving London, Lichnowsky reported Grey as saying: "The Emperor and M. Sazonov always expressed themselves in the most pacific manner, though it could not be denied that M. Sazonov had the desire that the Triple Entente should make a somewhat more robust appearance as a counterweight to the solid block of the Triple Alliance." Lichnowsky to Bethmann-Hollweg, 24 June; G 5. For Sazonov's desire to convert the Triple Entente into a triple alliance, see above, pp. 52–53.

‡ "England vor dem Kriege," a memorandum written in August, 1914, immediately after the ambassador's return to Germany; Fürst Lichnowsky, *Auf dem Wege zum Abgrund* (Berlin, 1927), I, 38. In the famous memorandum written in 1916 and published two years later, *Meine Londoner Mission*, Lichnowsky ascribes to Zimmermann, rather than to Bethmann, the statement that Russia was adding 900,000 men to her army, though he also says that the chancellor "complained about Russian armaments"; *ibid.*, I, 128.

and Herr von Bethmann had asserted two weeks before the murder, could a better one be found than the necessity of defending Serbia from too harsh demands on the part of Austria-Hungary? The excitable and unstable Emperor might easily surrender to his emotions and throw discretion to the winds. But the chancellor was not, like his master, prone to precipitate action, and he had clearly recognized the danger inherent in the Austro-Russian rivalry. It was to be expected, on his own showing, that he would weigh carefully any proposals submitted by the Austro-Hungarian Government and consider their possible effect on Russia. What the chancellor said in June, 1914, makes his post-war statement, "At the beginning of the crisis I assumed that even a Russian mind would shrink from taking the last fearful step except under extreme necessity,"* singularly unconvincing.

William II seems to have been greatly upset by the tragic end of a prince whom he had visited two weeks before; when the news was brought to him while yachting at Kiel, he is said to have exclaimed, "Now I've got to begin all over again!"†— whatever that may have meant. The imperial yacht was put about and the regatta stopped. On reaching shore the Emperor despatched two telegrams. To the Emperor Francis Joseph he said:

Completely overwhelmed by the news from Sarajevo, I beg You to accept the expression of my deeply felt sympathy. We must bow before God's decree which once more imposes heavy trials.

To Herr von Bethmann-Hollweg, who had sent the news, he replied:

The cowardly and execrable crime to which his Imperial

---

* T. von Bethmann-Hollweg, *Betrachtungen zum Weltkrieg* (Berlin, 1919), I, 132.

† R. Recouly, *Les heures tragiques d'avant-guerre* (Paris, n. d.), p. 20, quoting Jules Cambon, the French ambassador in Berlin, who had it from "a personage who was with the Emperor at that moment." According to another account, William remarked to the British ambassador, "It is a crime against Germanism [*das Deutschtum*]"; Beyens, *L'Allemagne avant la guerre*, p. 273.

Highness the Heir Apparent, my dear friend, and his consort have fallen victims, moves me to the depths of my soul.*

He then cancelled all his engagements and returned the next day to his capital. If his post-war recollections are correct, he wished to give up the cruise to Norway, being unwilling to leave the country "when the future was so unsettled"; the date of departure was actually postponed from 6 July to the 14th. But the chancellor represented that a sudden change of plans announced two months before would cause uneasiness in other countries and affect the stock exchanges of Europe. Wherefore, "with a heavy heart," the Emperor agreed to leave on the date arranged.†

For the week following the murder at Sarajevo, we have only one sure indication of his state of mind, but in that one record William II evidently revealed his innermost feelings, and he fairly let himself go in a manner that hardly betokened "a heavy heart." He has before him a report from his ambassador in Vienna,‡ on the views prevalent in the Austrian capital. Count Berchtold regrets that

the affair [the murder at Sarajevo] was so well thought out that very young men were intentionally selected for the perpetration of the crime, upon whom only a mild punishment could be inflicted.

"I hope not," notes William. Nevertheless, the ambassador hears expressed, "even among serious people, the wish that a thorough reckoning must be had with the Serbs once for all."

---

* Quoted by K. Jagow, "Der Potsdamer Kronrat," in *Süddeutsche Monatshefte*, XXV, 779 (August, 1928). A few days later he telegraphed to the Grand Duchess Louise: "This unspeakable misfortune has shaken me also to the depths. May God comfort the unfortunate children and the poor old gentleman."

† Kaiser Wilhelm II, *Ereignisse und Gestalten, 1878–1918* (Leipzig, 1922), p. 209; K. Jagow, *loc. cit.*, XXV, 783. On 5 July, Falkenhayn, the minister of war, informed Moltke, then at Carlsbad, that the chancellor "has not only raised no objections to the northern cruise, but has even advised it." Graf M. Montgelas, *Leitfaden zur Kriegsschuldfrage* (Berlin, 1923), p. 196.

‡ Tschirschky to Bethmann-Hollweg, 30 June; G 7. Received on 2 July, transmitted at once to the Emperor, and returned by him on 4 July.

"Now or never," is the imperial advice. Then he comes to what the ambassador himself is doing: "I take advantage of every such occasion to advise quietly, but very emphatically and seriously, against too hasty steps." These words the Emperor underscores, and then he delivers himself of the following:

Who authorized him to act thus? That is very stupid! It is absolutely none of his business, for it is solely Austria's affair what she intends to do in this matter. Afterward, if things go wrong, it will be said that Germany was not willing! Tschirschky will please drop this nonsense! The Serbs must be disposed of, *and* that right *soon!**

Taken by themselves, these wild words indicate no more than that William II was in one of his excitable moods—which were often succeeded by periods of pessimism and depression. But we have seen that in the autumn of 1913 he had pondered for several months the idea of a war launched by Austria-Hungary against Serbia, in case an understanding between those two states could not be reached, and in May, 1914, had said that he considered an understanding out of the question.† His com-

---

* Since the Emperor's comments were often acted upon, it is probable that Tschirschky was, in consequence, reproved for his conduct. Szögyény, the Austrian ambassador in Berlin, telegraphed to Berchtold on 8 July: "I was told at the foreign office that they had noted from a report of Herr von Tschirschky that he had been rather 'lukewarm' toward your Excellency. For this he had received a reprimand from Berlin." Gooss, pp. 39-40; *Ö.-U. A.*, 10,127. Count Montgelas, one of the editors of *Die deutschen Dokumente zum Kriegsausbruch*, declares that there is no record of a reprimand in the German archives, and argues that Szögyény must have got his impression from conversation with subordinate officials of the Wilhelmstrasse who referred to the fact of the Emperor's criticism; Montgelas, p. 174. The absence of documentary record in the archives scarcely proves that no reprimand was administered. It might have been conveyed by telephone, or in a private letter which did not get into the archives. Also, the subordinate officials would be a natural source of information on so delicate a matter. It is worth noting that Lichnowsky, writing in 1916, that is, before anything was publicly known about the supposed reprimand, said that when he was in Berlin just after the assassination, he "learned that Herr von Tschirschky had been reprimanded because he reported that he had counselled moderation in Vienna toward Serbia"; Lichnowsky, I, 128. The ambassador could not have heard of this reprimand on 29 June, 1914, but he visited the foreign office again on 5 July, and he could have been given the information on that occasion. His testimony certainly strengthens the view that Tschirschky was reproved in some manner. Whether or not this was the case, the latter person soon ceased (see above, pp. 269-270) to advocate caution at Vienna.
    † See above, pp. 171-172.

ments on the report of Herr von Tschirschky can therefore hardly be treated as a mere ebullition of the moment induced by indignation over the murder of his friend; rather they have to be considered as a serious expression of the opinion that the time had come to apply force. To what extent the Emperor's views influenced the foreign office, which had thus far been urging caution upon Austria-Hungary and a conciliatory attitude upon Serbia, and the chancellor, who, so far as is known, had not expressed his views, can be estimated only in the light of events about to be described.

POTSDAM, 5 JULY

On Sunday morning, 5 July, Count Hoyos arrived in Berlin with the memorandum of the Austro-Hungarian Government and the letter of Francis Joseph to William II; he handed over his documents and, as will be seen presently, explained his mission to the ambassador, Count Szögyény. The latter, as already instructed by telegram, sent word to the Emperor that Count Hoyos had brought a letter from the Emperor Francis Joseph, and was invited to Potsdam for luncheon. Count Hoyos himself proceeded to the Wilhelmstrasse for a discussion with Herr Zimmermann, to whom he gave copies of the documents. No minute of their conversation has been published.* Other official documents, however, record the terms in which certain proposals were presented. The protocol of the council of ministers held two days later at Vienna records that Count Hoyos had explained in Berlin the project of "a surprise attack on Serbia without any preliminary preparation," or, as it was again described in the council, "a surprise attack *sans crier gare.*" Count Berchtold's remarks in the discussion imply

---

* It was customary in the German foreign office for the secretary of state or his representative to make memoranda of conversations with foreign diplomatists; many of these documents are published in *Die Grosse Politik*. No such memoranda are contained in *Die deutschen Dokumente zum Kriegsausbruch*, apart from the formal record of three *démarches* by the British ambassador (nos. 496, 497, 522), although that collection is supposed to be complete. Quite possibly, in view of the extraordinary circumstances, no record was made of this conversation.

frankly that this was the plan which he favored and had presented to the German Government.* Count Hoyos also stated that "a complete partition of Serbia was under consideration" in Vienna.† He revealed, in short, how the programme hinted at in the letter of Francis Joseph was to be carried into execution.

Inasmuch as Herr Zimmermann had hitherto been advising moderation, he should have been shocked by these declarations of the Austrian diplomatist. He was, however, not in the least disturbed, saying that he "considered an energetic communication to Serbia . . . as a matter of course" and making no protest against the idea of partition.‡ His reaction is still more clearly revealed by his remarks to the German ambassador in London, whom he saw shortly afterward.

He told me [Prince Lichnowsky recorded] that a letter had just arrived from the Emperor of Austria to the effect that Vienna now intended to put an end to the intolerable state of things on the Serbian frontier by energetic action. The undersecretary seemed to think that, if war was now after all in-

* Protocol of the council of ministers, 7 July; A I 8. Zimmermann in 1919 remembered Hoyos as saying that "this time his government was going to act energetically on the Serbian question." Statement to the parliamentary investigating committee; *Zur Vorgeschichte des Weltkrieges*, I, no. 3. This innocuous statement, made five years after the event, can hardly stand against the contemporary evidence of Tisza, whose statement at the Vienna council was not denied by either Hoyos or Berchtold. Just what Hoyos meant by a 'surprise attack' does not appear from the meagre references to the plan. Taken by themselves, the words imply, and they were so understood by Tisza, an attack without warning, which would be possible only if made by troops instantly available; this, as we have seen (pp. 272–275), had been Berchtold's desire, which Conrad had opposed. Hoyos himself stated in 1928 that he could not remember exactly how he had broached the matter to Zimmermann. "But one thing I know definitely," he added, "namely, that an attack without a declaration of war certainly never entered into our calculations, and that if I spoke of prompt action, this was to be interpreted rather in the sense that we could not enter upon any diplomatic conversations with the European Powers about our right to proceed against Serbia and wished to present the other Powers with a *fait accompli*." K. Jagow, *loc. cit.*, XXV, 82–783, note 4. His guarded language amounts to an admission that he represented the policy of his government as a programme of war against Serbia; an attack would not be less in the nature of a surprise if it followed immediately on a sudden and unexpected declaration of war.

† Tschirschky to foreign office, telegram, 7 July; G 18. Zimmermann's post-war version was that Hoyos had said that "Serbia must be destroyed"; *Zur Vorgeschichte des Weltkrieges*, I, no. 3.

‡ Statement to the parliamentary investigating committee; *Zur Vorgeschichte des Weltkrieges*, I, no. 3.

evitable for us in consequence of the unfriendly attitude of Russia, it would perhaps be better to have it now rather than later.*

Herr Zimmermann was evidently under no illusions about the possible consequences of the Austrian action. He at once telephoned to the chancellor at Hohenfinow to inform him of the Austrian *démarche,* and Herr von Bethmann-Hollweg promised to come to Berlin that evening.†

But the interest of 5 July centres not so much in Berlin as in Potsdam, where Count Szögyény was received by William II to present the documents brought from Vienna. His Majesty read both the autograph letter and the memorandum, so the ambassador reported to his chief, "with the greatest attention."

He first assured me [continued Count Szögyény] that he had expected some serious step on our part against Serbia; but he had to admit that the statements of our most gracious master made him foresee serious *European* complications and therefore he could not give a definite answer until he had consulted the imperial chancellor.

The Emperor might well hesitate. The Austro-Hungarian programme called for "the isolation and diminution of Serbia," in order that the little state might be "eliminated as a factor of political power in the Balkans"—a policy that could be pursued only through warlike action, which was admirably calculated to bring about "serious European complications," and which the German Government had twice vetoed in the past two years.

The discussion was interrupted by luncheon, at which the Empress and other persons were present. When the discussion was resumed, Count Szögyény "once more called emphatic attention to the seriousness of the situation"; and this time Wil-

---

* Memorandum of August, 1914, "England vor dem Kriege." The passage was omitted by Lichnowsky in *Auf dem Wege zum Abgrund,* but was printed by F. Thimme, "Das Memoirenwerk Fürst Lichnowskys," in *Archiv für Politik und Geschichte,* VI, 42 (Heft 1, 1928), and in the English translation of the memoirs, *Heading for the Abyss* (London, 1928), p. 16.
† K. Jagow, *loc. cit.,* XXV, 783.

liam, without waiting for the arrival of the chancellor, authorized the ambassador to transmit to Francis Joseph the following message, which signified his personal approval of the Austro-Hungarian proposals:

In this case also we might rely on Germany's full support. He must, as he had said, first hear the opinion of the chancellor, but he did not in the least doubt that Herr von Bethmann-Hollweg would agree with him, especially in the matter of the action against Serbia. It was his (the Emperor William's) opinion that this action must not be delayed. Russia's action would doubtless be hostile, but he had been prepared for this for years; and should it come to war between Austria-Hungary and Russia, we could be assured that Germany would stand by our side with her accustomed loyalty. As things stood to-day, however, Russia was in no way prepared for war and would certainly think twice before appealing to arms, although she would incite the Powers of the Triple Entente against us and add fuel to the fire in the Balkans.

He understood very well that it would be hard for his Imperial and Royal Majesty, with his well-known love of peace, to march into Serbia; but if we had really recognized the necessity of war against Serbia, he would regret it if we did not make use of the present moment, which is all in our favor.

For the rest, the Emperor promised to see to it that King Carol of Rumania observed "a correct attitude"; and while "he had never had the least confidence in King Ferdinand of Bulgaria," he said that "he would not make the slightest objection to the conclusion of a treaty between the Monarchy and Bulgaria, provided care were taken that it contained nothing to offend Rumania." He would, he said, see the chancellor that very evening before departing for Norway. The ambassador concluded his report by saying that he himself would discuss the matter with the chancellor the next day.*

What strikes one instantly is that William II spoke of "marching into Serbia," although there is no mention of this in either the autograph letter or the official memorandum.

* Szögyény to Berchtold, telegram, 5 July; A I 6.

Obviously, Count Szögyény had been informed by Count Hoyos of Count Berchtold's plan for a surprise attack, or a seizure of Serbian territory by a prompt movement of troops, and had explained the matter to the Emperor. In fact, this is expressly stated by General von Falkenhayn, the Prussian minister of war:

His Majesty the Emperor and King summoned me to the New Palace this afternoon to inform me that Austria-Hungary appears determined not to tolerate any longer the plots hatched against Austria in the Balkan peninsula, and if necessary, to accomplish this end, to begin by marching into Serbia; even if Russia will not tolerate this, Austria is not disposed to abandon it.

His Majesty thought that he could deduce such an intention from the language of the Austrian ambassador when handing him a memorandum from the government in Vienna and an autograph letter of the Emperor Francis Joseph.*

The chief of the Emperor's naval cabinet, Admiral von Müller, was also informed, on that day or the next, of "the proposed advance of the Austrians into Serbia."† On this essential point, then, three independent witness agree.

Thus there can be no doubt that William II understood what Austria-Hungary proposed to do, or that in his own name and own authority he accepted its programme.‡ So far as the record shows, he did not inquire if Austria-Hungary had proofs of official Serbian complicity in the murder at Sarajevo; he gave his reply without consulting his government; he imposed no restriction on the projected action and he urged its immediate execution. He did, it is true, say that he must consult his chancellor, but he gave assurances of that gentleman's approval, and, without waiting to secure it, authorized the communication to Francis Joseph, including the promise of sup-

---

* Falkenhayn to Moltke, 5 July; Montgelas, p. 196.
† *Zur Vorgeschichte des Weltkrieges*, I, no. 12.
‡ The statement of Fay, II, 209, that "what this action of Austria's was to be, the Kaiser did not know definitely on July 5, and did not care to advise," is incorrect.

port in a war with Russia. He so fully committed himself that protest by the chancellor would be difficult and improbable. The ambassador, for his part, did not wait for the chancellor's approval, but telegraphed the Emperor's answer to Vienna at once. First in order of time, first in degree of authority among all his countrymen, the German Emperor thus sanctioned the course which Austria-Hungary desired to follow.

How serious the Emperor understood the matter to be is evident from the fact that, after the first conversation with the Austrian ambassador and before the luncheon, he caused his principal officials to be summoned to Potsdam.* The first to arrive, about 5 P. M., was General von Falkenhayn, the Prussian minister of war, who was responsible for mobilization and the material preparedness of the army.

According to the account of the ensuing conversation which the general sent to the chief of staff a few hours later, the Emperor informed the minister of war, as had already been noted, that "Austria-Hungary appears determined not to tolerate any longer the plots hatched against Austria in the Balkan peninsula, and if necessary, to accomplish this end, to begin by marching into Serbia." He then read aloud portions of the autograph letter and the memorandum. Following this, so General von Falkenhayn testified in 1919, the Emperor

pointed out how very serious consequences might ensue from the evidently firm determination of Austria-Hungary to put an end at last to the Great-Serbian propaganda, and in conclusion asked me the question whether the army was ready for all contingencies.

To this direct question, said the general,

I replied briefly and unconditionally, in accord with my conviction, that it was, and only asked on my part whether any other preparations were to be made. His Majesty answered just as briefly that they were not, and dismissed me.†

* K. Jagow, *loc. cit.*, XXV, 784.
† Statement to the parliamentary investigating committee; *Zur Vorgeschichte des Weltkrieges*, I, no. 17.

But Falkenhayn's biographer, who had the general's diary to work from, adds an important point. After mentioning the reading of the Austro-Hungarian documents, he says:

In view of the enormous possible consequences involved these documents raised the question whether Germany would in all circumstances fulfil her duty as an ally, which was answered in the affirmative. Falkenhayn thereupon urgently begged that adequate preparations for war [entsprechende Kriegsvorbereitungen] be made on the part of Germany. This was refused, in order not to disturb the diplomatic action.*

This statement throws a rather different light on the conversation: the Emperor was satisfied to know that the army was ready, and thought it politically inexpedient to alarm the other Powers.

General von Falkenhayn, for his part, later in the day personally wrote a "strictly secret" letter to General von Moltke, the chief of the general staff, who was taking the cure at Carlsbad. The letter is an illuminating document. After relating what the Emperor had told him about the Austrian plans —quoted above—the war minister continued:

His Majesty read me the letter [of Francis Joseph] as well as the memorandum [of the Vienna Cabinet], and so far as it was possible to form an opinion from hearing them read rapidly, I did not get the impression that the Vienna Government had come to a definite decision. Both picture the general situation of the Dual Monarchy as very black, as a result of the Pan-Slavist machinations. Both also represent it to be necessary that something should be done to stop them as soon as possible. But neither of them speaks of a military solution; rather they hint at "energetic" political action, such as the conclusion of a treaty with Bulgaria, for which they wish to secure the support of the German Empire.

This support is to be promised, with, however, an indication that it is Austria-Hungary's business in the first line to take the steps which its interests require.

*H. von Zwehl, Erich von Falkenhayn: eine biographische Studie (Berlin, 1926), p. 55.

The chancellor, who was also at Potsdam, seems to be no more confident than I am, that the Austrian Government is in earnest, although its language is more decisive than usual. . . . In no case, evidently, will there be any decision in the next few weeks. Considerable time will elapse before the treaty with Bulgaria is concluded. So Your Excellency need not curtail your stay at Carlsbad.

The reason for this advice is clear enough: the Emperor had forbidden any military preparations, in order not to alarm the Powers, and nothing would create more alarm than the sudden return from leave of the chief of the general staff. Falkenhayn, it may be noted, did not inform Moltke that he had "urgently begged" the Emperor to sanction "preparations for war"; and by confining himself to stating that the Austrian documents did not speak of "a military solution," which was quite true, he managed to draw a rather anodyne picture of the situation. On the other hand, and it is this which gives interest to his letter, he concluded as follows:

Nevertheless, I thought it desirable, although I have no instructions to do so, to let you know that the situation is acute, in order that you may not be quite unprepared for surprises which may in the end come about.*

The war minister, a subordinate of the chancellor, takes it upon himself to write privately to the chief of staff, who was on a level with the chancellor. Certainly an unusual proceeding. The impression left by Falkenhayn's letter is that, after his interviews with the Emperor and the chancellor, he was in a rather confused state of mind. But he was a confident and vigorous man, not afraid of responsibility, and precisely because he foresaw the consequences of the Austrian programme, if it were carried out, he took it upon himself to prepare the chief of staff for serious eventualities, without unduly alarming him. Unfortunately, we possess no indication of the reaction of General von Moltke to this communication.

* Falkenhayn to Moltke, 5 July; Montgelas, p. 196.

Herr von Bethmann-Hollweg reached Berlin in the middle of the afternoon, and was made acquainted by Herr Zimmermann with the Austrian documents. The two men then proceeded together to Potsdam, where they were received by the Emperor at about 6 P. M. in the garden of the New Palace. The chancellor, writing after the war, gave this account of the interview:

> The Emperor declared that he could not deceive himself about the gravity of the situation which had been brought about in the Danube Monarchy by the Great-Serbian propaganda. But it was not our business to instruct our ally what to do in regard to the Sarajevo crime. That matter Austria-Hungary must decide for herself. We should abstain from instigating or advising any action, all the more as we ought to strive by every means to prevent the Austro-Serbian difficulty from growing to the proportions of an international European conflict. But the Emperor Francis Joseph must understand, however, that we could not desert Austria-Hungary in time of need. Our own vital interests demanded the unimpaired maintenance of Austria. To draw Bulgaria into closer relationship seemed advisable, though Rumania must not be affronted by such action.
> These views of the Emperor were in line with my own opinions.*

The chancellor's recollection omits, however, one piquant and essential detail recorded by Herr Zimmermann, who relates that

> after Herr von Bethmann-Hollweg had briefly rehearsed to the Emperor the subject-matter of the Austro-Hungarian despatches, already made known to the latter by Count Szögyény, His Majesty spoke without waiting to hear the chancellor's proposals.†

William, it will be remembered, had assured Count Szögyény

* Bethmann-Hollweg, I, 124–125.
† Statement to the parliamentary investigating committee; *Zur Vorgeschichte des Weltkrieges*, I, no. 3.

that "he did not in the least doubt that Herr von Bethmann-Hollweg would agree with him" in promising Germany's support: he now made good this assurance by taking the words out of the chancellor's mouth. Whether Herr von Bethmann agreed with his master as fully as he professed, after the war, is open to doubt.* But he was confronted with an accomplished fact: the Emperor had already given his personal promise to the Austro-Hungarian ambassador. In any case, whatever may have been the chancellor's first reaction to the proposals of Vienna, he accepted the decision of the Emperor, and on the following day formally confirmed it.† In this brief conference at Potsdam the position of the German Government was definitely taken.

After the departure of the chancellor and the under-secretary of state, the Emperor received Captain Zenker, representing Rear-Admiral Behncke, the acting chief of the naval staff, who was away from his office when the summons arrived from Potsdam. Captain Zenker's conversation with the Emperor may be reported in his own words:

His Majesty the Emperor informed me, for transmission to my official superiors, that at noon on 5 July the Austro-Hungarian chargé d'affaires [sic] had inquired of him whether Germany would fulfil the obligations of her alliance in the event of an Austro-Hungarian conflict with Serbia and the strained relations with Russia that might perhaps result. His Majesty had promised this, but he did not believe that Russia would in-

---

* According to a well-informed German writer, "A few days after the audience, Herr Zimmermann boasted that he and the Emperor had 'stiffened' ['stark gemacht'] the hesitant chancellor. He had recalled Bismarck and his fundamental principle of defending the Danube Monarchy, for the sake of our own existence, with the pledge of the German Empire. The Emperor loved words of force. He supported Zimmermann in such lively fashion that Bethmann-Hollweg renounced his opposition. In any case, he knew also that the Emperor had already pledged himself to the Austrian ambassador." Fischer, pp. 68–69. No evidence is presented to support this story, which has consequently to be treated with reserve. It is, however, plausible.

† It is possible that Bethmann accepted the Emperor's views because he doubted, according to Falkenhayn, whether "the Austrian Government is in earnest, although its language is more decisive than usual" (see above, p. 298). But, as will be seen, he himself, on the following day, urged the Cabinet of Vienna to take prompt action.

tervene in behalf of Serbia, which had stained itself by an assassination. France, too, would scarcely let it come to war, as it lacked the heavy artillery for field armies. Yet, though war against Russia-France was not probable, nevertheless the possibility of such a war must be borne in mind from a military point of view.

Still, the High Seas Fleet was to start its cruise to Norway, as had been planned for the middle of July, as he was going to start on his journey according to schedule.

To my question whether the chief of the naval staff, who was then on leave, should be recalled, His Majesty replied in the negative.*

The last two paragraphs are in consonance with the intimation conveyed to the minister of war: no steps were to be taken which might put the other Powers on guard. Similarly, the opinion that Russia would not assist Serbia tallies with what William said to Count Szögyény. On the other hand, the Emperor did not tell Captain Zenker that he had urged prompt action on the part of Austria-Hungary.

Overnight some one—the Emperor himself or one of his suite—evidently recalled that neither the general staff nor the navy department had been informed of what had happened, for between 7 and 8 o'clock urgent telephone calls were sent to these two offices. Admiral von Capelle, acting secretary of state for the navy,—Admiral von Tirpitz being on leave,—arrived first. The Emperor walked up and down the garden, and gave the admiral a brief account of the events of the preceding day, adding, as the admiral remembered it in 1919, "something like the following":

He did not believe that a great war would develop. In his opinion the Tsar would not associate himself with the murderers of princes. Besides that, neither France nor Russia was prepared for war. The Emperor did not mention England. On the advice of the imperial chancellor, he was going to start quietly on his journey to the north, in order not to rouse any

* Zenker to foreign office, 8 November, 1919; *Die deutschen Dokumente zum Kriegsausbruch*, I, xvi.

apprehensions. Nevertheless, he wished to inform me of the strained situation, in order that I might consider it further.*

We shall see presently the implications of this significant final sentence.

As soon as Admiral von Capelle had departed, the Emperor received General von Bertrab, the chief of the map division of the general staff, who gives this account of the audience:

His Majesty the Emperor informed me personally, without any witnesses, of his conception of the situation created by the measures of Austria, in order that I, as the senior officer of the general staff at that time present in Berlin, might inform the chief of the general staff, who was then staying at Carlsbad, about it. The Empress, an adjutant, and a footman were present in the background. . . . No measures were arranged for either during or at the conclusion of the conversation. Indeed His Majesty made it quite clear that he did not consider it necessary to arrange for any measures, as he did not believe in serious complications as a result of the crime at Sarajevo.†

At the conclusion of the interview the Emperor entered his motor-car and started on his journey to Norway; his train left the Wildpark station at Potsdam at 9.15 the same morning and reached Kiel in the middle of the afternoon.‡

At Kiel the Emperor received at dinner on his yacht Baron Krupp von Bohlen-Halbach, the head of the great Krupp armament works, who had been advised from Potsdam on the previous day that the Emperor wished to see him.§ After the war Baron von Krupp testified that William had told him that "the

---

* Statement to the parliamentary investigating committee; *Zur Vorgeschichte des Weltkrieges*, I, no. 14.

† Bertrab to foreign office, 20 October, 1919; *Die deutschen Dokumente zum Kriegsausbruch*, I, xiv-xv.

‡ The Emperor's own account of the events of these two days reads thus: "The much-discussed so-called crown council of Potsdam on 5 July in reality never took place. It is an invention of malevolent persons. Naturally, before my departure, I received individual ministers, in order to let them report on the conditions of affairs in their departments. Likewise, no council of ministers was held, and there was no talk of preparations for war at any one of the conferences." Wilhelm II, pp. 209-210.

§ K. Jagow, *loc. cit.*, **XXV**, 784, 788.

political situation might become serious, in case—contrary to expectations—Russia and England should extend their protection to the Serbian regicides."* But on 17 July, 1914, he gave a more explicit account to a member of his board of directors:

> The Emperor had spoken to him of the conversation with the Austrians, but had characterized the affair as so secret that he [Krupp] would not have ventured to communicate even to his board of directors. . . . The Emperor had told him personally that he would declare war immediately if Russia mobilized. The Emperor's repeated insistence that in this matter no one would be able to reproach him again with want of resolution had produced an almost comic effect.†

The next morning William II sailed away to the Norwegian fiords and exercised no direct influence on German policy for the next three weeks.

The evidence of General von Falkenhayn, written down a few hours after his conversation with his master, and the later records of those who saw the Emperor on 5 July and 6 July confirm the official report which Count Szögyény telegraphed to his government, namely, that William II approved Count Berchtold's plan to take military action against Serbia and urged its immediate execution, and that he promised the unconditional support of Germany if Russia intervened on behalf of Serbia. It is also established that while he considered such intervention unlikely, he foresaw its possibility enough to summon the naval and military authorities and give them proper warning; and that he faced the prospect of a European war without hesitation.

On the afternoon of 6 July the promise of William II to

* Statement to the parliamentary investigating committee; *Zur Vorgeschichte des Weltkrieges*, I, no. 29.

† Dr. W. Muehlon, "Das Wiener Ultimatum an Serbien," in *Berliner Tageblatt*, 21 March, 1918, reprinted in *International Conciliation* (New York), September, 1918, p. 479. Dr. Muehlon recorded this conversation at the time, without, however, indicating the name of his informant. Cf. *Dr. Muehlon's Diary* (London, 1918), pp. 8-9.

Count Szögyény was confirmed by the German Government. Chancellor von Bethmann-Hollweg and Herr Zimmermann received the Austro-Hungarian ambassador and Count Hoyos, and the chancellor made a formal statement to the ambassador,* who telegraphed it at once to Count Berchtold. The statement was made verbally; but was none the less authoritative, and a report on the conferences in Berlin was taken to Vienna by Count Hoyos, who left for the Austrian capital the same evening.

Count Szögyény's telegram to his chief is perhaps the most important document of the crisis of July, 1914, for it records the answer of the German Government to the Austro-Hungarian overture.† It must therefore be quoted practically in full:

> In company with Count Hoyos, have just had a long conversation with the imperial chancellor and the under-secretary of state. Herr von Bethmann-Hollweg began by saying that the Emperor William had instructed him to express his best thanks for the autograph letter, which he would answer personally in a few days.
>
> He (the chancellor) was also authorized by his imperial master to define the position of the German Government with reference to the letter and the memorandum, as follows:
>
> The German Government perceives the dangers arising for Austria-Hungary, and for the Triple Alliance as well, out of Russia's plan for a Balkan league, and understands that the Cabinet of Vienna should be desirous of inducing Bulgaria to

---

* Statement of Zimmermann to the parliamentary investigating committee; *Zur Vorgeschichte des Weltkrieges*, I, no. 3.

† After the interview, Bethmann sent a telegram (G 15) to Tschirschky, informing him, in part, of what had happened. It was briefer and phrased in slightly different terms than the answer given to Szögyény. This document, however, was *not*, as is stated in Montgelas, p. 92, "the official German answer to the Austrian memorandum." Bethmann's telegram was for Tschirschky's "personal information and 'guidance [*Zu Ew. Exz. persönlicher Orientierung*]," not for communication to Berchtold. Bethmann, I, 127, says: "The general line we followed is clearly indicated in the reply to Count Szögyény, and was never abandoned." Furthermore, the Emperor William, in reply to the Emperor Francis Joseph, apologized for his delay in writing with the remark: "You will have received through your trusted ambassador . . . my assurance that you will find me and my empire standing faithfully at your side in this dark hour, in full accord with our old and tried friendship and with the obligations of our alliance. To repeat this assurance to you here is for me a joyful duty." William II to Francis Joseph, 14 July; G 26.

join the Triple Alliance formally; it is anxious, however, that this should be done in a manner—as indeed is contemplated—which will not prejudice our obligations to Rumania. The German minister in Sofia would therefore be instructed to negotiate in this sense with the Bulgarian Government, in case he were requested to do so by his Austro-Hungarian colleague. At the same time he (the chancellor) intends to instruct the German minister in Bucharest to speak openly with the King of Rumania, to inform him of the negotiations to be carried on in Sofia, and to call his attention to the fact that he ought to put a stop to the Rumanian agitation against us. He will also have the King told that in the past he has always advised us to come to terms with Serbia, but that, after the recent events, he recognizes that this is as good as impossible; and Rumania should take this into account.

With regard to our relations with Serbia, the German Government is of opinion that we must judge what is to be done to clear up the situation; whatever we may decide upon, we can always be sure that we shall find Germany at our side, as the ally and friend of the Monarchy.*

---

* Bethmann's telegram to Tschirschky (G 15) agrees with Szögyény's language about Bulgaria and Rumania. On the Serbian question, Bethmann said: "Finally, as far as Serbia is concerned, his Majesty, of course, cannot interfere in the questions now pending between that country and Austria-Hungary, as they do not lie within his competence. The Emperor Francis Joseph may, however, rest assured that His Majesty will [in all circumstances] faithfully stand by Austria-Hungary, as is required by the obligations of his alliance and of his ancient friendship." Before sending the telegram, which had been drafted by Zimmermann, Bethmann eliminated the phrase in brackets—"in all circumstances"—as if, on reflection, he felt that he had gone too far. But as Zimmermann was present at the conference with Szögyény and Hoyos, it may be presumed that he inserted the phrase "in all circumstances" because the words had been used by the chancellor. The limitation of the promise of German support to "the obligations of the alliance" also calls for remark. Taken literally, the words are meaningless: the Austro-German alliance did not bind Germany to support Austria-Hungary against Serbia, in fact there is not a word about Serbia in the treaty. We have seen, however (pp. 15–17), that the letters exchanged by Generals Conrad and von Moltke in 1909 and subsequent years created an obligation by which Germany promised, in case Austria-Hungary made war on Serbia and was in consequence attacked by Russia, to go to the assistance of her ally. The use of the words, "the obligations of the alliance," in July, 1914, to cover the contingency of an Austro-Hungarian action against Serbia affords the clearest proof of the binding character of the letters exchanged by the two chiefs of staff. The *nuances* between what Bethmann said to Tschirschky and what Szögyény reported Bethmann as saying were more apparent than real. Tschirschky himself, after hearing Szögyény's reports read, declared that they "correspond exactly with the tenor" of Bethmann's telegram (Tschirschky to foreign office, telegram, 7 July; G 18). But, if differences be thought to exist, as has sometimes been contended, it may be remarked that the statement made to Tschirschky for his personal information could not limit the formal answer given to Szögyény.

So far the chancellor had been replying to the questions raised by the Austro-Hungarian memorandum and the autograph letter. He then proceeded to give his opinion on what may be called the 'verbal proposals' of Count Hoyos. Count Szögyény's telegram continued:

In the course of further conversation, I learned that the chancellor, like his imperial master, considers *immediate action on our part* [*ein sofortiges Einschreiten unsererseits*] against Serbia as the best solution of our difficulties in the Balkans. From the point of view of international politics, he considers the present moment more favorable than some later time; he agrees entirely with us that we should notify neither Italy nor Rumania of an eventual action [*einer eventuellen Aktion*] against Serbia. On the other hand, Italy should be informed right away by the German Government, as well as by our own, of the plan to take Bulgaria into the Triple Alliance.*

The "eventual action" to be concealed from Austria-Hungary's allies could mean only an attack on Serbia.† After some further remarks about Bulgaria and Rumania, the German chancellor ended by warning Vienna against plans in Albania "which might endanger our relations with Italy and the continuance of the Triple Alliance."‡

* There is no mention of all this in Bethmann's telegram to Tschirschky. For obvious reasons, the German Government avoided referring in its own document to proposals made verbally by the Austro-Hungarian Government. The argument adduced by some writers that Szögyény, being old, must have misunderstood Bethmann or elaborated on his language, is an artificial hypothesis. Szögyény's telegram was published in 1919, more than a year before Bethmann's death; so far as is known to the writer, he never contested the accuracy of Szögyény's statement. The somewhat elaborate reasoning in Fay, II, 217, to prove that Bethmann could not have consented to keeping Italy in the dark is refuted by the simple fact that the German ambassador in Rome, when informed of the decision to support Austria-Hungary, was instructed not to mention the matter to the Italian foreign office. Jagow to Flotow, 11 July, telegram; G 33.

† Hoyos, p. 80, states that both he and Szögyény got the impression in Berlin that "the German Government was in favor of an immediate action against Serbia, although it clearly recognized the danger of a world war arising therefrom."

‡ Szögyény to Berchtold, telegram, 6 July; A I 7. In characteristic fashion, Bethmann, having encouraged his ally to violate Article VII of the Triple Alliance by taking action against Serbia without having secured previously the consent of Italy, was able to delude himself with the hope that Italy would be satisfied if her interests in Albania were not disregarded.

The two telegrams of Count Szögyény of 5 and 6 July (and the several statements of the Emperor William as well) leave no doubt that (1) the German Emperor and the German Government agreed to the proposals of Count Berchtold—all of them, written and verbal; (2) they promised unconditional support; (3) and they urged immediate action. The evidence of other official German and Austro-Hungarian records proves also that the German Government understood that Count Berchtold had in mind the partition of Serbia, and that this had not stood in the way of giving approval of his policy.* The Austro-Hungarian foreign minister had scored on every point, and to a degree that he apparently had not anticipated.† His telegram of acknowledgment instructed his ambassador in Berlin to convey his "warmest thanks" to the German Government.‡

True to its promise, the German Government promptly despatched instructions to its representatives in Rumania and Bulgaria. The minister in Bucharest was informed that the Emperor Francis Joseph, considering an understanding between Austria-Hungary and Serbia to have become "impossible," desired to draw Bulgaria into the Triple Alliance. The German Emperor had given his consent to this policy; but, since he "naturally attaches the greatest importance to the maintenance of the cordial and confidential relations arising

* The view generally taken of the German action is that it amounted to the giving of a 'blank cheque' or a 'free hand.' A distinguished American writer says: "They [the Emperor and his advisers] gave Austria a free hand and made the grave mistake of putting the situation outside of their control into the hands of a man as reckless and unscrupulous as Berchtold. They committed themselves to a leap in the dark. They soon found themselves involved, as we shall see, in actions which they did not approve, and by decisions which were taken against their advice." Fay, II, 223. The German Government did not give its ally a 'blank cheque' in the sense that it left Vienna a free hand to work out its programme. Vienna stated what its programme was: military action against Serbia. Berlin accepted that programme and promised to support it. In the days following 6 July, the question was, not whether the Austro-Hungarian Government would abuse the promise of support given by Germany, but whether it would be able, because of internal political difficulties, to go as far as it had indicated that it wished to go.

† He had told Conrad that he "expected Germany would leave us in the lurch"; Conrad, IV, 32.

‡ Berchtold to Szögyény, telegram, 8 July; A I 11. Memorandum of Jagow, 9 July; G 23.

out of the alliance with Rumania," he was prepared to insist, if King Carol so desired, that

> any agreement which might be made by Bulgaria with the Triple Alliance should not only be—which goes without saying—in harmony with the treaty obligations to Rumania, but should also expressly guarantee the territorial integrity of Rumania.

King Carol should also be asked "to consider whether, in view of the seriousness of the situation, he could not break away from Serbia and also take action against the agitation carried on in Rumania against the existence of the Danube Monarchy."* Since approximately half of the telegram dealt with Austro-Serbian relations, one may conclude that the detaching of Rumania from Serbia was considered to be as important as the programme of an alliance with Bulgaria.

This impression is more than confirmed by the instructions sent to the minister in Sofia, which read: "Your Excellency is authorized to support, *at his request,* any steps that may be taken in this direction [of bringing Bulgaria into the Triple Alliance] by your Austro-Hungarian colleague."† That limitation in italics is surely significant. Two days later the German Government learned that Count Berchtold had discarded, at least for the present, the project of a Bulgarian alliance, which he had represented, in a ten-page memorandum, as a matter of life or death for the Monarchy, on the ground that "Rumania might be disturbed by it."‡ Whereupon Herr von Jagow cancelled the instructions to the minister in Sofia in a three-line telegram without any explanations.§ It looks as if

---

* Bethmann-Hollweg to Waldburg, telegram, 6 July; G 16.
† Zimmermann to Michahelles, telegram, 6 July; G 17.
‡ Tschirschky to foreign office, telegram, 8 July; G 19. Berchtold offered another explanation to Szögyény (telegram, 8 July; A I 11) to the effect that Rumania "might adopt a very unfriendly attitude toward us in case we should go to war against Serbia"—which is significant of Berchtold's real purpose.
§ Jagow to Michahelles, telegram, 9 July; G 22. The instructions to Bucharest were also cancelled, but with a reminder of "the expectation that Rumania will fulfil her obligations as an ally to the full extent in the event of a conflict." Jagow to Waldburg, telegram, 9 July; G 21.

Count Hoyos had explained in Berlin that the Bulgarian alliance was a *pis aller* and was regarded by Count Berchtold only as the alternative to a military action against Serbia.

GERMAN PREPARATIONS

The Emperor, before starting for Norway, had forbidden General von Falkenhayn to take any military measures. Nor, so far as is known, were any orders issued to the army for war or in preparation for war.* They were not necessary. According to General Count von Waldersee, Moltke's deputy at the general staff,

There was nothing to initiate. . . . The arrangements for mobilization [*planmässigen Mobilmachungsarbeiten*] had been concluded on 31 March, 1914. The army was, as always, ready.†

Nor was this a post-bellum boast, for in the middle of July, 1914, he wrote to the foreign minister:

I shall remain here [Ivenack] ready to jump; we are all prepared at the general staff; in the meantime there is nothing for us to do.‡

"Nothing for us to do," "ready to jump": the words tell their

---

* Falkenhayn, Waldersee, the deputy chief of the general staff, General von Tappen, chief of the mobilization section of the general staff, Colonel von Tieschowitz, Moltke's first aide-de-camp, and General von Kress, the Bavarian minister of war, have affirmed that no preparations were made. Statements to the parliamentary investigating committee; *Zur Vorgeschichte des Weltkrieges*, I, nos. 17, 18, 21, 22, 23. For evidence that the normal routine of the German army was carried on, see *Zur Vorgeschichte des Weltkrieges*, II, 6–7, 63–66. The report sent to Paris (Cambon to Bienvenu-Martin, 21 July; F 15) that "the preliminary notices for mobilization, the object of which is to place Germany in a kind of 'attention' attitude in times of tension, have been sent out to those classes which would receive them in similar circumstances," is not confirmed by any available evidence. The French naval attaché was told this by the British naval attaché, who had heard a rumor to the effect that "preparatory notices about the possibility of mobilization have been sent to some German soldiers who are in the reserve." Bronevski to Sazonov, 22 July; *Красный Архив*, I, 164; R, 1925 6. B does not contain any such report.

† Statement to the parliamentary investigating committee; *Zur Vorgeschichte des Weltkrieges*, I, no. 18.

‡ Waldersee to Jagow, private, 17 July; G 74.

own story as regards German military preparedness during the crisis.

The action of Baron von Krupp is also not without interest. He was so impressed by the Emperor's statement at Kiel that he "discussed confidentially with two members of the directorate of Krupp's the question whether it was necessary to take any action toward reinforcing the supplies of the firm in case of mobilization." It was not necessary, for the great munition works had "a sufficient supply of materials on hand to guarantee the undisturbed continuance of the activity of the works for quite a long time, even if fully shut off" from outside sources.[*] Krupp's, like the army, could report itself prepared for war.

The naval authorities appear to have felt more need of immediate action. The Emperor, in telling Admiral von Capelle of "the strained situation," had asked him to "consider it further."[†] The admiral must have considered it rather quickly. Let us hear his own words:

Having returned to the imperial navy office [on 6 July], I called together the department heads and the chief of the central division—according to my recollection, Vice-Admiral Behncke, acting chief of the naval staff, also took part in the conference—and informed them of the Emperor's communication. We all agreed that, in view of the restrictions imposed —no political uneasiness, no employment of extraordinary financial means in the departments controlled by the imperial navy office, namely, the navy-yards (ship constructions, etc.), torpedo work-shops, artillery and mine depots, fortifications

[*] Statement to the parliamentary investigating committee; *Zur Vorgeschichte des Weltkrieges*, I, no. 29. "The view that a modern war could last only a short time prevailed in military as well as in business circles. This was justified by the fearful destructive power of modern weapons, which held out prospects of quick and decisive blows; likewise by the enormous loss of labor involved in calling the manhood of the country to arms and by the huge costs which were far in excess of the sums with which financiers and business men were hitherto accustomed to reckon; and finally by the instinctive feeling that the peoples of Europe would not let themselves be annihilated by submitting to the complete exhaustion of their physical and moral forces and the destruction of their economic and cultural values." K. Helfferich, *Der Weltkrieg* (Berlin, 1919), II, 43. Helfferich was in intimate touch with authoritative opinion.

[†] See above, p. 302.

(coast defense), clothing stores, commissary department, etc.
—no action was to be inaugurated.

According to my recollection, no official minutes were made
of this conference, nor did I give any notice of it to be included
in the reports or make a personal record of it for myself.
But, nevertheless, I certainly ordered the chief of the central
division, Rear-Admiral Hopmann, to arrange for the notification of the circumstances to Secretary of State Grand-Ad-
miral von Tirpitz then on leave.* This was in accordance
with the usual routine of the navy office. . . .

No military preparations or movements took place within
the domain of matters belonging to the imperial navy office
during this time [*i. e.*, before 23 July].†

Admiral Behncke was, as Capelle states, present at the conference, of which he gives the following account:

We were fully agreed that, with things as they were, it
was above all absolutely necessary to keep the affair secret,
and next, that no measures were to be taken that could occasion
any uneasiness, and that *only immaterial* [*intellektuelle*] *preparations* should at the time be made for meeting the situation
of a possible outbreak of war. It was agreed that the notice
should be given personally and by word of mouth to the higher
naval commanders and the chiefs of the dockyards on behalf
of the imperial navy office.‡

The testimony of both admirals is intended to convey the
idea that the German naval authorities did nothing out of the
ordinary with the view to a possible war. But three things
must strike the reader. (1) Capelle instantly summoned a
conference of the highest officials. (2) The matter was so important and secrecy so urgent that no minutes were kept, but
Admiral von Tirpitz was informed. (3) If no measures

---

* The information that reached Tirpitz at Tarasp, where he was on leave, was
that "the Austrian Government would approach Serbia with a demand for the
fullest satisfaction, and if this were not given, would march her troops into Serbia."
Tirpitz, *Erinnerungen*, pp. 208–209.

† Statement to the parliamentary investigating committee; *Zur Vorgeschichte
des Weltkrieges*, I, no. 14.

‡ Statement to the parliamentary investigating committee; *Zur Vorgeschichte des
Weltkrieges*, I, no. 19.

were taken by the navy department, it was not because the officials did not think them desirable, but solely because the Emperor had stipulated that the political situation was not to be
disturbed. One gets the very definite impression that the naval
officers grasped fully the significance of the information conveyed to them.

This view is confirmed by a study of the *"immaterial preparations"* made by the admiralty staff. Admiral Behncke describes
them as follows:

(*a*) A test, suited to the circumstances, of the measures established by the current mobilization practise. In making this
test the case of a possible war with Russia and France, without participation of England, was kept in mind.

(*b*) The making of a number of requisitions on the imperial navy office as a result of this test. These consisted of
measures to insure the timely preparation of war-ships and
smaller craft, and of their auxiliaries, without going noticeably
beyond the limit of peace measures or marking up a deficit
against our current peace budget.

(*c*) Direction of the movements of the High Seas Fleet
and of ships out of home waters according to the foreign
office's judgment of the situation.

The activities described under (*a*) consisted of work at the
staff and of verbal communications with the navy office and
commanders of the fleet and dockyards; they were, says Admiral Behncke, *"purely subjective."* The requisitions mentioned under (*b*) were made "by word of mouth"; on 25 July,
a written compilation, "enlarged by others of a similar nature
demanded by further measures," was sent in covering these
points:

1. The hastening to completion of new ships, torpedo-boats
and U-boats already almost finished and of such ships and
small craft in service as were laid up for repairs, as well as
the preparing for war service of all ships and small craft out
of commission. The budget allowance was not to be over-
stepped.

2. The completion of the Kaiser Wilhelm Canal and a test trip through by a battle-ship.

3. Enlarging the provision of fuel, etc. to the necessary volume.

4. Preparations for the provision of a number of auxiliary and store ships without incurring any immediate expense.

5. Putting into shape the naval flying forces.

Under (c) the movements of the High Seas Fleet were not interfered with, for "the naval staff felt sufficiently assured by the declaration of the foreign office that political developments would under all circumstances permit the timely return of the High Seas Fleet—six days before the possible commencement of war with England." But special orders were sent to certain ships on foreign stations. The *Scharnhorst* and the *Gneisenau*, which were on their way to Samoa, were instructed on 6 July to remain in Truk or Ponape, "to make possible a certain and constant communication with them." Three days later their commander, Admiral von Spee, was notified that war between Austria and Serbia was "possible"; in that case, said the telegram, "it is not impossible that the Triple Alliance will become involved," and on the following day England was mentioned as "a possible enemy" if it came to a general war.[*] Admiral Suchon, commanding in the Mediterranean, was informed that the situation was not free from anxiety;[†] his flagship, the *Goeben*, was ordered to Pola, an Austrian port, "a few days earlier than had been contemplated by her itinerary," and in the middle of July dockyard workers were sent there "to hasten the repairs to her boiler-tubes." The *Eber*, lying at Cape Town for repairs, "was notified in order that the necessary work might be adjusted to the political situation." Admiral Behncke represents the measures taken as going to the "very limit of military safety" in their "most complete inconspicuousness and self-restraint"; but the mere fact that

[*] Vice-Admiral E. Raeder, *Der Krieg zur See: der Kreuzerkrieg in den ausländischen Gewässern* [the official history] (Berlin, 1922), I, 62.

[†] Captain O. Groos, *Der Krieg zur See: der Krieg in der Nordsee* [the official history] (Berlin, 1920), I, 3.

any measures were thought necessary records sufficiently the impression made on the naval authorities by the Emperor's communication. Technically, up to 23 July, "no military movements were ordered or effected by the naval staff," but obviously everything was done that could be done which would not be interpreted as a sign of nervousness or reveal the preparations being made.* From 6 July onward the naval staff considered that preparations for an emergency were necessary.

On 9 July, four days after the Emperor's promise to Count Szögyény, the imperial chancellor sent for the minister of the interior, Dr. Clemens von Delbrück, who, though on leave from his office, happened to be in Berlin, in order to tell him that "Austria was planning to address an ultimatum to Serbia on account of the murder at Sarajevo." The minister's "first thought" was, "This means war!"† So he asked

whether the situation did not compel us to put into execution at once the economic measures arranged and prepared for the contingency of a possible war, especially the purchase of grain stocks in Rotterdam.

This the chancellor discouraged: he thought that it would be possible to localize the conflagration "in case war developed between Austria and Serbia," and "in any case it was not advisable that any measures should be initiated on our side that could be interpreted as preparations for imminent war." Moreover, the minister "was to observe absolute silence to everybody [except Herr von Jagow] about our consultation."

A week later, being assured by both Bethmann and Jagow that the political situation did not make his presence in Berlin necessary, Delbrück prepared to resume his vacation; but he was asked to "choose a resort from which [he] could reach Berlin in a few hours." Before leaving, the minister took the opportunity

* Statement of Behncke to the parliamentary investigating committee; *Zur Vorgeschichte des Weltkrieges*, I, no. 19.

† C. von Delbrück, *Die wirtschaftliche Mobilmachung in Deutschland 1914* (Berlin, 1924), p. 96.

again and again to go over all the measures necessary in case of war, with the under-secretary of state and the division chiefs concerned, and had particularly directed that they should go ahead with the purchase of the grain stocks just as soon as the foreign situation should make it advisable and possible.

Evidently, Dr. Delbrück was not satisfied by the assurances of the foreign office that "they would be able to prevent a general European war"; at least, he intended to take no chances. His narrative continues:

On 24 July my under-secretary of state besought me over the telephone to return to Berlin, where I arrived on the afternoon of the 25th. On my arrival I discovered that nothing had been done about the grain purchases up to that time, and on that account went to the secretary of the imperial treasury to ask for the necessary credits. He at first refused them to me, and only put them at my disposal after the chancellor, at my request, gave him instructions to do so. These instructions came too late, for, as I was shortly thereafter informed, *the Rotterdam market had been cleaned out.* Nevertheless, the stock of provisions held there had mostly reached Germany, as the wholesale dealers in the western part of the country, instructed by the proceedings of the Economics Committee, had opportunity at that time to buy it and bring it in.*

This Economics Committee was "formed of representatives of the agriculturalists, manufacturers, and business men for the discussion of economic conditions with the department of the interior"; and though there was delay in getting it organized in the spring of 1914, "the developments . . . were prosecuted with energy after the assassination at Sarajevo." It would appear, therefore, that the department of the interior refrained from purchasing the grain stocks officially, in order not to give the alarm, but arranged, through its Economics Committee, to have it done privately.†

* Statement to the parliamentary investigating committee; *Zur Vorgeschichte des Weltkrieges,* I, no. 27. According to Delbrück, p. 99, he reached Berlin on 24 July.
† There is no evidence of financial, as distinct from economic, preparation. The belief of the British commercial attaché in Berlin that "since the Morocco crisis (the middle of 1911) the whole financial policy of this country has been

In the light of the evidence brought together in this section, we are justified in thinking that the naval authorities of Germany and the officials responsible for the provisioning of the country in the event of war did not share the reassurances given them by the Emperor and the chancellor that a war between Austria and Serbia could be localized. Consequently, within the limits prescribed by the Emperor himself, they quietly took such steps as they could in preparation for a European war.

THE CALCULATIONS OF BERLIN

The action of the German Government, then, is perfectly clear. What were the motives which determined its policy and the view which it took of the international situation on

guided by only one consideration, viz., Germany's financial preparedness in case of war" (Oppenheimer to Goschen, 29 July, 1914; B 322), is amply confirmed by statements made to the parliamentary investigating committee of the Reichstag after the war by Herr von Havenstein, the president of the Reichsbank, and Dr. Meydenbauer, ministerial director of the Prussian ministry of finance in 1914; *Zur Vorgeschichte des Weltkrieges*, I, nos. 26, 28. But these gentlemen deny that any special steps were taken in July, 1914. On 18 July, says a British writer, "the Dresdner Bank caused a great commotion by selling its securities and by advising its clients to sell theirs. This was recognized as the first semi-official intimation of a probable European conflagration, and Berlin [*i. e.*, the Berlin stock exchange] became apprehensive." W. R. Lawson, *British War Finance, 1914-1915* (London, 1915), p. 178. This is hardly proof of fell design, even if the statement about the Dresdner Bank be true. According to Henry Morgenthau, the former American ambassador to Turkey, who claims to have got his information from his German colleague, Baron von Wangenheim, the Emperor William on 5 July asked "the captains of German industry" if they were "ready for war"; the financiers replied that "they must have two weeks to sell their foreign securities and to make loans." Mr. Morgenthau goes on to say that "all the great stock exchanges of the world show that the German bankers profitably used" the interval between 5 July and 23 July, and he cites as proof the "astonishing slumps in prices, especially on the stocks that had an international market," on the New York exchange. H. Morgenthau, *Ambassador Morgenthau's Story* (New York, 1918), pp. 85, 87. Fay, II, 177-180, subjects Mr. Morgenthau's figures of particular stocks to a careful analysis, and concludes that "it does not appear that the New York Stock Market affords any confirmation of the wide-spread story of German bankers demanding a two weeks' respite in which to turn American securities into gold in preparation for a war already decided upon." On the other hand, an examination of the trend of prices on the stock exchanges of Vienna, Berlin, Paris, Brussels, and London shows that "almost at once after the conferences at Potsdam, July 5 and 6, 1914, prices began to decline on various bourses, that this was noticed at the time, that a persistent reason then advanced was the tension over Serbian affairs, that the declines were at first most evident in Vienna and in Berlin, and that some of the selling elsewhere was at the time ascribed to German sources." R. Turner, "Sale of Securities in July, 1914," in *American Historical Review*, XXXV, 303-307 (January, 1930).

5 July? As it happens, the Austro-Hungarian ambassador to the German court, who had every reason to avoid any misrepresentation, on 12 July wrote a long despatch to his government in which he said:

The fact that His Majesty the Emperor William, and with him all persons in authority, urge us to undertake an action against Serbia which may eventually lead to war, needs some explanation.

It did need explanation, for the German attitude represented a complete *volte-face* from the policy followed for some years of preventing an Austrian military action against Serbia. So Count Szögyény proceeded to enumerate the "general political considerations and special ones inspired by the murder at Sarajevo" which he thought explained "the German way of thinking."

Germany [he said] has recently been strengthened in the conviction that Russia is preparing for war with her western neighbors, that she no longer regards war as a mere possibility of the future, but positively includes it in her political calculations. Still, this is a calculation for the future, for while she intends to wage war and is preparing for it with all her might, she does not propose it at the moment, or, to put the matter better, she is not sufficiently prepared for war at the present time.

It is therefore not absolutely certain [*ausgemacht*] that, if Serbia becomes involved in a war with the Monarchy, Russia would lend armed assistance, and, even if Tsardom should decide on this, it is just now not ready from a military point of view and not by any means so strong as it presumably will be in a few years.

Moreover, the German Government believes that it has sure proofs that England will not now take part in a war arising out of the Balkans, not even if this should lead to a passage at arms with Russia and eventually with France also. Not only have the relations of Germany and England improved so much that Germany believes it need no longer fear an openly hostile attitude on the part of England, but just now England is anything but desirous of war and not at all disposed to pull the chestnuts out of the fire for Serbia or, in the last analysis, for Russia.

Thus, in view of what has been said, the political constellation is, generally speaking, as favorable for the Monarchy as it ever can be.

Considerations of internal policy dictated by the murder also enter in. Hitherto a large portion of the population of the Monarchy was unwilling to believe in the anti-dynastic [*monarchiefeindlichen*] and separatist tendencies of some of our Serbs or in the agitation of this kind carried on from Serbia in the Monarchy. Now everybody in the Monarchy is convinced of it, and there is a spontaneous demand for energetic action against Serbia which will put an end to the Great-Serbian agitation once for all.

Similarly, the eyes of the whole civilized world have been opened. The crime of Sarajevo is condemned in every country, and it is understood that the Monarchy must hold Serbia responsible for it. And if Serbia's friends abroad will not, for political reasons, take position against her, it is probable that they also will not at the present moment stand up for her, at any rate not with armed forces.

For these reasons, in Count Szögyény's opinion, the German Empire, "with a clear perception of the opportunity offered, urges the Monarchy unreservedly to clear up its relations with Serbia, which Germany also feels to be untenable, in such a way as to stop the Pan-Slavist intrigues for all time."*

According to this analysis, the German action is to be explained by three considerations: (1) the feeling that for once the polyglot Habsburg state was united on a question of foreign policy and that the opportunity to take advantage of that unity should not be neglected; (2) the chance that a good case existed against Serbia; (3) the belief that, if this case were promptly exploited, other Powers would not interfere and that Austria-Hungary would therefore be able to score a resounding success which would impress the discordant elements in the state and dissipate certain centrifugal tendencies. To put it another way,

---

* Szögyény to Berchtold, 12 July; A I 15.

the German Government agreed with its ally that only drastic action against Serbia could save the Dual Monarchy from dissolution. And Count Szögyény had judged the situation correctly, for a few days later Herr Zimmermann gave expression to these same views in a conversation with the Bavarian chargé in Berlin.

Austria-Hungary [he said], thanks to her indecision and her easy-going ways [*Zerfahrenheit*], had really become the Sick Man of Europe, as Turkey had once been, upon whose partition Russians, Italians, Serbs and Montenegrins were waiting. A powerful and successful move against Serbia would make it possible for the Austrians and Hungarians to feel themselves once more to be a national power, would revive again the waning economic life of the country, and would set back foreign aspirations for years. To judge from the indignation at the murder which prevailed throughout the Monarchy, it looked as if they could be sure of the Slav troops. In a few years, if the Slav propaganda continued to develop, this would no longer be the case, as General Conrad von Hötzendorf himself had admitted.*

It was because "Austria was facing her hour of destiny," so Herr Zimmermann asserted, that Germany had promised her full support, "even at the risk of war with Russia."

The opinion of Count Szögyény, that the risk of war with Russia was minimized, seems to have been correct. Not only did the Emperor William, as we have seen, express to his officers the idea that Russia would not fight; Herr Zimmermann, who may have been instrumental in persuading the chancellor, cherished the same notion. To quote his observations to the Bavarian chargé:

If Russia is not determined on war with Austria and Germany in all circumstances, she can in this case—and this is the most favorable factor in the present situation—very well remain inactive, and justify herself to the Serbs on the ground that she approves of the kind of fighting which resorts to the throwing of bombs and the firing of revolvers just as little as other

* Schoen to Hertling, 18 July; Dirr, p. 6; D, supplement IV, no. 2.

civilized nations; this, especially, so long as Austria does not endanger the national independence of Serbia.

Both England and France, to neither of whom would war be desirable at the present moment, will exercise their influence on Russia in the interests of peace; 'bluffing' constitutes one of the favorite weapons of Russian policy, and while the Russian likes to threaten with the sword, yet he does not willingly draw it for the sake of others at the critical moment.*

If this view was correct, namely, that Russia was not ready, that she could not countenance regicide and could be bluffed into submission, partly by a show of German might, partly by the pressure of France and England, then the attitude taken by the German Government was both intelligible and shrewd. Russia would be forced to accept a severe diplomatic humiliation and her confidence in France and England would be severely shaken, if not destroyed; the Triple Entente would have become a broken reed. To accomplish this was doubtless one of the aims of the German Emperor and his chancellor when they agreed to the Austrian programme. But it is a striking fact that in the published German documents, the first report on the state of feeling in Russia after the murder at Sarajevo is dated 13 July;† nor is there any request to the ambassador in St. Petersburg for information. In other words, the Emperor and his government formulated their policy on a hypothesis which they were at no pains to check. Their omission is not less noteworthy in view of the fears which they had expressed, at the end of June, about the ultimate aims of Russian policy. Can it be that they were reconciled to the idea of a general war?‡

Certainly that is the impression created by some remarks

---

* Schoen to Hertling, 18 July; Dirr, p. 9; D, supplement IV, no. 2.
† G 53; received in Berlin, 16 July.
‡ An explanation sometimes offered of the German calculations is that because Russia had yielded to Austro-German pressure in 1908–1909 and again in 1912–1913, Emperor and chancellor expected her to yield again in 1914. It is a plausible explanation; but it must be said that there is no documentary evidence to sustain it except perhaps Zimmermann's remarks quoted above. Furthermore, such a conception of German reasoning runs counter to the ideas expressed by both the Emperor and the chancellor shortly before the murder with reference to Russian policy (see above, pp. 102–103).

made later in the month by Herr von Jagow, who, though not present at the consultations of 5 and 6 July, must have known what was in the minds of his associates. When reproached by Prince Lichnowsky for "risking the famous Pomeranian grenadier in support of Austria's marauding policy [*Pandourpolitik*],"* the secretary of state replied:

According to all competent observers, Russia will be ready to fight in a few years. Then she will crush us by the number of her soldiers; then she will have built her Baltic fleet and her strategic railways. Our group in the meantime will have become steadily weaker. In Russia this is well known, and therefore they are quite willing to have peace for a few years yet. . . . If localization cannot be secured and Russia attacks Austria, the *casus foederis* will then arise; we cannot abandon Austria. We stand in an isolation that can hardly be called proud. I do not desire a preventive war, but if the conflict should offer itself, we ought not to shirk it [*aber wenn der Kampf sich bietet, dürfen wir nicht kneifen*].†

It cannot be said that the German Government was 'spoiling for a fight' with Russia, but evidently it was not unwilling to participate if one were offered or to run the risk of starting it.

Count Szögyény's statement that "the German Government believes that it has sure proofs that England will not now take part in a war arising out of the Balkans" is borne out by the German evidence. To begin with, the Emperor, in his conversations at Potsdam with the naval officers, "did not mention England."‡ An even clearer indication is found in the conduct of the chancellor. On 16 June he had expressed the opinion that it would depend on the attitude of Germany and England whether an Austro-Russian conflict in the Balkans should develop into a European conflagration, and he had further remarked:

---

* Lichnowsky to Bethmann-Hollweg, 16 July; G 62.
† Jagow to Lichnowsky, private, 18 July; G 72. See also Naumann's statement to Hoyos on 1 July, quoted above, p. 267.
‡ See above, p. 301.

If we two come forward resolutely as the guarantors of European peace, which the obligations neither of the Triple Alliance nor the Triple Entente can prevent us from doing so long as we seek this object with a common purpose from the start, war will be avoided.*

Three weeks later Herr von Bethmann, so far from approaching Sir Edward Grey for joint action to prevent an Austro-Russian clash, not only sanctioned the violent course proposed by Count Berchtold, but carefully concealed the fact from the British foreign secretary. He would hardly have thus abandoned his own formula unless he believed that Great Britain could be left out of account. Defending his policy after the war, he said that he had believed that "England, when faced with the final decision, would value the peace of the world higher than her own friendships."† The ground for this confidence appears to have been the friendly and conciliatory attitude displayed by the British Government in the settlement of the Bagdad Railway question and the adjustment of colonial difficulties in Africa.‡ And, if Great Britain did not intervene at the beginning, she could hardly tip the balance of the conflict, for the German general staff expected to win the decisive battle over the French some three weeks after the commencement of operations.

The conduct of German policy down to 27 July leaves no doubt that British neutrality in the event of a general war was counted upon. Yet this attitude is hard to explain. The German ambassador in London, Prince Lichnowsky, almost from the moment of his appointment in November, 1912, had repeatedly and consistently reported his opinion that, although Great Britain did not desire war, she would be drawn into the struggle if Germany attacked France. These reports were,

---

* Bethmann-Hollweg to Lichnowsky, 16 June; G 2.
† Bethmann-Hollweg, I, 132.
‡ If it should come to a European war, said a high official of the foreign office in the spring of 1914, "we believe to-day that we can assume that England will not take part in it." Statement of Victor Naumann to the parliamentary investigating committee; *Zur Vorgeschichte des Weltkrieges*, I, no. 8, p. 45.

it is true, discounted.* But in the spring of 1914 the German Government secured copies of the notes exchanged in November, 1912, between the French and British Governments and† learned of the naval conversations begun between the British and Russian authorities. These documents were held to prove that Great Britain was bound to France and was binding herself to Russia. When Prince Lichnowsky reported Sir Edward Grey as saying that "there existed no agreements between Great Britain and her Entente associates which had not been made public,"‡ Herr Zimmermann declared:

There is nothing left to do but to give Lichnowsky some naturally very cautious hints concerning the secret but absolutely reliable reports coming to us *from St. Petersburg*§ which allow no doubt at all to arise as to the *existence* of permanent political and military agreements between England and France and as to negotiations leading to the same result which have already been started between England and Russia.||

Why, if this view was held, German officialdom should have clung to the notion that England would remain neutral,¶ is a

* See above, pp. 58–59.
† In a publication in the *Norddeutsche Allgemeine Zeitung* of 6 October, 1914, it was represented that the German Government obtained the notes in March, 1913, but the despatch is not reproduced in *Die Grosse Politik*.
‡ Lichnowsky to Bethmann-Hollweg, 24 June; G 5.
§ How the German Government obtained the documents is not known with certainty. It is said that Professor Theodor Schiemann, a personal friend of the Emperor and the contributor of articles on foreign policy to the *Kreuz-Zeitung* (republished annually, 1901–1914, under the title *Deutschland und die grosse Politik*) was able from 1908 to secure confidential Russian documents which he made use of in writing his articles. Another theory is that documents were secured through Benno von Siebert, a secretary of the Russian embassy in London, who was a Balt, *i. e.*, a German from the Baltic provinces of Russia. Siebert is said to have assisted the ambassador Count Benckendorff, also a Balt, who was not very familiar with Russian, in the translation and preparation of the embassy's correspondence; he kept copies of the more important documents and later published them under the title *Diplomatische Aktenstücke zur Geschichte der Entente-politik der Vorkriegsjahre* (Berlin, 1921).
|| Zimmermann to Bethmann-Hollweg, 27 June; G 6. The chancellor promised to see Lichnowsky, and did so on 29 June. The prince states that Bethmann did not then—or at any other time—inform him of the Grey-Cambon notes. Lichnowsky, I, 245–246. He ascribes the failure to give him such important information to the jealousy of Stumm, the director of the political department of the foreign office. The explanation is not very convincing, but there is no apparent reason why such facts were withheld from the ambassador.
¶ Zimmermann, it should be said, did not believe it. "Should it come to [a war between the Dual Alliance and the Triple Alliance]," he said to the Bavarian chargé,

complete puzzle. Such an attitude was on a par with the optimism professed in regard to Russia, and was just as lightly assumed.

In deciding to take the risk of war with Russia, Emperor and chancellor alike may have been influenced by the consideration that certain elements in Germany did frankly desire war. On 3 June, that is, several weeks before the murder at Sarajevo, Herr von Bethmann, discussing with the Bavarian minister in Berlin the idea of a preventive war, "which was demanded by many soldiers," said:

The Emperor has not conducted any preventive wars, and will not do so. But there are circles in the Empire which expect a war to bring about an improvement in the internal conditions of Germany, that is, in a conservative sense.*

Others were in favor of war because of the external situation. On 6 July Prince Lichnowsky, "speaking quite privately and on very delicate matters," told Sir Edward Grey that "there was some feeling in Germany . . . that trouble was bound to come and therefore it would be better not to restrain Austria and let trouble come now, rather than later."† Of even greater interest is the story reported from Sofia by the British minister:

I gather [he wrote] that General Markoff, the Bulgarian Minister in Berlin, wrote to King Ferdinand on *July 7th* that the Ballplatz were preparing a note of such a stiff nature for the Servian Government that no independent State could accept it: that the German Government had in no way endeavoured to persuade Count Berchtold to tone down the note, the wording of

"we should find our English cousins on the side of our enemies, inasmuch as England fears that France, in the event of a new defeat, would sink to the level of a second-class Power, and that the 'balance of power,' the maintenance of which England considers to be necessary for her own interests, would be thereby upset." Schoen to Hertling, 18 July; Dirr, p. 10; D, supplement IV, no. 2. He perceived, what his colleagues could or would not see, that while a Balkan war would not affect England, the moment a Balkan war became a European war, England would be as much interested as if the quarrel had arisen between Germany and France.

* Lerchenfeld to Hertling, 4 June; Dirr, p. 113. Cf. Bethmann-Hollweg, I, 21–23, where the chancellor complains of the agitation of the Pan-Germans.

† Grey to Rumbold, 6 July; E 32.

which was largely attributed in competent quarters to Count For-
gach, who has a special spite against the Servians. The General
further added that, in Berlin military circles, war between Austria, Servia and Montenegro was considered as a foregone conclusion; that they, the Germans, were absolutely prepared for
all consequences, whereas none of the Triple Entente powers
were ready. This letter reached the Palace on the 10th instant;
on the 11th instant Major von der Goltz, German Military
Attaché here, and son of the celebrated Field-Marshal von der
Goltz, was sent for to the Palace by the King's Chef de Cabinet,
and he left the same evening for Berlin. Major von der Goltz's
attitude had been very warlike ever since the assassination of
the Archduke Ferdinand, and before leaving he told two of his
friends that war between Austria and Servia was certain, but
that he was afraid that Russia would funk Germany at the last
moment.*

This story, the remarks of Prince Lichnowsky, and the chancellor's complaint must not be overemphasized: they merely
afford proof of the existence of chauvinistic currents which
would approve the course taken and which would make retreat
difficult if calculations went wrong. But the German Government was aware of these currents, and it may well have reckoned with them in formulating its policy.

To appraise that policy fairly is a most difficult problem.
At the moment Germany's official relations with her neighbors
were better than they had been for many years. There were
no issues pending with Russia or with France, and the long
controversy with Great Britain about African colonies and
the Bagdad Railway had been adjusted by treaties ready for
signature and publication. "We were," said Herr Zimmermann to the French ambassador on 31 July, "settling down
to what we thought were improved relations all round."† Even
if the commercial expansion which had been the wonder of the
world was slowing down and as a consequence unemployment
was threatening to become a problem,‡ the prestige of the

* Bax-Ironside to Nicolson, private, 29 July; B 653.
† Goschen to Nicolson, private, 1 August; B 510.
‡ Schmitt, *England and Germany, 1740-1914*, pp. 102-103, 114-115.

German Empire had not diminished. To the rest of the world, Germany's position seemed the most brilliant in Europe. With a population second only to that of Russia but far superior in intelligence and efficiency, with the most modern industrial organization, with an army generally considered the most powerful in the world and a navy surpassed only by the British, Germany was entitled, in the opinion of most observers, to face the future with confidence and security.

Yet, if one were so minded, the situation could be pictured in a different light. If France and Russia were momentarily quiet, French sentiment still remembered the lost provinces, Russian opinion was full of hostility to Germany; and, although Great Britain was inclined to friendliness, the naval question was only suppressed, not solved. Against these Powers stood, to be sure, the Triple Alliance, recently renewed and strengthened by military and naval conventions. But Italy's loyalty remained to be proved. Germany could feel sure of only one ally, an ally gravely weakened, however, by internal and external difficulties. To quote the German *White Book* of 1914:

If the Serbs continued with the aid of Russia and France to menace the existence of Austria-Hungary, the gradual collapse of Austria and the subjection of all the Slavs under one Russian sceptre would be the consequence, thus making untenable the position of the Teutonic race in Central Europe. A morally weakened Austria under the pressure of Russian Pan-Slavism would be no longer an ally on whom we could count and in whom we could have confidence, as we must be able to have, in view of the ever more menacing attitude of our easterly and westerly neighbors.*

Now that ally proposed to rehabilitate itself and conjure away unpleasant problems by a vigorous foreign policy. Was Germany to refuse her assistance and thus deprive herself of the advantage to be derived from a rejuvenated Austria-Hun-

* *Collected Diplomatic Documents relating to the Outbreak of the European War* p. 406.

gary? Herr von Jagow put the matter to Prince Lichnowsky
in forceful language:

After all, we are allied to Austria: *hic Rhodus, hic salta.* It
may be open to discussion whether we get our money's worth
from that increasingly disintegrating organization of states
on the Danube, but then I say with the poet—I think it was
Busch—"If you no longer like your company, look for another,
if you can find it." We have not yet established a relationship
with England that promises complete satisfaction, nor could
we, after all that has passed, arrive at it, if indeed we shall ever
be able to do so.

Austria, which has forfeited more and more prestige because
of a lack of a will to act, hardly counts any longer as a real
Great Power. The Balkan crisis has weakened her position
still more. . . . Austria intends not to tolerate the sapping in-
trigue of the Serbs any longer, and even less the continuously
provocative attitude of her small neighbor at Belgrade. She
now proposes to have it out [*auseinandersetzen*] with Serbia
and has informed us of this. . . . We have not driven her to
this decision. But we neither can nor ought to stay her hand.
If we were to do this, Austria (and we ourselves) could rightly
reproach us with having deprived her of her last chance to rehabilitate herself politically. Then the process of withering
away and of internal decay would be further accelerated. Her
position in the Balkans would be gone forever. You will doubtless agree with me that the complete establishment of Russian
hegemony in the Balkans is not tolerable for us either. The
maintenance of Austria and indeed of the most powerful
Austria possible is a necessity for us, for both internal and
external considerations. That she cannot be maintained forever, I willingly admit. But meanwhile we shall have to find
other combinations.*

* Jagow to Lichnowsky, private, 18 July; G 72. Lichnowsky protested in vigorous language against his chief's ideas. "I do not believe in a war with Russia. . . .
What interest, as a matter of fact, would Russia have in making war? So far as
my recollection goes, that is to say, as long as I have been in touch with diplomacy—and that is now nearly thirty years—I can remember that it has been said
that Russia was not ready, but would be ready in a few years, and that the general
staff was worried. And Russia was never ready when those few years had passed,
and so also will it be in the future. . . . I do not believe to-day that we shall have
to wage war with Russia if our policy is cleverly conducted.

". . . It is true, we have to protect Austria, but it is not to our interest to support her in an active Balkan policy in which we have everything to lose and nothing to gain. What advantage do you promise yourself from a strengthening of

Such reasoning is quite understandable. Moreover, the German Emperor and his government professed to believe that because Austria was under peculiar provocation and because each of the Entente Powers was confronted with domestic difficulties, no sharp opposition would be raised to the Austrian measures, however drastic. If their calculations were sound, they would score a notable victory which would consolidate the Triple Alliance and facilitate enormously the extension of German influence and power in the Balkans and Turkey. The chance for the Austro-Hungarian army to assert itself made a particular appeal to William II (if we may judge from his later utterances), and the attempt to suppress a nationalistic movement by force was conceived to be a natural and feasible method.

On the other hand, if the Dual Monarchy was really in so parlous a condition that it could be revived only by an active military policy which involved the danger of Russian intervention, which would in turn necessitate German participation, such a Power was worth very little as an ally.* Hitherto Germany had considered that aggression by Austria-Hungary against Serbia would bring war with Russia, and for that reason had refused to promise her support for such a course. Now she did this very thing. If the reasons of Austria-Hungary for taking such action were stronger than they had been in pre-

Austria's prestige in the Balkans or elsewhere? Austria's value as an ally depends above all else on her military capacity and not on her prestige abroad; and our position among the Great Powers is strong enough to insure the influence of the Triple Alliance group, even in spite of the diplomatic defeats of Count Berchtold. . . . Austria—I will not say a feeble, but a frightened Austria—is a very convenient ally for us to have; the diminution of Austrian influence in the Balkans has up to the present time been a factor of considerable advantage to our economic interests in that region. . . .

". . . I believe as little in the imminent collapse of Austria as I do in the possibility of mastering internal difficulties by an active foreign policy. The nationalistic feelings of the Southern Slavs and their craving for union cannot be destroyed by war and will perhaps be brought only the more violently to the surface. And it is by just such active proceedings on the part of Austria that the Balkan nations will be driven more and more under the ascendancy of Russia, while otherwise, as may be seen from the example of Rumania and Bulgaria, they have a tendency to try to stand on their own feet." Lichnowsky to Jagow, private, 23 July; G 161.

* Tschirschky had his doubts, which he expressed in a private letter to Jagow on 22 May, 1914; G. P., XXXIX, 364.

vious years, the German Government was none the less aware that it was playing with fire. The German *White Book* of 1914 contained this frank admission:

> We were perfectly aware that a possible warlike attitude of Austria-Hungary against Serbia might bring Russia on the field, and that it might involve us in a war in accordance with our duty as allies.*

In fact the very emphasis with which the German statesmen affirmed their readiness to fulfil their obligations as allies shows how clearly they recognized the danger. Nor was the chance that a general war might result from their policy considered a reason for rejecting or modifying that policy, and the promptness and completeness with which the Austro-Hungarian proposals were accepted can be explained only if the German Government was not greatly concerned whether war (under the conditions imagined, *i. e.,* on the assumption that Great Britain would remain neutral) came or not. It had a perfect right to adopt such an attitude, for war was a legitimate instrument of national policy, and every other government was equally prepared to fight rather than submit to a threat to national interests or to diplomatic humiliation. But William II and Theobald von Bethmann-Hollweg were the *first* responsible statesmen to take decisions which might have the most dire consequences. They may be acquitted of deliberate intent to precipitate a European war, but they did elect to put the system of alliances to the severest test and to spring a crisis of the first magnitude on Europe. It was they who took the gambler's plunge.

Appendix

THE STORY OF A 'CROWN COUNCIL' AT POTSDAM ON 5 JULY, 1914

War is a great breeder of legends, and that of 1914–1918 proved no exception. The German *White Book* of 1914 had stated that "the Imperial and Royal Government appraised [*sic*] Germany" of

* *Collected Diplomatic Documents*, p. 406.

its conception of the situation created by the murder at Sarajevo and "asked our opinion."* But the papers published by the German and Austro-Hungarian Governments contained no record of any such consultation. There was, accordingly, much curiosity as to when and how it had occurred. On 7 September, 1914, the *Nieuwe Rotterdamsche Courant* published the following article, dated 4 September, from its Berlin correspondent Dr. M. van Blankenstein:

From a trustworthy quarter I have heard a few more details about the preliminaries of the war which will serve to supplement those of my letter of 20 August, which I see has reached you in about two weeks.

The Archduke Francis Ferdinand was murdered on 28 June. Only a few days later the Austro-Hungarian Government informed Berlin that it was in a position to prove that the Serbian Government might have been able at least to prevent the murder. When people here had been made acquainted with these proofs, they were of the same opinion. Thereupon a crown council took place at Potsdam, on 5 July, if my informant remembers rightly. Austria had made known her intention of sending a punitive expedition against Serbia. In Vienna they could see no other possible way of putting an end to the intolerable state of affairs. Therefore they asked whether they could count on the assistance of Germany in the event of Russia's wishing to stand by Serbia.

This question was now discussed in the crown council. The military members warmly supported the idea of a very definite procedure, for reasons that I shall explain immediately. The Emperor and his civil advisers were, as always, strongly against any course which might involve war; nevertheless even they agreed that something must be done against Serbia.

In the end, it was decided to give Austria the assurance that it could count upon Germany, whatever the consequences might be of its procedure against Serbia.

The Emperor and the imperial chancellor refused to believe the danger of a general war very great. Their confidence was reinforced by the fact that they were counting on war at a definite time, that is, in February or March, 1916, and for the following reasons:

In 1916 the strategic railways in Poland would be completed. The Russian field artillery is already in excellent shape, but the siege batteries will not be ready for use for another year and a half; and numerous strong fortresses bar the way into the heart of Germany. France will introduce the automatic rifle in 1915 and be able

* *Collected Diplomatic Documents*, p. 406.

to make good the 1,800 metres by which its artillery falls short of the German in range.

So, up to 1916, there would still be time.

They count here on February or March, since these months are the most favorable for Germany's enemies for beginning a war. At the present moment a large part of the harvest has been gathered, and Germany can hold out. At the beginning of spring, however, the old harvest is nearly exhausted, and the growing of a new one can be prevented.

On the basis of these considerations the military members of the crown council pleaded for a very strong procedure on the Austro-German side. They hoped thereby to throw into confusion the fine calculations of those who rightly or wrongly were assumed to be the future enemies.

The Emperor, however, did not wish to play with fire, just as little as did Bethmann-Hollweg. That the military group was finally able to overcome the strong opposition depended on the argument that the enemy would not let its plans be thrown into confusion and would therefore take care not to make the Austro-Serbian conflict a general *casus belli*. When the council broke up, the decision had been taken to accede to the wishes of Austria. Strong optimism prevailed in the immediate entourage of the Emperor. The opinion that in view of future dangers the present had to be looked on as fairly secure had become a conviction.

The energetic plans of Austria—as I have pointed out in my report of 20 August—were kept strictly secret, probably in order to leave the other side not too much time for preparation. On 23 August [sic] we suddenly learned of the well-known ultimatum.*

The article passed almost unnoticed by the European press, for at the moment the Battle of the Marne was engrossing the attention of the world, and no one had much attention to spare for alleged diplomatic revelations.

Nothing more was heard of the story until on 21 January, 1916, the Paris *Temps* published the following over the signature of Hendrik Hudson, a "neutral returned from Germany, where he had resided for a fairly long time":

It was on 5 July that the German Government—which has dared to deny that it had premeditated this war—cold-bloodedly accepted the possibility of a European conflict. That is a detail which is little known in France, but about which no one in well-informed circles in Berlin is ignorant. On that day, when the

* This much of the article is translated into German in K. Jagow, *loc. cit.*, XXV, 790–791. The rest of the article deals with Russian policy.

diplomatists were leaving Berlin for their summer homes, there was a crown council in Potsdam at which the Emperor decided to give Austria carte blanche with reference to Serbia. The Emperor appears to have yielded at this moment to the strong pressure which his military entourage had been exerting upon him for a long time. Herr von Bethmann-Hollweg, although he was chancellor of the Empire, did nothing to keep him from this dangerous course. Never, during this crisis, did he find the courage necessary to set himself against the belligerent exhortations of the generals. . . .

Neither story appears to have called forth any denial on the part of the German Government.

In July, 1917, certain German socialists, delegates to the abortive Stockholm Peace Congress, referred to the story, and one of them, Herr Hugo Haase, alluded in the Reichstag on 19 July to the "meeting of 5 July, 1914."[*] Thereupon the London *Times* on 28 July published the following communication, "from a well-informed correspondent":

I have it on authority which is difficult, if not impossible, to doubt that the meeting referred to was a meeting which was held in Potsdam on the date mentioned.   There were present the Kaiser, Herr von Bethmann-Hollweg, Admiral von Tirpitz, General von Falkenhayn, Herr von Stumm, the Archduke Frederick, Count Berchtold, Count Tisza, and General von Hötzendorf. It appears that Herr von Jagow and General von Moltke were not present.

The meeting discussed and decided upon all the principal points in the Austrian ultimatum which was to be despatched to Serbia 18 days later. It was recognized that Russia would probably refuse to submit to such a direct humiliation, and that war would result. That consequence the meeting definitely decided to accept. It is probable, but not certain, that the date of mobilization was fixed at the same time.

The Kaiser, as is well known, then left for Norway, with the object of throwing dust in the eyes of the French and Russian Governments. Three weeks later, when it became known that England would not remain neutral, Herr von Bethmann-Hollweg wished to withdraw, but it was too late. The decision of 5 July was irrevocable.

On 30 July the *Nieuwe Rotterdamsche Courant* pointed out that it had already published an account of the meeting and republished its article of 7 September, 1914.

[*] His remarks were reproduced in the *Leipziger Volkszeitung* of 20 July.

The position of the *Times* forced the German Government to act. So it published, on 31 July, an official denial:

The information of the *Times* has been manufactured out of whole cloth in all its details. There was not, on this day or on any day of July, any common discussion of this kind, in the presence or the absence of the Emperor. We add, in contradiction to the assertions of the *Times,* that the German Government abstained from any intervention in the formulation of the Austrian ultimatum to Serbia and was entirely ignorant of the content of the ultimatum before it was presented.

Herr von Stumm declared that he had not been present at such a gathering, for he had left Berlin on 10 June and had not returned until 12 July.* Count Berchtold declared that the story was "absolutely imaginary." The belief that some kind of meeting had taken place was, however, confirmed by a statement in Prince Lichnowsky's memorandum published in March, 1918:

Subsequently I ascertained that, at the decisive conference at Potsdam, 5 July, the inquiry of Vienna received the unqualified approval of all the leading people, with the rider that it would not matter if war with Russia resulted. Thus it was expressed, at any rate, in the Austrian protocol which Count Mensdorff received in London.†

Meanwhile the story had been served up by way of Constantinople. On 26 September, 1915, the Italian minister Signor Barzilai, in a speech at Naples, stated that the Italian ambassador to Turkey had been told by his German colleague, Baron von Wangenheim, on 15 July, 1914, that "the note to Serbia had been so formulated as to make war unavoidable." The German Government thereupon denied that its ambassador had or could have made such a statement, "because he was as little informed beforehand as was the German Government of the text of the Austro-Hungarian ultimatum."‡ When the *Times* published its

---

* He reaffirmed this after the war to the parliamentary investigating committee; *Zur Vorgeschichte des Weltkrieges*, I, no. 35.
† Lichnowsky, I, 128. It is not clear what is meant by "the Austrian protocol." The letter of Francis Joseph to William II and the accompanying memorandum were communicated to Mensdorff on 15 July; *Ö.-U. A.*, 10,288. There is nothing, however, to indicate that he was sent a copy of the minutes of the ministerial council of 7 July or was informed about the decisions of his government.
‡ K. Jagow, *loc. cit.*, XXV, 795, 803-804.

article, Signor Barzilai returned to the charge. He published in the Paris *Matin* what purported to be the exact conversation between Baron von Wangenheim and Signor Garroni on 15 July, 1914:

WANGENHEIM: I'm back from Berlin! It's war!
GARRONI: War? Then it has been decided?
WANGENHEIM: Yes, in the course of a conference with the Emperor at which I was present.
GARRONI: But Serbia will yield. She will accept all the demands of Austria.
WANGENHEIM: That's impossible; the ultimatum has been drafted at Berlin in such a manner that it can't be accepted.
GARRONI: But does that mean then a European conflagration?
WANGENHEIM: Yes, that is what is desired in Berlin.

Likewise an American diplomatist, Mr. Lewis Einstein, who had been stationed in Constantinople in 1915, wrote to the London *Times* declaring that he had heard the same story from the Marquis Garroni and from "another diplomatist" as well.* No denials were forthcoming from Berlin.

"Another diplomatist" was Mr. Henry Morgenthau, who was American ambassador to Turkey from 1913 to 1916. Encouraged perhaps by the revelations in Europe, he proceeded to tell what he knew. In the New York *World* of 14 October, 1917, he stated that shortly after the German war-ships *Goeben* and *Breslau* had entered the Dardanelles (11 August, 1914) the German ambassador had revealed to him that "in the first half of the month of July a conference had taken place in Berlin at which the day for beginning the war had been fixed." The conference had taken place under the presidency of the Emperor; Wangenheim himself, Moltke, Tirpitz, and "the leading men of the German financial world, the directors of the railways and the captains of industry" had been present. All had declared themselves ready for war except the financiers, who asked for two weeks' delay in order to sell their foreign securities and put their affairs in order. The ambassador went on to say that the records of the New York Stock Exchange showed the effects of the sale of such securities. In *The World's Work* (New York) for May

* Letter of 3 August, 1917, published on 4 August.

and June, 1918, he offered a somewhat fuller version. He claimed
to have been struck by the absence of Baron von Wangenheim
from the memorial service held for the Archduke Francis Ferdinand on 4 July, 1914; he described the consultation of 5 July
as a 'crown council' (instead of as a 'conference'), and stated
that it had been held at Potsdam. Finally, in his memoirs published in the autumn of 1918, he gave the following account:

I have already mentioned that the German Ambassador had
left for Berlin soon after the assassination of the Grand Duke,
and he now revealed the cause of his sudden disappearance. The
Kaiser, he told me, had summoned him to Berlin for an imperial
conference. The Kaiser presided and nearly all the important
ambassadors attended. Wangenheim himself was summoned
to give assurance about Turkey and enlighten his associates generally on the situation in Constantinople, which was then regarded
as the pivotal point in the impending war. In telling me who attended this conference Wangenheim used no names, though he
specifically said that among them were—the facts are so important
that I quote his exact words in the German which he used—*"die
Häupter des Generalstabs und der Marine"*—(the heads of the
general staff and the navy) by which I have assumed that he
meant von Moltke and von Tirpitz. The great bankers, railroad
directors, and the captains of German industry, all of whom were
as necessary to German war preparations as the army itself, also
attended.

Wangenheim now told me that the Kaiser solemnly put the
question to each man in turn: "Are you ready for war?" All replied "yes" except the financiers. They said that they must have
two weeks to sell their foreign securities and to make loans. At
the time few people had looked upon the Sarajevo tragedy as
something that would inevitably lead to war. This conference,
Wangenheim told me, took all precautions that no such suspicion
should be aroused. It decided to give the bankers time to read-
just their finances for the coming war, and then the several members went quietly back to their work or started on vacations. The
Kaiser went to Norway on his yacht, von Bethmann-Hollweg left
for a rest, and Wangenheim returned to Constantinople. . . .

This imperial conference took place 5 July and the Serbian
ultimatum was sent on 22 July. That is just about the two weeks'
interval which the financiers had demanded to complete their
plans. All the great stock exchanges of the world show that the
German bankers profitably used this interval. Their records disclose that stocks were being sold in large quantities and that prices
declined rapidly. At that time the markets were somewhat puz-

zled at this movement, but Wangenheim's explanation clears up any doubts that may still remain. Germany was changing her securities into cash for war purposes. If any one wishes to verify Wangenheim, I would suggest that he examine the quotations of the New York stock market for these two historic weeks. He will find that there were astonishing slumps in prices, especially on the stocks that had an international market. Between 5 July and 22 July, Union Pacific dropped from 155½ to 127½, Baltimore and Ohio from 91½ to 81, United States Steel from 61 to 50½, Canadian Pacific from 194 to 185½, and Northern Pacific from 111⅜ to 108. At that time the high protectionists were blaming the Simmons-Underwood tariff act as responsible for this fall in values, while other critics of the Administration attributed it to the Federal Reserve Act—which had not yet been put into effect. How little the Wall Street brokers and the financial experts realized that an imperial conference, which had been held in Potsdam and presided over by the Kaiser, was the real force that was then depressing the market!*

Could anything be more convincing than the testimony of two German ambassadors? There was at the time no good reason for not believing what they said, or were reported to have said,† and this story of a Potsdam conference or crown council has been "an unconscionable time dying." Thus, M. Raymond Poincaré, writing in 1927, appears disposed to give some credence to it.‡ The account in the text, of what happened on 5 July, 1914, shows, however, that the story is grossly inaccurate and, in its more picturesque details, simply imaginary. Count Berchtold and General von Conrad were in Vienna on 5 July, Count Tisza in Budapest. Of the Germans supposed to have attended the conference, the ambassadors in Paris, Rome, Vienna, and St. Petersburg were, so far as is known, at their posts; the ambassador in London was in Berlin for a short time, but left for his post in the afternoon; Wangenheim, though on leave, was neither in Berlin nor in Potsdam, according to the statement of his widow.§ Tir-

* Morgenthau, *Ambassador Morgenthau's Story*, pp. 84–85, 87.

† The British representatives in Berlin and Vienna on 5 July, 1914, Sir Horace Rumbold and Sir Maurice de Bunsen, expressed their doubts privately in 1917, on the ground that the distinguished Austrians mentioned in the *Times* article could hardly have left Vienna or come to Germany without the fact becoming known. Oman, *The Outbreak of the War of 1914–1918*, pp. 16–17.

‡ Poincaré, IV, 196–199. See also R. Turner, "The Potsdam Conference: New Evidence Corroborating Ambassador Morgenthau's Account," in *Current History*, XXXI, 265–271 (November, 1929).

§ Montgelas, p. 172; Fay, II, 170–171.

pitz, Pohl, and Moltke were, as we have seen, on leave; Waldersee, Moltke's deputy, had gone to Hanover for a funeral.* There
is no evidence that any financiers or business men were present at
Potsdam on 5 July; on the contrary, the Emperor consulted Baron
von Krupp at Kiel on the following day. In short, most of the
persons alleged to have participated in the Potsdam Conference
were elsewhere on the day in question.

About equally veracious is Mr. Morgenthau's picture of the
crashing New York stock market. His figures have been shown
to be far wide of the truth.† It is true that the bourses of Vienna
and Budapest began to show a decline a week or ten days before
the presentation of the ultimatum to Siberia; but this was attributed to the rumors that had begun to fly about of impending
action.‡

There was, then, on 5 July, no crown council, no conference
in any formal sense—although there were numerous consultations
which had momentous consequences. But it is not without interest to trace the development of the story, which was not
concocted by Allied propaganda but had its origin in Germany.
In July, 1917, an official in the German ministry of the interior
supplied the following explanation:

On the evening of 5 July, Herr Stein, the correspondent of
the *Frankfurter Zeitung,* was at a well-known restaurant in Potsdam. A number of men came into the restaurant whom Stein at
once recognized as officers of high rank, especially as Moltke and
Conrad von Hötzendorf were among them. The officers went
into the room reserved for them. After a time, the manager of
the restaurant came to Herr Stein in some excitement. He said
that the waiter who was serving the officers had just told him
that they were talking of war with Russia, as though it were an
accomplished fact, and asked what Stein thought of that.

Herr Stein, when questioned, gave a rather different version:

He was sitting in the Kaiserhof Hotel in Berlin between ten
and eleven o'clock on the evening of 5 July, when one of the
employees of the hotel came to his neighbor and whispered to

* Statement to the parliamentary investigating committee; *Zur Vorgeschichte des
Weltkrieges,* I, no. 18.
† Fay, II, 177–180.
‡ Max Müller to Grey, 16 July; Bunsen to Grey, 21 July; B 81, 88.

him that a waiter, who was serving some officers of the Guards from Potsdam at an adjoining hotel, had heard that a meeting of Austrian and German diplomatists and military men had taken place that day at Potsdam—Szögyény, Bethmann-Hollweg, and Zimmermann were mentioned—and that the Emperor had given up his trip to Norway on this account.*

The story is also said to have been told at the royal stables in Berlin by an officer coming from Potsdam.† So it is not surprising that the correspondent of a Dutch newspaper picked up the tale.

Nothing more seems to have been heard of it in Germany until 1917. On 4 May of that year the Reichstag deputy, Dr. Oskar Cohn, a member of the Independent Socialist party, speaking before the main committee of the Reichstag against General von Falkenhayn, said:

Neither Herr von Moltke nor Secretary of State von Jagow, but certainly Herr von Falkenheyn took part in the crown council on 5 July, 1914, which was held here or in Potsdam and at which the Archduke Frederick and General Conrad von Hötzendorf were present. In the presence of Herr von Falkenhayn and on his insistence, the decision was there taken which was recorded in writing on the part of the Austrians. In this decision it was said that the ultimatum, the main points of which were then laid down, should be presented, "even though it involved the danger of war with Russia." Thus Herr von Falkenhayn was quite definitely a party to the decision to present an ultimatum, with which it was calculated to make the intervention of Russia the *dolus eventualis*.

Dr. Cohn's reference to an Austrian document appears to have been based on the statement of Prince Lichnowsky, whose memorandum he had seen. He was one of the delegates to the Stockholm congress, where he spread the story.‡

Neither the Marquis Garroni§ nor Mr. Morgenthau‖ reported to his government at the time his conversation with Baron von Wangenheim. But after the rupture between Italy and Turkey

---

* Montgelas, p. 171.   † K. Jagow, *loc. cit.*, XXV, 790, note 2.
‡ *Ibid.*, pp. 804–805, 814–817. The author made use of the minutes of the sessions of the main committee of the Reichstag.
§ Salandra, *La neutralità italiana*, pp. 117–118.
‖ There is no report on the matter in *Papers relating to the Foreign Relations of the United States, 1914, Supplement: the World War* (Washington, 1928).

in the summer of 1915, the former ambassador made a verbal statement to the Italian foreign minister, Baron Sonnino, who recorded it in these words:

Referring to the most recent Anglo-German discussions about the origins of the war and the respective responsibilities for the breaking of the peace, Garroni told that there could be no doubt of the firm intention of Germany during the month of July to push matters to the point of war, for she was convinced that, in view of the inadequate preparations of France and Russia, the most favorable moment for her had come. He had the best proof of it in a conversation with Wangenheim, the German ambassador in Constantinople, on 15 July. The latter had greeted him with the words, "Nous sommes à la guerre!" Asked why he thought so, he explained that Austria would shortly present to Serbia a complaint or a protest against the murder at Sarajevo which would be framed in such terms that it could not be accepted in any way and must lead to the worst. The Emperor of Austria had long hesitated to do so, but Germany had urged him and caused him to decide on it.

I asked Garroni if he had reported all this to the Consulta, saying that I had no knowledge of it, and that if he had done so, such a report would now have the greatest importance.

He replied that "he had not done so," because on the one hand his conversation with Wangenheim had been confidential, and because on the other he supposed that the government would be fully informed of it all by Berlin and it did not seem to him to be the correct thing to do out of consideration for Bollati [the ambassador in Berlin].*

To the Italian premier, the Marquis Garroni made a similar statement; adding that Wangenheim had returned "from a meeting of German ambassadors in Berlin."†

Did the Marquis Garroni invent this conversation? If so, he did it before his departure from Constantinople, for on 20 June he told the same story to an American diplomatist in Constantinople, Mr. Lewis Einstein, who recorded it in his diary:

I walked with Garroni to Nishastash. On our way we met W., who had just returned from Wangenheim. The latter is unwell and almost a nervous wreck. Garroni related to me that on July 15 last, the date of his birthday, Wangenheim, who had returned from Berlin the day before, called to congratulate him. He told

* Salandra, pp. 115–116. Memorandum of 1 September, 1915.
† Salandra's memorandum of 8 September; *ibid.*, p. 117.

him that the Emperor, alarmed by the Russian military preparations, had summoned a conference of ambassadors, generals, and leaders of industry. War had been irrevocably decided. The Archduke's murder was to furnish the pretext. An ultimatum would be presented to Serbia of a nature which she could not accept, and war would be declared forty-eight hours later. The German reasoning took into account the immediate crushing of France. There was greater uncertainty about England. Italy would be forced by German victory to fight with her. Such was the programme.

Garroni told me that, freshly arrived here, he did not like to wire this hearsay news to Rome, in spite of its source, as he was sure that his colleague in Berlin must have done so. During the days of apparent lull which followed, he was glad not to have done so, convinced that Wangenheim must have been mistaken. The Emperor's yachting trip to Norway, as was intended, misled Europe with the belief that nothing was impending. Rome remained in ignorance when the storm burst, and could do no more than declare her non-participation.*

M. Maurice Bompard, who was the French ambassador in Constantinople in 1914, states that the Marquis Garroni assured him in August, 1914, that their German colleague had told him the story.† There is, accordingly, ample evidence that the Marquis Garroni did not manufacture the story on his return to Rome.

In fact, it seems to have been current in diplomatic circles, for Mr. Einstein recorded on 5 May, 1915, that Wangenheim "was one of those summoned at the famous council, held early last July, when the Emperor turned to all the different leaders and captains of industry, and asked them if they were ready for war." He further stated that Wangenheim told the story to Mr. Morgenthau, from whom he himself heard it.§

There is, then, no reason to doubt that the German ambassador to Turkey did assert that a meeting was held at Potsdam or Berlin on 5 July at which it was decided to bring on a European war. What motive he may have had must remain a mystery,‖

---

* L. Einstein, *Inside Constantinople* (London, 1917), pp. 128-129.
† Poincaré, IV, 199; Bompard to K. Jagow, 26 March, 1928, in *Revue d'histoire de la guerre mondiale*, VIII, 48 (January, 1930). Bompard adds that "I did not myself hear Baron von Wangenheim speak of the crown council."
‡ Einstein, p. 24.
§ *Times* (London), 4 August, 1917; K. Jagow, *loc. cit.*, p. 797, note 4.
‖ According to the Austrian military attaché in Constantinople, Wangenheim was given to indiscretion and exaggeration. J. Pomiankowski, *Der Zusammenbruch*

for Baron von Wangenheim died before his story reached the
public or even the governments. Incidentally, the dates which
have been given show that the story was not fabricated after the
publication of the article in the London *Times*.

des Ottomanischen Reiches, pp. 49–50. In a letter of 20 November, 1929, to T. St.
John Gaffney (*Current History*, XXXI, 878, February, 1930), William II wrote:
"Certainly *neither* Morgenthau nor Page nor Garroni *invented* the Fable of the
'Potsdam Council' but they *propagated* it as an historical *true* fact. The *Lie* of
the 'Potsdam Crown-War-Council' was *concocted with all its exciting details by MY
OWN ! ! Ambassador*, pretending to have attended the Council *personally*, to give
more *probability* to his story !"

CHAPTER VI

THE DECISIONS OF AUSTRIA-HUNGARY

THE MINISTERIAL COUNCIL OF 7 JULY

THE telegrams sent by the Austro-Hungarian ambassador in Berlin on 5 and 6 July and the verbal report of Count Hoyos enabled the Cabinet of Vienna to judge accurately the attitude of its ally toward the Serbian problem. "Germany advises us to strike," and "will stand unconditionally by our side, even if our action against Serbia brings on the great war," Count Berchtold informed General Conrad on the morning of 7 July.* Count Berchtold was now in position to cope with possible opposition within his own government (hitherto he had only sounded certain officials confidentially and had not formally consulted the responsible authorities), and particularly with his principal antagonist, Count Tisza. At the latter's request, a ministerial council had been summoned for this very day, 7 July, to discuss the measures required by the situation in Bosnia-Herzegovina.† At this meeting the proposals submitted to the German Government and approved by it would be presented to the highest officials of the Monarchy. Since, however, Count Tisza had already registered his vigorous disapproval of this policy, an open conflict with him was likely to arise in the council, unless he could be won over beforehand; he was, in fact, in a position to veto the proposed course of action.

Count Berchtold accordingly invited to a conference, before the session of the council, the Austrian and Hungarian premiers and the German ambassador. Count Hoyos read to them the two telegrams from Count Szögyény reporting the promises of

---

* Conrad, IV, 42. Conrad at once requested the Archduke Frederick, now the commander-in-chief-designate of the army, to postpone a projected visit to Hamburg, and himself discussed with the chief of the operations section of the general staff the measures to be taken in the event of mobilization.

† Tisza to Berchtold, 3 July; H. F. Armstrong, "A Letter of Count Tisza's," in *Foreign Affairs* (New York), VI, 502 (April, 1928).

support given by the German Emperor and the German chancellor, and gave an account of his own conversation with Herr Zimmermann.* Tisza was dismayed; for obviously Berchtold, through Hoyos, had proposed to Berlin the very policy which Tisza had declined to approve, and, in addition, the partition of Serbia. The Hungarian premier refused to let his hand be forced and protested vigorously: so vigorously that, in the presence of the German ambassador, Count Berchtold was forced to disavow in part the explanations of his confidential emissary, and the ambassador had to telegraph to Berlin:

Count Berchtold and more especially Count Tisza wish it to be expressly understood that everything that Count Hoyos said in his conversation with the under-secretary of state is to be regarded as only his personal opinion. (This declaration refers particularly to the fact that Count Hoyos stated that a complete partition of Serbia was under consideration here.)†

Such stubbornness on Count Tisza's part was not a happy augury. But Count Berchtold was equal to the occasion.

Later in the day the ministerial council was held. Present,

* Tschirschky, in reporting to Berlin, stated that "Count Hoyos read us a memorandum that he had drawn up" of the conversation. The memorandum was not published in the post-war edition of the Austro-Hungarian documents, and is not preserved in the archives of the Ballplatz; Gooss, p. 35, note. The writer has been authoritatively informed that Hoyos had not drawn up a formal memorandum; he spoke from some notes which he had made. Later, the notes were lost.

† Tschirschky to foreign office, telegram, 7 July; G 18. Hoyos had, in fact, revealed the intentions of his government in reply to a question from Zimmermann; K. Jagow, *loc. cit.*, XXV, 788, note 2. He spoke of his own initiative and without authorization; but there is ample evidence that he was stating accurately the intentions of his superiors. According to Brandenburg, *Von Bismarck zum Weltkriege*, p. 413, "Count Berchtold had already expressed the same opinion to our ambassador." This fact is not recorded in the published documents; but Professor Brandenburg was allowed the free use of the German archives and often quotes from unpublished documents. The idea of partition was hinted at in the ministerial councils (see below, pp. 364–365), and was later openly discussed in the Austro-Hungarian embassy in London (cf. G 301). The writer also has private information which confirms the view that the plan to partition Serbia among her Balkan neighbors existed. Tschirschky's adroit phraseology—"Count Berchtold and more especially Count Tisza wish it to be understood"—contained the hint that Berchtold really maintained his position (which he had already made known) and that only Tisza really objected. It will be noted also that Berchtold disavowed only what Hoyos had said to Zimmermann, and not what Szögyény had said to the Emperor William. Berlin would therefore understand that Berchtold still held to his plan for military action against Serbia.

besides Count Berchtold, who acted as chairman, were the Austrian and Hungarian premiers, the common minister of finance Ritter von Bilinski, the common minister of war General von Krobatin, the chief of the general staff General Conrad von Hötzendorf, Admiral von Kailer as representative of the navy, and Count Hoyos as secretary. It was only on unusual occasions that the highest political and military authorities of the state were thus brought together.* The council was supposed to "concern itself exclusively with those measures of an internal political character which were to be taken in Bosnia and Herzegovina."† The protocol, however, notes, as a second subject, "the diplomatic action against Serbia," and the occasion was utilized by Count Berchtold to try to convert Count Tisza to the plan of a direct attack on Serbia.‡ Since the Austrian premier had not objected to Hoyos' language in Berlin and Conrad had suggested the plan, one gets the impression that Berchtold was obviously trying to overcome Tisza's opposition by sheer weight of numbers; certainly the elaborate debate which followed assumed the character of a demonstration of ministerial solidarity against the one recalcitrant.

The foreign minister opened the discussion by remarking that the consultation with Berlin had led to "a most satisfactory result, for both the German Emperor and the chancellor solemnly [*mit allem Nachdrucke*] promised the unconditional support of Germany in the event of a warlike complication with Serbia." In his opinion, the moment had come for a demonstration of power that would put an end to the Serbian intrigues once for all and stop tendencies that were now in full swing.

He was aware [he continued] that a passage-at-arms with

---

* According to Szilassy, p. 266, the new heir apparent, the Archduke Charles, was not invited, because of his pacific sentiments.

† Tschirschky to foreign office, telegram, 7 July; G 18. The *Fremdenblatt* announced the next day that merely the internal situation in the two provinces had been under consideration. Bunsen to Grey, 11 July; B 46.

‡ Bosnian affairs were indeed discussed at the end of the meeting, but about five-sixths of the protocol is given over to "the diplomatic action against Serbia."

Serbia might lead to a war with Russia.* At the moment, however, Russia was pursuing a policy of the long view which
aimed at a combination of the Balkan states, including Rumania, for the purpose of using them against the Monarchy
when the moment seemed opportune. So he was of the opinion
that we must take account of the fact that in the face of such
a policy our situation must become increasingly worse, all the
more so as failure to act would be interpreted by our Southern
Slavs and Rumanians as a sign of weakness and would
strengthen the power of attraction of the two neighboring
states.

The logical conclusion of what had been said was that we
should anticipate our enemies and by a timely reckoning with
Serbia put a stop to the movement that was already in full
swing, a result which it might not be possible to attain later on.

The events of recent years, he argued later on, had shown that
mere diplomatic successes had failed to strike at the root of the
problem. "A radical solution of the question raised by the
propaganda for a Greater Serbia, which is systematically oper-
ated from Belgrade and the corrupting effects of which are felt
from Agram to Zara, can be brought about only by the application of brute force."

Count Berchtold's ideas met with general approval, except
from Count Tisza. The Austrian premier quoted General Potiorek, the governor of Bosnia, to the effect that no measures
could be applied there "unless we deal Serbia a strong blow."†
The common finance minister, noting that "General Potiorek
desired war," expressed the conviction that "a decisive conflict
is unavoidable sooner or later" and that "a diplomatic success
would have no effect whatever in Bosnia, but would most likely
do harm." The war minister desired that mobilization should
be carried out as soon and as secretly as possible, and that an
ultimatum should be addressed to Serbia "as soon as mobiliza-

---

* The original version of the minutes read: "It was quite clear to him that war
with Russia would very probably be the consequence of our marching into Serbia."
Berchtold later changed this to the statement quoted in the text; Gooss, p. 52. The
discussion in the council shows that the other members regarded war with Russia
as probable.
† See above, p. 263.

tion is complete," after which war should be begun without a
formal declaration.* The minutes of the session record:

All present, except the royal Hungarian premier, were of the
opinion that a purely diplomatic success, even if it ended with
a resounding [*eklatante*] humiliation of Serbia, would be
worthless, and that therefore such far-reaching demands must
be made on Serbia as would make refusal certain, so that the
way would be open for a drastic [*radikalen*] solution by means
of military action.

Tisza, however, continued to oppose this precipitate course.
The Hungarian statesman said that he preferred a policy based
on the addition of Bulgaria to the Triple Alliance, and "called
attention to the terrible calamity of a European war in the
present circumstances." He would, he said, "never consent to
a surprise attack on Serbia without a previous diplomatic action," for this would create a bad impression in Europe. He
agreed that hard demands might be made on Serbia, "but not
such as cannot be complied with." Only if these demands were
refused by Serbia would he vote for warlike action, and even
in that case, Serbia, he insisted, must not be annihilated. "As
Hungarian premier he could never consent to the Monarchy's
annexing any part of Serbia."

The first impression created by Tisza's language is that he
was resisting the policy of Count Berchtold; and so he was.
But he had modified his position of 1 July, when he protested
against war at all: now he agreed to war if Serbia refused
"hard demands" duly presented in an ultimatum. He was, he
said, "anxious to meet the others half-way," and made clear
that he was standing, not on a matter of principle, but on a
method of procedure, for he now insisted only that "the demands to be addressed to Serbia were not to be such that our
intention of making unacceptable conditions could be clearly

---

* This might be regarded as still a third method of dealing with the problem
distinct from Berchtold's plan of a surprise attack, or Tisza's plan of an ultimatum
followed if necessary by war.

perceived."* Count Berchtold now accepted the Hungarian premier's view, for he dropped the plan of a surprise attack *"sans crier gare"* (as Tisza had put it) in favor of the alternative plan, that is, the presenting of severe demands to Serbia, in the form of an ultimatum, to be followed, if necessary, by military action. But on the very next day, quite regardless of Count Tisza, he privately informed General Conrad that an ultimatum, with demands which "it was to be supposed Serbia would refuse," would be presented in Belgrade on 22 July, "after the harvest and the conclusion of the investigation at Sarajevo."†

Just as the adroit foreign minister had gone over the head of the Hungarian premier by an appeal to Berlin, so now, having on his side the German Emperor, the German Government, the other ministers, the heads of the army and navy and the officials of the foreign office,‡ Count Berchtold set to work at once to win the consent of the Emperor to his policy and thus complete the isolation of Count Tisza. To prepare the ground, he sent to the Emperor, immediately after the council, a summary of the discussion. After stating that "a complete unanimity of opinion could not be reached," because "Count Tisza held the view that a warlike action against Serbia should be resorted to only if it proves impossible to humiliate Serbia diplomatically," Count Berchtold declared:

All the other members of the conference shared the opinion of myself that the present opportunity for a warlike action

* Also he apparently allowed to pass without protest Berchtold's summary of the discussion: "Though there were still differences of opinion between the members of the council and Count Tisza, still an agreement had been brought nearer; for the proposals of the Hungarian premier would in all probability lead to war with Serbia, the necessity of which he and all other members of the council had understood and admitted." The points of the projected ultimatum discussed concerned: "(1) punishment and expulsion of Serbian army officers involved in the Greater-Serbian propaganda; (2) apology of the Serbian Government for the language of M. Spalaykovich [Serbian minister in St. Petersburg]; (3) demand for an investigation into the procuring of the bombs; (4) dismissal of certain Serbian officials connected with the Pokrayats incident [see above, p. 251]; (5) passing of a new press law and proceedings against the *Piyemont;* (6) revision of the Serbian law relating to societies; (7) prohibition of distribution of journals hostile to Austria-Hungary in officers' clubs and public establishments." Gooss, p. 93, note 1.

† Conrad, IV, 61.   ‡ Szilassy, pp. 265–266.

against Serbia should be utilized, because our situation will only get worse by waiting longer, and the orientation toward Bulgaria, which has not yet got under way, even if it is successful, does not promise to offer an adequate compensation for the further deterioration which is certainly to be expected in our relations with Serbia and Rumania and in the internal political conditions connected therewith.*

Two days later, on 9 July, the minister proceeded to Ischl, where Francis Joseph was spending the summer, for a personal conference with the monarch.

Count Tisza, now fully aware of the situation being prepared for him, sought to record his position clearly by addressing to his master a second letter of remonstrance, which Count Berchtold obligingly took with him to Ischl. Tisza came to the point in the very first paragraph of this memorable document:

The very satisfactory news from Berlin, together with the quite justifiable indignation over the incidents in Serbia, has stimulated the intention of all the other participants in yesterday's ministerial conference to provoke war with Serbia, in order to have a final reckoning with this hereditary enemy of the Monarchy.

He had not been able, he said, to accept this plan in its entirety: "such an attack would, if human foresight does not deceive, cause the intervention of Russia and precipitate the world war." In such a war, the odds would, so General Conrad had said, be "rather to our disadvantage." As even the neutrality of Rumania was "very questionable," Count Tisza argued that it was necessary first of all to create "a more favorable constellation" for the Monarchy in the Balkans, toward which the first step must be the alliance with Bulgaria. For these, as well as for financial and social reasons,

I am unable, after painful and conscientious reflection, to share the responsibility for the military aggression that is proposed against Serbia.

He did not, he said, advocate "an inactive or unenergetic

* Berchtold to Francis Joseph, 7 July; A I 9.

policy" toward Serbia, but, in his opinion, "Serbia must be given a chance to avoid war by suffering a severe diplomatic defeat." After sketching his ideas of the demands that might be made, he concluded: "If Serbia yields to pressure, we must accept this solution of the difficulty *bona fide* and not hinder her retreat." He advised, in short, "a middle course which does not exclude a peaceful arrangement and will improve our chances, if war is indeed inevitable."*

But Count Berchtold had no intention of following such "a middle course." He confided to the German ambassador that in case Francis Joseph should adopt the views of the Hungarian statesman, he would advise the ruler "at least to make demands of such a nature that the possibility of their acceptance would be precluded."† Thus Tisza's own policy was to be turned against himself! Nor was this all. On this same day, that is, before proceeding to Ischl, Count Berchtold postponed, as we have seen,‡ the plan for a Bulgarian alliance which Count Tisza had represented to the Emperor as an alternative, or at least as the necessary preliminary, to a war against Serbia.

The Emperor Francis Joseph

On 27 June, the day before the murder at Sarajevo, the Emperor Francis Joseph had removed from Vienna to his summer

* Tisza to Francis Joseph, 8 July; A I 12. Tisza also drew up a short memorandum on the military situation which was apparently enclosed with the letter to Francis Joseph. He pointed out that, according to Conrad, the bulk of the army would have to be directed against Russia, only three corps being left to deal with Serbia and weak formations of second-line troops with Rumania. The Serbs would probably be victorious and no resistance could be offered to the Rumanians. The Russians would only have to wait until Austro-Hungarian troops were withdrawn to meet the advancing Rumanians. Bulgaria had not sufficiently recovered from the Balkan wars to be able to hold Rumania in check; moreover, a Bulgarian intervention would involve the *casus foederis* for Greece. *Ö.-U. A.*, 10,146, Beilage. Berchtold had asked Conrad (note of 1 July; *Ö.-U. A.*, 9976) for a statement on the military situation of the Monarchy, as affected by the attitude of Rumania, which he could transmit to Berlin along with the political memorandum. Conrad replied that the military plans had been based on the assumption that Rumanian forces would be available against Russia; now twenty divisions would be needed to insure the neutrality of Rumania, and they were not available. Note of 2 July; *Ö.-U. A.*, 9995.

† Tschirschky to foreign office, telegram, 8 July; G 19.

‡ See above, p. 308. The minister in Sofia was not informed of the proposed alliance; instead, he was summoned to Vienna for a conference. Berchtold to Tarnowski, telegram, 7 July; *Ö.-U. A.*, 10,107.

residence at Ischl, intending thereby, it is said, to avoid a meeting with the Archduke Francis Ferdinand on his return from the manœuvres in Bosnia. Equally indicative of his feeling toward the murdered prince was his language when the news of the tragedy was brought to him:

> Horrible! The Almighty does not stand for provocation! . . . A higher Power has restored the order that I unhappily was not able to maintain!*

To the last, he thought of his House and ignored the human element. It was perhaps the knowledge of the tense relations that had existed between Emperor and Archduke, as well as the advanced age of Francis Joseph, which explained the belief in diplomatic circles in Vienna that he would not approve an adventuresome policy toward Serbia. To quote the British ambassador:

> It is indeed generally assumed that the Emperor himself would with difficulty be moved to sanction an aggressive course of action leading almost certainly to international complications of the gravest kind.†

This opinion was, however, incorrect. In conversation with the German ambassador on 2 July, Francis Joseph expressed the hope that the German Emperor and the German Government "appreciated the dangers which threatened the Monarchy by reason of the neighborhood of Serbia"; and when Herr von Tschirschky replied that his emperor "would stand behind every firm determination arrived at by Austria-Hungary, His Majesty agreed eagerly with my every word and said that I was quite right."‡ This was not the speech of a man "absolutely opposed to war."§

Even more conclusive is the evidence of that invaluable and

---

* Margutti, pp. 147–148.
  † Bunsen to Grey, 13 July; B 55. The French ambassador was of the same opinion. Dumaine to Viviani, 8 July; *Affaires balkaniques*, III, 142.
  ‡ Tschirschky to Bethmann-Hollweg, 2 July; G 11.
  § As claimed by Margutti, p. 393, on the testimony of the court chamberlain Count Paar and the Emperor's Egeria Frau Schratt.

incorrigible witness, General Conrad, who was received by the Emperor on 5 July. The chief of staff urged that war with Serbia was inevitable. There followed this colloquy:

FRANCIS JOSEPH: Yes, you are quite right, but ought we to make war if others, especially Russia, may fall upon us?
CONRAD: But we are covered by Germany, aren't we?
FRANCIS JOSEPH: But are you sure of Germany?

His Majesty then explained that at Konopischt, three weeks before, the Emperor William had evaded the direct question of Francis Ferdinand;* but he added that a note had just gone to Germany demanding "a clear answer."

CONRAD: If the answer comes that Germany stands by our side, do we then make war on Serbia?
FRANCIS JOSEPH: Yes, indeed [*Dann ja*]. . . . But we must wait for the German answer.

And Conrad records as his impression of the audience: "His Majesty did not feel sure of Germany and therefore hesitated in his decisions."† Evidently the Emperor was fully aware of the import of the appeal made to Berlin. When Count Berchtold had his audience on 9 July, the German answer was at hand, to be used by the minister as an argument for his policy; and used it was. Count Berchtold informed the German ambassador the next day of the interview in these terms:

His Majesty the Emperor discussed the state of affairs with great calmness. First of all, he expressed his warm thanks for the attitude taken by our most gracious master and the imperial government. He stated that he was entirely of our [German] opinion that some decision must now be come to, in order to put an end to the intolerable conditions in respect to Serbia. His Majesty was quite clear as to the importance of such a decision.

When informed of the two methods of procedure proposed, the Emperor seemed to think that the difference between them

* See above, p. 169.   † Conrad, IV, 36–37.

might be bridged over; but he agreed that "concrete demands should be made on Serbia."* Count Berchtold was satisfied, for he confided to General Conrad:

He had found the Emperor quite determined and calm. His Majesty appeared to be in favor of action against Serbia and was worried only on account of possible unrest in Hungary.†

Tisza himself testified to the German ambassador a few days later that "Germany's unconditional siding with the Monarchy had decidedly a great influence on the attitude of the Emperor."‡ The aged monarch had consented not to end his days in peace.

The Conversion of Count Tisza

But until Count Tisza had been won over, Count Berchtold's programme could not be put into effect. On 14 July, however, the Hungarian premier yielded.§ At a conference with the foreign minister, he accepted the latter's policy, stipulating only for a declaration that "the Monarchy is not striving to acquire territory by the war, apart from small rectifications of frontier."‖ What caused him to change his attitude? In a speech

---

* Tschirschky to foreign office, telegram, 10 July; G 29. Berchtold then remarked to the ambassador: "He, the minister, could not deny the advantages of such procedure. The odium which would fall on the Monarchy from a surprise attack [*Überrumpelung*] on Serbia would be avoided and Serbia put in the wrong." This is further proof that Berchtold's original plan called for a surprise attack, and he would not have felt it necessary to justify himself to Tschirschky unless the German Government had been informed of the original intention.

† Conrad, IV, 70. The Bavarian minister learned that "Emperor inclines to sharper measures and finds support in Berlin." Tucher to foreign office, telegram, 11 July; Dirr, p. 126.

‡ Tschirschky to Bethmann-Hollweg, 14 July; G 49.

§ It is worth noting, however, that on the previous day, secret telegrams were sent to the representatives in Belgrade, Cetinje, and St. Petersburg calling attention to the instructions of 28 November, 1912 (see above, p. 134), which prescribed their conduct in the event of war. Berchtold to Giesl, Otto, and Otto Czernin, 13 July; Ö.-U. A., 10,229. The German Government was asked if it would take over the protection of Austro-Hungarian interests in Belgrade and Cetinje in the event of a diplomatic rupture. Berchtold to Szögyény, telegram, 13 July; Ö.-U. A., 10,236.

‖ Berchtold to Francis Joseph, 14 July; A I 19. On this same day, Tisza was requested by the minister of war to suppress the Serbian *sokol* societies in Croatia and to dissolve the Croatian diet; "this is the more important if we expect to have to face serious complications." Krobatin to Tisza, 14 July; Graf Stefan Tisza, *Briefe (1914–1918)* (Berlin, 1928), I, 41–42.

to the Hungarian parliament on 8 July, the day after the ministerial conference in Vienna, Count Tisza stated that while the
government would "do its duty in every direction," it would
take no precipitate action;* and this statement had been approved by the Hungarian Government.† Certainly nothing had
happened to relieve the fears he had expressed to General Conrad that "no serious resistance" could be offered to the Rumanian army in Transylvania.‡ The general situation had not
changed at all. And Tisza was not a weakling. A stern and unbending Calvinist, he had never been lacking in political courage and was always ready to fight for his convictions; he was,
in short, the most masterful personality in the Monarchy. Four
factors were apparently responsible for his change of front.

In the first place, the Emperor-King paid no attention to his
two letters, neithing sending an answer nor inviting their writer
to an audience; he simply noted on them *"ad acta F. J.,"* that
is,he consigned them to the archives!§ Of course, Count Tisza
might have resigned in protest—but such a course would only
have left Count Berchtold a free hand.‖

It was also evident that Tisza's political position was being
affected by the growing chauvinism in Hungary. The British
consul-general thought it worth while to analyze this in some
detail. Writing on 14 July, he said:

In Budapest there have been no violent anti-Serb demonstrations, but all classes of the population and the entire press without difference of shade of political opinion at once joined in
ascribing the origin of the Sarajevo outrage to Servian machinations. Not only the yellow journals but respectable Government newspapers, among them the *Pester Lloyd,* have in-

---

* Bunsen to Grey, 13 July; B 55.
† Fraknói, *Die ungarische Regierung und die Entstehung des Weltkrieges,* p. 35.
Two days later, however, Tisza asked the *ban* of Croatia to collect data for use
against Serbia secretly and as quickly as possible. Tisza to Skerlecz, 10 July; Tisza,
I, 39.
‡ Fraknói, p. 33.   § *Ibid.*, p. 34.
‖ Kanner, *Kaiserliche Katastrophenpolitik,* pp. 236–238, argues that Tisza, like
many of the great Magyar nobles, was as much the loyal servant of the king as he
was a Hungarian statesman, and was determined not to lose the royal favor. But
there is no proof that he preferred office to principle.

dulged in the wildest invective against Servia and the Servian Government. . . . Every day the *Pester Lloyd* dishes up for the edification of the public, under the heading "From the Servian Witches' Kitchen," the most violent extracts from the Servian newspapers.

He summarized his report with the remark that "here people of all classes talk openly of war with Servia, and certainly such a war would be most popular."* Moreover, in parliament the opposition was beginning to ask inconvenient questions and to press for action. Tisza was no more than human if he swam with rather than fought against these currents.

Furthermore, he was irritated by the language of Serbian diplomatists, notably M. Spalaykovich in St. Petersburg and M. Yovanovich in Berlin,† and by the provocative attitude of the Serbian press. Still another factor was the military situation. The chief of staff urged that

our diplomatic action must avoid everything that would delay action by protracted diplomatic negotiations and give our opponents time to take military measures which would place us at a disadvantage—which is always bad, but especially so in the case of Serbia and Montenegro.‡

This argument enabled Count Berchtold to point out to Count Tisza "the military difficulties which would result from hesitation."§

Finally, the influence of Germany was thrown into the scale.

* Max Müller to Grey, 14 July; B 70.
† Tisza to Francis Joseph, 8 July; A I 12. Spalaykovich gave an interview to the *Vechernoye Vremya* on 29 June, in which he asserted that the assassination of Francis Ferdinand had resulted from the discontent of Bosnia with Austro-Hungarian rule; that the Archduke had gone to Sarajevo in spite of warnings of danger; that there were no revolutionary organizations in Serbia; and that Serbs had had nothing to do with the shameful deed. Otto Czernin to Berchtold, telegram and despatch, 3 July; *Ö.-U. A.*, 10,016, 10,017. In the *Novoye Vremya* on 1 July, Spalaykovich indulged in sharp criticism of the Austro-Hungarian policy in Bosnia. Otto Czernin to Berchtold, 3 July; *Ö.-U. A.*, 10,018. Yovanovich appears to have spoken of the union of Serbia and Montenegro as impending, which Sazonov denied, calling the Serbian diplomatist a "fool." Otto Czernin to Berchtold, telegram, 6 July; *Ö.-U. A.*, 10,086.
‡ Conrad to Berchtold, 12 July; A I 14.
§ Berchtold to Francis Joseph, 14 July; A I 19.

Her advocate in Vienna was, as we have seen,* the advocate of strong measures. In conversation with his British colleague,

> Herr von Tschirsky [*sic*] said emphatically that [the relations between Austria and Servia] must be bad and that nothing could mend them. He added that he had tried in vain to convince Berlin of this fundamental truth. Some people in Germany still believed in the efficacy of a conciliatory policy on the part of Austria toward Servia. He himself knew better.†

If Herr von Tschirschky talked in this fashion to Sir Maurice de Bunsen, it is not difficult to imagine what tone he employed in the conference of 7 July. On the next day he called again on Count Berchtold to say that he had received a telegram from Berlin,

> in which his imperial master instructs him to declare emphatically that in Berlin action by the Monarchy against Serbia is fully expected and that Germany would not understand why we should neglect this opportunity of striking a blow.‡

Count Berchtold at once informed Count Tisza of what the ambassador had said, and added, as his own interpretation, that

> Germany would consider further negotiations with Serbia on our part as a confession of weakness, and this would damage our position in the Triple Alliance, and might influence Germany's future policy.§

---

* See above, pp. 269–270.   † Bunsen to Grey, 5 July; B 40.

‡ One of the editors of *Die deutschen Dokumente zum Kriegsausbruch* asserts that no such telegram was sent from Berlin or from the *Hohenzollern*, in which Tschirschky's imperial master was voyaging to Norway; Montgelas, pp. 172–175. Count Montgelas also states that nothing was found in Tschirschky's papers which would indicate the receipt by the ambassador of private instructions to speak in the sense noted by Berchtold. In the published documents there are no communications from the German Government to the ambassador between 6 and 11 July; which is extraordinary, considering the gravity of the matter. In the summer of 1928 Count Berchtold told the writer that Tschirschky had come to him holding in his hand what he, Tschirschky, said was a telegram from Berlin, and that Tschirschky had read out the statement quoted in the text; he did not, however, give Count Berchtold the telegram to read. Whether Tschirschky acted on his own initiative or whether through some secret channel not yet revealed he received the telegram in question, remains therefore a mystery.

§ Berchtold to Tisza, 8 July; A I 10.

This produced no immediate response from the Hungarian statesman. When he returned to Vienna on 14 July for another conference with Count Berchtold, a long report from Count Szögyény,* which was a powerful incitement to prompt and resolute action, was communicated to him.† According to this report,

Not only his Majesty the Emperor William but all the other persons in authority . . . are encouraging us emphatically not to neglect the present moment, but to proceed against Serbia in the most energetic fashion . . . in order to clear up our relations with Serbia in such a way as to put a stop to the Pan-Slavist agitation for all time.

This second appeal may well have been the deciding factor.‡

On this same day, 14 July, Count Tisza agreed to the plan of a short-term ultimatum, and "introduced a sharper tone in various places."§ Moreover, he went at once to the German embassy to announce his capitulation, and said to Herr von Tschirschky:

He had always been the one who advised caution, but every day had strengthened him in the conviction more and more that the Monarchy would have to come to an energetic decision, in order to prove its ability to exist and to put an end to the intolerable conditions in the southeast. The tone of the Serbian press and the Serbian diplomatists was so presumptuous as simply not to be tolerated. "It was very hard for me," said the minister, "to decide to advise in favor of war; but I am now

---

* Szögyény to Berchtold, 12 July; A I 15. See above, pp. 317–318.
† Fraknói, p. 36.
‡ At any rate Tisza stated some months later that "it should be emphasized that . . . we made our *démarche* in Belgrade upon the direct encouragement and the declaration of the German Government that it regarded the present moment as favorable for the ever more threatening reckoning with Serbia." Tisza to Tschirschky, 5 November, 1914; Tisza, I, 104. On 26 August, 1914, he wrote to his niece Margit von Zeyk: "My conscience is clear. The noose has already been put around our necks with which they would have strangled us at a suitable moment if we do not do it now. We could not do otherwise, but it hurts still that it had to be so." *Ibid.*, I, 62–63. The writer has discussed the problem with a number of persons who knew Tisza well, but found no agreement as to which consideration weighed most heavily with him. Probably all of them entered into his decision.
§ Tschirschky to Bethmann-Hollweg, 14 July; G 50.

firmly convinced of its necessity, and I shall work for the great-
ness of the Monarchy with all my strength.*

The visit to the German embassy at least shows what importance Count Tisza attached to solidarity with Berlin. It is
significant that he took pains to inform Herr von Tschirschky
that complaints of "indecision and delay" mattered little, "if
only they knew in Berlin that this was not the case." Taking
the ambassador by the hand, he said, "Together we shall now
look the future calmly and firmly in the face"; which evoked
from William II the enthusiastic appreciation, "Well, a real
man at last!"

BERLIN AND VIENNA, 5–19 JULY

Thus was Count Berchtold able, with the promise of German support in his pocket, to secure the acceptance by the Emperor Francis Joseph and Count Tisza, if not of his original
plan of a surprise attack on Serbia, at least of a note to the
Serbian Government of such a character that "the possibility
of its acceptance [so Berlin was assured] is practically excluded"† and "the probability of war [so Francis Joseph was
informed] must be reckoned with."‡ But before this happy
result had been achieved, the German Government, learning on
8 July of Count Tisza's opposition to the programme announced by Count Hoyos§ and two days later of his continued resistance,‖ began to fear that the Austrians, for all
their talk, would not exhibit the courage of their convictions.
Berlin accordingly began stimulating Vienna to action. "I was
able to ascertain," Count Szögyény informed his chief, "that
the secretary of state [Herr von Jagow] . . . is most decidedly of the opinion that the action proposed against Serbia

---

* Tschirschky to Bethmann-Hollweg, 14 July; G 49.
† Tschirschky to Bethmann-Hollweg, 14 July; G 49.
‡ Berchtold to Francis Joseph, 14 July; A I 19.
§ "I have the impression that Count Berchtold regards Count Tisza as an ele-
ment of encumbrance." Tschirschky to foreign office, telegram, 8 July; G 19.
‖ "The minister [Berchtold] complained again about the attitude of Count Tisza,
which made energetic action against Serbia difficult for him." Tschirschky to for-
eign office, telegram, 10 July; G 28.

should be taken in hand without delay."* Nor was this opinion confined to Herr von Jagow; it was quite generally held—by "not only his Majesty the Emperor William, but all the other persons in authority."†

His Majesty was indeed impatient. On 12 July he lamented that "it is taking a long time" for the Austrians to come to some determination, and quoted the dictum of Frederick the Great, "I am against all councils of war and conference, since the more timid party always has the upper hand."‡ When informed that the Austrian action would have to be delayed until 25 July, he exclaimed, "Too bad!"§ And these observations were communicated to the foreign office.

At Vienna, Herr von Tschirschky must have actually complained, for Count Berchtold felt it necessary to explain to him the reasons for delay:

We believe that we should delay the very energetic *démarche* contemplated in Belgrade until the President of the French Republic, who is now on the way to St. Petersburg, shall have left Russian soil. To start the contemplated action at a moment when the President is being fêted as the guest of the Tsar might naturally be interpreted as a political affront, which we wish to avoid. Furthermore, it seems to us unwise to take the threatening step at Belgrade at the very time when the peace-loving, hesitating Emperor Nicholas and the ever-cautious M. Sazonov are subject to the immediate influence of those two baiters Izvolski and Poincaré.||

Yet in spite of the assurance that "there was not a thought of hesitation or uncertainty" in Vienna,¶ Berlin was not satisfied. For Herr von Jagow, while professing to understand the explanation "perfectly," said that he regretted the delay "extremely" [*ganz ausserordentlich*];** and he took good care to inform the Ballplatz that an article of the *Norddeutsche Allge-*

---

* Szögyény to Berchtold, telegram, 9 July; A I 13.
† Szögyény to Berchtold, 12 July; A I 15.   ‡ Comment on G 29.
§ Comment on G 49. || Berchtold to Szögyény, telegram, 15 July; A I 21.
¶ Tschirschky to Bethmann-Hollweg, 14 July; G 50.
** Szögyény to Berchtold, telegram, 16 July; A I 23.

*meine Zeitung,** "intentionally written in a mild tone with an eye to European diplomacy," was not to be "wrongly considered as German deprecation of Vienna's determination."†
How little reassured the German Government was by the Austrian explanations is evidenced by a remark of the undersecretary of state. "It still seems very doubtful," said Herr Zimmermann on 18 July, "whether they will actually rise to the occasion in Vienna."‡

The motive behind this repeated pressure for prompt action was stated by Herr von Jagow to be the fear that "the sympathetic approval of this step and interest in it, not only in the Monarchy but in Germany as well, will be weakened by delay."§ Furthermore the German Government may well have believed that if only Austria-Hungary would strike while the memory of the murder was still fresh in the public mind of Europe, the attitude of the Powers of the Triple Entente would be more tolerant. Certainly the advantage of a *fait accompli* had been demonstrated when the Monarchy proclaimed the annexation of Bosnia in 1908 and was able to force a recognition of its action from the other Powers. Some further confidences of Herr Zimmermann, however, exhibit the action of Berlin in a less favorable light. "In Vienna," he explained to the Bavarian chargé, "they do not seem to have expected such an unconditional support of the Danube Monarchy on the part of Germany"; and he had the impression that "it is almost embarrassing to the ever timid and undecided authorities at Vienna not to be admonished by Germany to caution and restraint."‖

* See below, pp. 397–398.   † Jagow to Tschirschky, telegram, 18 July; G 70.
‡ Schoen to Hertling, 18 July; Dirr, p. 6; D, supplement IV, no. 2.
§ Szögyény to Berchtold, telegram, 16 July; A I 23.
‖ Schoen to Hertling, 18 July; Dirr, p. 7; G, Supplement IV, No. 2.
Even franker was the language used by Baron von Wangenheim at Constantinople. Explaining to his Bulgarian colleague that Germany was anxious for Austria-Hungary to recover her prestige, he said: "Therefore it is her firm determination not only to support action by Austria-Hungary in the present case, but also to encourage her. We have had enough of so much sleepiness on the part of Vienna. It is not enough that Serbia should be brought to her knees. Her humiliation must go so far that this state will find itself not only on its knees before Austria, but prostrate ['auf dem Bauche']." Toshev to Radoslavov, 21 July; KSF, VI, 232 (March,

During these two weeks the German Government let no opportunity pass to urge upon its ally the execution of the policy announced on 5 July.

THE FINAL DECISIONS

Finally, on Sunday, 19 July, another council of ministers was held, to discuss "the forthcoming diplomatic action against Serbia." Count Berchtold declared that he must object to any further delay because "people in Berlin are already beginning to get nervous and news of our intentions has already leaked out in Rome"; and "under the prompting of this declaration," continues the protocol of the meeting, "the council unanimously voted that the note should be presented at 5 P. M. on the 23d."

Before the meeting opened, the text of the note was "definitely settled" in informal discussion. The genesis of the note is worth tracing.*

Early in July two drafts had been successively prepared, according to which the Serbian Government was to be called upon to take strong and effective measures to put an end to the propaganda carried on in and by Serbia against Austria-Hungary, and to allow the co-operation of the Austro-Hungarian Government in the execution of these measures. These demands, which appear to have been formulated from a study of the evidence possessed by the Austro-Hungarian Government about the Great-Serbian agitation, were rather general

---

1928). Wangenheim also spoke in much the same sense to Pallavicini: "In Berlin they were now firmly determined to support us through thick and thin in Balkan affairs. But I could also deduce from his expressions that Berlin regarded the present moment as decisive for the Triple Alliance. Everything, so my interlocutor declared, would depend upon whether we should be in a position to secure a complete triumph over Serbia. If we should succeed in this, the possibility would also be revived, in the opinion of the German statesmen, of saving Rumania for the Triple Alliance. In the event of failure, so Baron Wangenheim let it be seen, the existence of the Triple Alliance would be considered in danger." Pallavicini to Berchtold, telegram, 16 July; Ö.-U. A., 10,303.

* Gooss, pp. 91–101; Musulin, *Das Haus am Ballplatz*, pp. 222–226. Dr. F. von Wiesner, "Der Sarajevoer Mord und die Kriegsschuldfrage," in *Das Neue Reich* (Vienna), 2 August, 1924; Dr. F. von Wiesner, "Meine Depesche vom 13. Juli, 1914," in Steinitz, *Rings um Sazonow*, pp. 167–186.

in character and did not refer specifically to the events of Sarajevo;* they represented, not a demand for the punishment of individuals guilty of murder or accessory to it, but the announcement of a political programme which was bound to produce great excitement in Europe. Accordingly the officials of the Ballplatz who were intrusted with the preparation of the note insisted that concrete demands must be formulated which, based on proved facts, could be justified before public opinion. But, as matters stood, the reports from the investigation at Sarajevo were lacking in precision, and sometimes conflicting.† Moreover, time was pressing, for it had been decided to present the note on 23 July. In order to ascertain the exact results of the investigation and, if possible, to secure evidence which from the point of view of international and criminal law would warrant strong demands on Serbia, Dr. Friedrich Ritter von Wiesner, one of the legal experts of the foreign office, was sent to Sarajevo on 10 July.

After three nights and two days of investigation and con-

* It is not without interest to note what the authorities allowed to leak out through the press, with the object of exciting public opinion in favor of the course contemplated. The *Bosnische Post* (Sarajevo) said that "the murders had been proved to have been organized and instigated by the Servian 'Narodna Odbrana' (National Defense); that a certain Miko Ciganovic distributed firearms and bombs in a Belgrade coffee-house to young men who expressed willingness to carry out the murder of the Archduke, and that Major Milan Pribicevic, of the Servian General Staff and Secretary of the 'Narodna Odbrana,' provided Ciganovic with the pistols and explosives." Jones to Bunsen, 4 July, enclosed in a despatch of Bunsen to Grey, 15 July; B 64. The *Neue Freie Presse* announced that two other accomplices (besides Printsip) had been discovered and arrested; declared that the statement of Grabezh implicated the Serbian general Yankovich, the president of the *Narodna Odbrana;* and quoted the *Budapesti Hirlap* to the effect that "the bombs came from the Serbian arsenal of Kraguyevats, where Chabrinovich, Printsip and the other conspirators obtained them." Finally, on 10 July, the *Neues Wiener Journal* professed to know that "the young Serbian murderers and their instigators stand not far from the Serbian court." Scott, pp. 49–50.

† Up to 7 July the picture was as follows: Seven persons—Printsip, Chabrinovich, Grabezh, Popovich, Chubrilovich, Mehmedbashich, Ilich—were involved in the plot; the first three had prepared it in Belgrade with Tsiganovich, who had given them weapons received from Tankosich, and instructed the conspirators in their use. The plot had been inspired by the Great-Serbian propaganda and in particular by the *Narodna Odbrana,* though the precise relation of the latter was not very clear, especially the share of Major Milan Pribichevich, its secretary (cf. *Ö.-U. A.,* 9991, 9992). Whether the Serbian Government was privy to the plot was not certain, although Potiorek insisted that it was. On 8 July, it was reported that Tsiganovich had passed the conspirators into Bosnia in some mysterious fashion and that he himself had left Belgrade on a month's leave.

sultation with the judicial, civil, and military authorities, Herr von Wiesner on 13 July telegraphed to Count Berchtold:

There is nothing to prove or even to lead one to suspect the complicity of the Serbian Government in the suggestion [*Leitung*] or preparation of the crime or the providing of the weapons. On the contrary there are many reasons for believing that this is out of the question.*

But he went on to say that there was "sufficient, though scanty" evidence to show that the Serbian propaganda in Bosnia was conducted "with the help as well as with the knowledge and approval of the Serbian Government." Furthermore the evidence of the accused persons left little doubt that "the crime was resolved upon in Belgrade and prepared with the co-operation of Serbian officials, Tsiganovich and Major Tankosich, who between them provided bombs, Brownings, ammunition and cyanide of potassium"; that the bombs came from the arsenal at Kraguyevats; and that the conspirators were "secretly smuggled across the frontier into Bosnia by Serbian officials." On the strength of this information, Herr von Wiesner recommended that the following demands be added to those already under consideration: (1) Suppression of the Serbian official agencies engaged in smuggling persons and goods across the frontier; (2) the dismissal of the frontier officials implicated in the plot; and (3) the prosecution of Tsiganovich and Tankosich.† He then started on his return

* After the war, Wiesner stated that as a result of his investigation in Sarajevo, he was reasonably sure that the Serbian Government had been informed of the plot; but he insisted on having proof, which was not available. Steinitz, pp. 184-185.

† Wiesner to foreign office, telegram, 13 July; A I 17. Before sending his telegram, Wiesner showed it to Potiorek, who disagreed with the conclusion that the Serbian Government was not involved. The general thereupon wrote a long letter to Conrad, in which he stated that proofs were at hand that "a number of Serbian officers on the active list and persons in high military positions played a leading part in these treacherous machinations." Though admitting that the army was not the government, he contended that in fact it amounted to a "rival government" [*Nebenregierung*] and that its conduct "was quite impossible without at least the knowledge and tolerance, if not the encouragement, of the official Serbian Government"; therefore, he argued, the opportunity should not be lost to "destroy the Serbian army with a vigorous hand." Potiorek to Conrad, 14 July; Conrad, IV, 82-85. Conrad received this letter on 16 July, two days after the conversion of Tisza; he does not say whether he sent it on to Berchtold; he did not refer to it in the ministerial council of 19 July.

journey to Vienna, where he arrived on the evening of 14 July, taking with him much material relating to the activity of the *Narodna Odbrana;* this material was later utilized for a memorandum circulated to the Powers in the latter part of the month.

Count Berchtold would have been in a stronger position *vis-à-vis* the European Powers if his agent had not exculpated the Serbian Government from direct complicity in the crime of Sarajevo; but since Count Tisza had agreed to a stern note and the German Government had been notified of this, the minister did not alter the character of the note, of which a third draft was prepared after the conference with Count Tisza on 14 July.* The only substantial effect of the Wiesner telegram was the addition of the demands recommended by him calling for the punishment of the individuals mentioned in it. Whether Count Berchtold showed the telegram to Tisza at their conference is not disclosed in any document; but, even if it were shown, it probably had no effect on Tisza's decision, for his language to the German ambassador shows that he had changed his mind for reasons of high policy, irrespective of the question of Serbian official complicity in the murder, and in such calculations the fact that the Serbian Government could not be proved guilty of the particular crime would be of small consequence. It was this third draft which, with certain alterations and emendations made desirable by Herr von Wiesner's researches, was adopted on 19 July. The note, in this form, presented an indictment of Serbia's general policy and only incidentally a demand for satisfaction for the murder of the Archduke.

This settled, the council had only to concern itself with the

---

* The Bavarian minister in Vienna, writing before the conversion of Tisza was known, said: "The possibility has to be reckoned with that the Serbian Government (on the assumption that it and not the military party is master of the situation) may accept all the demands of Austria-Hungary. In that event it will remain to be seen whether the determination to crush [*Wille zur Zerstückelung*] Serbia which prevails among a majority of the ministers is unshakable. But no chance will be given for any such change of mind and the contents of the note will be made unacceptable, so that it will be imperative to begin military operations immediately after the rejection of the demands." Tucher to the king, 14 July; Dirr, p. 127.

consequences of its action. The war minister, speaking of the
preparations for mobilization which he had inaugurated, stated
that

everything necessary would be submitted for the imperial sanction on Wednesday the 22d, and that agreement had already
been reached with the two governments in respect of the measures to be taken by the administrative authorities.

General Conrad promised Count Tisza that the garrisons left
in Transylvania, about which the Hungarian premier was nervous, should be "sufficiently strong to maintain order in case
of internal disturbances." Count Berchtold discounted the notion that Italy, out of irritation over being left uninformed
about the Austro-Hungarian action, might send an expedition
to Valona.

The only matter on which complete harmony did not prevail
was the fate of Serbia. Count Berchtold stated his position
thus:

If we were victorious in the event of a war with Serbia, we
should not, in the present political situation, annex any of
Serbia, but by the cession of as much of its territories as possible to Bulgaria, Greece, and Albania, and eventually to Rumania, endeavor to reduce its size so that it would no longer
be dangerous. The situation in the Balkans might change. It
was not at all impossible that Russia would succeed in overthrowing the present Bulgarian cabinet and in again bringing
to power there a government hostile to us; Albania was also
not yet a reliable factor. As director of foreign policy, he had
therefore to reckon with the possibility that at the end of the
war it might no longer be possible, in the circumstances then
existing, not to make any annexations, if we wished to bring
about better conditions on our frontiers than existed at the
present time.

The Austrian premier suggested that "Serbia might be made
dependent on the Monarchy by the deposition of the dynasty."
But Count Tisza would not agree:

The council of ministers must unanimously declare that the action against Serbia was not in any way connected with plans of aggrandizement on the part of the Monarchy and that no portion of Serbian territory should be annexed except for rectifications of frontier demanded by military considerations. He must absolutely insist that such a resolution be unanimously voted.

Accordingly, a resolution was passed to the effect that

As soon as the war begins, the Monarchy will declare to the other Powers that it is not conducting a war of conquest and does not plan the annexation of Serbia.

This respected Tisza's position with respect to annexation, and we shall see that this resolution was in due course communicated to the Powers. But at the same time a 'rider,' which was not communicated, was adopted which left Count Berchtold free to carry out his own policy. It read:

Of course, the rectifications of frontier which are strategically necessary, or the reduction of Serbia to the advantage of other states, as well as even an unavoidable temporary occupation of Serbian territory, are not excluded by this resolution.*

And this was accepted by the minister who, twelve days before, had forced Count Berchtold to disavow Count Hoyos for having talked in Berlin about "the complete partition of Serbia."†

---

* Conrad's comment on the resolution is illuminating. "On leaving the meeting I expressed myself to the minister of war on the matter of the territorial guarantee for Serbia: 'Well, we shall see. Before the Balkan war the Powers likewise talked about the *status quo*—after the war nobody bothered any more about it.'" Conrad, IV, 92.

† Tisza had not, in fact, maintained his position very long. In his second letter to the Emperor-King he said: "It is my opinion that after a successful war Serbia would have to be reduced by the cession of her conquered territories to Bulgaria, Greece, and Albania"—which was the view of Berchtold, except that he then desired Rumania rather than Greece to share in the spoils. In a note to the foreign office of 28 July, Tisza said: "I have often taken the opportunity to emphasize my conviction that we must firmly retain a free hand to advocate territorial changes in Macedonia"; Tisza, I, 43. On 10 August he wrote to Berchtold suggesting that in order to win over Bulgaria and Greece, Bulgaria should be promised Kavalla, while Greece should be indemnified in southern Albania and southwestern Macedonia; *ibid.*, I, 49.

Count Berchtold thereupon closed the meeting, with the statement that "fortunately complete agreement has been reached on all points."*

The text of the note having been determined, it was sent to the Austrian minister in Belgrade the next day by courier, with instructions to present it at 5 P. M. on 23 July; he was informed that "we cannot enter into any negotiations with Serbia with regard to our demands" and that only "unconditional acceptance" would prevent a diplomatic rupture. "Unconditional acceptance" was, however, not expected, for the minister was ordered to report by wire "the fact that Serbia had refused to comply with our demands or that the time limit had expired."† Conrad's dream was to be realized at last.‡

On the following day (21 July) Count Berchtold submitted the note to the Emperor. But a week before he had guaranteed to the German ambassador that "His Majesty will give his approval of it,"§ and so it turned out. Francis Joseph gave his sanction "without alteration" of the text;‖ indeed, after he had agreed to the proposed action against Serbia, he could hardly do otherwise. And he did so with a full realization of what was involved. Herr von Bilinski was also at Ischl on the day when Count Berchtold secured the monarch's approval, and he asked if the note might not have far-reaching consequences. "The Emperor, who was in good spirits, answered in his

---

* Protocol of the council of ministers, 19 July; A I 26.
† Berchtold to Giesl, 20 July; A I 28.
‡ It is interesting to note, as an indication of the expectations of the Ballplatz, that on 22 July, even before the note had been presented in Belgrade, Macchio, the second section-chief, or under-secretary, informed Tschirschky that "according to the Hague Conventions, the Monarchy would be bound eventually to present Serbia with a formal declaration of war," and requested that the German minister in Belgrade be allowed to present that document, since the Austro-Hungarian representative would have departed if the answer to the note was unsatisfactory. Tschirschky to Bethmann-Hollweg, 22 July; G 138. Berlin replied that "declaration of war through the instrumentality of our legation would create the impression in the public mind, which is not familiar with diplomatic usages, that we had *incited* Austria-Hungary to war." Jagow to Tschirschky, telegram, 24 July; G 142.
§ Tschirschky to Bethmann-Hollweg, 14 July; G 50. Forgách, when handing the text of the note to Tschirschky, remarked that "the imperial sanction has not yet been received, although, as a matter of fact, there is no doubt of its being given." Tschirschky to Bethmann-Hollweg, 21 July; G 106.
‖ Tschirschky to foreign office, telegram, 22 July; G 113.

abrupt way: 'Russia cannot accept it. We must not deceive ourselves, it will be a big war.' "*

Count Berchtold had pointed to German uneasiness as a convincing reason why the action against Serbia should not be delayed. But was public opinion ready for drastic measures? After the first excitement had worked itself out, demonstrations against Serbia had ceased, the newspapers had shown reserve, the bourse had manifested weakness. When, after the ministerial council of 7 July, certain papers professed to know that a peremptory diplomatic representation to Serbia had been prepared, the public mind was so agitated that official announcement was made declaring such statements to be entirely unfounded.† We know now that the statements, so far from being unfounded, were not far from correct; probably the government had inspired the statements in order to test public opinion. Opinion had therefore to be prepared. So the *Neue Freie Presse,* the most important newspaper in the country, which on 2 July had frowned upon wars of revenge, on 7 July, the day of the ministerial council, argued that the Monarchy ought not to limit itself to measures against the assassins. A week later it talked ominously of appealing to "the sword of veterans," and on 19 July, the day of the second council, it remarked that "of the Austrians now living only a few have seen war." On 16 and 17 July, the reactionary *Reichspost* quoted with approval extracts from Polish newspapers calling for war. The *Militärische Rundschau* argued openly for war: "Since we shall have to accept the contest some day, let us provoke it at once."‡ The plan of the Ballplatz, so the German ambassador explained, was "to hold the

---

* Kanner, pp. 250–251, on the authority of a personal communication from Bilinski. Conrad was told on 22 July that "the attitude of Ischl [meaning Francis Joseph] was very determined"; Conrad, IV, 95. According to Frau Schratt, Francis Joseph told her repeatedly that "he had not approved of the ultimatum at all and had allowed it to be sent only to please Germany"; Margutti, p. 394. But her testimony can hardly stand against the contemporary evidence of the Emperor's willingness to go to war with Serbia if German support was assured. If the old ruler really made such statements to Frau Schratt, it was obviously in order to justify his action after its unwisdom had been made evident by events.

† Bunsen to Grey, 11 July; B 46.   ‡ Dumaine to Viviani, 15 July; F 12.

press within bounds for a while" and "not to disturb the public mind prematurely."

At the same time care is being taken to give the widest possible circulation to the articles in the Serbian press by their complete reproduction, and attention is called to the fact that Serbia must have lost her standing in Europe entirely, through the demagogic intrigues which culminated in the assassination of the heir to the Austrian throne.*

The note to be sounded was that "the relations of Austria-Hungary with Serbia must be determined and regulated on the basis of the most dispassionate realism." If the Serbs did not exhibit "common sense and insight," reliance on "the methods used hitherto" would be "incomprehensible" to the peoples of the Monarchy.

The Serbian press certainly played into the hands of the official press bureau. The *Piyemont,* organ of the 'Black Hand,' proclaimed Printsip a "young martyr." The *Odyek* referred to the visit of Francis Ferdinand as a "brutal act" which was "bound to evoke brutal feelings of resistance, hatred, and revenge." The *Politika* described the Monarchy as "an anarchistic state," Vienna as "a city of criminals." The *Balkan* demanded that Austria-Hungary "be placed under international control"; the *Tribuna* advocated a boycott of its goods.† "I must say," observed the British ambassador early in July, "I think the Servian press is behaving shamefully."‡ The effects of such outbursts on Austrian opinion can easily be imagined. Tisza remarked to the German ambassador that "the tone of the Serbian press and of the Serbian diplomatists was so presumptuous as simply not to be borne."§ "Had the Serbian newspapers deliberately determined to solidify Austro-Hungarian opinion against the Serbian people and Government, they could scarcely have chosen a more effective method."‖

* Tschirschky to foreign office, 13 July; G 41A.
† For further selections, see Appendix 9 of the Austrian dossier; A II 48.
‡ Bunsen to Nicolson, private, 3 July; B 29.
§ Tschirschky to Bethmann-Hollweg, 14 July; G 49.
‖ Scott, pp. 54–55. Unless otherwise indicated, the press extracts given in the text are taken from chapter III, "The Drift toward War."

The Austrian official policy, however, bears much of the responsibility for the animosities of the press. It was the severe reprisals taken just after the murder against the Serb population of Bosnia which unchained the passions of the Serbian yellow journals,* and chauvinistic utterances from Belgrade were exclusively reproduced, although they were condemned by the Serbian Government. Furthermore, the results of the investigation at Sarajevo were doled out gradually, in order to whet the popular appetite and to arouse public opinion: without the Serbian Government being directly accused, the implications were that a wide-spread plot involving Serbian officials had been traced to Belgrade, and these revelations were energetically exploited by both the Austrian and the Hungarian press. "The nest of murderers is to be found in Belgrade, and public opinion," declared the *Neues Wiener Journal* on 10 July, "demands the fumigation of this lurking-hole of criminals." The *Pester Lloyd* took much the same line. The success of the government's tactics was indeed complete. "There is only one topic in the Vienna press," wrote the British ambassador on 17 July, "namely, when will the protest against Serbia be put in, and what will it contain?"† Only the *Zeit* and the *Arbeiter-Zeitung* stood out against the general current. It would, of course, be too much to say that official manœuvres were alone responsible for the conversion of public opinion from an attitude of reserve to one of desiring war: Vienna and Budapest could not be expected to take a dispassionate view of Serbia, and would have insisted upon some kind of punishment. But the government's hand was certainly not forced by public opinion; it determined its course, and then seemingly prepared the public for accepting that course.

THE CALCULATIONS OF VIENNA

In deciding on its course of action against Serbia, the Austro-Hungarian Government showed itself to be well aware

* Crackanthorpe to Grey, 10 July; B 45. The Serbian minister in Vienna complained of this to the Ballplatz. Yovanovich to Pashich, 3 July; S 12.
† Bunsen to Nicolson, private, 17 July; B 56.

of the possible, not to say probable, consequences. The protocol of the ministerial council of 7 July affords abundant proof that war with Russia was regarded as a likely result of a campaign against Serbia. Count Berchtold, it is true, credited Russian policy with taking a long view of the situation and argued that, because the Russian Government had not succeeded in recreating the Balkan League, it would not consider the moment propitious for intervention.* But Count Tisza thought otherwise, said so both in the council and in his communications to the Emperor, and, so far as published documents show, never changed his opinion. Reading between the lines of the protocol of the meeting, one is convinced that the other ministers agreed with their Hungarian colleague. The minister of war, General Krobatkin, said:

From a military point of view he must emphasize the view that it would be better to make war now rather than at a later date, since the balance of forces would be upset in the future to our disadvantage.

"Balance of forces" can refer only to the military strength of the Triple Alliance and the Triple Entente. The common minister of finance, Ritter von Bilinski, who "cherished" the conviction that a decisive conflict was inevitable sooner or later," declared:

On that question he had never doubted that in case of need Germany would stand by us, and he had, as early as November, 1912, received the most positive assurances from Herr von Tschirschky.

The Austrian premier, Count Stürgkh, referring to the "unconditional loyalty promised by our ally," remarked:

* One is entitled to doubt if this argument represented Berchtold's real opinion: his eagerness to secure German support for his policy, while explainable partly by his difficulty with Tisza, is intelligible, in the larger view, only by the realization on his part that action against Serbia probably involved war with Russia. This had been accepted as a basic premise by both Vienna and Berlin in previous Balkan crises. Before the council met, he had heard Tisza repeat his opposition to a bellicose policy; he had therefore to argue that this policy would not have the consequences which Tisza feared.

Count Tisza should appreciate the importance of this, and take into consideration the fact that a policy of hesitation and weakness will expose us to the danger that at some later date we may not be so sure of the unconditional support of the German Empire.

No minister, except Count Tisza, said flatly that war with Russia would result from the adoption of Count Berchtold's policy; but the emphasis laid on the promise of German support shows how greatly all the ministers were preoccupied by the eventuality which would involve that support. It is possible, of course, that they expected a demonstration of Austro-German solidarity to deter Russia from intervention.* But there is no mention of this in the protocol of the council, and in the afternoon session, during the discussion of the military arrangements necessary for the execution of Count Berchtold's policy, these direct questions were put to the chief of the general staff:

Whether it would be possible to mobilize first only against Serbia and then afterward, in case the necessity therefor should arise, also against Russia?
Where would battle be given to Russia?†

In other words, the question of war with Russia entered definitely into the calculations of the Austro-Hungarian statesmen. Naturally they hoped that Russia would stand aside. But, convinced as they were that war with Serbia was necessary, they were satisfied to know that Germany had

---

* Hoyos—writing after the war—reflects this view. The conviction obtained, he says, that "Russia was preparing methodically for war," and that the only way of avoiding a European conflagration was "to redress the balance between the Triple Alliance and the Triple Entente in favor of the Central Powers, while it was still doubtful whether the Russian armaments had been carried to that stage of preparedness which would justify the government in St. Petersburg in striking back." Hoyos, p. 83.

† Conrad replied—reluctantly, from fear of divulging military secrets (his statements were not incorporated in the protocol)—to the first question in the affirmative, provided that the mobilization against Russia began not more than five days after the mobilization against Serbia; a most important point, as will be seen later. To the second question he answered that the entire strength of the Monarchy would be available against Russia except the 5th and 6th armies, but that "the chances would not be favorable for us." Conrad, IV, 54–55.

promised her assistance; with this assurance they were prepared to face Russian intervention, if that was the price of
war with Serbia. According to the Bavarian minister, the
Ballplatz "was concerned lest the complete submission of Serbia would make a resort to force difficult, and was of the
opinion that, if Russia would not permit the localization of
the conflict with Serbia, the present moment was more favorable for a reckoning than a later one would be."* How reconciled, one might almost say indifferent, they were to a hostile attitude on the part of Russia is revealed by the failure
(at least in the published documents) of Vienna to ask its
representative in St. Petersburg about the currents of opinion
in Russia or the disposition of the Russian Government.†
So far as one can judge, the Austro-Hungarian statesmen and
generals were not greatly concerned about what Russia might
do.‡ Apparently they were persuaded that they could not
overcome the Yugoslav danger without a conflict sooner or
later with Russia, that from a military point of view the
situation would become more unfavorable with each passing
year on both the Balkan and the Russian fronts; they now had
the promise of German support, which had long been withheld and which might not be given again; and they were not
likely to find a better excuse for war than that provided by
the murder at Sarajevo.

* Tucher to Hertling, 18 July; Dirr, p. 129.
† The German ambassador in St. Petersburg asked the Austrian chargé if the
rumor was true that the chargé had been instructed to bespeak Russian support
for the execution of the Austrian demands on Serbia, and received "a categorical
reply in the negative." Czernin to Berchtold, 14 July; Gooss, pp. 82–83.
‡ The Russian ambassador in Vienna, M. Schebeko, made no secret, at least to
his friends, of his views. He told his British colleague that "an isolated combat with
Servia was impossible. . . . A Servian war meant a general European war." Bunsen to Grey, 5 July; B 40. In the middle of the month he declared that "Russia
would inevitably be drawn in," if, as the German military attaché averred, "the
hour of condign punishment for Servia is approaching." Bunsen to Nicolson, private, 17 July; B 56. What he may have said at the Ballplatz is not known, but it
is difficult to believe that his views were not known, for he postponed his summer
holiday "owing to the uncertainty of the situation." Bunsen to Grey, 19 July; B
156. He also pointed out that a communiqué had been issued in St. Petersburg
(see below, pp. 443–444) "expressing the conviction that the Austro-Hungarian Government would put forward no unreasonable demands, and that this had been
intended as a hint that it would be well for this Government to act with moderation."

It is not easy to take a fair and unprejudiced view of the Austro-Hungarian policy. The rulers of the Dual Monarchy appear to have believed in all sincerity that the integrity of the state was threatened by the propaganda emanating from Belgrade, and they feared its effects the more because they saw behind it, if not as the driving force, at least as the stalwart support, the mighty power of Russia. They rightly regarded the Serbo-Russian ambitions as fatal to the very existence of the Monarchy, and they would have been less than human had they not determined to prevent, if possible, the realization of those ambitions. To meet the serious provocation contained in the murder of the heir to the throne, prompt and effective measures were necessary and justifiable; the failure to establish the complicity of the Serbian Government in the Sarajevo crime did not seem a valid reason against proceeding either promptly or vigorously. To seize the opportunity for dealing with Serbia was, no reasonable person will deny, not only intelligible, it was natural.

On the other hand, the Austro-Hungarian statesmen never seem to have understood that the hostility of Serbia and the unrest in the Southern Slav provinces were in large part the natural consequences of their own foreign and domestic policy for a generation past; at least they never admitted any such responsibility. Perhaps they could not be expected to admit it. Nevertheless, this consideration is fundamental. If Serbia had provoked Austria-Hungary, the latter had in various ways and at various times done grave injury to the neighboring kingdom, and the ultimate aim of Habsburg policy was the destruction of Serbian independence.

Furthermore, the régime which Francis Joseph and Conrad von Hötzendorf, Count Berchtold and Count Tisza wished to preserve had become an unworkable anachronism. Its political system was based on the ascendancy of two minority races, its social arrangements lagged behind the demands of the twentieth century and bore most severely on those groups which were excluded from political power. All efforts to change the existing

system had failed; Francis Ferdinand was known to desire the
destruction of Dualism, but how he intended to accomplish it,
against the opposition of the Magyars, was problematical, and
he was intensely hated by the very people whose interests he
sought to promote. If it is not possible to estimate with accuracy the general attitude within the Monarchy toward the reign-
ing dynasty, there are indications that among certain groups
loyalty had been reduced to a skin-deep tolerance of existing
conditions until the death of the old Emperor, which in many
quarters was expected to produce a great upheaval.* And it is
certain that the foreign policy pursued for a number of years
was keenly disliked by most of the non-German or non-Mag-
yar elements; in 1914 those elements neither demanded action
against Serbia nor approved the official attitude. When, therefore, the ruling classes proclaimed the necessity of action to preserve the state, they were thinking primarily of their own privi-
leged position and were endeavoring to divert attention from
the rising tide of national discontent; and the prospect of dissolution which filled them with horror and dismay probably afforded a certain hope of relief to a majority of the people of
the Monarchy.

A balancing of these several points of view leads to the following judgment: Although Austria-Hungary was a worn-
out political entity, hopelessly torn by internal feuds and seriously threatened by external dangers,† yet it still existed as a
Great Power, with something of its old prestige, and its government, animated as governments naturally are by the desire
of self-preservation, was justified in demanding some kind
of satisfaction from Serbia for the affront offered by the murder at Sarajevo, even some definite solution of the threatening
agitation from across the border. In principle, the decision was
sound enough. But in their anger and desperation, the rulers

---

* "His life is so bound up with the peace of Europe that I dread anything that
must try his strength." Grey to Mensdorff, 29 July, 1914; B 15.
† "*Austria-Hungary's watch had run down.* . . . I believe to-day . . . that even
without the war the fall of the Monarchy would have happened, and that the assassination in Sarajevo was the first sign." Czernin, *Im Weltkriege*, p. 40.

of the Monarchy lost all sense of perspective. They were warned by the German ambassador that "Austria-Hungary does not stand alone in the world," that it was "her duty . . . to take the whole European situation into consideration,"* and they knew that too drastic action would precipitate a general war. These considerations they ignored, belittled, or defied: no matter which interpretation is preferred, their responsibility is heavy. In the first and second cases they were guilty of stupidity, which is unpardonable in politics; in the last case they were playing with fate. However much they might hope that their action might not be interfered with, they were aware their course was fraught with danger; nevertheless they accepted the risk willingly. Like their German ally, they took a gambler's chance. In such a situation responsibility is measured by the success or the failure of the throw.

GERMANY AND THE ULTIMATUM

The German Government, by immediately accepting, on 6 July, the Austro-Hungarian programme, had renounced all limiting control of its ally's course of action. It cannot therefore be logically criticised for failing to inform itself about the note which the Cabinet of Vienna proposed to address to Serbia.

Inasmuch, however, as the German foreign minister subsequently admitted that "he thought the note left much to be desired as a diplomatic document," and insisted that he "had had no previous knowledge of contents,"† thereby implying that if he had known of its contents he might have tried to get it modified, it is worth while ascertaining what the German Government did know about the note and what its attitude was.

The first information from Vienna in regard to the note was

* Tschirschky to Bethmann-Hollweg, 30 June; G 7.
† Rumbold to Grey, telegram, 25 July; B 122. Bethmann, I, 137-138, commenting on the charge that Germany did not trouble to learn the terms of the note, remarks: "Even to-day [1919] I am of the opinion that it would have been a mistake for us to have spared ourselves this reproach"; and then, on the next page, declares: "We did ascertain through Herr von Tschirschky the general lines of the demands that Austria would make on Serbia."

received in Berlin on 11 July. In a long telegram Herr von Tschirschky reported an interview with Count Berchtold:

At present the formulation of appropriate demands on Serbia constituted the principal source of anxiety here, and Count Berchtold said that he would be glad to know what they thought about it in Berlin. He thought that among other things, it might be demanded that an agency of the Austro-Hungarian Government be established in Belgrade in order to keep an eye from there on the Great Serbian machinations, perhaps, also, to insist upon the dissolution of the associations and the dismissal of some compromised officers. The respite allowed for the reply must be made as brief as possible, say forty-eight hours. . . . If the Serbs should accept all the demands made on them, it would prove a solution which would be "very disagreeable" to him, and he was still considering what demands could be made that would be wholly impossible for the Serbs to accept.*

Tschirschky added that "the minister complained again about the attitude of Count Tisza, which made energetic procedure against Serbia difficult for him": at the moment, therefore, Count Berchtold's programme might seem tentative and conditional. But on the following day the ambassador, in a private letter, "absolutely confidential," told a different story:

A closer agreement had been arrived at since yesterday with the president of the Hungarian council concerning the note to be directed to Serbia, and he hoped by Tuesday [14 July] to be able to determine on the final version of this document. So far as he could say to-day, the principal demands on Serbia would consist of the requirement that the king should officially and publicly proclaim, in a formal declaration, and through an order to the army, that Serbia discarded her Great Serbian policy; secondly, the institution of an agency of the Austro-Hungarian Government to see to the strict keeping of this promise, would be required.†

Berlin, then, was informed at this early date (11 July) of the general character of the note and of the intention to pre-

* Tschirschky to foreign office, telegram, 10 July; G 29.
† Tschirschky to Jagow, 11 July; *Zur Vorgeschichte des Weltkrieges*, I, 119–120.

sent unacceptable demands. On 18 July, Herr Zimmermann, in conversation with the Bavarian chargé, summarized its knowledge as follows:

1. The issuing of a proclamation by the King of Serbia which shall state that the Serbian Government has nothing to do with the Great Serbian movement, and fully disapproves of it.
2. The initiation of an inquiry to discover those implicated in the murder of Sarajevo, and the participation of Austrian officials in this inquiry.
3. Proceedings against all who have participated in the Great Serbian movement.
A respite of forty-eight hours is to be granted for the acceptance of those demands.*

Count Berchtold had said that "he would be glad to know what they thought in Berlin" about "appropriate demands."† But the German Government declined to express an opinion: "We can take no hand in the formulation of the demands on Serbia," said Herr von Jagow; "that is Austria's business."‡ This attitude was consistent with the position taken on 6 July and was maintained to the end. But it was maintained in full realization of the probable consequences of the Austro-Hungarian action. For Herr Zimmermann, when on 18 July he confided to the Bavarian chargé what he knew about the note, remarked:

It is absolutely plain that Serbia cannot accept any such demands, which are incompatible with her dignity as a sovereign state. Thus the result would be war.

Some concern may seem discernible in his next words:

What attitude the other Powers will take toward an armed conflict between Austria and Serbia will depend chiefly, ac-

---

* Schoen to Hertling, 18 July; Dirr, p. 5; D, supplement IV, no. 2. This despatch explains the statement of Count Hertling on 23 July to the French minister in Munich that the contents of the note were known to him, known, that is, before the note had been communicated to the Powers or published in the press; F 21.
† See above, p. 376.   ‡ Jagow to Tschirschky, 11 July; telegram; G 31.

cording to the opinion here, on whether Austria will content herself with a chastisement of Serbia, or will demand territorial compensations for herself. In the first place, it might be possible to localize the war; in the second, on the other hand, more serious complications would probably be inevitable.

But, although the danger of complications was frankly recognized, no effort was made by the German Government to secure from Austria an assurance that she would not take territory for herself.

On the contrary, both the German Emperor and the German foreign office assumed that Austria would take territory. When William II learned that Count Berchtold "was still considering what demands could be put that would be wholly impossible for Serbia to accept," he commented:

Evacuate the Sandjak [of Novi Bazar, which Serbia and Montenegro had acquired in 1913]! Then the row will be on at once. Austria must absolutely get that back at once, in order to prevent the union of Serbia and Montenegro and the acquisition of a seacoast by the Serbs! [He had supported this very programme in the spring of 1914!]*

This comment of the Emperor was received in the foreign office on 16 July. It may be a coincidence, but it is at least significant that on the following day Herr von Jagow wrote to Herr von Tschirschky reminding him that Count Berchtold and Count Tisza had repudiated Count Hoyos's statement in Berlin, that "Austria would have to proceed to a complete partition of Serbia." He then went on to say:

For the diplomatic handling of the conflict with Serbia, it would not be unimportant to know from the beginning what are the ideas of the Austro-Hungarian statesmen concerning the future status of Serbia, since this question will have a material influence on the attitude of Italy and on the public opinion and attitude of England.

* Tschirschky to foreign office, telegram, 10 July; G 29. One wonders if Szögyény had hinted something to William about the plans for the partition of Serbia.

That the plans of the statesmen of the Danube Monarchy may be influenced and modified by the course of events is indeed to be considered as a matter of course; nevertheless we may assume that the Cabinet of Vienna has already formed a general picture of the ends to be striven for even in the matter of territory. Your Excellency will endeavor, in conversation with Count Berchtold, to secure enlightenment on this matter, but in doing so, avoid giving the impression that we wished to put any obstacles in the path of the Austrian action or prescribe certain limits or ends. It would only be useful to us to be informed to a certain extent where the road may perhaps lead.*

Meanwhile, Herr von Jagow began to be curious about the note itself. Count Berchtold had promised to forward the definitive text on Sunday, 19 July, "even before submitting it to his own Emperor."† When that day arrived, the German foreign minister, without allowing time for its transmission, telegraphed for it. But he explained that his request was inspired solely by tactical considerations:

Your Excellency [so read the instruction to Tschirschky] will request immediate communication from Count Berchtold of text of proposed note to Belgrade, as well as any other announcements . . . in order that we can prepare in proper time for our *démarches* toward the other Powers.‡

This was followed up the next day by another request conceived in a similar spirit, Herr von Tschirschky being informed that

in order to facilitate the handling of our publicity, it would be the greatest advantage to us to be exactly informed not only of its contents, but also as to the day and hour of publication;

and the ambassador was asked to report by wire.§   Herr von

* Jagow to Tschirschky, 17 July; G 61.
† Tschirschky to Bethmann-Hollweg, 14 July; G 50.
‡ Jagow to Tschirschky, 19 July; G 77. The telegram was sent at 1.35 P. M. As the ministerial council in Vienna for the determination of the text was held at 9 A. M., not sufficient time had elapsed for the transmission in code of so long a document as the note.
§ Jagow to Tschirschky, 20 July; G 83.

Jagow was not too foresighted, as we shall see, in thinking of the necessity of justifying the note to the other Powers.

On this same day, 20 July, conclusive information was received from Vienna about the note. "Hoyos has just told me," said the counsellor of embassy there, "that the demands [to be made on Serbia] were really of such a nature that no nation which still possessed self-respect and dignity could possibly accept them."* A little later the news came that the note would be delivered to Tschirschky on the following day and sent on that evening.† Having received these final and drastic assurances, the imperial chancellor, without waiting for the note, addressed a circular despatch to the ambassadors in London, Paris, and St. Petersburg. In this document he offered a vigorous and hearty indorsement of the course being followed by Austria-Hungary; ratifying in advance the step about to be taken, he declared:

Neither the procedure nor the demands of the Austro-Hungarian Government can be regarded as otherwise than moderate and proper.‡

In similar fashion, Herr von Jagow, when on 21 July he asked Count Szögyény whether he "had yet received information from Vienna about the contents of the note," gave the ambassador "to understand clearly that of course Germany would stand by us with all her forces."§ In the light of all these statements, it is evident enough that the German Government, while in-

* Stolberg to Jagow, private, 17 July; G 87. In the first part of his letter Stolberg, who had gathered from Berchtold and Hoyos that "Serbia *can* accept the demands," complained that "if the people here really want a clearing up once for all of the relations with Serbia, as even Count Tisza in his recent speech indicated to be imperative, it is at least incomprehensible why they have not formulated such demands as would make a rupture unavoidable." A "so-called diplomatic success" would only confirm the current view that "the Monarchy is no longer able to act with vigor."
  † Tschirschky to foreign office, telegram, 20 July; G 88.
  ‡ Bethmann-Hollweg to Lichnowsky, Schoen and Pourtalès, 21 July; G 100. When first published in the German *White Book* of 1914 (no. 1), the despatch was dated *23* July, in order to obviate the charge that the German Government had declared the demands "moderate and proper" at a time when it claimed not to have known what the demands were.
  § Szögyény to Berchtold, telegram and despatch, 21 July; A I 39, 41.

different to the details, understood clearly the character and purpose of the note, had acquiesced in them, and had again committed itself to unflinching support of its ally.

Satisfied that the Austrian Government meant business, Herr von Jagow now addressed himself to the matter of staging the *démarche* in Belgrade. Count Berchtold had explained that "the sole reason" for the delay in sending the note was the visit of the French President to Russia, which was scheduled for 20–23 July; he wished to await the departure of M. Poincaré from St. Petersburg.

But so important a matter ought not to be left to chance, and Herr von Jagow therefore inquired of his ambassador in St. Petersburg at what hour M. Poincaré would leave Cronstadt on Thursday, 23 July.* The answer came that M. Poincaré's departure was arranged for 11 P. M.† Meanwhile Tschirschky had reported that the note would be delivered in Belgrade on Thursday afternoon.‡ There was danger of the whole plan miscarrying. So Herr von Jagow informed Vienna that M. Poincaré would not leave Cronstadt until 9.30 P. M., central European time, and pointed out that "if *démarche* in Belgrade is made to-morrow afternoon at five o'clock, it would thus become known while Poincaré is still in St. Petersburg."§ Count Berchtold returned his "warmest thanks" for this communication, and stated that the delivery of the note had been postponed for one hour.‖

Meanwhile Count Szögyény had become nervous under the pressure of Herr von Jagow for fuller information about the note. He accordingly telegraphed that "it was unconditionally necessary to make the contents known to the German Government, for the moment in strict confidence, before the note is communicated to the other governments."¶ It might give of-

* Jagow to Pourtalès, 21 July; G 93. He also inquired of Admiral Behncke, the chief of the naval staff; G 96.
† Pourtalès to foreign office, telegram, 22 July; G 108.
‡ Tschirschky to foreign office, telegram, 21 July; G 103.
§ Jagow to Tschirschky, telegram, 22 July; G 112.
‖ Tschirschky to foreign office, telegram, 23 July; G 127.
¶ Szögyény to Berchtold, telegram, 21 July; A I 39.

fense, he explained, if "we placed our ally on the same footing with the governments of the other Great Powers."* Count Berchtold's reply was that "for form's sake" the official communication to Berlin had to be made in the same way as to the other Powers, but that a copy of the note had already been given to Herr von Tschirschky.† The ambassador took this for an authorization to communicate the note to the German foreign minister, and did so on the evening of 22 July; at 8 P. M. the copy from Herr von Tschirschky was also handed to Herr von Jagow.

Herr von Jagow gives this account of his conversation with Count Szögyény:

I immediately expressed my opinion to the ambassador that the content seemed to me pretty sharp and to go beyond what was necessary. Count Szögyény replied that nothing could now be done about it, for the ultimatum had already been sent to Belgrade and was to be presented there the next morning while at the same time it would be published through the official telegraph agencies in Vienna. I expressed my astonishment to the ambassador that the decisions of his government had been communicated to us so late as to deprive us of the possibility of taking position about them.‡

But in 1914 he was of another opinion. "Herr von Jagow assured me," Count Szögyény then telegraphed to Vienna, "that the German Government agrees entirely with the contents of the note."§ Furthermore, Count Szögyény's statement that the note would be presented in Belgrade and published the next

---

* Szögyény to Berchtold, 21 July; A I 41.

† Berchtold to Szögyény, telegram, 22 July; A I 47. Tschirschky had in fact received the note from Forgách on 21 July and sent it on by post, probably from the fear that after its publication the secret of the German code would be revealed. It reached Berlin on the evening of 22 July. The communication was made in strict confidence, as, so Forgách said, "the Emperor's sanction has not yet been received." Tschirschky to Bethmann-Hollweg, 21 July; G 106. Curiously enough, Berchtold had telegraphed from Ischl that the note was not to be given to Tschirschky until 22 July, "as some corrections have to be made." Berchtold to foreign office, telegram, 21 July; A I 46. Forgách, however, had already acted.

‡ Jagow, *Ursachen und Ausbruch des Weltkrieges*, pp. 109–110. The book was written before the publication of *Die deutschen Dokumente zum Kriegsausbruch.*

§ Szögyény to Berchtold, 24 July; A II 6.

morning was at variance with Herr von Jagow's own information, for he knew that the note would be presented at 5 P. M. and would be published on Friday morning.* The German foreign minister himself had, as has just been seen, asked that the presentation be postponed beyond that hour. If he really believed the note to be too stiff, the least that he should have done would have been to challenge the accuracy of Count Szögyény's remark and to ask the ambassador to transmit to Vienna his objections to the note. In an age of telegraphs and telephones and with at least twenty-one hours at his disposal, there was certainly time for Herr von Jagow to have taken some action if he had wished to do so. The only plausible assumption is that he did not wish to do anything; and this feeling is strengthened by the fact that the circular despatch sent the day before, for ultimate presentation in London, Paris, and St. Petersburg, to justify the Austrian note was neither recalled nor modified. Once again the German conduct was consistent, for the German Government had promised not to interfere with the Austrian plans; but the German argument that the German Government at the last moment found the Austrian plans objectionable but was estopped by circumstances from interference, will not hold water.

Herr von Jagow's unreliability as a witness in the whole matter is further illustrated by his frequent denials of any knowledge of the ultimatum before it was formally presented to the German Government. Thus on 20 July he said to the Serbian chargé that he "was not acquainted . . . with the demands which Austria-Hungary intended to make";† which, as we have seen, was not altogether true. But even after he had received and read the text of the note, he continued to assert the contrary. On 23 July he telegraphed to Prince Lichnowsky that "we are not acquainted with the Austrian demands,"‡ and to his minister in Stockholm that "these demands are not known to

* Tschirschky to foreign office, telegram, 21 July; G 103.
† Jagow to Tschirschky, 20 July, telegram; G 91.
‡ Jagow to Lichnowsky, 23 July; G 126.

us."* The next day he affirmed to the French ambassador that "the Berlin cabinet had really been entirely ignorant of Austria's requirements before they were communicated to Belgrade."† And on the day following he repeated to the British chargé that "he had had no previous knowledge of terms of Austro-Hungarian note."‡ Not even with his own ally was the minister honest, for he telegraphed to Rome, on the very day when the note was officially communicated, that "we are not informed in detail about the Austrian note, nor do we wish to be."§

Such conduct was not only dishonest, it was foolish; for it permitted the French ambassador to express "surprise at seeing him [Jagow] thus undertake to support claims, of whose limit and scope he was ignorant,"‖ and to place the German Government in a false position. The French ambassador did not believe that Herr von Jagow was telling the truth; and, reading between the lines of his telegrams to London, one gets the impression that the British chargé was equally sceptical. Thus, from the very beginning of the crisis the German Government was handicapped by the suspicion it gratuitously created that it was not acting in a straightforward and dependable manner. At the moment this was not perhaps of great consequence, but the time was to come, a week later, when the Cabinet of Berlin was desperately anxious to have its professions believed; and, if they were not, it was partly because the insincerity displayed at the beginning of the negotiations had convinced the other Powers that the German Government had dissimulated its real part in the action of Austria-Hungary.

To sum up this stage of the story: the Austro-Hungarian Government having, upon consultation, found its ally unexpectedly receptive to the suggestion of a reckoning with Serbia, drew up a note which was desired and expected to precipitate a rupture. The German Government was kept informed in a

---

* Jagow to Reichenau, 23 July; G 123.
† J. Cambon to Bienvenu-Martin, 24 July; F 30.
‡ Rumbold to Grey, 25 July; B 122.　　§ Jagow to Flotow, 24 July; G 145.
‖ Jules Cambon to Bienvenu-Martin, 24 July; F 30.

general way of what was being prepared, offered no objections, and applied pressure in the interest of speedy action. Nearly twenty-four hours before any action was taken it learned precisely what was planned, took no steps to prevent that action, and did not modify a communication intended for the Entente Powers according to which the action was represented as right and proper. Although Austria-Hungary, as the Power taking action, must bear the immediate responsibility for the consequence, it is clear that she had not pursued her course without the encouragement and approval of her ally.

CHAPTER VII

DIPLOMATIC MANŒUVRES

In this fashion, then, Austria-Hungary and Germany determined to avenge the murder of the Archduke Francis Ferdinand. But the statesmen of Vienna and Berlin had resolved on something more than mere punishment for the crime: they proposed to effect nothing less than the humiliation and, one may fairly say, the practical subjugation of Serbia. With a view to forestalling as far as possible protests against their action on the part of the Triple Entente, or at least by Russia and France, the Central Powers decided to take Europe by surprise and to present their opponents with a *fait accompli*. They accordingly exerted every effort and exhibited much ingenuity, in the month following the murder, in concealing their intentions and throwing the other Powers off the scent. Not only was the fact of the Potsdam conversations successfully concealed,* but first hints and then positive assurances were given that the demands to be made on Serbia would be such that they could be accepted by that state.

The Assurances of Budapest and Vienna

As it happened, the Austrian parliament was not in session, and it could not have been convoked without suggesting that something serious was in the wind. But the Hungarian parliament was sitting, and before it Count Tisza delivered three speeches which merit close attention. On 8 July, the day after the first ministerial council in Vienna, he declared, in reply to an interpellation by Count Andrássy, that the inquiry into the crime at Sarajevo was still proceeding and it was not possible to say what would be done; though the government, he affirmed,

---

* "If there has been an exchange of views between Berlin and Vienna about the nature of the steps to be taken at Belgrade, the result has been kept absolutely secret." Rumbold to Grey, 18 July; B 63.

would "do its duty in every direction," it would not take precipitate action, and he even defended the loyalty of the majority of the Serbs domiciled in Hungary.* "The whole tone of Count Tisza's speech was peaceful and conciliatory," reported the British consul-general in Budapest, "and its tendency should be to contradict the warlike feeling which is in the air in this country and which must render all the more difficult the efforts of responsible ministers toward a peaceful settlement."†

Tisza was of course well aware of the policy that was being urged upon him from Vienna, but, since he had not yet agreed to it, he was justified in the language used. A week later, 15 July, he made another speech, the salient portions of which must be quoted:

The relations with Serbia must be cleared up in all circumstances, though in what manner, in what direction, and by what means, I cannot, in the nature of things, say, for it is a matter still under discussion.

I should like once more to emphasize that the government is penetrated with the consciousness of all the important interests which depend on the maintenance of peace. The government is not of the opinion that this clarification must necessarily lead to warlike complications. Above everything, I am not willing in this connection to indulge in prophesyings and will only remark that war is a sad *ultima ratio* to which resort must not be had until every possibility of a peaceful solution is exhausted. But every state, every nation, must be in a position and have the will to make war if it is to continue to exist as a state and nation.‡

The conclusion, however, was somewhat more peaceful, for it ran:

I must terminate my statement with the commonplace remark that political agitation and propaganda certainly exist, against which we must fight; this fight must be waged with energy; we must do all in our power to detect and destroy the root of the evil, but we must avoid all appearance of panic, all methodless and inconsequent activity, all superfluous talk.§

---

* *Times* (London), 10 July, 1914.　　† Max Müller to Grey, 14 July; B 70.
‡ Fraknói, p. 38.　　§ Max Müller to Grey, 17 July; B 82.

The speech made "a decidedly good impression" in Paris,* as
no doubt it was intended to do. Yet, on the previous day, Count
Tisza had accepted the programme of Count Berchtold and "had
even introduced a sharper tone at various places" in the note to
be addressed to Serbia.†

Even more disingenuous was the third and last speech on 22
July, which was to the following effect:

Count Tisza declared that he was still not in a position to
reply to questions addressed to him in regard to any contemplated action, but that he hoped to be able to make a detailed
statement very shortly. He explained that it would not be in
the interests of the country to open a discussion at the present
moment on the questions which formed the subject of the in-
terpellations. . . .
Count Tisza stated that the position of affairs was not such
as to justify the conclusion that a serious turn for the worse
was either certain or even probable; the foreign situation was
still uncertain and could be solved by peaceful means, though he
could not overlook the possibility of serious conflict.‡

Actually, the ultimatum had been despatched on 20 July to the
Austro-Hungarian minister in Belgrade for presentation on the
day following Count Tisza's speech. Attempts to mislead public
opinion in both Hungary and Europe could not go much
farther.

During these two weeks the authorities in Vienna took equal
pains to cover up their tracks. The irrepressible Conrad, who
was in high feather over the course matters were taking, suggested to Count Berchtold that "everything should be avoided
which might alarm our antagonists and cause them to take counter-measures; on the contrary, peaceful intentions should be
feigned."§ He was therefore told that "it would be well if you
and the minister of war were to go on leave for a time, in

---

* Szécsen to Berchtold, 18 July; Fraknói, p. 39; Ö.-U. A., 10,359.
† Tschirschky to Bethmann-Hollweg, 14 July; G 50.
‡ Max Müller to Grey, 23 July; B 157. Cf. also Bunsen to Grey, 23 July; B 85.
§ Conrad to Berchtold, ca. 10 July; A I 14. Ö.-U. A., 10,226, gives the date as
12 July.

order to give the appearance that nothing was impending."* They did so; and the ruse worked to perfection. The Italian ambassador in Berlin, who had been filled with "alarm," told his Austro-Hungarian colleague that he saw "a favorable symptom" in the fact that Generals Conrad and Krobatin had taken their "summer leave."† The British consul-general in Budapest was also taken in, for he wrote home:

If there were any immediate prospect of war or even of military preparation for war, it would not be possible for the Joint Minister of War, the Austrian Minister of the Landwehr, the Hungarian Minister of Honved, and the Chief of the General Staff all to be on leave.‡

Even the correspondent of the London *Times* in Vienna was reassured, and he connected the improvement on the bourse with the absence of the military officials.§ As late as 21 July, the permanent under-secretary in the British foreign office doubted "if Austria will proceed to any extreme measures—although [which shows how completely misled he was] Berlin is apparently anxious."‖ The duping of Europe seems to have been eminently successful.

For some time an impenetrable mystery surrounded the Ballhausplatz.¶ "We are left to conjecture what is the attitude of the Austro-Hungarian Foreign Office," wrote the British ambassador early in July, "from a few vague remarks by Count Berchtold, from newspaper articles, and from conversations

* Conrad, IV, 61. The German ambassador in Vienna reported this to Berlin, saying that "this is being done, so Count Berchtold told me, in order to prevent any uneasiness"; Tschirschky to Bethmann-Hollweg, 10 July; G 29. The German Emperor's comment was: "Childish!" as if he were not playing much the same game by going to Norway. The Austro-Hungarian military attaché in Constantinople, who was not informed of what was being prepared, records that he regarded the leave granted the two officers as "a deliberate move of the Vienna Cabinet to conceal its real intentions." Pomiankowski, *Der Zusammenbruch des ottomanischen Reiches*, p. 69.
† Szögyény to Berchtold, 16 July; A I 23.
‡ Max Müller to Grey, 16 July; B 81.
§ *Times*, 16 July, 1914.   ‖ Nicolson's minute on B 71.
¶ It is not without interest to note that the Bavarian minister in Vienna was told, in essentials, what happened in the council of 7 July, and that the intention to provoke war with Serbia by means of an unacceptable note was explained to him. Tucher to the king, 10 and 14 July; Dirr, pp. 125, 129.

with other persons more or less intimately connected with public affairs"; it was impossible, said Sir Maurice de Bunsen, to
obtain from the foreign minister "anything like an explicit
statement of his views on international affairs."* A week later
it was the same story:

Nothing . . . is really known at the present moment regarding the intentions of the Government, and it may well be that
they will hesitate to take a step which might lead to a position
of great international tension. . . . The Servian Minister at
Vienna states that he has no reason to expect that any threatening communication will be addressed to his Government.†

Then the veil was lifted a little. On 16 July, Count Lützow,
formerly Austro-Hungarian ambassador in Rome, invited Sir
Maurice de Bunsen to luncheon, and asked his guest if he
"realized how grave the situation was." The Count, who had
been to the foreign office the day before, went on to say:

A note was being drawn up and would be completed when
the Sarajevo inquiry was finished, demanding categorically that
Servia should take effective measures to prevent the manufacture and export of bombs, and to put down the insidious and
murderous propaganda against the Dual Monarchy. No futile
discussion would be tolerated. If Servia did not at once cave in,
force would be used to compel her. . . . Count Berchtold was
sure of German support and did not believe that any country
would hesitate to approve—not even Russia.‡

The ambassador thereupon telegraphed to London:

I gather that situation is regarded at the Ministry for Foreign
Affairs in a serious light and that a kind of indictment is being
prepared against the Servian Government for alleged complicity

---

* Bunsen to Grey, 5 July; B 40. At the moment Berchtold had not definitely
formulated his policy, but of course Bunsen did not know this.
† Bunsen to Grey, 11 July; B 46.
‡ Bunsen to Nicolson, private, 17 July; B 56. Bunsen discounted the news.
"I cannot yet believe," he added, "that Austria will resort to extreme measures,
but I think we have an anxious time before us." To Lützow he expressed doubts
"whether, if it really came to fighting, which I could not believe, Russia would allow Austria and Servia to have it out in a cockpit."

in the conspiracy which led to assassination of the Archduke. Accusation will be founded on the proceedings in the Sarajevo Court. My informant states that the Servian Government will be required to adopt certain definite measures in restraint of nationalist and anarchist propaganda, and that Austro-Hungarian Government are in no mood to parley with Servia, but will insist on immediate unconditional acceptance, failing which force will be used. Germany is said to be in complete agreement with this procedure, and it is thought that the rest of Europe will sympathize with Austria-Hungary in demanding that Servia shall adopt in future more submissive attitude.*

This was indeed ominous news, all the more so because a member of the Austro-Hungarian embassy in London spoke to an official of the foreign office at great length, "giving expression to very much the same views."†

The Austrian manœuvre may well have been an attempt to sound London on its attitude. But on the following day reassuring news was circulated in Vienna. Count Berchtold demurred to a remark by the Italian ambassador that the "situation was becoming grave," though he admitted that it was far from "serene"; the ambassador therefore told his British colleague that he did not believe that "unreasonable demands will be made on Servia," or that "either Minister for Foreign Affairs or Emperor would sanction such an unwise proceeding" as "a kind of ultimatum."‡ It was certainly a reasonable assumption that if Austria-Hungary's ally was optimistic, there was no cause for alarm. Moreover, the Austrian minister in Belgrade allowed it to be understood that

he is not personally in favour of pressing Servia too hard, since he is convinced that Servian Government are ready to take whatever measures can reasonably be demanded of them. He does not view the situation in a pessimistic light.§

---

* Bunsen to Grey, 16 July; B 50.   † Crowe's minute on B 50.
‡ Bunsen to Grey, telegram, 18 July; B 59.
§ Crackanthorpe to Grey, telegram, 18 July; B 57. As a matter of fact, the Austrian minister, Baron von Giesl, was the advocate of very strong measures. Giesl to Berchtold, 21 July; A I 37. He seems to have deliberately misled the British representative.

Accordingly, when the German ambassador discussed the situation with Sir Edward Grey on 20 July, he judged that the British foreign secretary "was still viewing the Austro-Serbian quarrel optimistically, and believed that a peaceful solution would be reached."*

Meanwhile, the Vienna Cabinet was also engaged in casting out feelers to discover the French attitude. On 20 July the French consul in Vienna drew up a memorandum as follows:

> From information furnished by a person specially well informed as to official news, it appears that the French Government would be wrong to have confidence in the disseminators of optimism; much will be demanded of Serbia; she will be required to dissolve several propagandist societies, she will be summoned to repress nationalism, to guard the frontier in co-operation with Austrian officials, to keep strict control over anti-Austrian tendencies in the schools; and it is a very difficult matter for a Government to consent to become in this way a policeman for a foreign Government. They foresee the subterfuges by which Serbia will doubtless wish to avoid giving a clear and direct reply; that is why a short interval will perhaps be fixed for her to declare whether she accepts or not. The tenor of the note and its imperious tone almost certainly ensure that Belgrade will refuse. Then military operations will begin.†

The information of the French consul turned out to be astonishingly accurate. Yet the French ambassador was allowed to believe that "the requirements of the Austro-Hungarian Government with regard to the punishment of the outrage, and to guarantees of control and police supervision seem to be acceptable to the dignity of the Serbians."‡ And when, under orders from Paris, he went to the Ballplatz to urge moderation, he was told by Baron Macchio, the under-secretary of state, that "the tone of the Austrian note, and the demands

---

* Lichnowsky to Bethmann-Hollweg, 20 July; G 92.
  † Extract from a consular report on the economic and political situation in Austria, 20 July; F 14.
  ‡ Dumaine to Bienvenu-Martin, 22 July; F 18.

which would be formulated in it, allow us to count on a peaceful result."*

To complete the story of deception, it may be noted that "in consequence of reassuring explanations made to him at the ministry of foreign affairs," the Russian ambassador left Vienna on 20 July for a fortnight's holiday.†

One can easily understand that the Vienna foreign office should, in the circumstances, have considered secrecy essential for the success of its programme;‡ and if it had kept its own counsel until the moment of action, it would not have laid itself open to criticism from the point of view of diplomatic etiquette. But the deliberate policy of lulling other governments into a feeling of security by assuring them that the demands on Serbia would be acceptable produced consequences disastrous to Austria-Hungary. For, when the note to Serbia was published, the Entente governments felt that they had been tricked and assumed an attitude of suspicion toward every statement emanating from Vienna.

The decision to present the note at Belgrade so that it could not become known until after the French president and the French premier had left Russia was also a move of doubtful wisdom. Count Berchtold's wish to delay the step "while the Emperor Nicholas and the Russian statesmen were under the influence of the two 'inciters' Poincaré and Izvolski,"§ was natural, for his procedure would take the Russian and French Governments at a disadvantage. But he might have foreseen that his procedure would be bitterly resented,|| and that, if MM. Izvolski and Poincaré were really "inciters," his conduct would certainly "incite" them.

---

* Circular of Bienvenu-Martin, 23 July; F 20. Cf. Bunsen to Grey, 23 July; B 90.
† Dumaine to Bienvenu-Martin, 22 July; F 18. Bunsen to Grey, 1 September; B 676.
‡ The ambassadors in London, Paris, and Rome were instructed to influence the press in favor of the Austro-Hungarian point of view. Berchtold to Mensdorff and Szécsen, telegrams, 9 July; Berchtold to Mérey, telegrams, 11, 13, and 16 July; Ö.-U. A., 10,158, 10,203, 10,245, 10,362.
§ Berchtold to Szécsen, telegram, 23 July; A I 57.
|| Circular of Bienvenu-Martin, 24 July; F 25. J. Cambon to Bienvenu-Martin, 24 July; F 29.

THE MANŒUVRES OF BERLIN

The Austrian game of hoodwinking the other European Powers was understood and was cleverly assisted by the German Government. Herr von Bethmann-Hollweg had advised the Emperor to undertake the journey to Norway, immediately after the Potsdam confabulations, "in order to avoid the attention that would have been aroused by his giving up an outing that he had for years been accustomed to take at this time of year."* This admission of the chancellor tells the whole story, but it is worth while to note how the Berlin officials utilized their august master as an instrument of their policy.

When William reached Bergen, the "draft of the customary telegram of congratulation for the birthday of the King of Serbia" was submitted to him. But he was boiling with indignation at the Serbs, and he knew very well what measures he had sanctioned against them. So he inquired forthwith of the foreign office "whether such a telegram appears necessary and unobjectionable at the present moment."† The question did honor to the Emperor's character, which revolted against such an exhibition of hypocrisy, but its point of view was not accepted in Berlin. On the same day, back came the answer that "the omission of the customary telegram would be too noticeable and might be the cause of premature uneasiness."‡ Nor was this a fleeting idea. A week later the Bavarian chargé was told that the government would explain to the Powers that

the Austrian action has been just as much a surprise to it as to the other Powers, pointing out the fact that the Emperor is on his northern journey, and that the Prussian minister of war, as well as the chief of the general staff, are away on leave of absence.§

---

* Bethmann, I, 136. Falkenhayn went on leave on 10 July; *Die deutschen Dokumente zum Kriegsausbruch*, I, xvi.
† Wedel to foreign office, telegram, 11 July; G 30A.
‡ Jagow to Wedel, telegram, 11 July; G 32A.
§ Schoen to Hertling, 18 July; Dirr, p. 8; D, supplement IV, no. 2.

And on the same day Herr von Jagow telegraphed for "exact particulars" about the Emperor's plans after 23 July; and he added:

As we wish to localize prospective conflict between Austria and Serbia, we cannot afford to alarm the world by the premature return of His Majesty, but on the other hand His Majesty must be within reach in case unforeseen circumstances should make important decisions (mobilization) necessary for us.*

Meanwhile His Majesty seems to have become somewhat alarmed, presumably because he learned from Tschirschky's reports of 14 July that the Austrians meant business and from a despatch of Pourtalès that the Russians were in an ugly mood.† On 19 July he advised the foreign office to warn the directors of the North German Lloyd and the Hamburg-American Line, the two most important German shipping companies, that the Austrian ultimatum would be presented on 23 July; for,

in view of incalculable consequences, which may come very suddenly, it appears desirable to His Majesty that the two great lines should be notified in time to make proper dispositions and to be able to issue orders to steamers now in foreign countries.‡

He also began to be worried about the German fleet, which was cruising in Norwegian waters. Later on the same day he telegraphed directly to the fleet:

The Emperor orders the fleet to be kept together until 25 July in such a manner that it can carry out quickly an order to break off the cruise. Entrance into Norwegian harbors is to

* Jagow to Wedel, 18 July; G 67.
† These documents, G 49, 50, 53, were sent on from the foreign office, and returned to it by the Emperor on 20 July.
‡ Wedel to foreign office, telegram from Balholm, 19 July; G 80. Jagow replied the next day that he had "confidentially informed Ballin [director of the Hamburg-American Line], who was here on a casual [sic: see below, pp. 399–401] visit," and had asked the director of the North German Lloyd to call on him the next day. Jagow to Wedel, telegram, 20 July; G 90.

take place only after first receiving special permission **direct** from the Emperor.*

Nothing could better reveal how fully the German Emperor appreciated the dangers of the situation created by his promise to Count Szögyény.

The order to the fleet was not to the liking of the chancellor. From his retreat at Hohenfinow he telegraphed to the foreign office:

His Majesty's order to keep the fleet together makes me fear that as soon as the ultimatum is refused, conspicuous fleet movements might be ordered from Balholm. On the other hand, in case of a crisis, a mistakenly chosen rendezvous for the fleet might be dangerous.

He therefore asked for the opinion of the naval staff.† In reply he was told that, in the judgment of the staff, the fleet need be recalled only six days before "the possibility of the outbreak of war with England";‡ to which the foreign office added that a prompt English decision to enter the war was "very unlikely."§ Thus fortified with the opinion of the responsible authority, the chancellor telegraphed to the Emperor on 23 July:

English fleet, according to information of the naval staff, is supposed to break up on the 27th and go into home ports. Any premature recall of our fleet might cause general uneasiness and be regarded as suspicious, especially in England.||

---

* Behncke to Jagow, 19 July; G 82.
† Bethmann-Hollweg to foreign office, 21 July; G 101.
‡ Behncke to foreign office, 22 July; G 111.
§ Jagow to Bethmann-Hollweg, 22 July; G 115.
|| Bethmann-Hollweg to Wedel, 23 July; G 125. At first the Emperor appears to have listened to this advice, for on the next day, the fleet was allowed to enter Norwegian ports and shore leave was granted. Naval staff to Jagow, 24 July; G 175. But the next morning, "on the strength of a Wolff report," he ordered the fleet to return home. Memorandum of Zimmermann, 25 July; G 174. Bethmann's prompt protest, on the ground that the British navy was taking "no unusual measures" and that Grey was "not considering direct participation by England in a possible European war," drew from the Emperor a flood of sarcastic comments. The British fleet, he exclaimed, "is already prepared for war, as the manœuvres have just shown,

The fact that such a message was sent on the very day when the ultimatum was presented in Belgrade needs no comment.

During these weeks a few hints were dropped to the press, enough to prepare German opinion, yet not sufficiently open to alarm the outside world. On 9 July, that is, after the decisions of Vienna were known to the Berlin foreign office, two inspired articles appeared. The *Kölnische Zeitung,* commenting on Count Tisza's speech in Budapest, remarked that "the calm and determination of this statement are fully understood here";* while the Berlin *Lokal-Anzeiger* affirmed that "official Germany would certainly not lag behind" Austria's determination to punish the parties guilty of the Sarajevo crime.† This was so mild that the British chargé in Berlin was content to report to London that "there is a consensus of opinion that Germany will and must stand by her ally in this matter";‡ which was hardly startling information. Ten days later, the *Frankfurter Zeitung,* which on 1 July had protested against forcible measures of revenge, expressed the view that if Serbia did not renounce her "Piedmontese" ambitions and accept the Austrian demands, war would result.§ But this could be discounted in view of the language of the *Norddeutsche Allgemeine Zeitung* of the same date: "It is increasingly recognized," wrote this semi-official organ, "that

and is mobilized." He had ordered the fleet to return home because of the mobilization at Belgrade [which is incorrect, because the Serbian mobilization was not ordered till the afternoon of 25 July]. "This *may* result in mobilization by Russia, *will* result in mobilization by Austria! In this case I must have my forces collected by land and sea. There is not a single ship in the Baltic. Besides I am not accustomed to undertake military measures on the strength of *one* Wolff telegram, but in accordance with the general situation, and that the *civilian* chancellor has not yet grasped!" William II to Bethmann-Hollweg, 25 July; G 182. This outburst reveals how clearly William realized the probable consequences of the Austrian action. In his memoirs he writes: "During my stay at Balholm I received only meagre news from the foreign office and was obliged to rely principally on the Norwegian newspapers, from which I got the impression that the situation was growing worse. I telegraphed repeatedly to the chancellor and the foreign office that I considered it advisable to return home, but was asked each time not to interrupt my journey." Wilhelm II, *Ereignisse und Gestalten, 1878–1918,* p. 210. The German documents show that very little news was sent to the Emperor. On the other hand, no telegrams from him to the chancellor and the foreign office have been published which exhibit any such uneasiness in the imperial mind.

* Rumbold to Grey, 11 July; B 44.   † Scott, p. 113.
‡ Rumbold to Grey, 11 July; B 44.   § Scott, pp. 114–115.

Austria-Hungary's desire to clear up her relations with Serbia is justified," and it continued:

> In this connection we share the hope expressed in more than one quarter that a serious crisis will be avoided by the Serbian Government giving way in time. In any event the solidarity of Europe, which made itself felt during the long Balkan crisis in maintaining peace among the great Powers, demands and requires that the discussions which may arise between Austria-Hungary and Serbia remain localized.*

These remarks were "intentionally written in a mild tone with an eye to European diplomacy," so Berlin informed Vienna in advance; certainly they would not "give the alarm prematurely."† In fact they merely echoed the hopes of most, if not all, of the foreign offices, and they made so little impression on the British chargé that he transmitted them by mail in a routine report.‡

Fully aware, however, of the projected 'bolt from the blue' and anxious to 'localize' the issue, the German Government determined to influence public opinion abroad by manipulation of the press, resorting to corruption if necessary. Twice the ambassador in London was instructed to remind the British press of the assassination of the king and queen of Serbia in 1903 and to create sympathy for the Austrian point of view.§ To the British press no suggestion of financial reward was to be made; but toward other countries there was no such squeamishness. The ambassador in Rome was bluntly asked "what sum" was needed for influencing the local press,‖ and the Vienna Cabinet was urged "to seek to influence the Italian press with money."¶ When Tschirschky reported that Vienna would welcome it "with real gratitude" if the German ambassador in St. Petersburg would help his Austrian colleague, who had "unlimited sums at his disposal," to get in

---

* Rumbold to Grey, 20 July; B 73.   † Jagow to Tschirschky, 18 July; G 70.
‡ Rumbold to Grey, 20 July; B 73.
§ Jagow to Lichnowsky, 12 and 15 July; G 36, 48.
‖ Jagow to Flotow, 15 July; G 47.   ¶ Jagow to Tschirschky, 21 July; G 97.

touch with the Russian press,* Count Pourtalès was instructed
to "assist Count Szápáry in finding intermediaries for the purpose of financially influencing the local press."† In this matter
the conduct of the German foreign minister was as shameless
as the activity of M. Izvolski in Paris.

Certain other manœuvres of the German Government are
equally illuminating. On 16 July the chancellor wrote to the
secretary of state for Alsace-Lorraine:

> We have reasons for assuming and are bound to wish that
> France, which is burdened at the moment with all sorts of
> troubles, will do everything she can to restrain Russia from
> intervening. This task will be made materially easier for the
> present wielders of power in Paris if the French nationalists
> find no cause for agitation out of which to make capital in
> the next few weeks.

Consequently, press polemics were to be avoided and irritat-
ing administrative measures should be postponed. And Herr
von Bethmann concluded with a rosy picture of what was to
be gained: "If we are successful not only in keeping France
quiet but in having Russia admonished to keep the peace, the
effect on the Franco-Russian alliance will be very favorable
for us."‡ Very favorable indeed! Unless Russia felt sure of
French support, she could not protest effectively against the
Austrian action, and she would resent deeply the defection of
her ally. The letter lends strong support to the view that an
important motive for the German promise to Austria-Hungary was the desire to disrupt the Triple Entente. Incidentally, it shows that in July, 1914, the German Government
considered the policy of France to be eminently pacific.

For the handling of Great Britain more positive measures
were considered necessary. On this same day, 16 July, Herr
von Jagow addressed a long letter to Albert Ballin, the direc-
tor-general of the Hamburg-American Line, who had long

* Tschirschky to Bethmann-Hollweg, 22 July; G 128.
† Jagow to Pourtalès, telegram, 24 July; G 143.
‡ Bethmann-Hollweg to Roedern, 16 July; G 58.

been a zealous supporter of an Anglo-German understanding. The shipping magnate was informed that "negotiations are going on between London and St. Petersburg for a naval convention, in which . . . a far-reaching military and naval co-operation is being sought by Russia." In order to "make a new attempt to cause the plan to fail" [direct diplomatic representations had already been tried], it was suggested to Ballin that he send a word of warning to one of his English friends, *e.g.,* Lord Haldane. More than that, a method of procedure was outlined:

You might write a letter stating that you had learned at Kiel [at the end of June, when the Emperor's annual regatta was held] that the announcement in the *Tageblatt* had some foundation of fact. Our naval circles were very much excited about it, and you foresaw that a new inevitable and intensive naval scare might result, with new and far-reaching provisions for the fleet. Even in the Wilhelmstrasse they were drawing long faces and asking themselves if the whole weary work of a *rapprochement* with England was now to fall hopelessly in ruins. The feeling that the ring of iron was closing about us more tightly every moment might finally even lead to serious consequences, in connection with the threat of the ever-increasing strength of Russia and the ever more aggressive tendencies of Pan-Slavism.*

In ordinary circumstances no great importance would be attached to this manœuvre. Ballin had acted before this as an intermediary in Anglo-German relations, and ostensibly he was now being asked merely to reinforce by a private warning what the German Government had already said officially. But the circumstances of the moment were not ordinary. The German Government was aware that a sudden and provocative diplomatic stroke was being prepared by Austria-Hungary; it had sanctioned its ally's plan in the expectation of British neutrality in the ensuing crisis; and now it was being informed by its ambassador that Sir Edward Grey was recommending moderation to the Cabinet of Vienna and that "sym-

* Jagow to Ballin, 15 July, despatched 16 July; G 56.

pathy here [London] will turn instantly and impulsively to the Serbs just as soon as Austria resorts to violence."* But all might still be well if the attention of the British Government could be diverted from the situation in the Balkans, where Great Britain had no direct interests, to the problem of the North Sea, which was of prime interest. Certainly the last sentence of Herr von Jagow's hints to Ballin suggests that the foreign minister hoped to intimidate the British Government into accepting the Austrian programme by the threat of a renewed naval competition and even of an ultimate appeal to arms.

On receipt of the letter, Herr Ballin, instead of writing at once to Lord Haldane, came to Berlin for a conference. He learned that "Austria would address a very sharp note to Serbia and that an answer dictated by Russia was expected." He was also told that "the reports of the German ambassador were not regarded as sufficiently reliable and complete," and he was asked to go to London to secure first-hand information about the political situation and the temper of English opinion. It was expected, obviously, that Ballin would be able to report more favorably than Lichnowsky was doing, and that he would influence opinion in high circles in the manner desired in Berlin. Ballin accepted the commission and went to London. In later days he complained that the Wilhelmstrasse had not been frank with him and had abused his intimate relations with British politicians; which would seem to be true.†

THE ATTITUDE OF ITALY

It is easy enough to understand why the Powers of the Triple Entente were kept in the dark about the intentions of the Austrian Government and why discreet steps were taken to handicap the possible action of France and Great Britain. But it may not be so evident, at first glance, why the decision was taken on 6 July not to inform Italy beforehand of the

---

* Lichnowsky to foreign office, telegram, 14 July; G 43. The ambassador repeated this opinion in another telegram two days later; G 55.

† Huldermann, *Albert Ballin*, pp. 300–301. Lichnowsky was not informed of Ballin's mission and did not hear of it until 1915. Lichnowsky, I, 247.

proposed action. We have seen that the treaty of the Triple
Alliance had been renewed in December, 1912, eighteen
months before its expiration, and that the alliance had presented a solid and effective front during the Balkan wars.
To such an extent had confidence—seemingly—been restored
between Italy and the Central Powers that in November, 1913,
an elaborate naval convention, marked "valid for 1914," had
been signed, and in March, 1914, a new military convention
arranged between the German and Italian staffs by which two
Italian army corps and three cavalry divisions were to join
the German armies engaged in a campaign against France.
It might be supposed that Germany and Austria-Hungary
would have valued the material assistance of Italy sufficiently
to refrain from any step which might give umbrage to their
ally. Moreover, Austria-Hungary's obligation was clearly defined, for Article VII of the treaty provided that action in the
Balkan Peninsula, by either Austria-Hungary or Italy, which
threatened to disturb the *status quo* required the previous
consent of the other Power.* Nevertheless the Austro-Hungarian Government proposed, and the German Government
consented, to ignore the solemn stimulation of the treaty.†

Count Berchtold later professed to be afraid that the Italian
Government, "in view of its Serbophile attitude, might easily
let something be known in Belgrade,"‡ and that "every hint,
even the slightest, would be immediately passed on to Russia";§
these fears were, as will be seen presently, not without justification.‖ But the real reason was, as the British ambassador

---

† Not only were the Austrian and German ambassadors instructed not to inform
the Italian foreign minister, the Marquis di San Giuliano, of the Austrian intentions: although the project of alliance with Bulgaria had been abandoned on 8 July,
both ambassadors were ordered to prepare the Italian minister for the conclusion
of such a treaty! Berchtold to Mérey, 12 July: A I 16. Jagow to Flotow, 11 July;
G 33.
‡ Stolberg to Jagow, private, 18 July; G 87.
§ Tschirschky to Bethmann-Hollweg, 20 July; G 94.
‖ It was only on the urgent representation of his ambassador in Rome that "in
order to prevent the Marquis di San Giuliano from taking personal offense," Count
Berchtold consented that the Italian foreign minister should be informed of the
Austro-Hungarian note on the day before its presentation in Belgrade. Mérey to
Berchtold, 14 July; Berchtold to Mérey, 15 July: A I 20, 22.

in Vienna put it, that "Italy would certainly have rejected the policy embodied in the note of July 23rd if she had been invited to indorse it."* Just a year before, Count Berchtold had sounded the Cabinet of Rome on the question of military action against Serbia, and had met with an uncompromising veto.† Now, assured of German support, he was going ahead with military action. Whatever Article VII of the alliance might specify about previous consultation and approval, he could not abide by its stipulations without endangering his whole plan.‡

In addition to this compelling reason, there was the further consideration that, notwithstanding the co-operation practised during the Balkan wars, the traditional animosities and suspicions of the two countries had flared up again in the spring of 1914. Incidents at Trieste arising out of the Austrian policy of encouraging the Slovene element against the Italian had led to irredentist demonstrations in Italy and debates in the Italian parliament against which the Austrian ambassador felt called upon to protest.§ In Albania, where the Prince of Wied was already facing an empty treasury and a tottering throne, Austro-Hungarian and Italian agents were working against each other, to the annoyance and disgust of Germany.‖ Likewise the Italian Government was thoroughly suspicious of Count Berchtold's opposition to the union of Serbia and Montenegro.¶ Early in July the Italian ambassador in Berlin, in the course of a long despatch devoted to Austro-Italian relations, said:

There is not a single question in which the interests of Italy

---

* Bunsen to Grey, 1 September; B 676.   † See above, pp. 136–138.

‡ "It was only by the creation of a *fait accompli* that it was probably possible to secure Italy's neutrality for a certain period which must lead Italy to participate in the war with or against us, according to the fortunes of the war. If he [Berchtold] had taken the Italian Government into his confidence as fully as he did the German, Italy would presumably have at once asked for the cession of the Trentino as compensation. In the existing circumstances, this demand would have been rejected as not open to discussion, and it would have come to a conflict which would have driven Italy to join our enemies much earlier." Hoyos, pp. 65–66.

§ *G. P.*, XXXIX, 404–409; Salandra, *La neutralità italiana*, pp. 44–50.
‖ *G. P.*, XXXVI, 595–741.   ¶ *G. P.*, XXXVIII, 325–361.

are not, or are not supposed to be, in contradiction with those of Austria, in which the policy of one government is not directed to watching jealously and more often to combating that of the other and to fortifying itself against it; they are inspired only by the conviction that what gives aid to the one must necessarily bring disadvantage to the other.*

What Austria-Hungary now proposed to do was so obviously contrary to the interests of Italy, whose policy it had been for a generation to oppose the extension of Habsburg influence in the Balkans, that Count Berchtold's unwillingness to forearm Italy by forewarning her was intelligible. To keep Italy in the dark was indeed the only sensible course to take.†

As a matter of fact, the Italian Government seems to have had an instinctive feeling‡ that Austria-Hungary would, after the provocation of Sarajevo, proceed to extreme measures, and it did not wait to be informed of the Austrian plans before indicating its attitude. Three times, on 12, 14, and 15 July, the Marquis di San Giuliano spoke to the German ambassador in Rome to urge moderation toward Serbia. "Austria," he said, "should not permit herself to be unfair in this matter."§ In the first place,

Italy would not be able to support the Austrian accusations without setting herself in opposition to the deep-seated convictions of the Italian people and to liberal principles . . . the Italian Government could never take up arms against the principle of nationality.

This meant that Italy would not, "in the event of serious complications," stand by Austria-Hungary,|| and that she would

---

* Bollati to San Giuliano, 8 July; Salandra, p. 52.
† Berchtold pressed his ambassador in Rome to influence the Italian press in favor of the Austro-Hungarian policy, authorizing him to spend 50,000 lire. Berchtold to Mérey, telegrams, 11, 13, 16 July; Ö.-U. A., 10,203, 10,245, 10,362. Mérey in reply pointed out that, quite apart from the hopelessness of trying to manipulate the Italian press, any effort to do so would reveal the intention of Vienna to take drastic action against Serbia, and he strongly advised against this course. Mérey to Berchtold, telegrams, 15, 18 July; Ö.-U. A., 10,290, 10,363.
‡ Cf. Mérey to Berchtold, telegram, 12 July; Ö.-U. A., 10,222.
§ Flotow to foreign office, telegram, 12 July; G 38.
|| Flotow to foreign office, telegram, 14 July; G 42.

not tolerate territorial acquisitions at the expense of Serbia.* Secondly, the action planned by Austria could "in no way lead to the desired result." Even if Serbia accepted the Austrian demands and suppressed the propagandist societies, "the agitation would simply change from a public to a secret character." Italian history, so the minister argued, ought to prove to Austria the futility of "police measures in such national questions"; and his opinion was that "if the Serbian question can be solved at all within the present status of Austria, it will only be possible by providing the Austrian Serbs with an interest in remaining part of Austria and in standing by Austria."† These remarks left the German ambassador under no illusions. "I have the impression," Herr von Flotow reported, "that it will be extremely difficult, not to say impossible, to persuade Italy to go with us in the event of European complications."‡

The reports of Herr von Flotow evidently impressed the German foreign minister. It is worth noting that Herr von Jagow was not in Berlin on 6 July when the German chancellor agreed to the proposal of the Austro-Hungarian Government that Italy should not be informed of the intended action. Now Herr von Jagow had served as ambassador in Rome before his appointment as foreign minister, and he was credited with understanding the Italians unusually well. Although he acquiesced in the policy adopted on 6 July, he was too experienced not to appreciate the importance of what the Marquis di San Giuliano had been saying and the warning of his own ambassador. He therefore took up, in a long despatch composed by himself, the task of making the dangers of the situation plain to Vienna.

There is no doubt in my mind [he wrote to Herr von Tschir-

* Flotow to foreign office, telegram, 15 July; G 51.
† Flotow to Bethmann-Hollweg, 16 July; G 73. It is interesting to observe that San Giuliano had learned the general character of the intended Austrian note. One may guess that Count Lützow had informed the Italian as well as the British ambassador in Vienna, or that the latter told his Italian colleague what he had learned.
‡ Flotow to Bethmann-Hollweg, 16 July; G 64.

schky] that in case of an Austro-Serbian conflict [Italy] will take a pronounced stand on the side of Serbia. A territorial expansion of the Austro-Hungarian Monarchy, or even an extension of its influence in the Balkans, will be looked upon in Italy with horror and as prejudicial to her position. . . . Quite apart from the fact that the policy of the government in Italy is dependent not inconsiderably on the voice of public opinion, the view mentioned above dominates the thinking of the majority of Italian statesmen. Whenever there has been question of a threat to Serbia on the part of Austria, I have been able to observe an extraordinary nervousness. Should Italy take the side of Serbia, the Russian disposition to act would, without question, be materially encouraged. In St. Petersburg it would be assumed that not only would Italy not fulfil her obligations as ally but would, if possible, turn directly against Austria-Hungary. The collapse of the Monarchy would indeed also open up to Italy the prospect of winning certain long-coveted territories.

In my opinion, therefore, it is of the *greatest* importance that Vienna should enter upon an exchange of view with the Cabinet of Rome concerning the aims to be followed in Serbia in the event of a conflict and keep it [Italy] on its [Vienna's] side, or—since a conflict with Serbia alone does not imply the *casus foederis*—keep it strictly neutral. According to its agreements with Austria, Italy has a right to compensation for every change in the Balkans that is to the advantage of the Danube monarchy. These, then, would constitute the object and the bait of the negotiations.

For form's sake Herr von Jagow mentioned Valona, but said frankly that "according to our information" this would not be considered "an acceptable compensation," and then boldly declared that "the acquisition of the Trentino is probably the only thing that would be regarded as ample compensation." He therefore instructed Herr von Tschirschky to have "a thorough and confidential discussion" with Count Berchtold. For the matter was really serious:

The attitude adopted by Italy will in any event have considerable influence on Russia's attitude toward the conflict with

Serbia; and should a general conflagration arise out of the latter, it would be of great military importance for us.*

Three days later, Herr von Jagow sent a second despatch to Vienna. Although this time he talked of Valona rather than of the Trentino, he closed on a serious note:

There can be no illusions in Vienna that an Austrian attack on Serbia will not only meet with a very unfavorable reception in Italy, but will presumably encounter direct opposition. For that reason I consider an early agreement between the Cabinets of Vienna and Rome urgently necessary, and I think that this would be materially simplified if Italy were engaged in Albania with Austria's consent.†

The Austro-Hungarian statesmen were deaf to argument, for they knew that they had the Germans at their mercy. The latter were reminded that they had consented to Italy's being kept in the dark: "they had admitted in Berlin that Hoyos, with whom this point had been discussed, was right." Count Berchtold "disclosed great optimism, seeming to think that Italy could not possibly be so despicable an ally as to turn against the Monarchy";‡ and Count Hoyos even denied Italy's right to compensation.§ On a second attempt, Tschirschky made

* Jagow to Tschirschky, "secret," 15 July; G 46. Jagow may have got the idea of using the Trentino as a bait for Italy from a recent despatch from Flotow. Early in the month the ambassador had discussed with San Giuliano the possibility that Austria-Hungary might consent to the union of Serbia and Montenegro in return for the cession of Mount Lovchen by Montenegro. At first the Italian minister used threatening language: "We [Germany] must not doubt for a moment that such procedure on the part of Austria would mean not only the end of the Triple Alliance, but an Italian war against Austria. This war would be prosecuted by every means, by stirring up revolution in Austria and with the help of the Serbs and Russians." But when the ambassador protested, San Giuliano declared that "the only possibility of making this eventuality acceptable to Italian public opinion would be a cession of territory in the Trentino to Italy." Flotow to Bethmann-Hollweg, 10 July; G. P., XXXVIII, 357–358.
† Jagow to Tschirschky, 18 July; G 68.
‡ The Austrian ambassador in Constantinople told his Bulgarian colleague that "Italy will act 'solidaire' with her allies." Toshev to Radoslavov, 21 July; KSF, VI, 231 (March, 1928).
§ Stolberg to Jagow, private letter, 18 July; G 87. In order to give the suggestion an unofficial character, it was presented by the counsellor of the embassy, Prince Stolberg, rather than by the ambassador. Schoen to Hertling, 18 July; Dirr, p. 11. Hoyos merely "listened in very friendly fashion" and mentioned the Dodecanese

use of "all the material" with which he had been supplied, but he might as well have argued with Conrad von Hötzendorf. Count Berchtold said flatly:

If Rome was unable at present to consider a practical and extensive Austro-Italian co-operation, well, there was no occasion at all for such a co-operation; Austria demanded neither co-operation nor support, but simply abstention from any hostile proceeding against an ally.

He thought that San Giuliano was bluffing; and he hoped to "make it possible for Italy to take her stand by the side of Austria" by a declaration that "Austria-Hungary had no territorial aggrandizement of any sort in view for herself as a result of her action against Serbia." But he could not allow himself, he said, to be intimidated by such news from Rome,* and he went so far as to hint that the Italian Government had got wind of the Austrian intentions through the indiscretions of the German ambassador.† By way of showing his annoyance with the German interference, Berchtold instructed Szö-

as "a possible compensation" for Italy; to which Jagow replied that "England would always be opposed to the complete surrender of the Dodecanese," and that consequently the Austrian consent would hardly be looked upon in Rome as a satisfactory compensation. Jagow to Tschirschky, telegram, 20 July; G 89.

* As a matter of fact, Berchtold had himself received much the same news from Rome. His ambassador reported that Italy would advise Serbia to accept and fulfil moderate demands on the part of Austria-Hungary, but that an armed conflict with Serbia would have disastrous consequences. "The traditional sympathies for Serbia here, Italy's aspirations in the Balkan peninsula, the danger of a European conflagration at a moment when her army is disorganized and her financial situation bad, and the terrifying prospect that after crushing Serbia we might recover our so greatly diminished prestige in the Balkans and eventually even secure territorial advantages—all this will automatically draw Italy and her sympathies to the side opposed to us. Article VII of the treaty of the Triple Alliance will be brought forward against us, theories about the equilibrium and the status quo in the Balkans and more particularly in the Adriatic will be adduced. Furthermore, by leaving Italy to one side and taking her by surprise, we shall touch a most sensitive spot, namely, the feeling that it is contrary to the traditions of Italy 'not to be on hand' [nicht dabei zu sein] in an important European action. . . . Only one thing seems certain to me: that in the event of a military reckoning with Serbia, our relations with Italy will for years—as at the time of the Bosnian crisis— take a very bad turn." Mérey, however, did not object to the policy of Vienna; he was content to point out its probable effect on Italy. Mérey to Berchtold, 16 July; Ö.-U. A., 10,308.

† Tschirschky to Bethmann-Hollweg, 20 July; G 94. Berchtold's version of the conversation is in A I 35. On the question of 'leakage' from the German embassy, see Mérey to Berchtold, 18 July, and Berchtold to Mérey, 20 July; A I 24, 33.

gyény to inform the German Government that "a discussion between Italy and the Monarchy about the interpretation of Article VII [of the treaty of the Triple Alliance] ought to be avoided at the present moment"!*

Indeed, in order to avoid a discussion, Count Berchtold assumed the offensive against Rome. In the expectation that the Marquis di San Giuliano would raise the question of Article VII, Herr von Mérey was provided with a long argument to prove that the Italian interpretation was not justified. Though not denying that an Austro-Hungarian action "in the Balkans" required the previous approval of Italy, Count Berchtold asserted that the phrase "in the Balkans" [dans les Balcans] referred only to territory belonging to Turkey (the wording had been adopted in 1887, when Turkey possessed large territories in Europe), and that therefore a temporary occupation of Serbian territory—which he admitted might be necessary—would not infringe the status quo envisaged by Article VII.† The ambassador was, however, to suggest to the Italian foreign minister that

instead of carrying on a judicial discussion of the interpretation of an article, it would be to the interests of both to consider the situation from the view-point of the great interests of Austria-Hungary and Italy as friends and allies.‡

And since "the Marquis di San Giuliano, with a just appreciation of the international situation, had repeatedly said that what Italy wanted was a strong Austria-Hungary," Count Berchtold submitted that at the present moment, when the Monarchy was proposing to clear up its relations with Serbia, "Italy's interests demand that she should side openly with Austria." A peaceful solution of the Austro-Serbian difficulty was, he averred, "quite possible"; but in any case, "the Cabinet of Vienna was far from thinking of a war of con-

* Berchtold to Szögyény, telegram, 22 July; Gooss, p. 121; Ö.-U. A., 10,479.
† Berchtold to Mérey, 20 July; A I 32.
‡ Berchtold to Mérey, 21 July; A I 42. Szögyény was instructed to make use of the same argument in case Jagow again urged a discussion with Italy. Berchtold to Szögyény, 22 July; A I 48.

quest or of the annexation of any part of Serbia," and the rumor of the *Temps* that "we are about to seize Mount Lovchen by surprise" was quite baseless.* In short, said Count Berchtold, they were convinced that they "could rely on the loyalty of Italy and her fidelity to the alliance."†

The result of this manœuvre "to show the greatest complaisance to Italy"‡ was somewhat curious. Mérey reported more optimistically than was to have been expected on his interview with San Giuliano. Although the Italian minister, said the ambassador, urged a policy of conciliation rather than one of violence, he declared his "determined intention to support us if our demands on Serbia are such that they can be legitimately complied with," promised to control the press after he learned the contents of the note to Belgrade, agreed to advise Montenegro to remain quiet, and asserted that he "had already advised Belgrade in a conciliatory sense." Such friendly language made the Austro-Hungarian ambassador feel that San Giuliano "does not expect war for the present, but believes that Serbia will give way" to pressure of the Powers.§ Count Berchtold replied by pointing out that Austria held the trumps against Italy: "the alliance, the declaration of territorial disinterestedness, the Albanian agreement, and, in

* The Italian ambassador and the Serbian minister in Paris expressed their fears that Austria might attack Mount Lovchen, "in order to secure a position dominating Montenegro and enabling them to prevent co-operation between Montenegro and Servia." Bunsen to Grey, 21 July; B 71. The *Messagero* declared that "no Italian Government would allow the Lovchen to fall into Austrian hands," and that the question was "an international one." De Salis to Grey, 26 July; B 652.

† Berchtold to Mérey, 20 July; A I 34.

‡ Tschirschky to foreign office, telegram, 21 July; G 104.

§ Mérey to Berchtold, telegram, 21 July; A I 43. On the same day Tschirschky informed Berchtold of a conversation with the Italian ambassador in Vienna, "who had expressed his conviction that the Italian Government would loyally fulfil its obligations as an ally in the dispute between Austria-Hungary and Serbia, and would stand by Austria's side, even if public opinion in Italy objected and raised its voice in protest." Memorandum of 21 July; A I 44. The Italian ambassador in London said just the opposite to Prince Lichnowsky. "It would be extremely difficult for any Italian Government to advocate, in opposition to the country, taking part in a war the object of which was perhaps the conquest or Austrianization of Serbia." But he added a remark which seemed to bear out Jagow's interpretation of Italian policy: "The war would run directly counter to Italian interests and could be undertaken only if Austria were to hold out prospect of adequate compensation." Lichnowsky to foreign office, telegram, 23 July; G 124.

the matter of Article VII, the Italian occupation of the Ægean Islands." Mérey was therefore not only to keep Italy loyal to the alliance, but to make clear that "separate action by Italy at Valona would create the most painful impression in the Monarchy" and "involve most serious [*grössten*] complications."* So he did not depart from the policy settled upon at the start.

The German ambassador in Rome got quite a different impression of the state of affairs; and rightly. On 18 July Herr von Jagow had represented to Signor Bollati, the Italian ambassador, that "the most practicable way of restraining Russia would be for the Triple Alliance to demonstrate its solidarity."† To this overture the Marquis di San Giuliano replied:

Italy is not bound to take part in an eventual war provoked by an aggressive action of Austria against Serbia which the entire political world will condemn; nor can we take any step favorable to Austria-Hungary without first being sure of the interpretation of Article VII of the treaty and until the question of compensation has been settled.‡

Consequently it is hardly surprising that Herr von Flotow, telegraphing on 22 July that San Giuliano considered the situation "extremely serious,"§ he begged for "any new con-

* Berchtold to Mérey, private, 21 July, sent 23 July; Gooss, pp. 125–127; *Ö.- U. A.*, 10,459.
† Bollati to San Giuliano, 18 July; Salandra, p. 71.
‡ San Giuliano to Bollati, 20 July; Salandra, pp. 70–71. It is possible to interpret this language as a hint that Italian participation might be purchased by the offer of adequate compensation, and a well-informed Italian historian has written: "The moment news of the Austrian ultimatum to Serbia arrived in Italy, the Italian Nationalists opened a campaign for Italian intervention on the side of the Central Powers and Italian forces began concentrating in the general direction of the frontiers of France. If, before hurling that ultimatum, the governments at Berlin and Vienna had come to an understanding with Rome, if they had offered Italy the Trentino with a proportionate share in the colonial fruits of victory, it is certain that an overwhelming majority, not of the Italian people, but of Italian statesmen, would have accepted such a proposition and forced the country into the war on the side of Austria and Germany." G. Salvemini, "Italian Diplomacy during the World War," in *Foreign Affairs* (New York), IV, 294 (January, 1926). This statement cannot at present be controlled. We shall see that German diplomacy did not give up its efforts to bring Italy into line until the very end.
§ Three days before he regarded it as "serious." Flotow to foreign office, telegram, 19 July; G 78.

siderations" which he might present to the Italian Government.* San Giuliano, he reported the next day, was not "entirely satisfied by Austria's assurances of disinterestedness," and Premier Salandra was demanding a discussion.†

It was evident that Italy could not be counted on if Austria-Hungary persisted in her course. But the German Government, either because it had already discounted the probable defection of Italy, or because, having met with one rebuff from Vienna, it did not care to risk another, did not provide Herr von Flotow with "any new considerations" or urge Count Berchtold to make concessions. It was content to let matters take their course.

Since the Italian Government has not published any documents for the crisis of July, 1914,‡ it has been necessary to analyze its views from other sources; and these sources, naturally, tell but little of any moves which the Italian Government may have been making as the crisis began to be foreshadowed. But they do provide a few indications which show how hopeless it was for Count Berchtold to expect Italian co-operation in or approval of his policy. The Austro-Hungarian minister himself complained that the Marquis di San Giuliano had sent instructions to his representatives in St. Petersburg and Bucharest "to bring it about indirectly that the respective governments should threaten Berlin and Vienna and thus prevent the Austrian action against Serbia."§ This may be an exaggeration; but there is no doubt that the Italian ambassador in St. Petersburg informed M. Sazonov of the nature of the intended Austrian action|| or that the minister in Bucharest requested the Rumanian Government to "make representations in Vienna in favor of the Austrian demands being made possible of acceptance by Serbia."¶

* Flotow to foreign office, telegram, 22 July; G 109.
† Flotow to foreign office, telegram, 23 July; G 119.
‡ Salandra, *passim*, gives a few documents.
§ Berchtold to Mérey, 21 July; A I 33.
|| Baron M. F. Schilling, *How the War Began in 1914: Diary of the Russian Foreign Office*, 3–20 July, 1914 [O. S.] (London, 1925), p. 25.
¶ Waldburg to foreign office, telegram, 23 July; G 135.

Still another indication of the Italian unwillingness to follow the Central Powers is found in the ingenious suggestion of the foreign minister to the British ambassador on 22 July:

The Marquis di San Giuliano said that as our two nations were associated with groups which were by force of circumstances likely to be ranged in antagonism, it seemed quite conceivable that, in the special circumstances of the case, we might arrange to "pair," like members of the British Parliament.

The ambassador did not commit himself to "this new form of counter-insurance"; but he wrote to his chief:

It is difficult for me to believe that some way will not be found here, if a conflict should arise, of evading the obligations of an alliance, the perils of which the present situation is calculated forcibly to illustrate.*

Thus, before the crisis was formally opened by the presentation of the Austro-Hungarian note, it was obvious that the Central Powers would suffer a sharp diplomatic defeat in their effort to secure Italian support for their action. They did not, however, alter their policy in consequence.

* Rodd to Grey, 22 July; B 161. The next day, Sir Rennell Rodd wrote even more frankly: "In view of the very grave consequences which may ensue, it is evident that the Italian Government are already preoccupied with studying the manner in which they can best find a plausible reason for not becoming involved." Rodd to Grey, 23 July; B 162.

CHAPTER VIII

THE TRIPLE ENTENTE

EUROPE was not unaccustomed to the assassination of high political personages. Anarchists had assassinated the President of the French Republic in 1894, the Empress of Austria in 1898, the King of Italy in 1900. In 1908 the King of Portugal and his eldest son had been killed in the streets of Lisbon. In Russia terrorism had removed one Tsar and more than one Grand Duke. The King of Greece had been murdered at Salonica in 1913. But not one of these tragic incidents had caused any international difficulty, for they were obviously the work of depraved individuals or protests against notorious misgovernment. The murder at Sarajevo, on the other hand, was regarded at once as having a grave international bearing; for the fact, speedily known, that the assassin was of the Serbian race and the rumor that the plot had been hatched in Belgrade gave every reason to fear that a new crisis would be provoked in the long and bitter rivalry of Austria-Hungary and Serbia.

Sympathy with Austria was indeed universal. "The assassination at Sarajevo," reported the German ambassador to Russia, "has, it seems, made a deep impression here, and condemnation of the shameless deed was expressed far and wide at the earliest moment."* The Tsarina is said to have wept without ceasing; M. Sazonov, calling at the Austrian embassy to express his sympathy, wrote on his card, *"Quel abominable crime!"*† and he assured the chargé that "the struggle against conspiracy was becoming more and more a common interest of monarchies."‡ Even the nationalist *Novoye Vremya* appeared to share the general indignation, for it published a number of telegrams expressing sympathy for the victims and the

---

* Pourtalès to Bethmann-Hollweg, 13 July; G 53.   † Scott, p. 159.
‡ Otto Czernin to Berchtold, 3 July; Ö.-U. A., 10,017.

414

House of Habsburg. In France, public opinion was too deeply absorbed in the parliamentary situation and in the impending trial of Madame Caillaux to pay much attention to an incident that was far away; still the press was not unsympathetic, and the *Temps* praised the dead Archduke for his devotion to duty. Across the Channel, where political murders have always been strongly condemned, there was genuine indignation. In spite of the distrust of Austrian policy which had grown up in late years, the Habsburg Monarchy still had many friends in England and it is not surprising that the British press, "basing their information upon reports coming from Austrian sources" (so the Serbian minister complained),* generally attributed the Sarajevo crime to Serbian revolutionaries. Sir Edward Grey expressed the official condolences of his government and his own personal sympathies in elevated and obviously sincere words;† Englishmen in general were not a little moved by the hard fate of the aged Emperor Francis Joseph, who had had to bear the loss, through violence, first of his son, then of his wife, and now of his heir.

In most countries, however, the real feeling appears to have been somewhat different. In Italy, according to the British ambassador, "while ostensibly the authorities and the press have been loud in their denunciations of the crime and full of sympathy with the Emperor, it is obvious that people generally have regarded the elimination of the late Archduke as almost providential."‡ The opinion in Paris was that "with the disappearance of his Imperial and Royal Highness a source of constant uneasiness has vanished."§ From St. Petersburg the British ambassador wrote:

Now that the first feeling of horror evoked by the assassination of the Archduke and his consort has passed away, the general impression would seem to be one of relief that so

---

* Boskovich to Pashich, 1 July; S 7.
† Grey to Bunsen and Mensdorff, 29 June; B 14, 15.
‡ Rodd to Grey, 7 July; B 36. The reports of the Austrian ambassador and military attaché were much to the same effect. *Ö.-U. A.*, 9988; Conrad, IV, 25.
§ Report of the Austrian military attaché, 4 July; Conrad, IV, 23

dangerous a personality should have been removed from the succession to the throne.*

The German ambassador got much the same impression, for he lamented that "not only in the press but among social circles one met with almost nothing but unfriendly criticism of the murdered Archduke, with the suggestion that in him Russia had lost a bitter enemy."† The best description of the situation would be what the Germans call *Schadenfreude.*

With such sentiments current in Rome, Paris, and St. Petersburg, any effort by Austria-Hungary to capitalize the death of Francis Ferdinand by making it an excuse for drastic action was likely to meet with difficulties. The British foreign office was probably justified in affirming, in 1914, that

both the governments and the public opinion of Europe were ready to support [Austria] in any measures, however severe, which she might think it necessary to take for the punishment of the murderer and his accomplices.‡

But there was no disposition to give Austria-Hungary a free hand to do as she liked: punishment for the crime was one thing, the subversion of Serbia quite another, and this point of view the Powers of the Triple Entente made no effort to conceal.

GREAT BRITAIN

The murder of Sarajevo occurred at a moment when British politics and opinion were more confused and uncertain than they had been since the days of the first Reform Bill. The approaching crisis in the struggle over Irish Home Rule entirely absorbed the activities of politicians and weighed heavily on the public mind. Party passions had reached such a pitch that London society was rent asunder; the government's attempt to use the army and navy as instruments of its Irish policy had

* Buchanan to Nicolson, 9 July; B 49.
† Pourtalès to Bethmann-Hollweg, 13 July; G 53.
‡ *Great Britain and the European Crisis*, Introductory Narrative, p. iii.

provoked threats of mutiny and aroused the most violent criticism from its opponents; many signs pointed to civil war as impending. As the month of July advanced, the situation became steadily worse, until finally the King himself intervened: at his suggestion a conference of the party leaders was opened at Buckingham Palace on 21 July in the hope of discovering a possible basis of compromise between the desperate factions.* A more unfortunate moment for the handling of a grave European crisis could hardly be imagined, and it is quite possible that knowledge of this situation contributed to the German belief that Great Britain would remain neutral if a European war should result from the Austrian action against Serbia.†

British opinion was divided on the question of the Sarajevo crime. If on the one hand papers so far apart politically as the *Morning Post* (Conservative) and the *Daily Citizen* (Labor) agreed in blaming Austro-Hungarian policy and holding it responsible for the catastrophe, on the other hand the majority of the press believed that the Dual Monarchy had a legitimate grievance and urged Serbia to afford satisfaction.

The British Government does not appear to have been greatly alarmed by the situation. Sir Arthur Nicolson, the permanent under-secretary of the foreign office, expressed the opinion on 6 July that, apart from the Albanian muddle, "We have no very urgent and pressing question to preoccupy us in the rest

* A brilliant picture of those days is given by Churchill, pp. 181–187; American Edition, pp. 191–198.

† The then prime minister, Mr. Asquith (later the Earl of Oxford and Asquith), states this as a fact: "There is no doubt that the possibility, and even the probability, of civil war in these islands was a factor that entered into the minds and affected the calculations of the military junta, which had already captured the control of the policy of the Central Powers. They had come to the definite conclusion that in the event of war Great Britain could be ruled out as a combatant." Asquith, *The Genesis of the War*, p. 149. The counsellor of the German embassy in London, Richard von Kühlmann, is supposed to have sent secret reports, behind the back of the ambassador, misrepresenting and exaggerating the difficulties of the British Government in Ireland, especially after a visit there in the early part of the summer. Cf. *The Autobiography of Margot Asquith* (London, 1922), II, 165. No such reports have been published. As a matter of fact, Herr von Kühlmann never visited Ireland, and he left London on 6 July, not to return until the beginning of August, during which period he "had no communication, neither verbal nor written, with the authorities in Berlin." T. Rhodes, *The Real von Kühlmann* (London, 1925), p. 13. There is no mention of Ireland in any available German document for July, 1914, and we have no record of what the German Government thought about Ireland.

of Europe"*—a remark which may be ranked with the classic statement of his predecessor on the eve of the Franco-German war.† Three days later he wrote:

I have my doubts whether Austria will take any action of a serious character, and I expect the storm will blow over.‡

Sir Edward Grey was equally optimistic. "The minister was in a thoroughly confident mood," noted the German ambassador on 9 July, "and declared in cheerful tones that he saw no reason for taking a pessimistic view of the situation."§ He himself has explained why he felt confidence:

For the first weeks [of July] the attitude of the Government in Vienna was neither extreme nor alarmist. There seemed to be good reason for the hope that, while treating the matter as one to be dealt with by Austria alone, they would handle it in such a way as not to involve Europe in the consequences.‖

As late as 15 July he told the Russian ambassador that he had not received any disturbing news from Vienna or Berlin, and, so Count Benckendorff thought, "did not appear very uneasy."¶

Yet if the British foreign secretary declined to grow alarmed, he had in fact made a significant statement to the German Government. Prince Lichnowsky, the German ambassador in London, had gone on leave at the end of June. In Berlin he found the chancellor and Herr Zimmermann complaining of Russian armaments; he learned that "Herr von Tschirschky had been reprimanded because he reported that he had counselled moderation toward Serbia in Vienna"; and, before returning to

* Nicolson to Bunsen, private, 6 July; B 19.
† "I had the honour," said Lord Granville in the House of Lords on 11 July, 1870, "of receiving the seals of the Foreign Office last Wednesday. On the previous day I had an unofficial communication with the able and experienced Under-Secretary, Mr. Hammond, at the Foreign Office; and he told me that, with the exception of the sad and painful subject about to be discussed this evening [the murder of some English gentlemen by brigands in Greece], he had never, during his long experience, known so great a lull in foreign affairs, and that he was not aware of any important question that I should have to deal with." 3 *Hansard*, CCIII, 3. War between France and Prussia began on 19 July, 1870.
‡ Minute on B 40.   § Lichnowsky to Bethmann-Hollweg, 9 July; G 30.
‖ Grey, I, 309; American edition, I, 299.
¶ Benckendorff to Sazonov, 16 July; Siebert, p. 827. There is no record of this conversation in the British documents.

London, he heard that "Austria intended to take steps against Serbia in order to put an end to an impossible situation." "At the moment," the Prince wrote several years later, "I under-estimated the importance of the news."* But he was so much impressed by what he had heard in his brief visit that immediately on his return to London on 6 July he went to see Sir Edward Grey.

The ambassador told the foreign secretary that he had found "anxiety and pessimism" in Berlin. In the first place, the Austrians were demanding "some humiliation for Servia," and it would be difficult for Germany to restrain them; secondly, there was "apprehension in Germany about the attitude of Russia, especially in connection with the recent increase of Russian military strength"; "a third thing was the idea that there was some Naval Convention between Russia and England," and "if there was such an understanding for co-operation directed against Germany, it would strengthen chauvinistic feeling in Russia, it would make Pan-German feeling quite irresistible, and lead to an increase of the German naval law."

All this was no doubt familiar to Sir Edward Grey, but then, so he recorded,

The ambassador went so far as to say that there was some feeling in Germany, based more especially upon the second and third things that he had mentioned to me this afternoon, that trouble was bound to come and therefore it would be better not to restrain Austria and let the trouble come now, rather than later. He impressed upon me more than once that he was speaking quite privately and on very delicate matters, but he was anxious to keep in touch with me.

Sir Edward replied that "no new or secret understanding existed," and "cordially confirmed" the Prince's observation that England "did not wish to see the groups of Powers draw apart."† But—and this is the main point of the conversation

---

* Lichnowsky, I, 127–128.
† On the other hand, "he did not," Lichnowsky noted, "directly deny that the [British and Russian] fleets would be in touch in the event of a general war." Lichnowsky to Bethmann-Hollweg, 6 July; G 20.

—he said, in conclusion, "I should like to talk the whole matter of your conversation over with you later on, when I have had time to consider it."*

The British foreign secretary was so impressed by the ambassador's communication that he made it the subject of a speech in the cabinet, and that body, so the ambassador learned from one of its members, was "no little dismayed at the possibility of another acute crisis in European affairs."† Evidently it authorized the foreign secretary to make a statement to the German ambassador, for three days later Sir Edward Grey sent for Prince Lichnowsky, and their conversation assumed an unusual character.

First of all, Sir Edward communicated the memorandum of their conversation on 24 June, in which he had said, *à propos* of British relations with France and Russia, that

there was no alliance; no agreement committing us to action; and that all the agreements of that character that we had with France and Russia had been published. On the other hand, . . . though we were not bound by engagement as allies, we did from time to time talk as intimately as allies.‡

Next, he informed the Prince that "conversations had taken place between the Military and Naval authorities of France and Russia and ourselves," that "they began in 1906." Everything, so Sir Edward insisted, "had been on the footing that the hands of the Governments were quite free," and he said he "supposed that Germany had her own Naval and Military arrangements with the other members of the Triple Alliance."§ He seemed to wish to minimize the importance of his com-

---

* Grey to Rumbold, 6 July; B 32.
† Lichnowsky, I, 42. His informant was Lord Beauchamp.
‡ Grey to Goschen, 24 June; B 4.
§ Lichnowsky replied, on this point, that "the Alliance remained as it was in Prince Bismarck's time: it was purely defensive and it did not include any Naval Agreement with regard to the Mediterranean." Actually, an elaborate naval convention had been concluded in the summer of 1913, which was "valid for 1914." Unless the Prince was deliberately lying, which there is no reason to suppose, his statement shows that he did not fully enjoy the confidence of his government, as he complained in his subsequent writings. Lichnowsky, I, 39, 245–247.

munication, for he denied more than once that there was "any Agreement that entailed obligations." But, in fact, Sir Edward Grey was revealing a jealously guarded secret, one that for years was kept from the British Cabinet itself and which at the moment was not known to Parliament or the public.

Thirdly, the foreign secretary adverted to the European situation. After informing Prince Lichnowsky [as the latter reported to Berlin] that he had "already been endeavoring, in case the Vienna Cabinet should find itself compelled as a result of the murder at Sarajevo to adopt a sterner attitude toward Serbia, to persuade the Russian Government to take the matter quietly and to assume a conciliatory attitude toward Austria,"* Sir Edward Grey said:

If Austria's action with regard to Servia kept within certain bounds, it would of course be comparatively easy to encourage patience at St. Petersburg;† but there were some things that Austria might do that would make the Russian Government say that the Slav feeling in Russia was so strong that they must send an ultimatum or something of that sort.‡

Sir Edward Grey's action was certainly remarkable, and since he reported it to the British chargé in Berlin in a despatch marked "secret,"§ it is not unreasonable to suppose that he desired to make clear to the German Government that excessive demands on the part of Austria-Hungary would bring about Russian intervention, and that in a European crisis, Great Britain, while not bound by obligations, was prepared to act as her interests required. Having thus delivered him-

---

* Lichnowsky to Bethmann-Hollweg, 9 July; G 30. For Grey's remarks to Benckendorff, see his despatch to Buchanan, 8 July; B 39.

† Grey had already said to Paul Cambon that "we must do all we could to encourage patience in St. Petersburg," a sentiment in which the French ambassador "cordially concurred." Grey to Bertie, 8 July; B 38.

‡ Lichnowsky's version reads: "Very much would depend, as a matter of fact, Sir Edward thought, on the kind of measures that were under consideration, and on whether they might not arouse Slavic sentiment in such a fashion as to make it impossible for M. Sazonov to remain passive under them." Lichnowsky to Bethmann-Hollweg, 9 July; G 30.

§ Grey to Rumbold, "secret," 9 July; B 41.

self, the British foreign minister took no further action until
20 July.

In the interval the Austro-Serbian question began to be discussed in the British press. On 16 July the *Times* published
a leading article entitled "Austria-Hungary and Servia." Referring to the demands of the Austrian press for the punishment by Serbia of any persons found guilty of complicity in
the plot and for guarantees that agitation should not be encouraged by the Serbian Government, it remarked:

We agree, and we would add that it is also, and in the first
place, a duty which [Servia] owes to herself. We do not doubt
that she will perform it.

It condemned the "reckless and provocative language" of the
Serbian press, and advised the Serbian Government to begin
"without delay" the investigation which Austria would surely
demand, to conduct it "fairly and openly," and to communicate the results to the Powers. But the article concluded with
a grave warning:

Austria-Hungary, for her part, must remember that nothing is to be gained and that everything may be imperilled by
the adoption of the kind of policy for which the military organs clamor. The Southern Slav question is probably the most
formidable and the most difficult of all the many arduous
problems which she has to face, and her relations with Serbia
are a branch, and an important branch of it. How it may be
solved, or what would be the best means of approaching it, are
questions too large for discussion at this moment. But it certainly cannot be solved in a sense satisfactory to Austria-
Hungary by force, or by menaces of force which irritate but
do not strike terror. Any attempt to meet it in that fashion
would constitute a fresh peril to European peace, and that, we
are convinced, the Emperor and his most sagacious advisers
very clearly perceive. Austria-Hungary has acted with self-
possession and with restraint hitherto. We earnestly hope that
she will continue so to act until the end. Her own history since
the middle of the last century contains some very impressive
warnings of the irreparable mischief which a sudden fit of

impatience may do to a policy that has been long and carefully followed under difficult conditions. Those warnings, we believe, she has taken to heart.*

The article was "much appreciated" in Berlin† (why, is a mystery!), but Prince Lichnowsky, who had already warned his government that "sympathies here will turn instantly and impulsively to the Serbs just as soon as Austria resorts to violence,"‡ understood its significance. "I repeat my opinion," he telegraphed to Berlin à propos of the article, "that if military measures are taken against Serbia, public opinion here will be united against Austria-Hungary."§

Unfortunately the effect of the *Times's* article was neutralized by the language of the *Westminster Gazette* the next day, which said:

* The Austro-Hungarian ambassador remarked that "on this occasion also Mr. Steed cannot altogether refrain from reading a lesson to the Monarchy, but this article is more favorable than anything that has come from his pen for a long time." Mensdorff to Berchtold, telegram, 16 July; *Ö.-U. A.*, 10,304.

† Rumbold to Grey, telegram, 20 July; B 73.

‡ Lichnowsky to foreign office, telegram, 14 July; G 43.

§ Lichnowsky to foreign office, telegram, 16 July; G 55. The article had an interesting sequel. On the day of its publication, the foreign editor of the *Times*, Mr. Wickham Steed, who had been its correspondent in Vienna from 1903 to 1913, was asked to dine the next evening with the London correspondent of the *Neues Wiener Tageblatt*. On his arrival at his host's house, he found assembled most of the members of the Austro-Hungarian embassy in London, as well as Mr. Sidney Low and M. Condurier de Chassaigne, the president of the Foreign Press Association in London. The discussion turned upon the Sarajevo assassinations, and the Austrian diplomatists presented their case against Serbia. Obviously the object of the meeting was to win over the *Times* to the Austrian cause. But Mr. Steed only asked inconvenient questions. So the next day, he was invited to luncheon with Count Mensdorff, the Austro-Hungarian ambassador, and, after repeated efforts to decline, accepted for Tuesday, 21 July. After the luncheon, the ambassador asked Steed to "use his influence in the British press to make the position of Austria-Hungary rightly understood." The journalist not only refused, but assured Count Mensdorff that "at the first shot you fire across the Save, Russia will cry 'Hands Off,'" and that Great Britain would "certainly" intervene if the conflict became general; to which Mensdorff replied, "I have the assurance that you will not intervene." Mr. Steed went forthwith to the foreign office and argued with a permanent official that "Sir Edward Grey or somebody ought to stump the country at once and make it clear that, if Austria-Hungary and Germany try to use the Sarajevo murders as a pretext for war, we shall be dead against them"; he was told that this would "spoil the diplomatic atmosphere" and got no encouragement for his idea. Convinced that Austria-Hungary was bent on war, Mr. Steed published in the *Times* the next day, 22 July, a cautious but firm warning under the caption "A Danger to Europe," which closed with the following query: "What chance is there . . . of 'localising' a war between German and Slav, between a Roman Catholic and an Orthodox Power in the Balkans; what prospect that such a war would end without disaster to the Dual Monarchy?" Steed, I, 404-411.

After the crime of Sarajevo, we cannot deny that Austria-Hungary has a *prima-facie* case for desiring to clarify her relations with Servia . . . the Government cannot be expected to remain inactive; and Servia will be well advised if she realizes the reasonableness of her great neighbor's anxiety, and does whatever may be in her power to allay it, without waiting for a pressure which might involve what Count Tisza calls "warlike complications."*

This was quoted at length in the Viennese press, which described it as a "warning addressed to Servia by organ of British Government,"† and the *Cologne Gazette* likewise expressed its satisfaction.‡ Even Prince Lichnowsky was encouraged by it. "In view of the friendly relations between the publisher, Mr. Spender, and Sir Edward Grey," he telegraphed, "it is easy to assume that the views of the minister have not been without influence, and that my repeated conversations with him have contributed to Austria's right to claim satisfaction being taken into consideration."§

As a matter of fact, the article was not inspired by the British Government, and Sir Edward Grey, learning that it was being taken in Vienna as "an encouragement to go ahead and fight,"

---

* On 15 July, Baron Franckenstein, a secretary at the Austrian embassy, called on Mr. J. A. Spender, the editor of the *Westminster Gazette*, to beg him to use his influence with the press against encouraging the Serbians to resist. The next day, Baron Schubert, of the German embassy, came on a similar mission. To both of them, Mr. Spender replied that "if it was a mere act of justice that was required, everybody would support Austria, supposing her proof to be as conclusive as he assured me." "It was impossible to resist the conclusion that something more than was disclosed, something that was beyond the simple act of justice, was contemplated, and that this something was known to both the Austrian and German ambassadors. I judged them to be extremely alarmed and anxious about the intentions of their Governments, and to be taking steps to soften the blow in this country. I thought the best I could do in the circumstances was to write in the sense in which I had spoken to Baron Franckenstein, and this I did on July 17th." J. A. Spender, *Life, Journalism and Politics* (London, 1927), II, 9–10. It will be remembered that Mensdorff was instructed to try to influence the British press (see above, p. 393); he reported hopefully on his efforts. Mensdorff to Berchtold, 17 July; Ö.-U. A., 10,335, 10,336.
† Bunsen to Grey, telegram, 18 July; B 58.
‡ Rumbold to Grey, telegram, 18 July; B 73.
§ Lichnowsky to foreign office, 17 July; G 76. About his relations with Grey, Mr. Spender writes: "The *Westminster* was widely quoted on the supposition that it expressed Grey's opinions and, as often as not, it was labelled in brackets as 'the organ of Sir Edward Grey.' The assumption was that it never could have expressed a positive opinion on foreign affairs without previous consultation with the For-

had the Austrian Government informed and himself told Prince Lichnowsky that he had not inspired the article.* But it may be doubted if these *démentis* made any impression or carried any conviction in Berlin and Vienna.

On 20 July Sir Edward Grey attempted once more to inculcate prudence in the Central Powers. He was not prejudiced in favor of Serbia. In his memoirs he writes:

Austria regarded Serbia's policy as provocative. Serbia regarded Austrian policy as menacing. What more probable than that Serbian fanatics had planned this crime on Serbian soil? So far, what Austria's opinion seemed to regard as certain, did not, to opinion in disinterested countries, appear to be improbable. Sympathy with Austria, my own sympathy certainly, was not diminished by this assumption.†

On 6 July he had said to Prince Lichnowsky that "surely [the Austrians] did not think of taking any [Serbian] territory."‡ He now asked the ambassador if he "had any news of what was going on in Vienna with regard to Servia"; and, on the ambassador replying in the negative, repeated the advice that Austria should "keep her demands within reasonable limits"; he hated, he said, the idea of war between any of the Great Powers, and that "any of them should be dragged into war by Servia would be detestable."§

eign Secretary. This, I imagine, would be a correct assumption in regard to many foreign newspapers. But it is seldom true of English papers, and certainly was not true of the *Westminster*. I cannot remember a single occasion on which Grey asked me to write an article or prompted me to say one thing and not another. Articles on foreign affairs were written, like others, on the spur of the moment and, I am afraid, without much thought of what the Foreign Office might think about them." Spender, I, 170.
  * Lichnowsky to foreign office, telegram, 20 July; G 92. There is no record in the British documents of such a communication to Vienna. On Bunsen's telegram (B 58), however, Grey minuted that the article "was not inspired by us at all," and this may have been passed on to the Austro-Hungarian embassy in London.
  † Grey, I, 309; American edition, I, 299.
  ‡ Grey to Rumbold, 6 July; B 32.
  § Grey to Rumbold, 20 July; B 68. Grey told Lichnowsky that he "had not heard anything recently, except that Count Berchtold . . . had deprecated the suggestion that the situation was grave, but had said that it should be cleared up." Actually, Grey had received Bunsen's forecast of the Austrian note (B 50; see above, p. 390), and this no doubt explains his question to Prince Lichnowsky; but Bunsen's news, of course, was private and unofficial. According to Lichnowsky's account,

The British minister, however, was ready to play fair. If he was urging Austria to show moderation, he was also disposed to give the same advice to Russia. So, after his conversation with the German ambassador, he telegraphed to St. Petersburg:

It is possible that Servian Government have been negligent, and that proceedings at the trial at Sarajevo will show that the murder of the Archduke was planned on Servian territory. If Austrian demands on Servia are kept within reasonable limits and if Austria can produce justification for making them, I hope every attempt will be made to prevent any breach of the peace. It would be very desirable that Austria and Russia should discuss things together if they become difficult.*

Two days later Sir Edward not only spoke in the same sense to Count Benckendorff, but also sketched what he thought might be done if he were in M. Sazonov's place.

It might be possible [Grey suggested] for M. Sazonof to send for the Austrian Ambassador in St. Petersburg; to refer to the statements in the press that Austria was going to make some demand on Servia; . . . and to ask the Austrian Government to take Russia into their confidence by telling them the extent and nature of their grievance against Servia, and what they felt it necessary to ask. It might then be possible for the Russian Government to get the Austrian demands kept within reasonable limits.†

he told Grey that Berchtold "would find himself obliged to demand satisfaction from Serbia as well as a guarantee for the future." Lichnowsky to foreign office, telegram, 20 July; G 92. The ambassador did not know the intentions of his government; at least there is no evidence in the German documents that he was ever informed of the decisions of Potsdam or the precise plans of Vienna. According to Paul Cambon, who got it from Grey, Lichnowsky said that "the German Government were endeavoring to hold back and moderate the Cabinet of Vienna, but that up to the present time they had not been successful in this." P. Cambon to Bienvenu-Martin, 22 July; F 19. He also said, in his report to Berlin, that Grey "was still viewing the Austro-Serbian quarrel optimistically." The ambassador was wrong, for on the following day Grey spoke to Cambon of the "great apprehension felt as to what Austria was going to demand of Servia." Grey to Bertie, 21 July; B 72. Since Lichnowsky also reported Grey as saying that a general conflagration must be avoided, Jagow concluded, so he told the Austrian ambassador in Berlin, that "England will endeavor, even in the last resort, to refrain from any belligerent intervention." Szögyény to Berchtold, telegram, 21 July; Ö.-U. A., 10,443.

* Grey to Buchanan, telegram, 20 July; B 67.
† Grey to Buchanan, 22 July; B 79.

The suggestion does honor to Grey's desire for peace; but the expectation that Austria-Hungary might be induced to show her hand to Russia appears in the light of our present knowledge of the disposition of Vienna, decidedly naïve.

Finally, the newly appointed British minister to Belgrade, Mr. Des Graz, was told that "it was not our business to take violent sides in this matter":*

If [the Austrians] proved that the plot to assassinate the Archduke Franz Ferdinand had been prepared and organized on Servian territory, and that Austria had real grounds for complaint against Servia, it would be possible for him to urge in Belgrade that the Servian Government really ought to give Austria the utmost assurances they could for the prevention of such plots against Austria being carried on in Servia in future.†

Obviously Sir Edward Grey was trying to approach the problem without prejudice and as a good European. On 22 July he let Prince Lichnowsky know that he would advise the Serbian Government "to accept the Austrian demands in case they were moderate and compatible with the independence of Serbia," and that he "was using his influence in St. Petersburg in behalf of the Austrian point of view." On the other hand, he made it clear that Germany was expected not to identify herself with demands "which are plainly intended to bring on war," or to "support any policy which makes use of the Sarajevo murder merely as an excuse for the realization of Austrian desires in the Balkans and the tearing-up of the treaty of Bucharest."‡

* On 17 July clear indications had been received of the temper of Serbia. "Present attitude of Servian Government is prudent and conciliatory. Servian Prime Minister has declared to Austrian Minister in unofficial conversation that Servian Government are prepared to comply at once with any request for police investigation and to take any other measures compatible with dignity and independence of State. But general feeling is that a demand on the part of Austro-Hungarian Government for appointment of a mixed commission of inquiry, for suppression of nationalist societies or for censorship of press, could not be acceded to, since it would imply foreign intervention in domestic affairs and legislation." Crackanthorpe to Grey, telegram, 17 July; B 53.

† Grey to Buchanan, 22 July; B 79. The instructions appear to have been given orally.

‡ Lichnowsky to foreign office, telegram, 22 July; G 118. There is no record in the British documents of any conversation between Grey and Lichnowsky on 22 July; Lichnowsky's telegram implies that Grey's views were conveyed to him indirectly.

If all the European governments had been as reasonable, there need not have been any war!

But on this very day the hopes which the British foreign minister had built on German willingness to co-operate with Great Britain in the interest of peace were seriously weakened. He received most ominous news from both Rome and Berlin. The British ambassador in the Italian capital reported that there was a "feeling of uneasiness at the German embassy":

> They seem to anticipate that the Austro-Hungarian Government is about to address a very strong communication to Servia, and fear that Servia, having a very swelled head, and feeling confident of the support of Russia, will reply in a manner which Austria can only regard as provocative.*

Later in the day there came an alarming telegram:

> [Italian] Minister for Foreign Affairs, who is in constant touch with Austrian Embassy, told me that he feared communication to be made to Servia had been drafted in terms which must inevitably be unacceptable.†

Much more disturbing was the revelation, at last, of the German position. Herr von Jagow, in conversation with the British chargé, after admitting that the article in the *Norddeutsche Allgemeine Zeitung* of 19 July‡ had been "practically drafted by himself," insisted that

> question at issue between Austria and Servia was one for discussion and settlement by these two countries alone without interference from outside. That being his view, he had not considered it opportune to say anything to Austro-Hungarian Government . . . in his opinion, Austro-Hungarian Government had shown great forbearance toward Servia for a long time past.§

* Rodd to Grey, private, 20 July; B 74.

† Rodd to Grey, telegram, 22 July; B 78. According to the Austro-Hungarian documents, no communication was made to San Giuliano about the note to Serbia until 23 July, but complaint was made that the Italian Government had got wind of it from the German embassy. Mérey to Berchtold, 23 July; Berchtold to Mérey, 20 July; A I 56, 33.

‡ See above, pp. 397–398.   § Rumbold to Grey, telegram, 22 July; B 77.

The situation was now only too clear. Not only was Austria-Hungary probably going ahead, but she was doing so with the connivance of Germany. Such, at any rate, was the opinion of Sir Eyre Crowe, the assistant under-secretary in the foreign office, who 'minuted' on the telegram from Berlin:

It is difficult to understand the attitude of the German Government. On the face of it, it does not bear the stamp of straightforwardness. . . .

They appear to rely on the British Government to reinforce the German and Austrian threats at Belgrade; it is clear that if the British Government did intervene in this sense, or by addressing admonitions to St. Petersburg, the much desired breach between England and Russia would be brought one step nearer realization. . . .

They know what the Austrian Government is going to demand, they are aware that those demands will raise a grave issue, and I think we may say with some assurance that they have expressed approval of those demands and promised support, should dangerous complications arise.

If Sir Eyre Crowe had had under his eyes the German documents published since the war, he could not have made a more accurate analysis of the situation. Henceforth, although he was the son of a German mother and was married to a German lady, he was to regard with suspicion every move of the German Government and to be the keenest critic of German policy.

In a last effort to save the situation, Sir Edward Grey sent for the Austro-Hungarian ambassador* in order to say to him, as the German ambassador was warned, that, if British influence was to be used at Belgrade,

Vienna must not bring forward charges *à la Friedjung* which cannot be proved, and the Austro-Hungarian Government must be in a position to demonstrate unequivocably the

* Mensdorff to Berchtold, telegram, 22 July; A I 54.

connection between the murder at Sarajevo and political circles at Belgrade.*

Count Mensdorff came on the next day, *i. e.,* 23 July, and had to listen to a long and pertinent warning, after he had explained privately the nature of the Austrian note.† Sir Edward said that a time limit in the note would be likely to inflame opinion in Russia, and, while declining to comment upon or criticise the explanations offered by the ambassador, "could not help dwelling on the awful consequences involved in the situation."

The possible consequences of the present situation were terrible. If as many as four Great Powers of Europe—let us say Austria, France, Russia, and Germany—were engaged in war, it seemed to me that it must involve the expenditure of so vast a sum of money and such an interference with trade, that a war would be accompanied or followed by a complete collapse of European credit and industry. In these days, in great industrial states, this would mean a state of things worse than that of 1848, and, irrespective of who were victors in the war, many things might be swept away.

He was, Count Mensdorff reported, "as cool and unprejudiced as ever, friendly and not without sympathy for our point of view"; but he made it clear that in his judgment a "mere explanation" would not satisfy St. Petersburg. He pointed out that "in a time of difficulties such as this, it was just as true to say that it required two to keep the peace as it was to

---

* Lichnowsky to foreign office, telegram, 22 July; G 118. The telegram evoked from William II some of his wildest comments, some of which are worth quoting. "This is a tremendous piece of British insolence. I am not called upon to prescribe *à la* Grey to His Majesty the Emperor how to defend his honor!" "Grey is committing the error of putting Serbia on the same plane with Austria and other Great Powers! This is unheard of! Serbia is a band of robbers that must be punished for its crimes! I shall not meddle in a matter about which the Emperor alone is competent to judge! I have expected this despatch and am not surprised by it! Real British reasoning and condescending way of giving orders, which I insist on having rebuffed!" The comments (made on G 121) were not received at the German foreign office until 27 July, but they help to explain the difficulty of Sir Edward Grey in securing German co-operation.

† Berchtold had authorized such a communication. Berchtold to Mensdorff, telegram, 23 July; A I 58.

say ordinarily that it took two to make a quarrel"; and therefore he recommended a direct exchange of views between
Austria and Russia*—which was exactly the advice he had
given to M. Sazonov. More Sir Edward Grey could hardly
have said,† and if, after these remarks, either Vienna or Berlin expected the British Government to recommend the Austro-Hungarian note in St. Petersburg, they were singularly
obtuse.‡

If the Austro-Hungarian ambassador received no encouragement from Sir Edward Grey, the Serbian minister fared
little better. When he asked Sir Arthur Nicolson for an
opinion on "the whole question" between Austria and Serbia,
he was told that "it was quite impossible to form an opinion,
having no data on which to base one." All that the permanent
under-secretary would say was that he trusted that the Serbian
Government "would endeavor to meet the Austrian requests in
a conciliatory and moderate spirit."§

Thus to the very moment that the Austro-Hungarian note
became known, the British Government, though more and
more alarmed, declined to commit itself or to take sides. It
gave much sound advice to the governments directly interested,
and in the circumstances it probably could not have done anything else. The country was concerned, not with the Austro-
Serbian quarrel, but with the Irish struggle, and would not have
understood a pronouncement of the government on the Euro-

* Grey to Bunsen, 23 July; B 86. Mensdorff to Berchtold, telegram, 23 July;
A I 59. The two accounts of the conversation tally unusually well, so that Berchtold was not deceived about Grey's views.

† While Mensdorff was with Grey, a telegram was received from St. Petersburg
saying that the French and Russian ambassadors in Vienna were being instructed
to give "friendly counsels of moderation" to the Austrian Government and implying that similar British representations were desirable. Buchanan to Grey, 23 July;
B 84. Nicolson judged this "not a judicious move," and Crowe thought that "any
such communication at Vienna would be likely to produce intense irritation, without any beneficial other effects." So no instructions were sent to Sir Maurice de
Bunsen to join in such representations. It was obviously hoped in London that
what Grey had said from time to time to Lichnowsky would be passed on to Vienna
by the German Government; but Berlin did not do so.

‡ Mensdorff understood the situation well enough. He informed Berchtold that
he feared Grey "would have much to say about the *démarche* having the character
of an ultimatum and about the time-limit." Mensdorff to Berchtold, 23 July; A I
59.

§ Memorandum of Nicolson, 23 July; B 87.

pean situation; indeed the cabinet itself had not yet considered the matter.* Unfortunately, sound advice was not wanted in Vienna or Berlin, and, as Sir Edward Grey pointed out to Prince Lichnowsky, the feeling of dislike with which Great Britain was at the moment regarded in Russia would prevent his representations from being very cordially received at St. Petersburg.† All that Sir Edward Grey could do was to wait.

If the British position is to be correctly and fully appreciated, it must be viewed, not primarily with regard to the situation in the Balkans, but from the angle of European politics generally. Negotiations over the final details of the Bagdad Railway settlement were being carried on with the German Government down to 22 July.‡ Much more important was the problem of Anglo-Russian relations. The Russians were resenting the exploitation of the Mesopotamian oil-fields by British companies. The British were complaining of the conduct of Russian consuls in Persia. This state of affairs was playing into the hands of the strong pro-German party in Russia, and the British Government had begun to fear that the Asiatic settlement embodied in the Convention of 31 August, 1907, might be imperilled or overturned. As a Russo-German understanding would have the gravest consequences for Great Britain, British policy was bound, by the nature of things, to proceed with the utmost care. "Russia is a formidable Power," Sir Arthur Nicolson observed about 20 July, "and will become increasingly strong. Let us hope that our relations with her will continue to be friendly."§ How much this consideration affected Sir Edward Grey's attitude to the Austro-Serbian question cannot be determined, but obviously it was not forgotten.

There was the further circumstance that, early in July, M. Sazonov, in his anxiety to allay what he called "the inveterate suspicion with which Russia is regarded in India and in cer-

---

* Private information.
† Lichnowsky to foreign office, telegram, 15 July; G 52.
‡ Cf. *G. P.*, XXXVII, 466–470.
§ Minute on B 66 (which dealt with the Russian army), received 20 July.

tain circles in England," had suggested informally a triple guarantee of their Asiatic possessions by Russia, Great Britain, and Japan.* Ten days later he renewed the proposal officially, and pressed for an answer.† Sir Edward Grey replied that he was "personally attracted" by the idea and would consult the Prime Minister and the cabinet "as soon as the Parliamentary and Irish situation gives them time."‡ Such a reply shows that, in spite of the difficulties in Persia, the British foreign secretary retained confidence in the Russian Government; he was not likely to be disabused of it by insinuations from Berlin or Vienna; and he would hesitate long before he would compromise the prospect of Anglo-Russian co-operation and harmony in Asia by supporting Austria-Hungary on the Serbian issue against the interests and wishes of Russia.§ Sir Edward Grey was prepared to be reasonable on the Austro-Serbian matter, and was anxious not to be drawn into it; but, if forced to take sides, he could not choose to stand by the Central Powers. Prince Lichnowsky was well aware of this, but he could not make his government understand it, or, if they did understand it, act accordingly.

FRANCE

France, like Great Britain, was passing through a political crisis in the early summer of 1914. Factional strife which for

---

* Buchanan to Nicolson, private, 9 July; *B. D.*, XI, xi.

† Buchanan to Grey, private and secret telegram, 19 July; *ibid.*, XI, xi.

‡ Grey to Buchanan, 20 July; *ibid.*, XI, xi.

§ The Austro-Hungarian ambassador understood the situation clearly. "From German sources I hear," he wrote early in July, "that in Russia they are becoming somewhat nervous about the *rapprochement* between London and Berlin, to which the understanding over the Bagdad Railway can only be helpful. To speak of a change in British policy, as they are perhaps disposed to do in Germany, seems to me, however, at least premature. . . . If I have always been of the opinion that the secretary of state is not at all disposed to enter upon any relationship of alliance with Russia—which he could not do in view of currents in the Radical party—I believe, on the other hand, that the maintenance of good and cordial relations with Russia remains, now as formerly, a cardinal principle of his policy. He has always, in opposition as well as when a minister, taken the line that Russia and England must come to an understanding on Asiatic questions, otherwise they would come to a point which must lead to one of the greatest and most regrettable conflicts in the history of the world. It is not to be assumed that Sir Edward Grey will now . . . accept a fundamental change in the principles of his policy." Mensdorff to Berchtold, 3 July; *Ö.-U. A.*, 10,013.

several years had been kept within reasonable limits had once more burst into full fury and was threatening to reduce French politics to chaos. The cabinet formed in December, 1913, was predominantly Radical; but, because of his alleged improper conduct during the Agadir crisis of 1911, when he had been premier,* the head of the Radical party, M. Joseph Caillaux, had been passed over in favor of M. Gaston Doumergue,† and M. Caillaux had to be content with the ministry of finance. But the murder of Gaston Calmette, the editor of the *Figaro,* in March, 1914, by Madame Caillaux had forced the resignation of the minister of finance. Thus a strong personal issue was injected into the situation, and the trial of Madame Caillaux promised to become a political event. In the elections of April and May, the Radicals suffered some losses. On the other hand, the Socialists gained considerably, and the alliance formed by Radicals and Socialists, while not possessing an absolute majority of the chamber of deputies, constituted the strongest 'bloc.' Confronted by this situation, M. Doumergue presented the resignation of his cabinet before the meeting of the new parliament on 1 June.

The selection of a new government proved a difficult task. The victorious groups, intent on an elaborate and costly programme of social reform, demanded the repeal of the three years' military service which had been restored in the summer of 1913. The President of the Republic, M. Raymond Poincaré, and the moderate politicians were strongly opposed to any such action, for they feared that it would gravely weaken the international position of France, but in the circumstances of the moment, M. René Viviani, the leader of the Republican Socialists, had to be commissioned to form a government. He was promptly threatened with the resignation of the French ambassador to Russia, M. Maurice Paléologue, who had just arrived from St. Petersburg, if the three years'

---

* He was accused of negotiating with Germany behind the back of the foreign office. The revelations, made in January, 1912, had led to the fall of the government and the appointment of Poincaré as premier.
† President of the French Republic since May, 1924.

service was abandoned.* M. Viviani assured M. Poincaré that he would maintain the law for the present, but he could not persuade his followers to follow him and returned his mandate. M. Alexandre Ribot, one of the veterans of French politics and the negotiator of the alliance with Russia, then tried his hand. He formed a cabinet, with the pacific Léon Bourgeois as foreign minister, but his categorical declaration in favor of the military law led to his overthrow within twenty-four hours. M. Poincaré would now have liked to resign,† but decided to appeal again to M. Viviani. This time success was achieved. Many of the Radicals were only half-hearted in their opposition to the three years' service, and in order to insure their participation in the new ministry, they agreed to a compromise: the three classes of soldiers then serving‡ would not be discharged, but the law might be modified if an adequate substitute for the existing system were devised. The Viviani ministry was given a vote of confidence on 16 June.

The new government, however, did not enjoy great prestige, for M. Viviani, who took the portfolio of foreign affairs, was without experience in that department. Although its declaration contained the usual solemn affirmation of solidarity with Russia, it was dependent on Socialist support for the execution of its domestic programme, particularly the introduction of an income tax. And not only did the Socialists dislike the Russian alliance,§ but about the middle of July they adopted in their annual congress a motion describing the General

---

* M. Paléologue, "La Russie des Tsars pendant la grande guerre," in *Revue des deux mondes*, 6th period, LXI, 228-229 (15 January, 1921).

† Poincaré, IV, 163.

‡ The original plan had been to retain for an extra year of service the class whose two-year term was about to expire. By this device the standing army would have been composed in 1914 of two-thirds trained troops, one-third recruits. Radical and Socialist opposition had necessitated the abandonment of this plan. As a substitute, it was decided to call two classes to the colors, the men of twenty and twenty-one years of age. But it is not correct, as sometimes stated, that *four* classes were serving with the colors in 1914.

§ The Austro-Hungarian ambassador noted that the cabinet "is dependent on a majority which is not disposed to warlike complications." Szécsen to Berchtold, 18 July; *Ö.-U. A.*, 10,358.

Strike, "simultaneously and internationally organized in the interested countries," as a "particularly efficacious" means of forcing governments to accept arbitration and of preventing war.* So peaceful did the intentions of the Viviani cabinet appear to be that the German chancellor thought it would be willing to restrain Russia from intervention in the Austro-Serbian crisis.†

In the summer of 1914 the relations of France and Germany were entirely correct and pacific. Two incidents, however, showed that the gulf between them had not been bridged. (1) When Jean Jaurès, the great Socialist leader, spoke in the chamber in favor of a *rapprochement* with Germany, the *Temps,* the organ of middle-class and conservative opinion, pointed out (8 July) that France had regained her diplomatic position in Europe by creating a group of Powers who were independent of German influence. "No Frenchman," it continued, "could subscribe to a political understanding with Germany which would bring the work of forty years to naught and abandon the path through which our diplomacy has recovered its liberty and security."‡ (2) The Prince of Monaco, who was desirous of promoting better relations between France and Germany, had proposed that M. Aristide Briand, one of the most prominent French politicians and a former premier, should go with him to the Kiel regatta at the end of June, and M. Briand seemed to like the idea. But both the President and M. Viviani objected. Because M. Briand was not a member of the cabinet, "he would find himself in a false position and expose himself to the danger

* Granville to Grey, 17 July; B 54.
† See above, p. 399. The cautious disposition of the new ministry is illustrated by its handling of a most delicate question. On 18 June Viviani learned that the resident-general in Morocco, General Lyautey, wished to take proceedings in a military court against two German residents on the charge of promoting desertion from the Foreign Legion. As the German Government declined to recognize the jurisdiction of the French military courts, General Lyautey was not allowed to act until it had been ascertained that one of the Germans was a naturalized Frenchman; the other was simply expelled from Morocco. Poincaré, IV, 169–171.
‡ Granville to Grey, 9 July; B 42. At a meeting of the League of Patriots held on 10 July to elect a president in succession to Paul Déroulède, Maurice Barrès made a chauvinistic speech declaring watchfulness necessary to prevent a Franco-German *rapprochement.*

of provoking unjust comment and fantastic conjectures." M. Poincaré asked him "what would be the use of going to Germany, talking with the Kaiser, and coming back without anything being changed?" So M. Briand declined the invitation.*

The Russian alliance continued to be the mainstay of French diplomacy. The new premier on 18 June authorized the French ambassador to Russia to tell the Tsar that

the three years' service would be maintained without change and that he would allow nothing to be done which might weaken or prejudice the alliance.†

During the month of July its value was several times pointed out to the French public. On 13 July a startling indictment of the deficient organization and equipment of the French army was made in a report by Senator Charles Humbert. The forts on the frontier were alleged to be poorly constructed; guns were said to lack ammunition; there was a bad shortage of boots. The French artillery was falling behind that of Germany, in numbers at least; in heavy guns especially, it was stated, the Germans possessed a distinct superiority. In the face of this dangerous situation, much comfort was derived from the excellent condition of the Russian army. The *Temps,* on 16 July, pointed out that Russia, with a population of 180,000,000, had only to take one soldier out of every hundred subjects to create a standing army of 1,800,000 men, and that this formula [which was also the German] was beginning to be applied; the dead-weight of these new masses of soldiers was bound, so it was asserted, to have its effect on the balance of power.‡

* Poincaré, IV, 168–169. According to the then German ambassador in Paris, "the plan had been knocked on the head by the French ambassador in St. Petersburg, M. Paléologue, President Poincaré's friend, who happened to be staying in Paris, and pointed out the danger of the Emperor William's attractions." Schoen, *Erlebtes,* p. 159; cf. Schoen to Bethmann-Hollweg, 8 June, 1914; *G. P.,* XXXIX, 258–259.

† Paléologue, *loc. cit.,* LXI, 231.

‡ Granville to Grey, 16 July; B 52. The Austro-Hungarian ambassador discounted this article. "I do not believe that at present the French public will wish for the active use of this much-praised military power in a European war." Szécsen to Berchtold, 18 July; *Ö.-U. A.,* 10,358.

Two days later the *Matin* predicted that by 1916 Russia would have increased the strength of its army on a peace footing to 2,245,000 men and was well on its way to becoming the greatest military power in history. For this reason, "Russian diplomacy is already adopting a new tone when it speaks to German diplomacy, and to-day Germany fears her eastern neighbor."* On 20 July the same paper's special correspondent telegraphed from St. Petersburg that the Russian army could be mobilized and concentrated in sixteen days as against ten needed by the German army; he added that while the recent revelations about the French army had made a disagreeable impression in St. Petersburg, they were not taken *"au tragique."*† In spite, therefore, of internal dissensions and difficulties, France could face a European crisis without the fear that Russia would leave her in the lurch. Likewise, she could support Russia without the danger that the Russian army would not be able to deal with its antagonists.

Owing to lack of French documents for the first three weeks of July, the attitude of the French foreign office toward the general international situation cannot be defined. But a remark of M. Jules Cambon, the ambassador in Berlin, is not without interest:

Matters as between France and Germany [he said to the British chargé] were by no means what they should be. The Germans were not behaving in a friendly way toward his country. The air would have to be cleared some time or other.‡

He, for one, was evidently not disposed to retreat before a German threat; no more was M. Poincaré; no more, for that matter, was the French public.

In the matter of the Sarajevo crime, the French press early began to take the side of Serbia. The *Temps,* which passed for the mouthpiece of the Quai d'Orsay, said on 2 July that "neither the Serbian Government nor the Serbian people are in

* Granville to Grey, 18 July; B 66.
† Bertie to Grey, 20 July; B 69.   ‡ Rumbold to Grey, 18 July; B 63.

any degree responsible for Austria-Hungary's mourning."* The *Journal* and the *Radical* criticised the policy of the Dual Monarchy toward the Southern Slavs. The *Humanité* on 1 July quoted a Socialist writer who said: "The only crime which I deplore is that which the Austrians have committed against the Serbs of Bosnia, and which has just received at Sarajevo its just reward"; and in the same issue Marcel Sembat, a well-known Socialist and pacifist, declared that Printsip and Chabrinovich were not political criminals, but "exasperated patriots." For the French press to agree in the interpretation of a foreign incident was as striking as it was rare. Some papers even suggested that Austria-Hungary might be planning to use the murder as an excuse for war with Serbia.†

The attitude of the French Government was correct and reserved. The President of the Republic despatched a telegram of condolence to the Emperor Francis Joseph on the day of the assassination.‡ But when the Austro-Hungarian ambassador came to thank him for this formality, M. Poincaré limited himself to expressing the conviction that "the Serbian Government would show the Monarchy the greatest complaisance in the judicial investigation and the prosecution of the accomplices"; if he added that "no state can divest itself of this duty," he was giving the ambassador to understand that Serbia should not be asked to go farther.§ The advice was given to Serbia to "preserve an attitude of calm and dignity in order to avoid giving cause for fresh accusations in Vienna."‖ Whether there was further admonition to investigate the conspiracy and offer satisfaction to Austria-Hungary is not known. The French

---

* The Austro-Hungarian ambassador characterized a series of articles in the *Temps* on Bosnia as "tendentious." Szécsen to Berchtold, telegram, 9 July; *Ö.-U. A.*, 10,159.

† Scott, pp. 184–185. "In spite of all chauvinistic baitings, French public opinion is very peace-loving. A state which, rightly or wrongly, is suspected of endangering peace, whether intentionally or only even by its general policy, will always be charged with aggression by the newspapers here." Szécsen to Berchtold, 12 July; *Ö.-U. A.*, 10,220.

‡ Poincaré, IV, 174.

§ Szécsen to Berchtold, 4 July; Gooss, p. 80; *Ö.-U. A.*, 10,047. Poincaré, IV, 191.

‖ Vesnich to Pashich, 4 July; S 13.

ambassador in Vienna gave his British colleague to understand, his country was "in sympathy with Servian aspirations";* whether that sympathy was manifested before the
presentation of the Austro-Hungarian ultimatum is a question that cannot now be answered.

Probably the attitude of France would be determined only
after consultation with Russia. As it happened, arrangements
had been made as far back as January for M. Poincaré to pay
an official visit to the Russian court in July, a ceremony which
was by tradition incumbent upon each President of the Republic, and M. Poincaré's visit was almost overdue. Accordingly, on 15 July, he and M. Viviani left Paris for Russia.

RUSSIA

Whether the Austro-Serbian dispute could be localized or
would expand to European dimensions depended on Russia.
Russia would protest against the Austrian action—of that there
was no doubt. But would she back up her protest by force?

The position of the Russian Government was one of no little difficulty. We have seen that its policy in the Near East was
dominated by the question of the Straits and Constantinople,
by the double desire to prevent their passing under the control
of another Power and to assure for Russia unrestricted passage from the Black Sea to the Ægean.† If this issue were
raised, Russia would certainly fight. But she had refused, in
1908–1909 at the time of the Bosnian crisis and again in 1912–
1913 during the Balkan wars, to draw the sword in behalf of
Serbia. Indeed, official Russia was prone to support the Serbs
or any other Balkan people only in so far as they would be of
service in the promotion of its own ambitions. If the Austro-Hungarian action did not imperil Russian interests at Constantinople, it might not evoke more than diplomatic protest.

But unofficial Russia was more impulsive. The liberation
of the Slav and Christian peoples of the Balkans from foreign
domination was ardently desired by wide circles, and the Tsar's

* Bunsen to Grey, 5 July; B 40.   † See above, pp. 83–88, 94–98.

government could never ignore this sentiment; it had, in 1908–
1909 and 1912–1913, only with difficulty resisted the pressure
of the Pan-Slavists for war in behalf of Serbia and Montenegro. As late as 23 May, 1914, the foreign minister, S. D.
Sazonov, had proclaimed in the Duma the principle of "the
Balkans for the Balkan peoples." If the Austro-Hungarian
action threatened the vital interests of Serbia, he would unquestionably be called on to make good his words. And perhaps he
was less disposed to resist such demands because the revolutionary current was beginning once again to manifest itself, and
in the event of internal disturbances the government would
need the support of all conservative elements. Furthermore,
during the previous crises the Serbs had been restrained by
promises, frequently renewed, that Russia, when ready for battle, "would do everything for Serbia."* It may also be noted
that certain Russian diplomatists, notably the minister in Belgrade, Nicholas Hartwig, were ardent supporters of the Slav
cause against Austria-Hungary.

Still another factor was bitter resentment against both Austria and Germany for their conduct ever since the annexation of Bosnia in 1908; although the ambassador in Paris, A.
P. Izvolski, is supposed to have been the incarnation of this
feeling, it was by no means confined to him. The desire that in
the next crisis Russia should stand up manfully to the Central
Powers was all but universal among the articulate classes.†
Moreover, many army officers, including, there is reason to
believe, the Grand Duke Nicholas Nicholayevich, the commander-in-chief-designate, confident in the strength of the rejuvenated Russian army, were entirely ready to measure its
strength against the less numerous forces of Germany and
Austria-Hungary. All in all, the situation was a most delicate
one, and, while both the German Emperor and the German
chancellor expressed the opinion that Russia would not rouse
herself to action, they did not, as we have seen, ignore the possibility of a conflict.

* See above, pp. 128–129, 135, 142.   † See above, pp. 101–102.

Russian opinion was greatly exasperated by the anti-Serbian demonstrations in Austria-Hungary which followed the assassination, and began to be critical. The *Petersburgsky Kuryer* asserted that the responsibility for the crime rested really, not with Serbia, but with those who had pushed Austria on in Bosnia and against Serbia, and that "in the name of considerations of humanity, Russia ought to fulfil her duty toward her brothers who find themselves under the yoke." The *Novoye Vremya* complained that the Jesuits wished the Serbs to be looked upon as assassins. The *Gazette* declared that Austria was defying half of Orthodox Europe, and that the "pogroms" made desirable the liberation of the Serbs and the other Slav nationalities from the German yoke. Early in July the *Russkoye Slovo* said bluntly that Serbia could not renounce her political independence, and that "in her struggle for freedom, Serbia will not stand alone."*

For some reason the Soviet Government, in publishing the diplomatic documents of the Tsarist régime, has neglected the period between the murder of the Archduke and the presentation of the Austrian note. What is known, therefore, about the attitude of the Russian Government during that period has to be derived from the documents of other governments. But the hints, though not very numerous, are clear-cut and concordant. Early in July, M. Sazonov sent for the Austro-Hungarian chargé to point out "in a friendly way" the danger of Russian opinion becoming irritated by the Austrian press campaign against Serbia; and when the chargé remarked that it might be necessary to search for the instigators of the Sarajevo crime on Serbian territory, the minister warned him "not to embark on such a course," saying that "no country has had to suffer more than Russia from crimes prepared on its territory."†

---

* Scott, pp. 161–163.

† Paléologue to Viviani, 6 July; F 10. The chargé's report of the conversation does not mention Sazonov's warning, and represents it as dealing chiefly with the utterances of the Serbian minister, Spalaykovich. He quotes Sazonov as saying that "he was a warm friend of the Monarchy." Otto Czernin to Berchtold, telegram, 7 July; *Ö.-U. A.*, 10,106.

Some ten days later, the Italian ambassador, the Marquis Carlotti, meeting at a social gathering Baron Schilling, *chef de de cabinet* of M. Sazonov, informed him that

he had the impression that Austria, calculating that Russia would indeed protest but would not decide to defend Serbia with force against an attack on the part of Austria-Hungary, was on the point of taking an irrevocable step against Serbia.

He added that if the Russian Government was not disposed, as Baron Schilling affirmed, to tolerate a move against the integrity and independence of Serbia, it should give an "unequivocal declaration" to this effect in Vienna. To this counsel Baron Schilling replied that such a declaration might be regarded as an ultimatum and would only make the situation worse, and he suggested that Italy and Germany might better try to restrain their ally.*

This incident was fresh in the mind of M. Sazonov when on 18 July he saw the Austro-Hungarian ambassador, who had returned to his post before the expiration of his leave† and had asked for an immediate interview. He told Count Szápáry that "he had been somewhat disquieted by the latest news from Vienna" and expressed the conviction that proofs of Serbian complicity would not be forthcoming.‡ If he did not, as the ambassador reported, indicate any anxiety about the form of the Austro-Hungarian demands, it was because Count Szápáry gave the most positive assurances that "Austria had not the least intention of aggravating her relations with Serbia." He was, so Sazonov told Schilling, "as gentle as a lamb," and the minister had not thought it necessary to "make any threats."§

But if care was taken to avoid brusque language which might irritate Vienna, a communiqué was issued to the St. Petersburg press to the following effect:

---

* Schilling, *How the War Began in 1914*, pp. 25–26.
† Sazonov, *Fateful Years, 1906–1916*, p. 151.
‡ Szápáry to Berchtold, telegram, 18 July; A I 25.
§ Schilling, pp. 26–27.

Russia hopes that Austria-Hungary will make no demand which threatens the national independence of Serbia. Moderate demands Russia will support.*

This, as the Russian ambassador in Vienna explained, was "intended as a hint that it would be well for this Government to act with moderation."† Thus, without resorting to formal representations which would certainly have been resented, the Russian Government did what it could to make its position clear at Vienna.

M. Sazonov appears to have had two conversations with the German ambassador, Count Pourtalès. In the first, on 13 July or earlier, he "could not find words enough with which to criticise the behavior of the Austro-Hungarian authorities for permitting the excesses against the Serbs." He protested against the assertion that the assassination was to be traced back to a Pan-Serb plot; nothing had been proved, he said, and "it was unjustifiable to the last degree to hold the Serbian Government . . . responsible for the crime," which, he insisted, was "only the act of individual and immature young men." He showed less enthusiasm for the idea of monarchical solidarity than Count Pourtalès was acustomed to find in him, and seemed possessed of an "unconquerable hatred" for Austria, a hatred which, the ambassador reported, "is more and more clouding all clear and calm judgment here." Count Pourtalès, who in the past had always regarded M. Sazonov as conciliatory and pacific, was evidently taken aback by the minister's stiffness.‡

At the second conversation, on 18 July, M. Sazonov again denounced the Austro-Hungarian policy.

There were [he said] very powerful and dangerous influences at work which were constantly gaining ground in both halves of the Monarchy and which did not shrink from the idea

---

* Scott, p. 163, quoting *Neue Freie Presse*, 17 July, and *Frankfurter Zeitung*, 18 July.
† Bunsen to Grey, 19 July; B 156. The Russian ambassador had, as early as 5 July, told Bunsen that "a Servian war meant a general war," for "Russia would be compelled to take up arms in defence of Servia." Bunsen to Grey, 5 July; B 40.
‡ Pourtalès to Bethmann-Hollweg, 13 July; G 53.

of plunging Austria into war, even at the risk of starting a general world conflagration. . . .

Previously the bellicose elements, among which clerical intrigues had also played an important rôle, had pinned their hopes to the late Archduke Francis Ferdinand. The death of the Archduke had in no way discouraged them; rather they were the ones who were inspiring the dangerous policy which Austria-Hungary was pursuing at the moment. . . .

The support of the Great-Serbian propaganda in Austria-Hungary by Serbia or by the Serbian Government had in no way been proved. A whole country could not be held responsible for the acts of individuals. Furthermore, the murderer of the Archduke was not even a Serbian subject. . . . The Vienna Cabinet did not have the slightest reason to complain of the attitude of the Serbian Government, which, on the contrary, was behaving with complete correctness. . . . .

Those people in Austria who were urging action against Serbia, would apparently not be content with making representations in Belgrade, but aimed at the annihilation of Serbia. . . . If Austria-Hungary was bent on disturbing the peace, she ought not to forget that in this case she will have to reckon with Europe. Russia could not look on indifferently at a move in Belgrade which aimed at the humiliation of Serbia. . . . In no case should there be any talk of an ultimatum.*

Even if allowance is made for the mercurial temperament which sometimes led the Russian minister to talk rather wildly, his tone was decidedly threatening; at the same time, no new policy was proclaimed, for, as we have seen, M. Sazonov had said unequivocally to the King of Roumania at Constanza that an Austrian attack on Serbia would led to Russian intervention and precipitate a European war.†

Count Pourtalès concluded his report by saying that M. Sazonov had informed the Italian ambassador that "Russia would not be able to allow Austria-Hungary to use threatening lan-

* Pourtalès to Bethmann-Hollweg, 21 July; G 120. Sazonov expressed the same views in his memoirs written in 1927; Sazonov, pp. 151–152.

† King Carol informed the German and Austrian ministers at his court of what Sazonov had said, and they in turn reported it to their governments. Waldburg to Bethmann-Hollweg, 11 July; G 41. Czernin to Berchtold, telegram, 3 July; Ö.-U. A., 10,007.

guage to Serbia or to take military measures." *"La politique de la Russie,"* said the minister, *"est pacifique, mais pas passive."*

The British ambassador was told the same thing. "In reply to a question of mine," Sir George Buchanan reported, "his Excellency [Sazonov] said that anything in the shape of an Austrian ultimatum at Belgrade could not leave Russia indifferent, and she might be forced to take some precautionary military measures."*

Whatever may be thought of the Russian policy, it is not open to the reproach of having concealed its sentiments and its intentions. The Powers of each group were informed frankly and before the crisis broke that Russia would fight if Serbia were attacked; if any of them chose to ignore this warning, the fault was not Russia's.

The Russian attitude was not, however, intransigent. If on the one hand he advised Belgrade that "the chief thing is for public opinion in Serbia to remain calm,"† M. Sazonov recognized on the other that Austria-Hungary had grounds for complaint and that it was incumbent on Serbia to afford redress. "If," he said to the British ambassador, "Austria could prove that the plot had been hatched in Servia there was no objection to her asking Servian Government to institute judicial inquiry, and this, he believed, Servia was ready to do."‡ Evidently he had been advising the Serbian Government in this sense. It would have been even better, no doubt, if he had urged the Serbs to begin an investigation without waiting for an Austrian request, for the inactivity of Belgrade played into the hands of Count Berchtold; but it was possible to argue, as did the Russian ambassador in Vienna, that the Serbian Government "had quite rightly . . . postponed taking any action until it should be in possession of concrete accusations against specified persons on which it could take effective action."§

All things considered, the conduct of the Russian Govern-

* Buchanan to Grey, telegram, 18 July; B 60.
† Spalaykovich to Pashich, telegram, 4 July; S 14.
‡ Buchanan to Grey, telegram, 22 July; B 76.
§ Bunsen to Grey, 19 July; B 156.

ment was cautious and reserved, and one is justified in assuming that its policy toward either Serbia or the Central Powers was not fully and finally determined until the conference with its French ally which was made possible by the visit of MM. Poincaré and Viviani. This began on 20 July, on the same day that the Austro-Hungarian note was despatched from Vienna for presentation in Belgrade on 23 July.

THE FRENCH VISIT TO RUSSIA, 20–23 JULY

MM. Poincaré and Viviani sailed from Dunkirk in the battleship *France* on 16 July and arrived at Cronstadt on the afternoon of 20 July. The latter has recorded their thoughts:

What were we going to say to the Tsar, to the Russian Government? Certainly we intended to talk about the state of Europe and the interests of our alliance. We were likewise—and M. Poincaré and I did not fail to do so—going to plead for a *rapprochement* between Russia and Sweden, which was complaining of certain isolated actions of the Russian naval attaché. Finally, we had to mention the complaints of England against the conduct of certain Russian consuls.*

They were, in fact, so much preoccupied by the question of Anglo-Russian relations in Persia, which were again becoming difficult and threatening to destroy the harmony of the Triple Entente, that they intended to make it "one of the chief subjects of conversation" with the Russian Government.† They were also worried by the obscurity of Austria-Hungary's intentions with respect to Serbia, but they received no disquieting news, and M. Poincaré declares that they "did not consider the likelihood of an early war."‡

The visit to the Tsar's court lasted from the afternoon of 20

---

* R. Viviani, *Réponse au Kaiser* (Paris, 1922), p. 81.
† Buchanan to Nicolson, private, 9 July; B 49. Poincaré, *Les origines de la guerre*, p. 201. The British ambassador in Paris complained to his Austro-Hungarian colleague (and one may presume, therefore, to the French foreign office) about the Russian conduct in Persia and the equivocations of Sazonov. Szécsen to Berchtold, 4 July; Ö.-U. A., 10,048.
‡ Poincaré, *Les origines de la guerre*, p. 200.

July to the late evening of the 23d. There was the usual round of state dinners, exchange of toasts, diplomatic receptions, military reviews. The atmosphere was charged with a certain tension, for the Austrian action was hourly expected. The Grand Duchess Anastasia, wife of the Grand Duke Nicholas, spoke to the French ambassador of "historic days." Her father, King Nicholas of Montenegro, had telegraphed her that "we shall have war before the end of the month." She produced a *bonbonnière* containing soil of Lorraine, and pointed to the table decorations of thistle, which was the flower of the lost province. During dinner she exclaimed:

War is going to break out. . . . There will be nothing of Austria left. . . . You will get Alsace-Lorraine back. . . . Our armies will meet in Berlin. . . . Germany will be annihilated.*

An engaging picture!

Read to-day in cold print, the toasts sound like "colorless foreign office jargon" [*fade verbiage du chancellerie*],† for they abound in such phrases as "the pacific desires of the two governments," "the equilibrium of the world," "the work of peace and civilization," "the same ideal of peace combined with strength, honor, and dignity"; there were also the usual references to the "indissoluble alliance" and its "beneficent action."‡ In short, the kind of thing that had to be said and was said whenever heads of allied states came together. But a good deal of warmth and feeling must have been put into the delivery of the speeches, for M. Paléologue subsequently qualified them as "four documents of great importance."§   M. Poincaré's diction and accent of authority greatly impressed his Russian hearers, who seemed to be saying: "That is how an autocrat

---

* M. Paléologue, *La Russie des Tsars pendant la grande guerre* (Paris, 1921), I, 14–15.
    † *Ibid.*, I, 5.
    ‡ The toasts may be read in full in Poincaré, IV, 241–243, 277–278, and in Schilling, pp. 113–116.
    § Schilling, p. 32.

ought to speak." In the interviews with the Tsar it was he who "directed the conversation,"* and a year later Nicholas II is said to have told a French politician that he could not forget the "firm language" which the French President had used.† The visit undoubtedly strengthened the feelings of intimacy and solidarity of the two allies.

The political results were considerable. The Russians evinced every disposition to relieve the tension with Great Britain in Persia. The Tsar admitted that Russian agents, "blinded by local preoccupations, sometimes too easily lost sight of general interests," and said that no issue must be allowed "to make any change in the good relations of England and Russia."‡ So Sir George Buchanan was able to send good news to London:

> President of the Republic told me yesterday that he had discussed Persian question with Emperor and Minister for Foreign Affairs, and that both had given him most satisfactory assurances as to the instructions which have been sent to Russian consuls. Emperor had declared in the most positive terms that he would [? omitted: not] allow Persia to cause division between England and Russia.§

This conciliatory temper in St. Petersburg was to have no little effect on the British attitude in the Austro-Serbo-Russian conflict now about to break.

The Tsar professed ignorance of the conduct of the naval attaché in Stockholm which had aroused the suspicion of Sweden, and asked if the increase in Swedish armaments might not indicate "the *arrière-pensée* of eventually taking sides against Russia, which, according to him, was the desire of Germany." It was agreed that M. Poincaré, who was to visit Stockholm, should convey to the King of Sweden the Tsar's desire for peace and friendly relations.‖

---

* Paléologue, I, 6.
† M. Cruppi, *Matin*, 26 August, 1915, quoted in Montgelas, p. 96.
‡ Poincaré, IV, 247.
§ Buchanan to Grey, telegram, 22 July; B 75.
‖ Poincaré, *Au service de la France*, IV, 239, 273–274. The Tsar's suspicions were not unwarranted. See below, II, chapter XXII, section seven ("The Small States").

In addition to these special points, a general agreement was reached between the French and Russian statesmen which was communicated to the British ambassador in these terms:

1. Perfect community of views on the various problems with which the Powers are confronted as regards the maintenance of general peace and balance of power in Europe, more especially in the East.

2. Decision to take action at Vienna with a view to the prevention of a demand for explanations or any summons equivalent to an intervention in the internal affairs of Servia which the latter would be justified in regarding as an attack on her sovereignty and independence.

3. Solemn affirmation of obligations imposed by the alliance of the two countries.*

In the Austro-Serbian crisis, then, France and Russia had agreed to pursue the same policy. According to M. Poincaré, neither Power had received any authoritative information of Austria-Hungary's intentions;† but the Italian ambassador believed that "Austria was on the point of taking an irrevocable step against Serbia,"‡ and the Serbian minister declared that he expected a "violent note" from Vienna and that if necessary Austria would create some incident which would furnish a pre-

---

* Buchanan to Grey, telegram, 24 July; B 101. This passage was omitted when the telegram was first published in the British *White Paper* of 1914. It was omitted on the ground that the British Government had no right to publish what had been agreed upon by the French and Russian Governments and which had been communicated in confidence. *B. D.*, XI, vi–vii. Nevertheless, there has been no little criticism of the omission, the argument being that the British Government was anxious to suppress evidence which might place France and Russia in an unfavorable light. As a matter of fact, the three points were revealed, if somewhat incidentally, in 1914. Point 1 is identical with the communiqué drawn up and published just before the departure of the French statesmen from Russia. Poincaré, IV, 279; Paléologue, I, 17. Point 2 is incorporated *verbatim* in the instructions sent to the French ambassador in Vienna. Viviani to Bienvenu-Martin, 24 July; F 22. Point 3 was not only stated publicly in the speeches of Poincaré and the Tsar, but was mentioned in the Russian *Orange Book* of 1914. Izvolski to Sazonov, 29 July; R 55. M. Poincaré protests against the argument that the three points involved a tightening [*resserrer*] of the alliance. "No agreement was signed. The Franco-Russian alliance was not modified, nor reinforced, nor tightened up." Point 3 was "only the supererogatory [*surabondante*] repetition of what the Russian and French governments had never ceased to proclaim from the beginning of the alliance." Poincaré, IV, 293–294.

† Poincaré, IV, 240, 243.   ‡ Schilling, p. 25.

text for attack.* Was it possible to take any useful step which might ward. off the danger?

Sir Edward Grey had expressed the view that "it would be very desirable that Austria and Russia should discuss things together if they become difficult."† On 21 July, the second day of his visit, M. Poincaré held a diplomatic reception at the Winter Palace, and the British ambassador seized the occasion to sound him on Grey's suggestion. But the French President rejected it:

His Excellency expressed opinion that a conversation à *deux* would be very dangerous at present moment, and seemed favorable to moderating counsels by France and England at Vienna.‡

M. Poincaré seems to have feared that such a conversation might prejudice mediation by the Concert of Europe;§ but, in fact, it would not be so dangerous as the pressure which M. Poincaré desired the Entente Powers to exert on Austria-Hungary, as he himself immediately discovered.

After Sir George Buchanan, the Austro-Hungarian ambassador was presented to the President. The latter proceeded to say that "Serbia was uneasy" and to express the opinion that Austria would not make demands which could not be justified by definite proofs. Count Szápáry replied coldly that the investigation was not complete, but that the Monarchy could not allow foreign governments to organize assassination of its sovereigns on their territory, a reply which convinced M. Poincaré that the Vienna cabinet intended to saddle Serbia with responsibility for the Sarajevo crime and to humiliate the offending state. He therefore reminded the ambassador that

Serbia had friends in Russia who would be astonished to learn of rigorous measures and that this surprise might be

---

* Poincaré, IV, 252. Buchanan to Grey, telegram, 22 July; B 76. Spalaykovich told the correspondent of the *Temps* that Poincaré had shown the warmest interest in Serbia, and seemed fully informed about the situation.
† Grey to Buchanan, telegram, 20 July; B 67.
‡ Buchanan to Grey, telegram, 22 July; B 76. Poincaré, IV, 252.
§ Statement of M. Poincaré to the writer.

shared by other countries in Europe which were friends of Serbia; there was accordingly the danger of a Balkan crisis which might lead to regrettable consequences.

But he hoped, he said in a more conciliatory tone, that Serbia would offer "every facility" to Austria-Hungary for the investigation and punishment of the crime; "with a little good will this Serbian affair can easily be adjusted."*

Conscious of the rebuff he had received, M. Poincaré concluded—rightly—that "Austria is preparing a *coup de théâtre* for us," and told his ambassador that "Sazonov must be firm and we must support him."† When the presidential party returned from the Winter Palace to the French embassy, they found a telegram from Paris, according to which "not only would Germany not oppose the brutal *démarche* planned by Austria but would associate herself with it."‡ No doubt this was discussed with M. Sazonov, for at the official dinner that night the Russian minister said that "it would be very difficult for Russia to mobilize, since the peasants were entirely taken up with working their fields." "But," continues M. Poincaré, "he was clearly putting this terrible eventuality out of his calculations quite as much as we were."§

As a result of his discussions with the French visitors, M. Sazonov, early the next morning, sent a long telegram to the ambassador in Vienna:

According to rumors current here, Austria is preparing to make various demands at Belgrade in connection with the events

---

* Poincaré, IV, 253–254; Paléologue, I, 10; Szápáry to Berchtold, 21 July, A I 45. Szápáry was quite indignant at Poincaré's conduct, and complained to his German colleague that the "President used language which, in consideration of the fact that he was addressing himself to a diplomat in a country in which he himself was a guest, could not but cause astonishment." Pourtalès to foreign office, telegram, 23 July; G 134. The German ambassador's conduct also caused some comment. "We were all struck," records the Rumanian minister in St. Petersburg, "by the sight of Count Pourtalès, the German ambassador. He was not, as we were, in full uniform, but in that informal costume [*petite tenue*] which the Russians call the '*vice-uniforme.*' When the British ambassador expressed his astonishment at this singular proceeding, he replied dryly that he reserved his full uniform for presentation to sovereigns." C. Diamandy, "Ma mission en Russe," in *Revue des deux mondes*, 7th period, IXL, 797 (15 February, 1929).
† Paléologue, I, 10.   ‡ Poincaré, IV, 256.   § Poincaré, IV, 258.

at Sarajevo. Please call the attention of the minister of foreign affairs, in friendly but energetic fashion, to the dangerous
consequences to which such a *démarche* might lead if it were to
be of a nature incompatible with the dignity of Serbia. It appears from my conversations with the French minister of foreign affairs that France is also preoccupied by any change which
might be brought about in the relations of Austria and Serbia and that she is not disposed to tolerate an unjustifiable humiliation of Serbia. The French ambassador has received instructions to advise the Austro-Hungarian Government to observe moderation.* According to our information, London also
condemns the intention ascribed to Austria of creating international complications in connection with this matter, and the
British Government has also ordered its representative in
Vienna to express himself in this sense.† I do not give up hope
that reason will prevail at Vienna over bellicose tendencies and
that timely warning given by the Great Powers will yet be able
to deter Austria from irrevocable measures. Before addressing yourself to Count Berchtold on this matter, please confer
with your French and British colleagues; but do not forget
that, in order to avoid any aggravation of the situation, the *démarches* which you may make ought not to appear to be either
joint or simultaneous.‡

This telegram, couched in courteous and conciliatory language, was a final warning to Austria that Russia must not be
ignored. Whether M. Sazonov expected any result from it, is
not known; having sent it, he took no further steps until the
news arrived of the presentation of the Austrian note in Belgrade.

For some reason, perhaps because of the pressure of the fes-
tivities in their honor, the French statesmen were rather slow
in sending similar instructions to their ambassador in Vienna.
It was not indeed until 1 A. M. on 24 July, nearly two days
later, that M. Viviani despatched from Reval, via the Quai

---

* Cf. circular of Bienvenu-Martin, 22 July; F 17.
† This was hardly correct. The British Government had been asked to associate
itself with the Franco-Russian *démarche*, but had not yet done so. See below, pp.

‡ Sazonov to Schebeko, 4 A. M., 22 July; Schilling, pp. 85–86. The telegram was
not received at the Russian embassy in Vienna until 3 P. M., the next day, 23 July,
too late to have any effect.

d'Orsay, an urgent telegram to M. Dumaine, informing him of the conversations between himself and the Russian foreign minister.

We found ourselves in agreement in thinking that we should not leave anything undone to prevent a demand for explanations or any summons [*mise en demeure*] which would be equivalent to an intervention in the internal affairs of Serbia, which the latter would be justified in regarding as an attack on her sovereignty and independence.

The ambassador was therefore instructed,

by means of a friendly conversation with Count Berchtold, [to] give him counsels of moderation, of such a kind as to make him understand how undesirable would be any intervention at Belgrade which would appear to be a threat on the part of the Cabinet of Vienna.

M. Dumaine was also asked

to discuss the matter with the Russian and British ambassadors, and to come to an agreement with them as to the best means by which each of you can make Count Berchtold understand without delay the moderation that the present situation appears to us to require.*

This language was somewhat stiffer than that used by M. Sazonov and reflects the tone, though hardly the literary style, of M. Poincaré. It was meant as a fair warning to Austria-Hungary of what she might expect if she persisted in the course that rumor assigned to her, but even before it was sent the Austrian note had been presented.

This fact, of course, was not yet known, and, in order to give added weight to their representations, both the Russian and the French Governments appealed to Great Britain to join in their *démarche*. Sir George Buchanan telegraphed to Sir Edward Grey,† and the Quai d'Orsay was instructed to "ask M. Paul

* Viviani to Bienvenu-Martin, 24 July; F 22.
† Buchanan to Grey, 22 and 23 July; B 76, 84.

Cambon to bring the advantages of this procedure to the notice
of Sir Edward Grey and to support the suggestion to this effect
which the British ambassador in Russia will have made."*
Thus the Triple Entente was to be united, if possible, against
the Central Powers; and, since the Italian Government had let
it be known in the Entente capitals that it disapproved of the
Austro-Hungarian procedure,† there was at least the chance,
if a bare one, that a united front on the part of the Entente
Powers would save the situation. If it did not, then France
and Russia were prepared to draw the logical conclusions, that
is to say, they would resist the Austrian pretensions by force.‡

It is worth noting that the demonstration of Franco-Russian
solidarity incident to M. Poincaré's visit failed to impress the
German ambassador. He telegraphed to Berlin:

The cool reception that President Poincaré met with on his
visit here attracts general attention. The great apathy can probably be attributed in part to the workingmen's strikes, which
have spread greatly in the last few days. More than half the
workingmen have stopped work. On account of the printers'
strike, a number of newspapers could not appear during Poincaré's visit. This has led to regrettable disturbances in which
the police and the Cossacks had to take a hand. . . .
At present strikes are taking place in other large cities besides St. Petersburg. They merit serious attention as symp-
toms of the embittered feeling which dominates the Russian
working classes, even if great importance is not to be attached
to them at the moment. However, in *the event of external
complications, they might cause the government serious embar-
rassment.*§

* Viviani to Bienvenu-Martin, 24 July; F 22.
† Carlotti's hints in St. Petersburg have already been noted. For Paris, cf. F 17;
for London, B 78 and G 124.
‡ The Russian minister in Stockholm, A. Nekludov, states that during the visit
of the French statesmen in the Swedish capital, M. Poincaré said to him: "We
are going through a truly alarming crisis; . . . I hope that we shall have a little
talk this evening." When Nekludov expressed the fear that "it means war," Viviani
replied: "It is terrible, terrible; *for if it means war for you, it most certainly also
means war for us.*" Nekludov, *Diplomatic Reminiscences*, p. 291.
§ Pourtalès to foreign office, telegram, 23 July; G 130. M. Poincaré writes:
"There were large crowds in all the streets through which we passed. A formidable
strike had, however, broken out in the last few days. The Grand Duke Nicholas

The words in italics are underlined by the German Emperor and approved by a laconic "Yes." The ambassador followed this with another telegram in which he said:

My Austro-Hungarian colleague believes that M. Poincaré is urging them on here to a conflict with the Triple Alliance; I assume rather that the President's statements [to Count Szápáry] were instigated by M. Sazonov, who is trying out a policy of bluff.*

Thus the German Government was encouraged to discount the effects of the French visit. What the French and Russian statesmen intended as warnings were regarded as vain and futile threats, and this illusion continued to be cherished by German diplomacy for some days.

The Austro-Hungarian Government likewise refused to be impressed. The Bavarian minister in Vienna, whose reports prove that he was accurately informed of the views of the Ballplatz, reported:

The toasts at Peterhof, especially those of the Tsar, are favorably regarded here, in so far as they reveal no encouragement of Serbia and justify the assumption that the Dual Alliance will permit a localization of the conflict.†

From every point of view, it was probably a most unfortunate accident that MM. Poincaré and Viviani were not in Paris, rather than in St. Petersburg, at this fateful time.‡

said that he thought the hand of Germany was to be detected in it, for she wished to turn the celebration of the Franco-Russian alliance into a fiasco. That, to be sure, is pure speculation. In any event, there was no question of failure or mishap. The spectators were numerous and raised frantic cheers for France. Popular enthusiasm did certainly seem to me less general and less deep than in London, but it was stronger than I had expected." Poincaré, IV, 249–250. For reports to Vienna on the strikes, see Szápáry to Berchtold, telegrams, 22, 23 July; *Ö.-U. A.*, 10,498, 10,547.

* Pourtalès to foreign office, 23 July; G 134. The Austro-Hungarian ambassador advised, however, that the consuls on leave should be ordered back to their posts. Szápáry to Berchtold, telegram, 22 July; *Ö.-U. A.*, 10,499.

† Tucher to foreign office, 21 July; Dirr, p. 130.

‡ On the day following the departure of the French statesmen, 24 July, Count Witte, the former Russian premier, who had been a consistent advocate of Russo-German friendship, talked at Bad Salzschlirf with an unnamed German. He sug-

Thus the stage was set for the great drama of the Thirteen Days, 23 July–4 August, 1914. The preparatory scene-shifting has been described in great detail because what was said and done by the several Powers before the presentation of the Austro-Hungarian note provides a more reliable clue to their real motives and purposes than actions and utterances called forth in the excitement of a stupendous crisis; also because each government, with the exception of the British, had decided before 23 July just what it would do and, as events were to prove, did not modify its position, even though one calculation after another was upset by the march of events. The situation on that fateful date may be summarized in this manner:

Austria-Hungary, assured of and encouraged by the promise of assistance from the German Empire, had determined on war against Serbia, and had devised a policy which made such a war unavoidable. Germany had accepted the programme of her ally, which had been carefully explained, not with the deliberate intent to precipitate a general European war, but with a complete willingness to accept such a war, if that were necessary for the execution of the Austro-Hungarian plan. Russia had decided, and announced, that she would resist by force any attempt on the part of the Dual Monarchy to diminish or unduly humiliate Serbia. France had proclaimed her solidarity with Russia. Thus, only retreat by one group or the other would permit a European war to be avoided. Italy, the third member of the Triple Alliance, had intimated to her allies that she would not follow them in a war against Serbia;* but

gested that the German Emperor and the Tsar should meet presently. "Now that the Peterhof meeting has taken place," he said, "the language employed by all the French and Russian papers will become more arrogant than ever. . . . If even now a meeting could be arranged between the two emperors, this would be of immense significance. The mischief-makers both in Russia and in France would be made to look small, and public opinion would calm down again. . . . Believe me, if this meeting comes off, the impression which the French visit has left on the Tsar will be entirely wiped out." He went on to say that "the personal relations between the Tsar and the [German] Emperor are not of an ordinary kind. They converse with each other on terms of intimate friendship, and each time the Tsar has had a chat with the Emperor he has been in better spirits." Witte's hint was not followed up on the German side. Huldermann, *Albert Ballin*, pp. 302–306.

*On the question whether Italy would have been willing to participate in return for adequate compensation, see above, p. 411.

whether she would remain neutral, or join the opposing group, was uncertain. Great Britain, the third member of the Triple Entente, had neither taken sides in the Austro-Serbian dispute nor decided what she would do if that dispute developed into a European conflagration. The attitude of these two Powers would profoundly affect the course of the diplomatic duel about to begin. But prompt decision by one or both of them was imperative, for the presentation of the Austro-Hungarian note and its subsequent publication created a situation between Austria-Hungary and Germany on the one side and Russia and France on the other in which peace could be preserved only if the odds were demonstrably weighted in favor of one group.

CHAPTER IX

THE AUSTRO–HUNGARIAN NOTE

SERBIA AND AUSTRIA-HUNGARY

In describing and analyzing the conduct of the Great Powers after the murder at Sarajevo, we have spoken only incidentally of the defendant in the case, Serbia. During the next weeks the little state, which was under suspicion of having been, in some way or other, connected with the tragedy, did little or nothing to clear itself or to facilitate a peaceful adjustment of the difficulty.

It will be recalled that the assassins of Francis Ferdinand claimed to have been inspired to their deed by resentment that his visit to Sarajevo had been set for 28 June. This day, the anniversary of the battle of Kossovo, when the mediæval Serbian kingdom had been overwhelmed by the Turks (1389), was particularly sacred to all Serbs; for Francis Ferdinand to come on such a day was deemed a national insult. But in 1914, now that the Turks had been defeated and the ancient battle-field itself recovered, the day was being celebrated with great solemnity as a "Festival of the Liberation." Under the auspices of the *Narodna Odbrana,* hundreds of Serbs were brought from southern Hungary, Bosnia and Dalmatia to participate in the ceremonies.* The people were in a highly wrought-up frame of mind, and friendliness to the neighboring Monarchy was not in their hearts, for the memory was still fresh of the veto imposed by Vienna on an Adriatic port and of the ultimatum of October, 1913.

News of the tragedy of Sarajevo was received in Serbia late in the day of its occurrence. It did not, according to the German minister, "arouse throughout the great masses of the people

* Hoflehner to Berchtold, 26 June, 7 July, Jehlitschka to Berchtold, 1 July; *Ö.-U. A.*, 9927, 9973, 10,104.

any feeling of special or heartfelt grief."* The Austro-Hungarian agents reported many painful scenes. At Belgrade, "people fell into one another's arms in delight," even after the Serbian Government had officially suspended the celebration;† at Prishtina, "the feeling which animated the fanatical crowd was . . . inhuman";‡ at Nish, "the deed was discussed . . . with obvious satisfaction."§ The judgment of the British chargé was that the news "produced in Belgrade a sensation rather of stupefaction than of regret":

The feeling most noticeable, especially among official circles, is one of apprehension lest too severe measures of repression should be exercised against the Serbs in Bosnia and in those parts of the Monarchy where the Serb element is preponderant. Such measures, it is feared, would excite public opinion in Servia and be made the occasion of anti-Austrian demonstrations which would not fail to bring about a tension in the relations between the two countries, and lead to serious complications.||

But as the weeks passed and no action was taken by Vienna, a feeling of confidence was created. "There is no longer any fear of being called to account," so the Austrian minister on 21 July advised his government, and the expectation was aroused that "in the immediate future the Habsburg state will fall to pieces"; "Austria-Hungary, hated as she is, now appears to the Serbs as powerless and scarcely worth waging war with."¶ It was this frame of mind which convinced the minister that "only the sharpened sword could reduce the hatred of the small neighbor to those limits which the interests of the Danube Monarchy unconditionally required."**

* Griesinger to Bethmann-Hollweg, 30 June; G 10.
† Storck to Berchtold, 29 June; Ö.-U. A., 9943.
‡ Jehlitschka to Berchtold, 1 July; Ö.-U. A., 9973.
§ Hoflehner to Berchtold, 6 July; Ö.-U. A., 10,084.
|| Crackanthorpe to Grey, 2 July; B 37. The first report was that the assassin was a Serbian from Belgrade. It is said that Pashich, who was dressing when the news was brought to him, took off his clothes and went to bed. A friend who found him there, thinking, was greeted with the words, "It is very bad. It is very bad. It will mean war." H. F. Armstrong, "Three Days in Belgrade, July, 1914," in Foreign Affairs (New York), V, 267 (January, 1927).
¶ Giesl to Berchtold, 21 July; A I 37.
** Giesl, Zwei Jahrzehnten im nahen Orient, p. 262.

The press, not restrained by any severe laws, indulged in reckless and vituperative language.* Twenty-six samples were collected by the Austro-Hungarian Government for the *dossier* which it later presented to the Powers;† some of the most provocative utterances have been quoted on page 368. Not only was Austria-Hungary abused and insulted, but the crime itself was glorified as an heroic and patriotic achievement. The Serbian minister in Vienna might point out that the utterances, which he condemned, were "partly accounted for, though certainly not justified, by the memory of innumerable attacks, couched in the most insulting language, which the Vienna press has been in the habit of making on the Servian people."‡ But they none the less, as we have seen, afforded the press of Vienna and Budapest the excuse to reply in kind and incite public opinion in the Monarchy to demand a rupture instead of a pacific settlement.

The Serbian Government, in its official organ, *Samouprava,* condemned the passions of the yellow press and asked it to cease from polemics;§ but without much success. Finally, M. Pashich was constrained to take refuge behind the assertion that the Austrians were quoting from papers "which are not the organs of any party or corporation," and to put forward the argument that, since in Serbia "the press is absolutely free," the government had no "constitutional or legal means" of control.‖ This was true; furthermore, so M. Pashich asserted to the German minister, "every attempt to increase the authority of the government and to provide it with the power of effective control had been shattered by the opposition of the Skupsh-

---

* The anti-Serbian demonstrations and excesses in Bosnia provided an excuse. Storck to Berchtold, 1, 7 July; *Ö.-U. A.*, 9963, 10,097. The *Politika* on 1 July laid the responsibility for the murder at Sarajevo on the Austro-Hungarian political methods in Bosnia and pointed out that the assassins and their forerunners were all Bosnians. Storck to Berchtold, 1 July; *Ö.-U. A.*, 9964, Beilage 2.
† A II 48 (in the 1915 *Red Book*, no. 19), appendix 9.
‡ Bunsen to Grey, 13 July; B 55.
§ Crackanthorpe to Grey, 10 July; B 45.
‖ Circular to Serbian legations abroad, telegram, 14 July; S 20. Loncharevich, *Jugoslaviens Entstehung*, pp. 555–564, prints a number of unabusive articles from the responsible party newspapers.

tina."* But the helplessness of the Serbian Government was, to say the least, unfortunate.

Officially, the Serbian Government repudiated the Sarajevo crime. The *Samouprava* on 29 June declared that "it could only be the work of some irresponsible maniac,"† and pointed out "how heavily this event falls on Serbia at a moment when such important and complex transactions with the Monarchy are nearing their solution."‡ On 3 July the same journal once more condemned the outrage, adding that

the crime is all the more regrettable in that it was detrimental to the interests of Servia, who is now convinced that it is to her interest to be on friendly terms with Austria-Hungary, and who sincerely desires the establishment of good relations with the Dual Monarchy.§

Of his own initiative the Serbian minister in Vienna not only expressed similar sentiments to the foreign office, but promised that his government "on its part will certainly and most loyally do everything to prove that they will not tolerate within their territory the fostering of any agitation or illegal proceedings."‖ The first attitude of the Serbian Government, then, was one of entire correctness.

This, however, did not last. When on 30 June the Austro-Hungarian chargé inquired of the Serbian foreign office what the government had done or proposed to do about the murder, the secretary-general, Dr. Gruyich, resented the question as "implying responsibility for the crime on the part of the Servian Government"¶ and replied that "the matter had not yet

* Griesinger to Bethmann-Hollweg, 8 July; G 32. The Serbian minister in Vienna requested Pashich to "induce the Belgrade press to be as moderate as possible in tone," and likewise begged the Ballplatz to control the Austro-Hungarian press. Yovanovich to Pashich, 1 and 3 July; S 9, 12.

† Crackanthorpe to Grey, 2 July; B 27.

‡ Griesinger to Bethmann-Hollweg, 30 June; G 10. The transactions referred to were the negotiations for the transfer to Serbia of the Oriental Railway which before the Balkan wars belonged to private Austrian interests; the negotiations were actually completed on 18 July.

§ Crackanthorpe to Grey, 4 July; B 35.

‖ Yovanovich to Pashich, 30 June; S 5. He added that Serbia "remained loyal to the desire to establish a sound basis for our good neighborly relations."

¶ Crackanthorpe to Grey, 2 July; B 27.

engaged the attention of the Serbian police."* Whereupon the Austrian diplomat "spoke very plainly"; with the result that Dr. Gruyich got into touch with the ministry of the interior, a number of searches and arrests were made, and a general investigation started.† "An interview of considerable violence" (as the British chargé described it) was not a happy start; relations between the foreign office and the legation were henceforth "very strained."

Nor, if M. Lyuba Yovanovich is to be believed, was the investigation of a kind to produce satisfactory results, although the German foreign office had advised Serbia to "neglect nothing in order to call to account those guilty of conspiracy."‡

When the Austrian stories arrived from Vienna [Yovanovich writes] to the effect that the assassins had received directions in Sarajevo from an official of the Serbian ministry of public works, a certain Milan Tsiganovich, M. Pashich asked M. Yotsa Yovanovich, then in charge of the department, who this official of his was; but M. Yotsa knew nothing about him, nor did anybody in his department. Under pressure from M. Pashich they at last unearthed Tsiganovich in some clerical post in the railway administration. . . . After that we heard from M. Yotsa that Tsiganovich had gone off somewhere out of Belgrade.§

---

* Storck to Berchtold, telegram, 30 June; *Ö.-U. A.*, 9950.

† Griesinger to Bethmann-Hollweg, 2 July; G 12. The Austro-Hungarian chargé had no confidence in any investigation which the Serbian police might undertake. Storck to Belgrade, 1, 3, 8 July; *Ö.-U. A.*, 9964, 10,004, 10,124.

‡ Lerchenfeld to Hertling, 2 July; Dirr, p. 118.

§ Yovanovich, *Кро Словенства*, p. 14; *The Murder of Sarajevo*, p. 7. It was reported to Vienna that three days after the murder at Sarajevo, Tsiganovich, at the request of the police, betook himself to Ribare and was given a month's leave. Storck to Berchtold, telegram, 7 July; *Ö.-U. A.*, 10,096. According to one Vladimir Kayganovich, a Serb from Slavonia, who claimed to have been persuaded by Milan Pribichevich to accept a commission in the Serbian gendarmerie, Tsiganovich's real name was Stefan Vecherinats; he was said to have come from Vinkovtse (in Slavonia), and to be employed in the tax department of the Serbian Government. Depositions of Kayganovich, 13, 17 July; *Ö.-U. A.*, 10,255, Beilage, 10,326, Beilage. Giesl, after investigating, replied that Tsiganovich was employed in a section of the railway administration which dealt with the taxes on railway employees. Giesl to Berchtold, telegram, 23 July; *Ö.-U. A.*, 10,525. A photograph of Vecherinats was sent to Potiorek, who was able to secure one of Tsiganovich. He reported that the two were not identical. Potiorek to Berchtold, telegram, 22 July; *Ö.-U. A.*, 10,505.

Nothing is known of any further investigation. The Austro-Hungarian minister was indeed informed that the Serbian Government was "prepared to comply at once with any request for police investigation and to take any other measures compatible with dignity and independence of State";* but the first move was left to Vienna.

Strictly speaking, the Serbian Government was within its legal rights. The crime was committed on Austro-Hungarian soil by subjects of the Habsburg Monarchy, and no formal complaint was lodged or demand made by the Cabinet of Vienna for action on the part of Serbia.† Still, "a decent respect to the opinions of mankind" and elementary political wisdom should have imposed on the Serbian Government the policy of instituting the most searching inquiry. There ought to have been a positive eagerness on the part of the Belgrade politicians to clear themselves of all imputations against the honor of the state and to fortify themselves against Austrian criticisms. There is no evidence of any such sentiments.

Perhaps at first they did not appreciate the gravity of the situation. M. Lyuba Yovanovich, while claiming to have been convinced that "Austria-Hungary would not be content with any kind of satisfaction and would declare war on us," states that the prime minister and his colleagues hoped that "we should somehow pull ourselves through this crisis."‡ This is borne out by the statement of Dr. Gruyich to the British chargé that "the Servian Government had certain knowledge that restraint would be exercised on Austria from Berlin."§ It is

---

* Crackanthorpe to Grey, telegram, 17 July; B 53.

† According to the *Politika* of 7 July, the Serbian Government had despatched a circular note to its representatives abroad repudiating any responsibility for the crime at Sarajevo and expressing the desire for good relations with Austria-Hungary. Storck to Berchtold, 8 July; *Ö.-U. A.*, 10,122. No such note is published in the Serbian *Blue Book* of 1914. "During the whole of this period, from the date of the perpetration of the outrage until to-day, not once did the Austro-Hungarian Government apply to the Serbian Government for their assistance. . . . They did not demand that any of the accomplices should be subjected to an inquiry or that they should be handed over to trial." Pashich to Serbian representatives abroad, telegram, 19 July; S 30.

‡ Yovanovich, *Крв Словенства*; pp. 15–16; *The Murder of Sarajevo*, pp. 8–9.

§ Crackanthorpe to Grey, 18 July; B 80. Crowe minuted that "it would be interesting to know who misled him [Gruyich]." Gruyich further stated that "should,

possible also that M. Pashich failed to appreciate the sensitive-ness of European opinion to political murder.

At the same time, the political situation in Serbia was, as the German minister recognized, "a very difficult one." M. Pashich was in the midst of a bitter electioneering campaign and, in spite of the tension with Austria-Hungary, felt it necessary to leave Belgrade on 19 July for a speaking tour in southern Serbia. As Herr von Griesinger explained to Berlin,

Every concession to the Monarchy will be charged against him by the united opposition as weakness. There is the further fact that military circles, blinded by their megalomania and chauvinism, are driving him to harsh measures which are quite out of keeping with his conciliatory disposition.*

Here exactly was the rub, for the election would determine whether the country was to be controlled by the Radical party or the military group of which the *Uyedinyenye ili Smrt* was the driving power. Until he had won the election M. Pashich was not strong enough to proceed to the limit against the 'Black Hand'—which fact made any thorough investigation of the Sarajevo conspiracy practically impossible. It was "on account of internal political considerations" (so the German minister thought) that the hard-pressed premier went the length of giving an outrageous interview to the *Leipziger Neueste Nachrichten* which was described by the Austro-Hungarian minister as "impudent" and strengthened his argument for drastic action.†

These circumstances may explain the inactivity of the Serbian Government; or it may have had a guilty conscience. But, warned by its ministers in Vienna‡ and London§ that a crisis

however, the worst come to the worst and Austria declare war, Servia would not stand alone. Russia would not remain quiet were Servia wantonly attacked, and Bulgaria would be immobilised by Roumania."

* Griesinger to Bethmann-Hollweg, 21 July; G 137.

† Giesl to Berchtold, 21 July; A I 37.

‡ "For the sake of her prestige, Austria-Hungary must take some action in the belief that she will thus raise her prestige internally as well as externally." Yovano-vich to Pashich, 15 July; S 25.

§ "No reliance should be placed in the ostensibly peaceable statements of Austro-

was approaching, it began trying to exculpate itself. The British chargé was told that

With regard to Chabrinovich, who had made the first attempt on the Archduke's life, it was already public knowledge that on his arrival in Belgrade recently the Servian Government had, as is usual in the case of Austrian subjects coming to reside in Belgrade, made the customary inquiry of the Austrian consulate as to his antecedents and had received satisfactory information on this point.* Of Printsip the Servian Government knew nothing.†

This was evidently felt not to go far enough; for when the chargé adverted to the advice of the *Times* that Serbia should undertake an investigation into the Sarajevo conspiracy, he was assured that "on publication of the result of the inquiry at Sarajevo the Servian Government would be fully prepared to comply with whatever request for further investigation the circumstances might call for and which would be compatible with international usage."‡

This was followed up by an appeal to the Powers. At the end of a long circular which offered an elaborate defense of the policy of the Serbian Government, M. Pashich affirmed his desire "to maintain friendly relations with Austria-Hungary, and to suppress every attempt against the peace and public safety of the neighboring Monarchy."

We will likewise [he continued] meet the wishes of the Austro-Hungarian Empire in the event of our being requested to subject to trial in our independent courts any accomplices in the outrage who are in Serbia—should such, of course, exist.

Hungarian official circles, as the way is being prepared for diplomatic pressure upon Serbia, which may develop into an armed attack." Boskovich to Pashich, telegram, 17 July; S 27. Boskovich may have been given some hint at the British foreign office, which had received Bunsen's forecast of the Austrian note. See above, pp. 390–391.

* On the truth of this assertion, see above, pp. 214–215.

† Which was hardly true, for at least Lyuba Yovanovich was acquainted with Printsip; see above, p. 210. Even if the Serbian Government was not aware of the plot before 28 June, it is difficult to believe that after the event it had not informed itself about the persons who actually perpetrated the crime.

‡ Crackanthorpe to Grey, 18 July, received 23 July; B 80. A telegraphic summary was sent on 19 July; B 61.

But we can never comply with demands which may be directed against the dignity of Serbia, and which would be inacceptable to any country which respects and maintains its independence.

Actuated by the desire that good neighborly relations may be firmly established and maintained, we beg the friendly governments to take note of these declarations and to act in a conciliatory sense should occasion or necessity arise.*

Such a declaration might have had some effect two weeks previously. As matters then stood, it fell quite flat.†

The bad situation was not improved by the sudden and spectacular death of the Russian minister in Belgrade. M. Hartwig was an ardent Pan-Slavist, who was commonly credited with inciting Serbian hatred of Austria-Hungary and holding out the hope of Russian help in the day of reckoning; and he was frequently and bitterly complained of by Austrian and German diplomacy. Curiously enough, he was passionately fond of the city of Vienna, and had established close personal relations with his Austro-Hungarian colleague, Baron Giesl. The latter happened to be on leave when the Sarajevo tragedy occurred, and did not return to Belgrade until 10 July. That same evening he was visited by M. Hartwig. The minister seemed to be breathing with difficulty, but was anxious for a political conversation. He assured Baron Giesl that the flag on the Russian legation had been kept at half-mast until the conclusion of the funeral ceremonies of the Archduke, in spite of rumors to the contrary,‡ and then asked what the Cabinet of Vienna proposed to do about Serbia. Baron Giesl replied that the punishment of the Serbian conspirators would be insisted upon,

---

* Pashich to missions abroad, telegram, 19 July; S 30.

† In London, Serbia was advised "to meet the Austrian requests in a conciliatory and moderate spirit." Memorandum of Nicolson, 23 July; B 87. At Berlin a sound snubbing was administered. Jagow told the Serbian chargé that Serbia "had done nothing to improve its relations with the neighboring monarchy," and said that he could well understand it "if at Vienna they are now going to strike a more energetic note." Jagow to Tschirschky, telegram, 20 June; G 94. Berchtold returned his thanks for the language used by his German colleague. Tschirschky to foreign office, telegram, 21 July; G 95.

‡ The statements that the flag was not at half-mast emanated from the Italian and British chargés. Storck to Berchtold, 6, 13 July; Ö.-U. A., 10,072, 10,235.

but that "the sovereignty of Serbia would not be touched." M. Hartwig appeared greatly relieved and was about to ask one more question when he suddenly collapsed. In a few minutes he was dead, from a heart attack.*

The news created a sensation in Belgrade, where fantastic stories began to circulate. According to one account, Hartwig had taken a "cup of tea" at the Austrian legation;† Baron Giesl overheard himself accused in a barber-shop of having brought back from Vienna an electric chair "which produces the instantaneous death of the occupier without leaving any trace!"‡ The general excitement produced rumors of possible anti-Austrian demonstrations on the king's birthday, 12 July; a number of Austrian residents fled across the river to Semlin or took refuge in the legation; and the Austro-Hungarian minister appealed to the government for protection, which was duly promised, although the need for it was denied by Pashich. Nothing happened in fact. On the following day, 13 July, Hartwig was given an imposing funeral which was attended by the Serbian Government and great masses of the people, without any disturbances;§ Baron Giesl and the Austrian military attaché were both present in uniform‖ and were "quite unnoticed."¶ But the incident was played up by the Budapest press,** to which the Serbian Government replied by asserting that "all these false reports are being purposely spread in order to arouse and excite Austro-Hungarian public opinion against Serbia."††

---

* Giesl, pp. 257–259.   † Crackanthorpe to Grey, 13 July; B 62.
‡ Giesl, p. 261.
§ Loncharevich, pp. 577–582, denies that there were rumors of anti-Austrian demonstrations and argues that they were invented in the Austro-Hungarian legation. The rumors reached the legation through a spy (Giesl to Berchtold, telegram, 12 July; Ö.-U. A., 10,213), but Giesl was reproved for speaking to Pashich on the basis of news from an unreliable person (Berchtold to Giesl, telegram, 13 July; Ö.-U. A., 10,230).
‖ Giesl proposed to attend in civil costume (Giesl to Berchtold, telegram, 11 July; Ö.-U. A., 10,192), but was ordered not to offend the diplomatic proprieties (Berchtold to Giesl, telegram, 12 July; Ö.-U. A., 10,212).
¶ Giesl, p. 261. Giesl to Berchtold, 14 July; Ö.-U. A., 10,256. Circular telegram of Pashich, 19 July; S 30. Griesinger to Bethmann-Hollweg, 21 July; G 137.
** Max Müller to Grey, 16 and 17 July; B 81, 82.
†† Circular telegram of Pashich, 14 July; S 21.

In Baron Giesl's opinion, Hartwig's death was a terrible misfortune.

Hartwig's side-remarks and statements during his visit indicated that he had none too high an opinion of Serbia's military strength; he was of the opinion that Serbia's army had not been adequately strengthened after the Balkan wars and that Russia was not ready at that time to conduct a great war. Armed action by Austria-Hungary against Serbia could lead only to the quick and complete subjection of the isolated country, and must therefore be prevented. In view of the influence which Hartwig enjoyed in St. Petersburg and of his preponderant position in Belgrade, he would certainly have succeeded in getting the Serbian Government to accept all of our demands unconditionally. Of course he would have had to promise a great and certain reckoning at a later time—perhaps in 1916 when the reorganization of the Tsar's army had been fully carried out, and Serbia would have to prepare her forces for this date. But if Hartwig had been alive on the critical day, 25 July, *the world war would not have broken out.**

The judgment is startling, but it may be correct. A certain confirmation is offered in Hartwig's exclamation, "Let us hope that it was not a Serbian,"† when he first heard of the crime at Sarajevo, a remark which hardly fits the theory that he was plotting with Dragutin Dimitriyevich and the 'Black Hand' to precipitate war.

All during this time the Serbian minister in Vienna was unable to penetrate the intentions of the Ballplatz;‡ which is not surprising, in view of what was being planned. But on 20 July he came to the conclusion that it was "highly probable" that "Austria was preparing for war with Serbia," and called attention to the military preparations being made "especially in the vicinity of the Serbian frontier."§ We do not know what impression this report made on the Serbian Government; so

---

* Giesl, p. 260.
† Griesinger to Bethmann-Hollweg, 30 June; G 10. The remark was overheard by the Italian chargé. Storck to Berchtold, 29 June; Ö.-U. A., 9943.
‡ Bunsen to Nicolson, private, 17 July; B 56.
§ Yovanovich to Pashich, 20 July; S 31.

far as is known, it did not recall the commander-in-chief of the army, Voivode Putnik, who was on leave at an Austrian watering-place.

There are only meagre indications of the advice which Serbia may have received from her friends and allies. The Italian information was to the effect that "Russia had been advising Belgrade to give way"*—how was not specified. Likewise the Rumanian Government "most urgently advised submission to Austria-Hungary."† Sir Edward Grey recommended the Serbian Government "to give to Austria the utmost assurances they could for the prevention of such plots against Austria being carried on in Servia in future."‡ If such admonitions were indeed rather vague, it cannot be said that Serbia was encouraged by her friends to resist the pressure of Vienna.

Serbia, for her part, as we have seen, was ready to begin an investigation when requested by Austria to do so, but there were certain things that she would not accept.

A demand on the part of Austro-Hungarian Government for appointment of a mixed commission of inquiry, for suppression of nationalist societies or for censorship of press, could not be acceded to, since it would imply foreign intervention in domestic affairs and legislation.§

Evidently the Serbs knew what to expect, and they were right, for these were the very points to which the Austro-Hungarian Government attached the greatest importance. It would be most interesting to know whether Count Berchtold was informed of this attitude of Serbia.

If the ravings of the press are put to one side (and the Austro-Hungarian press was as violent as the Serbian), the Serbian Government may be exculpated from deliberately aggravating the situation between itself and the Dual Monarchy; on the

---

* Flotow to foreign office, telegram, 14 July; G 42.
† Waldburg to foreign office, telegram, 23 July; G 135. Cf. also Czernin to Berchtold, telegram, 22 July; Ö.-U. A., 10,484.
‡ Grey to Buchanan, 22 July; B 79.
§ Crackanthorpe to Grey, telegram, 17 July; B 53.

other hand, it was guilty of a grievous blunder in not at once starting and pushing through with all speed an investigation of the antecedents of the Sarajevo crime on its own soil. But, in the long run, what the Serbian Government did or did not do probably made no difference. Austria-Hungary was determined to have war, and it is impossible to doubt that an excuse would have been found to make it.*

PRESENTATION OF THE AUSTRIAN NOTE

The Austrian note was, as we have seen, despatched from Vienna on 20 July for presentation on the 23d. Baron Giesl was to make clear to the Serbian Government that "the demands represent the minimum which we can ask if the present intolerable relations with Serbia are to be cleared up," that "we cannot enter into any negotiations," and that only "unconditional acceptance within the indicated time limit [48 hours] can relieve us of the necessity of proceeding to the logical consequences"; no extension of the time-limit was to be allowed for the explanation of the demands, and the minister was forbidden to give any explanation or interpretation. He was to say that he had "no information" about what "further steps" might be contemplated in the event of a rupture, but was to hint that Serbia would certainly be held responsible for the costs of the military measures which her "hostile attitude" had imposed on the Monarchy "in the last few years."† Baron Giesl

* On 23 July, the governor of the Boden-Credit-Anstalt, one of the most important Viennese banks, informed Berchtold of a conversation which he had had on the previous day with the Belgrade banker Benzion Bulley, who was "a special friend of Pashich and well informed about his intentions." Bulley made the following statement: "Serbia is entirely quiet, and no one is thinking of the possibility of war, for at present Serbia has only one desire: peace for many years, in order to pacify the new provinces. Without any doubt the minister-president Pashich, in reply to the demands to be made on Serbia, will exhibit the utmost conciliation possible, without regard to the politics of the street. A war can arise, then, only if Austria wishes unconditionally to bring it about at the last moment. But in that case a localization of it is considered as quite out of the question." Sieghart to Berchtold, 23 July; Ö.-U. A., 10,569. Since nothing more is known about this overture, its real significance cannot be determined. Berchtold merely wrote on Sieghart's letter, "Acknowledge with thanks"—and did not alter his policy.
† Berchtold to Giesl, 20 July; A I 28.

was further instructed that neither the absence of M. Pashich from Belgrade* nor even the resignation of the Serbian Government was to be accepted as an excuse for delay.† There must be acceptance *pure et simple* within 48 hours. These harsh instructions are additional proof that, as has already been shown, acceptance was neither expected nor desired.

One final effort was made to dissuade the Austro-Hungarian Government from too violent action. On 22 July, the day before the presentation of the note, the French ambassador in Vienna called at the foreign office to inform himself about the situation. According to the Austrian version,

he also discussed all the eventualities which might arise from an energetic step taken by us with the Cabinet of Belgrade, and painted in vivid colors the dangers of a war between Austria-Hungary and Serbia, especially in view of the fact that it might assume the character of a war of the Serbian race against the Monarchy.‡

He was told, so he reported to Paris, that "the tone of the Aus-

* Berchtold to Giesl, telegram, 21 July; A I 36.
† Berchtold to Giesl, telegram, 23 July; A I 63.
‡ Memorandum of 22 July; A I 53. The memorandum continues: "Nevertheless M. Dumaine concluded his remarks by saying that as a result of a short conversation with his Russian colleague about the matter in question, he was convinced that Russia was not disposed to make a strong stand for Serbia in the approaching conflict with Austria-Hungary or to vouchsafe her more than moral support. In the event of a passage at arms between us and Serbia, Russia would not, in the opinion of the French ambassador, intervene actively, but would endeavor rather to localize the war." M. Dumaine's account of this conversation has not been published. He appears to have had a certain sympathy with the Austro-Hungarian point of view, for he reported to his government that "growing condition of unrest in Southern Slav provinces of Dual Monarchy was such that Austro-Hungarian Government were compelled either to acquiesce in separation of those provinces or make a desperate effort to retain them by reducing Servia to impotency." Bunsen to Grey, telegram, 29 July; B 265. But it is very hard to believe that he expressed to the Ballplatz the view that Russia would not support Serbia, for his Russian colleague had said repeatedly that Russia would intervene in the event of an armed attack on Serbia. According to the British ambassador, "French ambassador spoke seriously yesterday to . . . Baron Macchio, on danger of provoking an armed conflict with Servia. Baron Macchio took his warning in good part, and led the French ambassador to think that moderate language would be used in the note." Bunsen to Grey, telegram, 23 July; B 90. Thus reassured, M. Dumaine may well have said that Russia would not intervene, for Sazonov had said, on the previous day, that "if Austria could prove plot to have been hatched in Servia there was no objection to her asking Servian Government to institute judicial inquiry, and this, he believed, Servia was ready to do." Buchanan to Grey, 22 July, telegram; B 76.

trian note, and the demands which would be formulated in it, allow us to count on a peaceful result."* But he was not told that the note would be presented the next day.†

On Thursday morning, 23 July, Baron Giesl, acting under instructions,‡ sent a secretary to the Yellow House (as the Serbian foreign office was sometimes called) to ask for an appointment at four o'clock that afternoon with M. Pashich, in order to deliver "an important communication." Usually diplomatists ask at what hour they may be received, but Serbia was to be spared nothing. As M. Pashich had not returned from his electioneering, it was arranged that Baron Giesl should be received by M. Pachu, the minister of finance, who had been entrusted with the foreign office during the premier's absence.

Of the members of the Serbian cabinet, only three, Lazar Pachu, Stoyan Protich, the minister of the interior, and Lyuba Yovanovich, the minister of education, were in town. After a hasty consultation, they decided to recall M. Pashich. He proved to be out of both telegraphic and telephonic reach, but finally was located by a gendarme, and started back to Belgrade in the afternoon.

A little before four o'clock the three ministers assembled at the foreign office to receive Baron Giesl. At 3.55 the latter's secretary appeared to say that the minister would not come until six o'clock, which was resented by the three Serbians.§ At the latter hour, Giesl appeared. He was received by MM. Pachu and Gruyich, the latter being present because the finance minister did not understand French. Saying,

I have instructions from my government to deliver you this note and to add that unless a satisfactory reply is given on all

---

* Circular of Bienvenu-Martin, 23 July; F 20.
† Bunsen to Grey, 1 September; B 676.
‡ Berchtold to Giesl, telegram, 21 July; A I 36.
§ The reason for the delay, which was of course unknown to the waiting Serbians, was the desire to postpone delivery of the note until so late an hour that it could not become known in St. Petersburg before the departure of MM. Poincaré and Viviani. Giesl was notified of the change of hour after he had made the appointment for four o'clock. Berchtold to Giesl, telegram, 23 July; A I 62.

points by six o'clock on Saturday, the day after to-morrow, I
shall leave Belgrade with all the personnel of my legation,

the Austro-Hungarian representative began to read the note.
But Pachu protested that he could not take the responsibility, in
the absence of Pashich; whereupon Giesl laid the note on the
table, and said that in an age of railways, telegraphs, and telephones and in view of the smallness of Serbia, it would be only
the matter of a few hours to arrange for the minister's return,
and that in any case that was the concern of the Serbian Government.   When Baron Giesl had departed, MM. Pachu and
Gruyich read the note and then showed it to the other ministers,
who were waiting in the next room.   Lyuba Yovanovich pondered awhile, and then exclaimed, "Well, there is nothing to do
but die fighting."   Certainly there was nothing to do at the moment but communicate the note to the Serbian ministers abroad
and to the foreign powers, and to await the return of M. Pashich, who did not arrive until the next morning.*

THE NOTE

The Austro-Hungarian note,† the most fateful document of
our time, began by quoting the declaration made by the Serbian Government on 31 March, 1909:‡

Serbia recognizes that the *fait accompli* regarding Bosnia has
not affected her rights, and consequently she will conform to
the decisions that the Powers may take in conformity with article 25 of the Treaty of Berlin.   In deference to the advice
of the Great Powers, Serbia undertakes to renounce from now
on the attitude of protest and opposition which she has adopted
with regard to the annexation since last autumn.   She undertakes, moreover, to modify the direction of her policy with re-

* H. F. Armstrong, "Three Days in Belgrade, July, 1914," in *Foreign Affairs*
(New York), V, 268–272 (January, 1927).   Giesl, *op. cit.*, pp. 266–267.   Giesl to
Berchtold, 23 July; A I 67.
† The note, the Serbian reply of 25 July and the Austrian comments of 27 July
are given, in parallel columns, in an appendix at the end of Volume II.
‡ The declaration was given by Serbia in order to prevent an attack by Austria-
Hungary, and was made to all the Great Powers; it brought to an end the crisis
provoked by the Austrian annexation of Bosnia-Herzegovina on 6 October, 1908.

gard to Austria-Hungary and to live in future on good neighborly terms with the latter.

This promise, said the Austro-Hungarian Government, had not been fulfilled: on the contrary, the Serbian Government had connived at "a subversive movement" which aimed to detach certain provinces from the Dual Monarchy. It had "permitted the criminal machinations of various societies and associations directed against the Monarchy"; had "tolerated unrestrained language on the part of the press, the glorification of the perpetrators of outrages, and the participation of officers and functionaries in subversive agitation"; it had "permitted an unwholesome propaganda in public instruction—in short, . . . all manifestations of a nature to incite the Serbian population to hatred of the Monarchy and contempt of its institutions."

The investigations of the Austro-Hungarian authorities were stated to prove that "the Sarajevo assassinations were planned in Belgrade; that the arms and explosives with which the murderers were provided had been given to them by Serbian officers and functionaries belonging to the *Narodna Odbrana;* and finally, that the passage into Bosnia of the criminals and their arms was organized and effected by the chiefs of the Serbian frontier service."

For these reasons the Serbian Government was required to publish in its *Official Journal* of 26 July, 1914, the following declaration:

The Royal Government of Serbia condemns the propaganda directed against Austria-Hungary, *i. e.,* the general tendency the final aim of which is to detach from the Austro-Hungarian Monarchy territories belonging to it, and it sincerely deplores the fatal consequences of these criminal proceedings.

The Royal Government regrets that Serbian officers and functionaries participated in the above-mentioned propaganda and thus compromised the good neighborly relations to which the Royal Government was solemnly pledged by its declaration of 31 March, 1909.

The Royal Government, which disapproves of and repudiates

all idea of interfering or attempting to interfere with the destinies of the inhabitants of any part whatsoever of Austria-Hungary, considers it its duty formally to warn officers and functionaries, and the whole population of the kingdom, that henceforward it will proceed with the utmost rigor against persons who may be guilty of such machinations, which it will use all its efforts to anticipate and suppress.

This declaration was also to be communicated to the army as an order of the day.

Moreover, the Serbian Government had to undertake:

1. To suppress any publication directed against Austria-Hungary.*

2. To dissolve the *Narodna Odbrana,* and to prevent the formation or activity of similar societies in the future.

3. To eliminate from the public schools all persons and all methods of instruction calculated to foment the propaganda.†

4. To remove all army officers and civil functionaries whom Austria might indicate as being guilty of propaganda against the Monarchy.

5. To accept the collaboration in Serbia of Austrian representatives for the suppression of the subversive movement.

6. To take judicial proceedings against accessories to the plot of 28 June who were on Serbian territory; delegates of the Austro-Hungarian Government were to take part in the investigation relating thereto.

7. To arrest Major Voya Tankosich and Milan Tsiganovich.

8. To prevent the illicit traffic in arms, and to dismiss and punish severely those officials who had assisted the Sarajevo conspirators to cross the frontier.

9. To explain the hostile utterances of Serbian officials, at home and abroad, concerning the crime of Sarajevo.

---

* According to Berchtold, "there are three precedents, in which the Serbian Government, without any hindrance from the press law and contrary to its wording, suppressed newspapers—in 1905 and 1907 the antidynastic papers *Narodni List, Oposizia* and *Otashbina,* and in 1910 *Republika*." Berchtold to Czernin, telegram, 24 July; *Ö.-U. A.,* 10,587.

† For a summary of nationalistic tendencies in Serbian school textbooks, see Storck to Berchtold, telegram, 8 July; *Ö.-U. A.,* 10,120.

10. To notify the Austro-Hungarian Government of the execution of the above measures.

Forty-eight hours were allowed for a reply.

Such was the famous note which, although not technically so styled, was by common consent called an ultimatum. In general, the remark of Sir Edward Grey,

> The note seemed to me the most formidable document I had ever seen addressed by one State to another that was independent,*

has commanded general assent. Even the German foreign minister admitted privately that "as a diplomatic document note left much to be desired,"† and he claims to have protested to the Austrian ambassador in Berlin that it was "pretty sharp."‡

The Serbian minister in Vienna, speculating on the possibilities of the situation, had pointed out that the Dual Monarchy could choose between two courses:

> Either to regard the Sarajevo outrage as a national misfortune which ought to be dealt with in accordance with the evidence obtained, in which Serbia's co-operation in the work would be requested, in order to prevent the perpetrators escaping the extreme penalty; or to treat the Sarajevo outrage as a

* Grey to Bunsen, telegram, 24 July; B 91.

† Rumbold to Grey, telegram, 25 July; B 122.

‡ See above, p. 382. The most level-headed German student of pre-war diplomacy is decidedly critical. "The categorical tone of the note, and the brief period of 48 hours allowed for a reply, emphasized the harshness of the whole proceeding. We know that this was not accidental, but that in Vienna they had purposely drafted the ultimatum in such a way that Serbia could not accept it, because they had from the beginning decided to resort to military measures." Brandenburg, Von Bismarck zum Weltkrieg, pp. 417–418. Some English newspapers, chiefly Radical in leaning, were disposed to think the Austrian demands not unjustified. Montgelas, pp. 196–197; Scott, pp. 215–221. Since the war, lenient views have been expressed by the French writer, M. Morhardt, Les preuves (Paris, 1924), pp. 70–105, and by the Canadian jurist J. S. Ewart, The Roots and Causes of the War (New York, 1925), II, 1043–1047. Fay, II, 273, writes: "One cannot say that the demands, though very severe, were excessive from the Austrian point of view. If they had been honestly calculated merely to exact punishment for those connected with the Sarajevo assassination and to obtain guarantees of security for the future, they might be regarded as justified. But having been deliberately framed with the expectation that they would be rejected, and that their rejection would lead to a localized war with Serbia, they must be condemned on both moral and practical grounds as one of the main causes of the World War. And Germany, in so far as she assented to them and indorsed them, must share in this condemnation."

Pan-Serbian, Southern Slav, and Pan-Slav conspiracy, with every manifestation of hatred, hitherto repressed, against Slavdom.*

In plain language, Austria-Hungary could, on legal and juridical grounds, demand punishment of the criminals; or she could put the whole matter on a political plane. For reasons which have already been discussed, she elected to do the latter. While her note did demand punishment of the guilty persons, it was in essence a political indictment of Serbia. But, by thus introducing political expediency as the motive of action, the Austro-Hungarian Government opened the way for other Powers to assert that their political interests were threatened by what it proposed to do and to resist its action, as, in all probability, they would not have done if the Monarchy had confined itself to demanding reparation for the crime. To project the future of Serbia into the discussion was a grave tactical blunder on the part of the Ballplatz, of which its opponents were not slow to take advantage.

Of the eleven demands—the publication of the declaration and the ten formally enumerated—nearly all involved some diminution of the sovereignty of Serbia. Nos. 6, 7, and 8 may be regarded as police measures incumbent on any law-abiding government and in large measure justified, although the second part of no. 6 was contrary to the Serbian constitution. No. 1 would involve a change in both the law and the constitution. The rest, by imposing certain actions on the Serbian Government, would prejudice its freedom of action. However effective they might promise to be for suppressing the Great-Serbian agitation, they were demands which an independent state could be expected to submit to only in the face of diplomatic isolation or military defeat.†

---

* Yovanovich to Pashich, 7 July; S 17.

† Baron Musulin, who actually drafted the ultimatum, writes: "In the formation of each point in the list of demands to be made upon Serbia, the question was asked whether the demand . . . would and could be accepted by Serbia, and in every single case the formulation of the text was declared complete only when the question had been answered in the affirmative. . . . In the foreign office no one believed that the

Before leaving the discussion of the ultimatum, it may not be out of place to indicate what the other Powers thought of it. Sir Edward Grey criticised two points in particular, the time limit and point 5. On the latter he said:

Demand No. 5 might mean that the Austro-Hungarian Government were to be entitled to appoint officials who should have authority in Servian territory and this would hardly be consistent with maintenance of independent sovereignty of Servia.

But he declined to discuss the merits of the dispute between Austria and Serbia, which, he said, was not "our concern."*

The acting French foreign minister, M. Bienvenu-Martin, likewise was struck by point 5, which he read over twice. He "admitted freely that the events of recent years and the attitude of the Serbian Government made energetic action on [Austria-Hungary's] part a matter that could be understood." But he declined to discuss the text.†

The secretary-general of the Italian foreign office thought that it was clever to quote the Serbian declaration of 1909 and agreed that Serbia must publish the declaration demanded; but he observed that "the acceptance of point 4 would be difficult for the Serbian Government." He seemed much impressed by the proofs of Serbian complicity, and admitted that the Austrian action was "purely defensive."‡ His chief, the Marquis di San Giuliano, was more critical, at least in what he said to the British ambassador:

He considers that, if the note was seriously meant in the sense that its text implies, it is a monument of absurdity. It

ultimatum would lead to war." Musulin, *Das Haus am Ballplatz*, pp. 225-227. It is possible that Musulin personally did believe this, but it is certain that Berchtold and Hoyos did not. The Austrian military attaché in Constantinople, considering it "out of the question that Serbia could accept the note in its entirety or that Russia could allow the subjugation of Serbia by Austria-Hungary," as soon as he read the note on 24 July, telegraphed to his family in Lemberg (Galicia) to proceed at once to Vienna and prepare for a long stay. Pomiankowski, *Der Zusammenbruch des Ottomanisches Reiches*, pp. 70-71.

* Grey to Bunsen, telegram, 24 July; B 91. Cf. Mensdorff to Berchtold, telegram, 24 July; A II 14.

† Szécsen to Berchtold, telegram, 24 July; A II 9.

‡ Mérey to Berchtold, telegram, 24 July; A II 8.

might have been drawn up by a policeman. Does the Austrian Government, he asked, still seriously think that racial instincts and national movements can be extinguished by police measures? If, on the other hand, it was meant simply as a declaration of war, then it is unnecessary to criticise it.*

What mattered, of course, was the opinion of Russia. In his first discussion of the note with the Austrian ambassador, M. Sazonov appears to have objected specifically to only two points. He "protested most vigorously against the dissolution of the *Narodna Odbrana* [point 2], a condition which Serbia could never accept. The minister further objected to the participation of the Imperial and Royal functionaries in the suppression of the subversive movement" [point 5].† This latter objection Count Berchtold sought to remove by explaining that Austria was "thinking of establishing in Belgrade a secret *bureau de sûreté* similar to the Russian establishment in Paris‡ and Berlin which would co-operate with the Serbian police and administrative authorities."§

At a second discussion on 26 July, M. Sazonov, according to Count Szápáry, said that, "of the ten points, seven were acceptable without great difficulties, but that the two points referring to the collaboration of the Imperial and Royal functionaries in Serbia [point 5] and the point [4] involving the dismissal of Serbian officers and officials *ad libitum* at our demand were, in this form, unacceptable."‖ Sazonov's own account reveals more extensive objections:

* Rodd to Grey, 27 July; B 648.
† Szápáry to Berchtold, telegram, 24 July; A II 17.
‡ Berchtold had received, at his request, information from his ambassador in Paris about the Russian establishment. Berchtold to Szécsen, telegram, 10 July, Szécsen to Berchtold, 18 July; Ö.-U. A., 10,181, 10,361.
§ Berchtold to Szápáry, 25 July, telegram; A II 38. It is a striking commentary on Berchtold's purposes that he did not communicate this explanation to Serbia, and he delayed the communication to Russia until it was too late for it to be passed on from St. Petersburg to Belgrade before 6 P. M. on Saturday, 25 July. It will be seen that the Serbian Government in its reply stated that "it did not clearly grasp the meaning or the scope of the demand." When Berchtold's explanation finally reached Belgrade, the demand was accepted. Lichnowsky to foreign office, telegram, 29 July; G 357. Szögyény to Berchtold, telegram, 30 July; A III 30.
‖ Szápáry to Berchtold, telegram, 27 July; A II 73.

Quite apart from the clumsy form in which they were presented, some of [the demands] were quite impracticable, even if the Serbian Government were to agree to accept them. Thus, for example, points 1 and 2 could not be carried out without recasting the Serbian press law and associations law, and to that it might be difficult to obtain the consent of the Skupshtina. As for enforcing points 4 and 5, this might lead to most dangerous consequences.* . . . Without regard to the other points it seemed to me that, with certain changes of detail, it would not be difficult to find a basis of mutual agreement, if the accusations contained in them were confirmed by sufficient proof.†

It is clear, then, that point 5, which called for the participation of Austrian officials in the suppression of the anti-Austrian tendencies in Serbia, was the principal stumbling-block;‡ point 4, which was really the corollary to point 5, also aroused suspicion, and points 1 and 2 were difficult. These questions will have to be kept in mind when we come to examine the Serbian reply.

The preparation of the Austro-Hungarian note may be considered as the prologue of the drama of the Thirteen Days. With its presentation at Belgrade, the curtain was raised for the first act.

* Sazonov appears not to have been satisfied by Berchtold's explanations about the *bureaux de sûreté*.

† Sazonov to Schebeko, telegram, 26 July; R 25.

‡ Mensdorff admitted tc Grey that this was the essential thing in the note. Grey to Bunsen, 27 July; B 188.

CHAPTER X

THE POWERS AND THE ULTIMATUM

THE Austro-Hungarian note to Serbia was published on 24 July. Outside of Austria-Hungary and Germany,* the note created a feeling of amazement and alarm, for its imperious tone, the sensational demands made on Serbia, and the short time limit foreshadowed, in the improbable event of an acceptance by Serbia, a diplomatic rupture and probably war. War between Austria-Hungary and Serbia! Ever since the Bosnian crisis of 1908–1909 European diplomacy had striven to prevent such a calamity, the consequences of which were incalculable and immeasurable. Now it loomed up, with fearful suddenness, as a most likely eventuality.

THE NOTIFICATION OF THE ULTIMATUM TO THE POWERS

The Central Powers, keenly aware of the impression which the violence of the Austro-Hungarian action was bound to make, had carefully planned their next steps. On the morning of 24 July the Austro-Hungarian ambassadors appeared at the foreign offices in the several capitals to present, along with an official copy of the note, a circular despatch in which the Cabinet of Vienna politely endeavored to construe its action in the

---

* The Vatican has to be included in the list of those who received the note favorably. The Bavarian chargé at the Holy See reported: "The Pope approves sharp action on the part of Austria against Serbia and does not have a high opinion of the Russian and French armies in case war with Russia should result. The cardinal secretary of state in any event hopes that this time Austria will stick to it; he did not know whenever she would be willing to go to war if she does not this time decide to use force against a movement stirred up from outside which has led to the murder of the heir apparent and which in the present situation constitutes a danger to her existence. The language also reveals the great anxiety of the Vatican with regard to Pan-Slavism." Ritter to Bavarian Government, telegram, 24 July; Dirr, p. 206. The papal secretary of state asked the Austro-Hungarian minister whether the investigation at Sarajevo had proved the complicity of Belgrade, for, he said, "since the murder of the king there had been no illusions in Catholic circles about the methods practised there." Schönburg to Berchtold, telegram, 24 July; Ö.-U. A., 10,612. Later he expressed approval of the "extremely sharp" note. Pálffy to Berchtold, 29 July; Ö.-U. A., 10,993.

most favorable light. The step at Belgrade had been taken, it was explained, "with a view to inducing the Serbian Government to stop the incendiary movement that is threatening the security and integrity of the Austro-Hungarian Monarchy" (what a confession for a Great Power to make!). The action was, so it was urged, "in full accordance with the feelings of all civilized nations," which did not tolerate regicide and were unwilling for "the peace of Europe to be continually disturbed by movements emanating from Belgrade." A *dossier* in support of the Austrian contentions was, so Count Berchtold stated, held at the disposal of the Powers.*

In addition, each ambassador had been provided with a special argument deemed fitting to the fancy of the government to which he was accredited. The attention of Rome was specially directed to the machinations of the *Narodna Odbrana*. In Paris it was stated that "France had always played the praiseworthy rôle of mediator in the conflicts between the two groups of Powers." London was reminded of "the converging tendency" of British and Austrian policy in the Near East and of the "moral complicity and criminal indifference" of the Belgrade politicians. To St. Petersburg the assurance was given that Austria-Hungary "feels no ill-will or hatred against Serbia" and that the action had been taken "only for reasons of self-preservation and self-defense"; also an appeal was made to the "feeling of solidarity among the great monarchies, who had

---

* Berchtold to ambassadors, 20 July; A I 29. The decision to present a *dossier* was taken on 9 July, and its preparation was intrusted to Wiesner, who made use of material gathered during his visit to Sarajevo (see above, p. 362). Comprising 57 pages, it was not available for distribution until 24 July, and then only in German; it was despatched by post on the following day, and was not presented at the several capitals until the following week. F. Ritter von Wiesner, "Das Memoire Österreich-Ungarns über die grossserbische Propaganda und deren Zusammenhänge mit dem Sarajevoer Attentat," KSF, VI, 492–593 (June, 1927). Berchtold sought to explain the delay by saying that the intention had been to present the *dossier* only in case Serbia refused the demands made upon her. Berchtold to Szápáry, 25 July; A II 42. In thus neglecting to transmit the *dossier* at the same time as the notification of the ultimatum, the Austro-Hungarian Government had ignored the advice of its ally, which had not only recommended the collection of material about the Pan-Slavist agitation but had said, "It would be best to publish this material—not in parts, but as a whole—shortly before submitting the demands or the ultimatum to Serbia." Jagow to Tschirschky, telegram, 11 July; G 31.

a common interest in defending themselves against regicide."*
In general, the language used was conciliatory and persuasive.

Very different in tone was the note which the German ambassadors in the Entente capitals delivered on the same day.
It began by rehearsing the conventional arguments why the
Monarchy must take action against Serbia, and then boldly asserted that "the course of procedure and demands of the Austro-Hungarian Government can only be regarded as equitable
and moderate" (although, it will be remembered, these demands were not known to the German Government in all the
details at the time the note was despatched from Berlin). But
since Serbia might refuse these demands and "allow herself to
be carried away into a provocative attitude toward Austria-
Hungary," the latter "would then have no choice but to obtain
the fulfilment of its demands . . . by strong pressure, and if
necessary by using military measures." The note then concluded:

> The Imperial Government want to emphasize their opinion
> that in the present case there is only question of a matter to be
> settled exclusively between Austria-Hungary and Serbia, and
> that the Great Powers ought seriously to reserve it to those
> two immediately concerned. The Imperial Government desire
> urgently the localization of the conflict, because every interfer-
> ence of another Power would, owing to the different treaty obli-
> gations, be followed by incalculable consequences.†

The note certainly offered "very strong support"‡ for the
Austrian position, and revealed the policy of the Central Powers. The Austro-Hungarian action was represented as morally
and politically necessary, yet as kept within "equitable and moderate" limits. The interference of other Powers was to be warded

---

* Berchtold to Mérey, Szécsen, Mensdorff and Szápáry, 20 July; A I 30.
† Bethmann-Hollweg to Lichnowsky, Schoen and Pourtalès, 21 July; G 100.
Pourtalès was also instructed to point out to Sazonov "the serious consequences
which might result for the monarchical idea if . . . the monarchical Powers should
not stand firmly by the side of Austria-Hungary." The note was presented to
the British Government in an English translation (B 100), which has been used
for the quotation.
‡ Minute of Clerk on the note; B 100.

off by bluff, by the threat of what would happen if the alliances were invoked. War was to be the alternative to acceptance of the Austro-Hungarian programme. And the moment was cleverly chosen. On this very day, British politicians in conference at Buckingham Palace separated without finding a solution of the Irish riddle; the French President and the French premier were on the high seas; the strikes were continuing in Moscow and St. Petersburg. The prospects for a great diplomatic victory might seem excellent if the Central Powers had correctly judged the European situation.

The Reception of the Ultimatum

In Rome, the note was to have been communicated a day in advance of its presentation in Belgrade.* But Count Berchtold's instructions, when he sent the text of the note to Herr von Mérey,† were interpreted by the ambassador to mean that the Italian Government was not to be informed after all until 24 July; consequently, although he saw the Marquis di San Giuliano on 22 July, he averred that he was still without information.‡ Meanwhile, Count Berchtold, perhaps realizing the obscurity of his instructions, telegraphed to Herr von Mérey to make the necessary communication on the afternoon of 23 July.§ But the ambassador had been taken ill, and the Italian foreign minister, who was suffering from gout, had returned from Rome to Fiuggi Fonte. The counsellor of embassy, Count Ambrózy, was therefore sent by automobile to Fiuggi,‖ where he informed San Giuliano of the presentation of the note and indicated its general character.¶ The note was not actually

---

* See above, p. 402.   † Berchtold to Mérey, 20 July; A I 30, 2.
‡ Mérey to Berchtold, telegram, 22 July; A I 50.
§ Berchtold to Mérey, telegram, 22 July; A I 49.
‖ Mérey to Berchtold, telegram, 23 July; A I 56. According, however, to Salandra, pp. 73–74, Ambrózy made his communication to the foreign office, which telephoned the news to Fiuggi. Perhaps Ambrózy went to both places.
¶ As no details were communicated, San Giuliano refused to make any comment, except to condemn the time limit, and to say, to the German ambassador, who had also fled to Fiuggi to escape from the heat of the capital, that he considered it against the spirit of the Triple Alliance "to enter upon such an action without first advising with the other allies." Flotow to foreign office, telegram, 24 July; G 136.

handed to the Italian Government until the morning of 24 July, that is, at the same time that it was given to the Entente Powers.*

The secretary-general of the Consulta, Signor di Martino, displayed considerable sympathy with the note, admitting that the Austro-Hungarian action was "purely defensive."† Later in the day, Signor Bollati, the ambassador in Berlin, told Herr von Jagow—according to the latter—that

Italy would maintain toward Austria the most friendly and benevolent attitude possible, and make no difficulties for her, always reserving the right to freedom of action and to her interests as based on Article VII of the treaty of the Triple Alliance.‡

But there must have been some misunderstanding or misrepresentation.

The text of the ultimatum was telephoned word for word from Rome to Fiuggi, whither the Italian premier had repaired at the request of the foreign minister.§ It was read to the German ambassador, who exclaimed, *"Vraiment, c'est un peu fort!"* There followed "a more or less excited conference" of the three men which "lasted several hours." Herr von Flotow was told roundly that since Austria had not come to an understanding beforehand with her ally "before entering upon a move so portentously aggressive, . . . Italy could not consider herself under any engagement with reference to the further consequences of this action." He was also told that Austria's denial of territorial ambitions had been made "only in a very

---

* A somewhat inaccurate explanation was offered to Tschirschky by Macchio. Tschirschky to foreign office, telegram, 25 July; G 187. When the Italian ambassador in Berlin complained, Jagow boldly denied that Germany had been previously informed of the ultimatum, and recalled that Italy had not given notice of her ultimatum to Turkey in 1911. Jagow to Flotow, telegram, 24 July; G 145. Szögyény to Berchtold, telegram, 25 July; Berchtold to Mérey, telegram, 26 July; A II 31, 53.
† Mérey to Berchtold, telegram, 24 July; A II 8.
‡ Jagow to Tschirschky, telegram, 24 July; G 150. The qualifying clause was interpreted in Berlin to mean that Italy's "policy would be directed toward trying to prevent any Austrian extension of territory." Jagow to William II, telegram, 25 July; G 168.
§ Salandra, p. 75.

conditional form," and that no Italian Government could combat the hostility of Italian and European public opinion to the Austrian note. The ambassador had therefore to conclude that

the only chance of holding Italy in line lies in offering her compensation at the right moment, if Austria attempts to possess herself of territory or to occupy the Lovchen.*

All this was, to be sure, only in line with what Herr von Flotow had been reporting for several weeks, and was hardly a surprise to Berlin; but it implied that the "benevolent attitude" promised by Signor Bollati was not likely to be worth very much in the ensuing crisis.†

The attitude of the Italian press was not more encouraging. The official and subventioned papers exhibited a formal acquiescence in the Austro-Hungarian action; and the *Popolo Romano* went so far as to say that Austria was altogether in the right, Serbia in the wrong.‡ But the independent press, from the *Corriere della Sera* (Milan) to the *Messagero* (Rome) and the *Mattino* (Naples) condemned the Austro-Hungarian note as at once prejudicial to good Austro-Italian relations and dan-

* Flotow to foreign office, telegram, 24 July; G 156. The instructions sent to Bollati, the ambassador in Berlin, as a result of this interview suggest that at the moment the Italian Government was ready to consider supporting the policy of its allies, provided adequate compensation was assured. "The fact that we are not bound by any such obligation [to support Austria in a war of aggression] does not exclude the possibility of our agreeing to take part in an eventual war whenever our vital interests require it. Given the political system of our country, such a participation would be possible only if the government were able to assure the country beforehand of a reward corresponding to the risks and of such a nature as to break down the resistance of public opinion to a war waged in the interests of Austria; . . . If we are not certain that our interpretation is accepted by our allies, we shall be forced to follow a policy opposed to that of Austria in all Balkan questions, except in the case of Albania, with respect to which special agreements exist between Italy and Austria." San Giuliano to Bollati, 24 July; Salandra, pp. 76–77. In communicating this to Jagow, Bollati stated confidentially that "Italy would demand the Trentino as compensation." Jagow to Tschirschky, telegram, 24 July; G 150.

† In view of the instructions sent by San Giuliano (see the preceding note), which were the basis of Bollati's communication to Jagow, it would appear that the ambassador tried to put the Italian attitude in as favorable a light as possible, or that the German foreign minister was afraid to tell Vienna the whole bitter truth.

‡ "The German ambassador states that he has made certain connections with the *Popolo Romano, Tribuna, Giornale d'Italia* and *Nazione;* he ascribes the very calm attitude thus far observed by the press in part to his work with it, partly with, partly without money." Mérey to Berchtold, telegram, 23 July; *Ö.-U A.*, 10,545.

gerous to the peace of Europe.* The German ambassador complained that the Austrian embassy had done nothing with respect to the press;† but, in spite of having 300,000 lire at its disposal, it could not win over the *Corriere della Sera.*‡ With both government and press critical of Austro-Hungarian policy, the Central Powers had no reason to expect effective help from their ally in carrying out their programme of localizing the dispute between Austria and Serbia.

At Paris the response to the *démarches* was perhaps slightly more favorable. According to the French version, the acting foreign minister instructed the political director of the Quai d'Orsay to point out to the Austro-Hungarian ambassador, when he presented the note, "the feelings of anxiety" aroused by the note and its short time limit, and to speak of the desirability of "soothing influence" being exercised on Austria and Serbia "in the interest of general peace."§ Count Szécsen, however, sent a much more optimistic report to Vienna. M. Bienvenu-Martin, he said, admitted that "it was the duty of Serbia to proceed energetically against any accomplices of the murderers of Sarajevo," and "avoided every attempt to palliate or to defend in any way the attitude of Serbia." He even, according to the ambassador, expressed the hope that "the controversy would be brought to an end peacefully in a manner corresponding to our wishes";‖ a statement scarcely in harmony with the view expressed to Count Szápáry by M. Poincaré and calculated to give Count Berchtold a wrong view of the French attitude.

The German ambassador, when he read the note of his government at the Quai d'Orsay, said that "the important matter" was the last paragraph, which referred to "incalculable consequences" if the alliances came into play. M. Bienvenu-Martin

---

* Rodd to Grey, 26 July; B 245.
† Flotow to foreign office, telegram, 25 July; G 167.
‡ Flotow to foreign office, telegram, 26 July; G 211. Flotow suggested that the Italian press might be influenced by announcements from Berlin that "Austria did not aim at territorial acquisitions but intended to clear up the relations with Serbia for reasons of internal policy." Flotow to foreign office, telegram, 25 July; G 196.
§ Circular of Bienvenu-Martin, 24 July; F 25.
‖ Szécsen to Berchtold, telegram, 24 July; A II 9.

pointed out the danger of requiring measures incompatible with the independence and dignity of Serbia, and, as an alternative, suggested the possibility of negotiation if "Serbia gave obvious proofs of good will." Austria, he remarked,

should not make it too difficult for third Powers, who could neither morally nor sentimentally cease to take an interest in Serbia, to take an attitude which was in accord with the wishes of Germany to localize the dispute.*

The political director, M. Philippe Berthelot, who was present at the interview, expressed the view that "the Serbian Government should at once declare its acceptance [of the Austro-Hungarian demands] in principle and ask for explanation and details on certain points."† The observations of the French minister were fairly reported to Berlin by the German ambassador, who added:

French Government sincerely shares the desire that conflict remain localized [at this point William II noted "Nonsense!"] and will exert itself in this direction in the interest of maintaining European peace.

Baron von Schoen also stated that "Serbia had been advised from here to concede as much as possible."‡ The French, for their part, drew the conclusion, which was conveyed to the Russian chargé, that "hope was not lost that the matter would be settled by negotiations between Austria and Serbia."§

This interview, which was conducted in a friendly spirit, had an unexpected and unfortunate sequel. On the following day the *Echo de Paris* published a statement of what the German ambassador had said, and then remarked:

This *démarche* is as much as to say: "Let Austria crush Serbia, otherwise you will have to reckon with Germany." It is, under the singularly paradoxical pretext of localizing the

* Circular of Bienvenu-Martin, 24 July; F 28.
† Szécsen to Berchtold, telegram, 24 July; A II 11.
‡ Schoen to foreign office, telegram, 24 July; G 154.
§ Sevastopulo to Sazonov, telegram, 24 July; G. von Romberg, *Die Fälschungen des russichen Orangebuches* (Berlin, 1922), p. 14; R 1925 15.

conflict, the menace of a collective humiliation for the Triple
Entente or the prospect of a general war.

It also alleged that this new *'coup d'Agadir'* had been prepared
at a moment when Great Britain and Russia were occupied with
Ulster and the St. Petersburg strike respectively and the heads
of the French Government were leaving Russia.* This sensational article at once brought Baron von Schoen to the Quai
d'Orsay to protest against the indiscretion and against the "distortion" of his language.† He denied that his words constituted a threat: "The German Government had merely indicated that they thought it desirable to localize the dispute, and
that the intervention of other Powers ran the risk of aggravating it."‡ The ambassador was assured that the foreign office
was not responsible for the indiscretion,§ and it was agreed that
the German embassy should issue a statement to the Havas
Agency to the effect that the Austro-Hungarian note was not
an ultimatum and that the German action had for its object
only the localization of the conflict.

But while the Quai d'Orsay interpreted Baron von Schoen's
action as signifying that "Germany is not seeking war at all
costs,"‖ the French press proceeded to exploit the incident. By
representing the German action as "in the nature of a warning
to France to remain quiet or to take the consequences," it was
deliberately trying, so the British ambassador thought, to stimu-
late French public opinion to range itself on the side of Russia.¶
"No one will believe," wrote M. Clemenceau in the *Homme
Libre,* "that Austria has acted otherwise than in full accord with

* Scott, pp. 190–191.
† Schoen to foreign office, telegram, 25 July; G 170. There was no distortion in
the statement ascribed to the ambassador. According to the paper, he had said
that the German Government approved the Austrian note to Serbia, that it hoped
that the discussion would remain localized between Vienna and Belgrade, and that
if a third Power intervened, the result might be grave tension between the two groups
of Powers. Bertie to Grey, telegram, 25 July; B 123. Scott, p. 190. This was an
accurate summary of the German note.
‡ Circular of Bienvenu-Martin, 25 July; F 36.
§ The British ambassador reported that "the *Echo de Paris* is known to be in
close relation with the Russian embassy." Bertie to Grey, telegram, 25 July; B 123.
‖ Sevastopulo to Sazonov, telegram, 25 July; Romberg, p. 16; R, 1925 24.
¶ Bertie to Grey, 27 July; B 193.

Germany,"* and this view was generally accepted. The *Temps* repeated the story, "which had already been denied once," that Serbia had warned Vienna of the plot.† In general, the press almost unanimously condemned the note and stated that evidently Austria-Hungary desired war.‡ There was also, outside of the Socialist papers, a general disposition to approve of the attitude which it was assumed Russia must and would take.§ The French press, then, was not impressed by the necessity of localizing the conflict, even though the Quai d'Orsay had shown a certain receptiveness to the idea.

In London the character of the Austro-Hungarian note had already been revealed by Count Mensdorff.‖ When he communicated the text, Sir Edward Grey once more commented adversely on the mention of a time limit, which, he pointed out, "could have been introduced at any later stage if Servia had procrastinated about a reply"; and declared that point 5 "would hardly be consistent with maintenance of independent sovereignty of Servia." Though admitting that many of the demands were justified, he refused to "discuss the merits of the dispute" or to listen to Count Berchtold's complaint that the Serbian Government had taken no action except to try to remove trace of the conspiracy.¶ He would, he said, concern himself about the matter "solely from the point of view of the peace of Europe," and he "felt great apprehension." "He repeated several times," Count Mensdorff telegraphed, "that he was greatly concerned about the maintenance of peace between the Great Powers." The only satisfaction vouchsafed was that he would enter into an exchange of views with the allies of Austria and Russia. The ambassador, it may be noted, apparently did not inform Sir Edward Grey of the *dossier* which Count Berchtold held at the disposition of the Powers, perhaps because he had not yet received it.**

---

* Scott, p. 189. † Szécsen to Berchtold, telegram, 25 July; A II 35.
‡ Schoen to foreign office, telegram, 25 July; G 169. § Scott, pp. 194–195.
‖ See above, p. 430. ¶ Berchtold to Mensdorff, telegram, 23 July; A I 16.
** Grey to Bunsen, telegram, 24 July; B 91. Mensdorff to Berchtold, telegram, 24 July; A II 14.

When the German ambassador came to make the *démarche* prescribed by his government, he found the British foreign minister "greatly affected by the Austrian note." Sir Edward Grey was, indeed, convinced that "a war between Austria and Servia cannot be localized,"* and he did not mince his words:

He said [so Prince Lichnowsky reported] that so far he had had no news from St. Petersburg and therefore did not know what they thought of the matter there. But he very much doubted whether it would be possible for the Russian Government to recommend the unconditional acceptance of the Austrian demands to the Serbian Government. . . .†
The danger of a European war, should Austria invade Serbian territory, would be immediate. The results of such a war between four nations—he expressly emphasized the number four, and meant thereby Russia, Austria-Hungary, Germany and France—would be absolutely incalculable. . . . What Sir Edward Grey most deplored, beside the tone of the note, was the brief time limit, which made war almost unavoidable.

Sir Edward could not see his way to exercise moderating influence at St. Petersburg:

I said that, in view of the extraordinarily stiff character of the Austrian note, the shortness of time allowed, and the wide scope of the demands on Servia, I felt quite helpless as far as Russia was concerned, and I did not believe any Power could exercise influence alone.‡

Hopeless, then, was the German expectation that British diplomacy would exert itself to localize the war. Not only that; Grey appealed to German diplomacy to abandon the position taken in the note which Lichnowsky had just presented.

Minute on B 100.
† Benckendorff had already told Lichnowsky that "he considered it scarcely possible to advise the Serbian Government to accept conditions which would reduce it to being a vassal of Austria. He did not think that the Russian Government was in a position to do this. . . . Public opinion would not tolerate it." Lichnowsky to foreign office, telegram, 24 July; G 152. Benckendorff said that he had not seen Grey, so that the latter was giving Lichnowsky an independent judgment. But what the Russian ambassador said should have reinforced Grey's warning.
‡ Grey to Rumbold, telegram, 24 July; B 99.

He told me [the ambassador telegraphed] that he would be willing to join with us in pleading at Vienna for a prolongation of the time limit, since perhaps that would offer a way out. . . . He further suggested that in the event of a dangerous tension between Russia and Austria, the four states not immediately concerned—England, Germany, France and Italy —should undertake to mediate between Russia and Austria-Hungary.*

Both of these proposals Grey asked Lichnowsky to transmit to his government,† and he himself communicated them to the British chargé in Berlin.‡ The British position was, in short, that "we can do nothing unless Germany is prepared *pari passu* to do the same."§ The tables had been cleverly turned on the German Government: instead of securing the promise of pressure on Russia to localize the war, it was told that it must put pressure on Austria-Hungary to prevent the war from starting.‖

In France, while the foreign office had shown reserve, the press was bitterly critical of the Austro-Hungarian action. In Great Britain, where the foreign secretary had practically condemned the Austrian note, the press was not unfriendly. Although the *Morning Post* denounced the note as a "challenge to the Triple Entente,"¶ the *Times* took quite a moderate view,** and the Liberal papers were even disposed to approve of

---

* Grey had already discussed the question of mediation with the French ambassador. Cambon desired mediation between Austria-Hungary and Serbia. At the moment Grey was considering only mediation between Austria-Hungary and Russia, "if Austria did move into Servia, and Russia then mobilized." Grey to Bertie, 24 July; B 98. See below, p. 514.

† Lichnowsky to foreign office, telegram, 24 July; G 157.

‡ Grey to Rumbold, telegram, 24 July; B 99.   § Grey's minute on B 103.

‖ Lichnowsky also reported that in the opinion of the foreign office (which he got from Sir William Tyrrel, Grey's private secretary), "Austria is underrating very much Serbia's power of resistance" and that "the attitude of Rumania is more than uncertain." There was certainly no lack of warning from London. Lichnowsky informed Mensdorff of his conversation with Grey. Mensdorff's summary, "Sir E. Grey is at one with the German Government in wishing to localize the conflict between us and Serbia" (Mensdorff to Berchtold, telegram, 24 July; A II 15), was misleading, for Grey had made clear to Lichnowsky that he did not believe the conflict could be localized.

¶Lichnowsky to foreign office, telegram, 25 July; G 165.

** Mensdorff to Berchtold, telegram, 25 July; A II 36. The *Times* on 25 July wrote: "It may be acknowledged that from the strict standpoint of international right any Power which suffers such treatment from a neighbour is entitled to end it by the

the note. The *Daily Chronicle* said that the note was "scarcely more drastic than the reasonable self-defense of the Dual Monarchy requires it to be," and that the most Russia "can wisely do is to advise Serbia to give way." The *Manchester Guardian* asserted that "if Austria has been overbearing toward Servia, at any rate she has some excuse," and characterized Russia's threat of war as "a piece of sheer brutality." The *Westminster Gazette* refused to imagine that "Servia will be so ill-advised as not to deal very respectfully and seriously with the charges made."* Such utterances from the organs of the party in power may have led Berlin and Vienna to discount the language of Sir Edward Grey. But Prince Lichnowsky telegraphed early on 25 July that the "general impression here [is] nothing but ruinous" [*geradezu vernichtend*],† and events were to bear him out.

What really mattered of course was the impression produced at St. Petersburg. The Austrian note reached the Russian foreign office from Belgrade early on the morning of 24 July. When M. Sazonov read it, he exclaimed, "That means a European war,"‡ and at once informed the Tsar of the note. Notices were sent out for a meeting of ministers to be held the same day, the foreign-office officials on leave were recalled, and the ambassadors to Paris and Vienna, who were in St. Petersburg, were ordered to return to their posts.

During the morning the Austro-Hungarian ambassador visited M. Sazonov to present the official text of the note and the official argumentation. The Russian minister listened to the reading of the document "in comparative calm," and tried to avoid committing himself. Then he said:

You want to make war on Serbia. . . . You are setting fire

threat of war, or even by war itself. But the Power which determines to exercise this right cannot expect others to own the justice of her action until she establishes it by something more than bare assertion. That is all Austria-Hungary has given us hitherto—except perhaps in the unpublished *dossier*." This was, of course, intended as a warning, if indeed a polite one.

* Scott, pp. 219–220.
† Lichnowsky to foreign office, telegram, 25 July; G 163.
‡ "*C'est la guerre européenne.*" Schilling, p. 28.

to Europe. It is a great responsibility that you are assuming, and you will see what an impression it will make in London and Paris and perhaps elsewhere.

But he did not refer to Russia's attitude, and while he criticised the form of the note and said that "a serious situation had been created," he left the impression upon Count Szápáry of being bowled over [*Niederschlagenheit*] rather than of being greatly excited.* The ambassador reported the conversation to his German colleague, who sent a reassuring telegram to Berlin.†

Reflection, however, seems to have tempered Count Szápáry's optimism, for later in the day he sent to Vienna a fuller report which was less encouraging.‡ M. Sazonov had protested against several points of the ultimatum, particularly against the presence of Austro-Hungarian officials in Serbia. "You will always be wanting to intervene again," he said, "and what a life you will lead Europe!" With regard to the *dossier,* he asked "why we had given ourselves this trouble, since we had already presented the ultimatum." He denied that the Austrian feelings "were shared by those of all civilized nations" and asserted that "the monarchical idea had nothing to do with the matter." He was, in fact, impervious to the ambassador's arguments. The latter was forced to recognize that, "in spite of his relative calm, the attitude of the minister, as was not to be otherwise expected, was thoroughly unaccommodating and hostile."§

Toward evening, after a ministerial council, which will be discussed presently, M. Sazonov received the German ambas-

---

* Szápáry to Berchtold, telegram, 24 July, 3.35 P. M.; A II 16.
† Pourtalès to foreign office, telegram, 24 July; G 148.
‡ He may have been impressed by the statement of Dr. Polly, the editor of the *St. Petersburg Political Correspondence,* who informed him of the effect of the Austro-Hungarian action on the Pechevsky Most [the Russian foreign office]. "Everything there was turned upside down; the excitement was great, for they thought that Russia could not leave Serbia in the lurch. M. Pashich would certainly accept everything, but then a revolution would get rid of him. Russia would not indeed intervene at once, but would make a *démarche* at Vienna in behalf of Serbia." Szápáry to Berchtold, telegram, 24 July; *Ö.-U. A.,* 10,618.
§ Szápáry to Berchtold, telegrams, 24 July, 8.25, 8 P. M.; A II 17, 18.

sador. In the interval he had discussed the situation with the
French and British ambassadors and the Rumanian and Serbian ministers, and the council of ministers had taken far-
reaching decisions. By this time the foreign minister was
"greatly excited." He accordingly spoke to Count Pourtalès
in the sharpest tones:

The minister . . . stated in the most determined manner
that Russia could not possibly allow the Austro-Serbian difference to be settled solely by the two parties concerned . . . he
could not consider the facts alleged by Austria-Hungary in
the note as in any way proved, rather the investigation filled
him with the greatest suspicion. . . . In case the facts asserted
should be proved, Serbia could give Austria satisfaction in the
purely legal question, but not, on the other hand, in the demands of a political nature.

The matter was, so M. Sazonov roundly asserted, "a European
affair," and he proposed that "the *dossier* of the investigation
should be laid before the Cabinets of the six Powers."

After noting that "my references to the monarchical principle made little impression on the minister," the ambassador
recorded:

In the course of the conversation, Sazonov exclaimed: "If
Austria-Hungary devours Serbia, we shall go to war with her."
From this it may perhaps be concluded that Russia will take up
arms only in the event of Austria's attempting to acquire territory at the expense of Serbia. The express desire to Euro-
peanize the question also seems to point to the fact that immediate intervention on the part of Russia is not to be anticipated.*

Count Pourtalès imparted his optimistic conclusions to his Austro-Hungarian colleague, and the latter telegraphed to Vienna:

I conclude that the minister had been previously instructed
by his imperial master to find a way out of the threatening
complications if possible.†

* Pourtalès to foreign office, telegram, 24 July; G 160. The ambassador sent a
fuller report by mail, which, however, adds little to our information. Pourtalès
to Bethmann-Hollweg, 25 July; G 204.
  † Szápáry to Berchtold, telegram, 24 July; A II 19.

Thus both the Austro-Hungarian and the German Governments were led to believe that Russia desired to negotiate and was not disposed to fight.

Now according to the Russian foreign minister's *chef de cabinet,*

Those who saw Count Pourtalès as he left the ministry state that he was very agitated and did not conceal the fact that the words of S. D. Sazonov and especially his firm resolution to offer resistance to the Austrian demands, had made a strong impression upon him.*

Moreover, in the diary which he wrote up in St. Petersburg during the crisis, Count Pourtalès recorded:

My conversation with M. Sazonov left me with the impression that the council of ministers, which had just preceded, had decided not to draw back before a sharp conflict.†

Yet in his report to his government he sought to minimize the significance of what M. Sazonov had said! How is so serious a dereliction of duty to be explained? Hardly by his subsequent statement that Sazonov's outburst about "devouring" Serbia was "the only time" that the minister "made any reference to the possibility of an armed intervention on the part of Russia."‡ Either he could not bring himself to admit that Russia might be in earnest,§ or he preferred to send the kind of report which he thought his government desired. In either case he committed a grave fault.

The ambassador's conduct on the next day was equally strange. The Russian Government issued an important *communiqué,* as follows:

Recent events and the despatch of an ultimatum to Serbia by Austria-Hungary are causing the Russian Government the

---

* Schilling, p. 31.
† F. Pourtalès, *Am Scheidewege zwischen Krieg und Frieden* (Berlin, 1919), p. 15.
‡ Pourtalès to Bethmann-Hollweg, 25 July; G 204.
§ The British ambassador, writing after the war, said that Pourtalès could not be persuaded that Russia was in earnest. Sir G. W. Buchanan, *My Mission in Russia and other Diplomatic Memories* (London, 1923), I, 198–199. Paléologue, I, 33, says much the same thing.

greatest anxiety. The Government are closely following the course of the dispute between the two countries, to which Russia cannot remain indifferent.*

So far as the published documents record, Count Pourtalès did not transmit this highly important announcement to Berlin. Furthermore, in the course of the day, he learned "from a reliable source" that, at the ministerial council of the day before, the principal question discussed was whether the internal situation would permit Russia to "look forward to external complications without uneasiness."

The majority of the ministers present are said to have expressed themselves to the effect that Russia did not need to shun complications of that nature on account of the internal situation.

This was surely most important information. Yet the ambassador, instead of telegraphing, was content to transmit it in a routine despatch.†

It is also a striking fact that neither Count Szápáry nor Count Pourtalès thought it worth while to inform their governments about the attitude of the Russian press. That attitude was nothing if not alarming. The correspondent of the London *Times* telegraphed:

Public opinion is incensed by what is considered the outrageous, brutal, and unjustifiable language of the Austrian ultimatum. Russian national sentiment would undoubtedly support the Government if mobilization were decided.‡

According to the British ambassador,

The Russian Press is unanimous in its condemnation of Austria's action against Servia and in assuming that it has been encouraged, or at least connived at, in Berlin. With the exception of the *Ryech* the press adopts a threatening attitude toward

---

* R 10. Austrian *Red Book* (1915), no. 15. Buchanan to Grey, telegram, 25 July; B 109.

† Pourtalès to Bethmann-Hollweg, 25 July; G 205. It was received in Berlin on the afternoon of 26 July, and not submitted to the Emperor until the next day.

‡ *Times*, 25 July.

Austria and urges the Russian Government to mobilize its frontier forces at once.*

Nevertheless Count Pourtalès presumed to write to the German chancellor that "local public opinion has thus far shown itself remarkably indifferent to the Austro-Serbian conflict."† One is constrained to think that the ambassador deliberately withheld from his government any news which would contradict the hypothesis that Russia would not move.‡ When we come to consider the action of the German Government on 25 July and the following days, we shall have to remember that it was misled by its own ambassador about the true situation in Russian official circles and public opinion.

To summarize the reactions of the other Powers to the Austro-German action, we may say that Italy was far from friendly, Great Britain sharply critical, France decidedly reserved, even if they had not formally taken position. The idea that the dispute should be localized was received, as an academic proposition, with sympathy, but nowhere was the conviction expressed that this would be possible. Russia, for her part, did not conceal her indignation, and publicly announced that she could not remain indifferent. If peace was to be preserved, diplomacy had no time to lose; it had in fact little more than twenty-four hours at its disposal.

RUSSIA'S DIPLOMATIC MEASURES

Convinced, as he told the British ambassador, that the step taken by Austria-Hungary "meant war," M. Sazonov immedi-

---

* Buchanan to Grey, 25 July; B 196. The extracts from the *Novoye Vremya*, *Petersburgsky Kuryer*, *Bourse Gazette*, *Svyet*, and *Russkoye Slovo* amply support the ambassador's summary. Cf. also Scott, pp. 164–170.

† Pourtalès to Bethmann-Hollweg, 25 July; G 204.

‡ Confirmation of this view was received from the German ambassador at Constantinople, who had spoken with his Russian colleague. Giers had said that "the Austrian demands on Serbia, if not justified, were comprehensible, with the exception of those which called for the active participation of Austrian supervisory officials in Serbia. This demand was equivalent to an invasion of Serbia's sovereignty. Therefore the situation was serious." But his language "was quiet and contained no threats." Moreover, "he had shortly before spoken to the grand vizier in a manner which gave the latter the distinct impression that Russia did not intend to intervene." Wangenheim to foreign office, telegram, 25 July; G 184.

ately on receipt of the ultimatum asked Sir George Buchanan to meet him and M. Paléologue at the French embassy. The Russian minister, who characterized Austria's conduct as "immoral and provocative," expressed the hope that

His Majesty's Government would proclaim their solidarity with France and Russia . . . he hoped that we would in any case express strong reprobation of Austria's action. If war did break out, we would sooner or later be dragged into it, but if we did not make common cause with France and Russia from the outset we should have rendered war more likely, and should not have played a "beau rôle."*

The French ambassador gave Buchanan to understand that

France would not only give Russia strong diplomatic support, but would, if necessary, fulfil all the obligations imposed upon her by the alliance.

Sir George said that he "could personally hold out no hope that His Majesty's Government would make any declaration of solidarity that would entail any engagement to support France and Russia by force of arms," and countered by two suggestions of his own:

. . . try to gain time by bringing our influence to bear to induce Austria to extend term of delay accorded to Servia.
. . . urge Servian Government to state precisely how far they were prepared to go to meet Austria's wishes.†

Balked in his plan to establish the solidarity of the Entente, M. Sazonov decided to adopt Sir George Buchanan's first sug-

* "I was profoundly convinced at the time, and am still convinced now, that had the British Government sided with Russia and France on the Serbian question from the first, Berlin would not have encouraged Austria in its policy of aggression, but would, on the contrary, have advised caution and moderation, and the hour of reckoning between the two hostile camps into which Europe was divided would have been postponed for years if not for ever." Sazonov, p. 180.

† Buchanan to Grey, telegram, "urgent," 24 July; B 101. Buchanan personally favored such a declaration as Sazonov desired, but knew that he could not give it. According to Paléologue, Buchanan said, "If the Conservative party were in power, I'm sure they would understand what our national interests so clearly require of us." M. Paléologue, "La Russie des Tsars," in *Revue des deux mondes*, 6th period, LXI, 248 (15 January, 1921).

gestion and secured the approval of the council of ministers, which met at three o'clock.* A telegram was accordingly despatched to Vienna requesting that "the period allowed for the Serbian reply should be extended," in order that the Powers might have "sufficient time" to study the Austro-Hungarian demands and "offer advice to the Serbian Government";† the other Cabinets were also asked to support this request.‡

Meanwhile a telegram adressed to the Tsar had been received from the Prince Regent of Serbia, in which Prince Alexander declared:

We are prepared to accept those of the Austro-Hungarian conditions which are compatible with the position of an independent state, as well as those to which your Majesty may advise us to agree. . . . We may be attacked by the expiration of the time limit by the Austro-Hungarian army which is concentrating upon our frontier. We are unable to defend ourselves, and we beg your Majesty to come to our aid as soon as possible.§

The Tsar did not reply to this appeal for some days.‖ Sazonov, however, telegraphed:

If Serbia is really in such a helpless condition . . . it would perhaps be better that in the event of an invasion by Austria the Serbs should make no attempt whatever to offer resistance, but should retire, and, allowing the enemy to occupy their territory without fighting, appeal to the Powers.¶

This was undoubtedly good advice, as far as it went, but it did not tell the Serbs what to do about their reply. M. Sazonov did indeed see the Serbian minister in St. Petersburg and advise "extreme moderation";** but we do not know what the

---

* Schilling, p. 30.   † Sazonov to Kudachev, telegram, 24 July; R 4.
‡ Circular telegram, 24 July; R 5.
§ The Prince Regent of Serbia to the Tsar, telegram, 24 July; R 6.
‖ According to the published documents; but see below, p. 532.
¶ Sazonov to Strandtmann, telegram, 24 July; Schilling, p. 86. Cf. also Buchanan to Grey, telegram, 25 July; B 125. The advice apparently reached Belgrade the same day. Crackanthorpe to Grey, telegram, 24 July, 8 P. M., B 107.
** Schilling, p. 31.

minister reported to Belgrade,* and the Russian chargé there appears to have received no instructions.† It was evidently the Russian policy to exercise no pressure on Serbia. M. Sazonov may have thought, in view of Prince Alexander's assurances, that pressure was unnecessary, unless he wished to advise the complete acceptance of the ultimatum; or he may have felt that war was inevitable and that pressure was therefore useless.

On the following day M. Sazonov renewed his appeal for a British declaration of solidarity. To Sir George Buchanan he said:

Unfortunately Germany was convinced that she could rely on our neutrality. With the exception of the *Times* nearly the whole of the British press was on the side of Austria. . . . He did not believe that Germany really wanted war, but her attitude was decided by ours. If we took our stand firmly with France and Russia there would be no war. If we failed them now rivers of blood would flow and we would in the end be dragged into war.‡

Not content with this, he himself telegraphed an appeal to London, in which he struck a somewhat different note:

We rely upon it that England will not delay to range herself definitely on the side of Russia and France in order to maintain that European balance for which she has always stood in the past and which in the event of Austria's victory will undoubtedly be broken.§

* The minister, after seeing Sazonov, told Pourtalès that the ultimatum "was not a question merely between Serbia and Austria, but a European question." Spalaykovich to Pashich, telegram, 24 July; S 36. No mention is made of what advice Sazonov gave the minister. According to an article of the *Novoye Vremya* of 23 October, 1914, as reproduced in the *Norddeutsche Allgemeine Zeitung* of 3 January, 1915, Sazonov assured Spalaykovich that "in no case would Russia tolerate an aggressive attitude of Austria toward Serbia," and stated that he had warned Pourtalès that the Russian Government would be forced to take the measures which it deemed necessary.

† Crackanthorpe to Grey, telegram, 25 July; B 111. The British chargé added: "It appears to me highly probable that Russian Government have already urged utmost moderation on Servian Government." The only evidence of this is what Sazonov said to Spalaykovich.

‡ Buchanan to Grey, telegram, 25 July; B 125.

§ Sazonov to Benckendorff, telegram, 25 July; Schilling, p. 87.

To raise the issue of the balance of power was to touch British diplomacy at its most sensitive spot.

In the same telegram, however, the Russian minister urged Great Britain, "as she is regarded in Vienna as being the most disinterested of the Powers,"* to "exert a moderating influence on Austria":

England should firmly and clearly make it understood that she considers Austria's action unjustified by the circumstances and extremely dangerous to European peace, the more so because she could easily obtain by peaceful means the satisfaction of those of her demands which are founded upon justice and are compatible with the dignity of Serbia.

In conformity with this view of Great Britain's high rôle, M. Sazonov also advised Serbia to address the British Government with a request for mediation.†

In the short time at its disposal, the Russian Government made a number of moves in the interest of peace, and could hardly have done more, short of advising Serbia to accept the Austro-Hungarian demands. But M. Sazonov told the British ambassador frankly that, unless Germany could restrain Austria-Hungary, the situation was "desperate":

Russia cannot allow Austria to crush Servia and become predominant power in Balkans, and, secure of support of France, she will face all the risks of war.‡

The German ambassador was living in a fool's paradise when on the same day he wrote to his chief that Sazonov "wishes above all things to temporize."§ This is the more evident when the Russian military steps are considered.

---

* Berchtold had himself recognized this. Cf. Berchtold to Mensdorff, telegram, 23 July; A I 61.
† Sazonov to Strandtmann, telegram, "urgent," 25 July; Schilling, p. 87.
‡ Buchanan to Grey, telegram, 25 July; B 125. In the version published in the British *Blue Book* of 1914, the words "if she feels" were inserted before "secure." This was one of the few serious bits of 'editing' in the British documents.
§ Pourtalès to Bethmann-Hollweg, 25 July; G 204.

Russian Military Measures

From the moment that the terms of the Austro-Hungarian note were known in St. Petersburg the Russian Government seems to have had little expectation that a general war would be avoided. M. Sazonov himself, as we have seen, exclaimed, *"C'est la guerre européenne."* It was taken for granted that Austria-Hungary would at once 'begin military operations against Serbia. A general of the Tsar's suite, conversing with General von Chelius on the afternoon of 25 July, remarked, when it struck six o'clock, "The guns along the Danube have probably already commenced their fire, for one only sends a note like that after the cannon have been loaded."* This idea was shared at the foreign office† and in the general staff.‡ Since the Russian Government was determined not to sit passive before an Austrian attack on Serbia, it at once decided to make preparations for military action. M. Sazonov, who had already hinted to M. Poincaré at the possibility of mobilization,§ at noon on 24 July expressed to Sir George Buchanan the personal opinion that "Russia would at any rate have to mobilize."|| In fact he appears to have discussed already the idea of a partial mobilization with General Yanushkevich, the chief of the general staff, for the latter sent for the chief of the mobilization section, General Dobrorolski, and inquired, "Have you everything ready for proclaiming the mobilization of the army?"¶

---

* Chelius to William II, 26 July; G 291. Chelius was the personal representative of the German Emperor at the Tsar's court.

† Sazonov was relieved when Pourtalès pointed out to him that "if Austria was really seeking a pretext for falling on Serbia, as he seemed to believe, we should already have heard of the commencement of some action on the part of Austria." Pourtalès to foreign office, 26 July; G 217.

‡ S. Dobrorolski, *Die Mobilmachung der russischen Armee 1914* (Berlin, 1922), pp. 17–18. The Russian original was published in Belgrade by the author, who was chief of the mobilization section of the Russian general staff, after the war; it is the most important source for our knowledge of Russian military measures. A French translation is available in the *Revue d'histoire de la guerre mondiale*, I, 53–69, 144–165 (April, July, 1923).

§ See above, p. 452. || Buchanan to Grey, telegram, 24 July; B 101.

¶ Dobrorolski, p. 18. Yanushkevich asked Dobrorolski for the documents concerning "the partial mobilization only against Austria-Hungary." "This mobilization," he said, "must not give Germany any ground for regarding it as a hostile

Accordingly, at 3 P. M. on that day, a conference of ministers was held. It was decided, subject to the approval of the Tsar:

To authorize the Ministers of War and Marine, in accordance with the duties of their offices, to beg your Imperial Majesty to consent, according to the progress of events, to order the mobilization of the four military districts of Kiev, Odessa, Moscow, and Kazan, and the Black Sea fleet.

To authorize the War Minister to proceed immediately to gather stores of war material.

To authorize the Minister of Finance to take measures instantly to diminish the funds of the Ministry of Finance which may be at present in Germany or Austria.*

It will be noted that the last two recommendations called for positive action, whereas the first merely laid down a principle: that mobilization of the four districts and the fleet was to be carried out if and when events required such a step.†

On the following day,‡ a ministerial council was held at Krasnoye Selo under the presidency of the Tsar; the Grand Duke Nicholas, the commander-designate of the army, and General Yanushkevich were also present. M. Sazonov is said to have argued that "only a military demonstration" could give effect to his diplomatic representations to the Central Powers.§ It was therefore decided in principle that thirteen army corps, i. e., the four southern military districts and the Black Sea and Bal-

act against herself." Dobrorolski declared that "a partial mobilization was out of the question"; but Yanushkevich, who had only recently been appointed chief of staff and apparently did not understand the details of mobilization, insisted, and ordered Dobrorolski to make a report "in an hour."

* R. C. Binkley, "New Light on Russia's War Guilt," in *Current History*, XXIII, 533 (January, 1926). The article gives the full text of the minutes of the session.

† Schilling, p. 30, states that these decisions were communicated to the French ambassador the same evening. Paléologue affirms, however, that Sazonov told him only of the decision to withdraw funds from Germany. "Can I certify to my government that you have not ordered any military measures?" asked the ambassador; to which the minister replied, "None, I assure you." Paléologue, I, 24–25. Perhaps Sazonov's statement was technically true, for measures had not been "ordered," only recommended to the Tsar.

‡ Dobrorolski, p. 21, gives 5 P. M. as the hour of meeting, but according to Sazonov's statement at the time, it was held in the morning. Buchanan to Grey, telegram, 25 July; B 125.

§ W. Sukhomlinov, *Erinnerungen* (Berlin, 1923), p. 358.

tic fleets [the Tsar himself inserted the word "Baltic" in the minutes] should be mobilized; but that it should be left to M. Sazonov to determine when the international situation required the mobilization to be actually ordered, and that he might continue to negotiate even if Belgrade were occupied by the Austrians.*

At the request of the general staff, four other steps, in a sense preparatory to and necessary for mobilization if it were resorted to, were determined upon:

1. The recall of troops from summer training-camps to barracks.

2. The promotion of cadets to officer rank.

3. The proclamation of a state of war, that is, of martial law, in fortresses and on the frontier.

4. The proclamation of the "period preparatory to war."† These measures were not left dependent on the. judgment of the foreign minister, but were to be carried out at once. Thus it is true to say that Russia began her military preparations before the Austro-Serbian rupture was known in St. Petersburg.

What were the real motives behind these decisions? So far as M. Sazonov is concerned, there is nothing to show that he intended to use the partial mobilization for any purpose except as a lever for compelling Austria-Hungary to submit to some kind of mediation, although, of course, he was determined to go to war if Austria-Hungary would not submit to mediation. He seems to have thought that the power given him to determine the moment of this partial mobilization left him in control of the situation; he certainly did not realize the military objections to any such measure, for he had later to be convinced by General Yanushkevich of its impracticability, after that soldier had had his own eyes opened by his subordinates.‡ The minister of war, General Sukhomlinov, had no use for partial

---

* Bienvenu-Martin to Viviani, telegram, 26 July; F 50. Paléologue's telegram reporting this information has not been published.

† Dobrorolski, pp. 20–21. Dobrorolski calls the last-named measure the "period preparatory to mobilization," but this is an error; Fay, II, 316, note 90.

‡ See below, II, pp. 95–96.

mobilization; but, writing after the war, he claimed not to have opposed it, on the ground that it was his "business to have the army ready for any political manœuvre designed by Sazonov" and because "Russia was never better prepared for war than in 1914." He implies, on the other hand, that the Grand Duke Nicholas, who "had the Tsar where he wanted him,"* was keen for war.†

Writing after the war, General Dobrorolski declared that, as a result of these decisions,

> The war was already a determined thing [*beschlossene Sache*], and the whole flood of telegrams between the Russian and other Governments represents only the *mise en scène* of the historic drama.‡

As a description of the subsequent course of events, the general's statement was entirely correct; whether he meant to imply a reckless determination to fight or only the expectation that Austria-Hungary would yield nothing and that war would therefore be necessary, is not clear. But, although from a military point of view Russia was not fully ready for war, for the 'great programme' of reorganization would not be completed until 1915 at the earliest,§ there is no doubt that the soldiers considered war unavoidable—unless, of course, Russia were to abdicate her position as protector of the Slavs—and pressed for adequate preparations to meet the danger; they regarded M. Sazonov's plan of exerting pressure on Austria-Hungary by a partial mobilization as both impracticable, because they had no plans for such a mobilization, and dangerous, because it would irritate the Central Powers without affording Russia the power required to enforce her wishes. For the moment they were unable to make their views prevail, for both the Tsar and M. Sazonov wished to try to bluff the Austrians into accepting a discussion of the Serbian quarrel; but the soldiers were left

---

* The Tsar is said to have declared, "We have stood this state of affairs for seven and a half years; now it is enough"; *Temps* (Paris), 29 July.
† Sukhomlinov, pp. 359-361.
‡ Dobrorolski, p. 21.   § Dobrorolski, p. 17.

with a powerful weapon which, as will be seen, they were not slow to use.*

The decisions of the council of ministers, which would involve the eventual mobilization of 1,100,000 men, were notified to the French and British ambassadors during the afternoon,† and began to be carried out the same day. At 8 P. M. General Yanushkevich summoned the departmental heads of the general staff and informed them of the decision "to answer the Austrian ultimatum in a manner worthy of Russia."‡ Shortly afterward the necessary orders began to be issued. The Tsar personally promoted the cadets of the military academy. By midnight the troops had been recalled to garrison. At 1 A. M. on 26 July the fortresses of Warsaw, Ossovyets, Novgorod, Brest-Litovsk, Ivangorod, Vilna, Grodno, and the mouth of the Dwina were placed on a war footing.§ A little later the inauguration of the 'period preparatory to war' was ordered throughout the whole of European Russia.‖ Some time during the day the bridges over the rivers near the frontier were placed under guard. By evening the governments [= provinces] of St. Petersburg and Moscow had been placed in a

---

* During these days when the question of mobilization was being discussed, strikes on a large scale were going on in St. Petersburg and all the larger cities of Russia. The German ambassador noted the fact that at the very moment when Poincaré was being welcomed at Krasnoye Selo with the *Marsellaise*, Cossacks were shooting down workmen in the suburbs of St. Petersburg for singing this anthem! (Actually the workmen were singing the *Internationale*.) Pourtalès to Bethmann-Hollweg, 23 July; G 130. It is possible that general mobilization was urged as a precaution against internal dangers. Cf. Pourtalès to Bethmann-Hollweg, 25 July; G 205.

† Buchanan to Grey, telegram, 25 July; B 125. Paléologue to Bienvenu-Martin, telegram, 26 July; Bourgeois and Pagès, *Les origines et les responsabilités de la grande guerre*, p. 39.

‡ Dobrorolski, p. 21. About the same time, the Tsar's chief equerry, Baron Grünwald, sitting next to General von Chelius at the banquet held after the review of the troops at Krasnoye Selo, said: "The situation is very serious. I am not permitted to tell you what was decided this noon. You will soon learn it yourself. But you can assume that it is very serious." Chelius to William II, 26 July; G 291.

§ Major G. Frantz, *Russlands Eintritt in den Weltkrieg* (Berlin, 1924), p. 56. Presumably the fortresses on the Austrian frontier were included in the same order, but nothing precise is known.

‖ The order to the commander at Warsaw was despatched at 3.26 A. M. Text in Frantz, appendix 91, p. 243, and in R. Hoeniger, *Russlands Vorbereitungen für den Weltkrieg* (Berlin, 1919), p. 81.

"state of extraordinary protective activity," a step taken ostensibly in view of strikes,* but, in the opinion of the British ambassador, "doubtless connected with intending [*sic; ?* impending] mobilization."† M. Sazonov tried to reassure Sir George Buchanan by saying that "no effective steps toward mobilization could be taken until Imperial ukase was issued";‡ which was true, but this circumstance did not prevent the execution of the preparatory measures.

The measure providing for a 'period preparatory for war' was not peculiar to Russia. Wherever the system of universal military service prevailed and armies had to be assembled by the mobilization of reserves, certain preliminary steps were considered essential before the formal order for mobilization was issued. Thus under the German system a 'state of danger of war' [*Kriegsgefahrzustand*], of which much will be said in later chapters, had first to be proclaimed. In Austria-Hungary a 'warning day' [*Alarmierungstag*] was announced. The French plans provided for a 'covering' [*couverture*] of the frontiers. The moment the international situation became tense, general staffs everywhere began to think of these steps which had to be taken if mobilization were to proceed quickly and safely, and, thinking as they must of national security and strategic advantage, they inevitably began to impress on the politicians in control of their governments the necessity of prompt action. Such action does not imply that the soldiers are anxious for war; they are simply anxious to have their military machines ready if war does come.

In the case of Russia, there was a special consideration which did not affect the other Great Powers. The vast extent of the Russian Empire and the paucity of railway communications made mobilization a slow business at best, in marked contrast with the speed attainable in other countries. It was generally calculated, in fact, that Russia would need six weeks for the

---

* The German ambassador noted that these were continuing, and William II commented, "Good." Pourtalès to Bethmann-Hollweg, 27 July; G 339.

† Buchanan to Grey, telegram, 26 July; B 155.

‡ Buchanan to Grey, telegram, 27 July; B 170.

completion of mobilization, whereas Austria-Hungary, whose schedule was the slowest of the other Powers, allowed only sixteen days. In such circumstances the nervousness of the Russian general staff and its anxiety to get its preparatory measures under way is quite intelligible.

The 'period preparatory to war,' which was defined in the law of 2 March, 1913, as "a period of diplomatic tension which precedes the beginning of war operations,"* involved two kinds of measures. The first series, which required no supplementary credits, included the institution of censorship, the appointment of army officers to take charge of railway-stations, and the organization of artillery parks and regimental trains. In the districts along the frontier, reservists might be called up (so far as the ordinary budget permitted), men whose time of service had expired might be retained with the colors, horses might be purchased, and the covering troops might be ordered to their war positions on the frontier. The second series of measures, for the execution of which special credits were necessary, provided for the protection of railways, the inauguration of defensive works on fortresses, and the calling up of reservists in the frontier districts if this had not been done under the first category. These latter measures were applicable at the discretion of the council of ministers. In addition, an elastic clause (no. 6) permitted the council to decide "whether still other measures in addition to those provided for in the lists are to be carried out during the period preparatory for war."

Two points must be noted with reference to the decision of 25 July to inaugurate the preparatory period. In the first place, the measures mentioned in the two lists were ordered to be taken simultaneously, instead of successively, so that a whole stage in the preparation was gained.† In the second place, the measures were applicable throughout the empire, no distinc-

---

* The text of the ordinance is given in Frantz, appendix 30, pp. 189–200. Cf. also an article by the same author, "Die Kriegsvorbereitungsperiode in Russland," in *KSF*, II, 89–98 (April, 1924).

† See the text, quoted in Fay, II, 314–315, note 87, from the original in the Hoover War Library at Stanford University.

tion being made between the German and Austrian frontiers, so that, while only a partial mobilization against Austria-Hungary was being prepared for, the preparatory steps would actually be taken along the German frontier as well; a fact which was to assume considerable importance in the next few days. Furthermore, the measures were applied to Siberia as well as to Russia in Europe, so that a general mobilization could be begun, if this were later decided upon, simultaneously from St. Petersburg to Vladivostok.

Up to the evening of 25 July, then, the Russian Government had not decided to go to war; on the contrary, it had made several suggestions in the interest of peace. But it had determined to oppose Austria-Hungary with force if that Power went to war with Serbia, and, in order to be able to intervene promptly, it had set in motion the machinery which would make mobilization possible if war did come. The French ambassador went to the railway-station at 7 P. M. to say good-by to A. P. Izvolski, who had been ordered back to his post at Paris.

On the platforms [wrote M. Paléologue in his diary] there is lively animation; the trains are crowded with officers and soldiers. Already it looks like mobilization. We quickly exchange impressions, and come to the same conclusion: *Cette fois c'est la guerre!*[*]

French and British Efforts at Adjustment

The Austro-Hungarian and German ambassadors in Paris, it will be remembered, had notified their governments on 24 July that France desired the localization of the Austro-Serbian conflict.[†] If they expected that the French Government would seek to restrain its ally, they were completely mistaken. In conversation with Sir George Buchanan on 25 July the French ambassador in St. Petersburg said that

he had received a number of telegrams from Minister in charge of Ministry of Foreign Affairs, that no one of them displayed

---

[*] Paléologue, I, 27–28.　　　　　[†] See above, pp. 488–489.

the slightest sign of hesitation, and that he was in position to give his Excellency [Sazonov] formal assurance that France placed herself unreservedly by Russia's side.*

This language was in keeping with what had been agreed upon by the French and Russian Governments earlier in the week during the visit of MM. Poincaré and Viviani. The position taken was analogous to that of Germany toward Austria-Hungary.

Nevertheless, in spite of the commitment, the Quai d'Orsay privately gave good advice to Serbia. M. Berthelot told the Serbian minister that "Serbia must try to gain time" by offering satisfaction on all the points not inconsistent with her dignity and independence, and she should ask for "full information" concerning the investigation at Sarajevo. But above all, she should "attempt to escape from the grip of Austria by declaring herself ready to submit to the arbitration of Europe."† All this was substantially what M. Sazonov had recommended.

In keeping with this desire to gain time, the French ambassador in Vienna was instructed to support the Russian request for an extension of the time allowed for the Serbian reply.‡ But the French foreign office was handicapped by the absence of the heads of the state and the government, and hesitated to take a positive line. Late on Saturday, 25 July, the acting foreign minister said to the British ambassador that "he had no suggestion to make, except that moderating advice might be given at Vienna as well as at Belgrade";§ which was certainly not very helpful.

---

* Buchanan to Grey, 25 July, telegram; B 125. Paléologue told the Italian ambassador that "France was ready to fulfil the obligations of her alliance in their entire scope"; the Entente Powers, he said, were "convinced of the futility of their endeavors," but would nevertheless "do everything possible to ward off a European catastrophe, or at least to make entirely clear who bore the huge responsibility for it." Carlotti to San Giuliano, telegram, 25 July; KSF, II, 164 (May, 1924).

† Circular of Bienvenu-Martin, 24 July; F 26. The German ambassador was told that "advice has been given to the Serbs to make all the concessions possible." Schoen to foreign office, telegram, 24 July; G 154.

‡ Bienvenu-Martin to Dumaine, telegram, 25 July; F 39.

§ Bertie to Grey, telegram, 25 July; B 127.

On the previous day, however, the French ambassador in London had proposed to Sir Edward Grey that

the British Cabinet might ask the German Government to take the initiative in approaching Vienna with the object of offering the mediation, between Austria and Serbia, of the four Powers which are not directly interested.*

Here was the root of the matter, for, as M. Cambon said, "it would be too late after Austria had once moved against Servia."† Cambon, like Grey, assumed that an Austro-Serbian war could not be localized, and pointed to the only way of preventing such a war, a way, however, which the British minister declined to follow until he had first spoken to the German ambassador. "It would be essential," he said, "for any chance of success for such a step that Germany should participate in it." Since Prince Lichnowsky on the same afternoon presented the German note declaring that the matter was solely for Austria-Hungary and Serbia to settle, Sir Edward Grey did not even mention Cambon's suggestion, and nothing more was heard of it for several days. M. Cambon, after talking with Sir Arthur Nicolson and Count Benckendorff, concluded that

the situation, therefore, is as grave as it can be, and we see no way of arresting the course of events.

To complete the story of French activity during these two days, a word must be said about the President of the Republic and the premier, who had put to sea late on 23 July. The next day they received a telegraphic summary of the Austro-Hungarian ultimatum, which they regarded as "a precipitate step" [*grave initiative*]. But not wishing, says M. Poincaré, "to push Serbia to a resistance which might bring about grave complications," M. Viviani telegraphed to the Entente capitals his opinion that

---

* P. Cambon to Bienvenu-Martin, telegram, 24 July; F 32.
† Grey to Bertie, 24 July; B 98.

1. Serbia should immediately offer every satisfaction compatible with her honor and independence;

2. She should request a prolongation of the 48-hour time limit;

3. The Entente Powers should support this request at Vienna, and

4. They should try to arrange that an international investigation should be substituted for the Austro-Serbian judicial inquiry in Serbia.*

The first three suggestions had already been anticipated. The last one was at least ingenious. Conceivably something might have come of it, and M. Viviani renewed it from Stockholm the next day. But it evidently did not find favor in London or St. Petersburg, for nothing more was heard of it. As the distinguished travellers received only fragmentary information of what was happening, there was little they could do except urge, as M. Viviani did, that France, Russia, and Great Britain should "search for a method [*examiner les moyens*] of preventing a conflict in which the other Powers might find themselves rapidly involved."†

To this task Sir Edward Grey had already been applying himself with great energy. First and last, he made five distinct efforts to save the situation. Convinced that the way to peace lay through Berlin, he immediately, as we have seen, approached the German Government with the request that it join with him in pleading at Vienna for a prolongation of the time limit and with a proposal that

the four Powers, Germany, Italy, France and ourselves, should work together simultaneously at Vienna and St. Petersburg in favor of moderation in the event of the relations between Austria and Russia becoming threatening.‡

It was essential, he saw, that Austria-Hungary should not pre-

---

* Poincaré, IV, 288.
† Viviani to Bienvenu-Martin, telegram, 25 July, 4.05 P. M.; Poincaré, IV, 307.
‡ Grey to Rumbold, telegram, 24 July; B 99.

cipitate military action. To make that danger less imminent, he telegraphed to Belgrade that

Servia ought certainly to express concern and regret that any officials, however subordinate, should have been accomplices in murder of the Archduke, and promise, if this is proved, to give fullest satisfaction.*

Thus all the Entente Powers were ready to admit that Serbia must make reparation to Austria-Hungary for any share in the crime at Sarajevo.

Late on the evening of 24 July the British foreign office was informed by Count Mensdorff that he was authorized† to explain that

the step taken at Belgrade was not an ultimatum but a *"démarche* with a time limit,"* and that if the Austrian demands were not complied with within the time limit his Government would break off diplomatic relations and commence military preparations (not operations).‡

This news was communicated at midnight to St. Petersburg and Paris, as "it makes the immediate situation rather less acute."§ A little time seemed actually to be gained.

In order that this prospect might be realized, Sir Maurice de Bunsen was instructed to support "in general terms" the request of the Russian Government for an extension of the time limit;‖ if too late to vary the time limit, then the Cabinet of Vienna was asked to give the Powers time to act "before taking any irretrievable steps."¶

* Grey to Crackanthorpe, telegram, 24 July; B 102. He added: "For the rest, I can only say that Servian Government must reply as they consider the interests of Servia require. . . . I cannot undertake responsibility of giving more advice than above, and I do not like to give that without knowing what Russian and French Governments are saying at Belgrade." Evidently, Grey did not intend to imperil the Entente; but for a minister who had said that the Austro-Serbian dispute was "not our concern," his advice to the Serbian Government represented a real concession to the Austrian point of view.
† Berchtold to Mensdorff, telegram, 24 July; A II 13.
‡ Communication by Austrian ambassador, 24 July; B 104.
§ Grey to Buchanan and Bertie, telegrams, 25 July, 12.10 A. M.; B 105.
‖ Sazonov's telegram was communicated to Grey by Benckendorff on 25 July; B 117.
¶ Grey to Bunsen, telegram, 25 July; B 118.

Lastly, Sir Edward Grey communicated to Prince Lichnowsky a forecast of the Serbian reply which was received from Belgrade three hours before the expiration of the time limit.* Since the reply had been drawn up "in most conciliatory terms" and met the Austro-Hungarian demands "in as large a measure as possible," Grey expressed the hope that

if the Servian reply when received at Vienna corresponds to this forecast,† the German Government may feel able to influence the Austrian Government to take a favorable view of it.‡

That same afternoon the German ambassador, who had the day before suggested that Serbia "must send at once a reply that was favorable on some points, sufficient to give Austria an excuse for not taking action immediately,"§ telegraphed both Grey's letter and the forecast to Berlin in English.‖ Up to the last minute the British minister (and the German ambassador) seized upon every chance that was offered to put in a word for peace.

But Sir Edward Grey evidently had little hope, for on the same afternoon, 25 July, he said to Prince Lichnowsky that "we should now apparently be soon confronted by a moment at which both Austria and Russia would have mobilized," and tried to impress upon him that "if Austria and Russia mobilized the participation of Germany would be essential to any diplomatic action for peace." And he warned the Prince that "we could do nothing."¶

The foreign secretary was not the only member of the

---

* Crackanthorpe to Grey, telegram, 25 July, received at 3 P. M.; B 114.
† The forecast read: "Servian Government consent to publication of declaration in 'Official Gazette.' The ten points are accepted with reserves. Servian Government declare themselves ready to agree to mixed commission of inquiry, provided that appointment of such commission can be proved to be in accordance with international usage. They consent to dismiss and prosecute those officers whose guilt can be clearly proved, and they have already arrested officer mentioned in Austrian note. They agree to suppress Narodna Odbrana."
‡ Grey to Lichnowsky, 25 July; B 115.
§ Grey to Rumbold, telegram, 24 July; B 99.
‖ Lichnowsky to foreign office, telegrams, 25 July, 6.09, 6.30 P. M.; G 186, 191A.
¶ Grey to Rumbold, telegram, 25 July; B 116.

British Government who felt concern. He had read the Austro-Hungarian note to the cabinet, which had spent the afternoon of 24 July in an inconclusive discussion of the Irish situation.* Its phrases and sentences deeply impressed the first lord of the admiralty, and, in the mind of that vigorous and imaginative gentleman,

The frontier of Fermanagh and Tyrone faded back into the mists and squalls of Ireland, and a strange light began immediately, but by perceptible gradations, to fall and grow upon the map of Europe.

After the cabinet meeting, Mr. Churchill returned to the admiralty, where he wrote out "a series of points [there were seventeen of them] which would have to be attended to if matters did not mend." The next morning he discussed the situation with his principal technical adviser.

As it happened, the entire British fleet had been mobilized and reviewed on 17 and 18 July. By this time the reservists had been paid off and dismissed to their homes. But the First and Second Fleets were still in being at Portland, and would remain so until 7 A. M. on Monday, 27 July. On Saturday, 25 July, there was, as Mr. Churchill decided, "nothing to do." "At no time in all these last three years were we more completely ready."†

The Powers of the Triple Entente had not been lacking in will or imagination to suggest how peace might be preserved. Advice to Serbia to accept the demands of Vienna as far as she could, to offer no resistance to armed invasion, to appeal to Europe; requests to Austria-Hungary to extend the time limit; invitation to Germany to restrain her ally and to join in mediation: surely in this plethora of proposals a compromise might be found which, while yielding legitimate satisfac-

---

* "At 3.15 we had a Cabinet, where was a lot of talk about Ulster, but the real interest was Grey's statement about the European situation, which is about as bad as it can possibly be . . . we are within measurable distance of a real Armageddon." Oxford and Asquith, *Memories and Reflections*, II, 8.

† Churchill, *The World Crisis*, pp. 193–194; American edition, p. 205.

tion to Austria, would not unduly offend the pride of Serbia. At least so it seemed to the foreign offices in St. Petersburg, Paris, and London, which, although surprised by the violence of the Austro-Hungarian note, did not oppose a blanket veto and supposed that the ordinary diplomatic processes would still be respected. They were aware, of course, that the acceptance of a compromise by the Central Powers would involve a reduction of the profits which they had promised themselves and even a diplomatic defeat at the hands of the Entente. On the other hand, they had endeavored to make clear what were likely to be the consequences of a refusal.

CHAPTER XI

THE SERBIAN REPLY

BERLIN, 24–25 JULY

THE Central Powers had asserted that the Austro-Serbian conflict must be localized. The Entente Powers had declared that it could not be localized, but had proposed a compromise. Would their offer be accepted? It would not be accepted, so far as the German Government was concerned, if it followed the lead of German public opinion. The attitude of the German press was not quite unanimous. It was natural for the Socialist *Vorwärts* to exclaim, "Because the blood of Francis Ferdinand and his wife have flowed, as the result of the shots of a crazy fanatic, shall the blood of thousands of peasants flow?" It was to be expected that the Social Democratic party should protest, in a flaming manifesto, against "the frivolous war-provocation of the Austro-Hungarian Government." Nor was it surprising that the Liberal *Frankfurter Zeitung* should criticise the "harsh and dictatorial" tone of the note and argue that Austria-Hungary had weakened her cause morally in the eyes of the world. What was remarkable was the unqualified denunciation of the Viennese policy by the Berlin *Post,* notoriously one of the most chauvinistic papers in Germany, and by the *Rheinisch-Westfälische Zeitung,* of Essen, which was supposed to be under the influence of Krupp's, the great munition firm. Both papers, which represented the Right politically, protested against the German Empire's being drawn into an Austrian war of conquest.*

But these were lonely voices. The German press as a whole expressed complete approval of the Austro-Hungarian note, argued for the localization of the conflict, and advocated unflinching support of the Dual Monarchy by the German Em-

* Scott, pp. 117–123. Bronevski to Sazonov, telegram, 25 July; R, 1925 21.

pire. The Berlin *Lokal-Anzeiger* on 24 July, in what were regarded in diplomatic circles as articles inspired by the German Government, said:

There will be no further question of haggling, bargaining or negotiating; the time for consideration, goodwill, hope, and confidence is past. Servia must make her choice quickly and without reserve. . . . The German people are relieved to feel that the Balkan situation is at last to be cleared up. They congratulate their ally on her resolute decision and will not fail to give proof of their loyalty and readiness to help in the difficult days which may possibly be in store for her. . . .

There is no going back either for the Dual Monarchy or for those who are determined loyally to fulfil their duties as allies if serious contingencies arise.*

At the same time the general view appears to have been that Russia would not intervene in behalf of Serbia.†

The German Government, then, could count on popular support for the policy it had adopted. Its tactics, so the French ambassador, M. Jules Cambon, thought, would be to play a game of bluff and to try to carry matters through with a high hand.‡ For the moment its cue was to do nothing, or as little as possible, as can be seen from the message sent late on 24 July to the Entente capitals:

It goes without saying that we are now unable to advise Vienna to draw back, now that Austria-Hungary, on her own initiative, has determined on sharp language.§

But the next day the German foreign office found itself forced to take position, for Sir Edward Grey had requested that it use its influence to secure an extension of the time limit.‖ To refuse

---

* Rumbold to Grey, 24 July; B 159. Cf. Bronevski to Sazonov, telegram, 24 July; R 7. Szögyény to Berchtold, telegram, 24 July; A II 7.
† *Times* (London), 25 July.
‡ Rumbold to Grey, telegram, 24 July; B 103. J. Cambon to Bienvenu-Martin, 24 July; F 30. Cambon thought that the only hope lay in pressure from Italy. Bronevski to Sazonov, telegrams, 24 July; R, 1925 13, 14.
§ Zimmermann to Schoen, Lichnowsky, and Pourtalès, telegrams, 24 July, 9.45 P. M.; G 153.
‖ See above, p. 493.

the request was to run the risk of offending the one Power which, it was hoped, might be willing to exert pressure on Russia: to do as Great Britain desired would mean putting a spoke in Austria's wheel. The conduct of the Wilhelmstrasse in this problem merits close attention.

At 1 P. M. on Saturday, 25 July, Herr von Jagow telegraphed to Prince Lichnowsky: "Have communicated proposal of Sir Edward Grey to Vienna," adding that, as Count Berchtold had gone to Ischl, a prolongation of the time limit was not to be expected.* Also he assured the British chargé that

on receipt of a telegram at 10 o'clock this morning from German Ambassador at London, he immediately instructed German Ambassador at Vienna to pass on to Austrian Minister for Foreign Affairs your suggestion for an extension of time limit, and to "speak to" his Excellency about it. Unfortunately it appeared from press that Count Berchtold is at Ischl, and Secretary of State thought that in these circumstances there would be delay and difficulty in getting time limit extended.†

The following points may be noted: (1) Prince Lichnowsky's telegram arrived at the foreign office at 1.16 A. M.,‡ although it is of course probable that Herr von Jagow did not see it until a more seasonable hour. (2) The German minister's information that Count Berchtold had gone to Ischl was derived, not from the press, but from a telegram from Vienna of the day before, according to which "Count Berchtold goes to Ischl at noon to-morrow";§ this telegram had been sent on to the Emperor by Jagow himself. (3) So far from transmitting Lichnowsky's telegram to Vienna "immediately," Herr von Jagow did not send it until 4 P. M.,‖ that is, not until long after Count Berchtold had left Vienna and when it was obviously

* Jagow to Lichnowsky, telegram, 25 July; G 164.
† Rumbold to Grey, telegram, 24 July; 3.16 P. M.; B 122. The conversation took place during the morning. J. Cambon to Bienvenu-Martin, 24 July; F 41.
‡ Note on G 157.
§ Tschirschky to foreign office, telegram, 24 July; G 151.
‖ Jagow to Tschirschky, telegram, 25 July; G 171.

too late to secure an extension of the time limit beyond 6 P. M.
(4) The instruction to Tschirschky to "speak to" Berchtold
about the British suggestion is lacking in the communication.
The 4 o'clock telegram, after the repetition of Lichnowsky's
message, contains only this:

> Have replied to London that I would communicate Sir E.
> Grey's proposals to Vienna. But, as the ultimatum expired to-
> day, and Count Berchtold was at Ischl, I did not believe that
> an extension of the time limit would be possible.

If Count Berchtold received this communication, he could
only construe it as an intimation that Berlin did not desire an
extension of the time limit. It is impossible not to see in the
whole manœuvre a deliberate attempt to mislead Sir Edward
Grey by making him think that Germany had in good faith
recommended his proposal to Vienna. Prince Lichnowsky had
urgently advised his government not to decline the British proposal:

> Otherwise we shall be reproached here for not having used
> every means for the maintenance of peace. Attitude of refusal
> might have a great influence on England's future position.*

And so it turned out. The German manœuvre was penetrated in
London, and aroused irritation and distrust.†

In order further to obviate the necessity of addressing Vienna, Herr von Jagow put off receiving the Russian chargé,
who had to present M. Sazonov's request for extension of the
time limit, until 4.50 P. M. on 25 July. The latter was therefore
constrained to communicate the request in writing, saying that
it was "of an uncommonly urgent nature" and arguing that
Austria "had declared its willingness to submit to the Powers
the grounds on which it bases its accusation."‡ At the interview Herr von Jagow once more explained that it was too late

---

* Lichnowsky to foreign office, telegram, 25 July, received 1.26 P. M.; G 165.
† Nicolson's minute on B 149.
‡ Bronevski to Jagow, 25 July; G 172. Cf. J. Cambon to Bienvenu-Martin,
25 July; F 42.

for a *démarche* at Vienna to have any effect and showed himself indifferent to M. Bronevski's hints of "possibly threatening consequences"; rather, he said, "Russia ought to be appeased by the assurances given Kudachev yesterday that Austria was not seeking any territorial acquisition"*—this from the person who had asked his ambassador in Vienna to find out what territorial changes the Austro-Hungarian statesmen had in mind.†

Prince Lichnowsky's telegram reporting Sir Edward Grey's hope that if the Serbian reply corresponded to the forecast received from Belgrade, "the German Government may feel able to influence the Austrian Government to take a favorable view of it," was received in Berlin at 9.25 P. M., and was transmitted to Vienna at 1.05 A. M. on 26 July.‡ When informing the British chargé that Herr von Tschirschky had been instructed to "pass on" the British suggestion, Herr Zimmermann said that

very fact of their making this communication to Austro-Hungarian Government implies that they associate themselves to a certain extent with your [Grey's] hope. German Government do not see their way to going beyond this.§

Now there is no evidence that the German Government did "associate themselves" with Sir Edward Grey's hopes; on the contrary not only was their whole policy from 5 July on incompatible with such a view, but their subsequent conduct showed that they did not desire Austria-Hungary to take a favorable view of the Serbian reply. Rather they merely wished to be able to say that British proposals had been "passed on" to Vienna.‖

---

* Bronevski to Sazonov, telegram, 25 July; R, 1925 20. The reference to the Austrian assurances was suppressed in R 14.
† See above, pp. 378–379. ‡ Notes on G 186.
§ Rumbold to Grey, telegram, 26 July, 7.35 P. M.; B 149.
‖ Tschirschky, discussing the matter with his British colleague, said that "it was all a sham, for Servia had ordered mobilization and retirement of Government from Belgrade before making her offer, thus proving that she well knew it to be insufficient to satisfy legitimate demands of Austria-Hungary." Bunsen to Grey, telegram, 26 July; B 150. Cf. Berchtold to Mensdorff, telegram, 26 July; A II 57.

In London the procedure of the German Government was not relished at all. Sir Eyre Crowe minuted on the report from Berlin:

Very insidious on the part of the German Government. I presume Sir E. Grey will say something to Prince Lichnowsky about this somewhat peculiar way of treating our suggestion that Germany should join in making a communication at Vienna.

The reproach was perhaps not quite fair, for the German Government was under no obligation to join with Great Britain in making representations at Vienna. But Crowe was right in suspecting the German Government of duplicity. Sir Arthur Nicolson, who had already convinced himself that "Berlin is playing with us,"* commented: "This is the second occasion on which Herr von Jagow has acted similarly," the first being the "passing on" of the request for extension of the time limit. From this time on German professions were regarded by the British foreign office with the deepest suspicion. Herr von Jagow's cleverness only reacted against himself.

How lacking in seriousness and sincerity were the representations which the German Government, in order to impress Sir Edward Grey, went through the form of making to Vienna, is revealed by a striking step taken on the same day (25 July). Before its action can be fully appreciated, some explanation of preceding events is essential. The original plan of Count Berchtold to launch a 'surprise attack' against Serbia, which Count Hoyos had explained at Berlin, had had to be abandoned: under pressure from Count Tisza, it was decided to present an ultimatum with "demands wholly impossible for the Serbs to accept." Count Berchtold promptly informed the German Government of this change of plan,† and Count Tisza subsequently let

---

* Nicolson to Grey, 26 July; B 144.
† Tschirschky to foreign office, telegram, 10 July; G 29. "Nor could he, the minister, deny the advantages of such a procedure. The odium of a surprise attack on Serbia, which would otherwise fall on the Monarchy, would thus be avoided, and Serbia would be placed in the wrong."

it be understood that "in case [Serbia] did not submit to all the demands, mobilization will follow."* Berchtold himself had previously explained that "sixteen days must be allowed for the mobilization."† By 15 July, accordingly, the German Government had been clearly informed of the change from a 'surprise attack' to the normal method of mobilizing before beginning military operations; there is no record of any objection offered by Berlin to this change, although it indicated its displeasure over the delay in drawing up the ultimatum.

Meanwhile the German general staff had been inquiring, through the military attaché at Vienna, about "the military intentions" of Austria-Hungary, and had been told as follows:

They intend to move six corps against Serbia and to undertake nothing in Galicia for the present. If Russia should intervene, they would break loose from Serbia and move all forces against the principal opponent.

This information, which was conveyed to the foreign office by the acting chief of the general staff,‡ indicated with precision the Austro-Hungarian plan, for without mobilization six corps could not be moved into Serbia. Nevertheless, as late as 23 July, the foreign office in Berlin professed not to know

whether they will first carry out mobilization in Austria— which would require from 12 to 16 days—or whether they will march into Serbia at once in order to put through their demands.§

Why such uncertainty should prevail is not evident.

On the next day, however, the German Government received a rude awakening. Herr von Tschirschky transmitted a request from the Ballplatz. Baron Macchio had submitted the following:

* Tschirschky to Bethmann-Hollweg, 14 July; G 49.
† Tschirschky to foreign office, telegram, 8 July; G 19.
‡ Waldersee to Jagow, 17 July; G 74.
§ Schoen to Hertling, 23 July; Dirr, p. 132.

According to the Hague Conventions, the Monarchy would be bound eventually to present a formal declaration of war to Serbia. This declaration of war would have to follow upon the completion of mobilization, immediately before the beginning of military operations.

But after the diplomatic rupture with Serbia, Austria-Hungary would have no means of presenting such a declaration. Would the German Government, Baron Macchio asked, be willing to transmit the declaration of war to the Serbian Government?* Herr von Jagow immediately telegraphed a refusal: to do so would "make it appear as if we had *incited* Austria-Hungary into the war."† Nevertheless, the prospect of having not only actual hostilities but even a declaration of war postponed for a fortnight was not relished, and when Count Szögyény came the next day to discuss the matter,‡ the irritation of the German foreign office was made known in no uncertain terms. The ambassador telegraphed to Vienna:

It is generally taken for granted here that an unsatisfactory answer on the part of Serbia will be followed immediately by our declaration of war, *as well as* by military operations.

People here consider every delay in beginning military operations as involving the danger of intervention by other Powers. We are urgently advised to go ahead at once and present the world with a *fait accompli*.

I share *completely* this view of the foreign office.§

Thus on the one hand the British ambassador in Berlin was being told that Herr von Jagow had passed on to Vienna Sir Edward Grey's request for an extension of the time limit of the ultimatum, and on the other hand the Austro-Hungarian ambassador was given to understand that his government was expected to declare war and begin military operations at once.

* Tschirschky to Bethmann-Hollweg, 22 July, received 24 July; G 138.
† Jagow to Tschirschky, 24 July, telegram; G 142.
‡ Szögyény had been informed from Vienna. Berchtold to Szögyény, telegram, 24 July, sent 25 July, 1.45 A. M.; *Ö.-U. A.*, 10,580.
§ Szögyény to Berchtold, 25 July, 2.12 P. M., telegram; A II 32.

This second *démarche* was destined to have momentous consequences, which will be explained in their proper sequence.

VIENNA, 24–25 JULY

In the Dual Monarchy the publication of the note to Serbia evoked almost universal expression of approval. In Vienna the language of the press left the impression that "the surrender of Servia is neither expected nor really desired."* The feeling was general that Europe would sympathize with the desire to punish the Serbs for their agitation and their crimes, and Russia was expected to remain quiet; only the Socialist *Arbeiter-Zeitung* uttered a warning that "the Pan-Slav current, if it swelled up strongly, might finally divert from its course the official policy of the Tsar."† In Budapest also the note was favorably received by the press, only the Socialist papers protesting against a step which they qualified as the work of the autocracy.‡ Although the general opinion was that Serbia could not accept the demands and that her day of reckoning had come, yet, so the British consul thought,

Probability of Russian intervention is denied or disregarded, and Government apparently expects that war will be localized, in spite of fact that they have prejudiced their case by their intemperance.§

Count Berchtold's first move was to talk with the Russian chargé, Prince Kudachev, who had asked for an interview (in order to present M. Sazonov's telegram of 22 July urging moderation)‖ and had been told to come at 11 A. M. The Austro-Hungarian minister explained to the Russian representative the reasons for the step in Belgrade: the necessity for the Monarchy to defend its integrity against Serbian agitation, the rooting out of an element dangerous to the peace of Europe, the

---

* Bunsen to Grey, telegram, 25 July; B 110.
† Scott, pp. 84–89.   ‡ Max Müller to Grey, 24 July; B 191.
§ Max Müller to Grey, telegram, 24 July; B 106.
‖ The French ambassador, who had belatedly received similar instructions, decided that, as the note had already been presented, such a communication would be out of place. Bunsen to Grey, telegram, 24 July; B 97.

strengthening of the monarchical idea. Count Berchtold further said:

There was nothing further from our minds than to humiliate Serbia, a proceeding in which we were not the least interested. Indeed it had been my endeavor to eliminate from the note everything which might create such an impression.

For sheer bravado this was truly magnificent. He concluded by giving the assurance that "we had no intention of acquiring territory, but wished only to keep what we had."

Prince Kudachev criticised the ultimatum on the grounds already familiar to us, but promised to report what Count Berchtold had said.* Then, when told that the Austrian minister would leave Belgrade in default of a satisfactory reply, he reflected some time, and said, "*Alors, c'est la guerre.*"†

These pleasantries, however, were not likely to impress Count Berchtold, who, in fact, had every reason to be satisfied with the situation. Count Szécsen had reported optimistically about the reaction of the French Government to the ultimatum,‡ and Count Szápáry had represented the Russian Government as hesitating.§ If indeed Count Mensdorff had found the British foreign secretary critical and reserved, still London was far away and at any rate not committed. Best of all was the news from Berlin. Count Szögyény declared that Herr von Jagow had assured him that "the German Government was in complete

---

* Kudachev to Sazonov, 26 July; Schilling, pp. 37–40; R, 1925 36. In this despatch he refers to telegrams of 24 July which have not been published.

† Daily report, 24 July; A II 23. Berchtold's version of the conversation was reported by Tschirschky to Berlin. Tschirschky to foreign office, telegram, 24 July; G 155. On the statement that "Austria would not lay claim to any Serbian territory," William II commented: "Ass! She *must* take back the Sandjak, otherwise the Serbs will get to the Adriatic." To the remark that Berchtold "was far from wishing to upset the balance of power either in the Balkans or in Europe," the German Emperor likewise took exception: "That will come about quite of its own accord, and must. Austria must become preponderant in the Balkans as against the little ones and at Russia's expense; otherwise there will be no peace." When we recall the part taken by the Emperor in the decisions of 5 July, such outbursts acquire a new significance.

‡ Szécsen to Berchtold, telegram, 24 July; A II 9.

§ Szápáry to Berchtold, telegrams, 24 July; A II 17, 18, 19. Berchtold could not know that his ambassadors were sending reports more favorable than the circumstances justified.

agreement with the terms of the note."* The attitude of the
Berlin press was also thoroughly satisfactory, especially the semi-
official language of the *Lokal-Anzeiger*.† Count Berchtold could
therefore go to Ischl on Saturday, 25 July, in order to be with
the Emperor Francis Joseph when the Serbian reply came, with
complete equanimity of mind.

Count Berchtold's departure left the Russian chargé in a
difficult position, for he had now received M. Sazonov's instructions to ask for an extension of the time limit. So he
telegraphed an "urgent request" to Count Berchtold *en route*‡
and then went to the Ballplatz to repeat it to Baron Macchio.§
Macchio replied that the note had not been communicated to the
Powers for their opinion on it; "but simply for their information, in accordance with the requirements of international etiquette." He did, however, promise to communicate the Russian
request to his chief; and did so.‖ Count Berchtold's reply, it
need hardly be said, was in the negative, but he pretended to
soften the blow a little by authorizing a statement to the Russian
chargé that even after the rupture of diplomatic relations a
peaceful solution was still possible if Serbia would accept the
ultimatum and agree to pay the cost of Austria's military measures.¶ One minor concession was indeed made to Russia, for
Count Szápáry was asked to explain to M. Sazonov that point
5 in the ultimatum involved the establishment in Belgrade of a
bureau de sûreté analogous to the Russian police establishments
in Paris and Berlin.** For the rest, however, Count Berchtold
was content to wait for the news from Belgrade.

* Szögyény to Berchtold, telegram, 24 July; A II 6.
† Szögyény to Berchtold, telegram, 24 July; A II 7.
‡ Kudachev to Berchtold, telegram, 25 July, 10.50 A. M.; A II 28.
§ Kudachev to Sazonov, telegram, 25 July; R 11.
‖ Macchio to Berchtold, telegram, 25 July; A II 29.
¶ Berchtold to Macchio, telegram from Lambach, 25 July; A II 27. The plan to
make Serbia pay the cost of Austrian military measures was suggested to Berchtold
by Conrad. Conrad, IV, 108. Kudachev informed Sazonov of the Austrian refusal
to extend the time limit, but did not mention what Berchtold had said about a
later acceptance of the ultimatum by Serbia. Kudachev to Sazonov, telegram,
25 July; R 12. It is quite possible that the telegram has been published only in
abbreviated form.
** Berchtold to Szápáry, telegram, 25 July; A II 38.

Meanwhile everything was made ready for immediate military action in the probable event of Serbia's refusing to accept the Austrian demands. Conrad told the Italian military attaché, on the evening of 24 July, who, presumably, informed his British colleague, that

arrangements for instant mobilization were complete, and orders would be issued, in event of non-receipt, or of unsatisfactory reply, without any interval.*

These plans called for the mobilization of eight army corps— the so-called 'B' [Balkan] mobilization. About midnight word was received from Agram (Zagreb) and Mitrovitsa that the Serbian mobilization had been ordered at 4 P. M. that afternoon.† On the strength of this news, Conrad asked Berchtold to order the mobilization for the next day, 25 July, without waiting for the Serbian reply. But as no further reports of Serbian mobilization were received, the mobilization orders were not issued.‡ Monitors were, however, despatched to the lower Danube.§ Everything now depended on the Serbian answer.

THE DECISIONS OF SERBIA

The Serbian premier, M. Pashich, returned to Belgrade at 5 A. M. on 24 July. During that day and the next the ministers, under the presidency of the Prince Regent, were in almost continuous session. They were surprised by the energetic tones and detailed demands of the Austrian note,‖ and did not hesi-

* Bunsen to Grey, telegram, 25 July; B 124. On 26 July the official Hungarian gazette, the *Budapesti Közlöny*, published 33 decrees ordering the mobilization of eight army corps, the military operation of railways, posts, telegraph and telephones, the nomination of royal commissioners, the suspension of constitutional liberties, etc. The decrees also appeared in the *Pester Lloyd* of the same date, as a supplement. The preparation of these decrees must have required some little time and have been ordered before the news was received of the rupture at Belgrade.
† Conrad to Berchtold, 24 July, midnight; A II 22.
‡ Conrad, IV, 109–110. Conrad to Berchtold, 24 July; Ö.-U. A., 10,633. According to E. Lavisse, *Histoire de la France contemporaine* (Paris, 1922), IX, 32, the mobilization order, when finally issued on 25 July, bore the date of 24 July.
§ Max Müller to Grey, telegram, 24 July; B 106.
‖ Giesl to Berchtold, telegram, 24 July; A II 3.

tate to let it be known that some points were unacceptable.* In particular they feared a military uprising if the required Order of the Day were issued to the army.† In despair M. Pashich appealed to the British Government to use its influence at Vienna to secure a moderation of the Austro-Hungarian demands.‡ The Prince Regent telegraphed to the Queen of Italy asking her to lend assistance to the dynasty,§ and above all to the Tsar, who was almost piteously besought to "be pleased to interest [himself] in the fate of the Kingdom of Serbia."‖ The Greek minister, in spite of the existing alliance, could give no assurance about the attitude of his government. The only comfort was the probability that Montenegro would march with Serbia.¶

On Saturday, 25 July, all preparations were made for the withdrawal of the government from Belgrade, the garrison departed in field kit, and at 3 P. M. mobilization was ordered.** The fact that mobilization was ordered before the presentation of the reply was promptly seized upon by Count Berchtold as proof that "no inclination for a peaceful solution existed in Belgrade."†† This seems exaggerated. But evidently the Serbian Government doubted whether their reply would satisfy Austria-Hungary and thought that war was likely to begin.

If the Belgrade Cabinet received from its European friends

* Crackanthorpe to Grey, telegram, 24 July; B 94.
† Griesinger to foreign office, telegram, 24 July; G 159.
‡ Crackanthorpe to Grey, telegram, 24 July; B 92. Pashich to Boshkovich, telegram, 24 July; S 35.
§ Griesinger to foreign office, telegram, 24 July; G 158. The Queen of Italy was the daughter of King Nicholas of Montenegro. The answer seems to have been "a polite reply saying nothing." Flotow to foreign office, telegram, 26 July; G 220.
‖ The Prince Regent to the Tsar, telegram, 24 July; S 37; R 8. There were rumors in Belgrade that on the evening of 23 July a long telegram promising support had been received from the Tsar and that the Prince Regent had shown the telegram in the officers' club. Giesl discredited the story. Giesl, *Zwei Jahrzehnten im nahen Orient*, pp. 267–268. So far as is known, the Tsar's answer to the Prince Regent was not despatched until 27 July; R 40.
¶ Giesl to Berchtold, telegram, 24 July; A II 4.
** Giesl to Berchtold, telegram, 25 July; A II 24. The statement of the German minister on 24 July (Griesinger to foreign office, telegram, 24 July; G 158) that "mobilization is already in full swing" is not confirmed by other evidence, unless it be the reports from Agram and Mitrovitsa (in Austro-Hungarian territory) on the basis of which Conrad had urged Austrian mobilization. See above, p. 530.
†† Berchtold to Mensdorff, telegram, 26 July; A II 57.

specific advice (we have seen that the Entente Powers urged moderation and conciliation) for the redaction of its reply, the fact is not known. The hypothesis that M. Berthelot of the French foreign office provided the draft of an answer,* while it may be correct, has not been proved. According to seemingly reliable information, the reply was written principally by Stoyan Protich, the minister of the interior.

Every word was discussed and rediscussed, and changes *ad infinitum* were made up to the last moment. . . . Even the final Serbian text as handed over to Dr. Grouitch [Gruyich] for translation and copying was so full of elisions and erasures and corrections and had so many little riders attached to it that only one who had been working on it could decipher the sense.†

As the definitive version was being copied, the typewriter broke down, no other machine was available, and three copies had to be made by hand.‡ They were finished at 5.50 P. M., and M. Pashich, taking one of them, walked to the Austro-Hungarian legation to present it in person.

He was received just before 6 o'clock by Baron Giesl, who records that the Serbian statesman, "a tall man, already past seventy, with quite gray hair and beard, was obviously conscious of the significance of the moment." In reply to Giesl's question about the content of the reply, Pashich answered in halting German:

* Morhardt, *Les preuves*, p. 71.
† H. F. Armstrong, "Three Days in Belgrade, July, 1914," in *Foreign Affairs*, V, 273–274 (January, 1927). According to a Serbian writer, who was living in Belgrade in July, 1914, as the representative of a Vienna newspaper, and who received his information from the chief of the press bureau of the Serbian foreign office, the Serbian Government was prepared to accept the Austro-Hungarian ultimatum if, at the expiration of the time limit, no answer had been received to the telegram addressed by the Prince Regent to the Tsar. Consequently the answer was so drafted as to permit of last-minute changes, according to the nature of the Russian response. He also states, on the authority of a former Serbian minister, that in the middle of the afternoon an answer arrived from Russia "which ran favorably," and that in consequence the Serbian Government issued the order for mobilization and prepared for war. Loncharevich, pp. 593, 596. Until more Serbian and Russian documents are published, the exact circumstances in which the Serbian reply was drawn up must remain uncertain.
‡ Even the copy handed to Giesl contained corrections, as can be seen from the facsimile of page 6 of the note which is reproduced in *Ö.-U. A.*, 10,648, Anlage.

We have accepted part of your demands. . . . For the rest we rely on the loyalty and chivalry of the Austrian general. We have always been quite satisfied with you.*

The Austro-Hungarian minister did not respond to this appeal, for his instructions were that "any acceptance which contains conditions or reservations must be considered in the light of a refusal."† Only a few moments were required to establish that the Serbian reply did not conform to this condition, and Baron Giesl had only to sign and send to Pashich the note, already prepared, stating that

The term fixed in the note which, by order of my government, I presented to his Excellency M. Pachu the day before yesterday, Thursday, at 6 P. M. having expired without a satisfactory reply having reached me, I have the honor to inform you that I am leaving Belgrade this evening with the staff of the Imperial and Royal legation.‡

At 6.15 the minister and his party drove to the station, which had been shut off by troops. The train left at 6.30. On arrival at Semlin, across the river, Giesl was called to the telephone, to hear Tisza, from Budapest, asking, "Must it really be?" [*Musste es denn sein?*], to which he replied shortly, "Yes." The departing minister himself telephoned to the Ballplatz, as he had been instructed to do, that the Serbian reply was unsatisfactory and he had broken off relations; that Serbian mobilization had been ordered three hours before, and that the government and diplomatic corps had retired to Krageyuvats.§ The train reached Budapest in the morning; Count Tisza was at the station, and, having read the Serbian reply, approved the rupture. In the afternoon Baron Giesl was received in Vienna by Count Berchtold.‖

At Ischl, on this eventful Saturday, the Duke of Cumber-

* Giesl, pp. 268–269.   † See above, p. 366.
‡ First published, in facsimile, by H. F. Armstrong, "Fateful Documents of the World War," in *Current History*, XXV, 92–93 (October, 1927).
§ Telephone message from Giesl, via Budapest, 25 July, received 7.45 P. M. A II 28.
‖ Giesl, pp. 271–272.

land and his family were the guests of the Emperor Francis
Joseph at luncheon. The old monarch was obviously disturbed:

> He kept walking up and down with a quick step and with
> his hands crossed behind his back. . . . One could see only too
> clearly that the Emperor was in such a state of uneasiness and
> excitement that he could scarcely master himself.

During the meal he scarcely noticed his guests. In the evening
the news of the rupture was received. The Emperor could only
exclaim, *"Also doch!"* His hand shook as he put on his glasses
to read the written announcement. "Well," he said, according
to his aide-de-camp General Margutti, "the rupture of diplomatic relations does not, however, mean war yet," and it was
only with difficulty that he finally sent for Count Berchtold.*
It is possible that Francis Joseph did for a moment regret the
course he had sanctioned. But when he received Baron Giesl
on 27 July, he said, "You could not have done otherwise. I
must also take even this on me."†

Isolated expressions, however, are far less important than
actions. At 9.23 P. M. on Saturday, 25 July, less than three
hours after the rupture, the Emperor issued the order for the
'B' mobilization, that is, for the mobilization of the eight army
corps intended to operate against Serbia, as well as of three
cavalry divisions. The first day of notification was to be 27
July, and actual mobilization was to begin on 28 July, a point
which will need to be remembered.‡ As Sazonov exclaimed to
Szápáry, Austria had "burned her bridges."

---

* Margutti, *Vom alten Kaiser*, pp. 401, 404.
† Giesl, p. 272.
‡ Conrad, IV, 122. Between 6.30 P. M. on 25 July and 1.50 P. M. on 26 July, the
British military attaché in Vienna sent three reports on Austrian military preparations to the war office. Bunsen to Grey, telegrams, 25 and 26 July; B 124, 136,
142. In the course of the three telegrams, the attaché mentioned all sixteen of the
Austro-Hungarian army corps, including those in Transylvania and Galicia, and
estimated the number of men available at 480,000, not including certain cavalry
divisions and the Landsturm troops. The impressions created by these reports
would be that mobilization was proceeding throughout the Monarchy. Austrian
writers claim that the order of 25 July involved only 23 infantry, 3 cavalry divisions and certain Landsturm brigades.

THE SERBIAN NOTE

By general consent the note handed to Baron Giesl went very much farther toward an accommodation of the Austro-Serbian dispute than was anywhere expected. The Serbian Government denied the charge that it had abetted the anti-Austrian agitation in its own country or in Bosnia-Herzegovina, but it agreed to publish in the *Official Journal* a declaration condemning such propaganda. It promised to modify the press laws and to amend the constitution; to purge the schools of propaganda; to accept such collaboration of Austrian officials "as agrees with the principle of international law, with criminal procedure, and with good neighborly relations"; to open an inquiry against the criminals of Sarajevo; to arrest Tsiganovich (Tankosich had already been arrested); to reform the administration of the frontier service; to give explanations of such utterances of Serbian officials as should be brought to its attention; and to give due notice of the execution of these measures. On one point only was there a definite refusal: the participation of Austrian officials in the judicial inquiry (point 5), but the offer was made to refer the entire dispute to the arbitration of the Hague Tribunal or of the Great Powers which took part in drawing up the declaration of 31 March, 1909.*

The note was not an integral acceptance of the Austro-Hungarian demands. Nevertheless, the governments of the Entente Powers, their respective public opinions, and, it may be added, the press of the United States, considered the reply not only as a remarkable submission to extraordinary demands but also as a satisfactory settlement, or at least as the basis of a settlement. Even the German foreign minister, who put off reading the note for several days, admitted that it provided "a basis for possible negotiation."† The course of subsequent events was profoundly influenced by the conviction in St. Petersburg,

* Note of the Serbian Government, 25 July; S 39; A II 47.
† J. Cambon to Bienvenu-Martin, 29 July; F 92.

Paris, and London that Serbia had done the handsome thing and that Austria-Hungary was acting most unreasonably in declining all discussion.*

The Austrian criticisms of the Serbian note were not formulated by Baron Giesl in order to have ground for declaring it unsatisfactory. They were drawn up in Vienna in the course of the next few days and give the appearance of having been composed with a view to justifying the *fait accompli* of the minister in Belgrade. They were embodied in a despatch which was not sent from Vienna until after the declaration of war on Serbia;† when this despatch, which was not telegraphed, was received in the Entente capitals, is not known, but it was never presented to the British Government, and there is no record that the French and Russian Governments ever received it. It is probably true that the document would have had little effect on the policy of the Entente Powers, even if it had been known to them. Nevertheless Austro-Hungarian diplomacy laid itself open to the reproach of making the alleged unsatisfactory reply the reason for declaring war on Serbia without waiting to explain why that reply was unsatisfactory.

The main Austrian objection appears to have been contained in the following passage:

Our grievance is that the Serbian Government has omitted to suppress the agitation directed against the territorial integrity of the Dual Monarchy, notwithstanding the obligations it entered into under the terms of the note of 31 March, 1909. . . . The contention of the Royal Serbian Government that utterances of the press and the activities of associations are of a private character and are beyond the control of the state, is plainly at variance with the institutions of modern states, even of those which have the most liberal regulations in this respect; these regulations, designed to safeguard public policy and right, impose state supervision upon both press and associations.

---

* On 27 July, after it became evident that Russia did not intend to leave Serbia in the lurch, Pashich told the Bulgarian minister in Belgrade that "if Serbia had known that she would be supported in this fashion, she would never have made the concessions which she had offered." Chaprashikov to Radoslavov, 27 July; *KSF*, VI, 245 (March, 1928).

† Circular despatch to all missions, 28 July; A II 96.

Moreover, the Serbian institutions themselves provide for such supervision.

It was not the first time that Austrian statesmen put forward this argument. Sixty years before, when Cavour was arousing the sentiment of Italians against the Austrian régime in Lombardy-Venetia by means of the Sardinian press, Buol, the Austrian foreign minister, demanded the suppression of the offending papers, and received much the same answer as that given by Nikola Pashich to Count Berchtold. History has passed judgment on that controversy. And when it is noted that the Austrian criticisms declared the passage of a new press law "immaterial" and an amendment to the Serbian constitution to be "of no use," it must be evident that Austria-Hungary was in substance demanding that Serbian public opinion should be made to Austro-Hungarian order.

With respect to the declaration to be published in the *Official Journal,* the Ballplatz complained that by specifying "all propaganda which *may* be directed against Austria-Hungary" and by inserting the words, "according to the communication of the Austro-Hungarian Government," Serbia was disavowing the existence of propaganda in the past and keeping its hands free for the future. The point seems rather petty, for the Serbian Government was ready to disavow "all idea of interfering or attempting to interfere with the destinies of the inhabitants of any part whatsoever of Austria-Hungary," and promised to prosecute all propagandists.

For the rest some flaw was found with the reply to nine of the ten demands. In some matters the Serbian language was evasive; the complaint that the Belgrade police had prevented the arrest of Tsiganovich was justified. But surely Serbia was entitled to demand *proof* that officials were guilty of propaganda, at which Vienna scoffed. With regard to the criticism that societies dissolved might be reconstituted under other names, it is to be remarked that the promise was given to dissolve all societies which might act against Austria-Hungary.

On the famous point 5 Serbia declared that she did not understand what was meant by the "collaboration" of Austrian officials—which Vienna qualified as "unintelligible." But statesmen as experienced as the British and Russian foreign ministers did not understand precisely what was involved, and Count Berchtold, as we have seen, thought it necessary to explain the matter to Russia. Why should Serbia have understood any more clearly? The Austrian contention that the Serbian Government misrepresented the distinction in point 6 between *enquête judiciare* and *recherches* and that only participation in the police investigation had been demanded, seems warranted; and since Serbia was willing to admit such collaboration as was consonant with international law, she might have strained the point and accepted this demand.

Whether the Serbian reply was conceived in a spirit of deceitfulness and evasion, as the Austro-Hungarian Government alleged, is a matter of personal opinion. But it may be pointed out that this was not the judgment of the two highest personages of the allied German Empire. On 30 July, after the German Government had had three days to study it, Herr von Bethmann-Hollweg said to the Prussian ministry that "the Serbian reply had in fact agreed to the Austrian wishes except on unimportant points."* And the German Emperor, when he had read the reply, commented:

A brilliant performance for a time limit of only forty-eight hours. This is more than one could have expected! A great moral victory for Vienna; but with it every reason for war disappears, and Giesl might have remained quietly in Belgrade!†

This verdict, particularly as it was given by the man who for several weeks had been clamoring for immediate military action against Serbia, seems conclusive. Moreover, William wrote to his foreign minister:

* " . . . dass die serbische Antwort bis auf geringe Punkte den österreichisch-ungarischen Desiderien tatsächlich zugestimmt habe." Minutes of the meeting of the Prussian state ministry, 30 July; G 456.
† Comment on G 271.

I am convinced that on the whole the wishes of the Dual Monarchy have been acceded to. The few reservations which Serbia makes in regard to individual points can, in my opinion, be cleared up by negotiation.*

This was the essential point. Even if the charge of Serbian complicity in the murder be considered proved and the most lenient view taken of the Austro-Hungarian demands, the Serbs had, as the German Emperor said, "announced *orbi et urbi* a capitulation of the most humiliating kind." If Austria-Hungary had been willing to negotiate on the basis of the Serbian reply, she could have demanded the rigid execution of the promises made, and, in default of Serbian performance, her diplomatic position would have been unassailable. Unfortunately for her, she had not expected so great a surrender on the part of Serbia, and she was determined not to accept a diplomatic solution. Thus she was forced, if she was to impose a military solution, to take the false step of ignoring a conciliatory overture which conceded nine-tenths of her demands.†

---

* William II to Jagow, 28 July; G 293.
† On 25 July, Professor Hold, the legal adviser of the Ballplatz, handed in a memorandum suggesting how the Serbian reply should be treated. If Serbia qualified her reply by any kind of protest, it should be rejected, on the ground that the declaration of 31 March, 1909, was thereby repudiated. "If Serbia announces her acceptance of our demands *en gros*, without any protest, we can still object that she did not within the prescribed time provide proofs that she carried out those provisions which had to be executed 'at once' or 'with all speed,' and whose execution she had to notify to us 'without delay.' " *Ö.-U. A.*, 10,706. Seton-Watson, *Sarajevo*, p. 264, thinks that this document proves Berchtold's anxiety "lest Serbia should, after all, swallow his impossible terms, or lest some other unforeseen incident should deprive him of all pretext for aggression." That Berchtold was anxious on this score, is probably true; but the editors of *Ö.-U. A.* state that the document in question was a spontaneous act of its author and seems not to have been submitted to Berchtold.